A workbook that helps you master the skills you will need to be successful in your courses . . . and beyond.

Containing many questions written in a similar format as on the licensing exam, *Connecting Core Competencies: A Workbook for Social Work Students* includes 300+ assessment questions.

Each chapter covers one of CSWE's 10 core competencies and includes:

- A detailed explanation of the competency

- Assessment questions that help you master the skills in the competency with multiple choice, short case vignette, and reflective essay questions.

Students: If your text did not come bundled with this printed workbook, you can purchase it at: www.mypearsonstore.com

MySocialWorkLab will help you develop the skills you'll need as a professional social worker.

Features include:

- **NEW! Hundreds of assessment questions**—multiple choice, case vignette scenarios and reflective essay—to help you monitor your progress in mastering the skills you will need as a social worker. And, they are written in a similar format as you will find on the licensing exam.

- Complete **eText** with audio files and **chapter tests**

- **Numerous videos** of real scenarios that you are likely to encounter as a social worker.

- **75 case studies** to help you apply theory to practice

- A **Gradebook** that allows you to monitor your progress on all assessment questions on the site

- **MySearchLab**—a collection of tools that help you master research assignments and papers

- And much more!

If your text did not come packaged with MySocialWorkLab, you can purchase access at: www.MySocialWorkLab.com

CSWE EPAS 2008 Core Competencies

Professional Identity

2.1.1 Identify as a professional social worker and conduct oneself accordingly.

Necessary Knowledge, Values, Skills

- Social workers serve as representatives of the profession, its mission, and its core values.
- Social workers know the profession's history.
- Social workers commit themselves to the profession's enhancement and to their own professional conduct and growth.

Operational Practice Behaviors

- Social workers advocate for client access to the services of social work;
- Social workers practice personal reflection and self-correction to assure continual professional development;
- Social workers attend to professional roles and boundaries;
- Social workers demonstrate professional demeanor in behavior, appearance, and communication;
- Social workers engage in career-long learning; and
- Social workers use supervision and consultation.

Ethical Practice

2.1.2 Apply social work ethical principles to guide professional practice.

Necessary Knowledge, Values, Skills

- Social workers have an obligation to conduct themselves ethically and engage in ethical decision-making.
- Social workers are knowledgeable about the value base of the profession, its ethical standards, and relevant law.

Operational Practice Behaviors

- Social workers recognize and manage personal values in a way that allows professional values to guide practice;
- Social workers make ethical decisions by applying standards of the National Association of Social Workers Code of Ethics and, as applicable, of the International Federation of Social Workers/International Association of Schools of Social Work Ethics in Social Work, Statement of Principles;
- Social workers tolerate ambiguity in resolving ethical conflicts; and
- Social workers apply strategies of ethical reasoning to arrive at principled decisions.

Critical Thinking

2.1.3 Apply critical thinking to inform and communicate professional judgments.

Necessary Knowledge, Values, Skills

- Social workers are knowledgeable about the principles of logic, scientific inquiry, and reasoned discernment.
- They use critical thinking augmented by creativity and curiosity.
- Critical thinking also requires the synthesis and communication of relevant information.

Operational Practice Behaviors

- Social workers distinguish, appraise, and integrate multiple sources of knowledge, including research-based knowledge, and practice wisdom;
- Social workers analyze models of assessment, prevention, intervention, and evaluation; and
- Social workers demonstrate effective oral and written communication in working with individuals, families, groups, organizations, communities, and colleagues.

Diversity in Practice

2.1.4 Engage diversity and difference in practice.

Necessary Knowledge, Values, Skills

- Social workers understand how diversity characterizes and shapes the human experience and is critical to the formation of identity.
- The dimensions of diversity are understood as the intersectionality of multiple factors including age, class, color, culture, disability, ethnicity, gender, gender identity and expression, immigration status, political ideology, race, religion, sex, and sexual orientation.
- Social workers appreciate that, as a consequence of difference, a person's life experiences may include oppression, poverty, marginalization, and alienation as well as privilege, power, and acclaim.

Operational Practice Behaviors

- Social workers recognize the extent to which a culture's structures and values may oppress, marginalize, alienate, or create or enhance privilege and power;
- Social workers gain sufficient self-awareness to eliminate the influence of personal biases and values in working with diverse groups;
- Social workers recognize and communicate their understanding of the importance of difference in shaping life experiences; and
- Social workers view themselves as learners and engage those with whom they work as informants.

Human Rights & Justice

2.1.5 Advance human rights and social and economic justice.

Necessary Knowledge, Values, Skills

- Each person, regardless of position in society, has basic human rights, such as freedom, safety, privacy, an adequate standard of living, health care, and education.
- Social workers recognize the global interconnections of oppression and are knowledgeable about theories of justice and strategies to promote human and civil rights.
- Social work incorporates social justice practices in organizations, institutions, and society to ensure that these basic human rights are distributed equitably and without prejudice.

Operational Practice Behaviors

- Social workers understand the forms and mechanisms of oppression and discrimination;
- Social workers advocate for human rights and social and economic justice; and
- Social workers engage in practices that advance social and economic justice.

Research Based Practice

2.1.6 Engage in research-informed practice and practice-informed research.

Necessary Knowledge, Values, Skills

- Social workers use practice experience to inform research, employ evidence-based interventions, evaluate their own practice, and use research findings to improve practice, policy, and social service delivery.
- Social workers comprehend quantitative and qualitative research and understand scientific and ethical approaches to building knowledge.

Operational Practice Behaviors

- Social workers use practice experience to inform scientific inquiry; and
- Social workers use research evidence to inform practice.

Human Behavior

2.1.7 Apply knowledge of human behavior and the social environment.

Necessary Knowledge, Values, Skills

- Social workers are knowledgeable about human behavior across the life course; the range of social systems in which people live; and the ways social systems promote or deter people in maintaining or achieving health and well-being.
- Social workers apply theories and knowledge from the liberal arts to understand biological, social, cultural, psychological, and spiritual development.

Operational Practice Behaviors

- Social workers utilize conceptual frameworks to guide the processes of assessment, intervention, and evaluation; and
- Social workers critique and apply knowledge to understand person and environment.

CSWE EPAS 2008 Core Competencies *(continued)*

Policy Practice   2.1.8 Engage in policy practice to advance social and economic well-being and to deliver effective social work services.

Necessary Knowledge, Values, Skills

- Social work practitioners understand that policy affects service delivery and they actively engage in policy practice.
- Social workers know the history and current structures of social policies and services; the role of policy in service delivery; and the role of practice in policy development.

Operational Practice Behaviors

- Social workers analyze, formulate, and advocate for policies that advance social well-being; and
- Social workers collaborate with colleagues and clients for effective policy action.

Practice Contexts
2.1.9 Respond to contexts that shape practice.

Necessary Knowledge, Values, Skills

- Social workers are informed, resourceful, and proactive in responding to evolving organizational, community, and societal contexts at all levels of practice.
- Social workers recognize that the context of practice is dynamic, and use knowledge and skill to respond proactively.

Operational Practice Behaviors

- Social workers continuously discover, appraise, and attend to changing locales, populations, scientific and technological developments, and emerging societal trends to provide relevant services; and
- Social workers provide leadership in promoting sustainable changes in service delivery and practice to improve the quality of social services.

Engage, Assess, Intervene, Evaluate   2.1.10 Engage, assess, intervene, and evaluate with individuals, families, groups, organizations, and communities.

Necessary Knowledge, Values, Skills

- Professional practice involves the dynamic and interactive processes of engagement, assessment, intervention, and evaluation at multiple levels.
- Social workers have the knowledge and skills to practice with individuals, families, groups, organizations, and communities.
- Practice knowledge includes
  - identifying, analyzing, and implementing evidence-based interventions designed to achieve client goals;
  - using research and technological advances;
  - evaluating program outcomes and practice effectiveness;
  - developing, analyzing, advocating, and providing leadership for policies and services; and
  - promoting social and economic justice.

Operational Practice Behaviors

(a) Engagement
- Social workers substantively and effectively prepare for action with individuals, families, groups, organizations, and communities;
- Social workers use empathy and other interpersonal skills; and
- Social workers develop a mutually agreed-on focus of work and desired outcomes.

(b) Assessment
- Social workers collect, organize, and interpret client data;
- Social workers assess client strengths and limitations;
- Social workers develop mutually agreed-on intervention goals and objectives; and
- Social workers select appropriate intervention strategies.

(c) Intervention
- Social workers initiate actions to achieve organizational goals;
- Social workers implement prevention interventions that enhance client capacities;
- Social workers help clients resolve problems;
- Social workers negotiate, mediate, and advocate for clients; and
- Social workers facilitate transitions and endings.

(d) Evaluation
- Social workers critically analyze, monitor, and evaluate interventions.

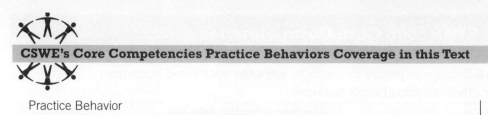

CSWE's Core Competencies Practice Behaviors Coverage in this Text

Practice Behavior	Chapter
Professional Identity (2.1.1)	
Social workers advocate for client access to the services of social work	2, 3, 8, 10
Social workers practice personal reflection and self-correction to assure continual professional development	1, 2, 3, 8
Social workers attend to professional roles and boundaries	2, 10
Social workers demonstrate professional demeanor in behavior, appearance, and communication	3, 10
Social workers engage in career-long learning	1, 3
Social workers use supervision and consultation	
Ethical Practice (2.1.2)	
Social workers recognize and manage personal values in a way that allows professional values to guide practice	1, 8, 10
Social workers make ethical decisions by applying standards of the National Association of Social Workers Code of Ethics and, as applicable, of the International Federation of Social Workers/International Association of Schools of Social Work Ethics in Social Work, Statement of Principles	1
Social workers tolerate ambiguity in resolving ethical conflicts	1, 6, 10
Social workers apply strategies of ethical reasoning to arrive at principled decisions	6, 8, 10
Critical Thinking (2.1.3)	
Social workers distinguish, appraise, and integrate multiple sources of knowledge, including research-based knowledge, and practice wisdom	7, 9, 11
Social workers analyze models of assessment, prevention, intervention, and evaluation	3, 4, 9, 11
Social workers demonstrate effective oral and written communication in working with individuals, families, groups, organizations, communities, and colleagues	3, 7, 9, 11
Diversity in Practice (2.1.4)	
Social workers recognize the extent to which a culture's structures and values may oppress, marginalize, alienate, or create or enhance privilege and power	4, 5, 7, 9, 10
Social workers gain sufficient self-awareness to eliminate the influence of personal biases and values in working with diverse groups	4, 7, 9, 10
Social workers recognize and communicate their understanding of the importance of difference in shaping life experiences	5, 7
Social workers view themselves as learners and engage those with whom they work as informants	4, 7, 9
Human Rights & Justice (2.1.5)	
Social workers understand the forms and mechanisms of oppression and discrimination	1, 2, 4, 5, 8, 10
Social workers advocate for human rights and social and economic justice	2, 4, 8
Social workers engage in practices that advance social and economic justice	2, 4, 5

CSWE's Core Competencies Practice Behaviors Coverage in this Text

Practice Behavior	Chapter
Research Based Practice (2.1.6)	
Social workers use practice experience to inform scientific inquiry	7
Social workers use research evidence to inform practice	3, 7, 11
Human Behavior (2.1.7)	
Social workers utilize conceptual frameworks to guide the processes of assessment, intervention, and evaluation	5
Social workers assess and apply knowledge to understand person and environment.	4, 5, 6, 11
Policy Practice (2.1.8)	
Social workers analyze, formulate, and advocate for policies that advance social well-being	1, 2, 6, 9
Social workers collaborate with colleagues and clients for effective policy action	1, 6, 9
Practice Contexts (2.1.9)	
Social workers continuously discover, appraise, and attend to changing locales, populations, scientific and technological developments, and emerging societal trends to provide relevant services	4, 5, 6, 7
Social workers provide leadership in promoting sustainable changes in service delivery and practice to improve the quality of social services	8, 6, 7, 11
Engage, Assess, Intervene, Evaluate (2.1.10(a)–(d))	
A) ENGAGEMENT	
Social workers substantively and effectively prepare for action with individuals, families, groups, organizations, and communities	2, 3, 9
Social workers use empathy and other interpersonal skills	9
Social workers develop a mutually agreed-on focus of work and desired outcomes	11
B) ASSESSMENT	
Social workers collect, organize, and interpret client data	9
Social workers assess client strengths and limitations	3, 9, 11
Social workers develop mutually agreed-on intervention goals and objectives	9
Social workers select appropriate intervention strategies	2, 9
C) INTERVENTION	
Social workers initiate actions to achieve organizational goals	2
Social workers implement prevention interventions that enhance client capacities	2
Social workers help clients resolve problems	
Social workers negotiate, mediate, and advocate for clients	9
Social workers facilitate transitions and endings	
D) EVALUATION	
Social workers critically analyze, monitor, and evaluate interventions	2, 3, 9, 11

| CONNECTING CORE COMPETENCIES **Chapter-by-Chapter Matrix** | | | | | | | | | |
Chapter	Professional Identity	Ethical Practice	Critical Thinking	Diversity in Practice	Human Rights & Justice	Research-Based Practice	Human Behavior	Policy Practice	Practice Contexts	Engage, Assess, Intervene, Evaluate
1	✔	✔			✔			✔		
2	✔				✔			✔		✔
3	✔		✔			✔				✔
4				✔	✔		✔		✔	
5				✔	✔		✔		✔	
6		✔					✔	✔	✔	
7			✔	✔		✔			✔	
8	✔	✔			✔				✔	
9			✔	✔				✔		✔
10	✔	✔		✔	✔					
11			✔			✔	✔		✔	
Total Chapters	5	4	4	5	6	3	4	4	6	3

FIFTH EDITION

Social Work Macro Practice

F. Ellen Netting
Virginia Commonwealth University

Peter M. Kettner
Arizona State University

Steven L. McMurtry
University of Wisconsin—Milwaukee

M. Lori Thomas
University of North Carolina—Charlotte

Pearson Education

Boston Columbus Indianapolis New York San Francisco Upper Saddle River
Amsterdam Cape Town Dubai London Madrid Milan Munich Paris Montreal Toronto
Delhi Mexico City São Paulo Sydney Hong Kong Seoul Singapore Taipei Tokyo

Editorial Director: Craig Campanella
Editor in Chief: Dickson Musslewhite
Executive Editor: Ashley Dodge
Editorial Product Manager: Carly Czech
Director of Marketing: Brandy Dawson
Executive Marketing Manager: Jeanette Koskinas
Senior Marketing Manager: Wendy Albert
Marketing Assistant: Jessica Warren
Media Project Manager: Felicia Halpert

Editorial Production Service: PreMediaGlobal
Production Manager: Kathy Sleys
Creative Director: Jayne Conte
Editorial Production and Composition Service:
  Saraswathi Muralidhar/PreMediaGlobal
Interior Design: Joyce Weston Design
Cover Designer: Kristina Mose-Libon/Karen
  Salzbach
Cover Image: Robert Llewellyn/Corbis

Credits appear on Page 410, which constitutes an extension of the copyright page.

Library of Congress Cataloging-in-Publication Data
Social work macro practice / F. Ellen Netting . . . [et al.].—5th ed.
    p. cm.
  Includes bibliographical references and index.
  ISBN-13: 978-0-205-83878-3
  ISBN-10: 0-205-83878-2
  1. Social service.   2. Social service—United States.   3. Macrosociology.
I. Netting, F. Ellen.
  HV41.N348 2012
  361.3'2—dc22

                                        2011009823

10 9 8 7 6 5 4 3 2 EBM 15 14 13 12

Student Edition
ISBN-10: 0-205-83878-2
ISBN-13: 978-0-205-83878-3

Instructor Edition
ISBN-10: 0-205-83880-4
ISBN-13: 978-0-205-83880-6

à la Carte Edition
ISBN-10: 0-205-00325-7
ISBN-13: 978-0-205-00325-9

PEARSON

Contents

Preface

Macro practice has come to mean many different things to different people, so we feel it is important to share our perspective at the outset. Over the years, we were intrigued to learn that previous editions of our text were being used at both graduate and undergraduate levels in courses on human behavior and policy practice as well as in courses on community practice and human service organizations. It is likely that a wide variety of curriculum designs and different ways of dividing curricular content accounts for the varying perspectives on how this book can be used. We are pleased that so many faculty have found a variety of uses for the book and its content, but we would also like to take this opportunity to clarify our perspective about the purpose of the book.

We are aware that the history of social work as a profession has been marked by shifts in and tensions between intervention with individuals and intervention with and within larger systems. Early perspectives on the latter tended to focus primarily on policy-level involvements (especially legislative processes). As the need for social work administration and management content, as well as community content, was recognized and incorporated into the curriculum of many schools of social work, this topic was also embraced as an area of concentration for those who wanted to work with and within larger systems. In order to manage oversubscribed curricula, students have often been forced to concentrate in *either* macro or micro areas, creating a false dichotomy, when social work of all professions is uniquely positioned to integrate both.

Therefore, as we taught our required foundation-level courses on community and organizational change, and as we worked with students and professionals in the field, we became aware of the changing dynamics of practice and expectations for practitioners. Both students and practitioners were working with populations such as homeless persons, members of teen street gangs, victims of domestic violence, chronically unemployed persons, frail elders, and other disenfranchised groups. Although social workers will always need casework and clinical skills to help people in need on a one-to-one basis, it was becoming increasingly evident to us that they were also expected to intervene at the community level. Typical activities included promoting the development of shelters, developing neighborhood alternatives to gang membership and juvenile incarceration, addressing chronic unemployment, and navigating the complexity of long-term care services as a community problem.

These activities are not new; many closely mirror the work of settlement-house workers in the early days of the profession. Yet, many social work students have traditionally seen themselves as preparing strictly for interventions at the individual or domestic level. It is unexpected and disconcerting when they find themselves being asked to initiate actions and design interventions that will affect large numbers of people and take on problems at the community or organizational level. A major goal of this book, then, is to recapture a broader definition of *social work practice* that recognizes the need for workers to be able to bridge these distinctions if they are to provide effective services.

When social work practice with macro systems is seen as solely the realm of administrators, community organizers, program planners, and others, a vital linkage to millions of people who struggle daily with environmental constraints has been severed. Social workers who see clients every day, we believe, are the ones who are most aware of the need for macro-level change. Macro practice, understood within this context, defines the uniqueness of social work practice. Many disciplines claim expertise in working with individuals, groups, and families, but social work has long stood alone in its focus on the organizational, community, and policy contexts within which its clients function. The concept of person-in-environment is not simply a slogan that makes social workers aware of environmental influences. It means that social workers recognize that sometimes it is the *environment* and not the *person* that needs to be changed.

Macro-level change may, but does not necessarily always, involve large-scale, costly reforms at the federal and state levels or the election of candidates more sympathetic to the poor, neglected, and underserved members of society. Sometimes useful macro-level change can involve organizing a local neighborhood to deal with deterioration and blight; sometimes it may mean initiating a self-help group and stepping back so that members will assume leadership roles. The focus of this book is on enabling social work practitioners to undertake whatever types of macro-level interventions are needed in an informed, analytical way and with a sense of confidence that they can do a competent job and achieve positive results.

Connecting Core Competencies Series

The new edition of this text is now a part of Pearson Education's *Connecting Core Competencies* series, which consists of foundation-level texts that make it easier than ever to ensure students' success in learning the ten core competencies as stated in 2008 by the Council on Social Work Education. This text contains:

- **Core Competency Icons** throughout the chapters, directly linking the CSWE core competencies to the content of the text. **Critical thinking questions** are also included to further students' mastery of the CSWE standards. For easy reference, page vi displays which competencies are used in each chapter, in a chapter-by-chapter matrix.
- **An end-of-chapter Practice Test**, with multiple-choice questions that test students' knowledge of the chapter content.
- **Assess your competence** at the end of each chapter by evaluating your mastery of the skills and competencies learned.
- **Additional questions pertaining to the videos and case studies found on MySocialWorkLab** at the end of each chapter to encourage students to access the site and explore the wealth of available materials. If this text did not come with an access code for MySocialWorkLab, you can purchase access at www.mysocialworklab.com.

Acknowledgments

As we finish this fifth edition, much has changed since our original 1993 publication. We are now scattered in four different geographical locations: Virginia, Arizona, Wisconsin, and North Carolina. In this edition we are delighted to add a new colleague (Lori Thomas) to our collaboration. We are indebted to the colleagues and students at the four universities where we have worked who have given us constructive and helpful feedback throughout the years. We especially want to thank Colleen Janczewski who took on the detailed task of incorporating competencies into each chapter. Also, we want to thank colleagues who provided feedback as they used our text at other universities. We appreciate as well the efforts of a number of reviewers who provided careful and thoughtful assessments of earlier drafts. For this fifth edition, these individuals are Jong Choi, California State University; Gary Norman, University of Houston; Tracy Soska, University of Pittsburgh; and Robert Vernon, Indiana State University.

To our former editor, Patricia Quinlin, we express our sincere appreciation for her oversight, patience, interest, and assistance as we began the revision of our text. To our current editor, Ashley Dodge, we thank her for working so hard to facilitate the many transitions we made during this edition and responding to our many questions along the way. To our project manager, Joseph Scordato, we extend a round of applause for his diligent oversight about details and his constant enthusiasm for the process.

Most of all, we thank those students and practitioners who, often in the face of seemingly insurmountable barriers, continue to practice social work the way it was intended. This book is dedicated to them. They intervene at whatever level is needed. They persist with what may appear to be intractable problems and work with clients who have lost hope until hope can be rediscovered and pursued. Their spirit and dedication continually inspire us in our efforts to provide whatever guidance we can for the next generation of social workers.

1

An Introduction to Macro Practice in Social Work

Core Competencies in this Chapter (Check marks indicate which competencies are covered in depth)				
✓ Professional Identity	✓ Ethical Practice	☐ Critical Thinking	☐ Diversity in Practice	✓ Human Rights & Justice
☐ Research-Based Practice	☐ Human Behavior	✓ Policy Practice	☐ Practice Contexts	☐ Engage, Assess, Intervene, Evaluate

MACRO PRACTICE IN CONTEXT

This book is intended for all social workers, regardless of whether they specialize or concentrate in micro or macro tracks within schools of social work. It is also designed to be an introduction to macro practice as a set of professional activities in which all social workers are involved. Although some practitioners will concentrate their efforts primarily in one arena more than another, all social workers encounter situations in which macro-level interventions are the appropriate response to a need or a problem. Therefore, we define *macro practice* as *professionally guided intervention(s) designed to bring about change in organizational, community, and/or policy arenas.*

This book is not designed to prepare practitioners for full-time agency administration, program planning, community organizing, or policy analysis positions. Social workers who assume full-time macro roles will need a more advanced understanding than this text provides. Nor is this a book on how to specialize in macro practice. Instead, it is designed to provide basic knowledge and skills on aspects of macro practice in which competent social work practitioners will need to engage at some time in their professional careers.

Experiences of Former Students

No matter what roles our former students assume after graduation, they are all involved in macro activities. Therefore, in preparation for each revision of this book, we talk with former students who are now practicing social workers, some of whom work directly with clients and some of whom are coordinators, planners, managers, administrators, organizers, and policy analysts in the United States and in other parts of the world. We also save emails from former students who keep us up-to-date and pose questions to us. We then include comments that illustrate the differences between students' expectations of social work practice and their actual experiences once they are working in the field.

For example, a social worker employed by a community-based agency on an American Indian reservation shared these thoughts: "Culture is so important to the work we do. I constantly have to ask indigenous people for advice so that I do not make assumptions about the people with whom I work. The concept of community and what it means to this tribe, even the value of the land as a part of their tradition, is so crucial. It is much more complex than I had assumed when I was in school." In her position, this social worker has come to appreciate what we taught about the false dichotomy between micro and macro social work. Although she works directly with tribal members, she is constantly assessing their environment, asking for advice, and recognizing the cultural context in which all her actions are embedded.

Another former student reinforced the importance of community. "The thing that has surprised me is how much I need to know about the community—people's values, where funding comes from, how to assess community needs. Even though I do direct practice, I am constantly pulled onto task forces and committees that have to deal with the broader community issues." This practitioner contacted us to share how the use of geographic information systems (GIS) was becoming critically important in her agency. She had learned to use GIS to locate pockets of need within the community, and she had used her findings to convince decision makers to re-target their programming to persons in greatest need.

One of our graduates, who decided to try a new location, sent an email from Australia where she, too, was recognizing the complexity of culture. She wrote, "I got a job as a family counselor in the Northern Territory here and it's way out in the bush, as they call it. If you're wondering how remote it is, look it up on the Web. My main job duties are to work with Aboriginal youth and families, especially those who have been affected by past government policies of assimilation by government officers who took Aboriginal or part Aboriginal people from their homes and placed them with white families or institutions simply because of their race. They call this population of people 'The Stolen Generation.' It's clinical-type work, but I'm in a new community-based organization, and we are desperate for books and reading materials on grant writing and fundraising. Can you help?" It is not unusual to receive emails similar to this one as practitioners suddenly recognize the importance of having skills in locating and accessing resources to keep human service programs operating.

These social workers focus heavily on local community concerns; others find themselves in policy-making arenas. One graduate sent the following email: "You were so right about the importance of having excellent writing skills and knowing how to persuade diverse audiences! I'm now a court program specialist in the State Supreme Court and I am amazed at how I have to constantly target various groups that I want to bring on board in assisting persons with disabilities. Sometimes I have to meet face-to-face first and do a lot of interpersonal convincing, but others want a legislative brief prepared before they will even see me. I am learning to be technologically savvy too. You would be amazed at how I can track legislation on-line and how I can mobilize constituencies through electronic advocacy networks. Those policy analysis and technological skills are coming in handy."

A graduate who secured a position in a county department of social service reported the following: "I'm hoping I'll eventually have enough wiggle room to go from child and adult protective services to the welfare-to-work area, which is my main interest. I think the political system is primarily involved in major policy issues and not implementation. They passed legislation and then expected the state and local delivery systems to implement the policy decision. I think on a micro level, legislators are concerned about the delivery of services to constituents, particularly if they receive a call. At the macro level, I am not as sure that there is a commitment to customer satisfaction. I believe more often that social services are viewed as a social control program. Do I sound cynical?" This practitioner recognizes how policy intent is often hard to implement in agencies and communities.

The realization that policy intent means little unless that policy can be implemented is an ongoing theme we hear from practitioners. One former student, now working as a hospice social worker, wrote, "With all of this talk about outcome-based measurement and evidence-based practice, I am having a hard time connecting the dots. All of my clients die, and if they don't, we have to discharge them from our program because they have lived more than their allotted six months. Ironic, isn't it? Policy demands that we discharge them, and then without the services we provide, you can rest assured that they will decline. I suppose a good intermediate outcome for our program is one in which patients steadily decline because if they get better, we can't serve them any more. To add insult to injury, it's hard to measure our ultimate outcomes when everyone eventually dies. I suppose that a 'good death' is our outcome, but how do you measure that concept? Would you like to help me with program evaluation here? It seemed a lot easier when we talked about it in class."

One of our former students, originally from Nigeria, returned to her country of origin to establish a mission house designed to improve the welfare of elders. She wrote, "From our preliminary studies here, poverty and health-related problems are the two most prevalent issues for elders. Then, add widowhood and you'll have a grim picture. There are cases of neglect arising primarily from the economic situations of family members. It is a case of being able to share what you have. If you have no food to eat, you cannot offer another person food. This is what we are trying to address in our programs here."

Compare this to what the former director of a social services unit in a U.S. hospital told us about elder care: "I have been here long enough to see the advent of diagnostic-related categories. This is the Medicare system's way of making sure older patients are discharged efficiently, and if they are not, the hospital has to pick up the tab." She went on to explain how social workers in health care are struggling to understand their roles, which are often limited by the services for which funding sources will authorize reimbursement. Understanding the way in which health-care organizations are changing, diversifying, and turning outward to the community has become critical for social workers who are encountering other professionals in roles similar to their own. As social work departments in health care and other organizations are decentralized into cost centers, social workers must understand why these administrative decisions are being made and find ways to influence future decision making. Many of these social workers entered health-care systems with the idea of providing counseling, but what they are doing is advocacy, solution-focused and crisis intervention, case management, and discharge planning. They are also encountering technological challenges in accessing and using large information systems.

Another student had this to say: "What makes this profession worthwhile for me is that there is a core of very committed people who really live up to the ideals of the profession. They're very talented people who could make a lot more money elsewhere, but they believe in what they're doing, and it's always a pleasure to work with them. Our biggest frustration has been that there are so many people (like state legislators, for example) who wield so much power over this profession but have no understanding of what social problems and human needs are all about. Even though professionals may have spent the better part of their careers trying to understand how to deal with people in need, their opinions and perspectives are often not accepted or respected by decision makers."

The clinical director of a private for-profit adoption agency added this view: "Unlike a lot of social workers, I work in a for-profit agency, and business considerations always have to be factored into our decisions. We have a fairly small operation, and I think the agency director is responsive to my concerns about how clients are treated, but I've still had to get used to the tension that can arise between making a profit and serving clients."

On a final note, a direct-practice student who graduated made this statement: "My education in social work taught me how little I know. I feel as if I have just scratched the surface. Learning is a long ongoing process. I work in a head injury center and what I learned from having had exposure to macro-practice roles is that you have to know the organization in which you work, particularly the philosophy behind what happens there. This is more important than I ever imagined."

These quotations tell a number of stories. First, the issues facing social workers in their daily practice are not limited to client problems. If social workers are to be effective in serving their clients, many problems must be recognized and addressed at the agency, community, and policy levels. Some of these problems require changing the nature of services, programs, or policies. Most require an understanding of funding issues and the complications caused by the economic recession since 2008. In social service programs, at least for now, social workers cannot look forward to additional funding or increased staff, but rather need to find ways to provide and hopefully even improve services with the same or fewer resources. Second, skills learned in classroom settings become critically important to practice success, whether they are writing, interpersonal, assessment, evaluation, or other skills. Finally, practitioners continue to learn as they move into their respective places of employment, often surprising themselves with their insights about policy intent, the use of technology, and knowing how to ask the right questions. We thank our former students for helping us illustrate the use of macro-practice skills across settings and arenas, and the importance of macro practice to the profession.

WHAT IS MACRO PRACTICE?

As defined earlier, macro practice is professionally guided intervention designed to bring about change in organizational, community, and policy arenas. Macro practice, as all social work practice, draws from theoretical foundations while simultaneously contributing to the development of new theory. Macro practice is based on any of a number of practice approaches, and it operates within the boundaries of professional values and ethics. In today's world, macro practice is rarely the domain of one profession. Rather, it involves the skills of many disciplines and professionals in interaction.

Macro activities go beyond individual interventions but are often based on needs, problems, issues, and concerns identified in the course of working one-to-one with service recipients. There are different ways to conceptualize the arenas in which macro social work practice occurs. Rothman, Erlich, and Tropman (2008) identify three arenas of intervention: communities, organizations, and small groups. We have selected communities and organizations as the arenas on which the majority of this text will focus, folding small group work in as a critical part of most interventions in both communities and organizations. *Small groups* are seen as collections of people who collaborate on tasks that move toward agreed-upon changes. It is our contention that small groups are often the nucleus around which change strategies are developed in both communities and organizations, and they are therefore more logically conceptualized as part of the strategy or medium for change rather than the focus of change.

Other writers focus on the policy context in which macro intervention occurs (Gilbert & Terrell, 2010; Jansson, 2011; Karger & Stoesz, 2009). The policy arena is well articulated in other social work textbooks that complement the content here (e.g., Cummins, Byers, & Pedrick, 2011). Organizational and community arenas are deeply embedded in political systems, which are typically the starting points for development of social policies. Although the creation and analysis of these policies is not our main focus, an understanding of how ideologies and values are manifested in local, state, and national politics is fundamental to macro change.

Locus of Involvement in Social Work Practice

Social work practice is broadly defined and allows for both micro (individual, domestic unit, or group) and macro interventions (organization, community, or policy). See Box 1.1. Social workers who undertake macro interventions

Box 1.1	Locus of Intervention
Locus	**Primary Focus of Intervention**
Micro	Individuals Domestic Unit Small Groups
Macro	Organizations Communities Policy

will often be engaged in what is called "policy practice" (Jansson, 2011) because policy change is so integral to what happens in organizations and communities. Given this division of labor, some professional roles require that the social worker be involved full time in macro practice. These professional roles are often referred to by such titles as planner, policy analyst, program coordinator, community organizer, manager, and administrator.

The micro service worker or clinical social worker also bears responsibility for initiating change in organizations and communities. Workers in micro-level roles are often the first to recognize patterns indicating the need for change. If one or two persons present a particular problem, a logical response is to deal with them as individuals. However, as more individuals present the same situation, it may become evident that something is awry in the systems with which these clients are interacting. The social worker must then assume the responsibility for identifying the system(s) in need of change and the type of change needed. The nature of the system(s) in need of change and the type of change needed may lead to communitywide intervention or intervention in a single organization.

Suppose, for example, the staff in a senior center discover that a number of elders in the community are, because of self-neglect, socially isolated and possibly malnourished. A caseworker could follow up on each person, one at a time, in an attempt to provide outreach and needed services. But this could take a long time and produce hit-or-miss results. An alternative would be to deal with the problem from a macro perspective—to invest time in organizing agency and community resources to identify older people who need the senior center's services and to ensure that services are provided through a combination of staff and volunteer efforts.

This may seem like a complex undertaking for someone who came into social work expecting to work with people one at a time. Although it is true that macro-level interventions can be complicated, we will attempt to provide a somewhat systematic approach that attempts to make such efforts more manageable. Remember, too, that these interventions are typically accomplished with the help of others, not alone.

A Systematic Approach to Macro Social Work Practice

Figure 1.1 illustrates an approach that can be used by social workers to identify, study, and analyze the need for change and to begin formulating solutions. Initial awareness that a problem exists may occur in a variety of ways. It might be brought to a social worker's attention by a client. A group of residents

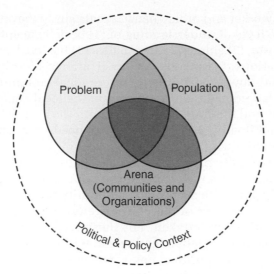

Figure 1.1

Macro Practice Conceptual Framework: Understanding Problem, Population, and Arena

within a neighborhood may present issues and concerns that need to be addressed. Issues in the workplace, such as the quality of service to clients, may surface and require organized intervention. Community problems may be so glaring that the need for change comes from many different directions. Regardless of how social workers identify change opportunities, they function in a political environment that cannot be ignored.

The three overlapping circles in Figure 1.1 illustrate the focal points of the social worker's efforts in undertaking a macro-level change episode. We will refer to these focal points as (1) problem, (2) population, and (3) arena.

Good social work practice requires understanding. To engage in macro practice to help a client who is addicted to alcohol, for example, the social worker must understand the problem (alcoholism), the background of the person addicted, the population (e.g., elderly, retired males), and the arena (community or organization) within which the problem occurs. Understanding communities and organizations adds a dimension of complexity to social work practice, but this understanding is a critical precursor to successful macro-level intervention.

In the course of developing an understanding of problem, population, and arena, the social worker will inevitably focus on the areas of overlap depicted in Figure 1.1. Continuing with the example of alcoholism among elderly, retired males, it would be important to review theory about how alcohol addiction develops, research reports from studies testing various interventions, and literature on the target population. As the change agent builds a body of knowledge about the problem and population, it becomes especially important to focus on the overlap between the two areas: alcoholism and its unique impact on elderly, retired males.

It is likewise important to understand how the phenomenon of alcoholism affects the local community (the overlap between problem and arena), and to what extent the needs of the population of elderly, retired males are understood and addressed in the local community (overlap between population and arena). Ultimately, in an episode of macro practice, the objective is to work toward an understanding of the area where all three circles overlap (alcoholism and its impact on elderly, retired males in a given neighborhood or town).

Policy Practice

Critical Thinking Question:
What are some strengths of micro practice that also help address complex problems in macro practice?

As the social worker and other change agents study the situation, they will gain at least some level of understanding of (1) basic concepts and issues surrounding alcoholism, (2) elderly, retired males, (3) the local community and/or relevant organizations, (4) alcoholism as it affects elderly, retired males, (5) alcoholism and how it is addressed in the local community, (6) how the needs of elderly, retired males are addressed in the local community, (7) available interventions and their applicability to both the population and community of interest, and finally, (8) the problem and needs of elderly, retired males in the local community who are addicted to alcohol.

Social and community problems and needs must also be addressed within a larger context that affects the problem, the population, and the community or organization. Dealing with social and community problems and needs effectively requires an awareness of the political environment within which the change episode will be undertaken. For these reasons, we have placed the three circles (problem, population, and arena) within a large dotted outer circle intended to depict the political environment. The importance of and the need for understanding the political and policy contexts within which macro-practice tasks take place cannot be overemphasized.

The Interrelationship of Micro and Macro Social Work Practice

Given the complexity of macro interventions, practitioners may begin to feel overwhelmed. Is it not enough to do good direct practice or clinical work? Is it not enough to listen to a client and offer options? Our answer is that professional practice focusing only on an individual's intrapsychic concerns does not fit the definition of social work. Being a social worker requires seeing the client as part of multiple, overlapping systems that comprise the person's social and physical environment. The profession of social work is committed to seeking social and economic justice in concert with vulnerable and underserved populations, and macro-practice skills are necessary in confronting these inequalities. For example, consider a woman reported for child neglect who lives in a run-down home with structural problems her landlord refuses to fix. A clinical intervention designed to strengthen her emotional coping skills might be useful, but that intervention alone would ignore the depth of the problem facing her. Social workers unwilling to engage in some macro-practice types of activities when the need arises are not practicing social work.

Similarly, social workers who carry out episodes of macro practice must understand what is involved in the provision of direct services to clients at the individual, domestic unit, or group level. Without this understanding, macro practice may occur without an adequate grounding in understanding client problems and needs. One example might be a social worker who conducts a community crime prevention campaign to combat high rates of petty theft in a neighborhood, unaware that most such acts are the work of a relatively small number of residents desperately in need of drug-abuse intervention. The interconnectedness of micro and macro roles is the heart of social work practice. In short, it is as important for social workers to understand the nature of individual and group interventions as it is to understand the nature of organizational, community, and policy change.

The interconnectedness of micro and macro roles is the heart of social work practice.

Because we believe that all social workers are professional change agents, we use the terms *social worker*, *professional*, and *change agent* interchangeably throughout this book. Social workers are always change agents because they are constantly identifying changes needed to make systems more responsive or sensitive to target populations. Indeed, change is so much a part of social work practice that one cannot separate the two. Other professionals may also see themselves as change agents, and it is important for the contemporary macro practitioner to collaborate and partner with those from other disciplines so that the knowledge of diverse fields can be used in planning effective change. *Professional* implies identification with a set of values that places the interests of the client first; a professional relies on knowledge, judgment, and skill to act on those values. Later in this chapter, we discuss the meaning of the professional values that unite social workers across roles, arenas, and areas of specialization.

THE FOUNDATION OF MACRO PRACTICE

Understanding the professional mission of social work that integrates micro and macro interventions and respects the practitioners who perform those roles is essential to recognizing why macro practice is important. Essentially, social workers have a mission to join the strengths of doing "both/and," being able to intervene with an individual service recipient and then skillfully moving into a larger system intervention that will make a difference in the lives of multiple individuals.

Similarly, the person-is-political perspective underscores the belief that individuals cannot be viewed separate from the larger society. The actions—or lack of actions—of individuals influence those around them and may have broad implications for others within an organization or a community. Thus, micro and macro roles are interconnected.

For those social workers committed to bringing about positive change not only for individual clients but for whole neighborhoods, organizations, and communities, the question becomes: How is it possible to meet all the expectations of a job and still be involved with larger issues?

In Chapters 3 through 11 of this book we will attempt to present the building blocks of a planned change model that makes it both possible and manageable to carry out episodes of change. Before we focus on a change model, it is necessary to develop a foundation for macro practice. That foundation is based on an understanding of the relevance of theories, models, and approaches; values and ethics; roles and expectations of a professional; and the historical roots of macro practice. In the remainder of this chapter we will introduce theories and models, values and ethical dilemmas, and professional identity. Chapter 2 will be devoted to a review of the history of macro practice in social work.

Theories, Models, and Approaches

Theories are sets of interrelated concepts and constructs that provide a framework for understanding how and why something does or does not work. *Models* are prescriptions based on theories that provide guidance and direction for the practitioner, whereas *approaches* are less prescribed. In other words, theories provide the tools for thinking about a problem or need, whereas models and approaches provide guidelines for action and intervention. In this book we develop a practice model of planned change that is fairly prescriptive and derives from systems theory. At the individual level, for example, theories provide explanations about the causes of various types of mental disorders, and practice models arising from these theories suggest ways of helping people affected by the disorders. On a larger scale, sociological theories may describe how communities, organizations, or societies function. A *practice model* for initiating change in communities and organizations (such as the planned change model presented in this book) illustrates how these theories can lead to specific actions.

One theory that seems to have considerable relevance at both the micro and macro levels is systems theory. Systems theory contends that there are multiple parts of any entity, whether it is a group, an organization, or a community. Entities can be best understood as systems with interconnecting components, and certain common principles help in understanding systems, whether they are as large as an international corporation or as small as a family. There are resources the system needs in order to function and they may come in the form of people, equipment, funding, knowledge, legitimacy, or a host of other forms. These resources interact within the system, producing something that becomes the system's product.

Consider a human service agency that targets gay and lesbian youth. The volunteers and staff, funding from various sources, teachers from local schools, concerned parents, and the youth themselves may all come together within this human service setting. Their relationships and interactions will determine whether the organization functions as a system or merely as a disparate assortment of parts. Functional systems have a dynamic interaction among components that holds them together. The interaction that holds this human service agency together may be the communication that occurs as teachers, parents, and youth come together; their bonding over an important cause; their shared commitment to the mission; and the desire to create a safer, more supportive environment for the youth. Systems expect conflict and have ways to cope when it occurs. For an agency dedicated to gay and lesbian youth, there will be strong community forces that do not agree with what the agency is doing, that seek to provide different interventions, and that even want to change the youth. Depending on the level of conflict, the system may have boundaries that are fairly rigid in order to protect itself from external forces. The product of this system would be youth who are better able to function in the larger environment and who have a sense of who they are.

Community researcher Roland Warren (1978) provided a good example of how systems theory can be applied to understanding communities. He built on the work of Talcott Parsons, a sociologist known for defining the characteristics of social systems. He also incorporated the work of others who described how community systems would differ from the groups and formal organizations to which systems theory had previously been applied.

Warren saw the community as not just one system but a system of systems in which all types of formal and informal groups and individuals interact. Given the diversity among groups and subgroups, communities have a broad range of structural and functional possibilities that do not conform to a centralized goal. The beauty of a community system is that it is a complex arena in which multiple groups and organizations with differing values may exist simultaneously.

Warren's contention that a system endures through time speaks to social work practitioners who work with groups committed to maintaining their communities and are grieving over the loss of what their communities used to be. For example, the physical land and the interactions that occurred on that land may render it sacred to Native American People. Similarly, an elderly widow who has lived on the same street corner for 60 years may hesitate to move even when increasing crime threatens her physical safety.

In an organizational arena, a systems approach reveals the complexity involved in recognizing multiple groups (e.g., professional staff, clerical staff, management, administration, board, clients, funding sources, neighbors, and others in the community) that have a stake in what that organization does and whom it serves. This theoretical perspective reminds the practitioner that organizations are complex systems embedded in larger community systems, all of which are interacting on a daily basis.

Warren also identifies the structure of internal and external patterns, which he labels *vertical* and *horizontal community linkages*. Vertical linkages connect community units (people, groups, organizations) to units outside the community. These linkages are exemplified by a human service agency with its headquarters in a different community that uses Skype to see its members face-to-face, by local chapters virtually connected through shared information systems with state and national umbrella organizations, and by public agencies having a central office external to the community from which they receive instruction. The concept of *vertical community* calls attention to the fact that many important decisions may be made by parent organizations outside the boundaries of the local community, and these decisions may or may not be in the best interests of the community. The *horizontal community* is geographically bounded and is represented by many linkages between and among organizations and neighborhoods that are located within the area, and, in most cases, serve the community. For example, the local nursing home may work with the neighborhood school to develop an intergenerational program for residents and children. This effort may also include a local bookstore that provides children's books, a bus driver who provides transportation, and a staff member from the local multigenerational center. These types of collaborative efforts, which are becoming increasingly common, illustrate the importance of the horizontal community as a concept. By distinguishing between types of relationships, Warren acknowledged the complex array of possible relationships within the community and with the larger society.

Boundary maintenance is also part of systems theory. Establishing boundaries is critical to system survival. If boundaries become blurred or indistinguishable, the community as a spatial set of relationships or the organization as a distinct entity may become less viable. For example, as congregations in local communities contract with government agencies to provide services to persons in need, the boundaries between what is an agency and a ministry may blur. Moreover, boundaries between long-established, faith-related, nonprofit organizations and congregations within the same faith may begin to overlap in unanticipated ways. Macro practitioners will witness the struggle for boundary maintenance in their work with communities and organizations. For instance, residents in a neighborhood that has just altered school attendance boundaries may face major changes in how they view their community. The annexation of previously unincorporated areas into the city limits may bring protesters to city hall. The reconfiguration of a planning and service area that alters agency's boundaries may mean that clients formerly considered part of one's community will no longer be eligible for service.

Thus, systems theory recognizes the importance of formal groups and organizations. For example, in dealing with child maltreatment, child protective service workers, law-enforcement officers, hospital emergency staff, teachers, public prosecutors, and others combine their efforts within a horizontal community to ensure that vulnerable children receive the highest levels of protection possible. However, it is equally important to recognize and acknowledge "informal linkages." For example, the social support that a female caregiver of an aged parent receives from other caregivers may not be formalized or highly visible in the community. Yet this linkage is vital to whether caregivers will be able to continue the caregiving role. Therefore, systems thinking is value-based thinking; what is selected for consideration will determine what is considered important. Because communities are complex, thinking of them as social systems involves balancing a number of variables that are in dynamic interaction.

Systems theory provides a set of assumptions that guide the planned change model in this book. It is important to note that there are multiple approaches to systems theory, some more open to change than others. We assume that social workers will encounter systems of every kind. Some organizations and communities will be more amenable to change than others, some will be more closed, and others will be more open to conflict. Being able to assess these arenas and their openness to change is central to the planned change process.

Underlying the planned change process is recognition of the values and ethical dilemmas that occur in macro practice. We now turn to those.

Values and Ethical Dilemmas

Values, which we define as those norms and principles that many or most members of a social system perceive to be important, are fundamental to social work practice. In some ways, values are similar to theories—they provide a framework for understanding and analyzing situations. Ethics are similar to models—they provide guidelines for practice. One can feel strongly about something, but acting on that feeling involves ethical behavior, which is the operationalization of that value.

Because codes of ethics serve as guidelines for professional practice, it is imperative that students know the content and limitations of written codes. For example, principle values in the National Association of Social Workers (NASW) Code of Ethics include service, social justice, dignity and worth of the person, importance of human relationships, integrity, and competence. The NASW Code of Ethics is intended to introduce a perspective that drives practitioners' thinking, establishes criteria for selecting goals, and influences how information is interpreted and understood. Regardless of which role the social worker plays—program coordinator, community organizer, political lobbyist, or direct practitioner—these professional actions are not value free.

Social work practice often presents *ethical dilemmas*, which can be defined as situations that necessitate a choice between competing but equally important values. For example, a social worker who values a child's right to a safe and secure environment must also value the parents' rights to have a say in their child's future. The public housing administrator who values the freedom of a disruptive resident to play loud music at top volume must also respect those in the building who value peace and quiet. Dilemmas are inherent in both situations. A choice between equally important values may have to be made when there are no easy or obviously "right or wrong" solutions.

Reamer (1995) notes that although social workers' views of values and ethics have matured, it would have been difficult in the profession's early years to predict the types of dilemmas contemporary society poses. For example, practitioners may deal with clients who are child molesters, spouse abusers, drug dealers who sell to children, people who commit hate crimes, and a host of other persons who act on values antithetical to those of the profession. Fortunately, the field of professional and applied ethics in social work emerged during the 1970s, and today there is energetic dialogue and a growing literature addressing the complex values issues that arise in social work practice (Reamer, 1995, 1998).

The NASW Code of Ethics lists six core values on which the ethical principles of social work are based: service, social justice, dignity and worth of the person, importance of human relationships, integrity, and competence. Realizing that many values have relevance to macro practice, we focus on the six from the NASW Code to illustrate ethical dilemmas that social workers face.

Service

Social workers are often simultaneously engaged in both direct and indirect practice, actions intended to help people in need and to address the social problems they face. Closely related to service is the concept of beneficence, which is based on the desire to do good for others, as well as not doing harm. Persons entering the field of social work will often say that they want to help others. This value is typically a primary motivator for those professionals who work in health and human service settings, reflecting their desire to find ways to serve others in making life more meaningful.

Beneficence requires that the professional view clients holistically. Jansson (2011) uses examples of a physician who treats a woman's presenting medical problem but does not consider her inability to afford a healthy diet, or a reputable attorney who assists with a divorce but does not consider the financial implications for the divorcee. Beneficence requires that the physician recognizes the woman's broader needs and refers her to a food bank or Meals on Wheels program, or that the attorney refer the client to a financial counselor.

Thus, beneficence means that all professionals must consider a client's multiple needs. This is particularly important for social workers, who are expected to bring a person-in-environment perspective to all their service interactions with clients. If social workers fail to perceive clients' broader needs, they have neglected the principle of beneficence and the call to be of service.

Social Justice

Ideally, social justice is achieved when there is a fair distribution of society's resources and benefits so that every individual receives a deserved portion. Social work is in the business of distributing and redistributing resources, whether they are as tangible as money and jobs or as intangible as self-efficacy or a sense of self-worth. Underlying the distribution of resources in society are value considerations that influence the enactment of laws, the enforcement of regulations, and the frameworks used in making policy decisions. Jansson (2011) points out that social justice is based on equality. With the many entrenched interests one encounters in local communities, it is likely that social workers will focus their efforts on oppressed target population groups and will always be discovering new inequalities. Since so many groups face problems related to having enough financial resources, social workers often extend the principle to include economic justice, often focusing on social and economic justice concerns.

Concerns about social and economic justice are exacerbated when clients cannot pay for services. As long as clients can pay, professional decision making may not conflict with the larger society because resources do not have to

Human Rights & Justice

Critical Thinking Question: Can you address issues of social justice and inequality without engaging in macro practice? Why or why not?

be redistributed. Conceivably, as long as clients can pay for professional services, professions can operate within the market economy. Private practice and
fee-for-service agencies conform to this approach. Quality care is exchanged
for economic resources, often in the form of third-party payments. The key to
this approach is that the client has insurance coverage or access to sufficient
personal funds.

This approach breaks down, however, when clients cannot pay. Many
social work clients are in problematic circumstances because their income is
inadequate to meet their needs and other resources are not available. Patients
with AIDS may find themselves unable to pay for care at the same time that
their needs increase because they are fired from jobs when news about their
disease becomes known. An older woman could avoid institutional care by
hiring an in-home caregiver, but despite having considerable lifetime savings,
medical expenses from her husband's terminal illness have left her with too
few funds to meet her own needs. A youth who has grown up in poverty
knows exactly what it means when the model breaks down. For that youth, a
broken model has been a way of life, and she or he has no reason to strive for a
better standard of living.

Health and human service systems are driven by considerations of
whether resources are available to pay for (or subsidize) the services clients
need. If resources are not available, the patient with AIDS and the older
woman may be forced to expend all their own resources before ending up in
public institutions, and the youth may continue in a cycle of insufficient education, housing, health care, and job opportunities. In this resource-driven
system, social workers may have difficulty maintaining a vision of the compassionate community in which mutual support is provided to all those in
need. These dilemmas face social workers because the profession is enmeshed
in issues of redistribution.

Dignity and Worth of the Person

Often called self-determination or autonomy, valuing the dignity and worth of
each person means respecting and honoring the right of that person to make
his or her own life choices. Concepts such as empowerment are built on the
value of dignity and worth, implying that power or control over one's life means
seizing the opportunity to make one's own decisions. As an example, the
pro-choice proponents in the abortion controversy advocate for autonomy, a
woman's right to choose. This stance conflicts with a number of religious
codes arguing the immorality of abortion and stating that the right of the
unborn child must be considered as well. Although autonomy may be perceived as individualistic and therefore more relevant to direct practice situations, one has only to be involved in the heated debate over abortion to realize
the ethical dilemma involved in situations where the autonomy of both parties
cannot be equally respected.

Importance of Human Relationships

Although it may be more time consuming and take more energy to include
clients in change processes, the NASW Code of Ethics is a reminder that the
dignity and worth of the person and the importance of human relationships
are core social work values. This means continually finding new and meaningful ways to facilitate consumer as well as citizen participation in organizational and community arenas. Nurturing relationships is an ongoing and
necessary challenge for the dedicated professional.

In macro-change opportunities the challenge is to include multiple stake-holders who may be both consumers and collaborators in the process. This challenge is grounded in the importance of human relationships, even when people do not agree. Technological advances help facilitate communication, particularly in mobilizing clients and providers to work toward a cause. Knowing how to engage clients and others in one's change efforts is critically important, and drawing from the evidence-based intervention literature is expected of the macro practitioner (see, e.g., Itzhaky & Bustin, 2005) so that useful strategies are identified to engage multiple constituencies in change opportunities. In addition, community information systems (CINS) are increasingly important tools for engaging others in training, evaluation, and efforts in interorganizational and community arenas (see, e.g., Hillier, Wernecke, & McKelvey, 2005). As new technological venues emerge, it will be necessary for the practitioner to keep up-to-date so that these tools can be used to communicate with and sustain the central importance of strong relationships with various constituencies.

Integrity

Integrity is based on trustworthiness. This principle implies that one's associates (e.g., colleagues, clients, and community groups) should be able to expect consistency in one's thinking and acting. Integrity gets to the character of the person. Professional integrity means that those persons who call themselves professionals will remember that the center of their practice is always the client. Social work is only one of many helping professions, but its unique contribution is to serve as a constant reminder that people are multidimensional and that they must be viewed in the context of their environments.

Professional integrity means that those persons who call themselves professionals will remember that the center of their practice is always the client.

In professional practice, integrity means that one does not simply do what one would like to do, but fits problems to solutions based on thorough analysis. Defining the problem to be changed requires integrating what clients have to say with what is known from scholarly research and practice results. This analytical process is dynamic and interactive, often causing the change agent to reframe the original problem statement. The process is also iterative, meaning that new information constantly requires rethinking. However, once the problem statement is agreed on, social workers must ascertain that their interventions have integrity in relation to the problem at hand. Interventions often require a creative imagination that goes beyond traditional approaches and that seek more fundamental change. Thus, it is hoped that the social worker will be imaginative, will think critically, and will use his or her best judgment as a professional in the process of planned change.

Competence

Professional social workers are expected to be informed and the macro practitioner will approach the need for change with an understanding and expectation that decisions will be based on as complete a set of data and information as time and resources allow. We recognize that there are multiple ways to regard systems, and it is important to carefully assess each arena in which social workers plan to carry out an episode of change. Competence implies that informed decision making is pursued in a systematic and scholarly manner, utilizing the best available theoretical, research-based, and practice-based knowledge. This approach, sometimes called Evidence-Based Practice (EBP), "requires an adequate knowledge base about the efficacy of interventions for selected client populations and problems" (Jenson, 2005, p. 132). The approach applies to whatever level of intervention the practitioner is addressing, whether individual, group, organization, or community.

In addition, systems theory that informs the planned changed model implies that there will be goals and outcomes, both of which are important steps in the planned change process. Our model of planned change assumes that there will be broadly defined goals to guide practitioners' efforts. Goals are usually long term and sometimes idealistic. However, goals provide a vision shared by clients and colleagues—a hope of what can be—and they assist the practitioner in maintaining a focus. The identification of these goals should be based on the best knowledge available.

From goals, we assume there will be outcomes defined as quality-of-life changes in clients' lives, based on the interventions planned by practitioners. Much of the history of social work practice has been focused on process— what the social worker does. Interventions of the future will be driven by outcomes—what change is expected to be achieved by and for the target population as a result of this change effort. Balancing the importance of process and the push for accountability through outcome measurement is part of competent, contemporary practice. It is also key to planned change intervention. Together, goals and outcomes are based on the best available evidence, guided by as complete as possible an understanding of the systems in which change will occur.

During the socialization process of preparing for professional social work practice, each person will have to determine how her or his personal values relate to the professional values being learned. Integrating one's personal and professional values is a part of professional identification, and leads to what Sullivan (2005) and others say about professions as communities of identity in which colleagues come together to work toward the civic good. Embracing that identity and approaching one's practice with integrity and competence will contribute to one's ability to join with others in pursuing the values of the profession.

Balancing the values of services, social justice, dignity and worth of the person, importance of human relationships, integrity, and competence demands an analytical approach to decision making and intervention. Inevitably, the macro practitioner will face ethical dilemmas that go beyond the bounds of the Code of Ethics. This requires that he or she have a strong professional identity. We now turn to three case examples that illustrate the dilemmas often encountered by social work practitioners.

THREE CASE EXAMPLES

Some of the aspects of social work macro practice that need to be understood by the student and the beginning practitioner can be illustrated by case examples. We selected the following examples because they contain similar themes but focus on different target population groups: children, elders and disabled persons, and persons who are homeless. As these cases and the workers' thoughts are presented, we encourage the reader to think about how macro-level change might be approached by beginning with a study of the *problem*, the *population*, and the *arena* within which change might take place. We also hope that these examples will illustrate both the systemic nature of social work macro practice and the types of value dilemmas confronting social workers.

Case Example 1   Child Protective Services

Child protective services (CPS) workers have responsibility for dealing with the abuse and neglect of children. When reports of alleged abuse or neglect come to the unit, the CPS worker is responsible for investigating the report and making decisions about the disposition of the case. It is a very demanding and emotionally draining area of specialization within the field of social work. One CPS worker several years ago took the time to record the details of a particular case, and also shared with us a list of dilemmas and contradictions he had encountered over the years, in the interest of helping new workers prepare for what they will face as they enter practice.

Friday, 10:40 A.M. Supervisor text messaged me about a report of neglect. She felt it should be checked out today because it sounded too serious to be left until after the weekend (as agency rules allow with some neglect allegations). According to the neighbor's report, parents have abandoned three minor children.

11:10 A.M. Got in my car and headed for the address on the intake form. I know the neighborhood well. It is the poorest in the city and unsafe at night. A high percentage of families receive some kind of assistance. Homes are run down, streets are littered, and any sense of pride in the community has long been abandoned.

11:40 A.M. The house at the address given is among the most run down in a seriously deteriorating neighborhood. The house has no front steps—just a cinder block placed in front of the door. Window casings are rotting out for lack of paint. There is no doorbell. I knocked. There was rustling inside, but no answer. I waited and knocked again. I walked around and peered through a window and saw a small child, about 3 years old I guessed, curled up in a chair. An older girl, about age 8 or 9, peeked out from behind a doorway.

I remembered that the oldest child was named Cindy, so I called out to her. After a bit of conversation I persuaded her to let me in. I quickly recognized that this would not be an ordinary case. A foul smell hit me so hard it made my eyes water. I used a tissue to filter the air. The worst odors were coming from the bathroom and kitchen. The water had evidently been shut off—toilets were not working and garbage was piled up. The kitchen was littered with fast-food containers, possibly retrieved from the dumpsters of nearby shops.

There were three very frightened children—Cindy (age 9), Scott (age 6), and Melissa (age 3). None would talk.

12:35 P.M. I made arrangements to transport them to the shelter and went back to the office to do the paperwork.

2:15 P.M. A previous neglect report revealed the following:

Father: Stan, age 27, unemployed, in and out of jail for petty theft, public intoxication, and several other minor offenses. Frequently slept in public parks or homeless shelters. Rarely showed up at home any more. Several police reports of violence against wife and children. Admits paternity for only the oldest child.

Mother: Sarah, age 25. Temporary Aid to Needy Families (TANF) recipient, high school dropout, never employed. Tests performed in connection with one attempt at job training revealed borderline retardation. Child care skills have always been minimal, but there is no previous history of abandonment of children. Whereabouts at this time are unknown.

3:35 P.M. Filed the appropriate forms with agency and the police. Entered field notes into laptop for the record. Children placed at Vista Shelter until a more permanent placement can be arranged. Emailed confirmation of placement to supervisor, copied to shelter staff.

Over the years, as this CPS worker dealt with similar cases, he kept a running list of the kinds of dilemmas, frustrations, and contradictions he and his colleagues regularly faced. These are excerpts from his list:

1. Abused and neglected children are the saddest victims of all. They brought nothing on themselves, yet their chances of success are extremely limited. Success, to a large extent, correlates with a child's ability to perform in school. A child's performance will be hindered by moving from shelter to foster home to home, changing schools, missing many days, lacking consistent parental support and help, having inadequate clothing and diet, lacking in self-esteem, and other barriers. We can predict failure, but we can't seem to do anything to change it. Could a macro-level preventive effort be launched that focuses on success for these children?

2. A disproportionately high percentage of lower socioeconomic status teens get pregnant and drop out of high school, go on welfare, parent poorly, and recycle many of their problems to the next generation. How can we interrupt this pattern? Current programs seem to focus primarily on survival in terms of shelter, food, clothing, and medical care, but do not change the behavior patterns. Can we develop a program to help young women make informed decisions during this highly vulnerable time in their lives and find ways to evaluate whether it works?

3. Lots of people in this wealthy country are worse off than lots of animals in this country. There ought to be minimum standards for food, clothing, housing, and medical care below which no one should be allowed to fall. Governments at all levels claim lack of resources and legislators seem bent on blaming the victims, when it is clearly a matter of priorities. Could we focus attention on this issue by organizing a panel of experts to establish these types of standards for our community and give them maximum publicity?

4. The corporate sector has reaped enormous benefits from our economic system. Gross national product continues to grow and many corporations are moving from a national to an international market. As a sort of a "return" or "payback" for their success, the corporate sector donates a few dollars to charitable organizations. Rarely do they get involved directly in the habilitation or rehabilitation of human beings, even though they control the means to self-sufficiency and success. If all employable people were somehow tied to a job with benefits, the need for income assistance and human services would be greatly reduced. Perhaps a few community-minded business owners would be willing to experiment with "adopting" families by providing employment, training, and scholarships.

5. Bureaucracy has a tendency to become an end in itself. Its manuals become a way of life for many of its employees. People in severe emotional pain bring their needs to our agency and we look up an answer in the manual and quote it to them. Worse yet, we send them to a website to access this information when they don't even have access to a computer. Sometimes all they want is to make contact with a human being, and they are unable to do so in our agency. Can we change this agency to make it more responsive to those it serves even though it is a large bureaucratic organization?

Case Example 2   Case Management with Elderly and Disabled Persons

Case managers work in a variety of public and private settings. They are responsible for screening potential clients, assessing client needs, developing care plans, mobilizing resources to meet identified needs, and monitoring and evaluating services provided. The case manager in this example works for a nonprofit agency in an inner-city neighborhood, where many of her clients have lived all their lives. She is assigned to the home and community-based long-term care unit, and carries a caseload of about 60 elderly and disabled clients. As part of the program evaluation, she was asked to keep a diary of what happened during a typical day. The following are excerpts from her diary.

Wednesday, 7:30 A.M. Arrived early to catch up on email and enter client data from previous day. Organized documents from eight cases, including two new care plans and five medical reports.

8:00–8:10 A.M. Mrs. Garcia, a 79-year-old woman, called. She was distraught over a letter received from the Social Security office, thinking it meant her benefits would be cut off. Explained that it was a form letter, indicating a routine change, not affecting the amount of her check. Knowing that she is often forgetful and has a hearing problem, made a note to make home visit tomorrow to be certain she understands what was said.

8:10–8:30 A.M. Met with Jim from In-Home Support Services. Mr. Thomas, a 93-year-old man, had fallen last night and was in Mercy Hospital. Homemaker had found him when she arrived at 7:00 this morning. He is not expected to live. Homemaker is very upset. Called his daughter and will plan to meet her at hospital later this morning.

8:30–9:30 A.M. Staff meeting regarding 10 clients discharged from City Hospital with inadequate discharge plans. Discussed how to work better with discharge planners from hospital because this situation continues to be a problem. As I left meeting, another case manager told me that my client, Mrs. Hannibal, had refused to let the home health nurse into her apartment.

9:30–9:45 A.M. Called Mrs. Hannibal, no answer. Called the lifeline program to meet me at her apartment.

9:45–10:00 A.M. Drove to Mrs. Hannibal's apartment. No one answered my knock, so got manager to let me in. Mrs. Hannibal had been drinking and was acting paranoid. Threw bottle at me and screamed, "No one is going to get me out of here. I'll never go to a home. I'll die first." Worked with lifeline staff to get Mrs. Hannibal calmed down. She is a 67-year-old widow. She goes in and out of the hospital every two months. Has a severe drinking problem.

10:00–11:00 A.M. Arrived at Mercy Hospital. Met Mr. Thomas's daughter. She was in tears, saying it was all her fault, that if he had been living with her this would have never happened. Talked with her regarding her father's desire to live alone, that this had been his choice. Contacted hospital social worker to work with daughter.

11:15 A.M.–12:00 P.M. Back to office. Entered notes on visits to Mrs. Hannibal and Mr. Thomas into computer. Called two new referrals, faxed documents to hospital, and set up appointments to do assessments tomorrow. Received call from Ms. Roman, age 83. She is lonely and wondered when I would be seeing her. Her partner of 40 years died last week and she is crying. Has no family. Assured her I would come see her on Friday.

12:00–12:30 P.M. Ate lunch with Adult Protective Services (APS) worker. Discussed abusive relationship of Mr. and Mrs. Tan, a couple in their 60s living in public housing. Agreed to work closely with APS regarding this situation.

12:45–2:00 P.M. Conducted in-home assessment for new client, Ms. Johnson. She was released from the hospital yesterday and is receiving home-delivered meals and

(Continued)

in-home nursing. Small house is a mess, roaches everywhere. Needs chore and housekeeping services, but there's a long waiting list. Called and cajoled volunteers at senior center to help her temporarily. Ms. Johnson was too weak to complete full assessment, will come back tomorrow.

2:30–3:30 P.M. Attended public hearing preceding the planning process for the Area Agency on Aging. Presented written and verbal documentation of problems in working with my caseload. Discussed the need for more flexibility in providing services to disabled clients under age 60. Gave examples of three clients on caseload who are in their 40s and have severe mobility problems.

3:45–4:15 P.M. Stopped by Sunnyside Nursing Home to see Mrs. Martinez. Has been my client for five years and was just admitted to Sunnyside. Doesn't know me and seems confused. Checked with facility social worker regarding what medications she is on and agreed to call physician regarding potential drug interactions. Made note to check with local long-term care ombudsman about any complaints against this facility. Also made mental note to check on Mrs. M's disabled daughter who is still in the home and will need supportive services previously provided by her mother.

4:45–5:15 P.M. Returned to office, found out Mr. Thomas had died. Called his daughter. Tried to call physician about Mrs. Martinez's medications but his nurse would not reveal any information to me because of the privacy act. I could tell she was angry that I would even suggest a medication interaction given my nonmedical background. Received call from home health aide referring client to us. Had to tell her that client did not qualify for our services, but referred her to a for-profit agency in town. Returned a call about assistive technology that might help several clients with disabilities.

5:15–5:30 P.M. Tried to clean up desk and catch a few emails. Decided to stop by and check on Mrs. Garcia on my way home.

Just as the CPS worker had kept a running list of the kinds of dilemmas he faced through the years, the case manager had kept a list of her dilemmas as well. In preparation for the Area Agency on Aging public hearing, she had updated the list in hopes something could be done to address her ongoing frustrations, particularly about persons with disabilities who were not yet 60 years old. Excerpts from her list follow:

1. So many of the older people I see have had problems all their lives. You can almost tell what's going to happen in their old age by what happens to them as they go through life. Drug and alcohol problems only seem to get worse. If someone had intervened when they began having these problems it would have been much easier, because the behavior patterns are set by the time I encounter them. I know people can change at any age, but it seems harder when one is under stress or facing hard times. Is there some way we could organize a prevention effort to prepare middle-aged people for their senior years?

2. Although some of our resources can be used to serve any older person in need, most of our funding is tied to income eligibility. Slots for people who aren't destitute are quickly filled and there is a long waiting list. So clients above the income eligibility level are referred to for-profit agencies or to other nonprofits that have sliding fee scales. The irony is that the ones who have set a little money aside are usually the same ones who get left out in the cold. These "notch group" clients can't afford to pay the full cost of services but fall just above our eligibility guidelines. It seems

that in our society if you aren't really poor or really rich, you had better hope your health holds out or you'll have nowhere to turn. Couldn't we organize this group to help each other and advocate for their own needs?

3. I'm concerned about our younger clients who have disabilities. So many of the places that claim to have the best interests of these clients at heart are not complying with the Americans with Disabilities Act. Water fountains aren't accessible, elevators are out of order, and ramps are poorly lit at night. I'm constantly reminding people who should know better that these policies are important. The problems caused by noncompliance are very demoralizing to our clients.

4. Working with Ms. Roman has reminded me how insensitive people are when partners die. I know there is new research on same-sex caregiving and resources on lesbian, gay, bisexual, and transgendered persons, but I haven't had time to fully explore these areas. I just know that when Ms. Roman went to the hospital to see her partner before she died last week, she was not treated as a family member and that her relationship was not respected as it should have been. What do I need to know in order to be more sensitive to diverse caregiving situations? How can I better advocate for my clients who are discriminated against in large systems?

5. I'm learning some revealing things about case management. Case managers attempt to coordinate what is really a nonsystem of services. If we had a real system we wouldn't need to pay people like me and we could put those resources toward client services. Even our professional organizations have bought into it. The National Association of Social Workers and the National Council on Aging have developed guidelines and standards for case management. There is even a credentialing movement for case management. We are investing a lot in institutionalizing case management when it often just covers up the real problem—that we don't have an accessible service delivery system in place. Until we get agencies in this community to collaborate in establishing a coordinated and accessible system of services, case management efforts will be of limited use. How can I work toward a more integrated system of care?

6. How does one maintain a client-centered perspective in a cost-obsessive environment? Working closely with health-care organizations has shown me the contrasts between the ideal and the reality of managed care. Ideally, managed care is supposed to view clients as whole people, recognizing that their psychosocial as well as medical needs must be addressed. In reality, many people view managed care simply as a mechanism for containing costs. As a case manager in a managed care environment, it's really hard to explain to higher-ups that case management can be intensive and long term and that it requires balancing advocacy and gatekeeping roles. How can I show administrators the effect that cost decisions have on clients' lives? What kind of documentation can I keep so that decision makers will benefit from what I know about my clients and so that I can adequately advocate for them?

7. Old people are not a homogeneous group. There are vulnerable subpopulations that get lost when one talks about "the aged." Most clients in my caseload are women who live alone and are often members of oppressed groups. Because many have been oppressed all their lives, they are practically "invisible" now. How do we familiarize policymakers with the unique needs of these clients? How do we persuade them to even care?

Case Example 3   Chronic Homelessness

A social worker was hired by a local nonprofit organization to coordinate the future efforts of key community stakeholders who had been meeting for over a year discussing the problem of chronic homelessness. The stakeholders were originally a part of a state policy academy sponsored by the U.S. Department of Health and Human Services to address the problems associated with homelessness. The policy academies were offered in several states and educated the stakeholders on different facets of homelessness and its potential solutions. The group from the social worker's state had participated in a policy academy on chronic homelessness, or long-term homelessness among individuals with disabilities. In the process, the group had decided to address the problem in a pilot community in the state. Members of the larger stakeholder group had become a steering committee for the pilot project.

The social worker was responsible for developing a *housing first* pilot project in the community. Housing first is an innovation in homeless services that differs from the traditional *treatment first* model. Housing first models assume that homeless individuals need the stability of permanent housing to succeed in services. Treatment first models assume that homeless individuals need services to become ready for housing. Participants in the policy academy had heard compelling evidence that housing first was a promising practice that was reducing chronic homelessness and the costs associated with chronic homelessness in several cities across the country. They had decided to focus their pilot efforts on chronic homelessness among individuals with a severe and persistent mental illness. After creating a steering committee and identifying a nonprofit to house the pilot program, the steering committee identified the social worker as the coordinator for the effort. Excerpts from the social worker's field notes follow.

Tuesday, 7:30 A.M. Arrived at the monthly board meeting of Metropolitan Supportive Housing Corporation (MSHC). The executive director of MSHC had been a member of the state policy academy and was now a member of the housing first steering committee. He had suggested that his organization would be willing to host the community's pilot program to address chronic homelessness. Last month, the board voted to administer the pilot program. In this month's meeting, I was introduced as the coordinator of that effort. I also updated the board on the status of the project since I started three weeks ago. I had spent much of that time reviewing the information that the policy academy members had received and meeting with steering committee members to discuss their goals for the project. I had also spent a significant portion of my first three weeks gathering information from the professional knowledge base on the problem of chronic homelessness and its potential solutions. The board seemed to appreciate my thoroughness, but I could tell that the executive director was ready to move toward action.

8:30–9:00 A.M. Went to my office to check my email and return phone calls. Set up two meetings with case managers at a local clinic for homeless individuals. I want to see how the service providers understand the problems faced by homeless adults experiencing serious mental illness. I also want to begin to better identify the strengths of the population—I've noticed that much of our conversations about these homeless adults are about their challenges, not about their resilience and strengths. Meeting with a variety of service providers will also help me gauge the support that direct service providers have for creating a housing first model in the community.

9:00–9:30 A.M. Prepared for three meetings scheduled for the day. Made copies of the handouts I had prepared yesterday for my lunch meeting with mental health service providers. The handouts detail the service models that are used for a variety of supportive housing programs around the country for homeless individuals with severe and persistent mental illness. Also put the finishing touches on a presentation for the

Chamber of Commerce foundation later today. Finished the registration paperwork for an upcoming conference on mental health recovery.

10:00–11:30 A.M. Met with the housing subcommittee of the original policy academy group. The committee included a commercial real estate agent, an architect, a general contractor, and housing staff from MSHC. The group reported on two older motels on a major bus route that could potentially be converted into efficiency apartments for chronically homeless individuals. Unfortunately, the owners of the two properties were unwilling to sell the properties at anything close to the price required by our budget. The subcommittee has now looked at 12 motels and believes that it is currently not feasible to utilize an existing motel for the pilot project. The group also questions the feasibility of constructing a new facility when the local government is already supporting two special needs housing projects, one of which is being constructed by MSHC. Because of financial commitments to these projects for the next two years, it will be difficult to obtain support for a new project any time soon. In addition, both of these projects struggled to get buy-in from their neighborhoods. All of the committee members express significant skepticism that this project can go forward as initially conceptualized. They recommend that the steering committee consider another housing model or postpone the project until the two other projects are completed.

11:30 A.M.–12:00 P.M. Drove to my next meeting thinking about the implications of the housing committee's recommendation. Would the political will to create this project end if the original model was not financially viable in this community? I'm concerned that if we postpone the project, we will lose political will to move forward. After all, this isn't a particularly popular population to serve—people often assume that these people are homeless because of bad choices and a refusal to address their addictions to alcohol and drugs. Made a note to myself to revisit the information about other housing first models that were introduced at the policy academy and to examine the professional knowledge base for alternatives to the original model the steering committee had proposed.

12:00–1:30 P.M. Arrived at a local diner for a lunch meeting with two local mental health service administrators, one of whom was a part of the original policy academy. The providers were concerned about the housing first model that the steering committee had chosen. The providers were particularly concerned about the low barrier, harm reduction philosophy of the program. How could we help these people if they weren't required to participate in services, quit using substances, and take the medication that would help them recover? How could we justify serving people who weren't willing to follow the rules while so many people were in need and willing to meet eligibility requirements? I listened to the administrators' concerns and assured them that I would relate them to the steering committee. I also discussed the success these models had achieved—success that surpassed traditional means of serving the population. I left the meeting wondering if this pilot project was doomed to fail.

2:00–3:30 P.M. Returned to the office to review information on other housing first models. Both the academic and practice literature suggested the effectiveness of a scattered site housing first model that had been successful in large urban areas for almost 10 years. Perhaps a scattered site model that used existing apartments could work if we could not locate a single site for a housing first residence. Created a table of the various models that included the location of the model, a description of the housing component, a description of the services component, and outcome measures or other evidence that suggested the model's success. Left a voicemail message for the executive director of a particularly successful scattered site model regarding his availability to do an educational event for members of the policy academy and the cost of

(Continued)

providing technical assistance. The table and the executive director's information will be a part of my presentation to the steering committee at next week's meeting.

4:00–5:00 P.M. Arrived at the offices of the Chamber of Commerce with the executive director of MSHC. The foundation director had heard about the pilot project and wanted to discuss the problem of chronic street homelessness from a business perspective and the possibility of supporting the pilot with a small seed grant. I had prepared a brief presentation that talked about the problem of chronic homelessness, the scope of the problem in the city, and the success of the proposed pilot in other cities. The foundation director relayed the concern of Chamber members who were concerned that visible street homelessness frightened potential customers. The executive director of MSHC noted that while that is a common perspective, homeless individuals are more likely to be victims of crime than to commit crime. Regardless, street homelessness will continue to be a problem until permanent housing solutions provide homeless individuals an alternative to the streets. The foundation director's body language suggested that he was pleased with the presentation and potential solution to visible street homelessness. He thanked us for coming and encouraged me to submit a letter of intent in their next funding cycle.

5:30 P.M. I drove home thinking of the day's events. On one hand, today's news was depressing. It seems like there are too many barriers to implement the steering committee's original model choice. On the other hand, there are other options and some support for the project from a high profile business organization. Tomorrow I will do additional research on scattered site housing first models and redevelop a budget to guide our discussion at next week's steering committee meeting.

The dilemmas experienced by this social worker are somewhat different from the previous two case examples. This professional was hired to coordinate a project that had been initially developed by a coalition of community stakeholders. Her direct practice background gave her considerable insight in understanding mental health and homelessness issues, yet her role as a coordinator of this community effort required a great deal of reflection. She outlined a number of questions and concerns.

1. This project has the initial support of a rather diverse group of key stakeholders from the homeless services sector, the mental health services sector, various offices of local and state government, the local hospital systems, and local law enforcement. How do I keep stakeholders involved and excited about this pilot project, particularly as we work through significant challenges? What level of detail should I provide the steering committee? To the original members of the state policy academy?

2. I have noticed that while we have representation from a variety of government and community organizations, we do not have representation from homeless individuals who have experienced serious mental illness. A central tenet of several of the housing first models for this population is that with support, people can recover from mental illness. If we are proposing a program that assumes recovery is possible, we should have meaningful representation from individuals who are in recovery and who have experienced some aspect of the problem we are addressing. How do we meaningfully include representatives in our decision-making and governance? How do I address those who are concerned about the ability of individuals with a serious mental illness to participate in the planning process?

3. In the three weeks I have worked for MSHC, I've noted a significant undercurrent of opposition to the housing first program model. At this point, I believe the opposition is around two philosophical tenets of the model—the belief that housing is a right and the emphasis on voluntary participation in services. Some stakeholders who attended the policy academy contend that housing as a "right" is too strong a political statement that the public will not support. Likewise, some stakeholders suggest that it might be irresponsible to use a harm reduction method regardless of the success of the model in other cities. "That philosophy won't sell here," they say. "We'll never get funders and the public behind a model that doesn't build in more accountability." The evidence of the model's success is overwhelming to me and the model is aligned with my professional values as a social worker. How do I address stakeholder concerns while preserving key components of the successful housing first models? How do I constructively manage this tension among stakeholders.

4. I am an employee of the MSHC, yet I am carrying out the objectives of the Housing First Steering Committee that is comprised of members from a larger state policy academy. I'm not always sure which organization or supervisor I work for. How do I define my role and the roles of others in this community effort? How do I ensure that MSHC is not the sole organization involved in this effort and that it retains its collaborative nature? How do I involve other organizations?

5. Housing first has been a high profile project in other communities and has been featured in their local newspapers and talk radio programs. The media coverage has been positive at times, but has also highlighted several instances where the program failed and a homeless person threatened his or her neighbors or was found sleeping in the street even after an apartment was provided for him or her. When should we involve the local media? Should we enlist their help as we try to raise funds to support the program or should we wait until we have a success story to highlight? How will we manage potentially negative coverage?

6. One of my responsibilities is to raise funds to start the pilot program but I also have to coordinate my grant writing efforts with the director of development at MSHC. I can only submit grants that are not in conflict with the ongoing fund development efforts of MSHC. This substantially restricts my ability to obtain the necessary funds to pilot this program. A program officer of one local foundation has indicated his interest in providing a three-year grant for the housing first program. This would require MSHC to postpone a submission to the foundation for five years (the foundation requires a two year hiatus between successful grant applications). The executive director of MSHC is hesitant to give up this MSHC funding source. How can I develop the funding streams to support this project when there is substantial competition for the grants, even within my own organization? How do I approach this subject with my executive director and members of the steering committee?

7. There's a lot of talk about capacity building, collaboration, effectiveness, and sustainability among coalition members, but they seem like buzzwords more than words with shared meanings. I know what the words mean to me but I'd do well to explore the professional

knowledge base and find out what is known about these concepts. It seems that we are trying to build capacity by engaging in collaboration among the organizations of key stakeholders. This raises a couple of questions: Are the organizations as excited to participate in the collaboration as their representative on the steering committee is? How will we sustain the collaboration over time?

SURVIVING THE DILEMMAS

Ethical Practice

Critical Thinking Question: What kinds of dilemmas do you anticipate facing in your future professional role?

[Some workers] ignore the larger issues . . . and relinquish the advocacy role. . . . The profession, then, ceases to be a calling and becomes "just a job."

We have presented these rather lengthy scenarios and the accompanying observations of the workers in an attempt to characterize the kinds of issues and problems social workers face almost every day. The nature of a capitalist system is that some people succeed economically whereas others do not. For the most part, social workers deal with those who are not able to care for at least a part of their own needs. It should be clear by this time that direct practice interventions alone cannot address large-scale community problems. Social workers must also master the skills involved in organizing people who may want change and have good intentions but need coordination and direction. Faced with these contrasts, a practitioner has a number of options, which can be categorized as follows:

1. **Develop a Strong Support System.** The types of dilemmas the practitioners in our case examples faced cannot be handled by one person, no matter how competent that person is. Social workers owe it to themselves to reach out to colleagues and friends, to make connections with persons from other professions, and to create opportunities to use formal and informal teams to solve tough interpersonal issues. No one has to work in isolation. Certainly one has to be careful about sharing confidential information about an agency or community problem that one is facing, but using close colleagues as a sounding board (and being available to others for the same purpose) is necessary to survive in a highly complex environment.

2. **Find Ways to Do Self-Care.** Some practitioners may burn out but remain on the job. Social workers can get caught in believing that they are working at impossible jobs. They stay in the system and feel powerless, accepting that they, too, are victims of the things they cannot control. They may do the basics of what has to be done with clients and ignore the larger issues, which means that they accept organizational norms and relinquish the advocacy role. This is a tempting option because taking on the larger issues can add many hours of work to an already busy week for what often seems like an impossible task. The profession, then, ceases to be a calling and becomes "just a job." One way to counter these tendencies is to engage in self-care behaviors. This means being intentional about nurturing oneself. For example, carve out time for the exercise class you know you have been meaning to take, but seem to never have time for. If reading for pleasure is something you just don't have time to do, find the time. Find ways to rest, to get away, to enjoy the outdoors, or do whatever renews you both personally and professionally.

3. **Prioritize Efforts.** Even social workers who are not burned out may become overcommitted and overwhelmed or develop excessively narrow perspectives or blind spots to matters they ought to consider.

These practitioners may remain very committed to clients but choose to ignore conflict or to engage in certain issues by focusing on a narrow area of expertise or assuming a set of responsibilities that establishes an independent base of power within the organization. This is certainly a strategy to use, but the downside is that focusing does not necessarily mean prioritizing. Focusing one's efforts may be important to getting things done, but occasionally set aside time to reprioritize so that a professional rut doesn't develop.

4. **Channel Energies.** Some social workers become activists, joining as many organizations and efforts as time and energy allow. Rejecting the norms of what are viewed as flawed organizations, these persons try to effect systemic change through whatever means possible. Adopting an independent stance from the organization in which he or she works, the social worker quickly becomes a maverick or "house radical." Often these persons become labeled as uncooperative and immature, losing credibility as they fight for change. Yet, they can also be a reminder of the broader issues, even to colleagues who are frustrated by their attitudes. Think about how to channel your energies so that the causes that really matter become the focus of your efforts.

5. **Join with Others to Initiate Change.** Building on a strong support system, social workers can go beyond interpersonal problem solving and join concerned colleagues, clients, and citizens to initiate change. Practitioners can apply professional knowledge and skill toward a systematic change effort designed to resolve at least a part of a problem and, hopefully, work toward its reduction and eventual elimination. This is an approach that can be taken by social workers who are committed to clients, community, career, and profession. Together with colleagues, workers form committees and task forces with the intent of changing organizational and community problems. Initiating feasible change means that the social worker must be selective, recognizing that not every problem is solvable and that choices must be made as to which will be addressed. Working toward change calls for sound judgment and discretion.

Much of the work done by social workers who seek to bring about change is what we refer to as macro practice, and is carried out with widely varying degrees of skill. The purpose of this book is to present a theoretical base and a practice model designed to assist the professional social worker in bringing about change in organizations and communities. Not only do we encourage readers to become change agents within the organizations and communities in which they will work, but we also believe that the value base of social work demands it. We believe, too, that surviving the dilemmas requires a strong professional identity. We now turn to an exploration of what that means.

Not only do we encourage readers to become change agents . . . but we also believe that the value base of social work demands it.

PROFESSIONAL IDENTITY

Professional identity is incredibly important at a time in which there is such rapid technological change, so many demographic shifts, and so many questions being asked about the effectiveness of higher education (Sullivan, 2005). Professional identity is a relational concept in that one identifies with a community of colleagues who share a common value base and whose joint efforts work toward "a way of life with public value" (p. 39). Lengthy lists of characteristics have been proposed to describe a "profession." Gustafson (1982) identifies three principal characteristics common to all professions: people-oriented purpose, extensive knowledge base, and mechanisms of control.

First, professions "exist to meet the needs of others" within the larger community (Gustafson, 1982, p. 508). This characteristic has led a number of writers to refer to professions as *callings* because they literally call members to contribute to the civic good. Professions are therefore client oriented and conform to a set of values that encapsulate the community good that is to be served. Activities designed only to serve the political or economic needs of powerful community members, even though they may be carried out by skilled individuals, do not qualify as professional endeavors.

Second, professions require mastery of a large body of theoretical, research-based, and technical knowledge. Having professional expertise means being up-to-date on what theories and practice models are available and integrating the best research evidence into one's practice. Thus, professional judgment derives from the ability to skillfully apply and discern the quality of the best knowledge available in a workable manner. Gustafson (1982) argues that professional practitioners prefer guidelines rather than rules because guidelines offer direction instead of rigid formulation. They allow professionals to exercise discretion and to use their judgment. However, professionals also carry enormous responsibility because what they decide and how they act will affect both their clients and the multiple constituencies previously discussed. Every choice is a value judgment.

Gustafson's third characteristic of professions is that they place many social controls on professional activities. In social work, these controls include the accreditation activities carried out by the Council on Social Work Education (CSWE) to ensure the quality and consistency of degree programs in social work; the sanctioning capacity of NASW; the NASW Code of Ethics, which provides basic value guidelines through which professional judgment is applied; and the credentialing and licensing requirements in various states. In short, there are many mechanisms for overseeing what occurs under the rubric of professional practice.

Certainly, each practitioner will have a vision of what the social work profession can be. The vision may be as broad as a higher quality of life for all and a better society, and may never be achieved as fully as one would like. Sullivan (2005) suggests that one major barrier to a shared vision is professional specialization. As the social work profession has developed (and as human service organizations have become larger and more bureaucratized), multiple specialties have emerged. For example, it is not uncommon to have social workers describe themselves as *psychiatric social workers*, *geriatric specialists*, *child welfare workers*, and so on. These specialties denote the target populations with whom these practitioners work. Just as common are terms such as *medical social worker* and *behavioral health specialist*, indicating a setting in which these professionals are employed. Terms such as *planner*, *community organizer*, *case manager*, and *group worker* describe actual functions performed by social workers. As will be discussed in later chapters, specialization offers attractive organizational efficiencies, and it can allow social workers to develop greater skill and expertise in particular areas of practice. On the other hand, it can also lead to tunnel vision, in which one begins to work within narrowly defined limits at the expense of a broader awareness of client needs.

Bureaucratization can be a barrier to professional vision. As professional organizations have developed and grown, as settings in which social workers

Professional Identity

Critical Thinking Question:
Why do you think that as your skill increases, so does your professional responsibility?

function have become multipurpose and diversified in their programs, and as communities have established numerous mechanisms that structure interaction amid units within those communities, it is easy to lose one's professional sense of the broader vision. Sometimes there are so many impediments to instituting change in an organization or a community that the change agent becomes frustrated.

Fabricant (1985) discusses the "industrialization" of social work practice, particularly in large public welfare agencies. In his discussion, he argues that social work is losing its aspects of "craft." A craft implies that the person responsible for beginning the professional task sticks with it until the end. For example, if a social worker provides intake for the client, that same social worker assesses the client, contracts with the client regarding a care plan, and persists in working with the client until the goals of that plan are achieved. This provides both the worker and the client with a sense of continuity, with ownership of the entire process, and with a shared understanding of what the outcome is to be.

As the nation's health and human service delivery systems have become more and more complex, as new actors enter the arenas, and as professionals specialize, it becomes rare for the practitioner to see an intervention from beginning to end. Many tasks have become more standardized and routinized; thus, social workers may feel bound by rules rather than directed by flexible guidelines that facilitate discretion and judgment. These changes can jeopardize the maintenance of a professional vision that transcends individual organizations and communities.

Although there are barriers to achieving an in-depth vision, we believe it is built on a commitment to serve diverse people within a society in which basic human needs are not always met and that at times actually denies support to some populations. The challenge is to work toward the development of comprehensive, effectiveness-oriented health and human service systems within local communities. This often requires the practitioner to understand situations without accepting "what is," to analyze dilemmas with the full realization that an ethical response is a choice among values, to envision competent and compassionate alternatives to what currently exists, and to skillfully use a macro-practice model to change "what is" to "what could be."

In many ways it is this commitment to the understanding and changing of larger systems that defines social work. Sullivan (2005) argues that the very nature of professionalism implies a responsibility to the larger society and to the common good.

SUMMARY

In this chapter we have provided the basic foundations on which students can build an understanding of social work macro practice. We defined *macro practice* as professionally guided intervention designed to bring about planned change in organizations and communities, and we began a discussion of the circumstances leading to the need for planned change. A conceptual framework was provided.

We used comments from former students who are now practicing social workers to illustrate how the circumstances that are often most important or troubling to social workers are not only client needs but also issues such as the management of their organization or the resources available within their communities.

Systems theory guides the planned change model that will be elaborated in subsequent chapters. Systems theory contends that there are multiple parts of any entity, whether it is a group, an organization, or a community. These parts have connections, some more closely aligned than others. There are resources the system needs in order to function and they may come in the form of people, equipment, funding, knowledge, legitimacy, and a host of other components. These resources interact within the system, producing something that becomes the system's product. We used Warren's classic work to focus on communities as systems in which there are both horizontal and vertical relationships.

The value base of social work is summarized most succinctly in the NASW Code of Ethics, which embodies the profession's orientation to practice. Intervening at any level presents ethical dilemmas that must be faced by the practitioner. In many cases no right or wrong answer is present, and the appropriate course of action is not at all clear. In such instances, the practitioner's job can be facilitated by analyzing the situation in terms of the six core values in the NASW Code of Ethics. *Service* (sometimes called beneficence) refers to the value of helping others. *Social justice* is assuring equal access to resources and equitable treatment. *Dignity and worth of the individual* (often associated with autonomy) refers to the value ascribed to an individual's right of self-determination. The *importance of human relationships* recognizes the value of connecting with others to improve quality of life and to facilitate change. *Integrity* and *competence* are values that implore professional social workers to be consistent and skilled in all that they do. Social workers engaged in macro practice may find that their job is one of balancing these values. In micro practice, for example, one must often temper the desire to help (and one's notions of how best to solve a client's problem) with a recognition of the client's need for personal autonomy. From a macro-practice perspective, social and economic justice considerations may demand that one focus not on individual helping but on attempts to alter macro systems that fail to distribute resources in a fair manner. These points were reinforced through three case studies showing how policies, program structures, resource deficits, and other macro-related criteria have much to do with social workers' ability to be effective in their jobs.

One way that social workers sometimes respond to these realities is to give up fighting against them. However, social workers who are skilled in macro practice have other options—to develop strong support systems, find ways to do self-care, prioritize efforts, channel energies, and use their understanding of macro systems to join with others to bring about needed changes in these systems. These skills are not and should not be limited to those who are working in traditional macro-practice roles such as administration or planning. Instead, they are critical for all social workers to know, including those engaged mostly in micro practice.

Working through these dilemmas aids in the development of a professional identity that incorporates both micro- and macro-practice aspects. Just as the profession must be built on social workers who are committed to making a difference in the lives of individual clients, these same workers must also be committed to making a difference in the systems within which clients live and on which they depend. In the chapters that follow we will provide a macro-practice model to guide social workers in undertaking change processes. But first, Chapter 2 will complete our introduction to the field by reviewing the historical background of social work macro practice.

Succeed with **mysocialworklab** PEARSON

Log onto **www.mysocialworklab.com** and answer the questions below. (*If you did not receive an access code to* **MySocialWorkLab** *with this text and wish to purchase access online, please visit* www.mysocialworklab.com.)

1. **Read the MySocialWorkLibrary case study: Golem, Albania.** Explain how vertical and horizontal linkages were influenced by the work of the community organization efforts in this city.

2. **Read the MySocialWorkLibrary case study: Professional Decision Making in Foster Care.** In the last paragraph, the author cautions that good social workers "seek self-awareness so they are not confusing their own needs with the needs of their clients." How can this advice about clients be applied to communities or populations?

PRACTICE TEST

The following questions will test your knowledge of the content found within this chapter. For additional assessment, including licensing-exam-type questions on applying chapter content to practice, visit **MySocialWorkLab**.

1. The person-in-environment concept means
   a. one must be aware of environmental constraints
   b. sometimes the environment needs to be changed
   c. focusing on environment means focus on the person
   d. you cannot remove the environment from the person

2. A vertical linkage connects community units with
   a. other internal community units
   b. small autonomous neighborhoods
   c. organizational agency connections
   d. units outside of the community

3. Horizontal linkage units are
   a. geographically located within the area
   b. connections with similar communities
   c. agreements between service agencies
   d. usually managed by the mayor's office

4. Which item below best describes social controls on a profession's activities?
   a. Code of Ethics sanctions
   b. A sense of "calling"
   c. A body of knowledge
   d. Professional conferences

5. Someone asks you, "Are you going into micro- or macro-level practice?" Based on the discussion in the beginning of this chapter, why is this not an easy question to answer?

ASSESS YOUR COMPETENCE

Use the scale below to rate your current level of achievement on the following concepts or skills associated with each competency presented in the chapter:

1	2	3
I can accurately describe the concept or skill.	I can consistently identify the concept or skill when observing and analyzing practice activities.	I can competently implement the concept or skill in my own practice.

_____ Can articulate the connection between working one on one with a client and working to solve community, systemic or societal problems.

_____ Can be mindful of the responsibility of social workers to protect human rights regardless of the specific focus of the job at hand.

_____ Can anticipate ethical dilemmas and demands and respond appropriately.

Can demonstrate a willingness to pursue opportunities for improving systems and communities, even if this means increased responsibility.

2

The Historical Roots of Macro Practice

CHAPTER OUTLINE

Core Competencies in this Chapter (Check marks indicate which competencies are covered in depth)				
✓ Professional Identity	☐ Ethical Practice	☐ Critical Thinking	☐ Diversity in Practice	✓ Human Rights & Justice
☐ Research-Based Practice	☐ Human Behavior	✓ Policy Practice	☐ Practice Contexts	✓ Engage, Assess, Intervene, Evaluate

TRENDS UNDERLYING THE EMERGENCE OF SOCIAL WORK ROLES

As noted in Chapter 1, social workers operate in a complex and rapidly changing society. To understand the problems and opportunities they face, it is important to be familiar with the historical trends that have shaped today's social systems and to recognize forces that will affect the evolution of these systems in the future. A framework for analyzing these past trends and current forces is provided by Garvin and Cox (2001), who call attention to (1) social conditions, (2) ideological currents, and (3) oppressed and disadvantaged populations. We will examine each of these in this chapter.

Social Conditions

Population Growth and Immigration

The first U.S. census in 1790 revealed a national population of less than 4 million. By 1900, this number had grown to almost 92 million, and the final total from the 2010 census estimated the nation's population at just under 309 million (U.S. Bureau of the Census, 2010a). The period of fastest growth was in the 1800s, when the nation's population increased by more than one-third every 10 years throughout the first half of the century, and, despite the death and destruction of the Civil War, continued to grow by more than 25 percent per decade during the century's second half. The rate of growth moderated after 1900, with increases diminishing to an average of about 10 percent per decade since 1960. Still, in raw numbers, the nation continues to add almost 30 million people to its population every 10 years.

Immigration has always been a critical element in population growth in the United States. One of the first great waves of immigrants occurred in the 1840s. To the East Coast came Irish and German immigrants fleeing famine and political upheaval; to the West Coast came Chinese workers seeking employment during the California gold rush. Successive waves followed from southern and eastern Europe as well as Asia, reaching a peak during 1900–1910 when immigrants totaled over six million and accounted for almost 40 percent of the nation's population growth. Although arrivals slowed after 1920, the proportion of population growth accounted for by immigration has again risen. For example, in 1970 there were 9.6 million foreign-born persons in the population. By 2009 the number had quadrupled to 38.5 million. This means that more than 11 percent of individuals in the United States were born outside its boundaries (U.S. Bureau of the Census, 2010b). Mexico is by far the most common external birth country, accounting for almost a third of the total, but the next three most frequent countries of origin—Philippines, India, and China—are all Asian nations (Pew Hispanic Center, 2007).

Industrialization

Accompanying the country's population growth was a rapid shift toward industrialization of its economy. Axinn and Stern (2008) use the production of cotton in the South to illustrate the effects of this shift. Total cotton production was only 6,000 bales the year before the invention of the cotton gin in 1793, after which it grew to 73,000 bales by 1800, and to almost 4 million bales near the start of the Civil War in 1860. In fewer than 70 years, mechanization thus helped to effect an almost 700-fold increase in production. This type of dramatic change transformed working life throughout the country. In 1820, for example, nearly 3 of every 4 workers in the nation were employed in agriculture, whereas in 2009 fewer than 1 in 300 labor-force members worked in the combined areas of farming, fishing, and forestry. Instead, the largest single occupational category was "Office and Administrative Support," which accounted for more than 22 million workers, or about 1 of every 6 persons in the U.S. labor force (U.S. Bureau of Labor Statistics, 2010b).

The economic opportunity produced by rapid industrialization was a key enabling factor for the rapid growth of the nation's population. The wealth generated by an expanding industrial economy meant that many more people could be supported than in previous agricultural economies. Trattner (1999) calls particular attention to the vast growth in national wealth that occurred following the Civil War. In the 40 years between 1860 and 1900, for example, the value of all manufactured products in the country grew sixfold and total investment in industry grew by a factor of 12.

Urbanization

The combination of population growth and industrialization brought about increased urbanization. As recently as 1910, over half the population still lived in rural areas, whereas by 2000, more than 80 percent lived in urban areas, including city suburbs (U.S. Bureau of the Census, 2001a). No U.S. city had a population of 50,000 at the time of the 1790 census, and 50 years later there were still only 40 communities in the nation that the Census Bureau considered urban. As of 1970 the United States had 150 cities with at least 100,000 residents (U.S. Bureau of the Census, 1970), and between then and 2009, this number almost doubled to 276 such cities (U.S. Bureau of the Census, 2010c). Most population growth initially occurred in the urban core of large industrial cities, whereas more recent increases have taken place in suburbs and medium-sized cities. Nevertheless, no U.S. city reached a population of 1 million until the 1880s, whereas by 2008, 54 percent of U.S. residents lived in the 50 metropolitan areas having populations of 1 million or more (U.S. Bureau of the Census, 2010d).

Change in Institutional Structures

As the United States became more urbanized and industrialized its social structure also changed, especially the system of organizations that meet people's needs. In the early 1800s, these organizations were usually few in number, informal, and small in scope (e.g., families, churches, and schools). Engaged primarily in agriculture and living in rural areas, people were forced to be largely self-sufficient and depended on organizations for a limited range of needs. With the advent of industrialization, however, new technologies were linked with advances in methods of organizing, and new patterns emerged. Of particular importance has been the rise of a complex system of highly specialized organizations. These range from accounting firms to computer manufacturers to adoption agencies, and they both reflect and embody the complexity of modern society. Their specialization allows them to do a few tasks efficiently and in great quantity, but they are dependent on other organizations for resources such as power, raw material, and trained personnel, even if they may not always recognize this dependence.

People in today's society benefit enormously from the output of these organizations, but like organizations, people are themselves more specialized in their roles. Instead of learning the range of tasks necessary for basic self-sufficiency, individuals in society now concentrate on learning particular skills that allow them to carry out particular functions—such as social work—that usually occur within or are provided by an organization. This allows both individuals and organizations to perform those tasks better and more efficiently, meaning that society as a whole is more productive. But a corollary effect of specialization is that individuals and organizations are no longer able to produce most of what they need on their own, and the level of interdependence within society is greater than ever before. Moreover, individuals who meet their needs through the roles they are able to fill are much more dependent on assistance from societal institutions. This is a principal reason for the development of social work as a profession.

Changes in broad social conditions that contributed to the development of social work thus included population growth, industrialization, urbanization, and changes in the institutional structure of society that led to increased specialization and interdependence. The institutional changes were particularly relevant to social work because they most directly influenced the development of services to people in need. Box 2.1 provides an overview of historical trends.

Institutional changes were particularly relevant to social work because they most directly influenced the development of services to people in need.

Ideological Currents

Not surprisingly, changes in broad social conditions coincided with considerable ideological change. Garvin and Cox (2001) identify several viewpoints that arose during the late 1800s in response to these conditions. These include *Social Darwinism, Manifest Destiny,* the growth of the labor and social justice movements (once called "radical" ideologies), and what is today called *progressivism.*

In the late 1800s, the English writer Herbert Spencer drew comparisons between Charles Darwin's biological theories and social phenomena. Applying the concept of survival of the fittest, he suggested that persons with wealth and power in society achieve this status because they are more fit than those without such resources. He also argued that in the biological world the random appearance of favorable traits leads to the gradual supplanting of less favorable traits, but in societies some individuals or groups remain inherently "inferior." Not surprisingly, this philosophy was embraced by many of the wealthy, who contended that little should be done for the poor and dispossessed on the grounds that such help would simply perpetuate societal problems (Bender, 2008).

Box 2.1   Historical Trends at a Glance

▶ **Population Growth and Immigration.** From fewer than 4 million in 1790, the U.S. population reached almost 309 million in the 2010 census. Today, more than 1 in 10 residents in the United States are persons who were born outside its boundaries.

▶ **Industrialization and Urbanization.** Most Americans 200 years ago were farmers living in rural areas. Now, fewer than 1 in 300 works in agriculture, 80 percent are urban dwellers, and more than half live in the 50 most populous metropolitan areas.

▶ **Institutional Structures.** Although largely self-sufficient when the nation was an agrarian society, Americans now live in a highly interdependent economy and social system. Most workers are extremely specialized, and relatively young professions such as social work have developed in response to the increased complexity of society.

The concept of *Manifest Destiny*, first coined by newspaper editor John L. O'Sullivan in 1845, described the belief that God had willed the North American continent to the Anglo-Saxon race to build a Utopian world. Such a world would fuse capitalism, Protestantism, and democracy, and in it Anglo-Saxon peoples were not to dilute their superiority by marrying members of other races (Jansson, 2009). Manifest Destiny was used to fuel westward expansion in the late 1800s and to justify seizure of lands from the American Indian groups already occupying them.

Partly as a reaction to the racism and classism inherent in these views, but also in response to the growing influence of Karl Marx and other socialist writers, the first flowerings of the labor and social justice movements appeared. The labor movement drew its strength from the appalling workplace conditions facing most industrial wage earners at the time. A goal of many writers and activists in the movement was to transfer industrial control from capitalists to trade unions (Garvin & Cox, 2001). Meanwhile, the growing number of poor people, their concentration in urban slums, and the desperate conditions in which they lived spurred the growth of what became the social justice movement. Its goal was and still is to mobilize, organize, and empower those who lack equal access to the nation's economic resources.

Progressivism is a complementary ideology that arose partly as a secular expression of Judeo-Christian values of egalitarianism and social responsibility, which were seen as ways to temper the excesses of laissez-faire capitalism. In this view, human rights supersede property rights, and society is seen as responsible for promoting the collective good. One of the early expressions of progressivism was scientific charity, which sought to harness what were seen as "natural" feelings of compassion for the poor to build private systems to provide one-on-one help (Bender, 2008). This view was to contribute to the rise of some of the earliest human service agencies—the Charity Organization Societies—in the late 1800s.

Box 2.2 provides an overview of the early trends discussed in this section.

Oppressed and Disadvantaged Populations

New social conditions, such as the changing face of the U.S. population and shifts in ideological currents, often intensified prejudicial attitudes and discriminatory behavior toward certain groups. As is often the case, these beliefs and actions were commonly directed toward groups already suffering the

---

Box 2.2   Historical Ideologies, Ideas, and Definitions

▶ **Social Darwinism.** The belief that income differences between rich and poor are natural and arise because the rich are more fit. A corollary is that services should not be offered to the poor since this would perpetuate the survival of those less fit.

▶ **Manifest Destiny.** The belief that North America was divinely intended for white Europeans, especially Anglo Saxons, to inhabit and control.

▶ **Social Justice Movement.** A broad term covering the philosophies of union organizers, anticapitalists, and social reformers who fought the excesses of the Industrial Revolution and advocated on behalf of laborers, immigrants, and the poor.

▶ **Progressivism.** A counterargument (in part) to social Darwinism that contends that as societies become more complex and individuals less self-sufficient, government must act to ameliorate the problems faced by those less able to cope.

harshest effects of rapid social change. The following sections focus on trends affecting populations whose members would later become important constituents for professional social workers.

Native Americans

In the 1800s and early 1900s, oppression of American Indians was governmental policy, enacted via war, forcible relocation, deliberate spread of disease, contravention of treaties, and confinement to reservations. The Removal Act of 1830 gave the federal government the right to relocate any native groups living east of the Mississippi River. For many tribes this meant virtual genocide. Relocation of the Cherokee nation in 1838, for example, led to immense loss of life from disease and exposure, becoming known as the Trail of Tears. Beginning in the 1890s, when many American Indian families had been forced onto reservations, generations of Native American youth were made to attend off-reservation boarding schools where the goal was to blend them into white society so well that their original cultural identity would be unrecognizable. The effect was often merely to damage Native American family life and alienate American Indian youth from their heritage (Coleman, 1999).

Latinos

More than 100,000 indigenous Spanish-speaking people in the Southwest became part of the United States following the Mexican-American War in 1848. The war began primarily as a result of U.S. military incursions into Mexico, and the Treaty of Guadalupe Hidalgo that ended it included specific protections regarding property rights and civil liberties for former Mexican citizens who became part of the United States. Nonetheless, many of these people were forced from their lands (Griswold del Castillo, 2001). Language was also a common tool of oppression, with Latinos being denied participation in voting and public education because they were not proficient in English. Following the Mexican Revolution in 1910, large waves of Mexican immigrants began to face similar barriers. During the Depression years of the 1930s, unemployment pressures and racism led to large-scale deportations of supposedly illegal residents, as many as 60 percent of whom were in fact U.S. citizens (Boisson, 2006).

African Americans

The Civil War won emancipation from slavery for African Americans, but equal treatment was slow to follow. The Freedmen's Bureau, set up in 1865 to assist the transition of freed slaves, was a rare example of federal involvement in the provision of social welfare services. In its brief six-year life, it assisted many former slaves in finding employment or gaining access to education and health care. But more typical of the Reconstruction era was the founding, also in 1865, of the Ku Klux Klan. Its reign of terror in the South lasted almost 100 years, effectively denying many freedoms African Americans had supposedly gained. In the courts, rulings such as the U.S. Supreme Court's landmark *Plessy v. Ferguson* decision of 1896 upheld the "separate but equal" doctrine that in essence made discrimination a governmental policy. Trattner (1999) notes that although advocates for better social welfare programs achieved important gains in the first decades of the twentieth century, these often had a much greater impact on poverty among white than among black Americans.

Asian Americans

On the West Coast, Chinese immigrants were often exploited as cheap labor, but when economic conditions changed they became targets of discrimination and hostility. An example is the 1882 Chinese Exclusion Act, which for more than 60 years outlawed all Chinese immigration to the United States (Orgad & Ruthizer, 2010). Meanwhile, immigration from Japan increased between 1890 and 1907, resulting in changes to California state laws that restricted the ability of Japanese residents to own or even lease property. Finally, in one of the most egregious examples of governmental discrimination by race, hundreds of thousands of Japanese Americans were forcibly relocated to internment camps during World War II.

Women

In the 1800s, the status of women had improved little from ancient times, and many women were often treated as little more than chattel. In the United States and other developing countries, outright subjugation had given way to a "fairer sex" stereotype of women as the repositories and purveyors of public virtue. This model was then used as a rationale for denying women access to education, employment, voting rights, and other benefits so that they would not be diverted from their role as moral guardians of society. Some women rose above this and began what has been termed the "first wave" of feminism (Gray & Boddy, 2010). Voting rights were the principal goal of this wave, but it also sought to overcome the homebound nurturer mold into which most women of the time were forced. Other women leveraged these stereotypes to aid in founding societies and associations that became the forerunners of contemporary human service organizations (Carlton-LeNey & Hodges, 2004; McCarthy, 2003). Nevertheless, advocacy for women's equal rights was often portrayed as a threat to women's domestic role, and this one-dimensional view of women as cloistered keepers of hearth and home delayed their progress toward full participation in society (DuBois, 1999).

Persons with Disabilities

Laws urging charitable and considerate treatment of persons with disabilities date from the Code of Hammurabi and ancient Judeo-Christian writings, yet in practice many societies have dealt harshly with their disabled members. Even in the relatively enlightened Greek and Roman cultures, accepted practices included infanticide, enslavement, concubinage, and euthanasia (Trattner, 1999). More recent societies have renounced these practices, but their treatment of persons with disabilities has still been affected by long-standing tendencies to view a disability as somehow the fault of the disabled or as punishment for unspecified sins. Terms such as *crippled* or *simple minded*, which have only recently faded from common usage, are instructive because (1) they describe disabilities through pejorative terms and (2) they define disability as some form of deficit vis-à-vis others in the population, although research has shown that persons with disabilities do not perceive themselves in terms of deficiencies (Wright, 1988).

In the United States after the Civil War, battlefield injuries were one of the few categories of disabilities receiving public attention. In 1866, the state of Mississippi spent one-fifth of its budget on artificial limbs for wounded veterans (Wynne, 2006), yet no public system existed in the state to serve the needs of persons with mental retardation. Even for veterans, available assistance was usually limited and did little to foster independence or integration with the rest of society. Not until the Veterans Rehabilitation Act of 1918 and the Civilian Vocational Rehabilitation Act of 1920 were federal programs established to promote greater participation and self-sufficiency. These were followed by income assistance programs created by the Social Security Act of 1935 (Percy, 1989).

Lesbian, Gay, Bisexual, and Transgendered Persons

Due to long-standing and widespread persecution, members of the gay and lesbian communities, along with persons of other sexual orientations, have historically been the most hidden of oppressed groups. In particular, homosexuality was often viewed through the lens of religious taboos, and some religious authorities placed it in the same category as willful murder as an example of a "mortal" sin. English law, unlike that of many other European countries, made homosexuality a crime as well, and as recently as 1816, English sailors were executed for the crime of "buggery" (Marotta, 1981). English legal codes on homosexuality were adopted in the United States, and, although not always enforced, were often used selectively as means of harassment. Finally, well into the latter part of the twentieth century, drawing in part on theories advanced by Sigmund Freud, gay men, lesbians, bisexual, and transgendered persons were considered mentally ill and could be forcibly subjected to hospitalization or other measures designed to cure their "perversions" (Crompton, 2003). Author Randy Shilts (1987) documented how these views contributed to the AIDS epidemic being viewed as a "gay disease" and thus eliciting a painfully slow response compared to what would have been the case if an equal proportion of heterosexuals had been affected.

The Development of Social Work

The oppression of ethnic minorities, women, disabled persons, and sexual minorities predated the development of the social work profession. The profession was thus born into an environment in which social change was needed. The effects of discrimination, ideological shifts, and economic and technological changes created social pressures that could not be indefinitely ignored, and the first organized efforts to respond to these pressures formed the basis for the creation of social work. Among such efforts were the Charity Organization Societies (COS) and the settlement house movement.

Local COS agencies, which began forming in the 1870s, were usually umbrella organizations that coordinated the activities of a wide variety of charities created to deal with the problems of immigrants and rural transplants who were flooding into industrialized northern cities in the United States in search of jobs. Ironically, Social Darwinism provided some of the philosophical base of the movement, as the "scientific charity" provided by COS agencies tended to be moralistic and oriented toward persons deemed able to become members of the industrial workforce (Axinn & Stern, 2008). Workers in the COS agencies were often volunteers, especially middle- and upper-class women, who served as "friendly visitors" to poor individuals and families. They tended to share idealistic goals of providing the poor with an opportunity to "better themselves," meaning that they typically viewed poverty as the result of individual failings and targeted their efforts toward reforming individuals rather than systems (Chambers, 1985). Although there was a gradual fading of the attitude that sufferers of problems such as oppression, poor health, or mental illness were somehow at fault for their plight, the focus of the COS movement on serving individuals on a case-by-case basis formed the foundation for social casework and for a modern array of micro-level interventions in social work.

At about the same time the COS agencies were developing, a different response to human need was employed by settlement houses. Conditions in the crowded slums and tenement houses of industrial cities in the late 1800s were as dire as any in the nation's history, and the goal of the settlement house movement, spearheaded by Jane Addams and others at Hull House in Chicago, was to attack these problems on a systemic level. This meant an approach that emphasized societal as well as individual and group reform. Many of the settlement houses served as religious missions and, like the COS members, did their share of proselytizing and moralizing. However, they were also more willing to meet their mostly immigrant constituents on their own grounds and to believe that chasms of class, religion, nationality, and culture could be spanned. In addition, their societal vision tended to be pluralistic—COS workers feared organized efforts such as the labor movement, whereas settlement leaders tended to support these endeavors. They also played prominent roles in the birth of organizations such as the National Association for the Advancement of Colored People, the Women's Trade Union League, and the American Civil Liberties Union (Brieland, 1987). Involvement in these sorts of efforts typifies what is now referred to as macro-level social work practice.

Women played a major role in building the foundations of social work in both the COS and settlement house movements. Three traditions of women's organizations and programs appeared in the early to mid-1800s: *benevolence*, *reform*, and *rights.* Starting in the late 1700s, women's benevolence primarily took the form of missionary work and the founding of orphan asylums to address immediate human needs. The rise of the reform tradition in the 1830s saw the creation of organizations to advocate for the abolition of slavery, closing of brothels, provision of sex education, and cessation of inappropriate sexual advances. In the 1840s through 1860s, a third tradition of feminist organizing arose around *women's rights* and produced groups such as the National Women's Suffrage Organization. The oldest of the three traditions—benevolent societies and charitable organizations—were forerunners of many of today's nonprofit health and human service agencies. The tradition can be traced to Isabella Graham and Joanna Bethune, a mother-daughter team who founded the Society for the Relief of Poor Widows with Small Children in New York in 1797 (Becker, 1987). Unfortunately, these early roots of today's macro practice have been given short shrift in historical accounts. Women who participated in benevolence have often been caricatured as ineffectual do-gooders, when in fact their efforts created a firm foundation for future service systems (McCarthy, 1990).

At the time, benevolent work was viewed as compatible with women's nurturing responsibilities, and even social change efforts were seen as an extension of domestic roles into the public arena (Chambers, 1986). Also, Trattner (1999) notes that because elected office was effectively denied to most women, an alternative chosen by many was to pursue their interest in social and political issues through involvement in the settlement houses and other efforts.

Box 2.3 provides a quick overview of how micro and macro practice developed.

Box 2.3 **Origins of Micro and Macro Practice**	
Micro	**Macro**
• Forerunners were COS agencies.	• Forerunners were settlement houses and state boards of charity.
• Guided by tenets of "scientific charity," focus was on improving the individual.	• Focus was on improving conditions for neighborhoods or other groups.
• Evolved into social casework.	• Evolved into community development and community organization.
• Influenced by books such as *Social Diagnosis.*	• Influenced by books such as *Case Studies of Unemployment.*
• Approach to practice influenced by clinical approaches such as Freudian psychoanalysis.	• Approach to practice influenced by mass-movement approaches of progressivists, trade unionists, and civil rights advocates.
• Influenced by disciplines such as medicine and psychology.	• Influenced by other disciplines such as sociology, economics, and political science.
• Motivated by desire to achieve professionalization of practice, including scientific knowledge base.	• Motivated by desire to achieve social reform.

Early Social Work Education

Service responsibility gradually began to shift from volunteers to paid employees. Workers in COS agencies emphasized the need for a systematic approach to the work, whereas workers in settlement houses demanded training on how to effect social change. Both traditions emphasized efforts to gather information systematically on neighborhood problems (Bricland, 1990), and the resulting need for skilled staff fostered the organization of schools of social work. The New York School of Philanthropy began in 1898 as a summer training program of the New York Charity Organization Society; the Boston School of Social Work was jointly founded by Simmons and Harvard colleges in 1904, also in response to prompting from local COS agencies (Trattner, 1999). Soon after, persons involved with the settlement house movement helped establish the Chicago School of Civics and Philanthropy in 1907 (Jansson, 2009).

Accompanying these efforts, a debate ensued over whether the fledgling profession should focus on macro or micro social work models. Macro models, concerned with fundamental social policy issues, demanded an academic curriculum based on social theory and an orientation toward analysis and reform. A parallel movement, represented by Jane Addams, emphasized training for political activism and promoted not only economic reforms but also a pacifist agenda (e.g., advocating peace negotiations instead of military involvement in World War I). In contrast, micro models focused on case-by-case assistance and required that caseworkers learn how to conduct fieldwork.

An important turning point in this debate was the 1915 meeting of the National Conference of Charities and Corrections. Abraham Flexner, a prominent national figure in medical education, was asked to address the issue of whether social work was truly a profession. He argued that social work still lacked key characteristics of a profession and could more appropriately be called a semi-profession, a view that is sometimes applied to careers in which women predominate. Flexner's six characteristics of a true profession were (1) professionals operate intellectually with large individual responsibility, (2) they derive their raw material from science and learning, (3) this material is applied practically, (4) an educationally communicable technique exists, (5) there is a tendency toward self-organization or association, and (6) professions become increasingly altruistic in motivation (Morris, 1983).

Some developments in the field tended to strengthen these characteristics. In 1917, for example, Mary Richmond published *Social Diagnosis*, which brought one-on-one casework practice to the fore and cast it firmly in a traditional, professional mold. By comparing casework assessments with diagnostic work, Reisch and Wenocur (1986) argue that the book opened the door to what is sometimes called the "medical model" in social work. The focus on diagnosis was further strengthened by the influence of Freudian psychotherapy, which became the dominant theoretical basis for casework practice throughout the next half century. On the other hand, Morris (2008) argues that the situation was more complex, and that social work continued to be involved in efforts at both micro and macro levels.

COMMUNITY ORGANIZATION AND SOCIAL REFORM

Although inconspicuous and not specifically professionally focused, the development of macro-practice models continued. By 1921, *The Community* by Eduard Lindeman had appeared, and at least five more books on the subject were written within the next 10 years. Organizational theorists such as Mary Follett and social work educators such as Lindeman called attention to the potential role to be played by small primary groups working to strengthen local areas within larger communities (Garvin & Cox, 2001). However, differences had already begun to arise concerning the appropriate focus of macro-level interventions. On one side were advocates of grassroots efforts to effect community change; on the other were those arguing for greater involvement in policy development and agency-based provision of services.

In addition, a social justice agenda emerged in the mid-1920s that reached a peak in the New Deal Era and was embraced as a part of professional identity in the early 1940s. Unionization efforts in the late 1920s and early 1930s resulted in social workers such as Bertha Capen Reynolds collaborating with other professions to reduce management abuses and ameliorate the impact of workforce reductions and pay cuts. Social workers also marched side by side with residents of urban slums, demanding improved housing conditions. These social workers were mostly young, held low-level positions (such as case managers and community action organizers), and did not strongly identify with "professional" social workers (Wagner, 1989).

Effects of the Great Depression

The Great Depression, which began with the stock market crash of 1929, became a watershed event in the history of macro practice. In the four-year period from 1929 to 1933 the gross national product of the United States fell by almost half, and the rate of unemployment reached 25 percent. The resulting impoverishment of vast segments of the population raised doubts about traditional notions that poor people were responsible for their own plight and should solve it through personal reform. As Axinn and Stern (2005) note:

> The depression demonstrated that one could be poor and unemployed as a result of the malfunctioning of society. The temporary relief programs developed to meet the exigencies of the depression acknowledged the existence of this kind of poverty and of a "new poor." The later permanent programs of the Social Security Act recognized the possibility of inherent societal malfunctioning. (pp. 174–175)

This was the point that settlement leaders, social reformers, and social justice advocates had long argued, and it was to play an influential role in the development of Franklin Roosevelt's New Deal programs. A number of social workers and agency administrators who had supported New Deal-like reforms during Roosevelt's term as governor of New York later assumed key positions in his presidential administration. Harry Hopkins, head of the Federal Emergency Relief Administration (FERA), and Frances Perkins, Secretary of Labor, were the most visible of these (Jansson, 2009).

Social Work and Social Change

In an atmosphere of sweeping change in the late 1930s, social justice advocates and mainstream social work leaders worked together more closely. The journal *Social Work Today* began to pay attention to social work practice, muting its traditional view that casework constituted a Band-Aid approach to human needs. Social justice elements remained identifiable as social work's left wing, but they were less dramatically differentiated from progressive but professionally oriented leaders. These shifts were enhanced by the achievement of mutual goals such as passage of the Social Security and National Labor Relations acts in 1935. The latter ensured labor's right to organize, strike, and bargain collectively, and it marked the beginning of a period of great success by the labor movement in organizing much of the industrial workforce in the country.

After the mid-1930s, large governmental agencies began to dominate the provision of human services, and the battle of social work roles shifted to this arena. Reisch and Andrews (2002) note that advocates of the casework model were well placed in many of these organizations and developed job specifications that largely excluded community organizers. However, members of the Rank and File Movement of social justice-oriented social workers also became involved in the public services arena, and they brought with them an emphasis on large-scale social reform (Wagner, 1989).

These developments in the 1930s and 1940s set the stage for later social movements. Although the 1950s were not a time of great tumult, key events occurred during the decade that would open the door for considerable social change in the 1960s. A landmark example was the 1954 *Brown v. Board of Education* decision by the Supreme Court that struck down "separate but equal" policies in public education. Ensuing efforts to ensure the ruling was applied in all schools and to overturn segregation elsewhere became the foundation of the Civil Rights Movement. Beginning with the Montgomery, Alabama, bus boycott in 1955, Martin Luther King Jr. and the Southern Christian Leadership Conference carried out a campaign of nonviolent resistance through sit-ins and demonstrations. Other groups, such as the Congress on Racial Equality (CORE) and the Student Nonviolent Coordinating Committee, sponsored "freedom rides" and trained young whites and blacks from elsewhere in the country to assist with organizing efforts in the South. Both the Voting Rights Act of 1964 and the Civil Rights Act of 1965 were passed largely as a result of these efforts.

In response to the struggles of blacks in the South and elsewhere, social change movements designed to help members of other traditionally oppressed groups began to appear. Cesar Chavez's United Farm Workers began organizing the predominantly Chicano field workers in the Southwest, and the La Raza movement sought to gain political power for Latinos through voter registration drives and other efforts that had worked well in the South. The American Indian Movement (AIM) called attention to governmental policies that often worsened rather than ameliorated problems in Native American communities. Books such as Betty Friedan's *The Feminine Mystique* (1963) became a catalyst for the Women's Movement, which sought to extend into the social and economic realms the equality women had gained in voting rights through the Suffrage Movement. Episodes of "gay-bashing" by citizens and police officers in New York City led to a disturbance in 1969 called the Stonewall Riot. This became a catalyst for the Gay Liberation Movement, the first large-scale effort to overcome prejudice and discrimination against homosexuals. Finally, the Counterculture Movement, student unrest (through groups such as Students for a Democratic Society), and protests against the Vietnam War helped make the late 1960s the most turbulent period of the century in terms of mass social movements. Participation in these movements provided on-the-job training for many community activists who later became professional social workers.

Also in the 1960s, expanded governmental social programs, although sometimes ill conceived, provided new opportunities for community-level interventions. One stimulus for these changes was renewed awareness of the plight of poor people, brought on in part by books such as Michael Harrington's *The Other America* (1962). John Kennedy's election in 1960 on a platform of social activism also played a part, resulting in initiation of programs such as Mobilization for Youth, inner-city delinquency prevention efforts, and (with an international focus) the Peace Corps. These efforts helped create and refine new models of community development (Trattner, 1999).

In 1964, Lyndon Johnson's call for a war on poverty led to the passage of a vast array of social welfare initiatives known collectively as the "Great Society" programs, after a phrase in one of his speeches of the time. These programs left a mixed legacy of results but provided an opportunity for testing macro-practice models. One of the most important examples was the Community Action Program (CAP), part of the Economic Opportunity Act of 1964, a keystone of antipoverty legislation. The goal of CAP was to achieve better coordination of services among community providers and facilitate citizen participation in decision making through "maximum feasible participation of the residents of the areas and the members of the groups being served" (U.S. Congress, 1964, p. 9). CAP agencies were created in neighborhoods and communities throughout the country, and residents were recruited to serve as board members or paid employees alongside professionally trained staff.

In their assessment of CAP initiatives, Peterson and Greenstone (1977) argue that the design and implementation of the programs largely undermined the first objective of improving coordination of services. However, CAP agencies achieved considerable success in their second objective of facilitating citizen participation, particularly by strengthening networks within African American communities that helped them gain greater political power. Other programs were less successful and in some cases resulted in harsh criticisms of social workers and their efforts. Within the field itself, however, accomplishments such as those of the CAP agencies helped to reestablish the importance of macro-practice roles.

Reflecting this trend, the Council on Social Work Education (CSWE) in 1962 recognized community organization as a method of social work practice comparable to group work and casework. In 1963, the Office of Juvenile Delinquency and Youth Development of the U.S. Department of Health, Education, and Welfare funded CSWE to develop a curriculum for training community organizers. Between 1965 and 1969, the number of schools of social work providing training in community organization rose by 37 percent, eventually including virtually every school in the country (Garvin & Cox, 2001). Community organization thus emerged as a legitimate part of social work practice.

THE ORGANIZATIONAL CONTEXT OF SOCIAL WORK

Communities are macro systems in which all social workers interact and for which practice models have evolved. However, communities themselves are largely composed of networks of organizations, and it is these organizations that usually assume responsibility for carrying out basic community functions. As such, organizations are a second type of macro system with which social workers must be familiar. We will examine many types of organizations in Chapters 7 and 8, but COS agencies, settlement houses, CAP agencies, and other such organizations that focus on the needs of society's have-nots fall into one group termed *human service organizations* (HSOs). Their history helps illustrate a pattern of shifting emphasis between centralization and decentralization of agencies and services.

England's Elizabethan Poor Law of 1601, the first written statute establishing a governmental system of services for the poor, adopted a decentralized approach to providing services. Under this law, assistance to the poor was a local function (as was taxation to pay for the assistance), and responsibility for service provision rested with an individual "overseer of the poor." This model was retained more or less intact in the American colonies, and until the 1800s, relief efforts for the needy were primarily local and small in scale.

The reformist period of the early nineteenth century began a slow transition to larger-scale services in the form of state-run asylums for dependent children, the mentally ill, and children and adults with mental retardation. Later, as population, urban concentration, and service needs increased, so did the diversity of both public and private programs. Eventually, it became apparent that some sort of coordinating mechanism was needed for these various efforts. Using Massachusetts in the late 1850s as an example, Trattner (1999) describes a hodgepodge of private facilities serving orphaned or delinquent youth, people with physical or developmental disabilities, those with mental illnesses, and others. Each institution tended to be independently governed, and lack of communication between them meant that critical information on matters such as standards of practice or treatment advances was infrequently shared. Trattner argues that this illustrates both the need for and value of having states assume coordination and regulatory roles.

The result was the creation of what became known as the State Boards of Charities, first in Massachusetts in 1863, then in another 15 states by the mid-1890s. These boards represented the first real involvement of state governments in centralized coordination of welfare services, and they helped establish standards for the administration of HSOs.

For about the next 65 years, much of the growth among HSOs took place in the private sector. The formation of the COS agencies and settlement houses was a partial recognition of the advantages of establishing standard service practices within the framework of a strong organizational base. Efforts were also made to expand public agency involvement in social welfare services during the Progressive Movement in the early 1900s. One example was the creation of the first state public welfare department in Illinois in 1917. Still, the focus remained on decentralized, private-agency services, and little growth occurred among HSOs in the public sector.

It was not until the Great Depression that public organizations for the provision of human services were established on a large scale. Roosevelt's New Deal programs created an infrastructure at the federal level designed to provide a governmental safety net to protect the poorest and most vulnerable from falling below a minimum standard of living. A key function of these programs was to distribute relief funds to states, and this helped spur the creation of state-level public welfare organizations. Some programs, such as FERA and the Work Projects Administration (WPA), were designed to respond to specific Depression-era problems and thus were relatively short-lived. Others, such as the Social Security Administration, formed the institutional basis of ongoing federal programs, and they continue to play major roles. With the creation in 1956 of the Department of Health, Education, and Welfare (now the Department of Health and Human Services), most of these agencies were combined into a single, cabinet-level organization through which federal insurance and assistance programs were administered.

Since its earliest stages, social work has usually been carried out from within some type of organization. These organizations have varied over time, as have the skills needed for effective practice within them. In the early years of social work education, for example, the focus was on preparing a limited number of macro practitioners to assume roles as administrators of small agencies, usually in the private sector. The skills needed included fundraising, working with voluntary boards, and supervising direct-service workers.

With the growth of large public bureaucracies and nationwide networks of private-sector agencies, the size and complexity of human service organizations changed, as did the role of macro practitioners within them. Trends such as the increased size of human service organizations, growing complexity and diversity of services, and changes in budgeting policies forced administrators to acquire new skills. Lewis (1978) calls particular attention to the growth of concern for fiscal accountability that first became a dominant issue in the late 1960s. He argues that these concerns forced social work administrators to shift from "problem solvers" to "managers." Implicit in this shift was a change in administrative orientation, moving away from external considerations of how best to deal with specific social problems and toward internal considerations such as budgetary compliance, operational efficiency, and more recently, information management. Concerns arose that if social work administrators do not acquire these skills, leadership of HSOs may pass to persons from other disciplines who lack training in individual behavior, social systems, and the interaction of person and environment.

Some writers also voiced concerns that administrative decisions in human service agencies might become so dominated by a focus on fiscal or operational efficiency that client needs and service effectiveness would be ignored. In response, Rapp and Poertner (1992) were among a number of voices calling for *client-driven* models of administration in which the achievement of desirable outcomes for clients became the primary criterion for decision making. The intent of this model was to view administrative practice in social work as a unique blend of managerial skills combined with broader knowledge of social problems and the means of addressing these problems. Patti (2000) has argued that the role of administrators in human service organizations is to fulfill instrumental tasks common to all managers (e.g., budgeting, acquiring resources, hiring and directing personnel) while remaining committed to improving the circumstances of those being served.

Professional Identity

Critical Thinking Question: How can a social work administrator promote social work values while leading a large bureaucracy?

CONTEMPORARY TRENDS

At the beginning of this chapter, we discussed major historical trends affecting the development of the social work profession. According to the model proposed by Garvin and Cox (2001), these trends are (1) social conditions, (2) ideological currents, and (3) oppressed and disadvantaged populations. In this section, we examine these areas in terms of their influence on current developments in the field.

Social Conditions

The effects of population growth, industrialization, urbanization, and changes in institutional structures have created a society that is different today than that in the early years of the profession. The changes have brought about profound improvements in areas such as health, income, and transportation, but not all aspects of the transformation have been ones to which members of society could easily adjust, and in some cases this has led to new social problems.

Poverty and Welfare Reform

In 1995, President Bill Clinton signed into law a set of sweeping changes to public assistance programs. The change was largely prompted by conservative charges that the existing system promoted welfare dependency and a bloated, bureaucratic service system. For example, Newt Gingrich, then Speaker of the U.S. House of Representatives, argued that government organizations in charge of programs to aid low-income children were simply "exploiting" them instead (Gingrich, 1995).

The key changes implemented by the Personal Responsibility and Work Opportunity Reconciliation Act (PRWORA) were the requirement that most recipients to find work and the placement of time limits on their eligibility for assistance. In 2006, 10 years after the act, considerable discussion and debate took place regarding its merits. Those viewing it as a success typically pointed to the following as evidence of its effects:

1. A dramatic drop (about 60 percent between 1994 and 2005) in welfare caseloads.

2. Increases of as much as 30 percentage points in employment among single and never-married mothers.

3. Increases of more than 100 percent among some subgroups in the proportion of income from employment in single-mother households.

4. Reductions of about one-fourth (from more than 20 percent to about 16 percent) in the number of children in poverty.

5. A reduction of about one-third between 1990 and 1999 in the poverty rate of single-mother households (Haskins, 2006).

Critics point to other results that cast doubt on the success of reforms. Parrott (2006) notes that drops in poverty rates for families and children mostly occurred before 2001, after which they began to rise. These rates increased most rapidly in the ranks of the poorest families and children, defined as those with incomes less than half the poverty rate. Other researchers studying larger economic trends have also raised concerns that the booming economy of the 1990s, not welfare reform, was responsible for increases in employment and decreases in poverty rates, and they, too, note with concern the reversal of those gains since 2001 (Murray & Primus, 2005).

Studies also suggest that many families fail to take advantage of benefits available to them not because of improved economic well-being but because of organizational barriers. Parrott (2006) found that more than half the drop in welfare caseloads in the late 1990s occurred less because families earned their way out of poverty than that they simply did not apply for help. A study by Wu and Eamon (2010) illustrates possible reasons for this, showing that families with meager resources who might benefit from help were often thwarted by insufficient information, bureaucratic barriers, and unreasonable eligibility criteria. Similarly, a study by Broughton (2010) found that most of the drop in welfare caseloads cited as evidence of success of welfare reform actually occurred as a result of "bureaucratic churning," efforts to deny applicants who, with help, might have qualified, and other means of restricting service access (p. 155). These problems do not appear to be restricted to large governmental agencies. Benish (2010) studied efforts in one state to transfer responsibility for services to the private sector and found that rules and regulations in the new non-governmental agencies became more rigid and inflexible than had been the case in older governmental agencies.

From a macro-practice perspective, these findings are useful in showing a de facto shift in the role of the federal government from poverty prevention to employment support. Holt (2006) calls attention to the growth of the Earned Income Tax Credit (EITC), which distributes federal funds in the form of tax refunds (often more than the amount actually paid) to low-income earners who file a return. From less than $2 billion in 1984, the program grew to about $57 billion in 2009 (U.S. Internal Revenue Service, 2010), and it continues to expand. Ironically, the Internal Revenue Service, which administers the EITC, might thus be said to have become a key agency for meeting the needs of poor people, a role for which many observers might question its suitability.

Box 2.4 provides a summary of the pros and cons of welfare reform. It is important for social workers to recognize how the shifts in federal policies can impact persons who live in poverty.

Income Inequality

In the midst of debates about poverty policy, many writers have become concerned about the increasing income gap between the highest-earning and lowest-earning households in the United States. In the four decades during and after World War II, the economy of the United States expanded rapidly, and households in poor and middle-income families (those at the 90th income percentile or below) enjoyed greater percentage increases in

Policy Practice

Critical Thinking Question: What are some ways PRWORA may espouse values similar to those of Social Darwinism? How is it different?

Box 2.4	**Summary of Pros and Cons of Welfare Reform**

Pros	Cons
• Welfare caseloads dropped dramatically in the first five years after passage of the reforms.	• Much of the caseload decline may have occurred because poor families assumed they would not qualify, not because they became less poor.
• More mothers joined the workforce.	• Jobs taken by many recipients who entered the workforce pay too little to allow real self-sufficiency.
• Work earnings as a percentage of household income rose sharply after the reforms, while income from welfare benefits decreased.	• Economic gains by poor families in the late 1990s may have been due to a strong economy rather than reform policies. Low-income families are now facing great hardship following the start of a recessionary period.
• Child poverty rates dropped after reforms were enacted, especially among black children, and some other indicators of child well-being also rose.	• Indicators such as child poverty, percentage of mothers in the workforce, and earnings from work among low-income families have worsened since about 2001.
• Children have benefited from the positive model of a parent who is employed and seeking to be self-sufficient.	• Conditions for the poorest of the poor have steadily worsened, as has the number of children in extreme poverty.

earnings than households in the top 10 percent. Since the late 1970s, however, income has increased substantially in the 10 percent of households with the highest earnings, while few gains have been made by households in the bottom 90 percent of income (Shaw & Stone, 2010). In 1977, for example, the highest-earning 10 percent of households received about one-third of all income in the United States, but by 2007 this figure had grown to the point that 10 percent of households earned about half of all income. This represented the greatest income disparity between the bottom 90 percent and top 10 percent of households ever recorded (Saez, 2010).

For about its first 35 years, the nation's post–World War II economic expansion benefited everyone, but for the past 30 years, it has benefited only the most affluent. For example, after adjusting for taxes and inflation, only the top fifth of households had meaningful income increases between 1979 and 1998, whereas the middle three-fifths stayed largely unchanged and the bottom fifth experienced a net *decrease* of 12.5 percent (Piketty & Saez, 2003). Perhaps most important for social workers to recognize about these trends is the fact that poor households are numerous and getting poorer. In 2007, about 61 million people lived in the 15.6 million households in the bottom fifth of income. Members of this group earned only 4.9 percent of all after-tax income that year, down from about 7 percent in 1979 (Sherman & Stone, 2010).

Income disparities become especially pronounced when examining the top 1 percent of income earners. In 1976, earners in this category received about 9 percent of all income, whereas by 2007, their share had grown to 21 percent (in other words, 1 of every 100 earners received more than 1 of every 5 dollars of income). Even more striking is the fact that two-thirds of new income generated by the economic expansion between 2002 and 2007 went to the top 1 percent of earners (Shaw & Stone, 2010). Much of this occurred because sources of income for the highest earners, including executive stock options and stock dividends grew rapidly (before the downturn that began in 2008), whereas other sources of income grew little. Most Americans receive their income in the form of wages and salaries, yet in early 2007, the proportion of all income earned from that source reached its lowest level since record-keeping began in 1929 (Aron-Dine & Shapiro, 2007).

Large disparities also exist between rich and poor with regard to net worth, which is the value of all assets minus the amount of all debts. In 1983, the wealthiest 5 percent of households accounted for 55 percent of all net worth, and this grew to 62 percent by 2007. The least wealthy 40 percent of American households accounted for just nine-tenths of 1 percent of net worth in 1983, and this dropped to two-tenths of 1 percent by 2007. Disparities are even greater if home values are excluded. In 2007 the wealthiest 5 percent of households held 72 percent of non-home wealth (up from 68 percent in 1983), whereas the least wealthy 40 percent of households accounted for −1 percent (compared to −0.9 percent in 1983). The negative values mean these households' average debt exceeded their non-home wealth (Wolff, 2010).

Disparities such as these can produce a variety of problems. Studies have shown that increased income inequality is associated with poorer infant health outcomes (Olson, Diekema, Elliott, & Renier, 2010), lower self-rated health status among adults (Hildebrand & Van Kerm, 2009), increased homicide risk (Redelings, Lieb, & Sorvillo, 2010), increased suicide risk (Huisman & Oldehinkel, 2009), political and community disengagement of low earners (Bernstein, Mishell, & Brocht, 2000), and many other concerns (Wilkinson & Pickett, 2009). Observers such as David Shipler (2005) argue that as the gap between the affluent and everyone else widens, more Americans will find themselves among the "working poor" who teeter constantly on the brink of disaster. He offers an example in which poor housing aggravates child health problems, which lead to higher medical costs, then late payments, then penalties or higher interest rates on an already undependable car. That, in turn, threatens the ability to hold down a job, which increases the likelihood that the family will have to remain in run-down housing. Even minor calamities can intensify a vicious cycle that becomes ever more difficult to escape.

These conditions affect many former welfare recipients who have replaced public assistance with work earnings, suggesting that reductions in welfare dependency have not been accompanied by increases in actual economic security. Box 2.5 provides an historical comparison of trends in income inequality.

Patterns of Affiliation and Identification with Community

A recurring question in community literature concerns whether communities are meeting the needs of their members and whether the traditional benefits of community living are in jeopardy. In 1978, for example, Roland Warren called attention to what he described as the "community problem," which involved a feeling among Americans that the communities in which they lived functioned less well than in the past and were subject to more frequent and serious disorders than before.

Fukuyama (1999) described what he termed a "Great Disruption" in countries within the developed world, where an unexpected growth of social problems occurred during a period beginning in the 1960s and extending into the 1990s. Among these problems were rising disruptions in family

Box 2.5 U.S. Income and Wealth Distribution in the Twentieth and Twenty-First Centuries		
Mid to Late Twentieth Century		**Twenty-First Century**
• 1940s to 1970s—poor and middle-income households had greater earnings increases than those in the top 10%	⇄	• 1980s to present—poor and middle-income households made few gains; earnings increased substantially in top 10%
• 1977—the highest-earning 10% of households received about one-third of all income	⇄	• 2007—the highest-earning 10% of households received about half of all income
• 1979 to 1998—households in the top fifth had sizable income increases; those in the middle three-fifths saw little change; those in the bottom fifth had a net *decrease* of 12.5%	⇄	• 2002 to 2007—households in the top 1% earned two-thirds of the new income from economic expansion
• 1976—households in the top 1% earned about 9% of all income	⇄	• 2007—households in the top 1% earned about 21% of all income
• 1979—households in the bottom fifth earned about 7% of all after-tax income	⇄	• 2007—households in the bottom fifth earned about 5% of all after-tax income
• 1985—the wealthiest 5% of households held 55% of all net worth	⇄	• 2007—the wealthiest 5% of households held 62% of all net worth
• 1983—the least wealthy 40% households held 0.9% of net worth	⇄	• 2007—the least wealthy 40% of households held 0.2% of net worth

systems (high divorce rates and high rates of births to single or very young mothers), increased crime, deterioration of inner cities, erosion of trust in traditional institutions and organizations, and generalized "weakening of social bonds and common values" (p. 56).

Putnam (2000) focused on changes in how people associate with each other, calling particular attention to falling participation in local membership groups as diverse as neighborhood bridge clubs, fraternal lodges, and college alumni chapters. Citing surveys showing substantial decreases in involvement in activities of such groups, he suggested that people are instead opting to affiliate with "tertiary associations" that might never actually hold meetings and whose members might never meet each other. Examples of such organizations include associations that support a political or charitable cause, and Putnam contends that relationships among members of such groups are more like those linking far-flung boosters of a sports team than those among members of a local club. In these situations, it is the cause rather than personal relations that ties members together.

Unlike Warren or Fukuyama, however, Putnam argues that these changes are not necessarily ominous. The fact that people affiliate in different ways than before does not necessarily portend a breakdown of social cohesiveness, but some members of society will inevitably adapt less well to rapid change than others.

Among the causes of the above changes are trends we have already discussed, including *urbanization* and what Warren (1978) called *loss of geographic relevance.* Large, complex cities offer many benefits, but they can also breed large, complex problems, and the very size and complexity of a city can interfere with solving these problems. For example, shared views of the common good are possible in small communities because their populations are relatively homogeneous and each person can be personally acquainted with many or all other residents. Small communities also share commonalities such as topography, growing conditions, and water supply. In contrast, cities can be so large that residents in one area share little with those in another in terms of economic base, political environment, lifestyle, or even climate and terrain. Likewise, it is impossible to get to know all of one's fellow residents in a large city, where most people one sees are often blurred faces passing by in vehicles or on busy sidewalks.

Still, many city dwellers love urban life and do not find it alienating. They may define "community" in different ways than in rural areas and apply the term to an apartment building, an ethnic enclave, a neighborhood surrounding a particular factory, church, or school, or even as an area of gang turf. As we will discuss, this means that social work at the local level in urban areas requires recognition of a complex arrangement of communities within communities.

Technological advances are also enabling the replacement of locality-based relationships with those that transcend geographic boundaries and make physical distance meaningless. The rapid proliferation of cell phones and Internet access paved the way for advances ranging from text messaging to blogs to videoconferencing to multiplayer gaming. Social networking sites have also grown with incredible speed. As of late 2010, Facebook alone had more than 500 million active users, and it is likely that users of other sites equaled or exceeded that total (Facebook Pressroom Statistics, 2011). These networks exist in cyberspace rather than physical space, so what Warren termed *extracommunity affiliations* now involve not only redefining "place" (e.g., as a web address rather than a street address), but redefining "community" as well.

Extracommunity affiliations are important not just to individuals but to organizations and institutions as well. An automobile assembly plant may be the major employer and economic engine in a small community, but despite its local prominence, its most important ties may be to the home office of its corporate owner in a city far away. A decision to close the plant, or a work stoppage at a supplier of critical parts for its assembly line, might happen far outside the community, but local residents could feel the effects quickly. Communities and their institutions are thus highly dependent on external ties, and the rapid development of new communication technologies sharpens that dependence and adds complexity to social work practice at the community level.

Changes in Organizations and Delivery Systems

In addition to community issues, contemporary developments in the structure of organizations are also important. One parallel between communities and organizations is that both have continued to become larger and more multifaceted. In organizations, this has often been accompanied by the *bureaucratization* of operations. The term *bureaucracy* has taken on a number of mostly negative connotations that, as we shall discuss in Chapter 7, may or may not always be accurate. We will refer to bureaucratization as the growth in size and structural complexity of organizations, including HSOs. This has been especially prominent in public agencies, which have generally continued to expand since the New Deal.

Bureaucratic organization is a means of structuring tasks and relationships among organizational members so as to maximize operational efficiency.

Specialization of task is one aspect of bureaucratization, and, as we discussed earlier, this type of change has helped spur vast increases in the productive capacity of modern industrial organizations. The problem with bureaucracies is that they sometimes become as machinelike as the tools they employ, and the result can be a dehumanizing environment for employees and unresponsive or ineffective services for those in need. This often grows more pronounced as organizational size increases, and large governmental HSOs have developed reputations (sometimes deserved, sometimes undeserved) for reflecting the negative aspects of bureaucratic structure. Even in small agencies, externally imposed regulations (such as for certain operational practices or financial procedures) may produce a service approach characterized by stringency and rigidity. Lens (2008) demonstrated that work requirements for clients seeking public assistance led line-level staff to adopt a "harsh and punitive" orientation resulting in denial of benefits or unjustified sanctions (p. 217). As we will discuss in Part IV, understanding how organizational structure and rules affect interactions with clients is essential for effective macro practice.

Beyond the issue of structure, a lingering topic of debate concerns which organizations should be responsible for providing services and how this should be financed. From the start of the New Deal through the War on Poverty, public agencies were created to provide human services ranging from mental health care to welfare benefits to child protective services. Beginning in the 1960s, however, proponents of *privatization* became increasingly influential. Privatization calls for reducing or ending direct provision of human services by public agencies and replacing it with *purchase of service (POS)* contracting, whereby governments pay private agencies (both nonprofit and for-profit) to provide those services. This trend might more accurately be called "reprivatization" because it involves returning human services to the sector in which they were mostly based prior to the New Deal.

Driven by a desire to reduce the size of government and to encourage competition and cost control, the amount of money flowing into POS has grown enormously. Kettner and Martin (1987) estimate that $263 million was spent on POS contracts to private, nonprofit agencies in 1973. By 2007, nonprofit organizations in the United States had expenditures of $1.3 trillion (Urban Institute, 2010). In 1997, social and legal service organizations nationwide drew more than half (52 percent) of their budget from government contracts, and if this proportion has remained constant, the value of POS contracts to nonprofits in 2007 was about $676 billion (Wing, Pollak, & Blackwood, 2008).

Within the POS model, decision making and financing functions remain with public agencies, but the actual delivery of services is shifted to the private sector. This can be attractive to service seekers because going to a local nonprofit agency may be viewed as less stigmatizing than asking for "government relief." Advocates of POS also argue that having agencies bid for contracts provides a variety of free-market benefits (e.g., minimizing costs, improving oversight) that would not occur if services were provided directly by the public agency in charge. To further advance the goal of service improvement, contracting agencies are now increasingly using *performance-based contracting*, in which agencies that receive contracts for services are required to meet specific targets for quantity or quality of services provided (Martin, 2005).

The question of whether privatization has had positive effects on the delivery of human services remains in contention. Critics complain that the narrow focus of POS contracts ignores important client problems and promotes an orientation toward solving problems after the fact rather than preventing them.

Others argue that the increased reliance of private agencies on government contracts threatens the independence of the private sector agencies and makes them more vulnerable than in times when their budgets were more diversified, especially when government cutbacks occur. In the early 1980s, for example, an economic slowdown led to decreased public funding, after which POS funds began drying up. Many nonprofit agencies, which had previously grown larger on public dollars, were suddenly faced with stiff competition for limited resources. In the health-care field, hospitals facing shortages of patients began diversifying into service areas other than primary health care, such as substance-abuse centers, home health, and others. For-profit organizations also began providing human services, and both they and private hospitals especially sought clients who could pay the cost of services from their own resources or through insurance coverage. Meanwhile, nonprofit agencies had traditionally served low-income clients by offsetting their costs with revenues earned from paying clients. But with government funds more scarce and paying clients being siphoned off through competition from hospitals and for-profit providers, the frequent result was cutbacks in services that fell most heavily on clients most in need (McMurtry, Netting, & Kettner, 1991). Nevertheless, the number of nonprofit organizations continues to grow faster than the rate of growth of organizations in the commercial sector, and as of the year 2005, nonprofits accounted for about 8 percent of wages and 10 percent of gross domestic product (GDP) in the United States (Wing et al., 2008).

The Information Age

Anyone who has used a computer or smartphone to make a purchase, schedule a flight, find a restaurant, send a message, locate an old friend, or make a new one knows that rapidly advancing information technology continues to make dramatic changes in our lives. Futurist Alvin Toffler predicted this trend more than 30 years ago, believing that it represented a major new form, or "Third Wave" of human society (1980). In his model, the first wave of social organization was the development of agriculture and the formation of communities it supported. The Industrial Revolution produced a second wave characterized by huge production gains, population growth, and urbanization. Each wave was marked by a particular commodity. In the first wave, it was agricultural products, and in the second, it was manufactured goods. In the third wave, it is information.

Information as a commodity comes in many forms—one example of which is knowledge, such as that acquired and used by professionals. If a farmer was the emblematic figure of the first wave and a factory worker that of the second, in the third it is professionals, who, as opposed to farmers or factory workers, provide services rather than physical goods. The shift to services is becoming increasingly profound, and in the past 50 years the service sector of the economy has grown far more rapidly than any other. This can be seen in changes over time in the share of GDP in the U.S. economy that is accounted for by the three principal sectors of agriculture, industry, and services. In 1947, the percentage of GDP accounted for by each was 8, 33, and 59 percent, respectively. By 2009, in contrast, these percentages were 1, 15, and 84 percent, respectively (U.S. Department of Commerce, 2010). More than four of every five dollars of wealth produced in 2009 thus originated in the service sector, which is also where the vast majority of new jobs have been created during the past few decades.

Economies in developed countries seldom grow because new resources are found but because better use is made of existing resources—human or material. When economists refer to "productivity," they typically mean the value of goods and services produced divided by the resources (human and material) available to produce them. With respect to services, an accounting firm might raise the number of tax returns it completes for customers by forcing its staff to work faster. This could not go far, however, before no one would stay with or join the firm. But if the firm computerized client data and also computerized most calculations its staff formerly did by hand, it could dramatically lower the time needed to complete each return and increase its productivity. This is exactly what has happened in accounting and many other fields in recent years. In 2002, for example, the U.S. Congressional Budget Office (CBO) examined the question of how much computer technology had to do with increases in productivity nationally. The results were that "CBO attributes *all* of the acceleration in [net productivity] growth during the 1996–2001 period to technological advances in the production of computer hardware" and the easier access to computer technology this caused (U.S. Congressional Budget Office, 2002, p. viii, emphasis added).

Advances in information technology are transforming the workplace in other ways as well. Increasing numbers of employees are staying home for part or all of the work week, carrying out their tasks over voice and data lines linking them to national and international networks. These changes have the potential to dramatically alter the nature of community life. At a minimum, they are likely to modify traditional commuting patterns by allowing more workers "go to the office" at home. Eventually they could reverse urbanization trends, contributing to smaller and more decentralized communities.

Social workers can expect the ongoing changes in information technology to have two types of effects on their own work. One is that the nature of the social problems they encounter will be altered, and the other is that the way they do their work will change. With respect to changes in social problems, we have already noted the income gap between high and low earners in the United States, and a looming shortage of skilled workers to fill information-related and other high-tech jobs is likely to further widen this gap. Carnevale, Smith, and Strohl (2010) project that almost 47 million new and replacement jobs will be created by 2018, and a college degree or other post-high school education will be needed for almost two-thirds of those. However, they also anticipate that the number of students who go to college and successfully acquire the necessary skills to fill these jobs will be more than 3 million fewer than actually needed. In the meantime, far fewer jobs will be created for others who lack postsecondary degrees. The result for them is likely to be underemployment or unemployment, and they will encounter particular difficulty finding work that pays a middle-class wage. This will further complicate the task of social workers who are attempting to assist society's poorest members, because few of those individuals will have the skills necessary to qualify for better-paying jobs.

The way social workers do their jobs is also changing. They compose reports, write progress notes, exchange messages with others internal and external to the organization, access client records, search for referral options, and perform a variety of other functions that define the technical details of their professional roles. Computers, data bases, and other information resources have become essential for these tasks. Smart phones and laptop or tablet computers can be used to take case notes, fill out forms, or administer assessment tools. In most cases they also provide wireless access to allow workers to email questions to a supervisor, search for referral agencies, or schedule appointments for clients. Access to agency files allows workers to search client records, upload forms and case notes, or input information used to monitor and evaluate services. They can also keep up with professional literature through online access to journals and research reports, post questions to members of a listserv who work in the same area of specialization, or visit websites that provide information on problems with which they are unfamiliar. Perhaps of greatest potential value to macro practitioners is their ability to download data on census tracts or access geographic information systems to plot the distribution of income, crime, age, health status, and many other variables on high-resolution maps of targeted areas. In other words, as in virtually all other fields, rapid change in computer and information technology will continue to change the way social workers do their jobs. Box 2.6 provides an overview of contemporary trends.

Ideological Currents

As with the discussion of broad social conditions, Warren's (1978) notion of "the community problem" offers a starting point for addressing contemporary ideological trends. One issue concerns community members' increasing difficulty in achieving a *sense of community*—the psychological feeling of belonging that is critical to both individuals and communities. This feeling should arise from individuals' awareness of their roles as useful contributors to the well-being of the community. In historic times, this usefulness was easy to see,

Box 2.6   Contemporary Trends at a Glance

▸ **Poverty and Welfare Reform.** Between 1996 (when major federal reforms were passed) and 2001, the number of welfare recipients dropped by more than half, but caseloads then began to stabilize. Poverty is now on the rise—especially child poverty—and children are more likely to be poor now than in the 1970s or 1980s.

▸ **Income Inequality.** Income gaps between wealthy and poor are widening, with the richest one-fifth of families in the United States gaining earning power in the past 20 years and those in the poorest 20 percent having lower earnings. In 2007, the top one-tenth of households accounted for more than 50 percent of all income earned, whereas the bottom one-fifth of households received less than 5 percent of all income earned.

▸ **Patterns of Affiliation and Identification with Community.** Members of society rely less on local relationships and are less closely tied to their communities than in the past. For example, they are less likely to join local membership groups and more likely to affiliate with national organizations whose other members they may never meet, and they now use social networking and other technology to maintain relationships over long distances. Also, their organizations and communities are much more affected than in the past by decisions made outside the local area.

▸ **Changes in Organizations and Delivery Systems.** Social workers are more likely than in the past to work in organizations, and these are more likely to have formal, bureaucratic structures. They are also more likely to be private rather than public agencies and to depend on purchase-of-service contracts.

▸ **The Information Age.** Computerization of many aspects of society means that the most valuable commodity is information. Moreover, most jobs now involve the production of services rather than food or manufactured goods. Only $1 of every $100 in the economy now comes from agriculture, while $4 of every $5 comes from services. From computer programming to health care, to a variety of social work functions, services are increasingly information driven and computer dependent.

as when a person was perhaps the only grocer, teacher, baker, blacksmith, or midwife in the community. In modern communities, however, people's activities may be so specialized that their contribution to the community good is apparent neither to them nor to other community members.

Loss of sense of community can produce feelings of *alienation*, which is often described as a sense of isolation from social groups with which individuals might naturally identify. People who experience alienation feel estranged or set apart from social and cultural connections, and they tend to be both less productive and less able to cope with the strains of daily living. Sometimes a vicious cycle can occur in which the complexity and impersonality of community living breeds alienation, and its sufferers in turn feel even less able to manage such complexity. Feelings of separation that are also part of the experience of alienation fall especially hard on members of historically disadvantaged groups who are already worse off than others in the community and may feel stigmatized because of that (Ohmer, 2010). A different effect of alienation can be the appearance of self-serving and antisocial behaviors in which concern for community good (in the absence of a clear perception of the community and one's role therein) is subordinated to individual interests. It is this phenomenon that has been labeled by some social commentators and political figures as a breakdown in "civility" in social relationships.

Social workers must also wrestle with tension between *individualism* and *collectivism*. This tension most often comes into play with regard to whether personal or group interests should guide behavior. American culture has typically valued and protected individual initiative, but in many other cultures individuals are more likely to define themselves in terms of membership in a group and to be motivated to advance the group as a whole. One line of research has explored the struggles facing people from other cultures when adapting to American norms, and this has included studies of Latinos (Parsai, Nieri, & Villar, 2010) and Asian Americans (Lau, Fung, Wang, & Kang, 2009). Difficulties also appear in other circumstances, however, and examples of groups where individual-versus-collective motivations clash include caregivers of older adults (Anngela-Cole & Hilton, 2009) and homeless youth (Thompson, Kim, McManus, Flynn, & Kim, 2007). Another aspect of the issue involves the question of where decision-making authority for designing programs should reside. As noted earlier, this is being played out in debates concerning whether state and local versus national authorities should control public programs. In general, political conservatives argue that local governments are best situated to discern local needs and tailor appropriate responses. Progressives argue for broad-scale programs that reduce inequities existing between communities and establish general standards for services or benefits.

A concept that is gaining particular attention for its explanatory power is *social capital*. This refers to the store of beliefs, values, and practices that are adhered to members of society and that contribute to the well-being of all. A society with high social capital, for instance, would be expected to have low crime rates because the majority of persons perceive the benefits of not preying on each other. Like economic capital (e.g., investable funds) or human capital (e.g., education or expertise), social capital is a measurable resource that can be considered part of the wealth of a society. A growing body of research suggests that greater social capital is associated with lower levels of poverty (Sun, Rehnberg, & Meng, 2009), lower mortality (Hutchinson, Putt, Dean, Long, Montagnet, & Armstrong, 2009), increased self-esteem and coping ability (Wahl, Bergland, & Løyland, 2010), more negative attitudes toward violence

(Kelly, Rasu, Lesser, Oscos-Sanchez, Mancha, & Orriega, 2010), and many other variables. The role of social workers can be seen as preserving and promoting social capital, but there is a lack of consensus as to what it is or how it can be increased. For example, both individualism and collectivism can be seen as aspects of social capital, but disagreement exists regarding proper balance between the two. Also at issue is whether, in the face of social disruptions Fukuyama (1999) described or the decline of forms of association noted by Putnam (2000), the nation's store of social capital is rising or ebbing.

A final note on ideology concerns not only what people believe but how they express those beliefs, especially in terms of the vehemence and one-sidedness of their messages. Observers in both the academic and public spheres, including President Barack Obama, have raised concerns that the positions being occupied and the rhetoric used to express them are often so polarized that the disagreement itself becomes all that matters (Allen, 2009). Other observers warn about the suppression of speech, especially in the workplace (Barry, 2007). The potential effect on communities and organizations of this *erosion of public discourse* is that some of the problems discussed earlier (e.g., loss of sense of community, alienation) are becoming worse while notions of collectivism disappear and social capital is lost. The question of how this issue should be defined and whether it is a serious threat was taken up by a commission at the University of Pennsylvania. In the introduction to their book on the commission's findings, Rodin and Steinberg (2003) conclude that incivility in public discourse has a long history, but modern communication methods can deliver it in larger quantities and greater variety than in the past. In addition, those with the harshest and most negative voices can use these methods to make their words stand out. On the other hand, the same innovative communication methods can be used to disseminate thoughtful and moderate messages if their senders become equally skilled in using these new methods.

Box 2.7 provides an overview of contemporary ideologies, ideas, and definitions.

Box 2.7 Contemporary Ideologies, Ideas, and Definitions

▶ **Sense of Community.** The degree to which community members identify with a community (either local or nonlocal) and feel a part of it.

▶ **Alienation.** A sense of estrangement from and lack of belonging to the rest of one's society. The absence of a sense of community is a common aspect of alienation.

▶ **Individualism versus Collectivism.** A continuum along which social policies may differ. Policies tilting toward individualism seek to place minimal constraints on personal freedom and individual volition, whereas policies favoring collectivism assume that some individual options must be limited to better serve the good of all.

▶ **Social Capital.** A public resource that is reflected in the willingness of individuals to behave in ways that further the cohesiveness of society and the well-being of its members. Social capital tends to be higher where alienation is low but people's sense of community is high.

▶ **Erosion of Public Discourse.** The fear that public debate is becoming both more polarized and more uncivil than in the past, and that the overall cohesiveness of society may be at risk as people become more entrenched in their views and less willing to listen to others.

Oppressed and Disadvantaged Populations

Much has been accomplished in the last 150 years to purge society of prejudice and oppression, which were often directed toward certain populations by official policy. Legislation, combined with gradual change in individual attitudes, has made overt discrimination based on race or ethnicity both illegal and, among most members of society, morally unacceptable. Women and persons with disabilities have also made strides in recent decades toward correcting the many ways in which they were treated as second-class citizens. People in the LGBT community have benefited from court decisions overturning state laws designed to criminalize intimate relationships among same-sex couples.

Still, discrimination and disadvantage have by no means disappeared. Despite decades of research to the contrary, for example, LGBT women and men are still vilified publicly for "deviant" or "pathological" behavior and are denied rights and opportunities that heterosexuals take for granted. Although women now outnumber men at both the undergraduate and graduate levels in U.S. colleges and universities, the average working woman still earns only about three-fourths as much from her work as does the average working man (American Council on Education, 2010; Institute for Women's Policy Research, 2010). And although blatant expressions of racism are now widely condemned, many racial and ethnic groups continue to suffer from lingering disadvantages caused by past racism and discriminatory practices.

Table 2.1 displays indicators of individual and family well-being in areas such as income, education, and health for each of five major racial/ethnic groups in U.S. society. In our discussion of the current status of these groups later in the chapter, we will call attention to a variety of these indicators. It should be emphasized that "disadvantage" is not "weakness" and the purpose of Table 2.1 is not to perpetuate a deficit model of portraying certain groups. Instead, we seek to make the point that access to and control of resources affords advantages to groups that enjoy such control. These are best illustrated by pointing out the lingering disadvantages affecting groups that have lacked such access and control. Because whites were most often those who exercised control, they will frequently be used as a reference group in our discussions.

Access to and control of resources affords advantages to groups that enjoy such control.

Terminology

Before proceeding with our discussion, it is important to note briefly the importance of language. Social workers need to recognize that terms used to define and distinguish special populations can be applied adversely in ways that reinforce stereotypes or isolate the members of these groups.

Abramovitz (1991) provides a glossary of terms to increase awareness about how common speech sends messages beyond those actually spoken. She offers as an example the phrase *feminization of poverty*, which calls attention to the economic concerns of women but may also imply that poverty is a new issue for women. She argues instead for the term *povertization of women*, which better reflects the long history of women's economic disadvantage. She also argues against the use of the sociological term *underclass*, which has been suggested as a replacement for *multiproblem*, *disadvantaged*, or *hard-to-reach* poor people, because of its stigmatizing connotations.

Common speech sends messages beyond those actually spoken.

Since the 1950s, growing attention has been given to employing more accurate and less historically laden language when referring to special populations. For example, among ethnic and racial groups, blacks adopted the term *black* as a preferred descriptor in the 1960s and 1970s, supplanting the

Table 2.1   Selected Indicators of Well-Being by Racial/Ethnic Groups

Indicator	Group (Percentage of Overall Population)				
	Black, non-Hispanic (12.1%)	Asian American (4.3%)	Hispanic (15.1%)	Native American (0.8%)	White, non-Hispanic (65.8%)
Income, employment, and food security					
Per-capita annual income in dollars[a]	17,711	29,447	15,063	17,292[b]	30,941
Percentage living below poverty line[c]	34.6	16.6	30.3	30.2[b]	19.2
Percentage unemployed at the end of 2010[d]	15.8	7.2	13.0	15.2[e]	8.5
Percentage of households with food insecurity in 2009[f]	24.9	*	26.9	*	11.0
Household composition					
Percentage of households headed by a single parent[g]	67	16	40	53	24
Percentage of children in grandparent-headed households[h]	7.6	2.2	3.3	*	2.5
Education (adults aged 25 and over)					
Percentage with less than high school degree	15.9	11.8	38.1	*	12.9
Percentage with high school degree only	35.4	19.4	29.3	*	31.2
Percentage with college or graduate degree	19.3	52.3	13.2	*	29.9
Housing and transportation					
Percentage living in same house as 12 months before[i]	78.1	80.0	78.2	80.6	85.9
Percentage living in house with moderate or severe repair problems[i]	9.6	4.5	7.7	7.0	4.0
Percentage relying on public transportation[h]	11.1	10.2	8.1	3.5	2.7
Health and behavioral health					
Infant deaths per 1,000 live births[j]	13.6	4.9	5.6	8.1	5.8
Percentage of persons aged 18 and over with health status of "poor" or "fair"[k]	18.2	9.0	14.7	20.1	11.9
Age-adjusted deaths per year per 100,000 in 2006[l]					
due to all causes	982.0	428.6	564.0	642.1	777.0
due to heart disease or stroke	480.9	222.6	284.7	266.2	378.2
due to cancer-related illness	298.5	142.6	151.3	161.8	256.3
due to accidents	62.3	25.8	51.8	93.8	67.9
due to homicide	21.6	2.8	7.3	7.5	2.7
Days in the past year with five or more alcoholic drinks, 2010[j]	12.6	8.8	19.9	*	27.7
Illicit drug use, past month[m]	9.6	3.7	7.9	18.3	8.8
Percentage of persons aged 16–64 with no usual source of health care[k]	16.4	18.1	28.3	23.0	13.5
Percentage with no health insurance at any time[k]	21.0	17.2	32.4	*	12.0

Except where noted, all data are from calendar year 2009 (U.S. Bureau of the Census, (2010d)).
*Data not available.
[a]U.S. Bureau of the Census (2011a)
[b]Estimated from 2005 data.
[c]Based on Definition 4 of poverty level. U.S. Bureau of the Census (2011b)
[d]U.S. Bureau of Labor Statistics (2011).
[e]Austin (2011).
[f]Nord, Coleman-Jensen, Andrews, and Carlson, (2010).
[g]Annie E. Casey Foundation (2010).
[h]2005 data.
[i]2007 data. U.S. Department of Housing and Urban Development (2008).
[j]2005 data. MacDorman and Mathews (2008).
[k]U.S. Department of Health and Human Services (2010a).
[l]2010 data. Centers for Disease Control (2010).
[m]U.S Department of Health and Human Services (2010b).

segregation-linked terms of *Negro* and *colored.* Since the Civil Rights Movement, the term *African American* has gained widespread use, and research indicates that African Americans are evenly divided between *black* and *African American* with regard to their preferred term (Sigelman, Tuch, & Martin, 2005). Among Native Americans, the term *Native American* has been promoted as more appropriate than *Indian.* However, the full phrase *American Indian* is considered appropriate to be used interchangeably with *Native American* (Native American Journalists Association, 2006). Some writers have proposed the term *First Nations People*, but it does not yet appear to have been widely adopted. The term *Latino* is used as a generic expression to represent persons of Latin American ancestry, including Puerto Ricans, Cuban Americans, Mexican Americans (who also use the term *Chicano*), and others. Advocates of the use of *Latino* or *Latina* contend that *Hispanic* (which was originally created by the U.S. Bureau of the Census) is appropriately applied only to persons with links to Spain (Gutiérrez & Lewis, 1999), but a survey by *Hispanic Magazine* (2006) found that *Hispanic* was preferred by about two-thirds of the more than 1,000 registered voters in the sample. About one-third percent chose to identify themselves as *Latino* (Granado, 2006). Finally, the term *white*, despite its common usage, is poorly defined, but it remains more broadly applicable than *Anglo* or *Caucasian.* Results from a study to determine the term they prefer to be used when describing their group showed that among whites, *white* was preferred by a wide margin (62 percent) over *Caucasian* (17 percent) (U.S. Bureau of Labor Statistics, 1995).

The term *persons with disabilities* is considered appropriate as a broad descriptor of individuals having different physical or mental capacities from the norm. The term *differently abled* has been advocated as a way to avoid categorizing members of this group in terms of their perceived limitations, but this phrase has not yet been commonly adopted. With respect to sexuality, *gay* and *lesbian* have been preferred terms for at least the past three decades, whereas individuals who are *bisexual* or *transgendered* have also become better recognized as distinct groups. Members of each group were previously referred to as being distinguished by their *sexual preference*, but the term *sexual orientation* is now considered more appropriate because it reflects research indicating that such orientation is innate rather than a matter of choice. The abbreviation *LGBT* (lesbian, gay, bisexual, and transgendered) has become commonplace and is now often expanded to LGBTQ. In some uses the additional letter stands for "questioning," referring to people who are uncertain about their sexual orientation. In others it stands for "queer," a once derogatory term that activists have embraced as a sign of defiance against discrimination. With respect to gender, some feminist writers have argued for use of the terms *womyn* or *wimin* on the basis that they are less derivative of "men," but as yet these terms have not gained wide use.

We recognize the importance of language, and it is our intent in this book to reflect that importance in our use of terms. Based on the preceding reviews, we will intersperse the terms *black* and *African American*, *Native American* and *American Indian*, and *Hispanic* and *Latino.* Our goal is to be sensitive to the convictions and wishes of as many people within diverse population groups as possible, and to reflect what is considered standard terminology by members of those groups. We hope the reader will recognize this as evidence of the dynamic, evolving nature of modern language.

Compared with earlier periods in our nation's history, the recent past has been marked by significant gains on the part of ethnic and racial groups, women, members of the LGBTQ community, and persons with disabilities in their struggle to achieve equal standing in society. Despite this progress, however, these efforts are by no means complete. Success in reducing societal acceptance of prejudicial attitudes and overt acts of discrimination must be balanced against the fact that these attitudes and behaviors have sometimes simply become more covert and thus more difficult to confront. Also, hard-won political victories have not always been matched by comparable economic gains, and for some groups conditions have in fact worsened.

Native Americans

Native Americans benefited in important ways from the social upheavals of the 1960s, with groups such as the American Indian Movement (AIM) helping to focus attention on the troubled relationship between tribal organizations and the federal government. As a result, tribal governments were able to diminish the paternalistic influence of agencies such as the Bureau of Indian Affairs and gain greater autonomy over their own operations. For example, the Indian Child Welfare Act of 1978 gave jurisdiction of child welfare cases to tribal rather than state courts, thus placing tighter controls on practices such as the adoption of Native American children by non-Native American families. Other examples of helpful federal legislation include the 1978 Religious Freedom Act, which recognized the legitimacy of the Native American Church, the 1988 Gaming Regulatory Act, which confirmed that tribes may create gambling establishments on reservation land if gaming of any other form is allowed in the state, and the 1990 Native American Grave Protection and Repatriation Act, which requires that artifacts removed from tribal lands be returned if requested.

Nonetheless, Native Americans have a more distinct cultural heritage than many other ethnic groups, and the struggle to simultaneously preserve this heritage and integrate with the rest of society has taken its toll. Poverty on some rural reservations is as pervasive and severe as anywhere in the country, and much remains to be done to improve economic conditions in these areas. Another concern is health care. The Indian Health Service (IHS), which was created to meet treaty-based federal guarantees for health-care provision to Native Americans, has a record of inconsistent and sometimes dramatically inferior care. In recent years it has also faced both budgetary cutbacks and controversy over the extent of its responsibility for providing services to urban as well as reservation-based populations (Westmoreland & Watson, 2006). The Indian Health Care Improvement Act, a part of the major health care reform legislation passed in 2010, is designed to help the IHS meet these challenges.

Many tribes have used casinos and gaming as a path toward economic development and reduced federal dependence. According to the National Indian Gaming Association (2010), for example, gaming on reservations created more than 600,000 jobs (directly or indirectly related to the industry) and generated almost $20 billion in revenues in 2009. Gaming revenues do not benefit all Native Americans, however, and in addition to those on reservations that have no gaming operations, poverty, joblessness, and other problems affect many Native Americans who live in cities or other areas away from concentrations of fellow tribal members.

Data in Table 2.1 illustrate these problems. In 2009, Native Americans had the second lowest per-capita annual income, the highest rate of poverty, and the second highest unemployment rate of all racial/ethnic groups. They also suffered the highest incidence of health that was only "fair" or "poor," and they had the highest rates of both alcohol and drug abuse. In their study of at-risk Native American youth, Waller, Okamoto, Miles, and Hurdle (2003) summed up the situation as follows:

> Institutionalized oppression of Native people is not just a historical artifact—it persists in contemporary life. Examples include federally-run, Eurocentric Indian health care, education, social service, and criminal justice systems that have always been and continue to be underfunded and poorly administered, resulting in culturally inappropriate and sub-standard services. Poverty, geographic isolation, and lack of access to needed resources further restrict the range of opportunities available. (pp. 80–81)

Latinos

The Hispanic population is currently growing faster than any other ethnic or racial group in the country, and this trend is expected to continue well into this century. By 2050, for example, Latinos are expected to number more than 130 million in the United States. This would represent about 30 percent of the total population, as compared to 9 percent in 1990 (U.S. Bureau of the Census, 2011c). Latinos tend to be younger than the rest of the population and mostly urban. As of 2006, about two-thirds (64 percent) were of Mexican descent, 13 percent were from Central and South American countries, about 9 percent were Puerto Rican in origin, and 3 percent were from Cuba (U.S. Bureau of the Census, 2011c). Population concentrations are in the West and Southwest for Mexican and Central Americans, the Northeast for Puerto Ricans, and the Southeast for Cuban Americans. Based partly on historic inequality and partly on the effect of many recent immigrants still struggling to gain equal economic footing, income among Latinos is much lower than for the population as a whole. As shown in Table 2.1, in 2009, Hispanics had the lowest per capita income of any major racial/ethnic group, along with the highest incidence of food insecurity. Because many Latino children have to learn English while in school, dropout rates are high, and the percentage of Latino adults who lack high school degrees is more than double that of any other group. Finally, lack of health insurance and regular access to health care affects a particularly high proportion of Latino households.

By far the most prominent and contentious issue involving Latinos is illegal immigration, mostly by Mexicans and Central Americans crossing the U.S.–Mexico border. Much of the debate centers on how illegal immigrants should be viewed. Should they be considered criminals and thus denied services, hunted energetically by law enforcement, and prosecuted or quickly deported when arrested? Or should they be seen as useful additions to the labor force and thus afforded access to basic services (e.g., health care, education, and human services) and allowed to work toward becoming citizens? Those on the "pro" side of the issue argue that illegal immigrants mostly take jobs that others refuse, allow businesses to prosper that otherwise might be unable to compete, keep prices in check by working for low wages, and represent the kind of residents the United States should welcome because of their determination and strong work ethic. Those arguing the "con" position contend that illegal immigrants take jobs that would otherwise go to citizens, receive services without paying taxes (such as straining already overcrowded school classrooms), and take money out of the economy by sending much of their earnings back to their home countries. Social workers, because of their commitment to human well-being, often take the side of ensuring that illegal immigrants and their families have access to basic services, whereas others fear that their "limbo" status in society makes them especially vulnerable to exploitation and abuse. Meanwhile, many average citizens feel economically threatened by illegal immigration and are vociferous in their opposition. Perhaps the best that can be said is that this issue is likely to remain difficult and divisive well into the future.

African Americans

For blacks, victories in the Civil Rights Movement of the 1950s and 1960s meant the rejection of segregationist practices that had prevailed since the Civil War. These gains helped spur electoral successes at both the local and national levels. Since the mid-1980s, five of the nation's six most populous cities—New York, Los Angeles, Chicago, Houston, and Philadelphia—have been led by an African American mayor, and Barack Obama's election as U.S. president in 2008 was an historic event. Nevertheless, grave concerns remain regarding the dramatic gap in economic well-being between African American families and others. In 2009, more than one-third of African Americans households lived in poverty, a rate well above the national average and almost two-thirds higher than that of whites (Table 2.1). A contributing factor is unemployment, which hit African Americans especially hard in the recession that began in 2008. At 15.8 percent, the jobless rate among blacks was almost double that of whites in 2009. Annual income was also low, as indicated by a per-capita rate among African Americans of $17,711, which is more than 40 percent lower than the comparable figure among whites (Table 2.1).

Poverty among African American children is even more widespread, affecting more than one in three (ChildStats.gov, 2010). Also, poverty and other historical disadvantages have had negative effects on the structure of black families, and, as Table 2.1 indicates, black children in 2005 were more likely than those in any other racial/ethnic group to live in a single-parent household or one headed by a grandparent.

Transportation is a key factor in finding and maintaining good employment, but in 2009, African Americans were more than four times as likely as whites to rely on public transportation, which is more time consuming and less flexible than commuting by car. With respect to housing, blacks were twice as likely as whites to occupy a house in poor repair. They were also more likely to be affected by residential instability (measured by the percentage of those living in a different house than 12 months before), which is a predictor of unemployment and other problems (Table 2.1).

Perhaps the most glaring indicators of African Americans' struggle to overcome past oppression and its consequences are in the area of health. As Table 2.1 shows, infant mortality rates are much higher among blacks than in any other racial/ethnic group, and they also have the second highest incidence of health that is only "fair" or "poor." Also striking are statistics from the Centers for Disease Control regarding annual death rates due to various causes. In 2006 (the most recent year for which data are available), African Americans' annual mortality rate from all causes was more than double that of the healthiest racial/ethnic group (Asian Americans). The gravest threats were heart and cardiovascular diseases and cancer or cancer-related illnesses. Also, because low income and lack of mobility often mean living in dangerous neighborhoods, African Americans in 2006 had a death rate from homicide that was eight times higher than that of whites (Table 2.1).

It is important to point out that results in Table 2.1 also show strengths among African Americans that typically receive little attention. Compared to other historically disadvantaged groups, for example, African Americans have a low proportion (about one in five) of persons age 16 to 65 who lack at least a high school education. Perhaps even more noteworthy is the fact that, corrosive stereotypes to the contrary, rates of illegal drug use among black adults is essentially no different from drug use among whites, and African Americans are less than half as likely than whites to engage in problem drinking (defined as the number of days per year in which five or more drinks were consumed).

Efforts continue within the African American community to confront problems and consolidate gains. An ongoing emphasis on strengthening basic institutions such as churches, families, and neighborhoods is one example of this, as are efforts to highlight the unique African American heritage through holiday celebrations such as Kwanzaa. Particular attention is being given to ensuring strong electoral representation, and the latest available Census figures placed the number of black elected officials nationwide in 2002 at 9,430, or more than six times higher than in 1970 (U.S. Bureau of the Census, 2011d).

Human Rights & Justice

Critical Thinking Question: What are the risks for social workers who may make assumptions based on these misinformed stereotypes?

Asian Americans

Public attention is often directed toward the educational achievements of Asian American youngsters, who, for example, led all other ethnic groups on indicators such as the percentage of students scoring "Proficient" on national tests in grades 4 and 8, SAT scores in the 12th grade, and rates of college completion (National Center for Education Statistics, 2007). Table 2.1 indicates that, as a group, Asian Americans have achieved other successes in areas such as income, employment, health, and low rates of substance abuse.

Still, evidence of such overall successes has sometimes masked problems facing particular Asian American groups, especially those of Cambodian, Laotian, and Hmong origin who are often among those most recently arrived in the United States and whose numbers have increased rapidly in the past three to four decades. Many were refugees who arrived destitute and without an existing community of prior immigrants available to assist in their transition to U.S. society. Once here, they had to adjust to a different culture and language, and most have had to struggle to overcome lingering problems of poverty, poor housing, and discrimination in hiring. Le (2006) notes that the "model minority" label attached to Asian Americans can sometimes be destructive in that it ignores the fact that it is a heterogeneous population within which some groups still face many social and economic challenges.

Women

Women's advancement has been marked by both progress and disappointment. One important gain was the development of women's groups such as the National Organization for Women (NOW), which was organized in the mid-1960s. NOW and other organizations formed the core of the Women's Movement, which had considerable success in calling attention to institutional sexism present in employment, government policy, and language. These efforts constituted what is known as the second wave of feminism (Gray & Boddy, 2010), and they led to many tangible gains, such as the narrowing of the difference in earnings between men and women. In 2009, for example, the value of median weekly earnings for women was 80 percent of the value for men. This was up from 62 percent in 1979 but slightly below the peak of 81 percent in 2005 and 2006 (U.S. Bureau of Labor Statistics, 2010a).

Collins (2010) notes that one of the most important pieces of women's rights legislation was the 1964 Civil Rights Act. It included anti-discrimination protections for women that were added as a joke by a pro-segregation Congressman, but to his surprise the additions were passed along with the rest of the Act. A disappointment for many was the failed attempt to add an Equal Rights Amendment to the U.S. Constitution. The amendment was designed to offer further protections against gender-based discrimination. It drew vociferous opposition by groups that believed it would undermine women's traditional roles, and in 1982, it failed due to lack of ratification by a sufficient number of states. One successful initiative was the 1994 Violence Against Women Act, which was reauthorized in 2006. It put in place programs to prevent domestic violence, improve law-enforcement response to acts of violence against women, and assist prosecution of offenses such as dating violence and stalking (National Task Force to End Sexual and Domestic Violence against Women, 2006). Another advance was the Lilly Ledbetter Fair Pay Act of 2009, which allows individuals to take action against employers for wage discrimination of the type that has often affected women (National Women's Law Center, 2009).

As with other historically disadvantaged groups, women still struggle to overcome gender stereotypes that cast them in nurturer/caregiver roles rather than simply as full participants in society. They also have considerable ground to make up in order to achieve parity in economic and career opportunities. As NOW President Kim Gandy (2005) noted, women continue to make up only a small minority of those in positions such as mayoral posts, partners in large legal firms, and corporate heads. They are greatly underrepresented in high-prestige, high-power jobs and overrepresented in those that pay poorly, making them much more likely to have incomes below the poverty line.

Persons with Disabilities

The Rehabilitation Act of 1973 and the subsequent Rehabilitation Act Amendments of 1974 were for persons with disabilities what the Civil Rights Act had been for other groups. The acts prohibited discrimination against anyone who currently had or had in the past "a physical or mental impairment which substantially limits one or more of such person's major life activities" (Rehabilitation Act of 1973). The Rehabilitation Act also was the first to require that public facilities be made accessible to disabled persons, and it laid the groundwork for the expansion of these requirements to all commercial properties through the Americans with Disabilities Act of 1990. Another example of related legislation was the 1975 Education for All Handicapped Children Act, which required children with developmental disabilities to be given access to mainstream public education rather than the traditionally segregated "special education" system. In 1990, the Education for All Handicapped Children Act was renamed the Individuals with Disabilities Education Act (IDEA), and it was reauthorized in 1997 and 2004 (O'Brien & Leneave, 2008).

The IDEA legislation and other initiatives share the general goal of *mainstreaming*, which is defined as providing assistance in such a way as to minimize the need for persons with disabilities to remain apart or operate separately from others in society. Unfortunately, efforts to measure success have progressed slowly. The nature of disabilities varies widely, as do their causes, thus people affected by a disability cannot be treated as a single group. This means that statistics on the well-being of members of this population are difficult to locate, and it is also difficult to determine whether efforts to maximize their participation in society are bearing fruit. Results from evaluations of mainstreaming efforts with disabled or emotionally disturbed children and youth have yielded mixed results. They suggest that factors such as intensity of preparation, involvement of parents and family, and student motivation are more important than problem severity in predicting success (Pitt & Curtin, 2004; Walter & Petr, 2004).

Lesbian, Gay, Bisexual, Transgendered, and Questioning/Queer Persons

As noted in the introduction to this section, the task of overcoming prejudice against lesbian women, gay men, and others in the LGBTQ population has been slow and difficult. Expressions of homophobic views or displays of what Corsini (2002) terms *heterosexism* remain surprisingly commonplace in a society that long ago ceased to tolerate such behaviors when directed toward racial or ethnic groups. The advances that have occurred have come about mostly from political activism. Lesbians, for example, were an integral part of the Women's Movement and have both contributed to and benefited from its achievements. Wilkinson and Kitzinger (2005) note that many gay males were inspired by the work of black civil rights leaders in the 1950s and 1960s, and this helped to foster the creation of organizations such as the Gay Liberation Front. A unique difficulty facing members of the LGBTQ population, however, is that in order to begin advocating for fair treatment, they must go through the process of recognizing their own sexual or gender identities and overcoming the fear or reluctance that often goes with such acknowledgment.

A major step in legal advocacy was taken with the 2003 U.S. Supreme Court decision that struck down a Texas law prohibiting consensual homosexual acts between adults. In effect, this negated all such laws nationwide, and it represented a significant victory in the struggle for equal rights. Another advance occurred in late 2010 when Congress voted to end the "don't ask, don't tell" policies of the U.S. military. These policies required that service men and women be dismissed simply for acknowledging being LGBTQ.

By far the most contentious issue affecting the LGBTQ community at present is the effort to secure legal recognition for gay and lesbian couples. As of this writing, same-sex marriage is legal and performed in five states (Connecticut, Iowa, Massachusetts, New Hampshire, Vermont) and in the District of Columbia. A number of others have civil union or domestic partnership laws that grant some but not all marriage rights to same-sex couples. At the same time, 30 states have passed laws expressly forbidding same-sex marriage. Also, the federal Defense of Marriage Act of 1996 prevents the federal government from recognizing same-sex unions, though in 2011 the Obama administration ceased enforcing many of its measures. Most observers expect same-sex marriage to remain a hotly debated and contested issue for the foreseeable future.

Lingering Problems

Two contrasting views can and often are held when assessing current circumstances affecting historically disadvantaged groups. One view sees progress in the way racism and, to a lesser degree, sexism are recognized and condemned both informally among society's members and formally through laws, operational rules, and new programs created to address old injustices. The opposing view sees lingering disparities in income, education, and health that continue to affect racial and ethnic minorities, stereotypes and paternalistic attitudes affecting women, neglect and ignorance affecting persons with disabilities, and reactionary legal initiatives designed to label LGBTQ citizens as aberrant and undeserving of equal protection.

The contrast between these views illustrates the way in which ideological differences seem to have become more sharply defined across the political spectrum, with the result that concepts of compassion and caring for vulnerable populations sometimes appear at risk of drowning in a sea of rhetoric. The task facing social workers is further compounded by the fact that their efforts are often portrayed as destroying individual responsibility and fostering dependency among those they serve.

Perhaps the most important point to keep in mind is that social programs tend to reflect the status quo because they address symptoms of oppression rather than causes. Professionals frequently assume they know the causes of oppression—and thus the needs of consumers—without directly asking the people they serve. During recent decades, efforts such as the social movements and citizen participation activities described earlier have taken steps to address the needs of special populations in a more comprehensive and consumer-involved manner. The task for practitioners remains that of (1) finding interventions that respond appropriately to the needs of these populations and (2) keeping in the forefront a genuine commitment to meeting these needs.

THE IMPORTANCE OF CHANGE

The development of social work macro practice has proceeded hand-in-hand with rapid changes in society. In fact, change is one of the few constants in modern life, and its effects are sometimes difficult to evaluate. Is fading participation in local membership groups evidence that people's connections to their communities are dying, or are we simply witnessing the replacement of old modes of affiliation and old definitions of "community" with newer ones? Does the gradual absorption of immigrants into the larger society represent a loss of their cultural identity, or by becoming a part of that society are they adding new flavors to it and guarding its variety and vibrancy? Is privatization a way to use market forces to lower costs and improve the quality of human services, or is it an intermediate step on a path toward abandonment of government responsibility for human services? Viewed up close, questions such as these are often difficult to answer, and sometimes it is only with the passage of years that a consensus begins to form.

In the meantime, social workers involved in macro practice must be aware that change is a constant force in society, and certain consequences of its presence can be anticipated. For lack of a better term, we will refer to these as *axioms of change*. They are:

1. Some individuals, organizations, and communities will be more welcoming to change than others.
2. Individuals, organizations, and communities will also vary in how well they cope with change.
3. Resistance to change may occur as individuals, organizations, and communities attempt simply to hold on to the familiar, but resistance may also be a rational response to changes that have negative effects.
4. The constancy of change, the fact that people and collections of people vary in how well they cope with change, and the fact that the change may be negative creates an ongoing need for social workers to assist at both the micro and macro levels.

Brager and Holloway (1978) list three types of change that affect health and human service providers: people-focused change, technological change, and structural change.

People-focused change centers on alterations in individuals' values, knowledge, and skills. Because it involves the values that underlie our attitudes and perceptions, people-focused change is often difficult. But in dealing with problems such as denial of rights or neglect of basic needs, social workers are commonly faced with the need to change people's values, knowledge, and skills.

Technological change refers to alterations in the process of *service delivery*—those activities and procedures that guide policy and program implementation. Since the days when COS staffers and settlement house workers demanded training to become more systematic in how they approached their work, professional technologies have evolved. As discussed earlier, advances such as smartphones, tablet computers, and access to an unprecedented array of databases and information-management tools have the capacity to both assist social workers and alter the way they do their jobs. For both good and ill, these changes tax practitioners' abilities to stay current in their methods, adapt to new service approaches, and apply new technologies in a humane way that does not depersonalize clients in the process.

Structural change deals with how units within a system relate to one another. Privatization of services exemplifies this type of change, in that it has the potential to fundamentally alter the process of meeting the needs of disadvantaged persons in society. However, its success requires that services not be driven solely by the criterion of expending the minimum resources possible. Instead, change must be managed in such a way that effectiveness is maximized at the lowest cost possible.

The ongoing nature of change and its occurrence in one or more of these three forms raises important questions. Because the effects of a particular change may not be clear for some time, what approach should macro practitioners use in deciding how to respond? How can the effects of individual, technological, or structural changes be anticipated? Is the change likely to be welcomed or opposed? Can new technologies with which the practitioner may be unfamiliar be used to assist in responding to the change? We believe that a planned change model can be employed to assist social workers in answering these questions and addressing problems in macro systems. Chapter 3 will introduce the basic elements of such a model by discussing how to identify macro-level problems and target populations.

Engage, Assess, Intervene, Evaluate

Critical Thinking Question: As a social worker, what do you feel "effective" structural change should look like?

SUMMARY

The need for social workers to be able to understand and practice in macro systems is based on both the history of the social work profession and the society in which it evolved. The effects of major social changes such as immigration, industrialization, and rapid population growth led to concentrations of people in large urban areas, where, for the first time, modern institutional structures such as highly specialized organizations began to arise. So, too, did modern problems of urban crime, unemployment, poverty, and blighted neighborhoods. Society's responses to these problems were affected by new ideologies. Social Darwinism provided a rationale for ignoring many of these problems (through the reasoning that people in need were weak and helping them would in turn weaken society) or to provide paternalistic and judgmental forms of assistance. However, services guided by progressivism and social justice concerns resulted in much more proactive helping efforts, such as the rise of the settlement houses.

The traditions of the COS agencies, with their emphasis on case-level practice, and the settlement houses, with their more community-oriented efforts, led to a dualistic professional model that continues today. Within this model, social workers must be able not only to perceive their clients as individuals with personal problems but also understand them as members of larger community systems, and they must be prepared to intervene at the community level as well.

In addition, social workers typically carry out their tasks from within formal organizations, and the structure of those organizations has much to do with the effectiveness of the tasks. Over time, human service organizations have tended to become more complex and more bureaucratized, meaning that they may be efficient but also rigid and unresponsive to clients. Other organizational trends such as reprivatization and the embrace of computers and information technology also present risks and opportunities for social workers. The acquisition of skills to bring about planned change within these environments may be a crucial factor in determining the social workers' ultimate effectiveness.

One recurring theme in this chapter was that understanding the development of modern macro systems and the social work profession requires knowing the history of oppressed and disadvantaged groups within society. Macro-level systems can either overcome or exacerbate institutionalized oppression, depending on how they are structured. For example, protections supposedly guaranteed to African Americans and Hispanics through the Emancipation Proclamation and the Treaty of Guadalupe Hidalgo were undermined by other economic and social policies that worked to maintain historical oppression. Complex urban, industrial communities produced vast wealth during the past century, but this was not always shared by ethnic groups segregated (formally or informally) in ghettos or on reservations. Highly bureaucratized organizations became efficient at processing individual clients in standardized ways, but they did not consistently advance in their ability to meet individual needs or avoid practices that actively or passively discriminated against particular groups.

Traditional debates about whether social workers should pursue casework, group work, or community organization seem less important in light of these realities. Macro systems pervade all types of social work practice, and the ability to recognize and redirect their influence is critical to all social workers, regardless of their primary role.

Social workers must be able not only to perceive their clients as individuals with personal problems, but . . . as members of larger community systems.

Log onto **www.mysocialworklab.com** and answer the questions below. (*If you did not receive an access code to* **MySocialWorkLab** *with this text and wish to purchase access online, please visit* www.mysocialworklab.com.)

1. **Watch the ABC video: Colorism.** Reflect on how language and lingering effects of racism have been perpetuated within the African American community.

2. **Watch the ABC video: Working Poor.** Describe the blend of the macro (social policy) and micro social work approaches referenced in the video that are aimed at supporting this working family.

PRACTICE TEST

The following questions will test your knowledge of the content found within this chapter. For additional assessment, including licensing-exam-type questions on applying chapter content to practice, visit **MySocialWorkLab**.

1. Which of the following is NOT TRUE about population growth and urbanization in the United States?
   a. more than half the population lives in just 50 large metropolitan areas
   b. the population is growing by about 10 percent per decade
   c. population growth was much faster in the past
   d. suburbs grew first, then the central cores of cities

2. Which of the following is true about micro and macro practice?
   a. both began at the government level
   b. social workers have always been involved in both types of practice
   c. focusing on one type eliminates the need to have skills in the other
   d. after the book *Social Diagnosis*, almost all social workers shifted to micro practice

3. Which of the following is true about the loss of geographic relevance in modern communities?
   a. tools such as cell phones and email allow people to form and maintain non-local relationships
   b. organizations depend less on others locally and more on non-local organizations
   c. the demise of local groups (e.g., civic clubs) doesn't mean that social capital is lower
   d. all of the above

4. Which is NOT TRUE of human service organizations since the New Deal era?
   a. they rely on fewer different sources of funds than in the past
   b. they have tended to become more bureaucratized
   c. many are private agencies doing what government agencies used to do
   d. professional staff are more likely to be specialists and less likely to be generalists.

5. Can the historical changes discussed in this chapter be classified using the categories of change discussed at the end of the chapter? Give examples to illustrate your points and indicate whether the categories are helpful in making sense of societal change.

ASSESS YOUR COMPETENCE

Use the scale below to rate your current level of achievement on the following concepts or skills associated with each competency presented in the chapter:

1	2	3
I can accurately describe the concept or skill.	I can consistently identify the concept or skill when observing and analyzing practice activities.	I can competently implement the concept or skill in my own practice.

_____ Can appreciate and apply the values of professional social work even if working in a large bureaucracy.

_____ Can determine historical patterns in current social policy and critically analyze laws and ideologies in terms of effectiveness.

_____ Can think creatively about strengths and strategies to serve disadvantaged and oppressed populations.

_____ Can anticipate political and systemic consequences of social change, especially with regard to vulnerable and disempowered populations and communities.

3

Understanding Community and Organizational Problems

Core Competencies in this Chapter (Check marks indicate which competencies are covered in depth)				
✔ Professional Identity	☐ Ethical Practice	✔ Critical Thinking	☐ Diversity in Practice	☐ Human Rights & Justice
✔ Research-Based Practice	☐ Human Behavior	☐ Policy Practice	☐ Practice Contexts	✔ Engage, Assess, Intervene, Evaluate

WHAT IS SOCIAL WORK PRACTICE?

Social work is a profession oriented toward action and change. People who practice social work commit themselves to serve as a resource for those who are struggling with *problems or needs*. People often find themselves in situations in which they have limited or no control over the changes that need to be made, even though they may well have the strengths and coping skills needed to solve their problems. When people with problems or needs request help or are willing to accept it, social work intervention is appropriate.

Problems and needs emerge in many forms. Some are personal or family problems that can be resolved within an individual or family context; others can be solved only by changing something within a larger system, such as a neighborhood, an organization, or a community.

The majority of social workers deal with change directly with clients, usually working with individuals one on one, or with families or small groups. Some practitioners focus on communitywide problems. Others work in the areas of planning, management, and administration of organizations. Regardless of the professional social worker's practice orientation, it is crucial that all social work practitioners support the position that although some problems can be resolved at an individual or family level, others will require intervention that takes on a broader scope, including the need to effect changes in organizations and communities.

This broad focus on arenas for change is a feature that makes social work unique among helping professions. When the arena for change is limited solely to casework with individuals and families, an assumption is being made. The assumption is that causal factors associated with the problem or need can be found only in some deficit in the micro system—the client, couple, or family coming for help—or in their abilities to access needed resources. Broadening the problem analysis to include organizations and communities recognizes the possibility or likelihood that in some situations the pathology or causal factors may be identified in the policies and/or practices of macro systems—communities and their various institutions. For example, an organization may fail to provide relevant and needed services, or may provide them in a narrow and discriminatory manner. Or some members of a community may find themselves excluded from participation in decisions that affect them.

Intervention in organizations or communities is referred to as *macro-level change*. Managing macro-level change requires a good deal of professional knowledge and skill. Poor management and flawed decision making in the change process can result in serious setbacks that can make things worse for those already in need. On the other hand, many positive changes in organizations and communities have been orchestrated by social workers and others who have carefully planned, designed, and carried out the change process.

It is not unusual for direct practitioners to have clients ask for help with problems that at first appear to be individual or interpersonal, but, after further examination, turn out to be macro-level problems. A family that loses its primary source of income, undergoes eviction, and finds that there is no low-income housing and a three-month waiting list to get into a homeless shelter represents a symptom of a community problem. Clearly, the family's immediate shelter problem must be resolved, but just as obviously, the community-wide lack of housing and emergency alternatives must be addressed.

A mother may describe the pressures put on her son to join a gang and become involved in the drug trade. The immediate need of this family can perhaps be met by building a support system for the boy designed to keep him in school, in a part-time job, and in constructive activities. However, this individual/family approach alone would not solve the problem for the many other families who must live daily with the same threats. In instances like these, micro-level interventions are inefficient (and often ineffective) ways to address macro-level problems. In some ways, using micro-level interventions to address a macro-level problem is similar to treating individuals who are suffering from a new flu strain one at a time rather than vaccinating the whole population before they contract the disease.

Social work students often express the concern that they came into the profession because of an interest in working with individuals and families, not with communities and organizations. This can sometimes present an ethical dilemma, because at times what a client or family most needs in the long run is macro-level change. This does not mean that the immediate need is not addressed. It also does not mean that the social worker is left alone to bring about community or organizational change. Macro practice is a collaborative effort, and change will rarely be immediate. But ignoring the need for change should not be considered a viable option.

The Role of the Social Worker in Macro Practice

Identifying and dealing with organizational and community conditions, problems, and needs present a complex set of challenges to a social worker. Over the years, the image of the change agent has developed around some of the early social change pioneers—people such as Jane Addams, a founder of the famous Hull House in Chicago and the second woman to be awarded the Nobel Peace Prize; Ida B. Wells, an African American journalist, newspaper editor, and a newspaper owner who was active in the Civil Rights and the Women's Rights movements; Dorothea Dix, a nurse, who, in the nineteenth century, became a reformer of prisons and mental health facilities; or Susan B. Anthony, a teacher, who, in the late nineteenth and early twentieth century, was a champion of suffrage, abolition of slavery, and equal rights for women. Others view change agents as super-organizers—people such as Dr. Martin Luther King Jr., who led the fight for civil rights during the 1960s, or Cesar Chavez, who, along with Delores Huerta, founded the United Farm Workers to protect the rights of migrant workers. Other, more recent organizers include Cathy Lightner, who, in 1980, founded Mothers Against Drunk Drivers; Ralph Nader, who founded Public Interest Groups on automotive safety, energy, the environment, global trade, health research, congressional oversight, and legal protection of civil rights; and Barack Obama, the first African American President of the United States. These leaders have served as role models and have had great success in bringing about social change through nationwide organization and exceptional political skill.

Most social workers have neither the resources, media exposure, charisma, experience, followers, or power that these leaders have had available to them. Yet, in spite of seemingly overwhelming challenges, social workers have been effective in bringing about positive changes in organizations and communities.

Effectiveness does not necessarily come from the power of personality or the ability to mobilize thousands to a cause. It can emerge from careful, thoughtful, and creative planning undertaken by a group committed to change,

Professional Identity

Critical Thinking Question:
What types of skills make social workers uniquely effective at macro-practice change?

along with the tenacity to see it through to completion. The change effort may be guided, led, or coordinated by a professional social worker, but those involved will represent a broad range of interests. Planned change is often incremental and cumulative. One particular episode of change may appear small and insignificant in view of the scope of the problem, but it should be recognized that others committed to positive change may be working on the same problem or need from a different perspective. Recovery from the terrorist attacks of September 11, 2001, is a good example. When faced with the enormity of the task, members of any one group could easily have felt that their contributions to recovery were insignificant. But taken together, the work of cleanup crews, the church groups that housed families and helped them rebuild their lives, the many thousands of volunteers who supplied needed services and support, the social workers who provided counseling services, and literally thousands of others all contributed to the renewal of communities and cities that would have been impossible or much delayed if the tasks had not been shared. These same types of shared responsibilities have also been cited as critical to recovery from the 2005 Gulf Coast hurricanes and the 2010 oil spill, especially given the slow and poorly organized responses from all levels of government. Although the one-to-one response with victim families is critically important, so too is the planning and organizing of the macro-practice role that enables large-scale recovery from crises and allows people to get on with their lives.

Planned change is often incremental and cumulative.

The Social Worker's Entry into an Episode of Macro-Level Change

As noted in Chapter 1, social workers find themselves drawn into episodes of macro practice through a number of different avenues, which we will refer to as (1) problem/need/opportunity, (2) population, and (3) arena. As the intervention becomes more clearly conceptualized and defined, political and policy contexts must also be taken into consideration. More will be said about these interacting factors later in this book, as the analytical and intervention phases of macro-level change are described. The following examples will illustrate these different points of entry into an episode of change.

- A social worker with a neighborhood service center may discover that among the many families served by the center are five or six single parents who have recently moved from welfare to work but are unable to find affordable child care. Working with this group's *problem or need* (children who need to be cared for while the parent is at work) as his or her point of entry into the episode of change, the social worker and others develop a plan for child care for the children of these single parents.
- A social worker working with a senior center discovers that assisted-living resources in the community are limited for low-income seniors. In this instance, the worker's point of entry into the episode of change may be through the *population* of low-income elders, helping them organize and approach the city council or the state legislature about the need for more options for low-income seniors who can no longer live alone.
- A social worker at a community center learns that many apartments in the neighborhood are being used as drop points for illegal immigrants, where they wait until they are sent to various communities across the country. Concerns are expressed about sanitation, safety, and exploitation. In this

instance the worker's point of entry into the episode of change may be the *community or neighborhood*, perhaps by sponsoring some communitywide meetings to discuss the impact, involving the appropriate community leaders and authorities, and working toward a resolution. This represents entry through the community *arena*.

The point is that in the practice of social work, one finds many avenues or points of entry that lead to the use of macro-practice skills. This chapter focuses on understanding *problem/need/opportunity*, one of the three domains through which social workers become involved in community and organizational change. Major tasks to be undertaken in understanding the problem/need/opportunity will be spelled out.

The model presented in this chapter and throughout most of this text is often referred to as a rational planning approach. It is based on a study of the current situation and a carefully developed and prescribed plan for change that leads to predetermined outcomes. In rational planning there is a type of linearity present in that the plan, when produced, goes from one step to the next until the established goal is achieved. This process is called "reverse-order planning" (Brody, 2000, pp. 77–78), establishing a goal and then backtracking to fill in the actions that need to occur to arrive at the selected goal. However, this is not the only approach to community and organizational change available to social workers. The alternative to reverse-order planning is "forward-sequence planning," which begins by asking where can one start rather than what one wants as the final result (Brody, 2000, pp. 77–78). These more interpretive planning processes and emergent approaches are elaborated in other textbooks (e.g., Netting, O'Connor, & Fauri, 2008) if you are interested in exploring alternative ways to plan. Rational approaches to change are typically preferred by funders and regulators; thus, it is important that the social worker be as certain as possible about the course of action to be taken in professionally assisted planned change, since there is often so much at stake. For this reason we recommend beginning with a rational planning approach and moving to these alternative approaches only when the social worker is confident that an emergent process is necessary.

In Chapter 1, Figure 1.1, we presented problem, population, and arena as three separate circles, each of which must be explored. In other words, in order to be effective in bringing about macro-level change, the social worker and collaborators must begin by becoming knowledgeable about (1) the problem, need, or opportunity; (2) the population affected; and (3) the locality or arena where the change will take place.

These three domains can also be thought of as three intersecting circles in which the most critical knowledge and information is at the points of overlap. Figure 3.1, originally presented in Chapter 1, illustrates how each of these domains has unique as well as overlapping elements.

In this chapter we will focus on one of the three circles: understanding the problem/need/opportunity. The following chapters will explore the remaining circles: understanding populations (Chapter 4) and understanding communities (Chapters 5 and 6) and/or organizations (Chapters 7 and 8) with and in which macro practice is carried out. This chapter and the next will be used to guide the practitioner into the study of a particular social, community, or organizational problem or need, as well as the study of a selected population. These chapters will present a conceptual framework for a model of macro practice and will specify a series of tasks necessary for collecting data and

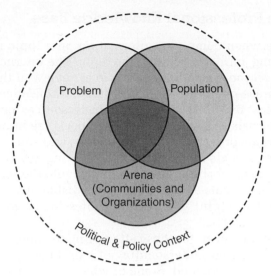

Figure 3.1

Understanding Problem, Population, and Arena

information. The actual data and information collected will come from a variety of sources, including interviews with people in the community or organization, census data, journal articles, textbooks, the Internet, research studies, and other resources.

Understanding organizations and communities and preparing a plan for intervention requires an understanding of some of the theories and concepts that help to explain the structure and function within these domains. Chapters 5, 6, 7, and 8, which focus on communities and organizations, will identify and describe some of the critical variables that must be understood and addressed in order to bring about change, regardless of the nature of the community or organization.

GUIDELINES FOR PLANNING CHANGE

For change to be initiated there must be an individual or a small group that recognizes the need for change and is prepared to take action. Within this core group, early decisions are made about collaboration and sharing of responsibility. Skills are needed in the areas of researching the professional knowledge base, quantitative and qualitative data collection, interviewing representatives of affected populations, and making an informed analysis based on findings. Remember that it is likely that the case to be made in favor of change will ultimately be taken to a decision-making body and possibly to a funding source. People who make decisions and allocate funds have a right to expect that those who come before them are knowledgeable, informed, and have "done their homework."

"Doing one's homework" in this instance means taking a disciplined, methodical approach to understanding the problem, population, arena, and political context of the proposed change. Referring to Figure 3.1 as a guide to our study of these domains, we first approach them as separate circles. This means that a social worker might, for example, look first at the problem/need/opportunity and attempt to understand everything he or she can about this domain within the limited time frame available.

Exploring the Professional Knowledge Base

There was a time when compiling information on a topic meant going to a library and scouring journal articles on the topic. The Internet has changed all that, and for this reason we no longer refer to a "review of the literature," but rather use the phrase *exploring the professional knowledge base.* The latest research, essays, case examples, and many other resources can be found online in professional journals and at other sites that specialize in problems or populations. Most journals provide a table of contents, and some provide abstracts as well. Resources can also be accessed by entering key words (e.g., "child neglect," "teenage alcohol abuse," or "dementia") into the search function and getting a list of types of data and information available. Articles in social work journals can also be helpful in directing professionals to useful resources (Roberts-DeGennaro, 2003).

It is important, however, for those attempting to compile a credible theoretical and research-based understanding of a problem or need to check the sources of information provided. Some of what is included on websites and other Internet resources may be opinion or conventional wisdom passed on without regard to authenticity. Internet sources should always be cited in the same way as journal articles, newspapers, news magazines, and other printed or electronic resources. The Social Science Data Resources website points out that one can find sound, useful data as well as bad, misinterpreted information floating around in this Information Age. To recognize the difference, the site invites users to visit another website called "About Stats," a product of the Statistical Assessment Service (STATS), a nonpartisan, nonprofit research organization in Washington, D.C.

Narrowing Down to the Most Useful Data and Information

While one project team is exploring the professional knowledge base, other individuals or teams can be gathering information from interviews with people in the organization or community that is the focus of the change effort. The intent is to understand as much as possible about the phenomenon itself—exploring the entire problem/need/opportunity circle from a scholarly perspective, while at the same time using information from those affected to help rule in or rule out various causal factors and other considerations.

Information on the overlapping areas of problem and population will often be found during the study. While attempting to understand teenagers, for example, we may come across studies on teenage violence. In most cases (but not all), these studies or summaries of existing knowledge about problem and population will be more informative than studies of problem alone or population alone. Each new finding is a potentially valuable addition to a body of knowledge that brings the change agent closer to understanding the problem. In this manner, the change agent and others involved in the change effort process gradually move toward understanding the problem and population as they currently exist in the local community, yet keeping in mind the fact that their understanding will always have its limitations.

Information and knowledge that will be of the greatest value to local decision makers will ultimately be found where the three circles in Figure 3.1 intersect. In other words, knowledge of how problem, population, and arena overlap will aid in understanding how these domains interact with each other to create the current situation and explain how it is unique to this local community.

In summary, the activities undertaken in the study phase of macro-level change include the following:

Problem

Explore the professional knowledge base to
- Conceptualize and define the problem or need.
- Locate relevant literature on theory related to causes and consequences of the problem.
- Compile relevant quantitative and qualitative data and other forms of information.

Interview those affected by the problem or need to
- Understand historical development at the local level.
- Identify major participants and systems.

Population

Explore the professional knowledge base to
- Know as much as possible about the population affected.
- Understand cultures and ethnic groups represented.
- Understand gender issues.

Interview those affected by the problem or need to
- Identify personal perspectives.
- Understand personal experiences in relation to the problem or need and attempts to deal with it.
- Understand how the problem or need is perceived by various groups within the organization or community.

Arena

Explore the professional knowledge base to
- Compile demographic and other data on the organization or community.
- Create useful maps of the community.
- Compile data on the problem or need and how it has been addressed by the organization or community.

Interview those affected by the problem or need to:
- Identify past experiences with the organization or community.
- Establish boundaries for the proposed change.
- Identify key decision makers and funding sources.
- Understand the many different perspectives on the etiology of the problem or need.

For all three studies (problem/need/opportunity, population, and arena), the core planning team will need to coordinate activities. These will include identifying various roles and responsibilities, assigning individuals according to their abilities, monitoring progress, and dealing with interpersonal, inter-group, and political dynamics.

We are not proposing an exhaustive exploration that goes on for years. There is rarely time or resources for such study, and responding expeditiously is often critical to success. However, plunging into a proposed solution without doing the necessary homework is equally risky. Our intent in this and the following chapters is to lay out a format for systematic study of each of the three circles in Figure 3.1 (as well as the political context, which will be discussed in Chapters 9 and 10) that can be accomplished within a reasonable

Engage, Assess, Intervene, Evaluate

Critical Thinking Question:
Why is it important to gather information about a problem and population from a variety of sources?

amount of time (a few weeks to a few months, depending on the people and the skills involved), beginning with a small core team of perhaps four or five people committed to bringing about needed change, and gradually expanding to others willing to carry out specific tasks.

UNDERSTANDING PROBLEMS AND OPPORTUNITIES

We have attempted to break down the understanding of what needs to be changed (to the extent this is possible) into three tasks:

> ♦ **Task 1:** Gather information from key informants in the community or organization
> ♦ **Task 2:** Explore the professional knowledge base on the condition, problem, need, or opportunity
> ♦ **Task 3:** Select factors that help explain the underlying causes of the problem

Community political and civic leaders, activists, and others are often so anxious to make change happen that they begin at the point of proposing solutions. Increased incidence of Driving Under the Influence (DUI)? Hire more police and increase penalties! More homeless families on the streets? Build a shelter. Increased numbers of teen pregnancies? Offer classes on the importance of sexual abstinence until marriage. These simplistic solutions will inevitably emerge in any episode of change. It is the responsibility of the social worker in a professionally guided change effort to make certain that a range of alternative perspectives and possible causes is adequately explored before proposing a solution.

There are several reasons for exploring multiple perspectives on the problem. First, leaping to quick solutions without adequate study is the antithesis of professional practice. In one-on-one counseling, for example, telling clients exactly how to solve their problems after only a brief introduction to the facts violates many ethical and professional principles. Second, quick and easy solutions are usually based on the assumption that the problem in question has one primary cause. In fact, as we will discuss in greater detail later in this chapter, virtually no social problem has only one cause. Many different factors come into play in the development of a social condition, and changing that condition almost always necessitates addressing more than one of these factors.

Take, for example, a community in which highway deaths due to alcohol have increased 18 percent in the past two years. How might the causes in this case be defined? One group will be convinced that the cause is lack of strict enforcement of existing laws prohibiting driving under the influence of drugs or alcohol, and may want to increase the budget of the police department to crack down on those who are driving while impaired. Another group will describe causes as easy availability of alcohol to teenagers, and may want to see increased penalties to those who sell alcohol to minors. Others will see alcohol abuse as a symptom of increasing stress or family breakdown, and may propose a campaign to promote activities that strengthen families. These represent just a few of the perspectives that might be introduced in an attempt to understand reasons behind driving under the influence of alcohol or drugs.

This early analytical work is an important part of the change process. We propose that change agents proceed with a set of tasks designed to gather as much useful information about the problem as is available. These tasks involve direct contact with those who have experienced the problem or need firsthand, as well as a systematic exploration of the professional knowledge base, data summaries, and perhaps a chronology of events leading to the current situation. This approach is designed to produce as thorough an understanding of the problem and population as possible in as short a time as possible, although there are limits to how short this time can be. A hurried and incomplete analysis can be worse than none at all.

These tasks can and should proceed simultaneously, which is where the coordinating work of the change agent becomes important. Those participating in the change effort who have the best credentials for entering the community or organization for the purpose of interviewing and data collection should be assigned to such tasks. Those who have demonstrated skill in searching and synthesizing theoretical and research resources should carry out this task. Those who work well with numerical data should plan to compile the necessary tables and charts. In the end, each of these separate tasks will contribute to a clearer understanding of the problem, need, or opportunity and will provide the basis for a well-designed plan of intervention leading to a positive solution.

A hurried and incomplete analysis can be worse than none at all.

Task 1: Gather Information from Key Informants in the Community or Organization

Understanding a macro-level problem or need in all its complexity requires skillful eliciting of information from a variety of people who have experienced the problem. Knowledge and sensitivity is required for this type of interview. The work done in macro practice in social work is not like that of a newspaper reporter gathering information for an article. A trusting relationship must be built so that those persons in the community or organization will develop a commitment to the changes needed and participate in the change effort. While it should be recognized that a macro-level intervention is not necessarily a research project, social workers can benefit from what ethnographers have learned about the study of a community. Fetterman (2009) points out that ethnography allows people to describe their own context in their own words.

A number of authors emphasize the importance of approaching the study of communities or organizations sensitively (Devore, 1998; Gutierrez & Lewis, 1999; Hyde, 2004; Lecca, Quervalu, Nunes, & Gonzales, 1998). A distillation of the work of these authors argues strongly for special attention to knowledge, values, leadership, and the helping process when working with problems, populations, or arenas where ethnicity, culture, gender, sexual identity, or other group identity factors may be relevant. A summary of considerations is presented here.

Knowledge and Values

Knowledge
- Knowledge of human behavior and the social environment, especially contemporary theories that incorporate ethnic, culture, gender, and other personal and collective identity considerations
- Knowledge about the effects of racism and poverty, especially on ethnic communities

- Knowledge of the agency or institution one represents and how it is perceived by the population of focus
- Knowledge of the ways in which the community, through its institutions (e.g., courts, school, law enforcement), has historically dealt with problems and needs faced by ethnic groups and other special populations
- Knowledge about how previous planned activities may have been imposed on the community without input or sanction from community members
- Knowledge of ethnic, gender, and other special population cultures and ways in which existing policies and standards either ignore or include issues important to them

Values
- Understanding social work values about people and issues of personal responsibility and social justice

Leadership

Group or Community Membership
- Ideally, leaders should be members of the groups or communities being organized
- The organizer serves as a facilitator and ensures incorporation of ethnic and gender perspectives

Ethnic/Gender Self-Awareness
- Leaders and participants in change affecting ethnic and/or gender groups and communities need to understand their own sense of identity in relation to ethnicity and gender

The Change Episode

Goals, Policies, and Practices
- Policies and practices should be consistent with ethnic, cultural, and/or gender considerations
- There should be agreement among the ethnic, cultural, gender, or other group participants on the results or outcomes desired
- Human and financial resources and other strengths available within the culture should be assessed

The points highlighted by the issues and questions raised are important ones. The organizer or change agent cannot simply enter a community or organizational culture without careful preparation and attention to the groups represented and to the professional knowledge base necessary to the intervention.

People who live or work in the place that is seen as needing change may not perceive the situation exactly as the change agent does. They may have important social support structures or resources unknown to persons outside that group. Their positions in the community or organization and their perspectives need to be respected. Cues should be taken from indigenous people as to appropriate roles and responsibilities in initiating a change effort.

Many changes involve cultural and ethnic considerations, so the preceding points should be incorporated early in any planned macro-level change. Also important is an awareness of the many ways in which culture can be manifested. For example, in an extended care facility there is a culture-of-care provision. In a high school, faculty, staff, students, and administrators will typically have developed an organizational culture over time. In these and other situations where the change agent is perceived as an outsider, the preceding principles can help the organizer or change agent build credibility and avoid mistakes.

The task of gathering information from key informants involves a number of activities, including (1) identifying the major participants, (2) identifying and defining the community or organizational condition or problem, and (3) preparing a chronology of significant historical events leading to the current situation. These activities will be discussed in the following sections.

Identify Major Participants

Questions to be explored for this activity include:

▶ Who first identified the problem? Are those initially involved still available? Are they still involved?

▶ What roles have local people played in past efforts at change?

▶ What individuals or groups support and oppose change?

▶ What individuals or groups have the power to approve or deny change?

Later in the process, after the community or organizational analysis has been completed, the change agent and others will identify the various systems involved and invite representatives of each of these systems to participate in selecting a strategy for change and organizing participants in a way that will maximize effectiveness.

However, the type of thorough identification of all systems to be undertaken later (see Chapter 9) is not the focus of this early selection of major participants. Rather, this effort is intended to identify key informants in an attempt to draw on the experiences of the most knowledgeable, as well as those best positioned to understand what has happened to date. Those gathering information should be aware that any single perspective may involve natural self-interest and lead to a biased or an incomplete understanding of the condition or problem. For this reason, multiple sources are to be preferred. A 2004 study proposes useful suggestions about ways in which professionals and community residents can work together to elicit important information (Ungar, Manuel, Mealey, Thomas, & Campbell, 2004).

Those who first identified the problem are important to the change process. For example, a community activist may have taken the lead in the past to ensure that health care for migrant workers is available. If this issue is revisited later in the process, it is important to understand the experiences and perspectives of the first initiator. Was he or she successful? Why or why not? Did he or she alienate any critical decision makers? How did he or she approach the issue, and what would he or she do differently? Has he or she brought certain biases or prejudices to his or her view of the situation? Who else was involved, and what were their roles and perspectives on the proposed change? Change agents are not obligated to utilize the same method or to affiliate with an earlier change effort, but they should at least be aware of the approach taken and the results achieved.

Those who first identified the problem are important to the change process.

Whether or not the current condition or problem has been addressed before, it is important that the change agent develop an understanding of which local individuals and groups support or oppose the change effort that is being considered. For example, a small group of staff within an organization may want to promote an aggressive affirmative action approach to recruitment and hiring in order to better reflect the changing demographics of a community. It would be a mistake to assume that all staff, managers, and administrators will favor this change effort. Rather than plan only with those who agree, change agents should encourage opponents to express their opinions. Working with the opposition can present some difficult ethical issues, but the skillful change agent will find ways to identify key local participants who favor and who oppose the change effort, and will make every attempt to keep the process open to all.

The third group of local participants to be identified is those individuals who have the power or authority to approve or reject the change that ultimately will be proposed. Within an organization, this will most likely be the chief executive officer (CEO) or the board of directors, but others throughout the organization may have an important say as well. In a community, the identity of decision makers will depend on the domain identified for change. If the focus is on a school or school district, decision makers will include principals, school board members, and others within the system. In a local neighborhood, key people will include city council members or city staff. Some exploration will be needed to determine who has this type of authority. When possible, it can be useful to have copies of local directories with phone numbers and email addresses of city personnel, school personnel, or others who may be involved. It is also helpful to have a complete briefing on local politics by someone who knows the organization or community so that key influential people are not left out, and so that alternative and opposing perspectives are understood. More will be said about this in Chapter 9.

Identify Community or Organizational Condition

Questions to be explored for this activity include the following:

▶ What is the difference between a condition and a problem?
▶ What does this community or organization consider to be its priority problems?
▶ In approaching an episode of change, how should the condition statement be framed?

A *condition* is a phenomenon that is present in a community or organization that may be troublesome to a number of people but that has not been formally identified, labeled, or publicly acknowledged as a problem. It is important that social workers understand whether a phenomenon is a condition that has not been formally recognized, or a problem that has been acknowledged by the organization or community. This status will affect where the social worker places her or his emphasis in early planning efforts. Ultimately, decision makers will have to acknowledge the existence of a problem (either willingly or reluctantly) if formal resources are to be dedicated to alleviating or eliminating the problem. An observer once noted that a condition becomes a problem when it is recognized by a significant number of people or a number of significant people.

Every organization and community is full of conditions as well as problems. Social consequences of urban living—such as traffic congestion, exposure to air pollution, dangerous neighborhoods, affordable housing, and other issues—can all be considered social or community conditions if no efforts have been mobilized to address them. Similarly, in rural communities, isolation, inaccessible health care, and a declining economic base can all be considered social conditions if they remain unrecognized by any formal or informal efforts toward resolution.

The same concept applies to organizations, where troublesome phenomena are present but have not necessarily been formally identified or labeled as a problem. For example, staff in a long-term care facility for elders may be concerned about what they consider to be overmedication of some of the residents. Similarly, program managers may recognize a trend to extend services to those who can pay while offering only a waiting list to those who cannot.

To be defined as a *problem*, a condition must in some way be formally recognized and incorporated into the action agenda of a group, organization, or community. This may mean, for example, that an elected official proposes a study of elderly suicide, or that a group of parents concerned about methamphetamine abuse lobbies for a city ordinance to regulate the sale of cold medicines containing pseudoephedrine (an ingredient used to make meth) within the city limits. It may mean that a task force within an organization is officially sanctioned to explore the effects of medication on residents in long-term care. Or it may mean that a neighborhood group experiencing high-speed traffic on their residential streets takes steps to bring about broader recognition of the presence of the condition and its problematic nature. Regardless of the form it takes, formal recognition is important for legitimization.

The distinction between a *condition* and a *problem* is significant to a social worker planning a macro-level intervention. If a condition has not been formally recognized in some way, the first task must be to obtain that formal recognition. For example, for many years homelessness was dealt with as a personal employment problem, family violence as a personal matter, and AIDS as a personal health problem. Most communities simply viewed these as existing conditions, not as social or community problems. When these conditions began to affect greater segments of society and reached the point at which they could no longer be ignored, national, state, and local community leaders began to identify them as problems and to dedicate resources toward their resolution. Once formally recognized and acknowledged as problems (usually as a result of persistent media attention), these conditions become candidates for organized intervention efforts. The creation of task forces for the homeless in cities across the country, child abuse and neglect reporting laws, and federal funding for AIDS research and services are results of recognizing conditions and defining them as problems.

One of the first tasks in problem identification, then, is to develop a *condition statement*. A condition statement must include (1) a target population, (2) a geographical boundary, and (3) the difficulty facing the population. Statements should be descriptive, as objective as possible, and based on findings to date.

Statements will be adapted depending on whether the condition exists within a community or in an organization. For example, a condition statement might be, "Domestic violence in Preston County is increasing." Generally speaking, the more precise the statement is, the greater likelihood of a successful intervention. This statement, for example, could vary from extremely general to very specific, as depicted in Figure 3.2.

A similar process within an organization would begin with a general statement. For example, an organizational condition might be that in a domestic violence shelter, resources are not being used efficiently and many residents are returning to their abusers. Quantitative data such as demographics, incidence, prevalence, or trends, and qualitative data focused, perhaps, on reasons for returning to abusers, would then need to be compiled to help pinpoint the condition as precisely as possible.

Condition statements are made more precise through a process of research and documentation of the nature, size, and scope of the problem. As one proceeds with subsequent tasks in problem analysis, the condition statement will

Critical Thinking

Critical Thinking Question: What are some potential consequences of not articulating a clear condition statement when planning for change?

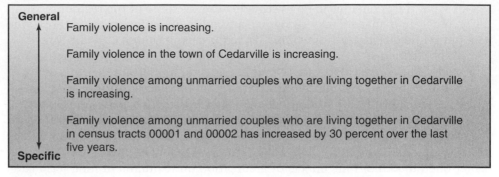

Figure 3.2
Sample Condition Statements

be refined many times as new facts and findings emerge. The statement may evolve into an identified problem on which there is consensus, or it may be perceived as a need or deficit. It is possible that a change effort can be developed around an opportunity, where there is no identified problem or need, but instead funding or resources become available. The change agent needs to recognize that consensus building is important no matter how the change effort arose.

Identify Relevant Historical Incidents

Questions to be explored for this activity include the following:

- Has the problem been recognized and acknowledged by any community or organizational members?
- If so, when was this condition, problem, or opportunity first recognized in this community or organization?
- What are the important incidents or events that have occurred from the first recognition to the present time?
- What do earlier efforts to address this problem reveal?

The next task is to compile a chronology of significant events or milestones that promotes understanding of the history of the community or organizational condition or problem. This shifts the focus to the area in Figure 3.1 where the problem and the arena overlap.

A condition or problem in any community or organization has its own history.

A condition or problem in any community or organization has its own history. This history can affect the ways in which people currently perceive the condition or problem. It is, therefore, important to understand how key people within the community or organization perceived the condition or problem in the past. If seen as a problem, how was it addressed? How effective were the attempts to alleviate the problem? Who were the major participants in any previous change efforts?

If one looks at the condition or problem merely as it is defined at present, much will be missed. Instead, it is crucial to determine the problem's history, particularly in terms of critical incidents that have shaped past and current perceptions of the problem. A task force might, for example, be concerned about a high dropout rate from the local high school. The following chronology of critical incidents could help the group to better understand factors that influenced the origin and development of important issues in the high school over the years.

2000   Riverview High School was a predominantly lower-middle-class high school with an 82 percent graduation rate.

2002   School district boundaries were redrawn, and the student body changed. For 30 percent of its members, English was a second language.

2004   Enrollment dropped 20 percent, and the graduation rate fell to 67 percent.

2005   Riverview High School initiated a strong vocational training program designed to prepare high school graduates for post–high school employment; the college preparatory curriculum was deemphasized.

2007   Enrollment increased; attendance patterns improved.

2009   Local employers hired only 32 percent of the graduates; unemployment rates among Riverview graduates one year later were as high as 37 percent.

2011   Enrollment dropped back to 2004 levels; the dropout rate reached 23 percent, its highest mark yet.

2012   Riverview High School was written up in the local newspaper as one of the ten worst schools in the state in terms of quality of education, retention rates of students, and post–high school employment. A blue-ribbon panel was formed to make recommendations to improve the quality of education.

Tracing these historical events lends insight into some of the incidents experienced by the faculty, staff, administration, students, and families associated with Riverview High School. In this case, the task force should expect to encounter a discouraged and cynical response to any sort of a "Stay in School" campaign. The critical incidents list indicates that many of the arguments for staying in school simply did not prove true for those who graduated.

When the employment, career, and financial incentives for remaining in high school are removed, the challenge to keep students in school is greatly increased. This means that the approach to organizational change needs to be tailored in a way that is relevant and meaningful to those who are intended to be the primary beneficiaries. This has clear implications for including in the change effort those who can, for example, positively influence the employment environment for graduates.

Exploring relevant historical incidents also helps establish the credibility of the change agent. Many people are simply not open to supporting change for their communities and organizations if those organizing the change effort are perceived as being "outsiders" who have not taken the time to become familiar with what has gone on in the past.

The types of critical incidents just described are generally gleaned from interviews or discussions with long-time residents, activists, community leaders, teachers, and social service agency employees. In tracing the history or antecedent conditions of an episode of change, the change agent hopes to discover (1) what happened in the past to call attention to the problem or need, (2) what the community's (neighborhood, city, county, state, private sector) response was to the attention focused on the problem or need, and (3) how successful or unsuccessful the response was and why.

based on census data include *USA Counties, Statistical Abstract of the United States,* and *State and Metropolitan Area Data Book,* all of which can be accessed online. Websites for these and other resources are identified in Figure 3.3.

State and/or county departments of social services, health, mental health, and corrections often collect data that can be useful in documenting the existence of social conditions or problems. Other sources include local social service agencies, the United Way, community councils, centralized data-collection resource centers, centralized information and referral agencies, law-enforcement

---

Monthly Catalog of United States Government Publications
Washington, DC: United States Government Printing Office (USGPO)
Available online as *Catalog of U.S. Government Publications*

American Statistics Index
Washington, DC: Congressional Information Service

CIS
Washington, DC: Congressional Information Service

Statistical Abstract of the United States
Washington, DC: U.S. Dept. of Commerce, Economic and Statistics
     Administration, Bureau of the Census
Available online: www.census.gov/statab/www/

County and City Data Book
Washington, DC: U.S. Dept. of Commerce, Economic and Statistics
     Administration, Bureau of the Census

State and Metropolitan Area Data Book
Washington, DC: U.S. Dept. of Commerce, Economic and Statistics
     Administration, Bureau of the Census
Available online: www.census.gov/statab/www/smadb.html

Health, United States
Hyattsville, MD: U.S. Dept. of Health and Human Services, Public Health
     Service, Centers for Disease Control, National Center for Health Statistics
Available online: www.cdc.gov/nchs/products/pubs/pubd/hus/hus.html

Mental Health, United States
Rockville, MD: U.S. Dept. of Health and Human Services, Substance Abuse,
     and Mental Health Administration, Center for Mental Health Survey.
Available online: www.samhsa.gov/news/newsreleases/011024nr.MH2000.html

Sourcebook of Criminal Justice Statistics
Washington, DC: U.S. Dept. of Justice, Office of Justice Programs,
     Bureau of Justice Statistics
Available online: www.albany.edu/sourcebook/

Digest of Educational Statistics
Washington, DC: U.S. Dept. of Education, Office of Educational Research
     and Improvement, National Center for Educational Statistics
Available online: www.ed.gov/pubs/stats.html

Figure 3.3
Resources for Data Collection

agencies, hospitals, and school district offices. The process of tracking down information is often similar to a scavenger hunt, where one clue leads to another until a point is reached where the quantity and quality of supportive data collected is sufficient to allow the persons initiating change to make their case.

In collecting supporting data, the change agent should think in terms of the entire "circle" of information needed to understand the presenting problem or condition. This means that data collection will not necessarily be limited to the *local* community, neighborhood, or organization that is the focus of the change effort. Although data on the smallest local units of analysis (such as the neighborhood or census tract) are certainly powerful in terms of supporting the argument that something must be done, data on the same conditions or problems at the county, state, or national levels can also be useful in providing a basis of comparison against which local figures can be judged.

Make the Data Meaningful for Interpretation

Questions to be explored for this activity include:

- What options can be used to display data?
- How should data be displayed in order to clearly and concisely make the case for change?

Comparative data are generally more useful than a single statistic, and several techniques can be used to collect and display comparative data. These include cross-sectional analysis, time-series comparisons, and comparisons with other data units. In addition to these data displays, techniques such as standards comparisons and epidemiological analysis can be useful (Kettner, Moroney, & Martin, 2008). Displays should be prepared and presented in a way that will tell the story effectively.

A number of graphic options are available, including line graphs, bar graphs, and pie charts. Thought should be given to which graphic display will have the greatest impact, given the data to be presented. Most of the graphics needed for these types of displays are a part of Microsoft Office Home Edition. This package includes Word (word processing), Excel (spreadsheets), Power-Point (presentations), and Access (relational databases). When job descriptions include a requirement for computer skills, in most cases ability to use these types of programs is expected.

Cross-Sectional Analysis. This approach involves collecting data at a single point in time and describing circumstances at the moment captured in those data. It usually focuses on a single population or sample. For example, a survey might concentrate on gathering information about a need experienced by a particular target population and display the percentage of the population who report a problem in this area, as illustrated in Table 3.2.

The data presented in Table 3.2 can be used to create a more dramatic visual effect by translating the data into graphic formats. Figure 3.4 illustrates age distribution in the form of a bar graph, which presents a picture of an aging population.

Figure 3.5 uses a pie chart to illustrate ethnic distribution. Side-by-side pie charts using census data 10 years apart could be used as a cross-sectional analysis as well as a time-series analysis.

As community or organizational conditions are identified, subpopulations can usually be assessed by demographic characteristics such as age, gender, and racial/ethnic group. The most serious limitation is that a cross-sectional analysis does not reveal changes over time.

Table 3.2　**An Illustration of Cross-Sectional Analysis, Examining the Percentage of Each Population Experiencing a Problem**

Variable	Population (%)	Housing (%)	Employment (%)	Nutrition (%)	Transportation (%)
Age					
0–18	11	5	N/A	5	N/A
19–30	21	14	7	9	16
31–64	28	17	11	8	19
65+	40	19	33	15	33
Gender					
Female	52	5	7	6	18
Male	48	16	24	11	17
Ethnicity					
White	42	10	5	4	7
Asian American	6	3	4	5	9
African American	34	17	11	12	15
Hispanic	14	7	10	9	11
Native American	4	11	23	8	14

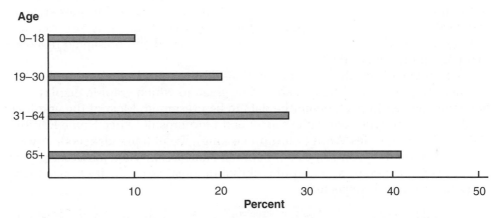

Figure 3.4

A Bar Graph Illustrating Age Distribution and Revealing an Aging Population

Time-Series Comparisons.　When available, data from repeated observations over time are preferred because they display trends. Assuming data were collected on an annual basis, a time-series comparison would look at trends in the variable(s) of interest. For example, the number of nonduplicated individuals requesting overnight stays in homeless shelters in a given city might be displayed in a line graph, as shown in Figure 3.6.

Statistics like these can help project need and cost into the future, based on assumptions about changes over time identified in a series of observations. Comparisons among these observations can provide the change agent with valuable information. For example, they can be used to document how client need is increasing, what the trends are for the next few years, why additional resources are needed, and the projected dollars necessary to fill anticipated need.

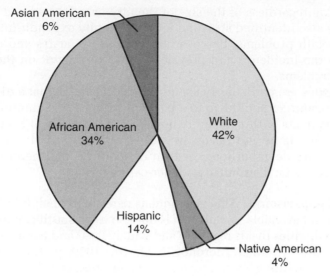

Figure 3.5

A Pie Chart Illustrating Ethnic Distribution

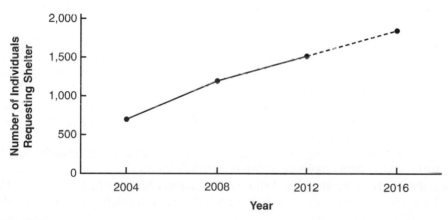

Figure 3.6

A Line Graph Illustrating a Time-Series Analysis of the Number of Individuals Requesting Overnight Shelter by Homeless Persons

Comparison with Other Data Units.   Even though cross-sectional analysis can provide a snapshot at a point in time, and time series can depict trends over time, questions might still be raised about the legitimacy of a problem, especially when comparisons are being made with other communities or organizations. For example, if a change agent is able to document a current teenage pregnancy rate of 22 percent in a community, and to show an upward trend over five years, a critic might reasonably ask if this rate is considered high or low. This is where comparison to other data units is helpful.

A wealth of both regularly and specially assembled information is available for use as supporting data. Over the past few decades, many federal, state, and local agencies have contributed to databases on rates per 1,000, 10,000, or 100,000 on a wide range of social, economic, and health problems. These statistics allow for comparison regardless of the size of the city or neighborhood in question. Studies have also identified state and local per-capita expenditures for various social and health problems. Based on these findings, states and cities can be ranked as to the incidence and prevalence of problems or on their efforts to address the problems.

Comparisons are particularly useful in making a case that a disproportionate share of resources should go to a particularly needy community. By comparing census tracts within a county on selected variables, it becomes readily evident that problems and needs are not always equally distributed across communities and neighborhoods within the county, and therefore resources should not always be distributed on a per-capita basis.

Standards Comparisons.   This technique is particularly helpful when comparative data are not available. A *standard* is defined as "a specification accepted by recognized authorities that is regularly and widely used and has a recognized and permanent status" (Kettner, Moroney, & Martin, 1999, p. 126). Standards are developed by accrediting bodies, governmental entities, and professional associations. For example, the Child Welfare League of America publishes comprehensive sets of standards related to community and agency programs for child abuse and neglect, adoption, and other child welfare services. Similarly, the National Council on Aging has developed case management standards. The National Association of Social Workers has developed standards for social work services in a wide variety of settings. Box 3.1 provides a brief example.

Where governmental units, accrediting bodies, and professional associations have defined standards, conditions considered to be falling below health, educational, personal care, housing, and other types of standards become more readily accessible as targets for change. Community leaders do not like the negative publicity that often results when services offered within their communities are described as being "below standard." These types of standards apply primarily to the quality of services being provided.

Standards of sorts may also be used to define a problem or population. For example, some cities have developed standardized criteria to define a homeless person or a gang member. Where such criteria have been established, they can be useful in interpreting existing records and compiling new quantitative data or other information.

Epidemiological Analysis.   This is a technique adapted from the field of public health, where an analysis of factors contributing to a disease helps to establish

---

Box 3.1   Selected Standards from NASW Standards for the Practice of Social Work with Adolescents

Standard 1. Social workers shall demonstrate knowledge and understanding of adolescent development.

Standard 2. Social workers shall demonstrate an understanding of and ability to assess the needs of adolescents; access social institutions, organizations, and resources within a community that provides services for adolescents and their families; and advocate for the development of needed resources.

Standard 3. Social workers shall demonstrate knowledge and understanding of family dynamics.

Note: These are three of ten standards and are listed here as examples. The entire listing can be found on the NASW website. Each standard has, in addition, a detailed interpretation that defines what is meant by terms contained within the standard.

Source: Excerpted from National Association of Social Workers (2005). *NASW Standards for the Practice of Social Work with Adolescents,* www.socialworkers.org/practice/standards/swadolescents.asp.

relationships even when a clear cause-and-effect relationship cannot be demonstrated. This approach can be applied not only to disease but also to social problems. For example, Piven and Cloward (1971) established relationships among the variables of poverty, poor education, poor housing, and welfare dependency. Although it cannot be said that any of these conditions *cause* welfare dependency, the relationship of dependency to the combination of factors is well established.

More recently, Sabol, Coulton, and Polousky (2004) examined variables influencing child maltreatment. In this study, the authors looked at age, race, and urban versus suburban location, and found that these factors could be used to predict the probability of a child being reported for an incident of maltreatment before his or her tenth birthday. In another study, Diala, Muntaner, and Walrath (2004) examined rural and urban location, demographic characteristics of age, gender, and race, and social class factors of education, household income, and wealth, and found that some relationships between and among these variables could be useful in predicting the probability of alcohol and drug abuse and dependence.

A useful feature of epidemiological thinking is that in analyzing problems it can help avoid simplistic cause-and-effect thinking. Although a single causal factor (e.g., poor education, poverty, or child abuse) may explain current problems faced by a small portion of the population, multiple factors in combination frequently help explain the problem or phenomenon for a much larger portion of the population.

Qualitative Data Displays. Qualitative data can also be presented in the form of tables and figures, allowing word data to tell a thematic story about the problem. Figure 3.7 provides an example from a qualitative study on faith-based advocacy organizations (FBAO). The organization was part of a study examining

Policy Area	Description	Issue Exemplars
First Amendment	• Preserving the wall of separation between religion and the state • Preventing public policy unduly influenced by singular religious viewpoints	• Prayer in government-funded public institutions • School vouchers • Religious curriculum in public schools • Charitable choice
Bias and Discrimination	• Opposing legislation that promotes bias and intolerance • Supporting efforts that encourage diversity	• Civil equality for same sex couples • Immigration • Hate crimes • Capital punishment
Health and Social Justice	• Representing those in need in the Jewish and broader community	• Medicaid expansion • Minimum wage • Reproductive choice • Stem cell research

Figure 3.7
An Example of How to Display Qualitative Data

the activities of FBAOs involved in lobbying on social welfare issues. The table illustrates the policy areas of one FBAO, using examples from the research as exemplars of the policy area.

Task 3: Select Factors That Help Explain the Underlying Causes of the Problem

Questions to be explored for this task include:

▶ From interviews with key informants, identification of important historical events, review of the professional knowledge base, and compilation of data, what appear to be the major factors that help in understanding the problem?

▶ Which expectations, at this point, appear to be the most logical ones to be addressed in this episode of change?

When those involved in the change effort have defined the problem; reviewed important historical events; completed a review of relevant journals articles, texts, and web resources; and compiled supporting evidence, they should have at least a beginning understanding of what it is that is causing the problem. The next step is to determine what cause-and-effect relationships must be dealt with in order to bring about needed changes. Preliminary identification of these factors is a necessary step in clarifying the change effort. Before distilling the data and information gathered, however, it is important to understand the types of causes or other considerations to be identified. Box 3.2 provides an example of causes or contributing factors about unsupervised children in a community.

When examining conditions or problems in the human services, there is often a strong temptation to identify lack of resources as a cause of a problem. For example, in studies focused on an organizational problem, causes often tend to be defined in terms of lack of operating funds, staff, adequate equipment and facilities, and so on. In defining a community problem, causes often are seen in terms of lack of resources for new programs or expanded services, such as more child-care slots, more training, and so on. In many cases, genuine resource deficits may exist, but we caution against superficial assessments that look to dollars as the only solution to every problem. There are several reasons for a more thorough approach.

First, resources have to do with the intervention or the so-called solution, and they should be considered only after a specific approach has been proposed and resource issues can be addressed in detailed, not general, terms. Second, "lack of resources" is so universal that it is relatively meaningless as a

---

Box 3.2   Example of Causes or Contributing Factors about Unsupervised Children in a Community

▶ There is an unusually high percentage of single, working mothers in the community.

▶ There are no after-school programs available in the community.

▶ Children in the community from single-parent families have few male mentors or role models.

▶ The community lacks a sense of cohesion; for the most part, people know few neighbors.

▶ No community-based organizations are currently addressing this problem.

part of problem analysis. Third, "lack of adequate resources" does not help explain underlying causal or contributing factors. The statement simply assumes that more of whatever is already being done will solve the problem. Additional resources in macro-level change can be critical to success, but the issue should be addressed later in the change process.

The types of causal or contributing factors to be addressed are those fundamental factors that explain why the problem emerged and why it persists over time. They are substantive factors that prevent progress toward solutions. Identifying these multiple causes helps clarify the complex nature of the problem. As a greater understanding of problem, population, and arena is achieved, these factors will be used to develop a working hypothesis of etiology or cause(s) and effect(s). This working hypothesis will then be used to guide the intervention.

Identification of possible causes is intended to help those who are exploring the need for change to focus their efforts, thereby increasing the chances of success. In most cases it is unlikely that all contributing factors will be addressed. Selection of a limited number of possible causes should lead either to a narrower, more limited focus or to collaboration with others, with agreement that each change effort will concentrate on different factors. For example, faced with a problem of unsupervised children in a community, a local church might agree to take responsibility for building mutual support systems among single mothers and strengthening the sense of community, whereas a local school may be willing to provide constructive, supervised after-school activities. At this point, however, these decisions would be premature. The purpose of identifying contributing factors is to arrive at an understanding of the problem that is as clear as possible.

SUMMARY

In this chapter we presented an approach to orderly, systematic, professionally assisted change. Critics may say that this approach takes too long and fails to seize the moment, and we acknowledge that part of the responsibility of a change agent is to make judgments about how and when to act. The study process can be streamlined or extended, depending on the complexity and duration of the problem. But simply ignoring the need for current information and proceeding to action may prove to be irresponsible and detrimental to the very people the change is intended to serve. A change effort worth undertaking is worth approaching systematically and thoroughly. In the next chapter we will explore what needs to be understood about the target population.

Framework for Understanding Community and Organizational Problems

Task 1: Gather Information from Key Informants in the Community or Organization

Identify Major Participants

▶ Who first identified the problem? Are those initially involved still available? Are they still involved?

▶ What roles have local people played in past efforts at change?

▶ Which individuals or groups support and oppose change?

▶ Which individuals or groups have the power to approve or deny change?

Identify Community or Organizational Condition

▶ What is the difference between a condition and a problem?

▶ What does this community or organization consider to be its priority problems?

▶ In approaching an episode of change, how should the condition statement be framed?

Identify Relevant Historical Incidents

▶ Has the problem been recognized and acknowledged by any community or organizational members?

▶ If so, when was this condition, problem, or opportunity first recognized in this community or organization?

▶ What are the important incidents or events that have occurred from first recognition to the present time?

▶ What do earlier efforts to address this problem reveal?

Task 2: Explore the Professional Knowledge Base on the Condition, Problem, Need, or Opportunity

Explore Relevant Theoretical and Research Resources

▶ What body of knowledge is considered key to understanding the condition, problem, need, or opportunity?

▶ What frameworks are useful in understanding the condition, problem, need, or opportunity?

▶ Where and how does one access the knowledge and information needed for this task?

Collect Supporting Data

▶ What data are most useful in describing the condition, problem, or opportunity?

▶ Where can useful quantitative data, historical records, agency-based studies, and other types of information be found?

Make the Data Meaningful for Interpretation

▶ What options can be used to display data?

▶ How should data be displayed in order to clearly and concisely make the case for change?

Task 3: Select Factors That Help Explain the Underlying Causes of the Problem

▶ From interviews with key informants, identification of important historical events, review of the professional knowledge base, and compilation of data, what appear to be the major factors that help in understanding the problem?

▶ Which explanations, at this point, appear to be the most logical ones to be addressed in this episode of change?

Succeed with PEARSON mysocialworklab

Log onto **www.mysocialworklab.com** and answer the questions below. (*If you did not receive an access code to* **MySocialWorkLab** *with this text and wish to purchase access online, please visit* www.mysocialworklab.com.)

1. **Read the MySocialWorkLibrary case study: A Qualitative Inquiry into Adult Child–Parent Relationships and Their Effects on Caregiving Roles.** Imagine you are designing services for the elderly who reside at home. As part of your research, identify 3–5 major factors from this reading that are potential barriers to adequate home care by a family member.

2. **Watch the ABC video: AIDS in Black America.** Imagine that the government was once again considering the idea of federal needle exchange program. Articulate the problem, population, and arena addressed through this policy.

PRACTICE TEST
The following questions will test your knowledge of the content found within this chapter. For additional assessment, including licensing-exam-type questions on applying chapter content to practice, visit **MySocialWorkLab**.

1. Which feature below makes social work unique among the helping professions?
   a. the broad focus on areas for change
   b. excellent psychiatric assessment
   c. emphasis on family dynamics
   d. specializations in child welfare

2. A worker decided to interview directors of agencies as major participants. These people most likely
   a. identified the problem in the first place
   b. represent people who attempted past changes
   c. will support planned community changes
   d. have the power to approve or reject change

3. A worker examines survey data on community problems including health, childcare, and employment at one point in time. The data reflect
   a. cross-sectional analysis
   b. time-series comparisons
   c. standards comparisons
   d. epidemiological analysis

4. When examining human services problems or conditions, it is most common to identify _____ as a cause.
   a. blaming the victim
   b. predominant policies
   c. lack of resources
   d. poor schools

5. You work in a domestic violence shelter that serves women with children. The shelter teaches independent living skills, parenting skills, and job readiness skills. Draft a clear, one-sentence statement of the problem, defining (a) the problem, (b) the target population, and (c) the geographical boundaries.

ASSESS YOUR COMPETENCE
Use the scale below to rate your current level of achievement on the following concepts or skills associated with each competency presented in the chapter:

1	2	3
I can accurately describe the concept or skill.	I can consistently identify the concept or skill when observing and analyzing practice activities.	I can competently implement the concept or skill in my own practice.

_____ Can apply clinical practice expertise to aid in understanding of complex social problems.

_____ Can identify a variety of sources of information that incorporates a diverse range of perspectives necessary to fully understand a community problem.

_____ Can fully articulate the problem, arena, and population rather than relying on overly broad statements about issues.

_____ Can interpret and synthesize information from multiple sources, setting the foundation to link micro and macro practice to meaningful research.

Understanding Populations

CHAPTER OUTLINE

Core Competencies in this Chapter (Check marks indicate which competencies are covered in depth)				
☐ Professional Identity	☐ Ethical Practice	☐ Critical Thinking	✓ Diversity in Practice	✓ Human Rights & Justice
☐ Research-Based Practice	✓ Human Behavior	☐ Policy Practice	✓ Practice Contexts	☐ Engage, Assess, Intervene, Evaluate

SELECTING AND STUDYING A POPULATION

Problems affect people. Solutions, if they are to be effective, must reflect an understanding of the people affected and the capacity to build on their strengths. If the professional change agent hopes to understand why problems exist and to help craft effective and meaningful solutions to those problems, she or he must understand the populations affected. For example, why do some individuals react to feelings of despair and commit acts of violence, whereas others commit suicide? The answer is likely complex, and the reasons may be different for teenagers than they are for adults or for older persons. How do people react to stress? The research may help explain that reactions can be affected not only by personal characteristics but also by social, cultural, and economic factors.

A particular target population may be implied or stated as a part of framing the problem. Focusing on a problem such as teenage pregnancy immediately narrows the population to young women between the ages of approximately 11 and 19. Elder abuse narrows the population to people who are usually over age 65 and in a vulnerable and dependent situation. In some cases, a population may be distinguished by shared race, ethnicity, or culture. For example, a focus on health disparities among African American women or resettlement barriers faced by Hmong immigrants suggests factors that may be central to understanding a population and the challenges they face. Change agents study and understand populations by interviewing key informants, completing a review of professional journals and texts, and using credible Internet resources.

In some cases the population may not be as clearly defined. For example, an episode of change may focus on a neighborhood. In this instance, it may be necessary to identify more than one population such as preschoolers, children, teenagers, young families, adults, and/or elders in multiple racial, ethnic, and cultural groups. When intervening at the neighborhood level, the analysis may be more heavily focused on *arena* (to be discussed in the following chapters), with less emphasis on the study of a specific population.

To conduct an analysis of the population in as efficient a manner as possible, we propose that the change agent engage in another series of tasks, which include the following:

1. Develop cultural humility.
2. Seek diverse perspectives.
3. Search the professional knowledge base on the target population.
4. Select factors that help in understanding the target population.

When these tasks have been completed, review the causes identified in relation to the problem (from Chapter 3) together with frameworks or explanations that help in understanding the population in item 4 above. Then speculation about possible cause-and-effect relationships occurs. We undertake these speculations in a fifth task:

5. Develop a working hypothesis of etiology about the problem.

But first, we begin by examining the role of diversity and difference in Task 1.

Task 1: Develop Cultural Humility

Most if not all episodes of macro-level change will involve populations that differ on some dimension from the social work change agent. For this reason, this chapter emphasizes listening to members of the target population and understanding a wide variety of theoretical perspectives and empirical evidence in order to develop an effective planned change intervention. But before a social worker engages in these learning activities, she or he must attend to personal attitudes regarding diversity and difference.

Questions to be explored for this task include:

▶ What are the power imbalances faced by this population group?
▶ What experiences has the social worker had with members of this population group?
▶ What self-identities and attitudes does the social worker bring to this situation?

Ideally, in each macro-level change effort there would be a change agent available who reflects the race, culture, ethnic group, gender, age group, and life experiences of the target population. This ideal should be pursued, but at times is not possible. Social workers find themselves the focal point or conduit for concerns representing many diverse perspectives, and it is expected that they will find ways to give visibility and voice to each perspective (Brooks, 2001).

If a social worker is a 23-year-old white or Hispanic woman working with an older African American or Asian person, she must recognize that her experiences are not the same as those of persons with whom she is working. In fact, the white or Hispanic social worker should not assume that her experiences are the same as those of someone who shares her ethnicity. Effective cross-cultural social work in this situation requires that the social worker be able to hear the voice of the older person and partner with him as they guide one another toward understanding and change.

To become effective in such cross-cultural situations, social workers have been encouraged to develop *cultural competence*. Cultural competence includes interrelated actions, thoughts, and even policies that are joined within a system or organization to facilitate effective cross-cultural work (NASW, 2000, p. 61). NASW (2001) recognizes cultural competence as both a process and a product that includes self-awareness and respect for diversity as well as effective practice behaviors on micro, mezzo, and macro levels.

Cross, Bazron, Dennis, and Isaacs (1989) identified six points on a continuum of competency. The authors suggested a process of growth that includes practitioner and agency awareness, knowledge, and skills. The authors' six points on the continuum are noted in Table 4.1 below.

The assumptions of cultural competence have been questioned in recent interdisciplinary scholarship, particularly the assumption that competence can ever truly be attained. In social work, scholars have noted the tensions and paradoxes of cultural competence. Johnson and Munch (2009) identified four paradoxes in current understandings of cultural competence. First, despite professional emphasis on *learning from* clients, models of cultural competence often espouse *knowing about* clients and assume specialized knowledge can be acquired about different client groups. Second, although ethical standards emphasize dignity and worth of individuals, descriptions of difference are by definition stereotypical and may overlook the uniqueness of each individual.

Table 4.1   Cultural Competence Continuum

Competency Continuum	Description
Cultural Destructiveness	▶ Attitudes, policies, and practices that are destructive to cultures are also destructive to individuals within cultures.
Cultural Incapacity	▶ The person, agency, or system lacks the capacity to help members of a cultural or ethnic group. ▶ The person, agency, or system does not respect the beliefs or traditions of the group being served.
Cultural Blindness	▶ The belief that culture is not important, that all people are the same. ▶ Use of helping approaches are seen to be universally applicable.
Cultural Precompetence	▶ The individual, agency, or system recognizes its cultural deficiencies and begins to make attempts to address them through outreach or hiring practices.
Cultural Competence	▶ Differences are accepted and respected. ▶ Self-assessment of staff and policies are made in relation to culture. ▶ Cultural knowledge and resources are expanded.
Cultural Proficiency	▶ Culture is held in high esteem. ▶ Cultural practice is enhanced by research. ▶ Cultural knowledge is increased.

Based on Cross, Bazron, Dennis, and Isaacs' (1989) six points of cultural competency.

Diversity in Practice

Critical Thinking Question: What is the difference between learning from clients and learning about clients? Why does this matter?

Third, the ethical value of self-determination may be undermined by a focus on the group. Finally, the authors questioned if competence can ever be achieved given (1) the lack of clarity about the definition and (2) the numerous unique combinations that comprise individual identities.

Social workers Yan and Wong (2005) questioned the assumptions of practitioner self-awareness embedded in most definitions of cultural competence. Social workers (and other health and human service professionals) are to explore their own cultural identities and prevent them from unduly affecting the practice situation. The authors questioned the implication that social workers can control the influence of their culture, yet clients are "passive cultural objects" (p. 185) who cannot exert such control. Citing Kondrat (1999), they advocate for a reflexive self-awareness that recognizes the self as affecting and affected by others, deemphasizing the subject–object distinction and emphasizing mutuality in practice situations.

In contrast to cultural *competence*, medical educators Tervalon and Murray-Garcia (1998) proposed cultural *humility* as the goal for cross-cultural practice. Unlike competence, humility does not suggest that one can master everything about a culture. Instead, it suggests an ongoing process that includes a continual commitment to learning and self-reflection, to altering the power imbalances in

Table 4.2   Critical Questions About Cultural Humility

Components of Cultural Humility	Critical Questions for Social Workers
Having a lifelong commitment to self-evaluation and critique	◗ How are my beliefs and values influencing how I view this person, group, or community? ◗ Have I identified and reflected on how my past experiences might influence how I view and treat this person, group, or community?
Attempting to redress power imbalances in the interaction and dynamics between social workers and a consumer of services	◗ Where is power located in this relationship? ◗ How am I using power in this situation? ◗ Am I using power "over" or power "with" this person, group, or community? ◗ How can I begin and sustain relationships that acknowledge and equalize power differences?
Developing mutually beneficial and non-paternalistic partnerships with communities	◗ How are community perspectives incorporated into this partnership? ◗ Have community representatives been a part of this partnership since its early stages? ◗ Were community perspectives sought before solutions were imposed?

Based on Tervalon and Murray-Garacia's (1998) components of cultural humility.

the interactions between helping professionals and service consumers, and to developing collaborative and equitable relationships with community members. Tervalon and Murray-Garcia and other critics of cultural competence recognize the importance of increasing knowledge and skills, but also recognize the limits and potential dangers of these behaviors if not accompanied by ongoing self-evaluative processes and relationship building.

For social workers who practice directly with individuals and families, each encounter with a client provides an opportunity to exercise cultural humility. For social workers who practice with organizations and communities, these opportunities are also readily available. Using Tervalon and Murray-Garcia's (1998) components of cultural humility, Table 4.2 provides critical questions to consider when faced with opportunities to develop and exercise cultural humility.

While we emphasize cultural humility in this text, we do not discount the value of the work that has been done to develop the concept and practices of cultural competence. Seeking to increase one's understanding of different groups and cultures is a goal worth pursuing and a task required by many professional bodies. Conceptual and empirical works on cultural competence are invaluable resources for professionals. For example, Organista (2009) proposes a practice model with Latinos that synthesizes previous models and methods of culturally competent practice. Using a range of theories and research, Organista contends that practice with Latinos should be attentive to four dimensions in order to practice competently: (1) increase service availability and access; (2) assess problems in the social and cultural context; (3) select culturally and socially acceptable interventions; and (4) increase service accountability (p. 300). These dimensions should assist practitioners as they assess and critique current practices and develop new practices with Latinos. The value of such an integrative model is that it provides a ready tool for practitioners as they work with one of the fastest growing minority groups in the United States.

We stress, however, that knowledge acquisition is only one dimension of ethical and effective cross-cultural practice. Drawing from Tervalon and Murray-Garcia (1998), such practice must also address power imbalances, mutuality in relationships, and critical self-awareness.

Knowledge acquisition is only one dimension of ethical and effective cross-cultural practice.

Task 2: Seek Diverse Perspectives

Full understanding of a population and the problems they face requires attention to a range of perspectives. Problems can be understood in a number of ways, including (1) experiencing the problem firsthand, (2) working closely with people who have experienced the problem, or (3) exploring the professional knowledge base about the problem. In considering these approaches, it is important to distinguish between the understanding and insight gained by personal experience as contrasted with other methods of learning about a population. For this reason, it is important to talk with persons who know about the problem firsthand.

Listen to Persons Who Have Experienced the Problem

Questions to be explored for this activity include:

- ▶ How do representatives of diverse groups affected by this problem or opportunity view it?
- ▶ Have diverse voices and perspectives been included in articulating and understanding the problem? If not, why?

In Chapter 3, the chapter on understanding problems, Task 1 encourages change agents to seek the perspectives of those experiencing the problem. Likewise, to better understand a particular population, the social work change agent must seek the perspectives of those who are members of the population. This activity is both an application of cultural humility and a prudent means to gather useful information to inform the planned change effort.

Further, if a person who identifies with the population is not already a part of the change effort, seeking input from members of the population may identify a representative or representatives of the population for participation in the planning and implementation of the change. Those who have direct experience with the problem or opportunity might not accept those without similar experience as spokespersons. People who have experienced life on public assistance may not be willing to accept a social worker as a representative of their feelings and needs. Likewise, someone living in an affordable housing development may be more likely to turn to a fellow resident as spokesperson. Describing the experiences that led to posttraumatic stress disorder in the wars in Vietnam, Iraq, and Afghanistan is more credibly done by someone who was there. People of a particular ethnic group may be able to speak for the experiences of their own group but not for another group. A person who is not transgendered may not be able to credibly represent a transgendered person. For these reasons, it is important to find spokespersons who are accepted and supported by their peers and who can help to articulate the perspectives of the group(s) involved.

The Importance of Inclusion. The importance of including population perspectives is reinforced by Weil, Gamble, and Williams (1998) when they point out that for community members to be empowered, community practice must be conducted "with" rather than "on" communities. The authors propose action research methods that involve simultaneous knowledge building, reflecting, and promoting change, along with four feminist-influenced approaches to community practice research: participatory action research, needs/assets assessment, empowerment evaluation, and demystification. These research approaches are discussed below in Table 4.3 and are examples of tools to consider in order to gain the diverse perspectives needed to better understand a population and the problems they experience.

The Use of Frameworks. Macro practitioners work with individuals and communities that vary along a number of dimensions including race, ethnicity, gender, socioeconomic status, and religion, among many others. In addition to talking to members of various populations, concepts and frameworks have been developed that help practitioners better understand the complexity of these intersecting dimensions and the relationship of a person's identity to majority culture.

Table 4.3   Descriptions of Feminist Influences in Research

Feminist-Influenced Research Approach	Description
Participatory Action Research	▶ Collaboratively involves members of the community in negotiating research topics, methods, and data analysis ▶ Minimizes the distinction between the researcher and those researched; the relationship is reciprocal, both teaching and learning from the other ▶ Action results from increased critical consciousness gained from the research process
Needs/Assets Assessment	▶ Provides data about the incidence of issues that are often "invisible" ▶ Provides data to be used by the community in advocacy work
Empowerment Evaluation	▶ Uses evaluation concepts, techniques, and findings to foster improvement and self-determination ▶ Assesses the effectiveness of different types of actions in meeting needs or solving problems ▶ Increases capacity to self-evaluate
Demystification	▶ Illuminates the "invisible" ▶ Lifts all voices up so that they can be heard

An early framework for understanding the complexities of cultural characteristics and the impact of those characteristics on the identity and well-being of individuals was Norton's (1978) *dual perspective*. The dual perspective views an individual at the center of two surrounding systems, which Norton called the nurturing system and the sustaining system. The *nurturing system* includes the values of parents and extended family or substitute family, by community experiences, beliefs, customs, and traditions with which the individual was raised. Surrounding the nurturing system is a *sustaining system*, represented by the dominant society and culture. The sustaining system also reflects beliefs, values, customs, and traditions.

Sustaining systems are made up of influential and powerful people, including for example, teachers, employers, and law enforcement and elected officials. Some segments of sustaining systems may reflect ageist, racist, sexist, or other prejudicial attitudes, and can therefore be perceived by diverse population groups as representing alien and hostile environments. Norton suggested that the more incongruence between a person's nurturing and sustaining systems, the more difficulty she or he would have. She urged social workers to take actions to support the nurturing system and educate and confront the sustaining system when needed.

Years earlier, W. E. B. DuBois (1903) coined the term *double consciousness* or *two-ness* to refer to the African Americans' awareness of their identity and the identity ascribed to them by the dominant white society. He and subsequent scholars recognized this dual consciousness both as a "special gift" and a powerful source of maladaptive identity development. As a gift or strength, double-consciousness recognizes the bi-cultural capacity of minority group members that function, by necessity, in both their own culture and the dominant culture. Members of the dominant culture rarely need and are seldom forced to experience and live within minority cultures. Along with that strength, however, is the risk that members of minority groups might internalize the stigmatized and stereotyped messages the dominant culture conveys about them.

More recently, theories of *intersectionality* have emphasized the complexity of multiple dimensions of difference that individuals occupy and the isms related to those dimensions in understanding identity development. Born out of Black Feminist scholarship (Hill Collins, 2000; Hooks, 1981, 1989), intersectionality suggests that gender alone is an insufficient analytic category to understand the experiences and identity of women of color. In fact, any singular category is inadequate. Instead, when considering life experiences and the development of identity, one must consider the interaction of multiple categories and isms. Specifically, everyone has a race, gender, and class, and these categorizations intersect to form complex identities. Identity is further developed by other differences including age, ethnicity, physical ability, and sexual identity.

The dual perspective, double consciousness, and intersectionality provide guidance when working with different population groups, particularly groups that are marginalized. Each of the concepts suggests that the best place to begin to understand a population is with the population itself, especially if the change agent is not a member of that population. In attempting to solve vexing social problems, the social work change agent should assume that oppressed or ignored groups have a better understanding of their culture than the change agent has about their culture. Related, the change agent should recognize that members of oppressed groups are more likely to understand and function within the dominant culture than members of the dominant culture are in minority cultures. People who live within a dominant society observe and experience, on a daily basis, the values, beliefs, traditions, and language of the dominant society through personal contact, television, newspapers, and other media. Representatives of the dominant society do not regularly observe and experience the values, beliefs, and traditions of non-dominant groups. A social worker must often help representatives of the dominant society understand the strengths and needs of the marginalized populations experiencing a social problem. For example, a young, black, special education student recently testified before the state legislative committee on his experiences with bullying. Special education students are by far the majority of victims. A social worker and a teacher identified this young man and made arrangements for his testimony so that his voice and experience could be heard by persons in decision-making roles.

Representatives of the dominant society do not regularly observe and experience the values, beliefs, and traditions of non-dominant groups.

Most programs and services, along with their underlying rationales, are designed from a dominant society perspective. Even the theories used to explain the problem and the research on which the practitioner builds hypotheses may reflect majority culture biases. Members of diverse ethnic and minority groups, on the other hand, may have different perspectives of the problem and how to resolve it. These perspectives are crucial in understanding a problem and creating effective solutions for change.

Consider, for example, a situation in which some of a community's elders are experiencing deteriorating quality of life. One culture may value the concept of extended family and wish to maintain elderly parents in the home, but family members may not be able to afford the expense of taking on another dependent. Another culture may value the independence and privacy of elderly parents, but its members may not be able to pay retirement-community prices. The community's influential and powerful leaders and decision makers may believe that government should not be involved, and that decisions about aging parents should be left to adult children. It is likely that these types of perceptions will be linked to factors relating to culture and/or gender and to nurturing-system/sustaining-system perspectives.

Listen to Population Allies and Advocates

Questions to be explored for this activity include:

- Who are the allies and advocates of this population group?
- What can be learned from allies and advocates about the history of experiences with the target population and the pressing problems and opportunities?

In addition to involving and listening to members of the population, allies with and advocates for the population may also assist the social work change agent in understanding the target population. An ally is a person of privilege who actively works to eliminate stigma and discrimination that occurs based on that stigma (Rosenblum & Travis, 2008, p. 473). Broido (2000) suggests that allies work to end oppression based on dominant members having greater privilege and power (p. 3). Allies work alongside individuals who are marginalized because of their race, ethnicity, gender, sexual orientation, disability, age, or other dimension of difference. Advocates are persons who argue for a cause or on another's behalf. A number of ally and advocacy organizations have been formed to confront oppression and support members of oppressed groups by advocating for change. For example, the organization PFLAG (Parents, Families and Friends of Lesbians and Gays) is an organization that engages and develops allies to advocate for equal civil rights and the health and well-being of sexual minorities. The National Council of La Raza is a national civil rights and advocacy organization that seeks to improve opportunities for Hispanic Americans. Local organizations that create opportunities for members of a target population and their allies to work together may be additional sources of information about a population.

If a social worker is attempting to understand a hidden population, or a population that remains out of public view for fear of physical or psychological harm, an ally may help arrange access to members of the population for research and participation. If a social worker is attempting to understand a population that is underage or experiencing the acute symptoms of a serious mental illness, an advocate can provide a voice for those who cannot, at that time, speak for themselves. Social workers are familiar with the advocate role and are often involved in advocating for groups that cannot advocate for themselves (National Association of Social Workers, 2000, 2001). The role of ally is discussed less but is a role premised on the assumptions of cultural humility—particularly shared power and non-paternalistic partnerships (Tervalon & Murray-Garcia, 1998).

Nygreen, Kwon, and Sanchez (2006) discuss the role of adult allies in the youth-led organizing efforts of urban youth. Noting that "urban youth" is a euphemism for marginalized, poor, minority youth, adult allies support youth efforts to engage their peers, change their communities, and in the process, challenge common stereotypes. Casey and Smith (2010) describe men who become allies in efforts to end violence against women and how they became involved in efforts to end violence against women. The men indicated that becoming involved as an ally in the fight to end violence against women was a process and that their involvement was influenced by an emotional connection to the issue, by opportunities to make sense of that exposure, and by invitations to join efforts to end violence against women.

Identifying and interviewing allies and advocates can supplement the information gained from the members of the target population. These key stakeholders should aid in understanding the history of experiences with the target population and the pressing problems and opportunities. If there have been relevant past experiences with this population, the change agent can compile a list of key actors and a chronology of interactions between the target population and the community or organizational representatives leading up to the present. These notes will help shape strategy and tactics later in the episode of change.

Whenever diverse groups make up a part of the target population and are expected to benefit from the change effort, credible expertise reflecting these different perspectives must be sought and incorporated into the problem analysis and intervention design. Involving target population members reflects professional ethical commitments and increases the probability that the target population will feel a sense of ownership of the proposed change (Armbruster, Gale, Brady, & Thompson, 1999; Hardina, 2003).

Task 3: Search the Professional Knowledge Base on the Target Population

Task 3 involves seeking additional information about the target population from academic and professional resources. When examining existing literature about a population, content areas should include at least an exploration of issues of growth and development of the population, diversity considerations, and external factors that affect the population.

In the model of problem analysis presented in Chapter 3, we proposed a review of the literature on the condition or problem. Likewise, when studying a population, the professional knowledge base is an essential source of information. The professional knowledge base includes the major contributions to a field of study, beginning with peer-reviewed professional journals in social work and related areas, books and monographs focused on the population, and reliable organizational resources. An Internet search can provide an overview of professional journals at websites such as *Social Work Abstracts*, *PsychINFO*, and *PubMed*. *WorldCat* is a valuable source of information on books. In addition to peer-reviewed scholarship and books indexed at the sites listed above, useful data and information may also be provided by groups representing populations such as the American Association of Retired Persons (AARP), the National Alliance to End Homelessness, the Children's Action Alliance, the American Cancer Society, and the National Alliance on Mental Illness (NAMI).

Local studies done within an agency or a community are also valuable sources of data. Although national studies tend to produce findings that are more widely applicable, local studies have the advantage of being specific to the agency or community and are therefore perhaps more precise and relevant to the population being studied. Agency employees and networks of service providers can be helpful in identifying local research projects that may be available.

An important part of the literature review should be devoted to identifying and applying relevant theoretical perspectives. Theories can be descriptive, helping to better understand the population group or prescriptive in helping the change agent know how to intervene (Mulroy, 2004; Savaya & Waysman, 2005). As opposed to the random listing of facts and observations, theories allow for categorizing one's findings, making sense out of them, and turning seemingly unrelated bits of information into explanatory propositions that lead to logical, testable hypotheses.

Different theories propose divergent explanations of a problem within a population and may suggest different possible interventions. Sometimes these explanations and potential interventions allow two different theories to merge and reinforce each other, but at other times each theory may conflict sharply with the rest. The change agent should be prepared to weigh these differing views and choose among them based on factors, such as

- Which seems to best fit the setting and population
- Which seems to have the greatest explanatory power
- Which has earned the most support in empirical tests of its predictive capacity and
- Which offers the richest range of testable hypotheses (usually in the form of possible interventions)

Theoretical principles should be critically evaluated for their biases and given credibility based on how thoroughly they have been tested, especially in relation to the problem and population being explored. Once selected as a framework for analysis, theoretical assumptions should be stated and shared with those involved in the change effort. This is intended to facilitate the achievement of a shared understanding of the problem and population(s) involved.

Framing problems and understanding populations is a professional undertaking that must be approached with care and sensitivity. Without careful attention to the multiple dimensions of problems and populations, descriptions and explanations may be overly simplistic and result in "blaming the victim" (Ryan, 1971). This is always a risk when attempting to understand why

Without careful attention to the multiple dimensions of problems and populations, descriptions and explanations may be overly simplistic.

a population is experiencing a particular condition or problem. The risk can be addressed, in part, by recognizing that factors ranging from human behavior and development to social relationships and structures contribute to robust explanations of problems and populations. The risk can also be addressed by recognizing the role of discrimination, stigma, and stereotypes in explanations of people and their problems.

In studying certain types of problems where human behavior is a factor, at least part of the focus of the study should be on what is known about the various stages of growth and development of the population. For example, problems such as eating disorders, substance abuse, interpersonal violence, and suicide may be understood in a particular population by considering stages of development over the life course.

In other instances, understanding the behavior of individuals within the target population is not as important as assessing the impact of the arena (community or organization) on its members. Organizations and communities can present barriers to full participation. Problems such as overutilization of emergency room services for routine health care or violation of zoning ordinances by housing multiple families in single-family units are examples of situations where the focus should be on understanding how the community or organization functions in relation to the target population. Whether the problem or population suggests attention to human behavior and/or social structures, the knowledge base on diversity and difference discussed previously will contribute to a better understanding of the factors that contribute to the population's experience of a problem.

Understand Concepts and Issues Related to Growth and Development

Questions to be explored for this activity include:

- What sources of the professional knowledge base are available on this population group?
- What theoretical frameworks are available that will help in understanding the target population?
- What factors or characteristics gleaned from the knowledge base on this population will be helpful in understanding the target population?

A useful starting point for understanding a population is a text on human growth and development. These texts are frequently divided into ages and stages of life. For example, Ashford, LeCroy, and Lortie (2009) organized their text on human behavior in the social environment around a multidimensional framework for assessing social functioning, including the biophysical, psychological, and social dimensions. The authors then explore phases of growth and development from pregnancy and birth through late adulthood. Hutchison (2010a&b) offers two volumes in which the changing life course and the person and environment are explored. Santrock (2010) has used the following chapter headings: Beginnings, Infancy, Early Childhood, Middle and Late Childhood, Adolescence, Early Adulthood, Middle Adulthood, Late Adulthood, and Death and Dying. These types of frameworks may be useful in organizing a study of the target population. For example, in attempting to understand a population of teenage methamphetamine users, a study might focus on adolescent growth and development, perhaps using selected biophysical, psychological, social, cultural, and gender characteristics that may, in some combination, contribute to the use and abuse of substances.

Theoretical perspectives may also assist in understanding a population's experience of a problem. One can draw from a range of traditional and alternative theories to do this. For example, focusing on the population of adolescents who drop out of high school, one might draw on the classical works of Skinner (1971), Erickson (1968), or Maslow (1943) to understand the behavior of the target population.

Using some of Skinner's most basic behavioral concepts such as reinforcement, extinction, or desensitization, one might examine the high school experience for selected students. It might be hypothesized that negative reinforcements in the form of poor grades and criticism lead to discouragement and poor attendance on the part of some students. These negative responses may also extinguish certain behaviors and limit the effort a student is willing to invest in academic success. In this case, efforts would have to be expended to discover what this group of students would consider positive reinforcement, and how the academic experience could be designed so that they could achieve success.

Erickson's concept of identity might cause one to focus on the need of high school youth for a positive self-image. The high school experience might then be examined to determine the degree to which it supports the development of a positive identity for some and destroys it for others. Activities would be designed to build self-esteem based on the hypothesis that increased self-esteem will act as a motivator to academic success.

Maslow, on the other hand, would examine the phenomenon of dropping out of high school in terms of the congruence between the high school experience and students' needs. The pertinent question would be whether the educational programs were appropriately tailored to meet the social, esteem, and fulfillment needs of students. Each level of need, once met, is no longer a motivator, so new challenges would have to be designed to achieve the goal of self-fulfillment.

Other traditional theorists provide additional perspectives on how adolescents deal with issues of self-identity as they grow and develop (e.g., Kohlberg, 1984; Marcia, 1993; Piaget, 1972). One can also draw from identity theories offered for various population groups including, for example, the Cross (1971, 1991) Model of Black Identity Development and Cass's (1979, 1984) Model of Homosexual Identity Formation. These two models are described briefly below.

Cross (1971, 1991) suggests a four-stage model of black racial identity development. In the first stage, *Pre-encounter*, the individual views herself or himself from a white frame of reference. In the second stage, *Encounter*, the individual confronts experiences that challenge a white frame of reference (i.e., acts of discrimination). In the third stage, *Immersion–Emersion*, the individual adopts a black identity and withdraws from interactions with other cultures, particularly the dominant white culture. In the final stage, *Internalization*, the individual develops self-confidence and security in her or his racial identity and embraces pluralism. Parham (1989) extended Cross's model by suggesting three ways of moving through the stages. First, a person can *stagnate* in any one of the stages. Second, a person can make *Stagewise Linear Progression (SLP)* through the four stages. Third, a person can *recycle* the stages and experience how it feels to struggle with racial identity and the action required to resolve that struggle.

Cass (1979, 1984) developed the Homosexual Identity Formation model based on her research of lesbian and gay individuals in Australia. In stage 1, *Identity Confusion*, the individual is aware of being different and that her or his behavior may be considered homosexual. In stage 2, *Identity Comparison*, the person realizes the she or he might be homosexual and feels alienated because of this possibility. In stage 3, *Identity Tolerance*, the individual accepts and tolerates the possibility of being homosexual and begins to seek community. In stage 4, *Identity Acceptance*, the person accepts her or himself as homosexual and increases efforts to create community. In stage 5, *Identity Pride*, the individual is proud of her or his identity and angry about heterosexism and heterosexist privilege. In stage 6, *Identity Synthesis*, the person is able to recognize heterosexual allies and integrate multiple aspects of her or his identity. Cass emphasized that individuals may progress through the stages at varying paces and some individuals may stop at a particular stage and not progress further, a process Cass referred to as *Identity Foreclosure*.

The two examples above suggest additional lenses through which to view the problems a population is experiencing. If the adolescents who are dropping out of high school are predominantly African American, perhaps members of that group believe that the school culture based on dominant culture assumptions are hostile to their own experience. Likewise, if those dropping out of high school are lesbian, gay, bisexual, or transgendered (LGBT) youth, leaving may be related to the lack of acceptance and fear she or he feels as someone with a developing awareness of her or his own identity. A number of other identity and developmental theories provide frameworks that help the social work change agent understand a population and its problems.

Understand Impact of Social Relationships and Structures

Questions to be explored for this activity include:

⯈ What structural and environmental forces are affecting this population group?
⯈ What theoretical frameworks are available that will help in understanding the interactions between members of the population and the larger social environment?

Understanding processes of growth and development contribute to the social work change agent's understanding of a population, but alone may be insufficient in understanding a population in relation to the problem(s) they are experiencing. Further, use of these explanatory frameworks alone may inaccurately focus attention and blame for a problem on the people experiencing it instead of on the contributing social factors. In addition to these individually focused explanatory perspectives, theories from sociology and social psychology can also provide insight on how social relationships and structures impact a population and how members of that population act and understand themselves.

Focusing on family homelessness, one might use role theory, agency/structure theories, and conflict theory to better understand families experiencing a housing crisis.

Role theory addresses the patterns of attitudes and behaviors typically associated with various positions in society (Turner, 1982, 1990). Roles may be related to gender or age (basic roles) or they may be related to a person's occupation or family positions (structural status roles). When a person fills a certain role, she or he is expected to conform to the behavior patterns associated with that role. For example, a woman is expected to act in accordance with the roles she holds as daughter, mother, and wife.

Role conflict may be experienced when one or more of the roles that a person holds conflicts with another role. Role strain may occur when one struggles to meet the expectations of a particular role. Single mothers in homeless

Human Behavior

Critical Thinking Question: How might role theory help inform your work with disenfranchised populations?

families may experience role conflict and strain as they attempt to be both an effective parent and provider. Emergency shelter regulations that do not allow dependent male children over a certain age force homeless mothers to contend with the stress of keeping their family together and providing housing for the rest of the family.

Sociological theories that bridge the concepts of agency (ability of individuals to act and create their own lives) and structural determinism (inability of individuals to act outside of constraining societal structures) can also be useful in understanding populations. Giddens (1979) proposed structuration theory to integrate agency and structure. He noted that the social practices performed by humans are recursive, that is, as they are repeated, social practices both create social structures and are conditioned by them. Bourdieu (1977) popularized the term *habitus* to refer to the recursive frameworks, often held unconsciously, that help humans function in everyday life. Conflict theory recognizes the inherent power differences among groups in society. Social problems in this perspective are viewed as the result of conflicts among various groups in society vying for control of important resources. Problems are not attributed to the individual, family, or social group, but to the exploitative practices of dominant groups that alienate nondominant groups.

These three theories are only examples of the many theoretical frameworks that may inform your understanding of a population. Along with the community and organizational theories noted in Chapters 5 and 7, respectively, sociological and psychosocial theories explain populations and the problems or opportunities in terms of the interactions between members of the population and the larger social environment.

Understand the Impact of Difference, Discrimination, and Oppression

Questions to be explored for this activity include:

- ▸ What stereotypes or generalizations confront this population group?
- ▸ How has this population group been discriminated against or oppressed?

Population groups that are recognized as different from the dominant culture are frequently stereotyped. *Stereotypes* are generalizations about a group that suggest that all members of that group are the same and will exhibit the same behavior (Rosenblum & Travis, 2008). For example, one stereotype of women is that they are not good at math. Asian students are often stereotyped as quiet, studious, and smart. Homeless individuals and people receiving public assistance are stereotyped as lazy and unwilling to work. Stereotypes about groups can stigmatize members of the group as unworthy and as having certain characteristics such as a disability or social class (Rosenblum & Travis, 2008). Link and Phelan (2001, p. 367) suggest that stigmatization occurs when the following five elements converge:

- ▸ Human differences are identified and then labeled.
- ▸ Cultural differences and values link labeled people to negative stereotypes.
- ▸ A separation of "us" and "them" develops, categorizing people as a group.
- ▸ Persons in the labeled group lose status and are discriminated against.
- ▸ Because they are stigmatized, the labeled population does not gain access to resources and is disempowered and excluded.

Difference that is stereotyped and stigmatized can result in discrimination and oppression. Discrimination refers to detrimental action or absence of action because of individual and group differences. Oppression includes everything from institutional discrimination to personal bigotry (Bell, 2007).

Stereotyping and stigmatizing others provides a rationale for discrimination and oppression. When a difference is construed as abnormal and wrong, individuals, programs, and institutions that identify as normal have a rationale to maintain their perspectives. The change agent must search beyond these normative descriptions of "different" groups to understand a population and its challenges. Social workers must recognize how a difference is portrayed and how dominant interpretations of that difference have resulted in discrimination and oppression. Oppression can occur around any dimension of difference, but common "isms" describing specific forms of oppression are defined in Table 4.4 and are discussed below.

Sexism is discrimination based on attitudes and assumptions about gender. Often these attitudes become barriers to community participation even though they are subtle and difficult to identify. Like other systems of oppression, they exist in the values, norms, and traditions of a society to be translated into local community activities. For example, as children are socialized in their educational, religious, and familial roles, they are given messages regarding what is considered appropriate for women and men. Bricker-Jenkins and Hooyman (1986) propose that social workers should examine patriarchy within the community. They suggest that the recording of history and the

Table 4.4	Systems of Oppression
System of Oppression	Definition
Ableism	An institutional, cultural, and individual system of disadvantage and discrimination against people who are considered physically or mentally unable to function as well as others
Ageism	An institutional, cultural, and individual system of disadvantage and discrimination against people who are old
Classism	An institutional, cultural, and individual system of disadvantage and discrimination against people who are at a lower socioeconomic level
Heterosexism	An institutional, cultural, and individual system of disadvantage and discrimination against people who are (or are perceived to be) lesbian, gay, bisexual, or transgendered
Racism	An institutional, cultural, and individual system of disadvantage and discrimination against people based on their race or perceived race
Sexism	An institutional, cultural, and individual system of disadvantage and discrimination against women because of their gender

establishment of myths that set direction for succeeding generations are parts of a patriarchal system in which experiences of women tend to be devalued as subordinate to those of their male colleagues.

The most serious type of oppression against women is violence (Jansen, 2006). Statistics on violence against women and resources to deal with this problem are available from such organizations as women's support groups, women's centers, and shelters for battered women (Busch & Wolfer, 2002). Access to employment and services may, in some instances, limit opportunities for women. Lack of services, such as child care and transportation, may limit access to employment. Inadequate transportation systems within the community may require women to transport children, limiting their abilities to be engaged in some types of employment as well as other pursuits in which they may have an interest (Fellin, 1995).

Racism is stereotyping and generalizing about people based on the physiological characteristics of their racial group. Ethnic groups share a common language, customs, history, culture, race, religion, or origin. *Ethnocentrism* implies that one's ethnic group is superior to others (Barker, 2003).

There are multiple theories that attempt to explain ethnicity, each examining different aspects of the dynamics of ethnic relations. Theories of assimilation focus on the process experienced by ethnic groups in becoming a part of the dominant society, but they do not always examine the conflict when differences clash. Therefore, ethnic pluralists react to the concept of assimilation and assumptions about the "melting pot," arguing that maintaining one's ethnicity is a way to cope with discrimination. Biological theories about ethnicity and human genetics have been highly controversial, often viewed as ethnocentric, even racist. Ecological theories have focused on competition for scarce resources as a critical force in ethnic relations and in leading to subjugation and domination. Stratification theories examine the distribution of power, whereas colonialism theories emphasize exploitation in which one part of society oppresses another (Barrera, Munoz, & Ornelas, 1972). Aguirre and Turner (2001) attempted to take the major principles of each theory, seeing ethnic discrimination in the United States as stressing several interrelated factors, including identifying with an ethnic group, perceiving threats that the ethnic group represents to others, stereotyping the group, determining the group's size and the group's positioning within the societal stratification system (p. 41).

The target population may encompass one or more racial or ethnic groups. Information on such factors as rates of employment, educational achievement, and socioeconomic status within these subgroups is important to understanding effects of institutional racism. Whether persons from different groups within the target population are involved in decision-making roles is an important indicator of sensitivity to ethnic and cultural issues. Services and other resources available to people from diverse ethnicities in the target population proportionate to their numbers in the community is another indicator.

Classism is a system of oppression based on persons' socioeconomic level. Cultural attitudes associated with classism frequently blame people who are poor for their own situation. These judgments are based on the assumption that those who are poor lack initiative and are unwilling to work to achieve a better socioeconomic status for themselves and their families. Such perspectives are sometimes reflected in the prejudicial language and popular culture stereotypes used to describe people from lower socioeconomic levels. Terms like *trailer trash*, *low class*, *ghetto*, *white trash*, and *redneck* impugn the character of individuals from lower socioeconomic levels. In popular culture, working-class people may be viewed as ignorant, whereas upper-middle-class lifestyles are seen as normal (Leondar-Wright & Yeskel, 2007).

Heterosexism is a system of oppression that privileges heterosexuality and discriminates against those who are or are assumed to be lesbian, gay, bisexual, or transgendered. *Homophobia* is a term used to describe irrational fears held by people toward individuals who have a same-gender sexual orientation. Homophobia, in the extreme, has taken the form of "gay bashing," a practice of physically beating gay people. In other forms, heterosexism and homophobia results in job discrimination, ridicule, and ostracizing. Like all prejudices (literally, "prejudgments"), homophobia blinds those afflicted with it to the individual qualities of lesbian women and gay men and causes them to be perceived only in the context of their sexual orientation. Homophobia, along with heterosexism, and heterocentrism (Appleby, 2007) like other systems of oppression, have an impact on every aspect of a person's life, including work environment, housing acquisition, access to health services, and religious and community life (Appleby, 2007).

Ageism is stereotyping and generalizing about people because of their age, and *ableism* is discrimination against those who are not considered physically or functionally able to perform as well as others. Although older persons are often perceived as being too physically or mentally limited to engage in ongoing community activities, only 4 percent of those persons over age 65 are living in nursing home settings (McInnis-Dittrich, 2002, p. 5). The vast majority of elders are capable of self-sufficiency and productive lives, yet they may be excluded from employment and from playing an important role in the community because of perceptions about their abilities. Older individuals may not be hired because employers are concerned about higher than average medical costs. The same treatment is often experienced by people (of any age) who have physical or functional limitations. Yet, older people vote at a higher rate than any other age group, contribute countless hours of volunteer time, perform with high dependability in positions of employment, and serve as potential resources to macro practitioners.

If age or disability is relevant to understanding the target population, statistics on the numbers and age ranges of those persons in the community should be compiled. How many persons are frail elders (over 85)? How many persons are physically disabled and what types of disabilities are documented? Is there adequate access to services that engage persons with disabilities in active community roles—transportation and outreach, for example? Are there support services (e.g., nutrition programs, homemaker, respite) that sustain these persons and their care partners?

Each of the "isms" discussed above does not exist in isolation, but rather intersect with other systems of oppression to further impact individuals and populations. For example, many of the "isms" intersect with classism to further marginalize members of affected populations. Persons at lower socioeconomic levels, particularly persons in poverty, are more likely to be a person of color or a woman. In addition, persons who are poor are more likely to be disabled than those who are not poor. As discussed earlier in this chapter, to understand a population, it is important not only to understand a target population's race, class, and gender, it is also important to understand how the systems of oppression associate with these and other categories of difference interact to exacerbate problems and subvert opportunities.

Different theoretical perspectives may propose divergent explanations about why and how discrimination and oppression occur and may suggest different possible interventions. Sometimes these explanations and potential interventions allow two different theories to merge with and reinforce each other, but at other times each theory may conflict sharply with the rest. The change agent should be prepared to weigh these differing views and choose among them based on factors, such as

- Which seems to best fit the setting and population
- Which seems to have the greatest explanatory power
- Which has earned the most support in empirical tests of its predictive capacity and
- Which offers the richest range of testable hypotheses (usually in the form of possible interventions)

Theoretical principles should be critically evaluated for their biases and given credibility based on how thoroughly they have been tested, especially in relation to the population being explored. Once selected as a framework for analysis, theoretical assumptions should be stated and shared with those involved in the change effort. This is intended to facilitate the achievement of a shared understanding of the problem and population group involved.

Human Rights & Justice

Critical Thinking Question: What are some ways that a theoretical perspective might be biased?

Task 4: Select Factors That Help in Understanding the Target Population

Questions to be explored in this task include:

- From review of the professional knowledge base on the target population and from listening to key informants, what appear to be the major factors that help in understanding the population?
- Which issues or needs, at this point, appear to be the most logical ones to be addressed in this episode of change?

When a review of the knowledge base and interviews has been completed, a beginning profile should begin to emerge. This profile will assist in understanding the target population and its perceptions and responses to the presenting problem or need. Factors relating to this population's needs or behaviors that must be dealt with in order to bring about needed changes should begin to become evident.

A study of single black mothers with young children examined the relationships between mothers' (1) low-wage employment, (2) self-efficacy beliefs, (3) depressive symptoms, and (4) selected parenting behaviors and children's cognitive and behavioral functioning in early elementary school years (Jackson & Scheines, 2005). Employment was related directly to higher self-efficacy, which in turn was associated with decreased depressive symptoms. Decreased depression was associated with frequency of contact with fathers, which in turn predicted more adequate maternal parenting and improved functioning for the child. The pattern of relationships that emerges here enables the change agent to begin to focus on specifics rather than attempting to address a large, complex generalized set of problems.

In another study, battered women's profiles were examined in relation to their help-seeking efforts (Macy, Nurius, Kernic, & Holt, 2005). The authors found distinctive profiles of needs and resources among battered women who seek various types of services. These types of studies illustrate ways in which exploration of a population and/or a problem can yield profiles that aid in understanding the particular needs or responses of the group being studied.

Ashford, LeCroy, and Lortie (2006) identify the following factors as being associated with preadolescents at risk of delinquency: (1) low expectations for education, (2) little participation in school activities, (3) low school achievement, (4) poor verbal ability, (5) truancy, (6) early stealing and lying, (7) heavy peer influence, (8) nonconformity, (9) hyperactivity and aggressive behavior, (10) lack of bonding with parents, (11) family history of violence, and (12) high-crime, high-mobility community (p. 412). If the population being studied includes this group, some of these factors might be used in compiling a profile that could be used in predicting certain outcomes.

Which, if any, of these factors associated with the particular population under study will be useful in understanding the population can only be determined within the context of an episode of change. Much will depend on the nature of the problem identified and the purpose of the intervention. When a list of relevant factors has been identified, the process is at a point where speculation can begin about etiology (cause-and-effect relationships).

UNDERSTANDING PROBLEMS AND POPULATIONS

It is now time to pull together what was learned in Chapter 3 and this chapter. The purpose of Chapter 3 was to guide the social worker through an analysis of the problem. In this chapter, we have examined in detail the population group most directly involved. The next step is to develop a working hypothesis, based on everything that has been learned.

Task 5: Develop a Working Hypothesis of Etiology About the Problem

When the problem- and population-analysis phases have been completed, a good deal of relevant quantitative data and other types of information will have been compiled and prioritized. The final activities under Task 4 involve distilling this information into a focused, shared understanding of the reasons behind the continued existence of the problem.

Etiology refers to the underlying causes of a problem. Speculating about the etiology of a problem is an attempt to arrive at an understanding of cause-and-effect relationships. As one begins to move into this territory, it is important to keep an open mind and let results from searches of the knowledge base, quantitative data, historical information, and the personal experiences of target population representatives inform an understanding of the problem. It is unlikely—in the analysis of social, community, and/or organizational problems—that there will be simple, linear, cause-and-effect relationships. It is more likely that there will be a variety of contributing factors, along with multiple views on what is relevant and applicable to the current situation.

It is unlikely—in the analysis of social, community, and/or organizational problems—that there will be simple, linear, cause-and-effect relationships.

Review What Was Learned in Both the Problem Analysis and the Population Analysis

Questions to be explored in this activity are:

▶ What are the major concepts, issues, and perspectives identified in the *problem* analysis?
▶ What are the major issues and perspectives identified in the *population* analysis?

Examination of history, theory, and research on the population and the problem come together at the point at which cause-and-effect relationships are postulated. The change agent looks for patterns of events or factors that seem to be associated so that a case can be made for a working hypothesis on selected causal or contributing factors. In the previous chapter, in exploring the problem of unsupervised children in a community, the following contributing factors were identified:

- There is a high percentage of single, working mothers in the community.
- There are no after-school programs available in the community.
- Children in the community from single-parent families have few male mentors or role models.
- The community lacks a sense of cohesion; for the most part, people know few neighbors.
- No community-based organizations are currently addressing this problem.

In many cases, alternative explanations of cause and effect are all logical and, in a sense, "correct," but they may apply to different groups within a given population. For example, all the following statements are probably logical explanations of why some adolescents exhibit delinquent behavior:

- Some adolescents feel neglected by parents.
- Some adolescents fail to bond with parents.
- Some adolescents are not able to succeed in school.
- Some adolescents choose peers who encourage delinquent activities.
- Some adolescents live in high-crime, high-mobility communities.

Thus, the decision that must then be made is not one of choosing the "correct" perspective on etiology but rather selecting the subgroup(s) to be addressed. As with most populations and problems, one understanding of etiology and one intervention does not fit all. There are multiple rational explanations, and ultimately one or more must be selected to serve as a framework for understanding the problem and the population.

A hypothesis of etiology should identify what the participants in the change process believe to be the most important and relevant factors contributing to the problem. This may be different from what was identified in the literature or may lead to a particular part of the literature that needs reexamination.

Practice Contexts

Critical Thinking Question: Why might your hypothesized etiology look different from those proposed in the literature?

Select Important Factors Explaining the Current Problem

Questions to be explored in this activity include:

- What are the causal factors that explain the problem?
- What are the results or effects of the causes identified?

Based on what was learned, a series of statements about probable effects of contributing factors can be generated. For example, in exploring the question of why some adolescents demonstrate antisocial behavior, including committing status offenses (acts that would not be offenses if they were adults, such as truancy or running away from home), a hypothesis of etiology emerges. Other factors could be added that focus on, for example, a specific subgroup of adolescent girls, or a group of Native American boys, in which case gender or cultural factors may be included in the hypothesis.

Another example arises from a growing concern about chronic homelessness among single adults. A study of the homeless services system may lead to the following findings:

- Permanent supportive housing is successful in ending homelessness for chronically homeless individuals with a serious mental illness.
- The majority of the system's programs are focused on emergency shelter.
- Affordable housing is limited.
- Few programs provide permanent supportive housing.
- Eligibility requirements for transitional and permanent supportive housing programs screen out a majority of chronically homeless individuals.
- Ability to remain in housing is linked to service success and program compliance.
- Mental health and substance abuse treatment services are limited.
- Trauma-informed services are rarely provided.
- Chronically homeless individuals who are not stably housed tend to over utilize hospital emergency rooms for health and mental health treatment.

A survey of the population reveals some of the problems and needs faced by individuals who are chronically homeless:

- Some believe that homeless programs do not respect them.
- Some are experiencing severe symptoms of a mental health disorder.
- Some are experiencing acute or chronic physical health conditions.
- Some have difficulty becoming clean and sober.
- Some suffer discrimination and rejection from service providers and community members.
- Some experience trauma because of current and previous experiences on and off the street.

Drawing on these findings from analysis of problem and population, relationships may be proposed between causes and their effects.

It should be clear from these examples that part of the job of creating a clearly focused macro-level intervention involves selecting some contributing factors and setting others aside, at least for the time being, unless enough resources are available to take on every factor within the same project. It is also possible that completely different factors could be identified within these examples if gender or cultural issues emerge during the course of the study. Each episode of change must find its focus within the context of the considerations and dictates of the local situation at the time.

Prepare a Hypothesis

Questions to be explored in this activity include:

- Based on the foregoing analysis of problem and population, what seem to be the dominant themes in understanding cause-and-effect relationships?
- How should the hypothesis of etiology be framed?

The hypothesis of etiology frames the change effort in a way that makes it focused and manageable. Example 1 in Box 4.1 leads to a working hypothesis such as the following:

When single, working mothers are unable to meet the needs of their adolescent children for parental guidance, and when adolescents lack a positive

---

Box 4.1 Selecting Factors from Analysis of Problem and Population: Example 1

Selected Factors Affecting Adolescent First-Offenders Who Commit Status Offenses:	**These Factors Appear to Lead to the Following Results:**
1. Some single working mothers have limited ability to meet the many needs of their adolescent children for parental guidance.	1. Adolescents whose needs for parental guidance are not met by parents may feel neglected.
2. Some adolescent children of single, working mothers lack male role models.	2. Lack of positive, male role models for some adolescents leads to bonding with older peers who may encourage delinquent behavior.
3. There are no after-school programs for adolescents in the community.	3. Absence of organized after-school activities for adolescents results in many hours of idle, nonproductive time every day, which may lead to participation in delinquent activities.

Box 4.2 Selecting Factors from Analysis of Problem and Population: Example 2

Selected Factors Affecting Chronically Homeless Adults with a Serious Mental Illness:	**These Factors Appear to Lead to the Following Results:**
1. The homeless service system focuses its resources primarily on emergency housing and services.	1. Little attention and few resources are directed to permanent supportive housing.
2. The eligibility criteria for existing permanent supportive housing screen out most chronically homeless individuals.	2. Chronically homeless individuals who can't qualify for permanent supportive housing programs live on the streets and in shelters.
3. Chronically homeless individuals tend to use and reuse hospital emergency rooms to meet health and mental health needs.	3. Chronically homeless individual's utilization of health and human services is fragmented and expensive.

---

male role model, and when no organized after-school activities are available for adolescents, it is likely that adolescents will feel neglected, will bond with older peers who may turn out to be negative role models, and will participate in delinquent acts during idle after-school hours.

Using the hypothesis for Example 1, the change agent will begin to think in terms of framing the intervention around identifying adolescent children of single, working mothers who have been involved in one or more delinquent activities and (1) dealing with their feelings of neglect, (2) finding positive male role models to serve as mentors to the adolescents identified, and (3) providing a program of organized after-school activities for the adolescents identified.

A hypothesis for Example 2 in Box 4.2 might read as follows:

When a homeless services system focuses the majority of its efforts and resources on emergency housing for the homeless; and when existing emergency, transitional, and permanent supportive housing programs "screen out" individuals who are chronically homeless and have a serious mental illness, and when chronically homeless individuals use and reuse hospital emergency rooms for health and mental health services, it is likely that the homeless service system will not develop permanent supportive housing programs, that chronically homeless individuals will not be able to access the permanent supportive housing programs that exist, and that chronically homeless individuals will overutilize expensive health and mental health services.

For Example 2, the intervention will focus on (1) redirecting existing resources toward permanent supportive housing, (2) developing eligibility criteria for programs that are more responsive to the needs of the population, and (3) coordinating immediate and routine health and mental health services to better respond to the health and mental health needs of chronically homeless individuals.

SUMMARY

Chapters 3 and 4 are intended to be companion pieces designed to lead the change agent through an orderly, systematic review of existing knowledge, research, data, information, historical perspectives, and other types of information that may be available on the problem(s) and the population(s) affected. The purpose of this compilation of knowledge and information is so that the change agent may develop a clear understanding of the many factors that may have led to the current situation. Based on a study and analysis of these factors, the change agent can narrow a broad, sweeping general definition of the problem to a small number of highly specific factors that lend themselves to intervention and problem resolution.

A complete study of problem and population involves many facets. These studies include a review of the existing professional knowledge base, personal interviews with local people affected by the problem, and a compilation of quantitative and qualitative data and information to back up the problem statement. Finally, all relevant knowledge, data, information, and other findings are narrowed down to a select few causal factors that become the focus of a working hypothesis of etiology. Once a consensus on the hypothesis is achieved among the participants, an analysis of community and/or relevant organization(s) is undertaken. These topics will be covered in the next four chapters.

Framework for Understanding the Target Population

Task 1: Develop Cultural Humility

- What are the power imbalances faced by this population group?
- What experiences has the social worker had with members of this population group?
- What self-identities and attitudes does the social worker bring to this situation?

Task 2: Seek Diverse Perspectives

Listen to Persons Who Have Experienced the Problem

- How do representatives of diverse groups affected by this problem or opportunity view it?
- Have diverse voices and perspectives been included in articulating and understanding the problem? If not, why?

Listen to Population Allies and Advocates

- Who are the allies and advocates of this population group?
- What can be learned from allies and advocates about the history of experiences with the target population and the pressing problems and opportunities?

Task 3: Search the Professional Knowledge Base on the Target Population

Understand Concepts and Issues Related to Growth and Development

- What sources of the professional knowledge base are available on this population group?
- What theoretical frameworks are available that will help in understanding the target population?
- What factors or characteristics gleaned from the knowledge base on this population will be helpful in understanding the target population?

Understand the Impact of Social Relationships and Structures

- What structural and environmental forces are affecting this population group?
- What theoretical frameworks are available that will help in understanding the interactions between members of the population and the larger social environment?

Understand the Impact of Difference, Discrimination, and Oppression

- What stereotypes or generalizations confront this population group?
- How has this population group been discriminated against or oppressed?

Task 4: Select Factors That Help in Understanding the Target Population

- From review of the professional knowledge base on the target population and from listening to key informants, what appear to be the major factors that help in understanding the population?
- Which issues or needs, at this point, appear to be the most logical ones to be addressed in this episode of change?

Task 5: Develop a Working Hypothesis of Etiology About the Problem

Review What Was Learned in Both the Problem Analysis and the Population Analysis

‣ What are the major concepts, issues, and perspectives identified in the *problem* analysis?
‣ What are the major issues and perspectives identified in the *population* analysis?

Select Important Factors Explaining the Current Problem

‣ What are the causal factors that explain the problem?
‣ What are the results or effects of these causes identified?

Prepare a Hypothesis

‣ Based on the foregoing analysis of problem and population, what seem to be the dominant themes in understanding cause-and-effect relationships?
‣ How should the hypothesis of etiology be framed?

Succeed with PEARSON mysocialworklab

Log onto **www.mysocialworklab.com** and answer the questions below. (*If you did not receive an access code to MySocialWorkLab with this text and wish to purchase access online, please visit www.mysocialworklab.com.*)

1. **Read the MySocialWorkLibrary case study: Please Don't Expect Me to Be a Model Minority Kid.** Imagine your agency is trying to develop a youth program in a predominately Korean neighborhood. What are some considerations you learned about Jane and her family that might help you plan your program? Based on what you read in the chapter, what type of perspective(s) will you seek out to inform your program?

2. **Read the MySocialWorkLibrary case study: Please Don't Let Our Mother Die: The Case of Asha Patel.** Form a hypothesis of etiology for depressed elderly immigrants from south Asia. (Of course, in practice you would have a more thorough understanding of the problem and population from a variety of sources prior to doing this!)

PRACTICE TEST

The following questions will test your knowledge of the content found within this chapter. For additional assessment, including licensing-exam-type questions on applying chapter content to practice, visit **MySocialWorkLab**.

1. When conducting a population analysis, which task below will most likely come last?
   a. develop a working hypothesis of etiology
   b. search the professional knowledge base
   c. seek diverse perspectives and ideas
   d. select factors that help in understanding

2. An agency decides to hire four new bilingual outreach workers. This best exemplifies
   a. cultural incapacity
   b. cultural precompetence
   c. cultural competence
   d. cultural proficiency

3. Simple, direct, linear cause-and-effect relationships are _____ when analyzing social, community, and/or organizational problems.
   a. unlikely
   b. predictable
   c. random
   d. probable

4. The hypothesis of etiology frames the change effort in a way that makes it
   a. focused and manageable
   b. acceptable to scientists
   c. easy to research
   d. possible to test

5. Imagine your next field placement is in an agency that serves homeless men with HIV. Reflect on your own experiences with this population, your self-identities and pre-existing attitudes about this group. Where might you look for allies and advocates?

ASSESS YOUR COMPETENCE

Use the scale below to rate your current level of achievement on the following concepts or skills associated with each competency presented in the chapter:

1	2	3
I can accurately describe the concept or skill.	I can consistently identify the concept or skill when observing and analyzing practice activities.	I can competently implement the concept or skill in my own practice.

_____ Can demonstrate cultural humility when considering problems within the context of populations.

_____ Can apply a range of theories that considers both person and environment.

_____ Can identify and refute theories and hypothesis of etiology that may be culturally biased.

_____ Can form hypothesis of etiology independently, using analysis techniques and diverse sources as discussed in this chapter.

5

Understanding Communities

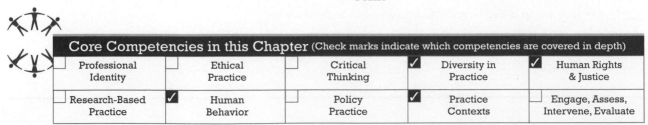

Core Competencies in this Chapter (Check marks indicate which competencies are covered in depth)				
☐ Professional Identity	☐ Ethical Practice	☐ Critical Thinking	✔ Diversity in Practice	✔ Human Rights & Justice
☐ Research-Based Practice	✔ Human Behavior	☐ Policy Practice	✔ Practice Contexts	☐ Engage, Assess, Intervene, Evaluate

INTRODUCTION

Communities are the arenas in which macro practice takes place, but they are so diverse that no one definition or theory seems able to capture their total essence. Terms such as *global community* and *world community* are used in contemporary society to refer to the complex array of relationships among the people of the world. Yet, when most people think about communities that are important to them, they usually think on a smaller scale—remembering where they grew up, identifying with where they live today, or focusing on relationships based on affiliations or interests rather than geographic proximity. These relationships may be bound by characteristics such as shared history, cultural values and traditions, concern for common issues, or frequent communication. Many people identify with multiple communities, thus making "*the* community" a misnomer. For many, affiliation with more than one community is an intrinsic part of who a person is.

Based on their life experiences, social workers will have their own perceptions of what a community is, along with expectations about what it should be. These perceptions and expectations will influence how they approach work in communities that are new to them, and it is important to recognize that experiences with and feelings about community as a geographic locality vary. Some communities will be viewed nostalgically, as desirable places, evoking warm memories. Other communities will be seen as oppressive, restrictive, or even dangerous to both residents and outsiders. At times, these differing views will be held about the same community, because each person's experience is unique. Community-based groups, ranging from youth gangs to garden clubs, represent attempts to create specialized communities of interest within geographical communities, sometimes in ways that intentionally run counter to the local culture.

Some observers believe that "community" as a geographically relevant concept began to erode with the expansion of suburbs in the 1950s and 1960s (Gerloff, 1992). Others see unlimited human potential lying dormant in inner-city communities that have been rendered dependent on social welfare organizations by an overzealous provision of services (Kretzmann & McKnight, 1993). One of the big issues we confront in this chapter is whether social workers are best served by looking at communities as places where people's interests are linked by geographic closeness, or whether—in an era of cell phones, email, instant text messaging, Twitter, Facebook, online interactive games, and any number of methods of easy long-distance communication—the whole idea of community needs to be radically redefined. Also, perhaps a problem confronting social workers in helping the poorest members of society is that they are forced to remain in a world where geographic proximity *does* matter because their environment is dangerous and lacks resources such as transportation, jobs, and child care. Conversely, proximity becomes ever less relevant to more affluent members of society who can afford the technologies that allow them to transcend geography. It may happen within a single episode of change that multiple definitions of *community* are needed to help keep commitments and relationships clear. For example, while the target of change may be a specific neighborhood (a geographically bounded community), those needed to support the change may be linked through concern and commitment, but may come both from the neighborhood and from across the entire city.

We believe that social workers have a responsibility to recognize that community can be a powerful medium for enfranchisement and empowerment when its potential is understood and skillfully brought to life. We also believe that social workers must recognize that problems and needs can often be addressed more effectively by dealing with them collectively than they can by dealing with them individually. The major focus of this chapter will be on understanding communities from a theoretical perspective as a first step toward better informed and more skillful community-level intervention.

Defining Community

There are many definitions of *community*, and we will provide only a sample here. As early as the 1950s, one scholar identified over ninety discrete definitions of *community* in use within the social science literature (Hillery, 1955). No matter what definition is selected, concepts such as *space*, *people*, *interaction*, and *shared identity* are repeated over and over again.

Even persons within the same community will differ in their perspectives of what that community is and what changes are needed.

Irrespective of the changes to be made in community arenas, the social worker will want to be aware of how persons affected by change define and perceive their communities. The social worker must understand alternative perspectives, recognize the assumptions and values that undergird these views, and understand how differing perspectives influence change opportunities (Gamble & Weil, 2010). It is also important to recognize that even persons within the same community will differ in their perspectives of what that community is and of what changes are needed. For example, it is not unusual within the boundaries of a community for one ethnic or cultural group to believe that schools are relevant and city services adequate to meet local needs, whereas another ethnic or cultural group believes they are irrelevant and inadequate.

One of the most cited definitions of community was provided by Warren (1978) who viewed community as the organization of social activities that affords people access to what is necessary for day-to-day living, such as the school, grocery store, hospital, house of worship, and other such social units and systems. Many people customarily think of social units as beginning with the domestic unit, extending to the neighborhood or to a voluntary association, and on to larger spheres of human interaction. Community may or may not have clear boundaries, but it is significant because it performs important functions necessary for human survival. Warren identifies five community functions, which we will discuss later. See Table 5.1.

Communities can be formal or informal, and the variable that usually determines the level of formality is *boundary clarity*. Cities and counties have clear boundaries, whereas neighborhoods are often less clearly defined, and a community based on common interests of its members may not have geographical boundaries at all. The boundaries may be based on a common interest, a cause, and even personal or professional characteristics that transcend space. The clarity of boundaries varies not only across different communities, but, as will be seen in later chapters, the presence of a formal boundary is often a key feature that differentiates organizations and communities.

Communities can exist within other communities, and they are often experienced in different ways by their members. Residents in a desperately poor inner-city neighborhood may be part of the same larger community as those who live in posh high-rise penthouses near downtown, yet they would likely define their "community" in sharply contrasting terms. When communities

---

Table 5.1   Warren's Definition of Community

Community is that combination of social units and systems that perform the major social functions relevant to meeting people's needs on a local level—Roland Warren (1978). Warren's social functions are:

Function	Definition	Example
Production, distribution, and consumption	Community activities designed to meet people's needs	Grocery stores, gas stations
Socialization	Learning prevailing norms, traditions, and values	Understanding how community members perceive the value of education
Social control	The process by which community members ensure compliance with norms and values	Establishing stringent eligibility requirements for public aid and social services
Social participation	Interaction with others in community groups, associations, and organizations	Local churches
Mutual support	Supportive functions carried out by family and community members in times of need	Neighbors helping neighbors during a natural disaster

exist within each other, they also intermingle in complex ways. The working mother in the poor neighborhood and the corporate leader in the penthouse may have little interaction with one another and may be opposed in their views on most "community" issues, yet they may sit next to each other on the subway train on which they both depend, and their interests in keeping it running on certain schedules and along certain routes may be identical. They might also support the same sports team or vote for the same mayoral candidate, meaning that commonalities and ways of grouping the two of them into the same "community" could be discovered in unexpected places.

As communities get larger, they may become more heterogeneous. As noted, the small community of penthouse owners is likely to be composed of individuals having much more in common with each other across a range of variables than the much larger community of subway riders. This means that smaller communities may be more cohesive and easier to organize for macro-level change than larger ones. However, sharp differences can exist even among members of relatively small communities, although, as discussed, commonalities may be found even among individuals from seemingly different communities.

Dimensions of Communities

Fellin (2001) contends that community occurs when people come together around common physical location, interests, cultures, and/or other identities. In this definition, it is important to note that this coming together may be intentional or might even be facilitated by a change agent who points out what people have in common (Knickmeyer, Hopkins, & Meyer, 2003). Fellin distinguishes three dimensions of communities: (1) a place or geographic locale in which one's needs for sustenance are met, (2) a pattern of social interactions, and (3) symbolic identification that gives meaning to one's identity. We will briefly examine each category.

Geographical, spatial, or territorial communities vary in how they meet people's needs, how social interactions are patterned, and how collective identity is perceived. Local communities are often called neighborhoods, cities, towns, boroughs, barrios, and a host of other terms. Smaller geographical spaces are nested within other communities, such as neighborhoods within towns or public housing developments within cities.

In earlier times, before people were so mobile and technology transcended space, communities were much more place bound. Today, however, considerations of space must be juxtaposed with other ways of conceptualizing community. Although we may operate within geographical jurisdictions, the influence of forces beyond the spatial boundaries is almost limitless.

Patterns of social interaction can occur in geographical communities, but can also be part of "nonplace" communities (sometimes called functional communities, relational or associational communities, communities of affiliation or affinity, or even communities of the mind). These nongeographical or functional communities bring people together based on a variety of identifications and characteristics including, for example, religion, race, or profession (Fellin, 2001).

Functional communities, which are examples of communities that are based on identification and interest, are formed when people work as a group to jointly address social problems (Gamble & Weil, 2010). For the social work practitioner, it is important to recognize and understand communities that are formed around shared concerns, such as AIDS, gun control, terrorism, disaster relief, and political loyalties. It is even more critical to recognize that these communities are formed around deeply held beliefs and values that may conflict with those of other communities. For example, faith-based communities or congregations that believe that being gay or lesbian is morally wrong may have a clash of values when encountering the gay and lesbian community. Similarly, professional communities that believe in social justice and advocacy for the poor may encounter political communities formed to reduce government spending and to terminate public assistance to those who are on welfare, regardless of need or capacity for self-sufficiency. Communities of interest based on social interaction are becoming increasingly politically active, and many people have warned of the polarizing effects of special-interest politics.

A functional community may exist when many disparate individuals are working toward a goal or advocating for a cause. Those same individuals may not be aware of the existence of organizations formed to address that goal. In some instances, there may not yet be more formal groups formed to work in a more organized fashion. The change agent's task may therefore involve making members of functional communities aware of one another and furthering the transition from functional community to formal organization. Thus, functional communities may form organizations that are more structured, with formally stated objectives and the resources, such as volunteers and staff, to get things done. An example is the number of persons in various communities and states who were frustrated over the conditions in the country's nursing homes. Citizen groups, families and friends of residents, and residents themselves were expressing concern in various localities, but they were not organized to make legislative change at the national level. The National Citizens Coalition on Nursing Home Reform was formed at the national level as an organizational

Table 5.2   Fellin's Dimensions of Communities

Dimension of Community	Definition	Example
Geographical Space—a place in which one's needs for sustenance are met	A community with defined boundaries where one expects to meet basic needs	A neighborhood in which families fulfill their basic functions and raise their children
A pattern of social interaction	A place or nonplace community of identification and interest	Relationships with others of the same ethnic group, regardless of location
Symbolic identification that gives meaning to one's identity	Attaching importance to groups and organizations as a means of helping to establish personal uniqueness	Identification with a religious group, a profession, or a cause

vehicle to raise the issues and concerns of residents and caregivers in long-term care facilities and to serve as a voice on Capitol Hill.

Fellin (2001) also identifies *a collective, symbolic relationship that gives meaning to one's identity* as a dimension of some place- and nonplace-based communities. In a complex society, people establish constellations of relationships that give meaning to their lives. For example, a social worker is likely to identify with others who have his or her occupation and professional training (a nonplace community), live in a neighborhood (a place community), and have close relationships scattered around the world (a personal network). Because each person will have a unique constellation of relationships, each person's definition of *community* will be distinctive. Often viewed as networks (or webs) of formal and informal resources, it is important for the change agent to recognize, respect, and understand these relationships and what they mean to the person's "sense of community." Methods such as *network analysis, ecological mapping, and concept mapping* are intended to reveal how individuals perceive their communities and to use those perceptions to develop community interventions. For example, Ridings and his colleagues (2008) used concept mapping to develop a conceptual framework of problems faced by African American male youth in Chicago in order to develop new outcomes for change. Community, then, can be seen as those spaces, interactions, and identifications that people share with others in both place-specific and nonplace-specific locations. Table 5.2 provides a summary of the types discussed, their definitions, and examples of each. The planned change model presented in later chapters will be applicable to both place and nonplace communities.

COMMUNITY FUNCTIONS

Communities are structured to perform certain functions for their members. In Table 5.1 we summarized Warren's (1978) identified five functions carried out by locality-relevant communities: (1) production, distribution, and consumption; (2) socialization; (3) social control; (4) social participation; and (5) mutual support.

Production, distribution, and consumption functions are community activities designed to meet people's material needs, including the most basic requirements, such as food, clothing, and shelter. In modern communities, families seldom produce most or all of what they consume. People are dependent on each other for these and other needs, including medical care, sanitation, employment, transportation, and recreation. The accepted medium of exchange for these goods and services is money, which becomes an important factor in defining the limits of consumption and comes into consideration in almost all community-change efforts.

A second function of community is *socialization* to the prevailing norms, traditions, and values of community members. Socialization guides attitudinal development, and these attitudes and perceptions influence how people view themselves, others, and their interpersonal rights and responsibilities. Attitudes and values also differ from community to community, and they vary across smaller communities that are nested within larger ones. To understand an individual or population, it is therefore critical to understand the norms, traditions, and values of the community or communities in which the person was socialized.

Social control is the process by which community members ensure compliance with norms and values. This is usually done by establishing laws, rules, and regulations, as well as systems for their enforcement. Social control is often performed by diverse institutions such as government, education, religion, and social services. Many social workers serve in practice settings in which they must constantly strive to balance their sometimes conflicting roles as helpers and agents of social control. Examples of such settings include schools, correctional institutions, probation and parole offices, and employment and training programs.

Communities may also exert subtle forms of social control through patterns of service distribution and eligibility criteria that regulate access to resources on the part of vulnerable groups. For example, case managers often find they must deny services due to limited resources. Concerns about these limitations may spur the practitioner to work toward change, only to discover that key policymakers have suppressed the demand for aid by keeping benefits low rather than providing the level of assistance needed to combat the presenting problem. Recognizing how social control can occur both overtly and covertly can be disillusioning, but is necessary for understanding both the impact of community values and the process of service delivery.

Social participation includes interaction with others in community groups, associations, and organizations. People are assumed to need some form of social outlet, and communities provide opportunities for people to express this need and to build natural helping and support networks. Some find their outlets in local religious groups, some in civic organizations, and some in informal neighborhood groups. Understanding the opportunities and patterns of social participation in a target population is helpful in assessing how well a community is meeting the needs of its members.

Mutual support is the function that families, friends, partners, neighbors, volunteers, and professionals carry out in communities when they care for the sick, the unemployed, and the distressed. As noted in Chapter 2, processes such as industrialization, urbanization, and increased mobility strained the capacity of traditional community units (e.g., families, faith groups, civic organizations) to meet the mutual-support needs of community members. This led to the growth of different community units, such as helping professionals and government-sponsored programs, that took over some of the roles previously left to informal and smaller-scale units.

Human Rights & Justice

Critical Thinking Question: In which of these community functions do you think social work clients are least active? Why?

When Community Functions Fail

In Warren's model (1978), these five functions define the purpose of a community. If all functions were performed in a given community in a manner that met the needs of all its members (in other words, if all consumption, socialization, social control, social participation, and mutual support needs were met in a healthy, positive, and constructive manner), the community would be considered optimally structured.

However, such an "ideal" community probably does not exist. Some religious communities in rural areas have fulfilled many of these functions in ways that minimize the need for intervention and change, but these are clearly exceptions. It is far more common to find these functions falling short of meeting the needs of at least some community members. This may be due to inadequate resources for distribution and consumption or to uneven distribution. Socialization may be tied to values imposed by some community members on others but not mutually shared. The social control function may not operate in an evenhanded manner and may even be oppressive. Social participation opportunities may be severely limited or available to some but not others. Mutual support functions may be undermined by a dominant value system that assumes individuals should be able to fend for themselves. In short, communities can be considered *healthy* or *unhealthy*, *functional* or *dysfunctional*, and *competent* or *incompetent* based on their ability to meet community needs. This may be particularly true for oppressed target populations within their boundaries. We hasten to say that rarely do we find a community that can be labeled so easily one way or another. Most communities are somewhere along a continuum between these pairs of descriptors.

Building on Warren's work, Pantoja and Perry (1998) provided a working model of community development and restoration. Citing production, distribution, and consumption as the economic area on which all other functions are dependent, they identify the remaining community functions as socialization, social control, social placement (participation), mutual support, defense, and communication. Defense and communication are additions to Warren's original list.

Defense is the way in which the community takes care of and protects its members. This function becomes important in communities that are unsafe and dangerous. Some communities have been labeled *defended communities* when they have to focus unusual amounts of effort toward looking after their members. The defense function can also be relevant to nonplace communities. One example is that defense is often critical among gay or lesbian persons because there are groups within the larger society that may seek to do them harm. Similarly, people of color in various communities have had to support one another in defending themselves against the effects of racial hatred.

Communication includes the use of a common language and symbols to express ideas. Although communication may be assumed as part of all functions originally identified by Warren, its identification as a separate function in contemporary society is important. As one example, debate about whether and how forcefully English proficiency should be demanded of immigrants has been a prominent aspect of the broader controversy over immigration in the United States. Similarly, the ability to communicate easily across the country and around the world through email and other rapidly expanding features of the Internet has vastly expanded the definition of *community* while simultaneously blurring its boundaries.

Table 5.3   Pantoja and Perry's Functions of Community

Function	Definition	Example
Production, distribution, and consumption	The areas on which all other functions are dependent	Small businesses that provide jobs and goods to a community
Socialization	Learning the prevailing norms, traditions, and values	Understanding how community members perceive their roles vis-à-vis local government
Social control	Ensuring compliance with norms and values	How law enforcement is administered
Social placement	Participation in activities significant to the life of the community	The extent to which parents participate in school-related functions
Mutual Support	Functions carried out in support of each other	The ways in which a community cares for its homeless
Defense	The way a community takes care of and protects its members	Block watch programs
Communication	Use of a common language to express ideas	The extent to which English proficiency is demanded of immigrant families

The assumption underlying the identification of functions is that communities serve the needs of members by performing these functions well. Conversely, when communities are dysfunctional (Pantoja & Perry, 1998) or incompetent (Fellin, 1995), people suffer and change needs to occur. According to Pantoja and Perry's framework, without a stable economic base the other functions, which are supportive, deteriorate, or are impaired. Therefore, it is important for the social worker to carefully assess how communities are functioning and how the needs of people are or are not being addressed. Table 5.3 provides an overview of community functions.

Functional definitions and understandings of community can also be useful in communities that are not geographically specific. For example, some people may have their communication needs met by keeping in touch with persons in different geographical areas. It is not unusual to have adult children of elderly parents who live miles apart calling daily to check on how their parents are doing. In professional communities, long-distance communication is carried out via telephone, fax, email, or text messaging on a regular basis. However, communication in this form requires access to the technology. In many communities this access is uneven, leading to what has been called *information poverty*. These communities are taking steps such as wiring whole cities for wireless Internet (McNutt, Queiro-Tajalli, Boland, & Campbell, 2001).

Functionalism "regards social structures (definable social entities that exist in relationship to other structures) and social functions (the roles, purposes, and uses of the entities) in a given social system as inextricably intertwined" (Harrison, 1995, p. 556). What this means is that *structures,* such as schools, synagogues, or political entities, are intermeshed with *functions,* such as teaching, providing leadership, or advocating for change. Understanding community requires analysis of structures and function *together*—not as separate entities. This notion is also relevant to social systems theory, to which we now turn in a discussion of how communities can usefully be viewed as social systems.

Understanding community requires analysis of structures and function together—not as separate entities.

DISTINGUISHING COMMUNITY THEORIES AND MODELS

One of the earliest efforts to conceptualize communities was the work of Ferdinand Tönnies (1987/1957), who discussed the constructs of *Gemeinschaft* and *Gesellschaft. Gemeinschaft,* which roughly translates as "community," focuses on the mutual, intimate, and common bonds that pull people together in local units. These bonds are based on caring about one another and valuing the relationships in the group in and of themselves. The group is valued, regardless of whether its members are creating a product or achieving a goal. Examples are the domestic unit, the neighborhood, and groups of friends. The focus of *Gemeinschaft* is on intimacy and relationship.

In contrast, Tönnies *Gesellschaft* refers generally to society or association. Examples of this concept are a city or government. *Gesellschaft* is an ideal type representing formalized relationships that are task oriented. In *Gesellschaft*-type relationships, people organize in a more formal way to achieve a purpose, task, or goal. Although they may benefit from the relationships that are established, the purpose of these social interactions is more restricted to the accomplishment of a particular end, to create some production, or to complete some task.

Sociologists in the late 1800s viewed *Gesellschaft* as representing all the negative forces pulling people away from traditional communities built on institutions such as the family and religion. It is important to recognize, however, that the contribution of Tönnies ideal types is to call attention to the differences between informal and formal systems and to the richness of their interactions. Social workers doing macro practice will find elements of both concepts in the communities with which they work. Tönnies work is considered a foundation from which community theory emerged in the 1990s.

Roland Warren's (1978) text on community synthesized the theories that existed up to the early 1970s and provided a valuable resource for identifying studies conducted up to that time. Warren characterized community as (1) *space*, (2) *people*, (3) *shared values and institutions*, (4) *interaction*, (5) *distribution of power*, and (6) *social system.* These themes will recur as we discuss community theory. Conceptualizations of community may be derived from each of these six themes.

Theories are sets of interrelated concepts that explain how and why something works or does not work for the purpose of enhancing our understanding. Sociological theories of community often describe how communities function. These *descriptive approaches* assist in analyzing what is happening within communities but do not provide the practitioner with methods to change a situation once it has been analyzed. Systems; human or population ecology; human behavior; and power, politics, and change theories will be discussed as sociological theories that assist in understanding how communities function. In contrast, a variety of community *practice perspectives and models* are intended to provide direction or guidance for persons wanting to change or intervene in a community arena. We will focus on strengths, empowerment, and resiliency perspectives, as well as capacity building and asset mapping as guides to practice.

Table 5.4 presents a general guide for distinguishing descriptive and prescriptive approaches, categorized by the use of these theories, perspectives, and models in place-based (geographical) and nonplace-based communities. Note that some approaches are helpful in analyzing both types of communities, whereas

Table 5.4	**Types of Theories and Perspectives by Types of Communities**	
Types of Theories/Perspectives	Place-Based (Geographical) Communities	Nonplace-Based Communities
Descriptive (to understand communities)	Systems Theories Human or population ecology Human behavior Power, politics, and change	Systems Theories Human behavior Power, politics, and change
Prescriptive (to guide practice)	Strengths, empowerment, and resiliency perspectives Capacity building and asset mapping	Strengths, empowerment, and resiliency perspectives

others are more geographically based. In the remainder of the chapter, we will present an overview of community theories that are helpful in understanding the environments in which practitioners find themselves, followed by an identification of practice perspectives and models that have emerged from these efforts and that provide *prescriptive approaches* (how-to guides for taking action).

SYSTEMS THEORY

In Chapter 1 we introduced Warren's (1978) position that social systems theory holds great promise for understanding communities. We also indicated that the planned change model in this book is based predominately on systems theory, and our discussion of organizations in Chapter 7 will also include information on systems theory.

Building on the work of Talcott Parsons (1971) and others, Warren applied social systems theory to communities. His description shows how the functions identified earlier are typically performed by various groups and organizations within local communities. Factories and stores carry out production and distribution functions, school and churches work to socialize community members, and so forth. These internal, *horizontal relationships* are complemented by *vertical relationships* that connect outside the community's geographical boundaries. For example, factories obtain raw materials from elsewhere, schools get books from national publishers, and many churches affiliate with larger denominations.

This situation has a number of ramifications. First, from a systems perspective, it means that communities are open rather than closed systems, and they are dependent on their external environment for certain resources. Second, not only horizontal but also vertical affiliations and interactions are critical for the community to function properly, and both must be understood in order to have a clear grasp of how the community operates. Third, just as certain groups or organizations play specific roles in carrying out essential community tasks, the community must carve out a role for itself in its larger environment that allows it to provide resources needed by other communities in return for acquiring the resources it needs. To use the language of systems theory, the community must establish the boundaries that define both it and its function within the surrounding environment.

Boundary setting and maintenance are critical to any system's survival. As boundaries become blurred or indistinguishable, the community as a spatial set of relationships weakens and becomes less able to fulfill its core functions. Boundaries are also important to systems within a community, and macro practitioners may often be able to witness diverse examples of the struggle for boundary maintenance in their work (Norlin & Chess, 1997). Youth gangs battling over neighborhood turf offer an obvious locality-based example of boundary conflicts, but others, such as efforts by gay and lesbian residents to secure legal recognition and benefits for their partners, may be less recognizable but are nonetheless boundary issues (Hash & Netting, 2007).

It is important, then, to recognize that there are multiple approaches to analyzing macro situations based on systems theory that can also be used for deeper understandings of how communities function. These include mechanical, organismic, morphogenic, factional, and catastrophic analogies (Burrell & Morgan, 1979; Martin & O'Connor, 1989).

A *mechanical analogy* views a social system as a machine in which all the parts work closely together, are well coordinated, and integrate smoothly. When one part of the system changes, it is expected that other parts will adapt to reestablish equilibrium. In this analogy, order is emphasized over change and conflict. If the practitioner approaches a community using this analogy, his or her task will be seen primarily as one of reducing conflict and restoring a sense of order, connectedness, and mutual purpose. For example, a local community whose members are comfortable with their lifestyles would be disrupted by an influx of immigrants from other cultures who represent difference. Instead of welcoming immigrants, the community members may impose strict boundaries, not be welcoming to outsiders, and work toward maintaining the status quo.

The *organismic analogy* comes from comparing social systems to biological organisms. Communities are viewed much like the human body, with each organ having a different function. This may sound familiar, given our discussion of community functions earlier in this chapter. Assuming that each unit within the community performs its respective role, the organismic analogy predicts that community members will work toward a common good. Parson's work on structural functionalism is primarily grounded in this analogy. It argues that structures arise to serve particular functions, and within the range of normal variability they should allow the community as a whole to function effectively and for community members to agree on what needs to happen. In practice, however, social workers often discover that consensus among diverse community members can be elusive. For example, immigrants coming into this type of community may find that they are cautiously welcomed, but only if they behave in ways that fully acculturate them into established community norms and maintain a sense of stability. As long as they agree to play by the established rules, conflict will be kept to a minimum (at least on the surface).

This leads to the question of what happens when there is conflict that cannot be overlooked, when there is seemingly no articulation of the parts or performance of the functions, or when harmony cannot be restored or perhaps never really existed. In this case, other analogies may need to be explored.

A *morphogenic analogy* is applicable when change is ongoing and the structure of the system is continually emerging. Fundamental change can occur in this type of situation because there may be no chance of returning to a former state of *homeostasis* (balance or equilibrium). This highly open approach to systems thinking means that change may be just as likely to be unpredictable as it is to be orderly. It is this unpredictability that requires the community practitioner to be open to clues about how things are changing and to be open to new possibilities. For example, immigrants arriving in this community can expect some conflict as community members adjust to one another's differences. Expectations will be that the community will change in some ways, and that the acceptable way to incorporate new members into the community will be through open dialogue and recognizing that the community will be changed in the process.

Similar to the morphogenic analogy is the *factional analogy* in which contentiousness in a community system is open and obvious. Conflict may be so basic in some community systems that change is likely to remain disorderly and subject to instability. Approaching this type of system with assumptions that order can be reestablished may be a set-up for failure. On the other hand, for the practitioner who can face conflict head-on, this type of community can be a stimulating challenge. Immigrants relocating to a factional community will find local groups in disagreement over how to handle their integration. Conflict will be a normal part of this community's operation, and groups will be trying to convince one another about what approaches should be taken. There will be no attempt to deny that change can be disruptive and debates over the pros and cons of immigration will be ongoing, sometimes heated.

Last, a *catastrophic analogy* is defined by contentiousness and conflict taken to extremes. Such a community system will be characterized by deep fissures and distress. Without order or predictability, there will be a sense of chaos in which no one can determine future directions. Communication may have broken down in the process and subsystems are warring. Intervention in this type of community would look different than it would from mechanical or organismic analogies. In catastrophic communities, there will be protests about how to handle immigration and what course the country (and communities) should take with the volatile issues surrounding immigration. The volatility might even lead to violence.

Our point is that depending on one's assessment of the community system and the degree of conflict, interventions will vary greatly, and in the case of immigration there will be much variation—from wanting to keep immigrants from relocating to a community all the way to full-blown conflict over how immigration should be handled.

In addition, it is important to recognize that communities are larger systems and that different views may coexist. For example, groups, organizations, and associations within the same community may embrace different analogies. In post-Katrina New Orleans, community groups differed in how they viewed the recovery effort. Differences over how the community system was perceived and varying levels of trust and expectations made the relief process challenging (Pyles & Cross, 2008).

Strengths and Weaknesses

Warren's work (1978) synthesized early research on communities, brought a systems perspective to the sociology of the community in the United States, and provided a framework for analyzing ways in which communities can fail in fulfilling one or more of their key functions. There are lessons that systems theory offers to community practice. Hardina (2002) calls attention to four such lessons:

- Changes in one aspect of a system produce alterations in other parts of the community.
- Actions in community subunits not only influence what happens within the unit, but within the larger system.

♦ Being able to identify how well a community functions means being able to compare its effectiveness to other communities.

♦ The push to return to a steady state in which everyone can participate in community life becomes a driving force in systems theory. (pp. 49–50)

As with any approach, systems theory has its critics, and their concerns often focus on the use of mechanical and organismic analogies through which assumptions are made about parts of systems working together to the benefit of the whole. Assumptions about common purposes, it is argued, ignore the role of unexplained change, conflict, and situations in which community members not only disagree but are deeply divided. These mechanical and organismic analogies are viewed as focused on preservation of the status quo and incremental change, even in the case of unresponsive or oppressive community structures desperately in need of correction. Applying the analogies inappropriately in this way is seen as a refusal to recognize the role of conflict and struggles for power inherent in community life (Martin & O'Connor, 1989). However, as pointed out earlier, there are other analogies of systems theory that do recognize conflict and change.

Even in systems approaches that view disagreements and clashes of viewpoints and interests as parts of human communities, on the whole, systems theory does not focus on power and politics. It provides limited understanding for community practitioners who must face uncertain dynamics among diverse participants. It also fails to explain how to engage community members, how to communicate, or how to use systems concepts to bring about change. Therefore, practice models derived from this theory base must draw from other human behavior theories and perspectives in guiding practitioners about power and politics, group dynamics, and interpersonal communication.

Stanfield (1993) suggests that it is critical to revise sociological concepts that view communities through the lens of structural-functionalism and processes such as socialization. He contends that this orientation promotes a *monocultural system perspective* that treats conflict as though it were something deviant. This leads to a view in which communities, associations, and structures created by population groups that do not conform to these accepted standards are seen as underdeveloped, dysfunctional, and pathological rather than as novel, inventive, and understandable responses on the part of segments of a community that have not been well served by its institutions or other members. Box 5.1 summarizes the strengths and weaknesses of systems theory.

Box 5.1 Systems Theory

Strengths	Weaknesses
Changes in one aspect of community produce changes in others.	Assumptions about common purposes ignore many considerations, including disagreements and deep divisions.
Actions in subunits affect the larger community.	Mechanical and organismic analogies are often viewed as preserving of the status quo.
Assessing community functions involves comparisons to other communities.	Systems models provide limited understanding of power and politics.
A push to return to a steady state becomes a driving force (Hardina, 2002).	Structural-functionalism and socialization promote a monocultural system perspective that views newly created structures as deviant.

HUMAN OR POPULATION ECOLOGY THEORY

Closely aligned with systems theorists are *human ecology* theorists, who also examine structural patterns and relationships within place-based communities. In the mid-1930s, a group of sociologists under the leadership of Robert E. Park at the University of Chicago examined local community spatial relationships. Human ecology theory emerged from this work, and is based on plant and animal ecology, which in turn has roots in Darwin's biological determinism. It was elaborated in the work of Hawley (1950, 1968).

Early human ecologists believed that if they studied one city well enough they could apply principles of what they learned to most other cities. Among these principles are three spatial concepts: the urban zone, the central city, and natural areas. Urban zones are large concentric circles surrounding a central city, whereas natural areas such as neighborhoods are smaller arenas in which social relationships develop. Both urban zones and natural areas are changing and dynamic. However, subsequent studies in other metropolitan areas revealed just how difficult it is to generalize. Other cities did not always show the same structural patterns.

Today, ecological theorists focus on the interaction of resident characteristics (e.g., age, gender, race), the use of physical space (e.g., housing, land use), and the social structures and technology within communities. An ecological approach views communities as highly interdependent, teeming with changing relationships among populations of people and organizations. For example, social workers have long studied issues of homelessness and inadequate housing in various communities, but research on home ownership possibilities for people with disabilities has been limited. Quinn (2004) reported on programs designed to offer home ownership possibilities for disabled community residents. From an ecological perspective, people with disabilities have often been confined to institutional or group home settings, whereas people without disabilities have had more freedom to choose their housing types. Social workers, however, can educate local communities about such possibilities as Home of Your Own Coalitions and work to change the relationship between resident characteristics, the use of physical space, and how the social structure of communities can integrate people who are disabled.

Human ecologists are particularly concerned about how place-based communities deal with the processes of competition, centralization, concentration, integration, and succession. Each of these processes can be viewed along a continuum (Fellin, 2001). For example, the degree of *competition* in a local community is about the acquisition or possession of land, jobs, votes, and other resources among competing groups, moving from low to intense (even contentious) depending on the power dynamics. The continuum of *centralization* to decentralization involves the degree to which groups and organizations cluster in a location close to what is considered the community's center or disperse beyond the area. Closely related is *concentration*, a process in which persons enter communities, whether through immigration or migration, and go from great to small numbers depending on how many people or organizations stay within a particular locale. The continuum of *segregation* to *integration* of population groups occurs as diverse groups either maintain or reduce their separation by characteristics such as race, religion, or age. The degree of community change can be placed along a *succession* continuum determined by the rapidity with which one social group or set of organizations

Diversity in Practice

Critical Thinking Question: How might a human ecologist view disproportionate unemployment in minorities living in an inner-city area?

Table 5.5	Human Ecology Characteristics and Issues	
Human Ecology	Characteristics	Issues
Individual units of a population are in competition, but also must cooperate to ensure that the community can support all its inhabitants (including plant, animal, and human life).	An organized population, rooted in the soil it occupies, and mutually interdependent on other inhabitants.	▶ Competition vs. cooperation ▶ Centralization vs. decentralization ▶ Concentration vs. dispersion ▶ Segregation vs. integration ▶ Succession vs. status quo

replaces another within the geographical area. For example, a social worker might need to know the history of a new immigrant group coming into a city. Initially, the group may concentrate in a particular area and compete for particular types of jobs in order to establish an economic foothold. At first, they may need to turn inward for mutual support and are isolated due to language barriers. They may also become highly segregated, unlikely to take advantage of existing services, and hard to engage even with diligent outreach efforts. Gradually—often only over generations—they integrate, and a new group moves in and starts a new cycle. For a summary of human ecology characteristics and issues see Table 5.5.

Advances in depicting these processes in geographical communities have paralleled the development of management information systems in organizations. *Geographic information systems (GIS)* use data to develop maps and graphics as tools to analyze local communities. Of particular relevance to social service providers, planners, and researchers is the ability to make thematic maps of their communities, geocode addresses, and perform spatial queries and analyses. Social workers can learn to extract and map census variables such as race, poverty, language, education, and health, as well as many other demographic variables, identifying concentrations of need in their communities (Coulton, 2003; Hillier, 2007). For example, a study of elders' characteristics and needs in a South Carolina county was undertaken to guide decision making about capital development in the coming years. The GIS component of the study was used to provide baseline information about older residents; identified public, nonprofit, and private resources available to elders in the county; and revealed gaps between older populations and community resources. Users of GIS data can pose questions such as how many elders live in a low-income community, and over time can see how things change within that same community. This ability to longitudinally examine community statistics is very helpful in assessing the effectiveness of interventions (Hirshorn & Stewart, 2003). These identified unmet needs were then used as a starting point for planning aging-related services in the county. Recognizing how the use of physical space can enhance access or create barriers to community resources is important, especially in communities with diverse population groups such as older adults (Hirshorn & Stewart, 2003) or homeless populations (Wong & Hillier, 2001).

Strengths and Weaknesses

Human and population ecologists are cousins of systems theorists. They share the goal of finding ways in which systems can become more harmonious and work better together. However, unlike their systems counterparts, these theorists

Human Behavior

Critical Thinking Question: What are some strategies that practitioners could use to avoid unintentionally alienating members of a community?

Box 5.2 **Human or Population Ecology Theory**	
Strengths	**Weaknesses**
Recognition that community groups are competing for limited resources.	No guidance for how to gain power for groups that do not have it.
Realization that groups without power must adapt.	Implication that physical environment essentially determines the social structure leaving little potential for change.
Recognition that the physical environment and social structures are interrelated (Hardina, 2002).	Considered by some as conservative and inherently somewhat fatalistic, assuming that there must be accommodation to existing environments.

recognize competition as an ongoing process for which conflict is an inevitable companion. Hardina (2002) identifies three community practice implications of ecological theory:

- Recognition that community groups are competing for limited resources, with survival of those with power
- Realization that groups without power must adapt
- Acknowledgment that social structures are heavily influenced by the physical environment, and changes in the physical can make a difference in the social

The recognition of relationships and their dynamics must be translated into guidelines for practice. Although competition is acknowledged and ecological theorists recognize power dynamics, they do not provide guidance for how to gain power for groups who do not currently have it. More important, assumptions that the physical environment influences social structures is somewhat deterministic, leaving the practitioner to wonder if an individual or even a group has the potential to make change within environments that are not conducive to the desired changes. Thus, like some systems theorists, human ecologists could be accused of being inherently conservative and somewhat fatalistic in assuming that populations and sets of organizations must find ways to adjust within resistant environments. Box 5.2 summarizes the strengths and weaknesses of human population ecology theory.

HUMAN BEHAVIOR THEORIES

Parallel to the focus on space, structure, function, and relationships among systems are the issues of how people behave in communities—how they understand and find meaning in relationships, what values guide their actions, and how their needs are determined. There are many ways to examine these factors, and we will address only a few here: interactions and values, collective identity, and needs.

Human behavior theories help social workers better understand why people do what they do, and this understanding is important to skilled practice. Whether communities are place or nonplace based, they are composed of human beings with multiple ways of viewing the meaning of interactions. When social work practitioners interact with community members, they are engaged in direct practice at the macro level. Knowing how to interact with individuals and groups within community arenas requires insight into why people act and respond as they do within context. Without this insight, actions may be misinterpreted, behaviors may hold little meaning, and practitioners may respond in ways that alienate the very community members they are trying to engage.

Interactions and Values

Beginning with rural communities and then expanding to urban environments, early anthropologists and sociologists explored how people related to one another. The Lynds' 1929 study of Middletown and its 1937 follow-up provided a cultural anthropological view of a small U.S. city (Lynd & Lynd, 1929, 1937). A subsequent study by West (1945) of the fictitiously named Plainville, Illinois, was similar to the Lynds' effort. These works were based on the assumption that rural communities were able to maintain "traditional" community values whereas cities were moving closer to a mass-society orientation in which competing values made life more complex. Similar distinctions and concerns continue to be expressed today, although the great majority of Americans now live in or near cities. The anthropological approach to community favored by the Lynds and West attempted to understand the daily lives of people, their behavior patterns, and their belief systems. What emerged from these and other case studies was recognition of the deeply held values that are inherent in community life.

Cohen (1985) views the community as rich with values, ideologies, and symbols that people have in common with one another but that also distinguish them from those who hold different beliefs. For example, the colors worn by a youth may symbolize certain values not easily recognized by someone who is not part of a particular culture. But wearing those colors into another community in which the colors are viewed as hostile can incite gang violence.

This relational view of community implies boundaries that are not necessarily tied to place. Boundaries may be physical, but they may also be racial, ethnic, linguistic, or religious. Boundaries may be perceptual, and may even vary among those who are part of the same relational community, just as persons who are not part of that community will perceive boundaries differently. Cohen (1985) explains that it is not the clarity of boundaries that are important (for they are always changing), but it is what the boundary symbolizes that is most crucial. For example, even though people may move out of a local community, the key phrases and words that they used in communicating with others will remain as symbols of their close relationships. Similarly, when a person with disabilities moves into a long-term care facility, the ties that are maintained with persons outside the home become symbolic of returning home.

Collective Identity

Clark (1973) proposes stepping back from the structural approaches to community and looking at the psychological ties that bind people in community. He suggests that community may be thought of as a shared sense of solidarity based on psychological identification with others. Going beyond social interactions, community rests in a sense of *we-ness* that can be either place specific or can transcend place. This approach lends itself to evaluating a community by measuring the strength of its members' perceived solidarity. This can be done whether the community is locality based, as in a neighborhood, town, or city, or whether it is affiliation based, as in a community formed by supporters of a political cause or members of an online chat group.

MacNair, Fowler, and Harris (2000) recognized psychological ties characteristic of communities in large social movements. Building on the work of Helms (1984), they developed a framework of diversity functions common to three movements by groups seeking greater equality in society: the African American Movement, the Women's Movement, and the Lesbian, Gay, and Bisexual Movement. These six functions are assimilation, normative antidiscrimination, militant direct action, separatism, introspective self-help, and pluralistic integration (p. 73). They represent approaches to organized change that reveal how different people identify with nonplace communities for different purposes.

Assimilation occurs when identity is tied to mainstream culture and the purpose of joining a movement is to become a part of the culture to which one has previously been denied access. *Normative antidiscrimination* is a confrontational approach that stays within legal parameters and is used to gain access to community institutions that were previously inaccessible due to oppression. *Militant direct action* is used to catch people off guard through activism, still with the intent of gaining a place within the community for persons involved in the movement. *Separatism* is an approach in which parallel communities are established and the identity of participants becomes tied to the alternative community. Because interaction with the mainstream is painful, norms emerge in association among members of the oppressed community and may be hidden from the mainstream. *Introspective self-help* is used when separatism is too difficult to maintain; thus, community members focus on self-development and self-mastery. Last, *pluralistic integration* occurs when groups form communities that are confident in their own cultural identities and do not give up their distinctiveness. They participate among and with persons from other cultures, without losing who they are. Collective identity, then, can take many different forms.

Needs

Amid these community interactions and values, community members have needs. Abraham Maslow (1962) developed a hierarchical framework for understanding human needs and factors that motivate human behavior. His hierarchy positions the most basic survival or physiological needs (e.g., food and water) at the base of a pyramid-shaped figure. One level above these needs are safety and security needs, followed by social or belonging needs, esteem or ego needs, and then, self-actualization needs at the highest level.

In Maslow's model, lower-level needs must be addressed before an individual can move to the next level. Any time a lower-level need is not being met, the person regresses down the hierarchy to satisfy that unmet need. Lower-level needs usually require a more immediate response and thus have higher urgency. Maslow also reminds us that a satisfied need is not a motivator.

This framework can be useful in assessing the needs of a target population, which can then be used to determine the adequacy of services available to them. The assessment task is one of defining more specifically the problems faced by the target population at each level and identifying the extent of met and unmet need in relation to each problem.

In discussing a community development perspective, Pantoja and Perry (1998) offer a slightly different view of human needs and dimensions. The authors begin with basic biological needs and then they discuss the need for love and belonging (which they consider a second level of *biological need*). After this comes the need for groups and relationships, particularly in times of emergency (*social*); for self-expression through symbols such as art and language (*cultural*); for learning from the past (*historical*); for the use of power (*political*); for viewing the past, present, and future through action, words, and movement (*creative/spiritual*); and for explanations that connect what happens in one's world through investigation and experimentation (*intellectual*). Their list of needs includes:

▶ *Basic biological needs* to have food, shelter, and clothing for survival and protection

▶ *Secondary biological needs* to have love, belonging and identity as a human being

▶ *Social needs* to engage in relationships, mutual aid, and support

▶ *Cultural needs* to use language, norms, values, and customs

▶ *Historical needs* to record the past and to use the past to explore the future

▶ *Political needs* to gain power, order, and control

▶ *Creative/spiritual needs* to use words, movements, and art to explain the unknown

▶ *Intellectual needs* to explore the nature of the environment, to investigate, and to experiment. (Pantoja & Perry, 1998, p. 227)

Theoretically, Pantoja and Perry provide a multidisciplinary typology that reveals the complexity of human needs within social context. Their original intent was to provide a sociological approach to analysis that would lead to deep understandings primarily of minority communities. But their ultimate intent was to build on this understanding so that these types of needs once understood could be addressed. Thus, their theoretical approach, which we have described, is designed to evolve one's understanding of diverse needs into a working model in which each human need is evaluated in light of how well community services and institutions function in meeting those needs.

In summary, Table 5.6 provides an overview of human behavior theories, their foci, and findings.

Table 5.6   Human Behavior Theories: Foci and Findings

Human Behavior Theories	Focus	Findings
Interactions and values	The daily lives of people; behavior patterns and belief systems	Deeply held values are inherent in some communities
	Values bind people together but also distinguish them from those who hold different values	It is not the clarity of boundaries that is important; it is the symbolic aspect of the boundary created by common values.
Collective identity	The psychological ties that bind people within a community	People feel a *sense of community* and a *we-ness* when there are psychological ties.
Needs	Understanding needs in a hierarchy from lower-order needs to higher-order needs	Higher-order needs cannot be met until lower-order needs are satisfied

Box 5.3 Human Behavior Theories

Strengths	Weaknesses
Examine how communities are formed and shaped by factors that motivate human behavior	Fail to provide a contextual understanding necessary to interpreting behaviors
Help to move past the "big picture" orientation of other theories and pick up on critical factors in the human interrelationships within a community	Often ignore the critical person-in-environment perspective
	Sometimes overgeneralize from the individual to the collective

Practice Contexts

Critical Thinking Question:
What kinds of contextual factors may strongly shape an individual's actions within a community?

Strengths and Weaknesses

Human behavior theories examine how communities are formed and shaped by factors that motivate human behavior. These include the drive to meet basic needs, the drive to affiliate, and the need to be guided by shared values once interactions reach a sufficient level of complexity. Without insight into why people feel and act as they do, community practitioners may see only the big picture, missing critical clues that will make the difference in whether trust and relationship can be established.

Human behavior theories look at the individual or the actions of individuals with others. However, critics of these theories caution that human beings are not robots and actions are situational. Viewing needs, values, interactions, and relationships without a contextual understanding can lead to misunderstandings about what certain behaviors mean. Theories that focus on individuals must be used with an eye to context so that the person-in-environment is paramount. A related criticism concerns the unit of analysis. Human behavior theories take the position that, if one wants to understand the behavior of communities, one must understand what motivates the behavior of individuals. If one can accurately predict how one member will behave in a given circumstance, it is suggested that one can then predict the likely path to be taken by a collection of actors following the same rules. The argument is that the whole is greater than the sum of the parts, so comparing whole community systems to one another and examining which differences between them predict which actions could be seen as a better approach than focusing on the individual's behavior. Box 5.3 summarizes the strengths and weaknesses of human behavior theory.

THEORIES ABOUT POWER, POLITICS, AND CHANGE

Given the diversity within communities, the focus of much of the literature has been on the process by which communities create and build bonds among people. However, it is important to recognize political and social dynamics within communities as powerful forces that can be oppressive as well as supportive.

In her community practice work, Hardina (2002) reviews three theories related to the acquisition of power: power dependency theory, conflict theory, and resource mobilization theory. Although *power dependency theory* has been primarily applied to organizational arenas in which organizations become dependent on donors (Blau, 1964), Hardina sees important implications for community practice:

▶ External forces may make demands that limit the abilities of local communities to initiate change.

▶ Consumers may be fearful to bite the hand that feeds them.

▶ Change occurs within the boundaries of an exchange relationship in which people feel obligated to support donors of resources. (p. 52)

In other words, local communities and units within local communities become "beholden" to external sources of resources. These sources include corporations that control whether to locate or keep a factory in a community. For example, in a town in the Plains states the largest employer was a meat packing plant. The plant depended heavily on migrant Latino workers who were often exploited because of language problems and their undocumented status. Civic leaders were highly resistant to efforts to initiate change on behalf of the workers, fearing a decision by the corporation to simply move elsewhere. Thus, one of the greatest sources of power in the economy of this small community was an external corporation.

Conflict theory typically views the community as divided into haves and have-nots, all competing for limited resources. A neo-Marxist view of conflict theory is that social services fulfill a social control function, providing just enough resources to keep the voices of dissent from becoming louder and maintaining the status quo (Hasenfeld, 1983). This casts social workers in the role of social control agents. Alternately, a perspective arising from the work of Alinsky (1971, 1974) might place social workers in the role of organizers who use unexpected sources of power in the hands of the have-nots to upset those in decision-making positions. Hardina (2002, p. 55) identifies basic assumptions of conflict theory as: (1) there is competition for resources; (2) the haves hold power over the have-nots; (3) oppression comes largely from the isms (e.g., racism, classism); and (4) the government as well as other vehicles of decision making are controlled by the haves. Conflict theory accepts the view that communities may be usefully analyzed in terms of who holds power and how it is applied, but it goes further in stating that differences in power and access to resources between the haves and have-nots inevitably lead to conflict and require an understanding of how to manage conflict in order to effect change.

Resource mobilization theory draws from both conflict and power dependency theories to address social movements and the reasons they occur. In order to mobilize, a collective identity (noted earlier under human behavior theories) must develop. Nkomo and Taylor (1996) summarize several theories that describe collective identity, including embedded group theory, social identity theory, race/gender research, organization demography, and ethnology (p. 340). Identity group members have common characteristics, shared histories, and have even experienced some of the same environmental change. In communities and organizations, identity group membership precedes organizational group membership. Nkomo and Taylor contend that identity must be understood as a complicated concept since individuals have multiple identities that may intersect into an amalgamated identity. Thus, when individuals come together as a community group, their identity (like all others) is constructed rather than something with which they were born. Collective identity then emerges and can change as context changes (Balser & Carmin, 2009; Mulucci, 1995).

Hardina (2002) identifies basic assumptions of resource mobilization as it relates to community practice:

▶ Social movements arise when groups are not represented in decision-making processes.

▶ Public recognition occurs when there is protest.

▶ Movements must develop an appropriate structure.

▶ Success is dependent upon establishing a collective identity.

▶ The better the organization's message, the more membership will increase.

▶ Fund raising is always a problem because members will have limited resources and accepting funds from others may lead to abandoning the radical nature of the cause. (p. 57)

Table 5.7 provides a quick overview of power dependency, conflict, and resource mobilization theory.

Table 5.7   Themes and Implications of Power, Politics, and Change Theories

Power, Politics, and Change Theories	Themes	Implications for Community Organizing
Power dependency theory	Organizations and communities are dependent on resources, often from outside sources.	▶ Consumers may limit change for fear of offending resource providers. ▶ Change may be limited to boundaries established within the relationship. ▶ Funding sources and providers of other resources external to the community may limit change.
Conflict theory	The community is divided into haves and have-nots.	▶ There is competition for resources. ▶ Haves have power over have-nots. ▶ People are usually oppressed because of prejudice and discrimination. ▶ Decision makers, including government, are controlled by haves.
Resource mobilization theory	Social movements need a collective identity.	▶ Groups not represented in decision making initiate social movements ▶ Public protests bring public recognition to an issue. ▶ Movements need a structure. ▶ Success depends on a collective identity for those involved in protest. ▶ Strength depends on the quality of the message. ▶ Funding without compromising the group's position is often a problem.

Understanding the Politics of Community Diversity

In Chapter 4, we discussed a framework called the dual perspective, which viewed the individual in a nurturing system that functions within the context of a larger sustaining system. The *nurturing system* is made up of those traditions and informal relationships in which the individual feels most familiar. The *sustaining system* is made up of traditions, beliefs, values, and practices of the dominant society. This framework is important in understanding how communities contain built-in conflicts. Persons who experience divergence between nurturing and sustaining systems will be aware of community politics, power, and change as part of their daily experience. Even when there is congruence between the nurturing and sustaining systems, it may engender a false perception that communities are benign or supportive of all their members. Because civic society is valued by dominant groups it reflects the values and norms of those in power; those same groups will resist the development of civil rights associations and other organizations that are dedicated to changing the status quo through political and economic empowerment.

To illustrate how norms of community are often taken for granted, Stanfield (1993, p. 137) points to the importance of civic responsibility and civic cultures in African American traditions. Historically, these traditions have been supported by institutions such as "civic associations, fraternal orders, and churches rather than businesses and finance institutions." Although European American communities have prided themselves on a civic culture rooted in production, distribution, and consumption (the economic function of community), African American communities have long been excluded from full participation in the dominant institutions within local communities. In addition, Stanfield points out that these communities did not just form in response to oppression, but also reflected unique cultural attributes.

Understanding the politics of different communities is critical to social workers as they interact with diverse groups. For example, the meaning of volunteerism in traditional U.S. communities translates to a formalized process through which volunteers are organized and coordinated, but that is a politically dominant view held by the sustaining system. This type of volunteering has seen resurgence in the declining economies of 2009 and 2010, with states and cities attempting to get volunteers to help with functions that were formerly performed by paid staff. Many states and local communities are attempting to keep parks and libraries open, for example, and to supplement many staff functions through the use of volunteers.

Stanfield (1993) contends that volunteerism in African American communities is so much an integral part of the informal nature of caring that it becomes a way of life. Yet, there is no calculation of in-kind contributions or records of volunteer time in this latter definition of volunteerism. It is not captured in anyone's log or volunteer record book. Put simply, it does not exist because it cannot be defined as "volunteerism" in traditional U.S. communities.

Another example of communities that do not conform to dominant criteria is provided by Kayal (1991) in his study of the gay men's health crisis in New York City. Kayal analyzes how volunteerism among those in the gay community became necessary at a time when government support was not forthcoming. He explains how members of the gay community responded to the problem of

AIDS, representing the way in which groups become committed to sharing the burden when crises arise. There are many more examples of groups that have formed locally and have responded to problems, but whose work has often not been recognized or valued within traditional understandings of community (e.g., Finn, 2005; Holley, 2003; Rogge, David, Maddox, & Jackson, 2005). Because social workers advocate with and for these groups, conflict is inevitable when intervening through macro practice.

Politics cannot be ignored as a part of understanding community. Feminist writers have long declared that the personal is political, indicating that every action or inaction that one takes is a political statement (Bricker-Jenkins & Netting, 2008; Lazzari, Colarossi, & Collins, 2009). There are multiple examples of various interest groups, some more formalized than others, interacting within local communities. In order to fully contextualize their work, social workers recognize the interplay of interest groups competing for resources within the community.

Strengths and Weaknesses

Understanding power and politics as part of community dynamics is critical to macro intervention. Theorists who focus on power, politics, and change are typically appealing to social work because they recognize oppression and are aware that conflict cannot be ignored. Their language is compatible with social work values and ethical principles, such as autonomy and social justice, and it resonates with social workers who want to make a difference.

Limitations within these theories are that although they may lead to better understandings about power and politics, they do not offer guidance on how to achieve one's ends without radical initiatives or how to judge when to act and when not to act. The nuances of finessing change are overwhelmed by the push to make change happen. There is no guidance for how to develop and use professional judgment so that targets of change are not alienated, because the assumption is that alienation will inevitably occur. Hardina (2003) indicates that even though these theories provide some guidance for how to deal with power and competition, they do not provide strategies for community organizers to use. Box 5.4 summarizes the strengths and weaknesses of theories of power, politics, and change.

Box 5.4 Theories of Power, Politics, and Change

Strengths	Weaknesses
Introduce important human factors into the understanding of communities and their dynamics.	Typically lack guidance on how to achieve ends without radical initiatives.
Help in understanding the role of power and politics as part of change.	Ignore details in favor of emphasizing the need to push to make changes happen.
Recognize oppression and make clear that conflict cannot be ignored.	Provide no guidance on how to avoid alienating targets of change.
	Do not present a full range of strategic options.

CONTEMPORARY PERSPECTIVES

In the 1950s and 1960s, sociological interest in and research on communities suffered a decline. It was assumed that mass society had replaced the concept of community (Lyon, 1987). This was part of a broader concern expressed by many writers that community has been lost and that there must be a search to regain, revitalize, and reinforce community. Many political candidates have also issued calls for decentralizing government, returning control to local communities, and reestablishing family values. Finally, "community lost" became a theme in the popular media, where people use words such as *helplessness* and *disempowerment* to describe their feelings about what is happening to community life.

Putting this in perspective, however, these concerns have waxed and waned since the Industrial Revolution. Hunter (1993) points out that social analysts have talked about the demise of local communities for decades and social pundits have feared the social decay of cities. He goes on to say that a number of researchers have reminded practitioners of the resilience of the informal relationships and structures that maintained human relationships long before the advent of modern society. What is hopeful about Hunter's reminder is that he recognizes and validates what was once viewed as nonrational, short-lived, unimportant, and invisible. The relationships that women with children formed in local neighborhoods, the plethora of self-help groups that emerged in the last decades, the nurturing systems of racial and ethnic minorities, the voluntary associations to which people flocked, the efforts of natural helpers, and the human bonds that transcend time and space, all maintain the functions and roles of community even when the formal structures suffer crises in credibility, integrity, or financial viability. Essentially, Hunter declares that those linkages that are so carefully delineated as "micro" and "macro" are intricately interwoven so that if one works with individuals, one must, by definition, understand community.

Strengths, Empowerment, and Resiliency Perspectives

In the mid-1980s and into the 1990s, community scholars regained what we believe to be a more balanced set of perspectives, indicating that *both* mass society and community are still relevant concepts. Since the turn of the century, reactions to Putnam's (2000) bestselling book on Bowling Alone brought new attention to the importance of community. Eikenberry (2009) contends that the way in which people engage in their communities and in civic activity may have changed.

We now highlight three interrelated perspectives that are particularly relevant in understanding positive attributes of communities: strengths, empowerment, and resiliency. The *strengths perspective* focuses on identifying the possibilities within individuals and communities, recognizing their assets rather than focusing on their deficits. Building on strengths, there is the potential for empowerment. *Empowerment* comes from within the individual or community as a whole when there is an "aha" realization that there are inherent strengths on which to build and that using those strengths can result in desired change. *Resiliency* is the capacity to maintain a sense of empowerment over time, to continue to work toward community betterment, and to resist the temptation to give up when there are conflicts, struggles, and set-backs—to bounce back time and again.

The *strengths perspective* was originally presented by Saleeby (1997). Whereas communities may not appear to be as functional or competent as one would wish, social work practitioners must be careful to recognize and assess the strengths within the communities in which they work. When addressing terrible social problems such as homelessness and violence, it can become too easy to write off entire communities as pathological and beyond assistance. Saleeby reminds us of words such as *empowerment*, *resilience*, and *membership* that can lift and inspire. Empowerment means assisting communities in recognizing the resources they have. Resilience is the potential that comes from the energy and skill of ongoing problem solving. Membership is a reminder that being a member of a community carries with it civic and moral strength.

For example, a social worker was hired by the State Department on Aging. Her role was to survey all nursing homes in the state and to determine how many had family councils. She discovered that most did not have active councils, and those that did were largely controlled by staff and administration. She recognized that this was a problem because it is well known that a "community presence" will mean residents within a facility receive more attention from staff. Without that community presence, older residents can become increasingly isolated. She did not deny that this was a problem, but rather than focusing on the problems inherent in developing effective family councils (and there were many), she began to list the strengths that could come from having a family council in a nursing home. Family members who often felt isolated would be able to link with other family members, communication between nursing home staff and families would increase, combined efforts of multiple family members would lead to identification of common challenges, and family members would be able to support one another. From a strengths perspective, the possibility of organizing family councils could improve the quality of life of caregivers and even potentially impact the quality of residents' care. Using this strengths perspective, she was able to convince family members and nursing home staff in facilities around the state that the strengths of added communication brought on by having active councils would benefit all parties and that it would better integrate facilities into their local communities.

Hardina (2003) traces the roots of the empowerment perspective to the concept of citizen participation and the War on Poverty. Having citizens engaged in community planning efforts was seen as a vehicle for social reform. Solomon (1976) refined the empowerment perspective when she acknowledged that empowerment emerged from recognizing the strengths and capabilities of individuals, groups, organizations, and communities in gaining control over actions to change repressive social structures that influenced their lives. Gutierrez and Lewis (1999, p. 11) contend that "empowerment practice must be focused at three levels: the personal, the interpersonal, and the political." In other words, individuals have to feel empowered in order to link with others to engage in change, and together the synergy of their joint efforts can make a difference. Mondros and Wilson (1994) identified four sources in the professional knowledge base that have contributed to the understanding of community power and empowerment: (1) theoretical debates over social protest and discontent, when it arises and why; (2) a growing body of literature that attempts to classify types of community organizations; (3) a descriptive body of knowledge describing social protest movements; and (4) an extensive literature on community organizing skills providing practical guidance about how to go about organizing.

Hardina (2003) provides an example of how an empowerment perspective can be translated into empowerment practice through the Independent Living

Movement (ILM). The ILM began in the 1940s when researchers recognized that the major difficulties imposed on persons with disabilities "rested in the negative social construction of disability" (p. 19). Since that time, the ILM established centers throughout the United States, and central to their practice is that consumers must make up 51 percent of their boards of directors, administrative, and service staff. Not only has the disability community recognized the strengths of their members but they also are empowered to utilize those strengths through the Independent Living Centers (ILC) located throughout the United States. Communities, like people, have great *resilience* (Lyon, 1987), the ability to continue to be empowered even in the face of seemingly overwhelming challenges. Breton (2001, p. 22) focuses on resiliency in neighborhoods, noting that resilient neighborhoods have a number of characteristics, such as: (1) trusting neighborhood networks, (2) residents that spring to action through voluntary associations, (3) stable local organizational networks, and (4) a social infrastructure with needed services available. Of particular relevance is the rapidly increasing literature on the communal nature of people and the resiliency of "the commons" even in times of great change (see, for example, Lohmann, 1992). Since the 1990s the concept of social capital has become a means of exploring power, privilege, and oppression in community settings (Portes, 2000) and is seen as helpful for community practitioners interested in better understanding human behavior within an environmental context (Aguilar & Sen, 2009).

Kretzmann and McKnight (1993) have studied resilient communities for years. They use a strengths perspective to develop a model of practice that focuses on community assets rather than limitations. They advocate for strengthening and empowering local community networks and provide detailed guidance for how to do what they call asset mapping. Green and Haines (2002) note that assets have always been available in local communities, but the focus has often been on problems. An assets approach is congruent with a strengths perspective and reframes community development as an empowering process rather than as a problem that needs to be fixed. Table 5.8 provides an overview of themes in strengths, empowerment, and resiliency perspectives.

An assets approach is congruent with a strengths perspective and reframes community development as an empowering process rather than as a problem that needs to be fixed.

Table 5.8	**Contemporary Perspectives**	
Contemporary Perspectives	Themes	Characteristics
Strengths	Communities are assessed in terms of their strengths rather than their deficits.	• Community intervention may emerge around a problem or need. • Assessments identify community strengths (asset mapping). • Solutions come from within the community rather than from "services."
Empowerment	Communities can gain control over decisions that affect them.	• People excluded from decisions gain their voice. • Resources go to the more powerful. • Leadership emerges and promotes an understanding of how decisions can be controlled locally.
Resiliency	Communities have great potential to rebound and to cope.	• Neighbor networks and trust are apparent. • Active voluntary associations participate in community life. • Stable organizational networks are maintained. • Adequate services are provided.

Capacity Building and Asset Mapping

Delgado (2000), Hardina (2003), Holley (2003), and others remind community practitioners that the strength of informal networks within ethnic communities is critical to capacity building efforts. *Informal units* are those that are not publicly incorporated as legal entities to deliver health and human services. Often, these units have not been recognized for their importance in the service delivery system, whereas they actually perform a vast assortment of mutual support tasks. They include the household unit, natural support systems and social networks, self-help groups, and voluntary or grassroots associations. We briefly examine each now.

Household Units

The household unit consists of those persons who share a common dwelling, whether they consider themselves families, significant others, friends, partners, or roommates. In the past, family was often seen as the same as household, but as more and more people live together without being related, the concept of household unit is a more helpful term (Smith, 1991). Service provision in this unit generally takes the form of caregiving and tends to fall heavily on women. For example, informal caregivers provide the vast majority of care for persons with disabilities and chronic conditions (Guberman, 2006). The potential for caregiver burden or strain suggests that mutual support provided by the informal system may require assistance from others within the community. Respite services are often needed in the interest of sustaining the physical and mental well-being of the caregiver.

In assessing the extent of service provided in household units within a given community, one should look for indicators of what is happening within private dwellings of members of the target population. For example, are identified caregivers within the community overburdened? Is there an identified need for respite services for caregivers of physically disabled, developmentally disabled and elderly persons, and/or young children? Are requests for live-ins and shared housing increasing?

Of particular concern is identifying the importance of the household unit for the target population. For example, if the target population is frail widows living alone, the household unit does not contain others who can assist. Not only are caregivers not available, but formerly active older women may suddenly find themselves alone after years of providing care to children and spouses. On the other hand, target populations such as inner-city children, who often live in crowded households where privacy is limited and tension is high, may draw support from siblings, peers, and parents. Respite for single mothers may be difficult to locate, and poverty may have reduced opportunities and life choices. Yet the household unit can be a critical source of support for these children, fragile as it may be. Recognizing the household unit as a source of community strength and developing services to support this unit can produce a double benefit in strengthening families and reducing the need for other support services.

Natural Support Systems and Social Networks

Often an unstructured, informal approach to mutual support will evolve as natural or social support systems develop. Most people are part of social networks, but this in itself does not constitute a natural support system. A natural support system, according to McIntyre (1986), exists when resources have actually been exchanged. The existence of natural support systems has been recognized for years. Recent studies and an emphasis on informal support have prompted a more intense examination, particularly in communities with high poverty rates (Saegert, Thompson, & Warren, 2001).

Because networks do not have established boundaries and depend on interaction between informal individuals and groups, they are likely to extend beyond the local community. Mutual support tasks may be provided by geographically dispersed, as well as geographically close, network members. Dispersed networks will depend on linkages such as transportation systems and telephones, and may therefore be vulnerable in times of crisis. Balgopal (1988) explains the importance of social networks in which relatives, friends, and colleagues form a support system and respond when there are crises. Social networks are emotionally sustaining and often assist with child care or looking out for neighbors.

Within the local community there are indicators of the extent of informal neighborhood groups and support systems. Neighborhood associations, child-care exchanges, and neighbor-to-neighbor interaction are indicators of the extent of support available within this unit.

Self-Help Groups

Self-help groups are one of the fastest-growing elements of community support. They have been formed to deal with a variety of personal and social problems and needs, including substance abuse, bereavement and loss, depression, parenting, and many other issues. A number of self-help groups (of which Alcoholics Anonymous is probably the best known) have formed national and international chapters and are recognized vehicles of service delivery.

Hutcheson and Dominguez (1986) acknowledge the importance of ethnic self-help groups in their research on Latino clients. Han (2003) reports a case study on domestic violence in a Korean community in California and the importance of using support groups as part of the prevention program. Because language and cultural barriers can arise in these and other ethnic populations, self-help groups assist in maintaining community identity and involvement.

Self-help groups are often viewed as being compatible with a feminist perspective as well. Such groups are directed at widows, women who have been exploited or abused, and caregivers. Mutual support provided through self-help groups may assist in protecting the mental and physical health of caregivers.

Depending on the target population identified, self-help groups may be of critical or only modest importance. For example, populations that already have access to the service system and its resources may find such groups less necessary, whereas populations struggling to have their needs recognized may find them extremely helpful.

Voluntary Associations

Smith (2000) identifies what he calls *grassroots associations* that form an interface between informal support groups and more structured service organizations. These associations are typically local in nature, autonomous, and composed of volunteers. Voluntary associations serve as a bridge between informal and formal components of a human service system and have been described as very closely tied to the values held by their members and to the causes about which they are concerned (Wollebaek, 2009). A *voluntary association* is defined as "a structured group whose members have united for the purpose of advancing an interest or achieving some social purpose. Theirs is a clear aim toward a chosen form of 'social betterment'" (Van Til, 1988, p. 8). Community groups such as neighborhood associations or local congregations fall within this category. Similar to self-help groups, voluntary associations vary in their degree of formalization. Because they are membership groups, a dues structure will often be in place. Therefore, their boundaries become more clearly defined than informal groups because there is a formal process for joining and providing financial support.

Voluntary associations have several characteristics. Members share a sense of community, which provides a collective identity. Social status may be enhanced by membership and social control may be exercised over members. A function of the association may be to enhance the well-being of its members in a supportive manner. If the association is strong, it may have a prominent profile from the perspective of nonmembers, though its influence may be positive or negative (Williams & Williams, 1984). For example, associations such as white supremacist groups can be powerful yet destructive forces within certain communities.

Voluntary associations are a study in both inclusiveness and exclusiveness. Williams and Williams (1984) discuss the importance of the black church in the development and growth of mutual aid societies. Historically, many mainstream activities beyond the church were closed to blacks who migrated to urban centers. "Blacks organized voluntary associations in the church in such forms as sick and burial societies, economic self-help groups, mission societies, and various secret and fraternal orders" (p. 21). Ethnic groups, lesbians and gays, and other oppressed people may use informal and mediating units to a larger degree than other populations. Neighborhood groups, self-help groups, and voluntary associations serve as a means of mutual support, as a place for clarifying perspectives, and as a focal point for action. In some cases these activities lead to recognition and wider support and to improved access to the existing formal units of human service delivery in a community. An interesting development in 2010 was the so-called Tea Party, an informal group of citizens who wished to express their displeasure with what they considered to be excessive spending and indebtedness at the federal level. Many local chapters have held rallies, and a national conference was held in early 2010. In assessing available services for a target population, it is important that the macro practitioner identify voluntary associations. Churches, unions, and professional groups are all potential sources of support for the target population. They may not be listed in human service directories, yet they may be the first source to which some people turn when in need (Wineberg, 1992). Trends in the development of what are called *giving circles* illustrate how community members form associations for the purpose of pooling their money and other resources for important causes. These types of fundraising ventures are particularly growing in communities of color and among women (Eikenberry, 2009).

Table 5.9 provides an overview of informal community units. Household units, natural support systems and social networks, self-help groups, and voluntary associations are all community units that interact in informal and sometimes more formalized ways. Capacity building and asset mapping are

Table 5.9   Overview of Informal Community Units

Informal Community Units	Composition	Examples of Support Provided
Household units	Persons who reside within the same dwelling	Informal caregivers of older adults and small children
Natural support systems and social networks	People within a community who exchange resources	People (natural helpers) who provide for a neighbor's need during a crisis
Self-help groups	People who come together to help each other with a problem or need that they share	Parents whose children have been killed by drunk drivers who provide mutual support to one another
Voluntary associations	People who unite for the purpose of advancing an interest	Neighborhood associations and resident councils

theoretical concepts that recognize the importance of understanding how these informal units are constructed, the ways in which they are viewed by community members, and the strengths they can bring to community interventions (Chaskin, Brown, Venkatesh, & Vidal, 2001; Hannah, 2006; Nye & Glickman, 2000). Communities rich in informal units have strong capacity, sometimes not previously recognized by community members. Macro practitioners are often engaged in pointing out just how many assets and strengths a community has so that mobilization efforts can occur.

COMMUNITY PRACTICE MODELS

Whereas theories of community provide an understanding for why communities do what they do, community action and community development writers seek to prescribe how change can occur in communities. Numerous community practice models have been and are being used by social workers to effect community change. These models are heavily grounded in the concepts and language of systems and ecological theories. A summary of the theories that influence many of the community practice models appear in Table 5.10.

There are many ways to approach community and social work practice models. As a beginning, Mondros and Wilson (1994) identify components typically found in practice models: (1) a change goal; (2) roles for staff, leaders, and members; (3) a process for selecting issues; (4) the target of the change effort; (5) an assessment of how cooperative or adversarial the target will be; (6) a change strategy; (7) an understanding of resources needed to produce change; and (8) an understanding of the role of an organization in the change process (p. 240). In this book we present a comprehensive practice model that includes all eight of these elements. This planned change model is elaborated in Chapters 9, 10, and 11 and is somewhat unique in that it can be used in both community and organizational arenas. Most well-known among community practice models are those by Rothman (2008), who proposes a multimodal approach that builds on the three intervention approaches he originally developed in 1968. These are (1) planning and policy,

Whereas theories of community provide an understanding for why communities do what they do, community action and community development writers seek to prescribe how change can occur in communities.

Table 5.10	**Summary of Contributions of Theories to Community Practice**
Theories	Contributions to Community Practice
Social systems	▸ Reveals that changes in one community unit will impact other units. ▸ Indicates that changes in subunits also influence the larger community. ▸ Allows comparisons between how different communities function. ▸ Recognizes that the push to return to a steady state will depend on the analogy used.
Human or population ecology	▸ Is particularly helpful with geographic communities intent on understanding relationships among units. ▸ Recognizes that community groups are competing for limited resources, with survival of those in power. ▸ Recognizes that groups without power have to adapt to community norms. ▸ Acknowledges the influences of the interconnections and mutual shaping of physical and social structures.
Human behavior	▸ Focuses on the individual within the context of community as the unit of analysis. ▸ Provides insight into relationships, interactions, values, and needs of individuals. ▸ Provides community practitioners with critical clues about the difference trust and relationship can make in community interaction.
Power, change, and politics	▸ Reveals the influence of external sources of resources on local communities. ▸ Views the community as divided into haves and have-nots. ▸ Focuses heavily on the isms. ▸ Recognizes the dynamics of social movements and their influence on community change. ▸ Acknowledges the role of power in all interpersonal transactions.

(2) community capacity development, and (3) social advocacy. Each type has three modes. Policy/planning includes rationalistic planning, participatory planning, and policy advocacy. Capacity development's three modes are capacity-centered development, planned capacity development, and identity activism. Social advocacy's three modes are social action, social reform, and solidarity organizing (p. 14).

The *planning and policy* approach is task oriented, a data driven approach in which persuasion with the "facts" prevail. It seeks to address and resolve substantive community problems through careful study of those problems and the applications of rational planning techniques. This approach also seeks to engage community members in the process, by hearing their needs and limiting the role of social planners to that of assisting the change process rather than imposing independently determined directives. In its purest form, the model assumes that logic will prevail over political bias. However, planners do not have to be politically naïve, and modifications can be made in the rational planning approach to include political considerations and advocacy.

The goal of *capacity development* is to develop the community's ability to become more integrated and cohesive through self-help, based on the assumption that broad cross-sections of the community need to engage in problem solving. Empowerment in this mode occurs through collaborative efforts and informed decision making by community residents. The focus is on process, building relationships, and solving problems so that groups can work together.

Capacity development fits well with approaches such as assets mapping, capacity building, strengths, resiliency, and empowerment. Its limitations are its time-consuming nature and its assumption that change can occur through consensus rather than confrontation. Thus, theoretical roots fit well with mechanical and organismic analogies of social systems.

The goal of *social advocacy* is both process and task oriented in that participants seek to shift power relationships and resources in order to effect institutional change. In this approach pressure is applied and conflict is expected. Beneficiaries of this type of intervention are often perceived to be victims of an oppressive power structure. Empowerment is achieved when beneficiaries feel a sense of mastery in influencing community decision making. Although the language of social action is often espoused by social workers, it is important to realize that this approach to community practice is based in conflict, power dependency, and resource mobilization theories of power and politics. The confrontation required in this model is energy draining and time consuming, and sometimes the focus on task becomes so important that process is forgotten. Because the outcome usually involves a win-or-lose scenario, social advocacy is difficult to complete without creating some enemies. We recommend that it be used when other approaches have failed to be effective.

Rothman is quick to point out that there are multiple ways in which these three modes can interrelate and overlap. Other writers have expanded on Rothman's work. For example, Mondros and Wilson (1994) identify three practice approaches that come under the rubric of the social action model: grassroots practice, lobbying practice, and a mobilizing approach. Political practice is added by Haynes and Mickelson (2006).

Gamble and Weil (2010) provide a larger range of community practice models (eight in all) that incorporate finer distinctions in methods and assumptions. These eight approaches are:

- Neighborhood and community organizing
- Organizing functional communities
- Social, economic, and sustainable development
- Inclusive program development
- Social planning
- Coalitions
- Political and social action
- Movements for progressive change

Gamble and Weil (2010) describe each of these models and place them in a matrix according to the following comparative characteristics: desired outcome, systems targeted for change, primary constituency, scope of concern, and social work/community practice roles (pp. 26–27).

These models reflect the many different ways in which social workers engage in community work. They range from locality-based grassroots community organizing in which social workers participate with indigenous groups to make change, to social movements that occur across geographical boundaries. Social movements, such as the Disability Movement (O'Brien & Leneave, 2008) or the Gay and Lesbian Movement (Adam, 1995), are usually broad based and include a wide range of people and perspectives (Meyer, 2010). Social movements remind practitioners of Warren's distinction between vertical and horizontal relationships because they often connect people from multiple communities (vertical) as well as develop local chapters (horizontal).

Our major caution is that readers recognize the absence of any "right" way to categorize community practice models, strategies, and tactics. Planned community change is a mixture of various approaches, based on a careful assessment of the situation to be changed. It is critical also to recognize that because situations and problems are constantly evolving, social workers must be flexible in altering their direction as new information emerges and reassessment occurs. Table 5.11 provides an overview of community practice models (Gamble & Weil, 2010; Kettner, Moroney, & Martin, 2009; Rothman, 2008).

Keep in mind that we have quickly introduced numerous models that are well developed in the professional knowledge base and can easily be accessed by the reader. You will be reminded of these community practice models and the concepts briefly introduced here when you get to chapters 9, 10, and 11 and are asked to focus on planned change interventions.

Table 5.11   Overview of Community Practice Models

Model	Basic Premise	Reference
Capacity development or neighborhood and community organizing	Focuses on development of community capacity and integration through self-help; very process oriented. Assets mapping and capacity building are used.	Rothman (2008)
Organizing functional communities	Brings together people focused on a particular cause to change people's behaviors and attitudes; not necessarily place based; focus designed to facilitate empowerment.	Gamble & Weil (2010)
Social, economic, and sustainable development	Prepares citizens at the grassroots level to focus on economic and social development that will last; uses intensive asset mapping, particularly in the economic arena, and builds capacity.	Gamble & Weil (2010)
Planning/policy	Engages participants in an interaction designed to address substantive social problems; uses skills of expert planners to guide process.	Rothman (2008)
Program development	Uses organizational base in which programs are designed to address community needs; uses skills of professionals in program design and intervention.	Kettner, Moroney, & Martin (2008)
Political and social action	Attempts to shift power relationships and resources in order to effect institutional change; strengths and empowerment perspectives dominate here.	Rothman (2008)
Coalitions	Joins multiple community units (e.g., organizations, groups) to build a power base from which change can occur.	Gamble & Weil (2010)
Movements for progressive change	Works outside existing structures toward social justice goals that will change existing societal structures; oriented toward broad-scale, structural (even radical) change.	Gamble & Weil (2010)

SUMMARY

This chapter provided an overview of community theory, perspectives, and practice models used by social workers. There are multiple definitions and types of communities. Three dimensions that were briefly examined are (1) geographical, spatial, or territorial communities; (2) communities of identification and interest; and (3) personal networks or an individual membership in multiple communities. Geographical communities are obviously place based, but communities of identification as well as personal networks may be both place and nonplace based. The planned change model presented in later chapters will be applicable to both place and nonplace communities.

One feature common to many community theories is their attention to structure and function. Five community functions were identified by Warren (1978): (1) production, distribution, and consumption; (2) socialization; (3) social control; (4) social participation; and (5) mutual support. Pantoja and Perry (1998) added two additional functions: (6) defense and (7) communication. Communities are seen as dysfunctional or incompetent when these functions are not adequately performed, especially the economic function. Approaches to community that employ systems theory also have their roots in the analysis of community structure and function.

Human ecology theories, originating with the work of Robert E. Park, view communities as highly interdependent and changing. People, their values, and their interactions were elements of the ecology of communities studied by early anthropologists and sociologists. This work also showed that communities reflect a collective identity rich with symbols, values, and ideologies that people hold in common.

Theories of community that focus on power, politics, and change as important variables are important for social work practice. The person-in-environment perspective tends to lead social workers to view communities as political arenas in which the power of dominant groups necessitates a change so that underserved population needs can be addressed. Understanding the politics of different communities is critical to social workers seeking to assist underserved groups.

Last, contemporary community theory and practice reveal a new interest in rethinking the value of community as an arena for future study. Strengths, empowerment, and resiliency perspectives were followed by capacity building and assets mapping approaches to community practice. A brief overview of community practice models was presented as a way to introduce the reader to the multiple strategies used to foster community change and to prepare the reader for thinking about the planned change model in this book.

Succeed with **mysocialworklab**

Log onto **www.mysocialworklab.com** and answer the questions below. (*If you did not receive an access code to* **MySocialWorkLab** *with this text and wish to purchase access online, please visit* www.mysocialworklab.com.)

1. **Read MySocialWorkLibrary case study: Volunteer Experiences with the Neighbors Helping Neighbors Program.** Using Mondros and Wilson's approach to practice models, try to articulate the eight components in the NHN program.

2. **Read MySocialWorkLibrary case study: Chelsea Green Space and the Power Plant.** Pay particular attention to the section entitled, "The Campaign Against the Power Plant." What kind of community practice model do you think Green Space embodies? (There may be more than one.)

PRACTICE TEST The following questions will test your knowledge of the content found within this chapter. For additional assessment, including licensing-exam-type questions on applying chapter content to practice, visit **MySocialWorkLab**.

1. An adult protective services worker warns a family that they may be liable for prosecution for elder abuse. This is:
   a. socialization
   b. social control
   c. social participation
   d. mutual support

2. Communities generally have both horizontal and vertical linkages. This means that they are usually ___ systems.
   a. open
   b. closed
   c. permeable
   d. differentiated

3. A social worker finds that residents in a community need protection from violence. Which Maslow needs category is this?
   a. esteem
   b. social
   c. safety
   d. survival

4. Which practice modality most likely connects vertical and horizontal community connections?
   a. social planning
   b. program development
   c. grassroots action
   d. social movements

5. Roland Warren (1978) states that a community is "that combination of social units and systems that perform the major social functions" relevant to meet people's needs on a local level. Does it help a macro social worker to understand community? Does it encompass all types of communities? Why or why not?

ASSESS YOUR COMPETENCE Use the scale below to rate your current level of achievement on the following concepts or skills associated with each competency presented in the chapter:

1	2	3
I can accurately describe the concept or skill.	I can consistently identify the concept or skill when observing and analyzing practice activities.	I can competently implement the concept or skill in my own practice.

_____ Can apply community theories and models to problems regarding how individuals living in heterogeneous communities experience diversity.

_____ Can articulate how different social functions of a community may be strengths or sources of oppression for community residents lacking power.

_____ Can understand how individuals and groups behave and can engage members of a community without alienating or offending individuals.

_____ Can anticipate external contexts that may influence the behavior of a community member.

6

Assessing Communities

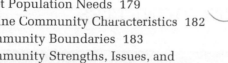

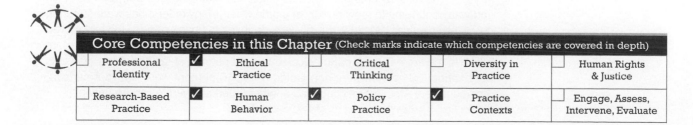

Core Competencies in this Chapter (Check marks indicate which competencies are covered in depth)								
	Professional Identity	✔	Ethical Practice		Critical Thinking		Diversity in Practice	Human Rights & Justice
	Research-Based Practice	✔	Human Behavior	✔	Policy Practice	✔	Practice Contexts	Engage, Assess, Intervene, Evaluate

INTRODUCTION

Setting out to understand a community is a major undertaking. Long-time residents may say, "I've lived in this town for 40 years and I still can't figure it out!" By what means, then, can a student or a practitioner hope to assess something as complex as a community, much less propose ways to change it? And what if, unlike neighborhoods, towns, or cities, one is trying to assess a non-place community that has no geographical boundaries?

There is no single, universally accepted method for understanding all the elements that make up a community. Instead, for the macro practitioner, understanding means gathering as much information as possible in a particular area of interest or concern, within the time available, and making the best-informed decisions the information allows.

There are three reasons why macro practitioners need a systematic approach to conceptualizing and assessing communities and their strengths and social problems. First, the person-in-environment view, which is central to social work practice, requires consideration of how individuals function within larger systems. A person's community has much to do with his or her values, beliefs, problems to be faced, and resources available, so it is difficult to see how social workers can be effective without understanding community influences. The framework for community assessment presented here is designed to assist in conceptualizing the arena within which people experience hope and draw strength, as well as face oppression and frustration. Note the word *assist,* which means that this framework does not have to be used in lock-step fashion. Instead, it is a versatile tool that can be adapted to the circumstances at hand.

Second, community-level macro change requires an understanding of the significant events in the history and development of a community that influence the ways in which people view contemporary issues. Without this knowledge, the practitioner will have a deficient understanding of important factors such as values, attitudes, and traditions, along with their significance in either maintaining the status quo or allowing for change.

Communities constantly change.

Third, communities constantly change. Individuals and groups move into power, economic structures change, as do sources of funding, and citizens' roles and expectations change. A framework for assessing communities can be helpful in recognizing and interpreting these changes.

TWO COMMUNITY VIGNETTES

VIGNETTE 1   Canyon City

Located in the western United States, Canyon City had a population of 60,000 people in 1975. The most recent data indicated that it had now exceeded 300,000 residents and was continuing to grow rapidly at a time when many older cities were suffering population declines. Because the city was inhabited by many people who had moved to the western Sun Belt to follow job opportunities, most of its residents were not native to the area. Census data indicated that 20 percent of Canyon City's residents were Latino, 60 percent were non-Latino white, 10 percent were Native American, 5 percent were African American, and another 5 percent were Asian American.

Encountering the Community. A recent social work graduate took a position in a multiservice agency in Canyon City. One of her tasks was to develop a program to address the needs of battered women in the community. Data from the police department and various other sources revealed a high incidence of domestic violence within the community relative to other communities of similar size. The social worker was new to Canyon City, having lived in another part of the country most of her life. She viewed this chance to assess and understand the community with great anticipation.

She began her work by talking with a number of police officers, social workers, and others who had expertise in domestic violence. Through these contacts, she was able to locate a few women who were willing to talk with her confidentially about their situations. She learned that each woman perceived the situation somewhat differently. Based on numerous conversations, the social worker found that there was a general sense of isolation within the community. Neighbors often did not know one another, and newcomers felt it was hard to form friendships or to feel they were part of a community. Given both the growth and the rapid turnover of Canyon City's population, this was not surprising. It appeared to the social worker that people tended to focus on their own problems and dwell on them within a narrow range of family or friends. The social worker soon found herself looking hard for evidence of any community strengths on which to build.

However, when she got beyond individual interviews and reached out to organizations, she found that Canyon City had many strengths. First, community members seemed willing to acknowledge the problem and were anxious to address it. The social worker encountered few people who denied that something needed to be done. Second, there was diversity within the community that made for a rich mix of customs, traditions, and values. Third, there were several women's groups in Canyon City willing to volunteer their efforts to whatever program was developed. Fourth, a local foundation was willing to fund a project if it was well designed.

Narrowing the Focus. In the course of collecting data and defining boundaries, the social worker determined that the problem of domestic violence was being addressed in some parts of the community but not others. Although there were three battered women's shelters within the city, each tended to serve only a limited area. A counseling service for domestic violence victims was available, but only to those who could afford the service. In particular, few Latinas were served by either the shelters or the counseling service. This led the social worker to narrow her focus toward the needs of these women.

The social worker knew she had to take care to recognize the diverse cultural traditions and beliefs of this target population. A number of models were available for developing shelters, safe homes, and services for white middle-class women, but few focused on women of color. The social worker also learned that Latinas in the community often provided shelter for one another, but this often imposed great financial burdens on the host and guest. She began to talk with the women about how to design a program that would be sensitive and relevant to identified needs.

In the process, she also discovered additional community strengths. There was a strong sense of community among many Latinas who had lived in the area most of their lives. There were associations of women that were not identified in any listings of services or programs because they were not as formalized as other groups. This informal network was

(continued)

VIGNETTE 1   Canyon City (*Continued*)

a source of pride in the community, yet these relationships were not known or understood in the larger community. Two Latino churches had identified domestic violence as their focus of concern for the coming year and were willing to work with the social worker and her agency. Also, a support group for women of color had been meeting in one of the churches for several years.

Mobilizing Resources. After a few weeks the social worker realized that there were more resources in the community than she had originally anticipated. However, she also discovered that there were definite locations of power. Community leaders among the women of color were not visible in the larger community and were often left out of any local decision-making processes. Within her own agency, the social worker found that members of the board of directors were not certain they wanted to focus on women of color because the board hoped to serve the needs of all women in the community. The foundation was willing to fund a project that would focus on Latinas' needs, but its board members wanted to be assured that the funds would be used to do something innovative rather than duplicating an existing model. Also, the foundation was willing to fund the project only if it would be self-sufficient within three years. The women's shelters that were already open were cautious about supporting the new program concept for fear that it might call attention to their failure to serve many women of color in the past. The women's support group in the local church was concerned that the group would lose its focus and become part of a bigger project that would take members away from their feeling of closeness and intimacy.

It was the social worker's job to continue to collect information and to determine the project's feasibility. Although this was time consuming, she continued to hear the perspectives of various women who had been battered and to include them in the development of a community project.

VIGNETTE 2   Lakeside

Lakeside was a planned community developed in the 1930s. The downtown area was built around a small lake, surrounded by weeping willow trees. The Baptist, United Methodist, and Presbyterian churches sat side by side along the lake front, forming what was known as "church circle." Each of the Protestant denominations had a children's home, and the Methodist Home for Orphaned Children, built in 1902, was a local landmark.

The population in Lakeside during the 1930s was approximately 20,000 people. The majority of employees worked for a company manufacturing major office products, making Lakeside "a company town." Other businesses in town manufactured paper, building supplies, and various other products.

Assessing Major Changes. By the 1990s, Lakeside had grown to 75,000 persons, and the community was going through a number of changes. Many residents had moved to the outskirts of town and had taken jobs in a larger city nearby, creating problems for the economic base of Lakeside. The various manufacturing companies had experienced layoffs, which made community residents feel uncertain about job security and advancement. One company had closed its doors completely. As manufacturing technologies changed, needed skill sets also shifted. Front page news in the *Lakeside Gazette* focused on how local persons were being laid off, whereas new employees with different skills were being recruited to come to the local plants. Both the paper company and the chemical plant had been bought by Canadian companies that were bringing in their own executives. Job competition was becoming much more intense.

Three housing developments for elderly and disabled persons had been built downtown. Two assisted living facilities had been completed, and two more were in process. The Methodist Children's Home began providing services to elders as well as to children, because orphans were few in number but the number of older persons was increasing.

Although Lakeside had been a haven for Protestant families and diversity had been limited, the population was changing. In 1930, the only religious groups other than the Protestant congregations were one Catholic church and one synagogue. By 2005, there was a mosque, two African Methodist Episcopal Zion churches, and a number of new groups that had split off from the original mainline churches. The population was also more racially and ethnically diverse. Whereas in 1930 only 20 percent of the downtown population was African American, by 2005 this figure had grown to 60 percent. The church circle remained a centerpiece in the community around the lake, but many of the members commuted to church from outside the city limits.

Witnessing the Impact of Change. A social worker at the Methodist Home was assigned to work with older persons and persons with disabilities in Lakeside. Her role was to build community and to develop strong support networks for clients. She found that many of her clients lived in the three housing developments in Lakeside and several more were residents in the assisted living facilities. The two target populations of older and disabled persons were diverse. With respect to age, for example, elderly residents ranged from 60 to 105 years, and persons with disabilities ranged in age from 25 to 95. The housing developments were 55 percent African American, 2 percent Latino, and 43 percent white, whereas the assisted living facilities were predominantly non-Latino whites.

The majority of the residents had lived in Lakeside all their lives and knew many of the other residents but this was changing as new employees came to Lakeside and relocated their aging parents to their new community. There was a large senior citizens center housed in an old department store that had moved to the mall, and the center was trying to reach out to newly relocated elders who had moved to Lakeside.

The social worker was pleased to learn about these strengths, but she was also aware of the problems that had emerged in Lakeside. There was a definite sense of racial tension in the town. There was also tension between the old and the young persons with disabilities who were living in the same apartment buildings. Older clients complained about loud music and partying at all hours of the night. Younger persons were frustrated by "being forced" to live with old people. Most major stores in the downtown area had relocated, and although mobile community members tended to shop at the mall, persons without transportation were forced to walk to the few remaining downtown stores, where prices were high and bargains were few. Getting Social Security checks cashed at the one downtown grocery store meant paying a five-dollar fee for cashing privileges.

Amid these tensions and concerns, widespread fear of crime had also emerged. Two older women who lived alone had had their purses snatched. In a small community,

(continued)

VIGNETTE 2   Lakeside (*Continued*)

this was the "talk of the town," and no one felt safe anymore. Elderly women who lived in the downtown area were being cautioned to keep their doors locked at all times, not to let strangers in, and to call 911 if they had any reason to be suspicious of anyone. A neighborhood crime watch association had been organized, and volunteer escorts were available in the evening hours for anyone having to go out alone. The police department had contacted the social worker so that they could work together, and the senior center was holding self-defense classes. The social worker heard older residents complain over and over again that Lakeside just wasn't the community they had known.

Implications of the Vignettes

Communities change, and it is not unusual for residents to grieve over the loss of what has been. Some changes are planned, such as the deliberate attempts in Vignette 1, to develop a project that would address the needs of Latinas who have been abused. Other changes are unplanned, such as the way in which the "planned" community of Lakeside's downtown area changed. Canyon City addresses a substantive problem (violence against Latinas), and Lakeside faces issues of how to meet the needs of an increasing number of older people and persons with disabilities, as well as how to remain viable as an economic center.

The two vignettes offer a glimpse at what social workers in community practice arenas experience. In Canyon City, the social worker encountered a growing city with much diversity. In Lakeside, the social worker found a city that was changing in different ways. However, both practitioners discovered strengths and problems, tensions and frustrations. Both found that the inclusion of multiple perspectives was important but also complicated the analysis. For example, in Vignette 1, the social worker had to deal with the power dynamics between a possible funding source, local women's shelters that were already established, and Latinas whose voices were not always heard. In Vignette 2, the social worker encountered interracial and intergenerational tensions among residents of a changing downtown neighborhood.

In Chapter 5, we identified three dimensions of communities: (1) geographical, spatial, or territorial; (2) identification and interest; and (3) collective relationship that gives meaning to one's identity. Although both vignettes are geographically based, they include elements of all three types of community. They also illustrate how place and nonplace communities can overlap. Canyon City is a "place" or geographical community. Yet bonds of identification within ethnic groups in this community require special consideration. The Latino community has connections that are stronger than geography, and much of the tension in creating a special shelter is tied to nonplace communities of identification and interest, as well as meaningful collections of relationships that provide meaning and identity. Similarly, Lakeside is a place or geographical community, but within its domain are persons who are moving in from the outside. Their collective relationships that give meaning to their lives may be scattered across other locations from which they have come. These nonplace community ties will not cease when employees and their aging parents move to Lakeside, even though geography separates them from others. In addition, within Lakeside there are communities of symbolic identification that are different, yet at times overlapping, for older and disabled persons. These two groups are tied to differing, and sometimes competing, communities of interest that are much more broadly based than the town of Lakeside. For example, persons with disabilities have formed national networks that advocate for consumer-directed care whereas older adults are connected by a national movement calling for civic engagement that is part of the "Age Wave" in a graying society.

Each vignette requires asking many questions in order to know how to intervene. This chapter provides a systematic approach to questions with which one might begin to assess communities like Canyon City and Lakeside from the perspective of the target populations served. Keep in mind that some questions in this framework may be useful in some communities and not as useful in others. The identified tasks do not have to be used in the order presented. The point is to find a way to begin to assess a community and to generate additional questions that will provide further direction.

FRAMEWORK FOR COMMUNITY ASSESSMENT

In any situation in which an assessment is called for, whether for an individual, family, or entire community, it is helpful to use a framework that can help guide the process. With respect to assessing communities, the work of Roland Warren (1978) again provides a useful starting point. He proposes that communities can be better understood if selected community variables are analyzed. Of particular interest are variables that represent characteristics that can be used to differentiate one community from another. For example, some communities are larger than most, some have greater diversity or different kinds of diversity or racial/ethnic mixes, some are wealthier than others, and some are more technologically advanced than others. A first step in assessing a community can be to create or adapt a framework that will help make comparisons on variables such as these from one community to another.

Building on Warren's work, we have identified three tasks that incorporate an eleven-step framework to be used in assessing a community. In subsequent chapters, we will present methods for planning changes based on this assessment. The framework is shown in Table 6.1.

Task 1: Focus on Target Populations

Many approaches to community assessment contend that the community must be understood in its totality to the greatest extent possible before intervention is planned. We propose, instead, that the task be narrowed by first selecting a target population and that the community be understood from the perspective of the concerns and needs of that population. We will define a *target population* as those individuals, families, and/or groups who are experiencing a problem or need and for whose benefit some type of community change is being considered.

The choice of a particular target population is a choice of values. In every community there are multitudes of groups with varying needs, but in most community change episodes it may only be possible to effectively address one group at a time. Also, the social worker must realize that in focusing on a single target population he or she is making a choice to examine the community from a specific perspective (though in the interest of richer understanding it will be helpful to periodically examine the community from the perspective of

Policy Practice

Critical Thinking Question: Why is it problematic to start planning only after ensuring that a community is understood in its entirety?

The choice of a particular target population is a choice of values.

Table 6.1   The Community Encounter Framework

Task	Variable	Activity
1. Focus on a target population	People	1. To identify the population or subgroup.
	Characteristics	2. To understand the characteristics of target population members.
	Needs	3. To locate data and information on target population members.
2. Determine community characteristics	Space	4. To identify geographical boundaries of the community toward which a change effort is to be targeted.
	Social problems	5. To establish a profile of problems affecting the target population within the community.
	Values	6. To observe and understand dominant values affecting the target population within the community.
	Oppression and discrimination	7. To recognize ways in which the target population has been formally or covertly restricted by powerful persons and/or institutions.
3. Identify community structure	Power and resource availability	8. To recognize stakeholders and where power (and the accompanying resources) is located in addressing target population needs.
	Service-delivery units	9. To identify informal, mediating, and formal units that deliver services to target population members.
	Patterns of resource control and service delivery	10. To determine who provides and who controls resource delivery to the target population in the community.
	Linkages between units	11. To identify connections between service-delivery units or gaps in which connections need to be made in order to serve target population needs.

other target populations). For example, existing reports on community issues and populations may predetermine what target group practitioners can serve, with only limited opportunity to familiarize themselves with other community needs and concerns.

We suggest that a community be analyzed and understood from this limited perspective because (1) people who become involved in community change often hold full-time jobs, and it is not unusual that macro-level intervention responsibilities are added on top of those jobs, and (2) there is a practical limit to the amount of information that can be gathered or analyzed in macro-level interventions. Although we do not disagree that ideally everything possible should be known and understood about a community in advance, limits on time and resources mean that responsible change efforts can usually be initiated only by narrowing the parameters of community assessment.

Identifying a target population can be a difficult task because populations are varied and often have indistinct boundaries. We may define ourselves as part of a geographical or place community based on location (e.g., the town where we live), but ethnicity (e.g., the Latino community), religion (e.g., the Jewish community), commitment to a position (e.g., the pro-choice community), profession (e.g., the social work community), avocation (e.g., the environmental movement community), and many other designations may be nonplace communities. Also, as this list suggests, each individual may be part of many different communities (both place and nonplace) at once.

It is also important to note that there are critical differences between urban, suburban, and rural communities. This approach may be particularly difficult in a rural community where members of the target population are geographically dispersed. We also caution the reader not to assume that the target population can be disengaged or isolated from the larger community, even though one may focus on the target population for the purpose of the change episode. Members of the target population may already feel isolated from the larger community, so the actions of the social worker should avoid reinforcing this perception, while working to strengthen ties and reduce isolation.

Viewed graphically, a community might appear as a series of overlapping circles, representing important elements or reference groups within the community. A given individual could then be represented in a space formed from the overlap of the unique combination of elements relevant to that person, as illustrated in Figure 6.1.

The first step for someone attempting to understand a community is to identify the community members on whom he or she will focus: the *target population.* A target population can be narrowly or broadly defined, but the more precise its definition, the more feasible a full understanding of it becomes. Oftentimes the target population is obvious because they are a group that a social worker's agency wants to serve better or to reach out to for the first

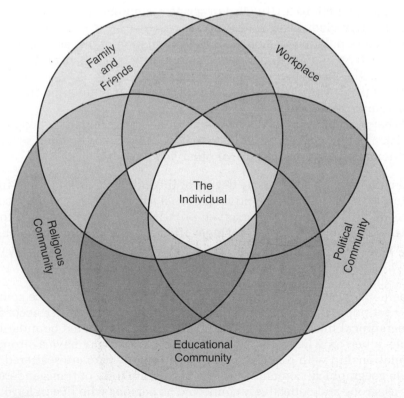

Figure 6.1
The Individual within the Community

time. In this case, the social worker may have the backing of their place of employment or even be tasked to assess this population's needs.

For example, the target population for a particular community assessment could be "people with domestic violence problems who live in Canyon City" or it could be "Latina women who have been the victims of physical abuse by spouses or significant others within the past two years in Canyon City." One is more inclusive, the other more focused. It is probably advisable, at early stages of the analysis, that a broader definition be adopted, with the expectation that it may be narrowed as a clearer understanding of needed change emerges.

Once a target population has been identified and the definition appropriately narrowed, other variables in the community are explored and examined from the perspective of that group. For each variable to be explored, we will identify a task intended to bring clarity to the collection of data and information. We will next focus on questions to be asked about the population. Finally, we will propose some questions to be asked about the target population's community that will aid in understanding each dimension and in comparing it to other communities. Although this framework contains a number of tasks, the process of analyzing a community requires the social worker to go back and forth, returning to refine previous tasks as new data are gathered. Accordingly, the social worker is urged to employ the framework as an interactive guide rather than a rigid formula for community assessment.

Identify the Target Population

Questions to be explored for this activity include:

- What populations are in need of services, and how can they be accurately identified?
- Which population will be the target population of this assessment?
- Is this target population part of a community that is geographical, interactional, symbolic, or a combination?
- What priority is given to the needs of this target population in the community?
- What percentage of the target population is represented by people at risk of being underserved due to their race/ethnicity, gender, sexual orientation, age, disabilities, or other factors?

All communities suffer some degree of inequitable distribution of income, opportunity, political representation, personal safety, or other social resources. This means that multiple underserved populations can be expected to exist, and not all can be addressed by a single effort. The initial task facing a social worker when assessing a community is to determine the group that will be selected as the target population, recognizing that a large variety of populations might be in need of his or her efforts.

One note of caution is in order here when it comes to nonplace communities. Target population groups may not define their community according to the geographical lines established by planners and designated boundaries. For example, a person who self-identifies as transgender may have a strong symbolic relationship with other transgendered persons who are scattered across multiple geographical communities. Yet, the community of transgendered persons is as strong and collectively connected as persons who live in local neighborhoods, perhaps even more so. Thus, the practitioner who is working with the transgender community will be engaged with a population group that is more vertically connected than horizontally based, as are other groups within geographical communities.

One distinction that may be helpful in this process is offered by Rossi, Lipsey, and Freeman (2004), who distinguish between *populations at risk* and *populations at need.* A population at risk is one in danger of developing a particular problem, whereas a population at need is one in which the problem already exists. In a population at risk, change efforts may be oriented toward prevention; in a population at need, the change may be more focused on intervention or treatment. In the case of a neighborhood plagued by youth gangs, for example, the social worker may identify the target population as those youth who are at risk of joining a gang, in which case the goal may be to stop this from happening. Alternatively, youth already in gangs may be identified as the target population, in which case efforts might be focused on ways to free them from these gangs or divert the gangs from criminal activity.

A further task facing the social worker in selecting a target population is establishing criteria for deciding which community members are inside or outside this population. In the youth gang example, the social worker may decide to focus on kids at risk of joining a gang. After some study, he or she might propose that the criteria for being considered part of the target population would be to attend one of seven schools serving the neighborhood, to be between 10 and 14 years of age, and to belong to a particular ethnic group that has established gangs in the community. These criteria establish what Rossi and colleagues (2004) call the *boundary* of the target population, and they point out that two types of errors can occur in the boundary-setting process.

One error is *overinclusion,* which happens when a boundary takes in too many people. That might occur in this case if both males and females are included in the target population, when in fact few females actually join gangs. Overinclusion might also occur if ethnicity is not considered, because almost all gangs are ethnic based. Among the consequences of overinclusion is the expenditure of scarce resources on community members who do not need them. On the other hand, *underinclusion* occurs when community members who need services are not taken within the boundaries of the target population, such as children under age 10 who may nonetheless be recruited by a gang. One of the consequences of underinclusion can be failure to intervene successfully because too few community members are reached.

Ethical Practice

Critical Thinking Question: Do you think under- or overinclusion is worse? Why?

People who are identified as being in a target population are consumers of services, and ideally the services provided are designed to meet their needs. However, it is important to recognize that people's needs are always changing. This requires a human service system that has flexibility to respond to changing needs. Because the characteristics of community residents vary, there may be subgroups that require special attention. For example, if a community has a high proportion of retirees, one can expect that many of the services will address the needs of older people. If services are not available, the delivery system may not be adequately meeting community needs.

For the sake of discussion, consider the following seven target populations that could be used for planning purposes. Funding may be clustered around these categories:

- Children
- Youth
- Families
- Young and middle-aged adults

- Elderly adults
- Developmentally disabled persons
- Physically disabled persons

Obviously, these groups are neither exhaustive nor mutually exclusive. In addition, there are many subgroups that fall within each category. For example, if the target population is children, it is important to recognize that children come from families of all socioeconomic statuses, racial and ethnic groups, and locations within a community. In other words, identifying a target population as simply "all children" may lead to many problems associated with overinclusion.

Although we have identified seven categories of people who may have some common characteristics and needs, individual communities will have their own definitions of target populations. The social worker should determine how the community categorizes client groups for planning purposes. Local and regional planning agencies, United Ways, community councils, and associations of agencies often produce agreed-on classification schemes for data collection and planning purposes, and the social worker will need to decide whether to keep these definitions in establishing target population boundaries or to establish new definitions. Each approach can be expected to have certain advantages and disadvantages.

Understand Characteristics of Target Population Members

Questions to be explored for this activity include:

- What is known about the history of the target population in this community?
- How many persons comprise the target population and what are their relevant characteristics?
- How geographically contained or dispersed are members of this group?
- How do persons in the target population perceive themselves and the history of their group?

Demographic characteristics provide helpful information, but there are also attitudinal differences, assumptions, and worldviews that may be harder to identify within and between target population groups. It is these differences among target population members that the macro practitioner must attempt to understand. This usually begins with an examination of available demographic data, which refers to variables such as socioeconomic status, age, race, and gender. Information of this sort can often be found online from the U.S. Census Bureau, which within cities break down the information by geographic units called tracts. Such divisions are relatively small and often incorporate as few as 3,000 to 8,000 people, making it possible to categorize community units as small as an individual neighborhood. Using this type of source, it is important to identify areas of poverty and high need, as well as to determine whether the target population is heavily concentrated in certain areas or is spread across an entire city or county.

The practitioner may find that there are a small number of members of the target population concentrated in a particular area, yet if one expands their reach there are many more persons in the target population across multiple geographical communities. Knowing how geographically contained or dispersed a target population is important when one plans an intervention. For example, it may be hard to convince a funding source that enough people will be served if one defines boundaries too tightly, but if one joins with agencies in other communities across the city, county, or state, then the scope of the problem may be evident.

In addition to gathering data-based information, it is also necessary to talk with people who understand the history of a target population as perceived by its own members. Generally, how do people in this target population (and others close to them) perceive their concerns, problems, issues, and/or needs? Do they tend to see them in terms of a need for empowerment, freedom from oppression, access to opportunity, removal of barriers, need for resources or services, and/or need for protection? These types of questions focus on the perceptions that target population members have about themselves in the context of their community. For example, the Latina women in Canyon City may view their history differently than the women who are currently being served in domestic violence shelters. Hearing directly from them may raise the possibilities of alternative interventions that are more sensitive to cultural differences (e.g., working through a local Latino Catholic church where trust has already been established). Similarly, in Lakeside, the older persons who have lived there all their lives and the newly arrived elders who moved to be near their children will have different historical experiences. The sensitive practitioner will take the time to understand how different characteristics of target population members and their life experiences may contribute to a variety of attitudes and values. Bellah, Madsen, Sullivan, Swidler, and Tipton (1985) explain the importance of a community as a collection of people who are interdependent and who share in making decisions and in the activities of daily practices. These types of communities take time to develop since they require a shared history and jointly held memories. Examining the characteristics of the target population and identifying where they are located, together with gathering information from the perspective of people in the target population, completes the second task in the community encounter.

Assess Target Population Needs

Questions to be explored for this activity include:

- What are feasible and appropriate ways to locate needs assessment data and other relevant information about the target population?
- What unmet needs are identified by persons in the target population?
- What is the history of efforts by persons in the target population to express their needs to others in the community?
- How do persons in the target population perceive their community and its responsiveness to their needs?
- Do community members outside the target population perceive that their needs are different from those of members within the target population?
- Do some members of the target population experience greater unmet needs due to their race/ethnicity, gender, sexual orientation, age, disabilities, or other factors?

Eight general methods of approaching a needs assessment have been discussed in the literature. They include:

- Gathering opinions and judgments from key informants through community forums, public hearings, face-to-face interaction, and focus groups;

- ▶ Collecting service statistics such as utilization, waiting list, and caseload data;
- ▶ Locating epidemiological studies (of the origins of problems);
- ▶ Finding studies of the incidence and prevalence of problems;
- ▶ Using social indicators (e.g., unemployment, crime);
- ▶ Conducting or locating surveys of population group members, providers, and others;
- ▶ Conducting secondary analyses of existing studies;
- ▶ Any combination of the above. (Meenaghan & Gibbons, 2000, p. 8)

The preferred approach in assessing need within a particular population is to use existing data. Original data collection is expensive and time consuming and is usually beyond the scope of the macro practitioner unless a particular change effort has widespread community and financial backing. Table 6.2 summarizes the advantages and disadvantages of using various approaches.

Ideally, the macro practitioner would like to know (1) the number of people in the target population who are experiencing each problem and (2) the number of people who are being served by existing resources. The first number minus the second number represents the target population's unmet need. Unmet needs, inadequately met needs, or inappropriately met needs are typically the focus of macro-level change efforts.

With special population groups that require multiple services, classification schemes are often based on the concept of a continuum of care. A continuum

Table 6.2   Needs Assessment Methods: Advantages and Disadvantages

Method	Description	Advantages	Disadvantages
Gathering opinions and judgments from key informants	Community forums Public hearings Face-to-face interaction Focus groups	Provides opportunities to hear directly from the target population	Often difficult to locate people who fully understand the issues; also time consuming
Service statistics	Utilization and rates Waiting lists Caseload data	Provides information from those who serve the target population	Is limited by what is collected and how well data are managed
Locating epidemiological studies (of the origins of problems)	Analyzing existing data	Data are already collected and usually accessible	Analysis is restricted by what data were collected
Finding studies of the incidence and prevalence of problems	Reporting what previous studies have found	Studies have already been conducted and findings are available	Generalizability of findings may be limited
Social indicators	Reviews of data such as income, age, occupation	Data are available and provide broad overview of community	Indicators do not provide detailed information
Conducting and locating surveys	Interviews with community members	Provides broad overview of needs	Requires great time and expense

Table 6.3   **Continuum of Long-Term Care Services by Category**

In-Home Services	Community-Based Services	Institutional Services
Outreach	Case management	Alcohol and drug treatment
Information and referral	Transportation	Rehabilitation
Comprehensive geriatric assessment	Senior centers	Psychiatric care
Emergency response system	Senior discount programs	Swing beds or step-down
Companionship/friendly visiting	Recreational activities	units
Telephone reassurance	Caregiver support groups	Skilled nursing care
Caregiver respite services	Self-help groups	Extended care
Homemaker and chore services	Counseling	
Household repair services	Foster homes	
Personal care	Adult care homes	
Home-delivered meals	Shared housing	
Home health	Congregate housing	
In-home high-technology therapy	Wellness and	
Hospice	health promotion clinics	
	Geriatric assessment clinics	
	Physician services	
	Adult day care	
	Mental health clinics	
	Outpatient clinics	

of care consists of a broad menu of services from which items can be selected to address the specific needs of certain individuals or groups. Ideally, each menu will vary based on what is needed for the target population served. Table 6.3 provides one way of classifying continuum of care services for those persons requiring long-term care, with in-home services being the least restrictive care environment and institutional services being the most restrictive.

Need is an elusive and complex concept that must be understood from a variety of perspectives. What we have discussed thus far are individual needs experienced by many people. When one person is hungry, it is an individual problem; when hundreds of people are hungry and the community is not prepared to assist, it is a social problem. When needs outstrip resources, it is a communitywide problem and may require a human service response. More food banks, more homeless shelters, or more employment training services may be needed. It is important to note, however, that just because data collected indicate a particular need, it does not necessarily follow that these data, combined with other types of information, will translate into widespread support from the community. It is also important to recognize that just because a need is being addressed does not mean that the service provided is what is needed. For example, a large metropolitan city in the Southwest experienced sustained high temperatures throughout July. So unrelenting was the heat that it dehydrated vulnerable people to the point of death. On closer analysis, it was discovered that a low-income home energy assistance program was in place, but the city did not have the resources to provide air conditioning. More funding was allocated to cold weather states for winter heating than to states with warm climates, somehow missing the fact that hot climates had emergency energy needs as well.

Some needs may require something other than a human service response and may even demand a redesign of structures and systems. As discussed in the previous chapter, structure and power are important variables for understanding community. When communities suffer from inferior housing, transportation, or schools, or an inadequate economic base, the issue may be more than simply individual problems on a large scale and may need to be viewed as a collective need. For example, after the Gulf Oil Spill of 2010, the magnitude of collective need required large-scale action from outside the local community.

It is assumed by most social scientists that communities should seek to ensure adequately functioning systems of service and sufficient support to enable their citizens to achieve basic standards for quality of life. This includes an economic base that produces jobs and income, affordable housing, adequate transportation, sound public health practices, quality education for children, public safety, and freedom to pursue obligations and interests without fear. When these conditions are absent, a service response (more money, more resources of any kind) may provide temporary relief without dealing with fundamental structural problems.

The long-term need may be for group empowerment, a collective sense of dignity, full participation in decisions that affect the lives of people in the community, self-direction, or self-control. Assessing collective need requires understanding the history and development of the community, an ability to compare economic and social problem data to other communities, and sensitivity to the needs and aspirations of those who are part of the community. Collective need may also have to be addressed at another level, such as the state legislature or U.S. Congress. The focus can remain on the local community and actions can be taken locally, but the point of intervention may be outside the community. Similarly, in a nonplace community, the locus of intervention may be at the state or national level (extralocal) simply because the community transcends geographical lines (Milofsky, 2008).

When the collective need for empowerment, participation, control, and other such factors is identified or expressed, the role of the macro practitioner is different from the role taken when the need is for a human service response. These roles will be discussed in Chapters 9 through 11.

Task 2: Determine Community Characteristics

In communities with severe and/or urgent social problems, the scope of intervention may have to be narrowed in order to address problems in depth.

Characteristics of a community can be assessed in a number of ways, and in this task we focus on *boundaries; strengths, issues,* and *social problems;* and *values.* Size can be calculated in terms of the amount of space covered, by the number of people within a community's boundaries, or both. Geographical boundaries established for macro-level interventions can range from neighborhood to county or even larger. Boundaries of nonplace communities may be more difficult to determine because members may be scattered across multiple locations, but the practitioners still need to know what they must do to intervene appropriately. Whether a community is place or nonplace bound, it is important to consider the strengths of its members and of its culture. We emphasize strengths first because it is often too easy to simply profile social problems as a way to determine community characteristics. In communities with severe and/or urgent social problems, the scope of intervention may have to be narrowed in order to address problems in depth. Keeping strengths in mind, as issues and problems are recognized, may help the practitioner maintain a sense of balance (Green & Haines, 2002). Community strengths are assets from which one can draw (Kretzmann & McKnight, 1993). In addition, understanding dominant values is important in determining community expectations and the "fit" of various population groups with one another. Value characteristics will provide clues to the practitioner about what is important to community members. Clearly, the boundaries, strengths, issues, social problems, and values of the community will affect the nature of the macro-level analysis and, ultimately, the intervention.

Identify Community Boundaries

Questions to be explored for this activity include:

- What are the boundaries within which intervention on behalf of the target population will occur?
- Where are members of the target population located within the boundaries? Are they highly concentrated or scattered? Are the boundaries geographically, interest, and/or identity bound?
- How compatible are jurisdictional boundaries of health and human service programs that serve the target population?

Earlier in this chapter, we discussed the establishment of criteria for inclusion of individuals in a target population, a process sometimes referred to as *boundary setting.* Another, more common use of the term *boundary* refers to the lines determining the geographical area occupied by a community. For a social worker involved in a macro-level intervention, one important consideration has to do with the extent of the area to be included. If resources are available to focus on the entire city or county, then these may be appropriate boundaries in that instance. If, however, the effort is to be undertaken by a small committee of volunteers who have limited time and resources, it may be better to focus the encounter on the part of the city or even a neighborhood in which there appears to be the greatest need for intervention. In nonplace communities, boundary setting may be around the numbers of members of the target population who can be served rather than their geographical location.

Establishing boundaries for a macro-level intervention is done by determining the characteristics (age, year in school, presence of a problem), the geographical area of residence, or the shared interests of a target population. For most interventions in which boundaries involve geographic space, we recommend beginning with clearly recognizable units, such as a city or county, and then narrowing the focus to smaller areas if appropriate. This is not intended to indicate that an intervention at the state, regional, or national level is inappropriate, but for the vast majority of interventions a level of county or smaller will be most relevant and practical. For nonplace interventions, establishing a manageable number of persons who can be served in a pilot approach may be a way to begin.

Figure 6.2 illustrates the boundary-setting process. Knowing that one cannot address all target population needs within large arenas, the encounter focuses on the target population within a manageable part of the broader community.

A target population or community defined by the area its members occupy may be a small section of the inner city or a large rural area containing scattered farms. The notion of community as space is applicable to mostly Latino *barrios* that have reasonably well-defined boundaries within a large metropolitan area. Spatial concepts of community are also applicable in less densely

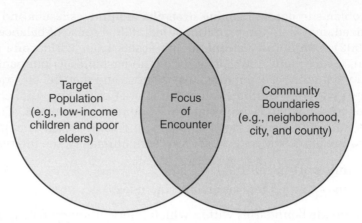

Figure 6.2
Setting Parameters for the Community Encounter

populated areas, but they may be more difficult to determine. This was noted by a Navajo social worker who explained how difficult it can be to determine spatial boundaries on a reservation where there may be no street systems, property information, and signs indicating county lines, or well-defined human service areas. In a way, this student was experiencing the overlap of place and nonplace communities. The reservation was so dispersed that the major consideration needed to be identification as a tribal member rather than where each person actually lived.

Another characteristic important to understanding community as space are the jurisdictional units established by various government agencies for planning and service provision purposes (e.g., school districts or mental health catchment areas). Because the macro practitioner's focus is frequently limited to a designated geographical area, mapping overlapping jurisdictional units can be important and useful. For example, a change agent may be working with residents of a particular county to establish a prenatal health-care campaign for pregnant teens, only to discover that he or she is dealing with representatives from multiple city governments as well as the county government. Determining who is responsible within what geographical domain can be extremely important politically. Similarly, a practitioner hired by a mental health clinic may find that the clinic's catchment area overlaps parts of three school districts, requiring letters of agreement with multiple school boards. Being able to anticipate and adjust to these circumstances will aid in both planning and implementation of the change episode. When possible it may be helpful to set boundaries congruent with established jurisdictional units because data and information will be organized within these boundaries, whereas working across existing boundaries may limit one's ability to compile the necessary information.

In nonplace communities, establishing boundaries will vary depending on how organized the nonplace community is. For example, if one is trying to address the needs of gay, lesbian, bisexual, and transgendered persons, many of whom may not want other community members to know who they are, locating the target population may be difficult without assurances of confidentiality. Chances are that the target population will not conform to geographical parameters, and boundaries will have to remain somewhat fluid depending on who feels comfortable making their sexual orientation known. Conversely, in a community of interest based on getting the word out about a devastating disease such as Alzheimer's, the practitioner may have a ready cadre of advocates from the ranks of persons who have had experience with the disease in their families. They may be willing to join forces to work toward change, relieved to tell their stories to the larger public. These boundaries may also be fluid, expanding as more people join the cause from different locations. In both cases, neither community conforms to strict geographical boundaries, but they are held together by the boundaries of shared identities.

Identify Community Strengths, Issues, and Problems

Questions to be explored for this activity include:

- What data sources are available, and how are these data used within the community?
- Who collects the data, and is this an ongoing process?
- What are the community's strengths?
- What are the major community issues?
- What are the major social problems affecting the target population in this community as perceived by their spokespersons?
- Are there subgroups of the target population that are experiencing major social problems?
- To what extent are these problems interconnected, and must some be solved before others can be addressed?

Macro-level interventions tend to be conceptualized and organized around a selected population and a specific problem they are experiencing. For example, a social worker might discover a lack of child-care options for teenaged parents who wish to return to school, or an increasing problem of malnutrition among isolated elders, or a community made up primarily of African Americans and Latinos who believe their requests are not receiving a fair hearing by the city council.

Often overlooked are the strengths (sometimes called *assets*) of a community. For example, the social worker who has discovered a lack of child-care options may also discover a strong kinship network and that grandparents are active in their grandchildren's lives. The increasing problem of malnutrition may overshadow the fact that a number of area congregations are ready and willing to provide meals to older people. And African Americans and Latinos who feel that the city council is willing to be responsive to their issues may have strong motivations to have their voices heard, have a strong sense of community identity, and be eager to mobilize. It is important for the practitioner to identify strengths that may make the difference in determining whether a community can address its issues and problems. Green and Haines (2002) suggest community assets can be categorized into five areas: *physical, human, social, financial*, and *environmental capital*. The practitioner may wish to use these categories to assess strengths in a particular situation.

Identifying strengths, issues, and problems helps in two ways: (1) It enables the macro practitioner to appreciate the full range of possibilities as well as difficulties experienced by the target population, thereby helping to prioritize needs and (2) it should help in proposing more realistic solutions. For example, sometimes there are resources to address a transportation need and in doing so, a bigger problem of access to services can be addressed.

Social problems are negatively labeled "conditions" recognized by community residents. Identified social problems will vary by community and target population. Sometimes there are conditions that have not been labeled as problems. It may be the social worker's task to bring these conditions to the attention of people in power so that they are recognized as social problems. This is not always easy because community residents may have a great deal invested in denying that there is a problem. *Issues* are points over which there are disagreements. Community members may disagree over whether something is a problem, over how resources are to be used to address a problem, or a host of other points. It is helpful to know what the points of disagreement are.

The purpose of establishing a profile of strengths, issues, and problems is to understand the conditions affecting the target population. This requires both direct contact and searching the professional knowledge base. Direct contact with people who can articulate the problems and needs of the target population gives the practitioner a first-person interpretation of issues. The professional knowledge base adds theoretical background as well as practice and research findings based on the experiences of others with the same or similar populations and problems.

We cannot emphasize strongly enough the importance of original, authoritative sources in understanding a target population. Populations must be understood in terms of their diversity. In family practice, for example, the meaning of family—husband–wife relationships, parent–child relationships, aging grandparents' roles—may differ from one culture to the next. Similarly, the ways in which members of the gay and lesbian community define family may differ radically from traditional community values. In border states many people are expressing strong opinions on illegal immigration. People who live on the border (mayors, law enforcement people, and citizens) are vocal and critical of those who do not take the time to consult with persons who live with the problem every day and have important insights into how immigration should be addressed. A target population will not be adequately understood if these potentially widely divergent views are not respected and taken into consideration.

Once major social problems defined by community members have been identified, one can begin to determine their incidence and prevalence. Incidence is defined as a phenomenon actually occurring over a period of time (Kettner, Daley, & Nichols, 1985, p. 72). For example, fifteen students may have been arrested for drug use in the local high school in the most recent academic year. Prevalence is tied to the number of cases of the phenomenon that exist within a community at any one time (Kettner et al., 1985, p. 72). For example, current estimates indicate that drug use among teenagers is as high as 50 percent.

Social indicator data may be helpful in gaining a broad overview of social problems at the national, regional, state, and local levels. In this way, the community's social problems can be comparatively assessed. Other professionals in the community, or at the county or state level, can also be valuable sources of information. They may have firsthand experience with the target population, or their organizations may have conducted surveys or collected statistics of specific social problems. Accessing the websites of these organizations may reveal valuable and useful information.

Understand Dominant Values

Questions to be explored for this activity include:

▶ What cultural values, traditions, and beliefs are important to the target population as individuals or as a whole?

▶ What are the predominant values that affect the target population within this community?

▶ What groups and individuals espouse these values, who opposes them, and are there value conflicts surrounding the target population?

▶ How do people in this community feel about giving and receiving help?

▶ What are the predominant shared perspectives in this community on inclusion of the target population in decisions that affect them?

In the previous chapter, we discussed the importance of values in gaining a basic understanding of community. *Values* are strongly held beliefs and *community values* are beliefs that are strongly held by persons who make up the community. These values are often reinforced by the associations and organizations with which community residents affiliate.

The idea of shared values requires refinement in today's changing world. At one time, communities without divisions of labor (e.g., farming communities) were more likely to have shared value systems. Early community values had a great deal to do with such issues as self-sufficiency, taking care of one's own family needs, and minimal reliance on government services. Even today political differences are often defined in terms of one set of beliefs being framed around minimum standards of care for all versus an alternative set of beliefs focused on individuals and families receiving only the standards of care they can afford.

As people specialized, community members had limited understanding of what other persons in the community did for a living. In addition, differentiation of interests and associations occurred as society shifted from primary (face-to-face groups such as families and neighbors) to secondary groups (more formalized groups and organizations). Local associations became chapters of national organizations, tying their members into an extracommunity network. Technological advances made it possible to maintain contact with others who were geographically dispersed.

Given these changes, one must take care not to assume a single, common, shared value system in contemporary communities or among members of a target population. For example, if the target population comprises persons who have been abused, members of that group will cut across all socioeconomic levels and a host of other differences. They may have completely different perspectives on how abuse is defined and how they define healthy relationships.

Depending on the selected target population, practitioners will find a host of value perspectives. For example, if the target population is people with AIDS, some persons in the community will feel strongly that such people deserve the best possible care and comfort, whereas others will react in fear, not wanting people with AIDS in their local acute and long-term care facilities. Similarly, if the target population is pregnant teenagers, value conflicts may arise between community residents who believe that teenagers should be given contraceptive information and those who believe that this information will only encourage sexual activity.

Jansson (2009) sees value clarification as critically important in asking questions about social welfare responses to various target population groups. He poses questions such as:

▶ Should the target population receive services and on what terms?

▶ For what needs and problems is a community responsible, and what target population needs should receive priority?

▶ What strategies should be used to address specific target population strengths, issues, and problems?

▶ Should the community give preferential assistance or treatment to the target population?

These value clarification questions may be answered differently depending on the population targeted within the community. This series of questions implies that some populations may be valued more than others; that is, some may be perceived as "deserving" and others as "undeserving." There may be an outcry to treat drug-addicted infants, whereas their addicted mothers may be treated with disdain. Homeless families may be perceived as down on their luck, whereas homeless alcoholics may be seen as "bringing this on themselves."

Depending on the target population group, there may be subgroups within the larger whole that are viewed differently. Recognition of the importance of diversity will lead the macro practitioner to check carefully the values of each ethnic or racial group affected; the possible different perspectives of women and men in the target population; and the perspectives of representatives of gay, lesbian, bisexual, and transgendered groups if they are affected by the change. It is wiser to take the time to be inclusive of a wide range of values than to find out, too late, that a change effort is not working because differing perspectives were overlooked. Change agents should go into this values-clarification exercise understanding that they may not always like what is discovered about community values or even target population members' values, but struggling with value conflicts will give change agents some understanding of how much the community is committed to addressing the needs of the target population. These efforts often provide vivid illustrations of one segment of the community considering something a problem while others view it as a condition or merely a fact of life.

As one begins to form an understanding of major community value perspectives, one must take care to recognize the fit (or lack of fit) between target population perspectives and dominant community perspectives. Are target population perspectives taken into consideration when decisions are made that affect them? Recognizing value differences and power discrepancies is an important part of the community assessment process.

Regardless of the target population identified, there will be differences between this population and other groups within the community. There will also be differences within the target population. Potential differences include gender, social class, spiritual and religious beliefs, sexual orientation, age, and physical and mental ability.

The "dynamics of difference" (Cross, Bazron, Dennis, & Isaacs, 1989, p. 20) may involve cross-cultural exchanges where groups with diverse histories and values interact. There is always the possibility of misunderstanding and misinterpretation when this occurs. "Both will bring culturally-prescribed patterns of communication, etiquette, and problem-solving. Both may bring stereotypes or underlying feelings about serving or being served by someone who is different" (Cross et al., 1989, p. 20). For example, professionals who serve elders may rationalize why they do not serve many Latino clients by stereotyping Latino families as taking care of their own and therefore needing few formal services. This oversimplification may ignore the fact that one-fourth of the Latino families in a local community are poor, and caring for an older family member is a tremendous financial burden. It also ignores the fact that all Latino elders do not have other family members residing in the community.

Differences may be subtle or taken for granted, yet they may influence the way in which members of the target population communicate with one another and with other groups. The National Association of Social Workers

(NASW) has developed standards for cultural competence in social work, and these standards are particularly relevant when it comes to recognizing community differences. Cultural competence is a process in which human beings and their systems are sensitive, respectful, and responsive to all persons' cultures, affirming their differences in a way that values their worth and preserves their dignity (NASW, 2006, p. 4). Feminist scholars encourage the recognition of gender differences (e.g., Netting, O'Connor, & Fauri, 2009), and Tannen's research indicates that men and women speak in "genderlects" that comprise "cross cultural communication" (1990, p. 18). For example, a male social worker was assessing a community's responsiveness to single mothers with young children. He attended several support groups for the target population and was frustrated that all they did was talk without coming to a consensus on what they wanted from the larger community. He assessed part of the problem as an unwillingness on the part of the target population to face up to their problems and to work on solutions. The women in the support group, however, felt that this was an opportunity to process their thoughts and feelings. They did not view the group as a place to immediately resolve problems. The group was a place to make connections and to achieve intimacy. Note how the support group performed a nurturing function in light of the larger demands of the sustaining community system. Also, observe how important it is to be culturally sensitive to gender, recognizing the strengths of this nurturing system in supporting the women.

Identify Formal and Covert Means of Oppression and Discrimination

Questions to be explored for this activity include:

- What differences are observed among members of the target population?
- What differences are observed among other groups within the community?
- Are there barriers (e.g., organizations, rules, procedures, and policies) that inhibit the target population from becoming fully integrated into the community?
- To what extent are the perspectives of people of color; women; gay men, lesbians, and transgendered persons; older persons; and persons with disabilities sought in decisions affecting the target population?

Oppression occurs when severe constraints are placed on any group (sometimes consciously, but oftentimes unconsciously), thus restricting the group's ability to compete and making them vulnerable to exploitation (Barker, 1995, p. 265). Oppression focuses on differences, the assumption being that some group is lesser than, not as good as, or less worthy than others. Oppression is based on differential power, the power to set the terms and to limit others' choices (Appleby, 2007). Quite often oppression takes the form of hiring people similar to oneself because it is more comfortable, or giving contracts to people who are part of an "inner circle" rather than giving new contractors a chance.

Some people are uncomfortable with differences, and because they assume that one way must be better than another way, they look on differences as a problem to be solved. An alternative perspective is that differences reflect a variety of ways to view the world, to believe, and to behave. Social workers can employ differences as potential strengths within a target population, but they must remember that differences often include alternative definitions of a successful outcome. For example, in the women's group just described, the social worker was frustrated because he believed the group members were not solving their problems. For the members, however, the group itself was something of a solution. It provided a forum in which single mothers could share their concerns and find understanding and support. This forum could, in turn, serve as a foundation on which additional solutions might be built, but in the manner and at the pace that suited members of the group, not the group leader.

Areas around which oppression often occurs are gender, race, ethnicity, sexual orientation, age, and ability. Depending on the target population, all of the resulting "isms" or selected ones may be relevant. In many cases, the target population may be persons affected by one of the "isms" (Appleby, Colon, & Hamilton, 2007), as previously defined in Chapter 4.

Up-to-date data combined with information from the professional knowledge base give the practitioner a grounding in what is known about community differences. It also provides background for future needs assessment data collection and a solid foundation on which to pursue community change.

Identifying value conflicts is critical to recognizing oppression and discrimination.

Identifying value conflicts is critical to recognizing oppression and discrimination. Values may be based on prejudices, those prejudgments that community residents have about the target group that are not grounded in systematic evidence. The issue of systematic evidence is one that needs to be treated with care and sensitivity. Many people still believe that every individual essentially controls his or her own destiny and that hard work and persistence will overcome any barrier or limitation. This belief is reinforced when severely disabled persons accomplish incredible physical feats or severely deprived persons make it to the top.

These accomplishments become "evidence" for local, state, and national leaders that those who need help are simply not trying hard enough. People who hold this belief look at what they consider to be systematic evidence and deny that their beliefs are prejudices. What is overlooked here, however, is generations of differential treatment that have made it difficult for people of color, women, persons with physical and developmental disabilities, and others to have equal access to economic resources and self-sufficiency. An alternative view is the capabilities perspective (Sen & Williams, 1982) in which it is recognized that not all people have the opportunity to start at the same place and that consideration must be given to what it takes to get to the place where they can compete with others (Nussbaum, 2006). So, for example, when a job is available and a homeless person chooses not to take it, one person will see that as evidence that he is lazy, whereas another will recognize it as a response to a lifetime of hopeless, discouraging, dead-end jobs in which skill development was never a possibility. For some, the pain of life on the street is less than the pain of hopelessness in their share of the workplace. In this situation, a practitioner using the capabilities perspective will know to start from where the client is and design a change effort that respects the homeless person within his or her context.

Prejudices are intimately tied to values and may affect how a person feels. *Discrimination* is acting out those prejudices. These actions can be observed in the differences in quality of life between the target population and the rest of the community.

For example, older minority women who live in poverty face triple jeopardy—they are old, female, and poor. Their experience points to generations of blocked opportunities, discrimination, and neglect. Serious damage is done to the fabric of the country, and therefore to the fabric of its communities, when any group of people is discriminated against as a whole category, when an individual is treated only as a member of a group, and when individual differences are disregarded. To many who are victims of this attitude, the message is that it does not matter how hard they work, how honest and law-abiding they are, or how much they play by the rules; they can never escape discrimination and oppression because they are lifetime members of the group. Thus, recognizing discriminatory behavior is important in assessing the community.

Task 3: Identify Community Structure

The third task in the pursuit of understanding a community is to identify its structure. Different structural domains will be important, depending on the defined problem and the needs of the target population. Recall the overview of community practice models in Chapter 5 in which a variety of models were identified, each depicting different organizing structures. For example, one might focus on the city if the problem is homelessness or focus on the school district if the problem is a high dropout rate. The domain may be a mental health catchment area or the planning and service area of an Area Agency on Aging. The goal is to ground the macro practitioner in recognizing the distribution of power, the provision and allocation of resources, and the patterns of service distribution that affect the target population within the domain of the targeted community. The practitioner will need to know how community groups advocate for, participate in, and engage in service provision.

Part of the community's structure is its human service system and the programs it offers persons in need. Table 6.4 identifies the types of units that should be considered when assessing service provision in a community. These units, taken together, comprise the total health and human service delivery system within the community, and they operate interdependently. A community, depending on availability of resources, may emphasize the provision of services through one set of units more than another. For example, in a resource-poor community, reliance on informal units may be a necessity until publicly funded formal services can be obtained. However, elements of informal, mediating, and formal service units will be found in each community. The astute practitioner will carefully assess all avenues of service delivery for the target population.

Recognize Sources of Power and Resource Availability

Questions to be explored in this activity include:

▶ What is the domain or jurisdiction involved, given the target population and problem?
▶ Who controls the funds?

Table 6.4   Units within the Health and Human Service Delivery System

Informal Units	Mediating Units	Formal Units
Household units	Self-help groups	Voluntary nonprofit agencies
Neighborhood groups	Grassroots associations Voluntary associations	Public agencies For-profit agencies

▶ Who are the major community leaders within the domain identified who will respond to the concerns of the target population? Who will oppose their concerns?

▶ How accessible are services for the target population?

Originally, primary groups, composed of families, friends, and neighbors, performed the functions necessary for community survival. This was the concept of *Gemeinschaft* referred to in Chapter 5. Businesses and government have gradually assumed many of these functions and a more formal provision of services has occurred, reflecting the concept of *Gesellschaft.* The most obvious change occurred during the New Deal era in the mid-1930s when government reluctantly responded to the social welfare needs of a post-Depression society. At that time, the balance between public and private service provision shifted, with public dollars taking over an increasing share of human service funding.

Urbanization and industrialization have greatly affected the social, political, and economic structures of this country. One of the major areas of impact, noted by Warren (1978), was the separation of one's working life from where he or she lives. Because of this change, people who hold power change, depending on the way in which a community is defined.

As local (horizontal) and extracommunity (vertical) ties have expanded, so has bureaucratization and its accompanying impersonalization. Bureaucratic structures are usually adopted by government, businesses, and voluntary organizations as size of population increases. Funding patterns can lead to power brokers external to the community. Being the major source of funding for local service efforts implies the ability to influence and direct provider decisions regarding target population needs. For example, the specialized volunteer-run, community-based agency that once served the neighborhood may have been transformed into a multiservice agency with many paid staff members. This means that there may be a number of leaders within the health and human service system, all representing different sectors (e.g., government, nonprofit, for profit). In addition, the larger multiservice organization may have multiple funding sources, including federal, state, and local government funds; United Way; private contributions; and fees. Each source must be satisfied that its expectations are being met.

Viewing the community from a power perspective requires identifying the formal and informal leaders within a community. It also means examining their effectiveness. Assessing the political climate requires reading the local newspaper and talking with local community leaders to determine the top-priority issues competing for funding. If a legislative change is needed, it is necessary to identify who may be willing to take the lead on issues affecting the target population.

Community power has been viewed from three perspectives: (1) an elitist structure, (2) a pluralist structure, and (3) an amorphous structure. An *elitist* approach assumes that a small number of people have disproportionate power in various community sectors and this power remains constant regardless of the issue. A *pluralist* perspective implies that as issues change, various interest groups and shifting coalitions arise. This perspective increases as more special-interest groups develop within the local community. The *amorphous* structure implies no persistent pattern of power relationships within the community (Meenaghan, Gibbons, & McNutt, 2005). Understanding the community's power dynamics will enable the practitioner to evaluate the community for this task.

Related to community structure is the issue of available resources. Communities can be described as *resource rich* or *resource poor* when it comes to providing for the needs of the target population. Although it is important to consider resources in connection with power, it is also important to compile information on resources so that appropriate sources will be targeted in pursuit of community change.

There are many types of resources to consider. Resources may be tangible, such as a welfare check, or symbolic, such as caring or social support. Resources can include status, information, money, goods, or services. Most early community encounters will focus heavily on the more concrete resources that are exchanged (money, goods, services) because tangible resources are easier to define and observe. However, as the professional becomes more actively engaged in community practice, there will be more opportunities to learn about symbolic exchanges (status, information) that are equally important to members of the target population.

Resources may be available from a variety of domains. King and Mayers (1984) have developed Guidelines for Community Assessment designed for use in analyzing community resources. They suggest that when assessing community resources available to a particular population, a number of domains be explored. Within each domain, questions of policy, practice, eligibility, location, and participation must be addressed in order to determine how available each resource is to the target population. Their domains are:

- Health
- Welfare
- Education
- Housing
- Recreation
- Employment
- Business
- Religion

For example, if the target population is low-income children, resources to be explored would include Medicaid (health), child welfare services (welfare), school programs (education), public housing, child-care programs provided by parents' places of employment, corporate community service initiatives (business), and faith-based groups involved in serving their communities (religion). One would want to ask: How effective are these systems in meeting the needs of the community's children and satisfying the expectations of the community? How do programs within each of these domains relate to one another?

Service accessibility is affected by a number of variables, including population density, distribution of service need, ability of area residents to pay for services, existence of competition among service providers, and transportation options available to consumers. Population density is important because service sites tend to arise where enough prospective service recipients are available to ensure steady demand. This is why accessibility is often dramatically more limited in rural areas and thinly populated suburbs than in cities. Similarly, services tend to gravitate toward areas of need; thus, child-care centers will be more common where there are concentrations of families with children, whereas senior centers will be more common where more older adults congregate. Gaps arise when no single group predominates, when demographic characteristics are changing rapidly, or when information is scarce regarding population characteristics and needs.

Services also tend to be located where consumers can pay, even if the service is offered by nonprofit organizations. For example, in recent years many cities have experienced high rates of hospital closures in low-income neighborhoods. These hospitals may be run by charitable organizations and may have existed for many years, but the combination of high costs, lack of health insurance or other resources on the part of local residents, and high demand for costly emergency care may render it financially impossible for the hospital to remain open. Nonprofit organizations must also compete with for-profits for paying customers, and this often leads to steering services and service locations away from those most in need. Finally, low-income residents of a community who require a particular service may still be able to reach it if public transit or other transportation resources are in place. However, transit systems are usually better developed in the most densely populated parts of a community and increasingly scarce in suburbs or newly developed areas. The social worker will need to be aware of these dynamics and the ways they interact in order to understand variations in service accessibility from one part of a community to another.

Having examined the resources available to the target population, those involved in community assessment should examine the human service delivery system.

Examine Service-Delivery Units

Questions to be explored in this activity include:

- ▶ What informal units (e.g., household, natural, and social networks) are actively engaged in service delivery to the target population?
- ▶ What mediating units (e.g., self-help groups and voluntary or grassroots associations) are actively engaged in service delivery to the target population?
- ▶ What formal service delivery units (e.g., nonprofit, public, for-profit) are actively engaged in service delivery?
- ▶ Are there differences in service delivery that appear to be based on race or ethnicity, gender, sexual orientation, disability, age, or religion?

In Chapter 5 we discussed the importance of informal and mediating units in understanding communities. Household units consist of persons who reside within a common dwelling, whether they consider themselves families, significant others, friends, partners, or roommates. Natural support systems evolve around mutual support, going beyond purely social networks, and engaging in resource exchange. Assessing these informal and mediating units is somewhat difficult simply because they are "informal," and therefore less accessible. Yet, any information that can be gathered will be helpful because it is often these less-visible activities that make a quality difference for people in need.

Formal vehicles of health and human service delivery are interconnected in numerous ways. For example, one might become a member of the Alliance of Information and Referral Systems (AIRS), which is an umbrella organization for providers of information and referral programs and seeks to enhance the capacity of local service networks (AIRS, 2006). The AIRS program might put you in touch with other communities and how they organize their service-delivery units. We will briefly examine service-delivery units according to three types of auspice: nonprofit, public (governmental), and for-profit (commercial).

Nonprofit Agencies.   As voluntary associations become more formal, they may become incorporated as nonprofit agencies, recognized as publicly chartered tax-free organizations. There are many types of nonprofit agencies, but we will focus on nonprofit human service agencies. Nonprofit agencies are formal vehicles of health and human service delivery (Kramer 1981). They are often viewed within local communities as the agency of choice—a voluntary initiative that targets a specialized clientele. This traditional view is based on the early U.S. welfare system, which arose from a profusion of agencies sponsored by various religious and secular groups. In recent years the professional knowledge base concerning nonprofit organizations has rapidly expanded and is worth exploring (see, for example, Hasenfeld, 2010; O'Connor & Netting, 2009).

Nonprofit agencies provide many different services within local communities. Although all nonprofit agencies using government funding serve clients without regard to race or gender, a growing number of agencies are specifically designed to serve the special needs of ethnic communities and families, women who are victims of discrimination and/or violence, and other groups underserved by more traditional agencies. The macro practitioner should identify which nonprofit agencies serve the target population and whether they have particular service emphases.

Public Agencies.   The public sector consists of federal, state, regional, county, and city government entities. When the mutual support function is performed by government, it is referred to as *social welfare*. The U.S. social welfare system has been described as a scattered, unpatterned mixture of programs and policies that does not work in a systematic way and is not easy to understand (Karger & Stoesz, 1990, p. 167).

By the time federal programs are operating within the local community, they have usually gone through several levels of bureaucracy. Depending on the structure, which will vary by program type, there may be several extracommunity levels through which dollars have flowed. There may be regional as well as state mandates, rules, regulations, and procedures that instruct local providers regarding what they can and cannot do. Local decision making and autonomy will vary depending on the policies that drive a particular program. In short, extracommunity sources have a definite influence on the local delivery of public services.

In assessing a community's human service system, it is important to gain knowledge about policies and programs that affect the target population. For example, working with elders means that one must be familiar with the Older Americans Act, which explains that there is a designated state unit on aging in every state and a network of area agencies on aging (AAAs). Every state must have a three- to five-year plan for elder services, and each AAA must have a local plan. Therefore, every community in the United States will be included in a plan that addresses elders' needs. Experience suggests, however, that this does not mean that every community *meets* the needs of their older members. Resources will be limited and the actual implementation of the plan will include the use of Older Americans Act funding, in partnership with other public and private initiatives. In addition, many communities have waiting lists for services, and state commitments to carrying out the objectives of the federal legislation vary.

If one's target population is single mothers receiving assistance from Temporary Aid to Needy Families (TANF), the social worker will need to know that states vary in what income is counted against benefits received. States also establish their own needs standard for families in that state. Therefore, although TANF is a large public assistance program developed at the federal level, state-level decisions influence what benefits families will receive. To be effective, the social worker will need to understand how federal and state governments interact, how community attitudes toward TANF recipients influence clients, and what the findings of TANF evaluations are (Tilbury, 2007).

In assessing the distribution of public resources across an entire community, including the funding of social service programs, it is important once again to examine community practices from the perspective of specific populations. Voluntary associations often serve as advocates for their members and have had varying degrees of success in influencing the allocation of resources. In many communities elders have been highly successful in these efforts, but attention to the needs of children varies. Ethnic groups have exercised increasing political power over the last few decades but still find, in many communities, that their interests and needs are considered a low priority. For example, some communities press for hiring bilingual social workers to address the needs of a growing multilingual constituency, but many agencies have workers who can only communicate in a rudimentary way with non-English-speaking clientele (Engstrom, Piedra, & Min, 2009). Groups representing lesbian, gay, and transgendered persons have increasingly taken up causes such as funding for AIDS research and have participated in the political arena to influence allocation of resources, but they still face widespread discrimination.

Understanding the political system within the community is a challenge. In the United States, jurisdiction over health and human service programs is distributed across cities, counties, and states. Social workers must contend with federal statutes, regulations, administrative rules, and funding formulas, as well as identify state and local laws and funding procedures (Jansson, 2011).

Professional colleagues, however, can provide perspectives on types of services and whether government is truly addressing the needs of the target population. For example, for macro practitioners working in a public housing development, social workers in other developments will be helpful in interpreting how regulations assist as well as constrain their efforts. Locating colleagues in similar settings is important to developing a professional support system to aid in coping with public policies, procedures, and rules.

Practice Contexts

Critical Thinking Question: How can you work within jurisdictional boundaries to improve problems with scopes extending far beyond these boundaries?

For-Profit Agencies.   Corporate foundations have played a major role in funding programs that benefit local communities, and many corporations have long provided employee benefits addressing health, human service, and retirement needs. Indeed, a growing number of social workers are involved in the corporate workplace through employee assistance programs (EAPs). These programs have developed as corporations realize that productive employees are those who are supported in all aspects of their lives. In an aging society, some large corporations have created eldercare support networks for employees caring for aged parents.

In the last decade, the actual delivery of health and human services has been increasingly carried out by for-profit corporations. For example, the majority of U.S. nursing homes are for-profit organizations. These shifting patterns were first noticed in the health-care arena, when proprietary hospitals began competing with traditional nonprofit providers (Marmor, Schlesinger, & Smithey, 1987). Public financing of health care through private mechanisms was only the beginning. As profit-making corporations bid for public contracts, competition with nonprofit organizations increased. Twenty years ago, our discussion of the health and human service systems would have focused almost entirely on the government and nonprofit sectors and their partnership. Today, the term *mixed economy,* including government, nonprofit, and for-profit services, is an accurate description (Marwell & McInerney, 2005).

If all these entities making up the structure of a community's social welfare system present a somewhat confusing picture to the student or new practitioner, that confusion is understandable and shared by many. If one looks at structure as a continuum, at one extreme might be the public education system and at the other the entrepreneurial or business system. Education is highly organized with increasingly more challenging curricula at each level from kindergarten through graduate education. In any community if a parent wishes to have the educational needs of his or her child met, the appropriate educational services can usually be located in relatively short order. The business sector, on the other hand, is made up of large and small organizations where someone perceived a need and proceeded to design some sort of a procurement and delivery system. There is not necessarily any order to it, and finding a particular product or service to meet a need may be a very lengthy process. Human services is somewhere in the middle. Every community includes certain services mandated by some level of government, but there is nothing to prevent an individual from perceiving a need and providing a service as a volunteer, non-profit, or for-profit organization. The result is often a very complex web or network of services designed to meet the needs of a given population, and a beginning exploration of agencies' websites may be time well spent.

Given the complexity of the formal service delivery system, the purpose of this assessment is to gain a better understanding of what organizations are providing services to the target population in this community. Having a general idea of what nonprofit, public, and for-profit agencies are available to the community leads to an examination of how they work together, as well as how they relate to the informal units within the service delivery system.

Identify Patterns of Influence, Control, and Service Delivery

Questions to be explored for this activity include:

- What groups, associations, and organizations (both extra- and local community) advocate for and provide assistance to the target population?
- How is resource distribution to the target population influenced by interaction (both electronic and face to face) within the community?
- What limits are placed on services to the target population, and who establishes these limits?
- What roles do citizens and consumers play in the control of services to the target population?

When assessing patterns and levels of participation, it is important that the macro practitioner distinguish between citizen and consumer-client participation. There are many citizens who, for reasons of altruism and conviction, are committed to fighting for the rights of the poor and oppressed. They bring a certain perspective to the discussion and make a contribution to constructive change in communities. However, it should not be assumed that interested citizen advocates represent the same perspective as those persons directly affected by the problem. Representatives of the target population should, whenever possible, be sought out to represent themselves in their own words; it should not be left to professionals and other concerned citizens to speak for them.

When dealing with the question of control over service availability to a target population, there can be both intracommunity and extracommunity sources of control—referring to whether the organization's headquarters are within or outside the community. In practice, external and internal patterned interactions tend to develop as community units work together. Examples of extracommunity sources of control are state and federal government funding of community-based health clinics. Resources are typically allocated through contracts that include regulations and performance expectations. Thus, various human service agencies within the local community interact with these extracommunity public entities. Relationships internal to a community have an important part in linking community subsystems together. Organizations with similar interests often form loosely knit federations to accomplish certain functions where there are common interests. For example, several women's groups may form a coalition to establish a battered women's shelter or a political action committee.

Not only are there horizontal relationships that tie one to local informal and formal groups and organizations within the community but also numerous vertical ties that transcend geographical boundaries. Local community autonomy may be reduced as extracommunity forces influence what one does and how one thinks. The importance of extracommunity forces on the target population within the local community must be considered in order to understand service distribution patterns. On the other hand, extracommunity forces may actually strengthen communities by providing more options and additional resources as well as requiring performance expectations so important to accountability.

How powerful the controlling entities become in a community often depends on the extent of citizen involvement. Before the Internet, citizen participation was primarily a face-to-face proposition, but today entire webs of relationships can develop sight unseen given multiple forms of electronic access. Citizen participation can take the form of a number of roles, including reviewing and commenting on various materials such as reports and proposals. This review process may be carried out electronically, in committee meetings, through requests for feedback from selected individuals, or through public hearings. Advising and consulting involves giving opinions about what needs to be done, whereas an advisory role usually involves a more formal ongoing mechanism such as a United Way advisory council or planning committee. Although advisory committees do not have the power of policy boards, they can have a strong voice because of their access to decision makers. In addition, their opinions may proactively affect proposals rather than simply reacting to programs designed by others. Governance occurs when citizens and consumers are placed in positions of control over decisions, such as policy statements, or become members on boards of directors. These types of positions allow for the greatest amount of control by citizens and consumers. For example, a consumer who serves on the governing board of a family service agency may convince other board members that quality child-care services for single mothers should be a top agency priority.

One cannot assume that citizen participation automatically goes hand in hand with changes practitioners initiate within the community. The concept of citizen participation is essential to democracy, but it will often involve groups who disagree with one another. Just as citizens may comprise the local board of planned parenthood, there are citizens who believe that some of the services offered by this agency are morally wrong. Whenever interested citizens and consumers participate in community activities, these types of clashes should be expected.

Simply knowing what groups and agencies are available is not enough. It is important for the macro practitioner to know whether they actually work together so that target groups do not fall through gaps in the service delivery system. Thus, the last task in the assessment process examines the linkages evident to the practitioner and requires a judgment as to whether these interacting units truly comprise a system that is responsive to multiple needs.

Determine Linkages between Units

Questions to be explored for this activity include:

- How are the various types of service units generally connected?
- What are the established linkages between units that serve the target population within *this* community?
- Where are linkages between service units obviously needed but not currently established?
- Are the interests of people of color, women, gay men, lesbians, transgendered persons, and other oppressed groups represented in the network established through linkages between units?

If there are multiple agencies with overlapping relationships and numerous types of services, is there a glue that holds the community's delivery system together? Certainly there may be competition among units, but there will also be connections. Just as the individual is embedded in a social network, group and organizational units are imbedded within a service community. These relational patterns may change over time.

Human Behavior

Critical Thinking Question: How might personal relationships play a role in how large agencies work together?

A number of writers have created typologies of how organizations relate to one another. Tobin, Ellor, and Anderson-Ray (1986) have identified five levels of interaction between human service agencies within the community: communication, cooperation, coordination, collaboration, and confederation. Bailey and Koney (2000) identify four levels: affiliation; federation, association, or coalition; consortium, network, or joint venture; and merger, acquisition, or consolidation. Table 6.5 provides an adaptation of these various categories, each of which are discussed next.

Communication. Communication can be formal or informal. Information and referral exemplifies formal communication that happens between units on a daily basis. Communication designed to increase interagency information and understanding may be enhanced through the use of websites such as the social networking site The Facebook, brochures, pamphlets, and media. In this sense, it is an affiliation process. Informal communication occurs between units as groups meet to discuss community issues, as staff engage in email exchanges or even talk about their programs at conferences. Although communication is assumed to occur, breakdowns in the delivery system often happen because this process of sharing information across units is not nurtured and there are so many ways to communicate that it may be hard to track these relationships. Often, written agreements are developed as a reminder of the importance of constant communication as staff change within organizations and new groups are formed within the community.

Cooperation. Cooperation occurs when units within the community agree to work toward similar goals. A local private child-care center may work closely with a public human service agency. Both want to provide support for single

Table 6.5	**Five Levels of Interaction Among Service Providers**		
Level of Interaction	Type of Relationship	Characteristics	Level of Provider Autonomy
Communication	Friendly, cordial	Sharing of ideas between units, including consultation	High
Cooperation	May be defined as an affiliation	Working together to plan and implement independent programs	High
Coordination	Could be a federation-, association-, or coalition-type relationship	Working together to avoid duplication and to assist one another in sharing information, advertising for one another, and making referrals	Moderate
Collaboration	Could be a consortium, network, or joint venture	Joining together to provide a single program or service, with shared resources	Moderate
Consolidation		Merging into one entity	Autonomy relinquished

Sources: Adapted from the works of Tobin, Ellor, & Anderson-Ray (1986) and Bailey & Koney (2000).

parents with young children, yet these units provide different resources. Social workers at the child-care center meet with staff at the human service agency once a month to discuss common concerns and to maintain a sense of continuity for parents who are clients of both agencies. The practitioner needs to know that these linkages are established and should also be actively involved in establishing them.

Corporate volunteerism represents a cooperative linkage between the for-profit and nonprofit sectors. The Levi Strauss Company provides an example. In U.S. communities in which Levi Strauss factories are located, there are community involvement teams. In one southeastern city, the company encouraged its employees to become actively involved with a multicounty nonprofit home aide service for elderly and physically disabled persons. Employees donated time to painting and repairing the homes of older shut-ins, as well as provided friendly visits to the agency's clients. If the target population is older widows, the social worker needs to know that the corporate sector is willing to address client needs.

The concept of corporate volunteerism is manifested in a number of ways (Brudney, 2005). A business may subsidize its employees by giving them release time to do community service work. Other companies will loan employees to human service agencies for a specified period of time so that the expertise required for a project can be provided at no cost to the agency. As employees near retirement, the for-profit sector often provides preretirement training in which postretirement volunteer opportunities are presented. In this way, the for-profit sector actually performs a recruitment function for the nonprofit service delivery system.

The interchange between the for-profit and nonprofit sectors also occurs in the form of corporate cash and in-kind contributions. Computer manufacturers may donate hardware to a local service agency, assisting in computerizing its information system. Restaurants donate food to homeless shelters. A local for-profit nursing home may open its doors to older community residents who live alone in a large metropolitan area during a time of anxiety over a crime wave. In a community, what cooperative efforts exist between service units within different sectors that focus on the target population's needs? Are race, ethnicity, gender, or sexual orientation factors that need to be taken into consideration in assessing service system interactions? Are any of these interests left out when they should be included?

Coordination. Coordination implies a concerted effort to work together. Often, separate units will draft agreements, outlining ways in which coordination will occur. Federations, associations, and coalitions may be formed.

In a continuum of care system that attempts to address the needs of such populations as older persons, those with disabilities, or people with AIDS within the community, coordination is necessary. As consumers exit the acute-care hospital, discharge planners work to develop a care plan. This requires knowledge of and close coordination with local service providers. Service plans often include a package to support the exiting client's needs—mobile meals, visiting nurses, and homemaker services. Depending on the level of disability and the length of time expected for recovery, this service plan may make the difference between returning home or convalescing in a long-term care facility. Extensive coordination is required.

The growth of case management within local communities reflects the need for interunit oversight as consumers receive services from multiple units. Case management programs attempt to provide a coordination function so that service delivery flows across informal and formal providers of care. Where there are case managers serving the target population, it is useful to learn how they view the relationships between service units that serve the target population and where they see gaps.

Collaboration. Collaboration implies the concept of a joint venture. Joint ventures are agreements in which two or more units within the community agree to set up a new program or service. This usually occurs when no one separate unit within the community is able or willing to establish the new venture alone. Consortia and networks are typically established for collaborative purposes.

For example, a local senior citizens center identified the need for home repair services for many of its participants. Because older persons tend to own older homes, repairs were often needed. The center did not have the resources to begin this program alone, but by working with a community action agency within the community, a home repair service was sponsored jointly by the center and the agency. Eventually, the home repair service became a separate unit and was incorporated as a nonprofit organization.

Coalition building is another form of collaboration. A coalition is a loosely developed association of constituent groups and organizations, each of whose primary identification is outside the coalition. For example, state coalitions have been formed in efforts to prevent child abuse. Community organizations, voluntary associations, public agencies, and interested individuals have joined forces to work toward a common goal—a safe environment for the nation's children. In coming together, a new voluntary association is formed. Even though the diverse members of this coalition represent various interests across community units, their collaboration on child welfare concerns provides a strong and focused network for change.

In some communities, agencies created to serve the needs of a special population collaborate to assess need, to examine the fit between needs and services, and to present a united front and a stronger voice in pursuing funding for programs. Many federal and state contracts require active collaboration or partnerships, even encouraging the sharing of staff and hiring of coordinators in order to ensure full participation. Requests for proposals (RFPs) from private foundations typically require grantees to be specific about how they will collaborate with others.

Confederation.   Units within the community may actually merge, often when one or both units become unable to function autonomously. A *horizontal merger* occurs, for example, when two mental health centers consolidate into a single organization. A *vertical merger* occurs when a hospital absorbs a home health provider. A *conglomerate merger* occurs when units within the community form a confederation of multiple smaller units under a large umbrella agency. These actions are generally limited to nongovernmental agencies.

Agency interaction inevitably involves competition and conflict. Change agents learn to cope with competition and conflict on a regular basis. These types of interactions will be discussed in Chapters 7 and 8 of this book.

Overall, the preceding tasks may be approached as a series of general questions to be applied to the task of assessing services in a community. Having looked at the community, consider these overriding concerns:

- Is the community generally sensitive to the needs of the target population?
- Are target population needs adequately assessed in this community?
- Is there a "continuum of care" concept or framework that guides service planning and funding for target population needs?
- How adequate is funding to meet target population needs in the community?
- Are services appropriately located for target group accessibility?
- What is the degree of cooperation, collaboration, and competition in providing services to the target population?
- What gaps in services and problems affecting the target population have been identified in the process of conducting this assessment?
- How does the race or ethnicity, gender, or sexual orientation of the target population, or some people in the population, affect the need for and provision of services?

SUMMARY

We began this chapter by discussing three reasons why macro practitioners need a framework for assessing communities. First, social work in general and macro practice in particular require an orientation toward the person-in-environment perspective. In this chapter, the community in which the target population functions comprises the environment. Second, communities change and professionals need a framework for understanding these changes. We have discussed three tasks that provide insight into how the target population is served within the community. Third, macro-level change requires an understanding of the history and development of a community as well as an assessment of its current status.

The community assessment provides one method of analyzing what has occurred and is occurring within the designated arena. Skilled macro practice requires (1) focused and precise data collection; (2) analysis of historical trends; and (3) a thorough understanding of qualitative elements that reflect human experiences, interactions, and relationships.

The assessment process begins with the definition of a target population. Following this, the human service response is explored, and collective needs are considered. Sources of help are then addressed, including informal sources such as households and social networks and mediating sources such as self-help groups and voluntary associations. Formal sources of services include nonprofit, public, and for-profit providers, and both the nature and orientation of services may differ in important ways across these auspices. Determining the competence of these systems in combining to meet needs in an effective way is the final consideration.

Based on data and information accumulated in the process of assessing a community's human service system, the macro practitioner must finally exercise professional judgment in evaluating the adequacy of resources devoted to the target population within the community. If the assessment has been thorough and productive, the practitioner will have gained enough understanding of what occurs within the community to identify and begin assessing needed change on behalf of the target population.

Framework for Assessing Community

Task 1: Focus on Target Population

Identify the Target Population

▶ What populations are in need of services, and how can they be accurately identified?

▶ Which population will be the target population of this assessment?

▶ Is this target population part of a community that is geographical, interactional, symbolic, or a combination?

▶ What priority is given to the needs of this target population in the community?

▶ What percentage of the target population is represented by people at risk of being underserved due to their race/ethnicity, gender, sexual orientation, age, disabilities, or other factors?

Understand Characteristics of Target Population Members

▶ What is known about the history of the target population in this community?

▶ How many persons comprise the target population, and what are their relevant characteristics?

▶ How geographically contained or dispersed are members of this group?

▶ How do persons in the target population perceive themselves and the history of their group?

Assess Target Population Needs

▶ What are feasible and appropriate ways to locate needs assessment data and other relevant information about the target population?

▶ What unmet needs are identified by persons in the target population?

▶ What is the history of efforts by persons in the target population to express their needs to others in the community?

▶ How do persons in the target population perceive their community and its responsiveness to their needs?

▶ Do community members outside the target population perceive that their needs are different from those of members within the target population?

▶ Do some members of the target population experience greater unmet needs due to their race/ethnicity, gender, sexual orientation, age, disabilities, or other factors?

Task 2: Determine Community Characteristics

Identify Community Boundaries

▶ What are the boundaries within which intervention on behalf of the target population will occur?

▶ Where are members of the target population located within the boundaries? Are they highly concentrated or scattered? Are the boundaries geographically, interest, and/or identity bound?

▶ How compatible are jurisdictional boundaries of health and human service programs that serve the target population?

Identify Community Strengths, Issues, and Problems

▶ What data sources are available, and how are these data used within the community?

▶ Who collects the data, and is this an ongoing process?

▶ What are the community's strengths?

▶ What are the major community issues?

▶ What are the major social problems affecting the target population in this community as perceived by their spokespersons?

▶ Are there subgroups of the target population that are experiencing major social problems?

▶ To what extent are these problems interconnected, and must some be solved before others can be addressed?

Understand Dominant Values

▶ What cultural values, traditions, and beliefs are important to the target population as individuals or as a whole?

▶ What are the predominant values that affect the target population within this community?

▶ What groups and individuals espouse these values, who opposes them, and are there value conflicts surrounding the target population?

▶ How do people in this community feel about giving and receiving help?

▶ What are the predominant shared perspectives in this community on inclusion of the target population in decisions that affect them?

Identify Formal and Covert Means of Oppression and Discrimination

▶ What differences are observed among members of the target population?

▶ What differences are observed among other groups within the community?

▶ Are there barriers (e.g., organizations, rules, procedures, and policies) that inhibit the target population from becoming fully integrated into the community?

▶ To what extent are the perspectives of people of color; women; gay men, lesbians, and transgendered persons; older persons; and persons with disabilities sought in decisions affecting the target population?

Task 3: Identify Community Structure

Recognize Sources of Power and Resource Availability

▶ What is the domain or jurisdiction involved, given the target population and problem?

▶ Who controls the funds?

▶ Who are the major community leaders within the domain identified who will respond to the concerns of the target population? Who will oppose their concerns?

▶ How accessible are services for the target population?

Examine Service-Delivery Units

▶ What informal units (e.g., household, natural, and social networks) are actively engaged in service delivery to the target population?

▶ What mediating units (e.g., self-help groups and voluntary or grassroots associations) are actively engaged in service delivery to the target population?

- What formal service delivery units (e.g., nonprofit, public, for-profit) are actively engaged in service delivery?
- Are there differences in service delivery that appear to be based on race or ethnicity, gender, sexual orientation, disability, age, or religion?

Identify Patterns of Influence, Control, and Service Delivery

- What groups, associations, and organizations (both extra- and local community) advocate for and provide assistance to the target population?
- How is resource distribution to the target population influenced by interaction (both electronic and face to face) within the community?
- What limits are placed on services to the target population, and who establishes these limits?
- What roles do citizens and consumers play in the control of services to the target population?

Determine Linkages between Units

- How are the various types of service units generally connected?
- What are the established linkages between units that serve the target population within this community?
- Where are linkages between service units obviously needed but not currently established?
- Are the interests of people of color, women, gay men and lesbians, and other oppressed groups represented in the network established through linkages between units?

Succeed with **PEARSON** **mysocialworklab**

Log onto **www.mysocialworklab.com** and answer the questions below. (*If you did not receive an access code to* **MySocialWorkLab** *with this text and wish to purchase access online, please visit* www.mysocialworklab.com.)

1. **Watch the Core Competency video: Advocating for Human Rights and Social and Economic Justice.** Is there any overt or covert oppression or discrimination that may be at work at a systemic level? What kind of policy changes may help?

2. **Read the MySocialWorkLibrary case study: An Alzheimer's Male Caregivers' Support Group.** What other services may help these caregivers? Identify the system or community supports (informal or formal) that are potential providers, and identify issues that may limit service accessibility for this population.

PRACTICE TEST

The following questions will test your knowledge of the content found within this chapter. For additional assessment, including licensing-exam-type questions on applying chapter content to practice, visit **MySocialWorkLab**.

1. When assessing a community, the authors recommend that a framework should be used
   a. as an interactive guide
   b. as a rigid static formula
   c. with multiple frameworks
   d. with supportive census data

2. According to the authors, which approach is preferred when assessing need within a particular population?
   a. use existing data
   b. gather new data
   c. generate historic data
   d. verify ancillary data

3. Shelter workers count the homeless people on the street in a certain area at 3:00 a.m. This is measuring
   a. incidence
   b. prevalence
   c. risk severity
   d. service usage

4. A team of case managers from different agencies meets monthly to avoid duplicating services. This is most directly
   a. cooperation
   b. coordination
   c. collaboration
   d. confederation

5. It is much easier to identify formal agencies in the community than it is to locate the multiple sources of informal support; yet, recognizing the importance of both is necessary. How might you learn about informal systems in a community? How might informal systems vary by population group?

ASSESS YOUR COMPETENCE

Use the scale below to rate your current level of achievement on the following concepts or skills associated with each competency presented in the chapter:

1	2	3
I can accurately describe the concept or skill.	I can consistently identify the concept or skill when observing and analyzing practice activities.	I can competently implement the concept or skill in my own practice.

_____ Can consider multiple aspects of community identity and identify the major priorities, important voices, and strengths found within them.

_____ Can effectively define community parameters in program planning, minimizing both over- and underinclusion.

_____ Can actively engage multiple systems and constituencies within a community when working on a planning effort.

_____ Can apply clinical knowledge about human behavior to personal interactions within inter-agency partnerships in order to promote meaningful collaborations.

7

Understanding Organizations

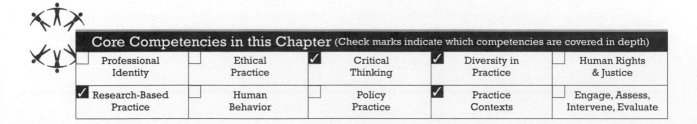

Core Competencies in this Chapter (Check marks indicate which competencies are covered in depth)				
☐ Professional Identity	☐ Ethical Practice	✔ Critical Thinking	✔ Diversity in Practice	☐ Human Rights & Justice
✔ Research-Based Practice	☐ Human Behavior	☐ Policy Practice	✔ Practice Contexts	☐ Engage, Assess, Intervene, Evaluate

INTRODUCTION

We live in a society of organizations. Whether they are large or small, formally or informally structured, it is organizations that carry out the core functions of our social order. As noted in previous chapters, prior to the Industrial Revolution most individuals lived in rural, agrarian settings in which they were personally responsible for meeting their basic needs. People built their own houses, drew their own water, grew their own food, made their own clothes, cared for their own aged, and attended, as best they could, to their own mental health needs. In modern times, however, the great majority of people live in large, complex, urban and suburban communities, where people's needs are met by specialized organizations, such as supermarkets, restaurants, department stores, municipal utilities, construction companies, schools, hospitals, and social welfare institutions.

Organizations also comprise the building blocks of larger macro systems, and individuals engage society through these organizations. Communities are critical societal units, yet individuals tend not to interact directly with their community but with organizations that make up the community. In fact, communities often can be understood not just as masses of individuals but as networks of organizations. Communities provide the superstructure within which organizations interact, but it is organizations that carry out most basic community functions (see Chapter 5). As sociologist Talcott Parsons (1960) noted, organizations may be seen as a type of social invention designed to allow a group of people to accomplish something that one person alone could not. Macro practice that involves working with communities therefore inevitably requires an understanding of organizations as well.

Of still further importance is the fact that most social workers, as well as most members of society, carry out their jobs from within organizations. In organizations other than the workplace, social workers usually have a consumer–provider relationship, and they are free to turn to alternative organizations if the relationship is unsatisfactory. Workplace environments, however, involve a different type of relationship that is not as easily terminated, and the need for a paycheck may force the social worker to persevere in a less-than-satisfactory relationship with the organization.

The organization may also be one that does not function well. Over time, agencies can stagnate, lose sight of their mission and goals, and begin to provide services that are unhelpful or even harmful to clients. This can occur because of inadequate resources, poor leadership, poor planning, inappropriate procedures or structures, or a combination of these factors. Social workers in these situations may have the option to leave, but doing so can create other dilemmas. We believe that professional social workers have an obligation to attempt to correct problems in their organizations for the benefit of both their clients and themselves. Just as agencies can lose a sense of mission and direction, so too can they regain it. The path to change begins with an understanding of the organization itself—its history, underlying theoretical principles and assumptions, and causes of current problems. The major focus of this chapter will be on understanding organizations in general.

Over time, an organization can stagnate, lose sight of its mission and goals.

The path to change begins with an understanding of the organization itself.

Defining Organizations

Organizations will be defined here as collectives of individuals gathered together to serve a particular purpose. The key word in this definition is *purpose.* Parsons (1960) contends that organizations are both defined and differentiated from other social constructions by their focus on achieving a particular objective or outcome.

As noted in previous chapters, the goals that people organize themselves to accomplish span the full range of human needs, from obtaining food, water, and shelter to achieving growth of the self. Goals may focus on production and profitability, as is usually the case in profit-making enterprises, or, as in human service agencies, the goal may be to improve the quality of life of persons outside the organization (e.g., helping someone resolve a drinking problem, or providing in-home services to help elderly persons prolong independent living). In each case, the organization exists because, as a collective, it makes possible the accomplishment of tasks that could not be completed as well or at all by a single individual.

As we discussed in Chapter 2, today's society was made possible in large measure by the rise of an "organizationalized" structure. This point is made by Etzioni (1964) who notes that from birth (typically in a hospital) to death (under the care of a hospital or hospice, followed by services handled by funeral home) and at almost all points in between (schools, churches, employers, etc.) we interact with and depend upon organizations throughout our lives.

This ubiquity of organizations is true in human services as well, and as social workers our roles within, interactions with, and attempts to influence organizations define much of what we do.

Clients often seek help because they have been unable to obtain education, employment, assistance, or other resources from organizations in their community. In turn, the services social workers provide often involve interacting with these same organizations on clients' behalf or helping clients improve their own ability to interact with these organizations. This is closely related to the basic social work function of case management mentioned in Chapter 6. Doing this well requires considerable effort spanning a range of agencies and service systems. Social workers with little or no idea of how organizations operate, how they relate to each other, or how they can be influenced and changed from both outside and inside are likely to be severely limited in their effectiveness.

Using Theory

Understanding organizations requires reviewing theories that seek to explain them. Organizational theories address how organizations arise, why they take certain forms, and how they operate. As with all theories, their value is judged by the accuracy with which they describe things (organizations) and predict events (organizational behavior). The best theories are those that offer the simplest summary of a phenomenon, cover the widest range of variation within it, and predict how it will act in the most accurate and verifiable ways. This usually involves *identification* of variables that characterize or bring about the phenomenon and *explanation* of how these variables interact.

As will become apparent, there are many different organization theories, and each emphasizes certain variables (e.g., organizational type or managerial style) or explanatory principles (e.g., organizations as open systems or organizations as cultures). By the end of the review, readers may feel overwhelmed by the number of different theories, unsure of how they are applied, or uncertain about which one(s) to choose. Thus, it may be helpful to keep in mind a few basic questions that serve as reminders of what the theories are intended to accomplish. These include:

- What variables emphasized by different theories are of greatest importance in my organization?
- Does my organization resemble or differ from those used as examples in the theories being discussed?
- Does my organization deliberately structure itself or operate in ways promoted by certain theories?
- Which theory best describes the structure of my organization? Which seems best able to predict its actions or decisions?
- Which theories help me understand how my organization differs from others?

Our review is by no means complete, as there is such a large body of theory and research that full coverage is beyond the scope of this book. Instead, we will present a brief review of the most important schools of thought about organizations, a summary of the main tenets of each school, and the strengths and weaknesses of each school, proceeding in roughly chronological order.

Theories as Frames and Filters

Bolman and Deal (2008) discuss the importance of "framing" in making sense of organizations. The picture captured within a frame offers one view of reality, but no frame captures everything, and understanding grows as multiple frames are examined. Each theory we will review frames organizations in a certain way, and the frames themselves fall into larger groups. Bolman and Deal identify four such groups that represent metaphors used to describe organizations. For some theories the metaphor is a *factory*; for others it is a *family*, a *jungle*, or something like a *temple* or *carnival*. We will describe each metaphor and refer to them at different points in the chapter to show similarities in the way theories frame organizations.

Another distinction we will offer is between *descriptive* and *prescriptive* schools of thought. Descriptive approaches are intended to provide a means of analyzing organizations in terms of certain characteristics or procedures. They often reflect a sociological approach to organizations, which seeks to understand organizations as social phenomena. In contrast, prescriptive approaches are designed as how-to guides, and their goal is to help build better organizations. Not surprisingly, because managers play important roles in deciding how to build and operate an organization, most prescriptive theories are part of the literature on management and leadership.

Table 7.1 illustrates these and other distinctions among various schools of thought about organizations. Primary theorists associated with each school are shown in the left column, after which the date of the first published work in each area appears. Also shown are the key concepts associated with each school, along with distinctions relating to whether each theory approaches organizations as *open systems* or *closed systems.* Open-system perspectives are concerned with how organizations are influenced by interactions with their environments, whereas closed-system approaches are more concerned with internal structures and processes.

Table 7.1   Comparative Dimensions of Key Organizational Theories

Theory (Theorist)	Dimension				
	Earliest Date	Metaphor*	Approach	Key Concepts	Conception of Organization in Environment
Bureaucracy (Weber)	1894 (approx.)	Factory	Descriptive	Structure Hierarchy	Closed
Scientific and universalistic management (Taylor; Fayol)	1911	Factory	Prescriptive	Efficiency Measurement	Closed
Human relations (Mayo)	1933	Family	Prescriptive	Social rewards Informal structure	Closed
Theory Y (McGregor)	1960	Family	Prescriptive	Higher-order rewards	Closed
Management by objectives (Drucker)	1954	Factory	Prescriptive	Setting goals and objectives	Closed
Organizational goals (Michels; Selznick)	1915		Descriptive	Goal displacement Natural systems	Closed
Decision making (Simon; March)	1957	Jungle	Descriptive	Bounded rationality Satisficing	Closed
Open systems (Katz & Kahn)	1966		Descriptive	Systems theory Inputs/outputs	Open
Contingency theory (Burns & Stalker; Morse & Lorsch; Thompson)	1961	Factory	(Varies)	Environmental constraints Task environment	(Varies)
Power and politics (Pfeffer; Wamsley & Zald)	1981	Jungle	(Varies)	Political economy	Open
Organizational culture (Schein, Cross, Weick, & Morgan)	1985	Carnival, temple	Prescriptive	Values, beliefs, diversity, sense-making, metaphor	Open
Quality-oriented management (Deming)	1951		Prescriptive	Consumer/quality Process focus	Open
Evidence-based management (Rousseau; Pfeffer & Sutton)	2002	Factory	Prescriptive	Data collection, analysis, feedback	Open
Organizational learning (Argyris & Schön; Senge)	1990	Carnival, temple	Prescriptive	Learning organiza-tion, systemic understanding	Open

*Bolman & Deal (2008)

Theories offer views of organizations from different perspectives, and any given view may sharpen the focus on one part of an organization while blurring others. Astronomers know that objects in space glow at different wavelengths, and they use filters to shut out some parts so that others can be seen. Galaxies that appear ordinary in visible light may show spectacular features in infrared. Organizational theories may be thought of as filters, restricting the glare from some areas so others come into view. We suggest that readers return to Table 7.1 regularly to help keep track of the distinctions between different schools of thought, especially with respect to the organizational variable(s) each theory emphasizes.

BUREAUCRACY AND ORGANIZATIONAL STRUCTURE

Organizational structure refers to the way relationships are constituted among persons within an organization. As we discussed earlier, one of the advantages of organizations is that individuals working in concert can accomplish much more than the same number of individuals working independently. This occurs when the activities of members of a group are coordinated in such a way that the work of one supports or enhances that of the others. Organizational structure is the means by which this coordination is achieved.

Individuals working in concert can accomplish much more than the same number of individuals working independently.

Even in informal task groups, members usually do not all attempt to do the same activities. Instead, they divide the responsibilities for tasks among themselves. Recognizing that members also have varying skills and interests, efforts are usually made to match individuals with tasks. Finally, to help ensure that everyone is working toward the common goal and supporting others' efforts, at least one individual in the organization usually takes on a management role. These aspects of organizational functioning—including task specialization, matching of person and position, and leadership—are examples of structural characteristics that are common to virtually all organizations and that provide a means by which they may be analyzed and understood.

Among the earliest and most important conceptual work on organizational structure was that of German sociologist Max Weber. Weber coined the term "bureaucracy" and applied it to a particular form of organization. The *bureaucracy* is an "ideal type," meaning that it is a conceptual construct, and it is unlikely that any organization fits perfectly with all the characteristics of a bureaucracy. The bureaucracy typifies descriptive organizational theories in that it provides a model against which organizations can be compared, after which they can be described in terms of the extent to which they fit this model. Also, because many of the organizations Weber described *were* factories, his work corresponds to that metaphor. It should be noted that Weber did not conceptualize the bureaucratic model as a goal toward which organizations should strive, but as a way to understand organizational structure and variation among organizations.

The following characteristics of a bureaucracy are adapted from Weber (1947 [1924]) and subsequent summaries of his work (Rogers, 1975). They include:

1. Positions in the organization are grouped into a clearly defined hierarchy.
2. Job candidates are selected on the basis of their technical qualifications.

3. Each position has a defined sphere of competence. In a hospital, for example, a physician has exclusive authority to prescribe medications, but a financial officer determines the vendor and the quantity of bulk purchases.

4. Positions reflect a high degree of specialization based on expert training.

5. Positions typically demand the full working capacity (in other words, full-time employment) of their holders.

6. Positions are career oriented. There is a system of promotion according to seniority or achievement, and promotion is dependent on the judgment of superiors.

7. Rules of procedure are outlined for rational coordination of activities.

8. A central system of records is maintained to summarize the activities of the organization.

9. Impersonality governs relationships between organizational members.

10. Distinctions are drawn between private and public lives and positions of members.

Figure 7.1 shows the structure of a large human service organization these rules might produce. Under a single executive selected for his or her technical

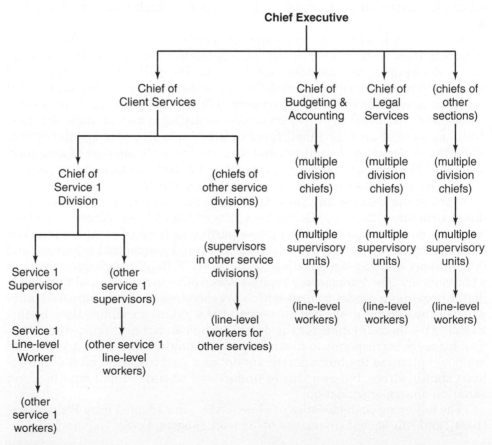

Figure 7.1

Example of Bureaucratic Structure—Human Service Organization competence, the organization is divided into sections by tasks such as client services, budgeting and accounting, and legal services. These are further subdivided by function so that most line-level workers in each supervisory unit perform one particular function, those in the next unit a different function, and so forth. The structure resembles a wide, flat pyramid in which there are many people at the line level and few at the administrative level.

Weber was interested in this organizational model because he believed it reflected a change in the values of society as a whole. In fact, his work began with a more general concern about the way power is legitimized in social relations—why people consent to do the will of others. He used *authority* as the term for power wielded with the consent of those being led, and he identified three major forms:

1. *Traditional Authority.* The right to govern bestowed on kings, emperors, popes, and other patrimonial leaders. This type of authority rests in the ruler's claim to historic or ancestral rights of control. It is associated with long-lasting systems and can be passed from generation to generation of rulers.

2. *Charismatic Authority.* Dominance exercised by an individual through extraordinary personal heroism, piety, fanaticism, martial skill, or other traits. Systems based on this type of authority tend to be unstable and transitional.

3. *Rational/Legal Authority.* Power assigned on the basis of the ability to achieve instrumental goals. This type of authority derives from the legitimacy given to rational rules and processes and from expertise rather than hereditary claims.

Bureaucracies are the embodiment of rational/legal authority, and the fact that they have become a dominant organizational model reflects societal movement away from systems based on traditional or charismatic authority.

Strengths. Bureaucratic structure is designed to help an organization complete its tasks by maximizing the *efficiency* with which those tasks are carried out. Weber (1947) argues that the bureaucratic model has proliferated because it makes organizations more efficient, and he believes that organizations using bureaucratic principles have the same advantage over other organizations that mechanized work has over manual work.

As bureaucracies evolved, this technical superiority helped bring about the Industrial Revolution, which led to immense growth in the size and complexity of manufacturing, distribution, and other commercial organizations.

Critical Thinking

Critical Thinking Question: Could an organization promote the positive aspects and minimize the negative aspects of bureaucracy. How?

Box 7.1 Weber's Theory of Bureaucracy Structure

▸ **Purpose.** Descriptive

▸ **Key Features.** Bureaucracies emphasize efficiency of operation. Decision making is done at the top, and authority to do so is based on expertise rather than inherited authority. Tasks are specialized, organizational relationships are impersonal, and a "by-the-book" orientation restricts individual discretion.

▸ **Strengths and Weaknesses.** Organizations with bureaucratic structure are efficient at repetitive tasks such as mass production of material goods, but they can be dehumanizing. Also, they are less efficient at variable tasks, in unpredictable environments, and with staff who must exercise professional judgment.

It also provided a blueprint for vast governmental institutions, from the military to large agencies responsible for various health and human services. Bureaucratic organization helped these organizations serve far more people than before, as evidenced by the tens of millions who receive Social Security payments, Medicare, and other benefits.

In some ways, the practice of social work fits well with bureaucratic organization. For example, the profession encourages job specialization based on expertise and the promotion of individuals as they accumulate skills and seniority. The profession also subscribes to the belief that people's abilities count for more than who they know or how well liked they are, and fame or fortune outside the organization do not count for more than the person's competence. In other words, although we do not often think of it in such terms, social workers and the settings in which they work have embraced many fundamental principles of bureaucratic organization.

Weaknesses.   Despite the technical merits of bureaucracies, describing an organization as "bureaucratic" typically conjures images of a vast, impersonal, monolithic body that is anything but efficient. Most organizations go out of their way to avoid being called bureaucracies, and in everyday usage the term is almost always negative. Why is this so? Weber did not believe that the bureaucracy was a model for poor organization, and research has shown that bureaucratic structure can indeed contribute to greater productivity and efficiency. The answer is that as bureaucratic structure became more prevalent it showed not only its benefits but also its limitations.

The machinelike qualities to which Weber called attention can be perfectly suited to manufacturing firms but disastrous in organizations in which the goal is not to process raw materials but respond to human needs. One example of the ways bureaucracies can go wrong was offered by Merton (1952) in his study of employees of bureaucratic organizations. He found that over time, workers' concern for doing their job well became secondary to meeting procedural and paperwork requirements. Merton called this mindset the "bureaucratic personality." He also coined the term 'trained incapacity" to describe the ways in which bureaucratic personalities lose focus on the needs of those they serve. He saw the problem as an inevitable consequence of tightly structured chains of command and pressures for rule compliance that eventually force on all workers the realization that their interests are best served not by doing the job well but by doing it "by the book."

To further the study of how bureaucracies fall short of maximal functioning, various observers have gone beyond structural elements to address factors such as goals, decision-making processes, technology, and the role of the individual within the organization. Their work forms the basis for many schools of thought that followed Weber and that will be reviewed here. Questions have also been raised about whether racial or ethnic minorities and women are disadvantaged in bureaucratic organizations, or whether the bureaucratic model reflects a male orientation to organization or provides advantages to males (Gorman & Kmec, 2009). As employees are promoted through lower and middle levels to upper-level administrative positions, white males have often dominated the highest levels and denied access to others. This phenomenon has been referred to as the *glass ceiling*. Women and minorities can reach a level at which they have a view of functioning at the top but cannot get there because those who select persons for top positions often value sameness and fear diversity.

MANAGEMENT THEORIES

Scientific and Universalistic Management

Some of the earliest writings on managing tasks and functions in the work-place were by Frederick Taylor, a U.S. industrialist and educator whose principal works appeared in the first two decades of the 1900s. Taylor had been both a laborer and a mechanical engineer, and he wanted to identify management techniques that would lead to increased productivity. He also believed many organizational problems were tied to misunderstandings between managers and workers. Managers thought workers were lazy and unmotivated, and they mistakenly believed they understood workers' jobs. Workers thought that managers cared only about exploiting workers, not about productivity.

To solve these problems, Taylor (1911) developed what came to be known as *scientific management*, which derives its name from his emphasis on the need for managers to analyze the workplace scientifically. One of the first steps is to complete a careful study of the work itself, usually by identifying the best worker and studying that person. The goal is to find the optimal way of doing a job—in Taylor's words the "one best way"—to develop the best tools for completing it, fit workers' abilities and interests to particular assignments, and find the level of production the average worker can sustain.

The next step is to provide incentives to increase productivity. Taylor's favorite tool for this was the *piece-rate wage*, in which workers are paid for each unit they produce. In this manner, more units are produced, unit cost is reduced, organizational productivity and profitability are enhanced, and workers earn more.

Taylor was seeking an industrial workplace in which the traditional animosity between management and labor could be overcome by recognition of the mutual aims of each. His points in this regard are summarized by George (1968):

1. The objective of good management is to pay high wages and have low unit production costs;

2. To achieve this objective management has to apply scientific methods of research and experiment . . . in order to formulate principles and standard processes that would allow for control of the manufacturing operations;

3. Employees have to be scientifically placed in jobs where materials and working conditions are scientifically selected so that standards can be met;

4. Employees should be scientifically and precisely trained to improve their skill in performing a job so that the standard of output can be met;

5. An air of close and friendly cooperation has to be cultivated between management and workers in order to ensure the continuance of a psychological environment that would make possible the application of the other principles. (p. 89)

As can be seen from these principles, Taylor's interests were as much in the area of organizational psychology as in traditional management theory. Subsequent to his work, other writers focused more narrowly on Taylor's concern with maximizing organizational productivity, and they began to ask whether broader principles could be identified that encapsulated the ideals of rational management. These writers eventually became known as the *universalistic management* theorists. A prominent member of this group was French industrialist Henri Fayol, who focused on specifying the structural attributes of organizations that managers should develop and promote. Scott (1981) and others have suggested ways in which Fayol's ideas can be condensed into a few characteristics that describe organizations which adopt his management principles. These include:

1. *Pyramidal Shape:* Hierarchical management advocated by Fayol produces a structure having a single decision maker at the top and a gradually widening chain of command similar to that illustrated in Figure 7.1.

2. *Single Supervisor:* Each person reports to only one immediate superior.

3. *Restricted Span of Supervision:* No supervisor is responsible for more than a moderate number of subordinates, usually six to eight.

4. *Autonomy in Routine Performance:* Subordinates are responsible for routine matters covered by standard rules; supervisors are responsible for unusual circumstances not covered by those rules.

5. *Specialization by Task:* A division of labor exists within the organization through which similar functions are grouped together (e.g., those that are similar in terms of purpose, process, clientele, or location).

6. *Differentiation of Line and Support Functions:* Line functions are those that are central to the completion of core organizational tasks; staff functions are supportive or advisory.

Although somewhat broader in scope, the outcomes intended from the application of these principles were similar to the goals of scientific management. These included stability, predictability (especially with respect to the manufacturing process), and maximum individual productivity. Also, although these writers were prescriptive management theorists—whereas Weber was a descriptive sociological observer—it is not difficult to see that a manager adhering to these principles would create an organization that incorporated many characteristics of a bureaucracy.

Strengths.   Although it clearly is not a manufacturing enterprise, social work has adopted a number of "scientific" approaches to practice. For example, many social workers have specialized roles, and within these they follow procedures and protocols for serving certain types of cases. Also, as part of the profession's commitment to research-based practice, individual social workers are expected to study the progress of clients in their caseloads by using methods

---

Box 7.2   Scientific and Universalistic Management Theories

▸ **Purpose.** Prescriptive

▸ **Key Features.** Although not influenced by Weber, these theories essentially describe how to create a bureaucracy from the management side. Again, the emphasis is on efficiency, top-down control, and specialized work. Managers are also responsible for studying the work itself and teaching staff the "one best way" of doing each job.

▸ **Strengths and Weaknesses.** Organizations managed by these principles can achieve the original goals of stability, predictability, and efficient production, but, as with bureaucracies, the result can be an oppressive and monotonous workplace.

such as single-subject designs. In a similar way, requirements for outcome evaluation have placed more rigorous demands on the design of interventions and the measurement of success. Although these trends do not embrace the most mechanistic aspects of Taylor's notions, they echo his concern for operations based on careful analysis of the work itself.

Weaknesses. The works of Taylor and Fayol were subsequently criticized for what Mouzelis (1967) termed a "technicist" bias; that is, both writers tended to treat workers as little more than cogs in a wheel. This is the ultimate extension of what Bolman and Deal (2008) term the "organization-as-factory" metaphor. In reality, of course, no two people, and no two workers, are exactly alike; thus, the "one best way" of doing a job may be unique to the person doing it. In fact, forcing the same approach on all workers may decrease both productivity and worker satisfaction. Also, because these approaches addressed means for increasing the output of workers, they were subjected to considerable criticism (especially by writers in the labor movement) for facilitating the exploitation of workers by management.

Because both Taylor and Fayol were interested primarily in industrial organizations, their work was usually thought to have limited applicability to human service organizations during the first few decades in which social work began drawing on management theories. For example, the predominant approach to allocating work responsibility followed that of physicians, that is, assigning "cases" or clients to social workers who had a loosely structured mandate to employ their professional skill to meet client needs. As a result, the focus of scientific and universalistic management on precision, measurement, and specialization of function fit poorly with this type of job design.

Human Relations

As the field of organizational management and analysis grew, the works of Taylor, Weber, and others were criticized for their focus on rational, structural approaches to understanding organizations. The earliest of these criticisms addressed Taylor's assumptions about factors that motivate organizational actors. Critics took issue with the notion that workers are oriented to the instrumental goals of the organization and respond most readily to material rewards (e.g., piece-rate wages) designed to further those goals. One such group sought to test Taylor's principles concerning productivity enhancement. Its members eventually concluded that organizations must be viewed as social institutions, and it is social factors—friendship, belongingness, and group solidarity—that are most important in understanding how organizational actors behave.

Often referred to as the *human relations school*, this view had its origins in the so-called Hawthorne studies conducted in the 1920s. Experimenters placed a group of workers in a special room and varied the intensity of the lighting and other environmental factors to observe the effect on productivity. Initially they found that the greater the intensity of lighting, the more productivity rose. However, when they reduced the lighting, expecting to find reduced productivity, they found that productivity continued to grow even in dim lighting. The researchers concluded that the cause of the increase in productivity was *social factors.* Workers appeared not to respond to the lighting but instead to the fact that they were members of a group for which they wanted to do their part, and it was this sense of social responsibility that prompted better performance.

Practice Contexts

Critical Thinking Question: Discuss the pros and cons of using scientific management for the helping process in human service organizations.

Subsequent experiments on the effect of social factors on organizations, including many from the field of industrial psychology, examined broader questions about the behavior of groups. The basic tenets of the human relations approach that developed from these findings are detailed below (adapted from Etzioni, 1964):

1. *It is not the physical limits of workers that determine output levels but expectations among workers themselves regarding what levels are reasonable and sustainable.*

2. *The approval or disapproval of coworkers is more important than monetary rewards or penalties in determining how workers act, and coworker approval or disapproval can negate or enhance monetary rewards.* Studies found that workers who were capable of producing more would often not do so. The reason seemed to be that they were unwilling to exceed what the group as a whole could do, even if this meant a reduction in their earnings.

3. *Individual employees' behaviors or motivations tend to be less important than those of employees as a group.* Attempts by management to influence workers' behavior are more successful if aimed at the whole group rather than at individuals because the latter may be unwilling to change unless accompanied by everyone.

4. *The role of leadership is important in understanding social forces in organizations, and this leadership may be either formal or informal.* On a factory floor, for example, there may be an official foreman (formal leader) and a respected worker to whom others listen (informal leader). Informal leadership influences behavior in ways that can either amplify or negate formal leadership. In addition, organizations tend to function better if formal and informal leaders are the same.

Important implications of these tenets include the idea that individuals may be equally or more likely to draw satisfaction from social relationships in the organization than from its instrumental activities. Also important is the notion that workers' willingness to follow management comes from their willingness to follow members of the work group. The key to making effective changes in organizational operations thus lies not in rules and formal structure but in the quality of personal affiliations and the coherence of informal structures. Managers who succeed in increasing productivity are most likely to be those who are responsive to the social needs of workers.

Another writer associated with this school, Mary Parker Follett (2005 [1926]), noted that social relations also come into play with regard to how managers treat their subordinates. Arguing that "probably more industrial trouble has been caused by the manner in which orders are given than in any other way" (p. 153), she urged managers to recognize that workers remain people rather than parts of a machine, and retaining basic standards of interpersonal communication would ultimately facilitate productive functioning.

Strengths.   Human relations theory has had an important effect on organizational thinking. With respect to management practice, its tenets have provided a counterbalance to the formalized and often rigid approaches of other management theories. It has also influenced descriptive approaches by serving as a reminder of how the needs and interests of individual employees can be critical determinants of organizational behavior. Later theories would develop around genuine empowerment for employees, but human relations management eventually died out as an approach to running an organization when it was recognized that a happy workforce was not necessarily a productive one, and other variables began to enter the equation. Nevertheless, human relations called attention to factors such as teamwork, cooperation, leadership, and positive attention from management that remain relevant today. Its emphasis on these aspects of interpersonal relations made it the first of several schools of thought to employ what Bolman and Deal (2008) term the "family" metaphor of organizations.

Weaknesses. Criticisms of the human relations school fall into two major categories. First, a number of writers have raised concerns about the methodological soundness of studies on which these views are based. For example, the original Hawthorne experiments have earned an infamous place in the history of research methodology. The term *Hawthorne effect* refers to the fact that experimental subjects may perform in certain ways simply because they know they are being studied. In this case, workers in the Hawthorne plant may have raised production not because of lighting or a sense of group solidarity but because of self-consciousness about being observed. Other critics have argued that the design of these studies was such that expectations about economic incentives might still have influenced the subjects, further undermining the supposed effect of social factors (Sykes, 1965).

A second line of criticism argues that it is possible to overestimate the importance of social factors in organizations. For example, various studies have indicated that informal organizational structures may not be as prevalent or powerful as human relations writers suggest, that democratic leadership is not always associated with greater productivity or worker satisfaction, and that economic benefits *are* important to many employees. Also, Landsberger (1958) argued that emphasizing worker contentedness at the expense of economic rewards could foster an administrative model that is even more manipulative and paternalistic than might be the case with scientific management. This is because human relations theory, like other management approaches of the time, concentrated power and decision making at the top and was never intended to empower employees or assist them in gaining genuine participation in the running of the organization. If people were treated more humanely under human relations management, it was because proponents believed this would lead to greater productivity, not because of a desire to create a more democratic workplace. Finally, an emphasis on strengthening personal/social relationships within the workplace may also have disadvantaged some groups of employees over the years. Social relationships within organizations play a role in identifying and securing jobs and promotions for people, but women and ethnic minorities have often been excluded from personal networks that control these rewards.

Theory X and Theory Y

Later writers drew on the work of human relations theorists but incorporated them into more general frameworks addressing human motivation. One example is the work of Douglas McGregor (1960) who adopted Abraham Maslow's hierarchy of needs as a framework for understanding workers' actions. To McGregor, organizational actors were not just social creatures but *self-actualizing* beings whose ultimate goal in organizations is to meet higher-order needs. To illustrate this point, he identified two contrasting approaches to management that he labeled "Theory X" and "Theory Y." *Theory X* includes traditional views of management and organizational structure such as those of Taylor, Weber, and others, which, McGregor argued, make the following assumptions about human nature:

1. The average human being has an inherent dislike of work and will avoid it if [he or she] can. (p. 33)

2. Because of this human characteristic of dislike of work, most people must be coerced, controlled, directed, [or] threatened with punishment to get them to put forth adequate effort toward the achievement of organizational objectives.

3. The average human being prefers to be directed, wishes to avoid responsibility, has relatively little ambition, wants security above all. (p. 34)

These assumptions led to what McGregor sees as the domineering, oppressive aspects of Theory X management.

In contrast, *Theory Y* assumes that the task of management is to recognize workers' higher-order needs and design organizations that allow them to achieve these needs. Its assumptions are that:

1. The expenditure of physical and mental effort in work is as natural as play or rest.

2. External control and the threat of punishment are not the only means for bringing about effort toward organizational objectives. [People] will exercise self-direction and self-control in the service of objectives to which [they are] committed.

3. Commitment to objectives is a function of the rewards associated with their achievement.

4. The average human being learns, under proper conditions, not only to accept but to seek responsibility.

5. The capacity to exercise a relatively high degree of imagination, ingenuity, and creativity in the solution of organizational problems is widely, not narrowly, distributed in the population.

6. The intellectual potentialities of the average human being [in modern organization] are only partly utilized. (pp. 47–48)

The critical feature of this approach is its break from the management-dominated orientation of previous theories in favor of placing decision-making power with lower-level actors. Such loosely structured organizations are seen

---

Box 7.3   Human Relations and Theory Y

▶ **Purpose.** Prescriptive

▶ **Key Features.** These theories assume that workers are motivated by factors other than wages. Human relations theorists noted that social relations among staff can enhance production, and they sought to enhance performance by promoting group cohesion and adding social rewards to the range of reinforcements available in the workplace. Others added needs such as self-actualization to the list of additional motivating factors.

▶ **Strengths and Weaknesses.** Managers are more likely to recognize workers' higher-order needs (beyond merely a paycheck) and expand their awareness of potential motivating factors. Flawed early research overestimated the effect of social influences on production, and the model continued to place discretion and authority solely in the hands of administrators. Later writers argued that increased worker participation would enhance both productivity and workers' ability to meet their needs.

as best for promoting productivity by allowing employees to meet higher-order needs through their work.

Strengths.   McGregor's analysis was supported by the research of Frederick Herzberg (1966). Herzberg studied motivation among employees, dividing motivational elements into two categories: *extrinsic factors* and *intrinsic factors.* Factors extrinsic to the job include wages, hours, working conditions, and benefits. Intrinsic factors have to do with motivators that lie within the work itself, such as satisfaction with successful task completion. Herzberg discovered that, in the long run, extrinsic factors tend to keep down the levels of dissatisfaction with the job, but they do not motivate workers to work harder. Only intrinsic factors, such as the ability to use one's own creativity and problem-solving skills, motivate employees to become more productive. Herzberg's work helped foster ongoing interest in *job redesign*, which, broadly defined, seeks to increase the intrinsic rewardingness of work. Research has shown that appropriate job design positively influences not only productivity in industrial settings but effectiveness in service-related realms (Hakanen, Schaufeli, & Ahola, 2008; Leana, Appelbaum, & Shevchuk, 2009). In addition, better job design has been linked with decreased absenteeism (Pfeiffer, 2010), decreased turnover (Simons & Jankowski, 2008), and increased job satisfaction (Chang, Chiu, & Chen, 2010).

Weaknesses.   Results of other studies indicated that there are limits to how loosely structured an organization's operations can become and still function effectively. Morse and Lorsch (1970) found that organizations in which tasks were loosely defined and variable appeared to fit well with Theory Y management styles. However, those in which tasks were predictable, repetitive, and required great precision functioned better when organized according to principles McGregor labeled as Theory X. The importance for social work of McGregor's work is that social workers' tasks are often loosely defined and seemingly well suited to Theory Y management, yet many human service organizations are still operated with a Theory X mentality. Ultimately, no single management model applies equally well across all types of organizations, and it was this lesson from their 1970 study that prompted Morse and Lorsch to outline the foundations of contingency theory, which is discussed later in this chapter.

Management by Objectives (MBO)

Fundamental to the conceptualization and functioning of an organization is *purpose*, a commonly shared understanding of the reason for existence of the organization. In most cases, purpose has to do with productivity and profit. Taylor, Weber, and human relations theorists all stressed a different approach to the achievement of purpose, but all made certain assumptions about purpose in organizations.

Peter Drucker (1954) proposed that purpose was often assumed by theorists to be clearer than it actually was; thus, a key function of management was to establish what it is that an organization seeks to accomplish. He suggested that organizational goals and objectives should be made the central construct around which organizational life revolves. Instead of focusing on structure, precision, or efficiency and hoping for an increase in productivity and profit, Drucker proposed beginning with the desired outcome and working backward to create an organizational design to achieve that outcome. Termed *management by objectives (MBO),* this approach involves both short-range and long-range planning, and it is through the planning process that organizational structures and procedures necessary to achieve an outcome are established.

Drucker identifies several elements of MBO's strategic planning process. *Expectations* are the hoped-for outcomes, and an example might be the addition of a new service or client population in an agency, or it might be an improvement in the number of clients served or results of their services (e.g., an increase of 25 percent in client satisfaction over current levels). *Objectives* are means of achieving expectations, such as the steps that must be taken to add or improve programs. *Assumptions* reflect what is presumed about how meeting the objectives will achieve expectations (e.g., that the use of better service techniques will improve outcomes).

Other elements in the process include consideration of *alternative courses of action*, such as the costs and benefits of making no changes. Also, the plan must take into account what Drucker terms the "decision structure," which represents the constraints that exist on how much the plan can do, and the "impact stage," which addresses costs associated with implementing the plan and limitations it may place on other initiatives or operations. Finally, once implemented a plan will have *results*, and the result of an MBO process is measured by the extent to which actual outcomes match the original expectations.

Strengths.   One major advantage of MBO is its emphasis on producing clear statements, made available to all employees, about expectations for the coming year. Techniques are also developed for breaking goals and objectives into tasks, and for monitoring progress throughout the year. An organization that follows MBO principles tends to improve collaboration and cooperative activity.

Many modern approaches to management include various aspects of MBO in their model. For example, organizations often require the development of an annual plan in which goals and objectives in each programmatic area are made explicit. Also significant has been the growth of attention paid to *outcomes*, both in commercial and human service organizations. Social work as a profession was for many years primarily concerned with *process* in the development of its practice approaches. Management by objectives, together with the accountability movement, establishes program outcomes as the major criteria for determining funding and program continuation.

Weaknesses.   Management by objectives adopts a particularistic approach to leadership in which, according to some critics, the attention of managers is concentrated on the trees rather than on the forest. In other words, management

---

Box 7.4 Management by Objectives (MBO)

▶ **Purpose.** Prescriptive

▶ **Key Features.** MBO argues that management must ensure the continuing presence of clear goals and objectives for the organization. Once these are in place, the task of management becomes one of decision making regarding how best to achieve each objective. Success is measured by the extent to which objectives were achieved.

▶ **Strengths and Weaknesses.** MBO focuses attention on results and reorients management toward the question of how to accomplish desired outcomes. On a day-to-day basis, however, consideration is given mostly to small steps necessary for reaching intermediate objectives, which may lead to a loss of awareness of eventual end goals.

requires large-scale strategic thinking in addition to small-scale tactical thinking, yet MBO focuses mostly on the latter. Another criticism is that, although it is sometimes admirable to be clear and direct about organizational expectations, the concept of building organizational life around goals and objectives has its drawbacks. Objectives can serve simply to reinforce existing power structures within an organization (Dirsmith, Heian, & Covaleski, 1997), and, as we will see in the next section, the stated goals of an organization can be subverted by efforts to promote unstated goals.

ORGANIZATIONAL GOALS AND THE NATURAL-SYSTEM PERSPECTIVE

One theme made explicit in Drucker's MBO model is the assumption that organizations should be directed by rational actions designed to achieve certain goals. This assumption began to be questioned by writers concerned about whether rational, goal-directed, formalized structures are the best way of serving organizational goals, and whether these goals provide a clear direction. In fact, the idea that the goals of an organization and its members could gradually change had been present in organizational literature for some time.

In the early 1900s, Robert Michels (1949 [1915]) examined political parties as examples of large modern organizations. Noting the rise of oligarchies, or small groups of key decision makers, within the parties, he suggested that these and other organizations have identifiable life cycles that proceed through the following steps:

1. The organization develops a formal structure.

2. The original leaders move into positions at the upper levels of the hierarchy.

3. These individuals discover the personal advantages of having such positions.

4. They begin to make more conservative decisions that might not advance their original cause as forcefully as before but that are less likely to jeopardize their own security or that of the organization.

5. The organization's original goals are pushed aside, and it becomes mostly a means for achieving the personal goals of upper-level administrators.

Michels called this the "Iron Rule of Oligarchy," concluding that it is an unavoidable fate of large organizations that adopt bureaucratic approaches to structuring themselves.

Philip Selznick (1949) found a related mechanism in his study of the early years of the Tennessee Valley Authority (TVA). The TVA was a New Deal-era agency created to promote economic development in the poverty-stricken Tennessee River valley. While its most visible accomplishments were large public works such as dams and electrification projects, it also sought to replace ossified political structures with new ones built through grassroots organizing. Because of its enormous scope and rather vague goals, the TVA delegated decision making to subunits responsible for projects in local areas. In this way, its aims became vulnerable to *cooptation* by the same local authorities it had sought to replace. Their involvement brought needed influence, but their own goals began to turn the organization in unintended directions. The TVA increasingly became a structure for serving goals defined by the interests of local units rather than its original aims.

Writers such as Etzioni (1964) refer to this process as "goal displacement." The formal goals of the organization—*stated goals*—and those of decision makers—*real goals*—may be very different, but through mechanisms such as cooptation, growth of oligarchies, and development of the bureaucratic personality, it is usually stated goals that are displaced by real goals representing the interests of decision makers. Selznick (1957) saw this as part of a larger process he called "institutionalization." An institutionalized organization takes on a life of its own that may have more to do with the interests of its own participants than with the instrumental goals it is supposedly serving.

Several points are worth noting here. First, Weber viewed the bureaucratic model as the embodiment of rational behavior, but he viewed rationality as the process of determining how best to serve organizational goals. Theorists such as Selznick point out that organizations are run by people, and it is those people who decide what goals to serve. People, in turn, are biological organisms, and organisms seek first and foremost to preserve themselves. Those who run an organization also seek to preserve it, so the organization acts as a *natural system*—an entity that is aware of its own self-interest and acts to protect itself.

In addition to applying the *organization-as-organism* metaphor to processes such as goal displacement, Bolman and Deal (2008) would add their metaphor of *organization-as-jungle*. In a jungle's constant battle for survival, animals that are not predators are usually prey. To the extent that this is the case within an organization, it is not difficult to see how protecting and advancing oneself becomes more important than serving lofty but sometimes vague organizational goals. It is also not hard to see how oligarchies form and seek to bend the organization toward their interests rather than toward its stated goals.

Strengths.   Recognition of the importance of organizational goals, particularly survival goals, has proved to be an important contribution to the development of organizational and management theory. These views have also had considerable influence on the study of human service organizations, such as a well-known analysis of the March of Dimes (Sills, 1957). Organized originally to unify the efforts of volunteers attempting to raise money for polio research, the March of Dimes became one of the vanguard organizations in the fight

---

Box 7.5   Organizational Goals and Goal Displacement

▶ **Purpose.** Descriptive

▶ **Key Features.** Writers in this school point out that organizational actors tend to be driven more by personal than organizational goals. Organizations can thus be redirected to serve the self-interests of administrators or others. Also, because organizations are made up of many individuals, they act less like rational systems than organic (natural) ones, seeking to protect themselves just as individuals do.

▶ **Strengths and Weaknesses.** Viewing organizations as organic systems helped draw theoretical attention away from its earlier focus on internal factors, such as structure or management style, and reorient it toward issues of how organizations interact with their environments. This made organizational behavior a new focus of attention. Still, some findings showed that goal displacement and the rise of self-serving administrations is not inevitable in bureaucracies, and variables such as information flow may determine whether this occurs.

against polio nationwide. These efforts were eventually successful in that funding from the March of Dimes helped lead to Jonas Salk's development of the first polio vaccine. This and subsequent vaccines proved to be so effective that polio quickly became a rare problem, which meant that the activities of the March of Dimes were no longer needed. Having successfully achieved its goal, the organization could simply have disbanded, but it did not. Instead, it took on a whole new cause—birth defects—and its efforts shifted toward solving this new problem.

Sills contends that this is the behavior that would be predicted by the natural-system (organization-as-organism) model. The survival imperative prevails even if it means the system must alter its original reason for existence. The result is not necessarily bad, because in this case an organization with experience in countering public health problems was able to turn itself toward new challenges. However, as we will review at greater length in the next chapter, organizations with too strong a focus on their own survival can cease to be effective in providing services.

Weaknesses.   Physicists are accustomed to searching for laws to describe physical phenomena, but there are few relationships in the social realm that are predictable enough to justify the term *law*. Not surprisingly, research on the behavior of groups has raised doubts about whether goal displacement and the rise of oligarchical control are inevitable. For example, instances have been found of bureaucratic organizations in which oligarchies failed to arise (Katovich, Weiland, & Couch, 1981; Borkman, 2006). One important factor in these cases appeared to be that the flow of information remained open, and sufficient transparency of decision making was maintained to prevent the rise of a dominant elite. In addition, Leach (2005) documented cases in which oligarchies arose in nonbureaucratic organizations, a finding that casts doubt on the assumption that goal displacement is specific to that type of structure.

DECISION MAKING

Although natural-system perspectives were gaining prominence, other writers continued to explain organizations as rational systems by exploring the process of *decision making*. One of these, Herbert Simon (1957), began by changing the unit of analysis from the organization to individual actors and focusing on their decision making. A strong influence on his thinking was the work of psychologists who studied the importance of stimulus-response connections as explanations for human behavior. He believed organizations can be conceptualized as aggregations of individual decisions within them, and organizational behavior as decisions made about how to respond to certain stimuli.

March and Simon (1958) argued that the key to understanding organizational decisions is to recognize that there are constraints that limit decision making. They termed this phenomenon "bounded rationality" and identified three major categories of constraints:

1. Habits, abilities, and other personal characteristics that individuals bring with them into the decision-making process and that influence their actions in certain ways, irrespective of the circumstances surrounding a specific decision;

2. Loyalties toward a certain group (inside or outside the organization) that has values which conflict with the values of the organization as a whole; and

3. The inability of the decision maker to know all the variables that might influence the decision or all possible consequences of the decision.

Because every decision carries some risk, decision-making in organizations may be thought of as a risk-management process. The goal of the decision maker is not necessarily to achieve a perfect outcome, since this may never be possible. Instead, the decision maker seeks to reduce uncertainty as much as possible in order to make a decision that has a reasonable likelihood of producing an acceptable outcome. March and Simon called this "satisficing," and they argued that understanding how satisfactory outcomes are pursued via decisions made in the context of bounded rationality is key to understanding organizations.

Subsequent works expanded on these ideas in several directions. Cyert and March (1963) suggested that decision making in aggregate is a process of bargaining between individuals and units having different views and goals. The eventual actions of the organization can be understood as the outcome of these ongoing negotiations among organizational members. March and Olsen (1976) proposed a "garbage can" analogy to describe the rather chaotic process in which decisions emerge from a mixture of people, problems, ideas, and "choice opportunities" that are unique to every organization and situation. Interactions among these elements are considered the primary determinants of the eventual decision, and rationality is viewed as playing a relatively minor role.

Strengths.   Management theorists such as Taylor assumed that adherence to a few basic organizational principles would consistently lead to maximum productivity. Simon and others countered this view by showing that (1) the role of managers is not just to order workers' tasks but also to make strategic decisions and long-term plans and (2) the quality of these decisions is closely linked to the soundness of the information on which they are based. The most efficiently structured organization may still fail if it makes the wrong choices about future directions. Writings of decision-making theorists, though now 50 years old and more, continue to be heavily cited in the literature, and current research supports their argument that information deficiency constrains and shapes management decisions (Bae, 2008; Desai, 2010).

Box 7.6 Decision Making

▸ **Purpose.** Descriptive

▸ **Key Features.** Much of what organizations are and do is the product of decisions made by individuals throughout the hierarchy, but especially at the administrative level. These decisions are only as good as the information on which they are based, however, and complete information needed to make informed decisions is seldom, if ever, present. Because of this lack of information, organizations can never be fully rational. Decision makers thus learn to *satisfice*, meaning they do not expect optimal outcomes but merely acceptable ones.

▸ **Strengths and Weaknesses.** These writers showed that the quality of other aspects of management is irrelevant if the quality of decision making is bad. They also accurately anticipated the computer age, which demonstrated the importance of information as an organizational commodity. The better the quality (though not necessarily quantity) of information available, the better the decisions and, eventually, the outcomes. The drawback to this approach was that it remained inwardly focused and failed to give sufficient attention to the larger environment in which an organization operates and in which its decisions are made.

In addition, decision-making theory has had a substantial impact on organizational analysis through its concern with information access and quality. This concern coincided with the advent of computers, and it has played a part in the rapid growth of interest in information management in organizations. The basic idea is that information systems, augmented by the unique data-processing capabilities of computers, can be used to reduce the uncertainty that decision makers must confront and increase the likelihood that they will make effective decisions.

Weaknesses. As a means of understanding organizations, the decision-making approach has a number of limitations. For example, in a critique of March and Simon's work, Blau and Scott (1962) argued that the model focuses too narrowly on formal decision making, ignoring the interpersonal aspects of organizations and the influence that informal structures can have on decisions that are made. Champion (1975) noted that little attention is paid to situations in which a particular individual may not seek overall rationality but personal or local-unit gain. Most important, the decision-making model has been criticized for its focus on internal factors that lead to particular decisions. This emphasis ignores the fact that often it is influences external to the organization that are most important to eliciting and determining a decision. In fact, growing attention toward the importance of external factors provided the impetus for the next important developments in organizational theory.

ORGANIZATIONS AS OPEN SYSTEMS

Understanding Open Systems

In learning about practice with individual clients, most social workers are introduced to systems theory. This approach is based on the work of biologist Ludwig von Bertalanffy (1950), who believed that lessons learned in fields such as ecology, which concerns organisms' interdependence with their surroundings, provide a way to conceptualize other phenomena as systems engaged in environmental interactions. In this light, individual clients are viewed not as isolated entities driven by internal processes but as social beings whose personalities and behaviors emerge from constant interaction with the world around them. As *open systems*, clients both give to and draw from elements external to themselves. Understanding this ongoing process of exchange with critical elements of their personal environment (e.g., culture, community, and family) is key to understanding clients. In Chapter 5 we discussed how this *organismic analogy* has been extended to communities, and in the 1960s, various writers began to argue that it applies to organizations as well.

One influential example was the work of Katz and Kahn (1966), who noted that earlier theorists approached organizations as though they were closed systems that could be understood simply by studying their internal structure and processes. This approach corresponds to the *mechanical analogy* also mentioned in Chapter 5, and Katz and Kahn considered it naïve. They argued that organizations must be understood as open systems surviving through a constant exchange of resources with organizations and other entities surrounding them. The design and functioning of the system is shaped by the exchanges through which it acts on and responds to its environment.

As illustrated in Figure 7.2, systems are made up of collections of constituent parts (whether cells comprising an organism or people comprising

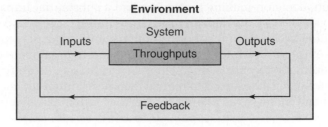

Figure 7.2
The Open-Systems Model

an organization) that receive *inputs*, operate on them through some sort of process called the *throughput*, and produce *outputs*. In human service agencies, inputs include resources such as funding, staff, and facilities. Clients who request services are also important inputs, as are the types and severity of the problems for which they seek help. More subtle but also vital are inputs such as values, expectations, and opinions about the agency that are held by community members, funding agencies, regulatory bodies, and other segments of the environment.

Throughput involves the services provided by the agency—often referred to as its *technology*—and the way it is structured to apply this technology to inputs it receives. *Output* refers to the organization's products. In industrial firms this is usually some sort of material object; in social work agencies it is the completion of a service to a client. As we will discuss, the important aspect of service output is often defined as an *outcome*, which is a measure of a quality-of-life change (improvement, stasis, or deterioration) for a client.

A further element of many open-systems models is a *feedback* mechanism, which is a defining characteristic of what are called *cybernetic systems*. A cybernetic system is self-correcting, meaning that it is able to garner information from its surroundings, interpret this information, and adjust its functioning accordingly. Biological organisms exist as cybernetic systems because they adapt themselves to changing conditions in their environments. Organizations are also cybernetic systems, and it seems impossible to envision one that could survive without gathering information on environmental conditions and taking steps to adjust. Manufacturers must constantly react to changing demand for their goods, and their survival often depends on the ability to adapt quickly by making more fast-selling items and cutting production on those that are not selling. Likewise, human service agencies must provide needed and relevant services or they will go out of business. This process of receiving feedback from the environment and adapting to fit external conditions is at the heart of the open-systems approach.

Strengths.   From Weber through Simon, theorists prior to Katz and Kahn implicitly assumed that the key to understanding an organization lay within, and that is where they directed their attention. The open-systems view dramatically redirected writers' attention to external environments and the way organizations must be viewed as dynamic entities constantly involved in exchanges with those environments. This view is a natural fit for social workers who are taught to understand clients from a *person-in-environment* perspective. It also echoes the profession's focus on research-based practice, which is necessary to ensure that services remain relevant. For example, in response to a given problem in a community, the social worker might conduct a needs assessment, use

---

Box 7.7 Organizations as Open Systems

▶ **Purpose.** Descriptive

▶ **Key Features.** This theory broadened and extended the natural-systems perspective by showing that all organizations, like all organisms, are open systems. Open systems acquire resources (*inputs*) from their environments, such as funds, staff, and clients, and they return products or services (*outputs*) to the environment. Understanding organizational actions thus requires viewing them as part of a larger environment in which and with which they carry out these exchanges.

▶ **Strengths and Weaknesses.** Organizational behavior can be explained as efforts to make beneficial environmental exchanges, and organizations act in ways that seek to reduce uncertainty and make their environments as predictable as possible. This makes organizations themselves more predictable. Still, there are limits to how far the comparisons between organizations and organisms can be extended. A full understanding of how organizations act requires examining both their interactions with their environments and the interactions among their members.

---

the data to design a program to address the problem, implement the program, then gather new data to evaluate and refine it. This meshes well with the input-throughput-output model elaborated in the open-systems view.

Weaknesses.   Most concerns raised about the open-systems perspective echo those directed earlier at Selznick's natural-systems view, which is that the analogy linking organizations to individual organisms can sometimes be overdrawn. Although both organizations and organisms exist within a larger environment, and both engage in exchanges with that environment, organizations are themselves composed of individuals whose goals may differ from those of their organization. The throughput phase of environmental interactions in an organization thus involves the interactions of many organizational members, which adds a new layer of complexity to the model.

Contingency Theory

Partly in response to the new perspectives offered by open-systems thinking and partly because of doubts about one-size-fits-all management theories, a new outlook began to take shape in the 1960s. Its basic premise was that different organizations face different circumstances, so they may need to structure themselves in different ways. Known generally as *contingency theory*, this approach can be boiled down to three basic tenets. Two were proposed by Galbraith (1973), and the first of these, which directly disagreed with Taylor, suggested that there are many ways to organize rather than just a single "best way." The second acknowledged that some ways of organizing are better than others, so effort must be expended to find at least an acceptable approach. Scott (1981) added a third, open-systems principle, which stated that the organization's environment determines which way of organizing works best under present conditions. The unifying theme across all three principles is that the nature of the organization and its management scheme depend on many factors unique to that organization, so expecting to be able to manage a human service agency in the same way as an auto-assembly plant, for example, would be naïve.

Morse and Lorsch (1970) took issue with views such as those of McGregor that decentralized, humanistic management models should be the preferred approach across most organizations. Their research showed that high organizational effectiveness and a strong sense of personal competence can be found in organizations with relatively rigid rules and structure. Similarly, some organizations with a loose structure and high individual autonomy were not always effective or satisfying to their workers. The key variable to which results pointed was the nature of organizational tasks. Organizations with predictable tasks, such as manufacturing firms, fared best with a tightly controlled structure. Those with less-predictable tasks (in this case a research and development role) appeared much better suited to a loose structure and management style.

A typology of these differences was proposed by Burns and Stalker (1961), who distinguished between two forms of management that they labeled "mechanistic" and "organic." Mechanistic systems, which reflect characteristics of bureaucracies as described by Weber and the managerial techniques laid out by Taylor, are commonly found in organizations having relatively stable environments. Organic forms occur in unstable environments in which the inputs are unpredictable and the organization's viability depends on responding in ways that are less bound by formal rules and structures. Table 7.2 compares and contrasts characteristics of organic and mechanistic organizations.

Lawrence and Lorsch (1967) also noted that the stability of the environment is a critical contingency on which an analysis of organizational structure and leadership should rest. Models such as Weber's bureaucratic system are better at explaining circumstances in stable organizational environments, while the human relations model appears to work better in situations of environmental turbulence. Incorporating some aspects of the decision-making approach, they also called attention to the importance of certainty versus uncertainty in determining organizational actions. Stable environments allow for greater certainty in structuring operations; thus, a human service agency that deals mostly with clients having a particular problem (e.g., a food bank) is expected to have fairly routinized operations and formal structure. Conversely,

Table 7.2   Elements Of Mechanistic Versus Organic Organizations

Variable	Mechanistic Organization	Organic Organization
Focus of work	Completion of discrete tasks	Contribution to overall result
Responsibility for integrating work	Supervisor of each level	Shared within level, across units
Responsibility for problem solving	Limited to precise obligations set out for each position	Owned by affected individual; cannot be shirked as "out of my area"
Structure of control and authority	Hierarchic	Networked
Location of knowledge, information	Concentrated at top	Expertise and need for information assumed to exist at various levels
Character of organizational structure	Rigid; accountability rests with individual	Fluid; accountability is shared by group
Content of communication	Instructions, decisions	Information, advice
Direction of communication	Vertical; between supervisor and subordinate	Lateral and also across ranks
Expected loyalty	To supervisor, unit	To technology, outcome

Source: Adapted from Burns and Stalker (1961).

organizations that deal with a wide variety of clients and unpredictable client problems (e.g., a disaster-relief organization) can be expected to be structured loosely and have a much less "by-the-book" approach to operational rules.

James Thompson (1967) agreed that a key issue in organization–environment interactions is the degree of uncertainty in the environment, and he noted that organizations seek predictability because this allows the creation of rational (logically planned) structures. However, because environments are never perfectly predictable, an organization that structures itself too rigidly will not survive long. Understanding how an organization has structured itself to respond to environmental uncertainty is therefore critical to understanding it as a whole.

Similar to Morse and Lorsch, Thompson focused on organizations' technology. As illustrated in Figure 7.3, he described three levels of functioning: (1) the technical core, (2) the managerial system, and (3) the institutional system. The *technical core* includes the structures and processes within an organization's boundaries that allow it to carry out the principal functions for which it was created (such as the manufacture of an object or the delivery of a service). Theoretically, the technical core works best when environmental inputs never vary and the same work can be done in the same way repeatedly. But because environments are constantly changing, the rational organization seeks to accommodate to such variations without endangering its most vital elements (the technical core). The *managerial system* includes those structures and processes that manage the work of the technical core. The *institutional system* deals with interactions between the organization and the environment.

Adaptive responses to environmental change are crucial in Thompson's analytical model, and he hypothesized that these fall into a three-part sequence: (1) actions to protect the technical core, (2) actions to acquire power over the task environment, and (3) actions to absorb key elements of the environment by altering organizational boundaries. Actions to protect the technical core involve responses that allow the organization to contain necessary changes within itself, such as by increasing or decreasing output, hiring or laying off staff, or shifting resources among different internal units.

The *task environment* is the term Thompson uses to describe external organizations on which an organization depends, either as providers of needed input (money, raw materials, and client referrals) or as consumers of its output. If internal responses are unsuccessful in adjusting to change, the organization will attempt to alter its relationships with members of the task environment to

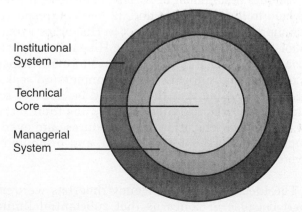

Institutional System

Technical Core

Managerial System

Figure 7.3
Thompson's Organizational Model

gain more control over the change. Examples of this might include negotiating long-term funding agreements or arranging for regular referral of clients (e.g., a residential treatment center may become the exclusive provider of treatment for a particular school district).

Finally, if the organization cannot adapt to change by any of these methods, Thompson predicted that it would seek to incorporate into itself parts of the environment that relate to the change. For example, a human service organization that serves substance-abusing clients whose costs are paid by contracts with a public agency would be endangered if funding priorities shifted toward prevention rather than treatment. If a smaller agency in the area appears to be in line for much of this funding, the older, larger agency may seek to acquire the smaller one in an effort to maintain its funding base. But because such a move involves changing at least part of the older agency's technical core, this response would likely occur only after other tactics were tried and proved inadequate.

Strengths.   Contingency theorists accepted the premise of the open-systems model that the environment is critical in understanding how organizations behave. They also argued that organizations develop their structures not so much through the application of management principles as by being forced to react to ever-changing environmental conditions. These ideas continue to have considerable influence on organizational analysis, and research continues to demonstrate the applicability of contingency theory principles. For example, Katz, Batt, and Keefe (2003) demonstrated how contingency theory was able to predict accurately the process of revitalization of a large national labor union, a type of organization not typically used to illustrate the theory's principles. Similarly, Fernandez and Wise (2010) document episodes of the "ingestion" of needed technology in response to environmental change, as predicted by Thompson.

Another example of how environmental contingencies explain organizational actions can be seen in the attention being paid by various companies and agencies to the growing diversity of the U.S. workforce. As noted earlier, employees and the knowledge and skill they possess are important inputs that organizations draw from their environments. A report from the U.S. Bureau of Labor Statistics (2009) estimates that, between 2008 and 2018, the number of persons in the workforce nationwide will increase by 8 percent overall. The number of white, non-Hispanic workers, however, is projected to increase by only 6 percent, whereas the number of African American and Asian American workers is projected to increase by 14 and 32 percent, respectively. The projections are even more striking with respect to Hispanics versus non-Hispanics, with the labor-force participation among Hispanics expected to increase by 33 percent compared to the 4 percent increase for non-Hispanics. If organizations fail to constantly monitor their environment and seek to adapt to its changes, it might be expected that little would be done to respond to this trend. Fortunately, many organizations are adapting their recruitment methods, technology, office locations, training procedures, and even rules of interpersonal conduct in an effort to attract, retain, and promote members of an increasingly diverse workforce.

Weaknesses.   The ideas of the contingency theorists were not universally accepted, in part because of concerns that substantial limitations remain regarding the ability of administrators to rationally assess and respond to

> ## Box 7.8   Contingency Theory

> ▶ **Purpose.** Descriptive
> ▶ **Key Features.** A one-size-fits-all approach to organizational analysis or management is doomed to fail because organizations have different purposes and exist in different environments. The question is not how closely an organization adheres to a particular form (e.g., the bureaucratic model) but how and how well it structures itself to accommodate to its unique environment. Also, contingency theory calls attention to an organization's *technology,* referring to the ways it carries out its tasks. Predictable environmental input and routine tasks are amenable to more traditional, hierarchical structure, whereas unpredictable environments and nonroutine technology require less rigid structure.

> ▶ **Strengths and Weaknesses.** Contingency theory has influenced many subsequent works, and its contention that organizations must be understood in terms of how they structure themselves in response to their environments remains widely accepted. Most concerns about this approach address the role of decision makers. Although proponents argue that their response to the environment tends to be planned, predictable, and based on the rational application of management principles, critics contend that the evidence for this is scarce and that responses to environmental change are often unstructured and reactive rather than planned.

external environments. For example, Millar (1978) raised doubts about Burns and Stalker's proposal that rigid structures are suitable for some contingencies, whereas loosely linked structures are a better fit for others. He argued that "mechanistic" types of organizations may not be appropriate even when the environment is stable. This is due to the dehumanizing aspects of most mechanistic structures. He also raises doubts about contingency theory's assumption that rationality will prevail in these organizations, noting that there is little basis for assuming that individuals will always give priority to organizational goals over any others.

Also, Thompson himself offered the caveat that the processes he described took place under "norms of rationality," meaning that organizations which do not use rational analytical processes in adapting to environmental change might act in unpredictable ways. The problem is that rationality is an elusive notion, particularly when considering that different organizations in different circumstances may respond in varying ways to environmental turbulence. In commercial firms it may be "rational" to protect the interests of shareholders by maximizing profitability, but equally rational to keep profits and dividends modest in order to emphasize long-term investment. Likewise, actions such as stiffening eligibility criteria may be rational for a for-profit human service agency wishing to protect its earning capacity, but irrational for a nonprofit agency wishing to protect its mission of serving even clients who cannot pay. Similar organizations facing similar circumstances may choose different courses of action based on their interpretation of the circumstances; thus, the predictability of organizational actions remains limited.

CONTEMPORARY PERSPECTIVES

The history of organizational and management theory has been, in many ways, the history of a search for insights into the best ways to organize and manage—a search for the theory that will unlock the secrets of productivity. As we have attempted to show, the theme was different for each new theory. For Weber it was structure, for Taylor it was precision, for human relations theorists it was atten-tiveness to social factors, for Drucker it was a shared sense of direction, for Simon it was the process of decision making, and for Thompson and others it was cop-ing with environmental changes. Following the analogy we offered at the start of the chapter, it could be said that each theorist examined organizations through an eyepiece with a different filter than others.

A major contribution of contingency theory was the idea that no one theme or set of variables was right for every situation. For contingency theorists, when asked the question, "What is the best way to manage an organization?" the correct answer was, "It depends." Every organization is made up of a unique mix of variables, and contingency theorists argue that there can be no single formula for optimal structure and management style. The direction the organization takes will depend on its environment and on the nature of its core structures and processes.

Whether or not its tenets are always accepted, it is probably fair to state that the contingency approach has been a springboard for contemporary thinking about organizational and management theories. Recent decades have witnessed the introduction of a number of alternative perspectives. Although none has dominated the field, each contributed to our ability to analyze organizations and understand how they are structured and led. Certain terms are prominent in this literature, including *power, culture, vision, empowerment, quality, values,* and *information. Leadership* also became the term of choice over *management,* though both are acknowledged as having their place. The following discussion will briefly introduce the reader to a sampling of themes from the organiza-tional literature of the 1980s through today.

Power and Politics

Jeffrey Pfeffer (1981) argued that organizational actions are best understood in terms of power relationships and political forces. He defined *power* as the abil-ity to influence actions and *politics* as the process through which this influ-ence is used. Asked where power originates, Pfeffer would contend that it arises from an individual's position within the organization, meaning that power and organizational structure are closely tied.

To illustrate the relationship of power and structure, Pfeffer compared three models of organizational analysis: (1) the bureaucratic model, (2) the rational-choice model, and (3) the political model. The *bureaucratic model* is based on the classic Weberian approach that assumes an organization both acts and is structured in a manner that maximizes its production efficiency. Pfeffer's criticisms of this model were essentially the same as those detailed earlier. The *rational-choice model* derives from the work of decision-making theorists such as Simon. Pfeffer agreed with their points concerning con-straints on rational decision making, but he noted that these models still assume that decision making is oriented toward a clear organizational goal, whereas in most organizations a range of goals and motivations may exist. Pfeffer urged the use of a *political model* of structural analysis, which calls attention to the manner in which organizational actions may be either instru-mental (serving the presumed goals of the organization as a whole) or parochial (serving the perceived self-interest of a particular individual or organizational unit). These goals may differ, as does the power of the deci-sion maker to effect his or her choice of action. Pfeffer thus believed that organizational actions must be understood in terms of the complex interplay of individuals working together—sometimes toward mutual goals and sometimes toward personal goals—in a manner analogous to what happens in the political arena.

Along similar lines, Wamsley and Zald (1976) argued that structure and process in organizations is best understood in terms of the interplay of political and economic interests, both internal *and* external to the organization. *Political* means the processes by which the organization obtains power and legitimacy. *Economic* means the processes by which the organization gets resources such as clients, staff, and funding.

The goal of the *political economy* perspective was to incorporate much of the work of previous schools into a more general conceptual model. Within this model, elements such as individual interests and goals, the power wielded by the holders of these interests, and environmental resources and the relative influence of those who control them are all seen to interact in a way that creates the unique character of an organization. This character is not static but changes as the political economy of the organization changes.

An example of how these ideas build on and extend previous work can be gleaned from our earlier discussion of the weaknesses of Thompson's model. Pfeffer would argue that Thompson, in assuming that "norms of rationality" govern organizational actions, fails to account for the fact that both instrumental *and* parochial concerns are being addressed. Individuals who have the power to choose a particular organizational action will make their decisions based not solely on what is best for the organization but also on what is best for themselves. Consider an administrator deciding between two new programs that have been proposed. Thompson's model suggests that the one that best responds to demands in the organization's environment will automatically be favored. Pfeffer suggests that the administrator might choose the other program if, despite meeting organizational needs less satisfactorily, the administrator believed it was the one that might best further his or her career or maintain his or her position within the organization. This mixing of interests is what Pfeffer as well as Wamsley and Zald refer to as the *political context* of organizations. Their point is that organizational behavior can be understood as the outcome of decisions by individuals who have acquired decision-making power, and these decisions will reflect their assessment of what is politically and economically wise for both themselves and the organization. With respect to the metaphors proposed by Bolman and Deal (2008) this fits the "jungle" model, in that the organization is seen as an environment of competing interests where those holding the power determine whose interests are given priority.

The topic of power has also been discussed with respect to its effect on ethnic minorities and women in organizations. For example, evidence suggests that the gap in pay between white males and others does not arise solely from the fact that white males typically occupy better-paid positions. Instead, it also appears to result from white males holding power that allows them to protect their earnings advantage. Castilla (2008) demonstrated that merit pay systems designed to award salary adjustments on the basis of job performance could be manipulated to benefit those in power. Cohen (2007) found that having a higher proportion of women in an organization had little effect on correcting the male/female wage gap. What did begin to narrow the gap was having at least a few women in positions with high prestige and influence. This supports Pfeffer's contention that power and influence—rather than procedures or numbers—determine how organizations behave.

Organizational Culture

Elements of Culture

The concept of *organizational culture* has also shaped the development of contemporary theories. Many different writers have used a familiar expression to define organizational culture, describing it as "the way we do things around here." It may also be thought of as the "unwritten rules" of what constitutes intelligent behavior in an organization, or the shared values that people hold.

A prominent writer on the subject, Edgar Schein (2010), explains that an organizational culture develops through shared experiences. Newly formed organizations are heavily influenced by leaders who bring their perspectives to the organization and around which assumptions and beliefs emerge. A certain amount of time must pass for shared experiences among those in the organization to produce the sort of mutually accepted ideas and practices that can be termed organizational culture. Also, leadership and culture are intimately related, and understanding what assumptions leaders bring to organizations is central to analyzing how change occurs.

The connection of leadership to organizational culture has been explored in numerous ways. For example, feminist scholars have analyzed the processes of empowerment and collective action within organizations and the effect these processes have on changing cultural assumptions within organizations. Ecklund (2006) found that the prevailing culture in religious organizations was a principal determinant in whether opportunities arose for leadership by women. Similar influence on gender equalities resulting from organizational culture and leadership has also been documented in settings such as engineering firms, non-governmental service organizations, and the military (Davis, 2009; Bastalich, Franzway, Gill, Mills, & Sharp, 2007).

Organizational culture is important in understanding any organization, and Schein (2010) notes that it is something which is "visible" and "feelable." When entering an organization, one quickly perceives that established patterns occur within that system even if they are not explicitly stated. The social worker who assumes a new place in an organization must be aware that these patterns may be so central to organizational functioning that they are taken for granted by members of that organization. When violated, members may respond emotionally because they are so invested in the "way things have always been done." This is why Bolman and Deal (2008) link the organizational culture perspective with their "temple" metaphor. An organization's culture is much broader than climate, ideology, or philosophy. It is a sense of group identity that permeates decision making and communication within the organization.

Writers continue to expand the organizational culture model in many directions. Cameron and Quinn's (2006) "competing value framework" proposes that elements of more than a single culture may exist within an organization, and competition between these cultures, while often a source of strife, may also be a source of dynamism and a path to needed change. O'Connor, Netting, and Fabelo (2009) found evidence of this in human service agencies. Testing for the presence of four orientations or "paradigms" proposed by Burrell and Morgan (1979), respondents to their survey reported that aspects of two or more contrasting cultural elements were often present within their agencies. Patterns showed more homogeneity of culture in public agencies and less in younger agencies, but most agencies incorporated elements of presumptively incompatible paradigms. Among other implications, the authors note that the results suggest that social workers are able to tolerate some levels of ambiguity in organizational culture and may see benefits in doing so, such as when keeping alive prospects for change in a culture that appears hostile toward change.

Organizational culture has also been linked to organizational commitment. The latter tends to be high in organizations where the culture is viewed as strong, easy to perceive, and mutually supportive of and supported by organizational actors (Mathew & Ogbanna, 2009; Meyer & Parfyonova, 2010). In turn, high organizational commitment is a strong predictor of job satisfaction and employee retention (O'Donnell & Kirkner, 2009; Ohana & Meyer, 2010). It has also been linked to lower levels of emotional exhaustion, a primary component of burnout (Glisson, Dukes, & Green, 2006).

Diversity as an Element of Culture

In many organizations the culture was dominated by a particular gender group (usually men), a particular racial/ethnic group (usually whites), and a particular socioeconomic class (usually wealthy elites). As with much of the rest of society, organizations were far from level playing fields, and, to an even greater degree than in the rest of society, those in power were able to shape rules, structures, and operations in ways that preserved their privileges. As Brazell (2003) notes, change came about only as social action and large-scale social movements began to change society as a whole. The Civil Rights Movement, the Women's Movement, and the Disability Rights Movement are examples of efforts that heightened awareness of discrimination and made it less likely to go unchallenged. The movements also helped establish antidiscrimination laws that extended new legal protections into the workplace. In addition to these forces, changing economic conditions and better access to education sent women into the workforce in unprecedented numbers, whereas changing demographics, such as the rapid growth of the Latino population, made the workforce more heterogeneous.

In an early work on diversity in organizations, Roosevelt Thomas Jr. (1991) identified three forces acting on organizations in the United States:

1. The need for corporations to do business in an increasingly competitive global market
2. Rapid changes in the United States that are increasing the diversity of its workforce
3. The demise of the "melting pot" concept in favor of a recognition that diversity is a strength rather than a weakness

Thomas believed that effective management of diversity is crucial to improving productivity. This is because, in a global economy, organizations with a diverse workforce are more likely to be those with novel ideas and adroit responses to changing circumstances.

Cross (2000) notes the usefulness of the organizational culture approach for developing methods of harnessing and managing diversity. To the extent that culture in organizations involves a shared set of understandings about "how things are done," those understandings must incorporate the differing frames of reference that diversity entails. To illustrate, Cross describes an exercise carried out in one commercial firm to identify the outlook, opinions, motivations, and expectations of employees that helped comprise its organizational culture. Employees were asked to generate an exhaustive list of the company's norms, and this was then reduced to a shorter set of statements with which all

Diversity in Practice

Critical Thinking Question: How might diversity management also help strengthen social workers' abilities to work with diverse client populations?

employees were asked to indicate their level of agreement. Cross discovered broad agreement about the existence of a norm that the company was among the best at what it did, and this norm was also seen as positive by almost all participants. However, although participants agreed about the overarching importance of short-term profit, most saw the norm as counterproductive because it tended to favor only white men in upper-level positions. Similarly, all groups were frank in noting that a common norm in the organization questioned the ability of employees of color. Although all participants agreed this was negative, all also reported that it had been difficult to erase.

Carr-Ruffino (2002) sums up many of the key points of diversity management by arguing that administrators must take the lead in changing an organization's culture toward one that embraces diversity. To accomplish this, she proposes six strategies or responsibilities that administrators must assume:

1. Promote tolerance.

2. Be a role model of respect and appreciation.

3. Value empathy (for example, by training oneself to see things through others' eyes).

4. Promote trust and goodwill.

5. Encourage collaboration (to break through cliques and promote interaction among organizational members).

6. Work toward synthesis (seek to benefit from new insights offered by bringing diverse perspectives to bear on an issue).

7. Create synergy (use diversity to achieve as a team more than the sum of what could be achieved by individuals working alone). (pp. 118–119)

In Chapter 8 we will provide a framework for analyzing the culture of an organization with respect to its friendliness to diversity. The framework addresses many of the elements in Carr-Ruffino's list and adds others. These include culture-reinforcing elements such as a mission statement that embraces diversity and a participatory approach to decision making.

Pursuing Excellence

Another important management theme linked to organizational culture was the "excellence" theme, pioneered by Thomas Peters and Robert Waterman (1982). Both authors, after working at a management consulting firm, became leaders of a project on organizational effectiveness. They created a definition for what they considered excellent companies, then selected sixty-two for study. They also immersed themselves in the philosophies and practices of excellent companies and discovered that the dominant themes were elements of organizational culture such as a family feeling among employees, a preference for smallness, a preference for simplicity rather than complexity, and attention to individuals. In effect, they found that management practices in these organizations focused on personal elements such as those noted by human relations theorists and McGregor's Theory Y.

Peters and Waterman also concluded that, although a rational organizational base built on collection and analysis of data is indispensable, the analytical process must be flexible and take into account a wide range of considerations, including the individual person. Rational approaches, they argued, need to stop viewing human actors as a "necessary nuisance" and instead build on the strengths brought into a system by employees.

Their findings were organized into eight basic principles that have become the focal point of the "excellence approach" to management:

1. *A Bias for Action.* A preference for doing something—anything—rather than sending a question through cycles and cycles of analyses and committee reports

2. *Staying Close to the Customer.* Learning preferences and catering to them

3. *Autonomy and Entrepreneurship.* Breaking the corporation into small companies and encouraging them to think independently and competitively

4. *Productivity Through People.* Creating in all employees a belief that their best efforts are essential and that they will share the rewards of the company's success

5. *Hands-On, Value Driven.* Insisting that executives keep in touch with the firm's essential mission

6. *Stick to the Knitting.* Remaining with the business the company knows best

7. *Simple Form, Lean Staff.* Few administrative layers, few people at the upper levels

8. *Simultaneous Loose/Tight Properties.* Fostering a climate where there is dedication to the central values of the company, combined with tolerance for all employees who accept those values

Peters and Waterman's work is often considered part of the larger organizational culture literature, with its focus being on creating an excellence-oriented culture. In human services, as operational orientations have moved closer to a provider–consumer relationship, the authors' findings and the principles derived from them have grown in importance. Public as well as private agencies recognize the link between quality of the work environment and quality of the organization's products. In addition, strategies to cope with uncertain environments have included forming flexible and collaborative relationships with others in order to survive and grow.

It should be noted, however, that the goal of maximizing excellence and service effectiveness by fine-tuning management practices can be elusive. An example is offered by Herman and Renz (2004), who studied fifty-five nonprofit agencies to determine the effect of new management practices on service quality. Results failed to show that the new techniques had been effective, although different constituencies tended to differ on their ratings of effectiveness. Echoing warnings first voiced by contingency theorists, the authors concluded that the "right way" of managing in one organization may be the wrong way in another, and successfully matching management style to the organization may have a greater impact on service effectiveness than adhering blindly to any particular management dogma.

Sense-Making

In addition to the "excellence" theme, another body of work that meshes well with the organizational culture model is the analytical approach termed "sense-making." Proposed by Karl Weick (1995), this model is based in part on communications theory, which is concerned with how people process information and make sense of what they see around them. Its relevance to organizations and its connection to organizational culture come from the assumption that individuals draw clues from their environments, engage in internal conversations designed to make sense of these clues, then form conclusions about what they have seen and heard.

Weick, Sutcliffe, and Obstfeld (2005) describe various aspects of this process. First, sense-making arises as a natural effort by individuals to process what is going on around them, which at first may seem random and disordered. Events are "bracketed" (differentiated from others and categorized), after which the category into which they are placed is labeled, again using some form of internal shorthand. Sense-making is retrospective (meaning that it requires interpreting events *after* they occur), and the necessity to act typically precedes sense-making done to gauge the results of the action.

To understand the value of the sense-making approach, it is helpful to keep in mind that organizations may be seen as collections of individuals who are constantly engaged in sense-making to allow them to meet the expectation that they work together toward mutual goals. We noted earlier the definition of organizational culture as "the way things are done around here," and people's understanding of how things are done arise from their sense-making processes within the organization. Weick and colleagues (2005) describe sense-making as small-scale mechanisms that in time can lead to large-scale changes, meaning that the shared understandings and modes of operation comprising organizational culture develop from ongoing thought processes on the part of each individual. At a larger level, leaders of an organization engage in sense-making processes to evaluate the position of the organization as a whole within its environment.

A theme related to sense-making is offered by Gareth Morgan (1986), who emphasizes the value of metaphor in understanding organizations. Morgan notes that metaphor was often used (explicitly or implicitly) by earlier organizational theories, and he considers it a valid heuristic tool (that is, a device or method used to help understand something). Weber deliberately compared bureaucracies to machines, Morgan notes, and this metaphor was also used by Weber's critics to decry the mechanistic and impersonal aspects of bureaucracies. For open-systems theorists the metaphor of choice was *organization-as-organism*, and it was from this metaphor that descriptions and studies of the "survival instinct" of organizations arose.

Morgan's ideas fit comfortably with the use of "culture" as a metaphor to describe how organizations work. The concept of culture is used by anthropologists seeking to differentiate societies of people on the basis of their shared beliefs, values, and histories, and Morgan considers this a similarly valid tool for differentiating organizations. This view has been supported by studies showing that the metaphor of organizational culture can be used by managers to reinforce shared perceptions among members of organizations (Gibson & Zellmer-Bruhn, 2001) and to promote team building (Kang, Yang, & Rowley, 2006).

Quality-Oriented Management

Shortly after World War II, U.S. college professor W. Edwards Deming traveled to Japan to assist with a proposed national census there. He stayed to help Japanese managers, who were working to rebuild the country's industries, and learn new ideas for control of the manufacturing process as a means of improving the quality of goods produced. Two important outcomes arose from this work. First, within only thirty years, Japanese management techniques had gained such a reputation for effectiveness that they were being re-imported to the United States and touted as a model for improving U.S. management. Second, Deming and others realized that principles being used to improve manufactured goods could be applied to service organizations as well. These were the earliest stirrings of a set of related movements that featured a focus by management on quality and ongoing quality improvement. Two of the most influential schools of thought associated with this approach are *Theory Z* and *Total Quality Management.*

Theory Z

Due in part to the quality-control procedures they had perfected, Japanese firms in the late 1970s and early 1980s began capturing markets long dominated by U.S. businesses. This aroused curiosity about how Japanese companies had overcome their prior reputation for poor products and were now setting worldwide standards of quality.

William Ouchi attempted to capture Japanese-style management in his 1981 book, *Theory Z.* The message of the title was that the philosophical and theoretical principles underlying Japanese management went beyond McGregor's conceptualization of Theory Y. An organization in Japan, said Ouchi, was more than a structural or goal-oriented entity—it was a way of life. It provided career-long employment, intermeshed with the social, political, and economic systems of the country, and influenced organizations such as universities and public schools, even to the lowest grades.

The basic premise of Japanese-style management was that involved workers are the key to increased productivity. Although this may sound similar to the human relations school, that was only partly so. The Japanese were concerned about more than whether workers felt that their social needs were met in the workplace. They wanted workers to become a demonstrable part of the process through which the organization was run. Ideas and suggestions about how to improve the organization were regularly solicited and, where feasible, implemented. One example was the *quality circle*, where employees set aside time to brainstorm ways to improve quality and productivity.

In contrast to U.S. organizations, Japanese organizations at the time tended to have neither organizational charts nor written objectives. Most work was done in teams, and consensus was achieved without a designated leader. Cooperation rather than competition was sought between units. Loyalty to the organization was extremely important, and it was rewarded with loyalty to the employee.

These approaches had considerable influence, and among the organizations that were early adopters of these principles were several research and development offices in the U.S. military (Chenhall, 2003). Even more interesting is the fact that, although Ouchi and others were promoting Japanese adaptations of quality-oriented management, a parallel movement in the United States that also had roots in Deming's work was beginning to gain attention.

Total Quality Management

A U.S. writer, Armand Feigenbaum, coined the term "total quality" to describe management practices designed to direct all aspects of an organization's operations toward achieving and maintaining maximum quality in goods or services. Feigenbaum developed many of the principles of this approach independent of Deming's work and at about the same time, beginning with a book published in 1951. But it was not until the 1980s that the work of these and other writers gained prominence and began to be known under the general title of *total quality management* or *TQM*.

In its definition of TQM, the American Society for Quality emphasizes that the fundamental orientation of TQM is toward maximizing customer satisfaction. This definition is useful in two ways. First, it highlights the breadth of applicability of the concept of quality, which is intended to apply not only to, for example, a machine that holds up under years of use but also to services that are accurately targeted toward meeting the needs of the purchaser. The second way the definition is useful is in its reference to customer satisfaction. Defining quality as satisfaction imposes a requirement that organizations stay in touch with their customers, use the information gleaned from them to assess performance, and fine-tune their operations based on this input. Table 7.3 presents a typology by Martin (1993) that compares these and other TQM principles with traditional management approaches.

Although some principles in the table are unique to TQM, others reflect earlier schools of thought. For example, TQM adopts McGregor's view that workers are more productive if they are allowed discretion in determining how the job is to be done. The model also favors using quality circles and other team-building

Table 7.3   Comparison of Traditional American Management Principles with TQM Management Principles

Traditional Management Principles	American Total Quality Management (TQM) Principles
The organization has multiple competing goals.	Quality is the primary organizational goal.
Financial concerns drive the organization.	Customer satisfaction drives the organization.
Management and professionals determine what quality is.	Customers determine what quality is.
The focus is on the status quo—"If it ain't broke, don't fix it."	The focus is on continuous improvement—"Unattended systems tend to run down."
Change is abrupt and is accomplished by champions battling the bureaucracy.	Change is continuous and is accomplished by teamwork.
Employees and departments compete with each other.	Employees and departments cooperate with each other.
Decisions are based on "gut feelings." It is better to do nothing than to do something wrong.	Decisions are based on data analysis. It is better do something than to do nothing.
Employee training is considered a luxury and a cost.	Employee training is considered essential and an investment.
Organizational communication is primarily top–down.	Organizational communication is top–down, down–up, and sideways.
Contractors are encouraged to compete with each other on the basis of price.	Long-term relationships are developed with contractors who deliver quality products and services.

Source: L. L. Martin, *Total Quality Management in Human Service Organizations,* copyright © 1993 by Sage Publications. Reprinted by Permission of Sage Publications, Inc.

approaches described by Ouchi. In other cases, though, TQM explicitly rejects prior theoretical views. Among these are bureaucratic (rule-oriented) structures, which TQM adherents view as a threat to the flexibility needed to respond to consumer input and engage in ongoing quality improvement. Saylor (1996) also notes that TQM is incompatible with Drucker's management by objective (MBO) guidelines, since TQM considers customer satisfaction a moving target. This again demands a continual process orientation designed to anticipate and adapt to new customer needs, whereas MBO, Saylor argues, focuses on achieving static outcomes that may ignore the changing needs of customers.

Because TQM has its origins in commercial manufacturing firms, its applicability to human service organizations in the public or private sectors may be questioned. However, results of studies in which TQM principles were applied in human service agencies suggest that this concern is unfounded (Kelly & Lauderdale, 2001; Williams, 2004). In addition, Moore and Kelly (1996) have suggested that TQM principles can be useful if tailored to the unique needs of the organization when implemented. Among the elements of TQM, those they believe can benefit human service agencies are (1) using quality circles to improve staff involvement and make services more relevant, (2) using careful measurement practices to monitor whether consumer needs are being met, (3) hiring and training staff in ways that ensure front-line staff have both the skills and interests necessary for their jobs, and (4) having management staff that can define a quality orientation and move the organization toward that goal.

Evidence-Based Management

One recent movement in management thought focuses on the tendency of people to make decisions based on personal experience, overall impressions, and "instinct" or "gut feelings." Managers and administrators often operate this way, and experienced leaders can be in great demand because they are assumed to have gained good "instincts" through years of on-the-job training. Proponents of evidence-based management (EBM) do not deny that experience has merit, but they caution against assuming that managers can make good decisions based on "practice wisdom" alone (Bolman & Deal, 2008).

In defining EBM, Rousseau (2006) emphasizes its goal of improving results by combining three elements: findings from empirical research, expertise of administrators, and information regarding the preferences of service users. Problems usually arise, she contends, because decision makers typically rely only on their own experiences and fail to systematically collect and use information from the other two sources. Briggs and McBeath (2009) trace the origins of this approach to the accountability movement that appeared first in the health-care arena and then spread to other sectors, and they and other advocates of EBM acknowledge that in many ways this returns to ideas put forth by Frederick Taylor and the scientific management school 100 years ago. However, Pfeffer and Sutton (2006) note that Taylor called for decisions to be made by managers and then imposed on workers, whereas EBM calls for the entire organization and all staff within it to adopt an orientation toward more informed decision making. The process is also seen as not merely collecting data for its own sake but gathering it systematically, evaluating it carefully, using it to choose a course of action, and reexamining the decision once its results are known.

In describing the new model, Sutton (2006) offers a variety of anecdotes and examples that highlight the false assumptions managers often hold and the mistakes they make in the decision-making process. The following list summarizes some of the most common of these:

1. Assuming the right answer can be discerned without careful investigation
2. Assuming that published research findings are not applicable to practical decisions
3. Overgeneralizing isolated problems to the organization as a whole
4. Overgeneralizing solutions and applying them to all operations instead of testing to see which ones work in which conditions
5. Failing to analyze assumptions to be sure they fit the evidence
6. Failing to analyze evidence systematically and without bias
7. Failing to seek out bad news and treat it as useful evidence
8. Failing to use scientific methods of data analysis to separate useful data from mere piles of numbers
9. Failing to continually reexamine and refine decision-making processes
10. Failing, when things go wrong, to conduct post-mortems and learn from their results

Research-Based Practice

Critical Thinking Question: What strategies may make it easier for managers in human service organizations to use evidence-based management?

To illustrate these failures, Pfeffer and Sutton (2006) point to a particular type of management decision—the choice to merge with another organization. Mergers happen for many reasons, such as to increase capacity, acquire new capabilities, absorb potential competitors, or increase market share. They occur in both nonprofit and for-profit organizations; since 2005, the value of all mergers in the United States has averaged almost $6 trillion per year worldwide and almost $2 trillion per year in the United States (Institute for Mergers and Acquisitions, 2011). Despite the zest for mergers these figures reflect, Pfeffer and Sutton note that up to 70 percent of mergers fail to achieve desired results, and few organizations have been able to complete large numbers of them successfully. Still, a few companies, such as Internet infrastructure provider Cisco Systems, have completed scores of successful mergers, and Pfeffer and Sutton believe this is due to the company's use of evidence-based management. This included carefully studying the research literature on mergers to formulate principles about when they succeed or fail. It also included a system for evaluating the company's own mergers in order to learn why some worked better than others.

These steps may seem obvious as ways of making management decisions, and a question naturally arises as to why they are not more commonly followed. Studies point to a wide variety of reasons, but two examples offer insights into why bad managerial decision making persists. The first has to do with the fact that decisions, once made, have their own inertia and are notoriously hard to reverse, especially by the decision makers themselves. This arises from their desire to avoid looking foolish by second-guessing their own work, even to the point of looking still more foolish as a result of problems caused by their decisions. In fact, managers often become more, rather than less, invested in bad decisions, and this may lead to further mistakes. This phenomenon is described in a classic article by Brockner (1992), who viewed it as slavish and unwavering devotion to actions that didn't work. Political scientists have pointed out the frequency of this phenomenon among politicians wedded to flawed domestic policies or foreign military entanglements.

A second reason why faulty decision making persists is offered by Kovner and Rundall (2006), who contrast clinical decision making with managerial decision making. In fields such as medicine, the consequences of poor clinical decisions can be both rapid and dramatic with regard to the health of patients, as when a serious illness is misdiagnosed. In contrast, the consequences of management decisions, whether good or bad, may take years to be known and may be much harder to ascribe to a particular decision. For this reason, the culture of carefulness, precision, feedback, and reliance on research that has arisen in clinical practice within many fields is far less powerful or widespread in management.

To correct this problem, Kovner and Rundall (2006) offer a guide for managers seeking to improve their decision making. It begins with following basic principles governing all research-based endeavors, including identifying the question to be answered, reviewing the theoretical and empirical literature, and evaluating the rigorousness of available research in terms of the validity of measures and strength of study designs. Results then need to be organized in a way that they inform the decision(s) to be made, after which the final step is to bring the information to bear on the decision itself.

In addition to these steps, most writers would add one further step. This would be to gather information about the results of the decision, then re-apply it in a loop to ensure that ongoing assessment and, if necessary, revision of decisions becomes a basic part of the decision-making process. This helps illustrate an often-noted link between successful use of EBM and the development of the "learning organizations" discussed in the next section.

Results from studies of evidence-based management principles have provided some empirical support for this approach. Collins-Camargo and Royse (2010) found that the presence of an organizational culture that promotes evidence-based practice, combined with effective supervision, positively influences workers' perception of their self-efficacy. In the health arena, Friedmann, Lan, & Alexander (2010) found that an orientation on the part of managers toward EBM principles was positively associated with their willingness to adopt new techniques for drug-abuse intervention that had received strong support in empirical studies. Findings such as these appear promising with respect to the ongoing diffusion of EBM practices, but whether the approach will prove to be a lasting addition or a short-lived repackaging of old ideas may not be known for some time. It is worth noting, however, that evidence-based practice continues to be an important trend in micro-level social work, and the parallel aims of EBM suggest that the two approaches may prove to be mutually reinforcing.

Organizational Learning

In our discussion of the open-systems approach we noted that organizations are cybernetic systems, meaning they gather information from their environment and use it to decide on their next actions. Acting on input in this way involves "single loop" learning, while taking action and then monitoring its effect to alter later actions is termed "double loop" learning. For organisms the action/feedback/learning process tends to be immediate and comparatively straightforward: a small hand extending to a countertop and encountering a cookie yields one lesson; the same small hand encountering a hot stove yields another. Argyris and Schön, in two books on organizational learning (1978; 1996), called attention to the constant way in which organizations receive feedback from their environment and attempt to correctly interpret it. They also noted that this feedback is often less immediate and more ambiguous than in the case of organisms. As Senge (1990) explains, organisms receive feedback directly, whereas in an organization it may be one division that takes an action (e.g., a decision by the purchasing department to buy a cheaper part) but a different division that encounters the feedback (such as the consumer complaint or warranty departments).

In addition to horizontal (department-to-department) distance between decision and effect, there is also vertical distance. Most of us have been in situations where we or others around us have bemoaned being the lowly "grunts" suffering the consequences of decisions made by higher-ups. This dynamic leads to two serious problems. First, decisions gone wrong cause deterioration of morale, which in turn initiates a "blame game" cycle in which everyone in the organization thinks everyone else is responsible for things that go bad. Second, because the effects of a decision—good or bad—tend to be out of sight of the decision maker, more and more decisions are made in the absence of information about their effects. Bolman and Deal (2008) refer to this as "system blindness." Its key characteristics are a delayed feedback loop in which information about decisions filters back to management only slowly, and short-term thinking, in which managers begin to favor decisions that make them look good at the moment even if they have long-term negative consequences.

Peter Senge is mostly closely associated with the concept of the "learning organization," because in his 1990 book he proposes that the solution to the above dynamic is to build organizations that mirror the learning process of a single organism. Organisms have nerve pathways that rush information quickly from one part of the body to another, and body systems work in tandem to, for example, quickly withdraw the small hand from the hot stove. Senge's learning organization has similar capacities. It is oriented toward gathering, processing, and sharing information both vertically and horizontally. It also places responsibility for creating the learning organization on leaders. They must provide guidelines, incentives, and examples to staff members to help develop the pathways and procedures needed for rapid movement and absorption of information. They must also become fully familiar with the organization that results from this process—replacing system blindness with "systemic understanding."

The concept of "learning organization" seems to mesh well with the outlook of many administrators and staff members in human service organizations, and Senge's work continues to be cited frequently in this literature. In addition, findings tend to confirm that Senge's ideas are well received when implemented. Latting, Beck, Slack, Tetrick, Jones, Etchegaray, and da Silva (2004) found that the problems of mistrust across vertical levels of a human service organization can be overcome if administrators begin with efforts to create a learning- and innovation-oriented climate within the organization and then move to employee-empowerment efforts supported by supervisors. In their study these efforts were rewarding with increased organizational commitment on the part of employees. This is consistent with results from a study by Beddoe (2009), who found that even in a time of relatively high environmental turmoil social workers in a human service agency were receptive to efforts to adopt the learning-organization model. Receptiveness was diminished, however, to the extent that the change was perceived as a top–down mandate rather than a grassroots-led innovation. Finally, Bowen, Ware, Rose, and Powers (2007) examined educational settings and developed a measure of a school's

Box 7.9 Contemporary Theories

▶ **Purpose.** Most approaches are prescriptive and focus on offering detailed guidelines for both structure and management.

▶ **Key Features.** These theories often build on ideas from earlier works that have been generally accepted. All assume, for example, that environmental circumstances are critical to understanding organizational behavior, that no one structure works equally well for all organizations, and that the personal interests of individuals within organizations powerfully influence how they operate. Contemporary theories tend to differ in their choice of variables that have been ignored or underestimated in prior work. Examples of these include *power* and its exercise through political relationships within organizations (Pfeffer), *culture* (Schein), *sense-making* (Weick), *diversity* and the increasing heterogeneity of the workforce (Cross),

quality and the orientation of management toward consumer satisfaction (Deming), scientific analysis of information to enable decisions that are more evidence based (multiple authors), and the fostering of an organizational orientation toward learning from and responding to the environment (Senge).

▶ **Summary.** Organizational theory continues to evolve, as new theories either supplant older ones or build on their strong points and extend them in new directions. As in the past, many contemporary ideas arose first in studies of commercial firms, and some are easier to adapt to social work organizations than others. Also of note is the fact that work from fields as diverse as political science, biology, and engineering have influenced contemporary organizational theories. Given the increasingly interdisciplinary nature of scientific work, this trend is likely to continue.

capacity to function as a learning organization. Results validated the ability of the instrument to measure theoretically predicted organizational performance. This offers empirical support not only for the validity of the measure but also for Senge's conceptualization of how learning organizations operate.

Analysis of Contemporary Theories

The perspectives discussed here come together in interesting ways. Clearly, one trend coming out of the 1980s was the move toward a better, more thorough understanding of organizational culture. Often this begins with an identification of the locus of power and an understanding of the effectiveness of various individuals or groups in exercising political and leadership skills. These factors, together with the development of an organization-wide sense of shared purpose and ways of operating, make up what has come to be understood as organizational culture. As Morgan (1986) points out, "culture" can in turn be used as a powerful metaphor for understanding how people come together in an organization to define and pursue mutual goals.

An increasingly important factor in the development and evolution of organizational culture is the diversity of the workforce. Organizations of the future will continue to grow more diverse, and this means they will need to continuously address the question of whether their culture embraces this diversity and uses it in ways that benefit both the organization and its individual members.

The notion of quality has become a criterion for designing structures and processes as well as for evaluating organizational success. Whether this will bring about genuine change, however, may depend on how "quality" is defined. In his discussion of goal displacement in organizations, Selznick (1949) argued that one starting point for this process is "unanalyzed abstractions," which are touted by management as being noble goals but may have little real meaning in practice. (References by politicians to powerful but often vague symbols such as "freedom" or "patriotism" are other examples of such abstractions.) If "quality" becomes merely another unanalyzed abstraction, it is likely to have little long-term effect on organizations.

Still, advocates of quality-oriented management argue that it represents truly new ideas due to its emphasis on process rather than exclusively on outcomes. Through this process orientation, they contend, fundamental changes can occur in the way organizations work. Such changes may include increased involvement by line staff in the design of procedures and services. They might also include a definition of quality operations that effectively incorporates workforce diversity as an organizational resource.

The interest generated by evidence-based management principles reveals a widespread desire to ensure that "quality" is not simply an abstraction but a continuously measured effect of operations. In addition, documenting and maintaining this effect must take precedence. If organizations cannot demonstrate that they provide quality services, then it should be immaterial whether, for example, their staff feels empowered by management. The goal of creating "learning organizations" is compatible with evidence-based management principles, in that the flow of information required to successfully implement an evidence-based management approach can only be achieved in the type of data- and communication-sensitive learning organization described by Senge and others.

Or, finally, there continues to be considerable evidence that no "one-size-fits-all" approach to organizing will be found. In Burns and Stalker's language, we may find that some organizations must indeed move away from a mechanistic structure and design toward a more organic approach. For others, however, it may be found preferable to avoid entrepreneurial, *laissez-faire* styles of management in favor of more circumscribed, even mechanistic, approaches. As contingency theorists are fond of saying, "It depends." The most useful organizational and management theories and approaches for today's human service agencies will depend on such factors as mission; objectives; target population served; personal, family, and social problems addressed; types of persons employed; the state of the art of treatment or intervention; and the clarity of outcome expectations. All things considered, what faces us is a compelling challenge for the application of new knowledge and the discovery of new approaches to understanding and managing organizations, particularly those in which social workers operate.

SUMMARY

The goal of this chapter has been to introduce theories about organizations that may help social workers make sense of the organizations in which and with which they work. These theories can be understood partly in terms of how they differ among themselves (Table 7.1). Some (such as scientific management and the human relations school) are prescriptive models, meaning that they provide guidelines on how to organize. Others, such as the bureaucracy and the decision-making model, offer conceptual strategies for analyzing organizations and their operations.

The theories can also be differentiated in terms of their approach to explaining organizational behavior. Some adopt a rational approach in which behavior is seen as the result of logical decision making about how to achieve instrumental goals. Others employ a natural-systems approach, in which the organization is seen as analogous to a biological organism and its behavior as responding to survival and self-maintenance needs.

Theories also differ as to whether they adopt a closed- or open-systems perspective regarding the role of the organization's environment. Closed-systems approaches implicitly focus on internal structure and processes within organizations and tend to pay little or no attention to the role of the environment. Open-systems models emphasize organizations' dependence on their environment and adopt analytical strategies that view internal structure and process as the product of interactions with the environment.

Each theory can also be understood in terms of one or a small group of organizational variables toward which it directs attention. These include structure (the bureaucracy), productivity and the role of management (scientific and universalistic management), social interactions and self-actualization (human relations and Theory Y), organizational goals (the institutional school and management by objectives), strategic choice (the decision-making model), environmental interactions (contingency theory), the exercise of power and political influence (the political economy model), organizational culture, quality (Theory Z and TQM), and applying research principles to inform decision-making (evidence-based management). As is often the case with theory building, many of the models arose from criticisms of earlier works and attempts to correct their flaws. Nonetheless, even the earliest theories retain considerable merit, and a critical task in organizational analysis is to extract from each model its most valuable insights and apply those to the task at hand.

As we will see, organizational analysis in human service organizations has already produced a substantial body of literature that can be helpful to macro practice. Chapter 8 reviews this literature and discusses means for applying it to specific problems that often arise in human service organizations.

Succeed with PEARSON mysocialworklab

Log onto **www.mysocialworklab.com** and answer the questions below. (*If you did not receive an access code to* **MySocialWorkLab** *with this text and wish to purchase access online, please visit* www.mysocialworklab.com.)

1. **Read the MySocialWorkLibrary case study: When an Internship Experience Goes Wrong.** The author views Grace's lack of resources and organizational experience through Ecological Systems Theory. After reading the section in this book about open systems, what can you add to the author's analysis?

2. **Read the MySocialWorkLibrary case study: Trauma-Organized Versus Trauma-Informed Organizational Culture.** List several ways in which human service organizations, and the social workers who work in them, are different from other types of organizations and employees. Based on this case study, which organizational theories seem to fit best? Which ones do not seem appropriate?

PRACTICE TEST
The following questions will test your knowledge of the content found within this chapter. For additional assessment, including licensing-exam-type questions on applying chapter content to practice, visit **MySocialWorkLab**.

1. Which of the following is NOT TRUE of Weber's bureaucratic model of organization?
   a. It embodies a commitment to rational/legal authority.
   b. It functions best in predictable environments with standardized inputs.
   c. It is unsuitable for any type of human service organization.
   d. It is an "ideal type" that probably doesn't exist in pure form in the real world.

2. Open-system theories
   a. consider organizations to be analogous to biological organisms
   b. believe that operating funds are always the most important environmental input
   c. focus on hierarchical relationships among organization members
   d. all of the above

3. Which of the following is NOT TRUE of Taylor's guidelines for management?
   a. criticized by Human Relations theorists who said people aren't motivated only by money
   b. criticized by Decision Making theorists who said poor information always limits efficiency
   c. criticized by Contingency Theorists who said there is seldom only "one best way"
   d. criticized by Evidence-Based Management theorists who said Taylor was scornful of research.

4. Which of the following emphasized the value of customer satisfaction?
   a. the Natural Systems perspective
   b. TQM
   c. Theory X
   d. Management by Objectives

5. Think of an organization with which you are familiar. List some of its norms (e.g., "how things are done around here."). Divide your list into norms shared by most people in that organization and those that are not. Are any of them in conflict or harmful to the organization as a whole?

ASSESS YOUR COMPETENCE
Use the scale below to rate your current level of achievement on the following concepts or skills associated with each competency presented in the chapter:

1	2	3
I can accurately describe the concept or skill.	I can consistently identify the concept or skill when observing and analyzing practice activities.	I can competently implement the concept or skill in my own practice.

_____ Can assess organizational models and critically analyze positive and negative aspects to various organizational approaches.

_____ Can explain the differences between human service organizations' mission, employees, and clients and those of other organizations, and the implication of these differences on organizational structure and change.

_____ Can integrate diversity and other social work values beyond work with clients and into the very structure of the organization.

_____ Can develop policies and strategies where social work evidence is actively applied and a culture of learning and knowledge-seeking prevails throughout the agency.

8

Assessing Human Service Organizations

Core Competencies in this Chapter (Check marks indicate which competencies are covered in depth)				
✓ Professional Identity	✓ Ethical Practice	☐ Critical Thinking	☐ Diversity in Practice	✓ Human Rights & Justice
☐ Research-Based Practice	☐ Human Behavior	☐ Policy Practice	✓ Practice Contexts	☐ Engage, Assess, Intervene, Evaluate

INTRODUCTION

Having reviewed in Chapter 7 a variety of approaches to understanding organizations in general, we now focus on human service organizations (HSOs), where most social workers are employed. These organizations have unique characteristics that distinguish them from other types, and social workers must understand these differences in order to employ their macro-practice skills effectively. The distinguishing features of HSOs are not always clear-cut, so we begin with a discussion of ways in which these organizations are defined.

Hasenfeld (1983) notes that HSOs operate in some way on the people they serve, and though they may distribute or even produce certain goods (as in a food bank or housing cooperative), their focus is on improving the quality of life of their constituents, consumers, or clients. Of course, many kinds of organizations work with or on people, and service providers from boutiques to barber shops to bistros are carefully designed to enhance at least the perceived well-being of their clients. Does this make them HSOs? Hasenfeld (1983) says no, contending that the defining feature of HSOs is that they are designed to promote human welfare. More specifically, they must conform to societal expectations (both implicit and explicit) that the services they provide not only help clients but enhance the overall welfare of the public. Agencies whose activities cannot be legitimized in the context of these expectations cannot be considered HSOs.

A great many organizations may still be encompassed within this definition, and to make sense of such variety one important consideration is the auspice, or sectoral location, of the organization. As we discussed in Chapter 6, HSOs may be classified as one of three types, corresponding to the three major sectors of the economy: public, nonprofit, or for-profit. These are important distinctions because the mission, service orientation, and nature of practice within an organization may vary substantially across sectors. On the other hand, distinctions between organizations in each sector have decreased in the past 20 to 30 years, and at the same time the need for intersectoral cooperation and joint ventures among organizations in different sectors has increased (Darlington & Feeney, 2008; Gronbjerg, 2001; Poole, 2008). In this chapter, we will discuss the concept of "sector" as one variable worth considering when assessing human service organizations, but we do so with the caution that the lines differentiating sectors have become increasingly blurred, and many human service organizations may be difficult to classify as belonging to only one sector or another.

TWO VIGNETTES OF HUMAN SERVICE ORGANIZATIONS

The following vignettes illustrate the issues and problems encountered by social workers in governmental and nonprofit settings in the Canyon City and Lakeside communities we introduced in Chapter 6. Vignette 1 focuses on a large public child welfare agency and its development within Canyon City. The concerns the agency encounters involve factors such as the growth of bureaucracy and a hierarchical organizational structure, the role of elected officials, frustrations concerning slow change processes, constrained creativity, and barriers to client services.

The second vignette describes a medium-sized, nonprofit, church-affiliated agency established in the 1930s at the time the Lakeside community was first developed. As times change, the organization grows through the receipt of government grants and contracts. Issues related to working with boards of directors and sponsoring groups, attempts to address the needs of multiple constituencies in an increasingly regulated environment, and the use of volunteers are illustrated.

We hope these vignettes will show how social workers can begin to analyze circumstances in their own agencies or others with which they interact. Immediately following the vignettes we will discuss some of the issues raised and present a framework for assessing HSOs.

VIGNETTE 1   Canyon County Department of Child Welfare

Creating a Dynamic Organization. Canyon City is the county seat of Canyon. The Canyon County Department of Child Welfare (CCDCW) had long considered itself a unique and innovative organization. Created in the early 1960s, its initial years of development came during a time when national attention was focused on the creation of high-quality human service programs designed to address both client needs and community problems. The department's director was hired after an extensive national search. She built a strong reputation as a person who ran successful programs and was well liked by the community, her staff, and clients.

The director took the job at CCDCW because she was excited by the challenge of building a department from scratch with more-than-adequate resources made available from federal, state, and county governments. She hired staff members who, like herself, were committed to teamwork, collaboration, and problem solving. Middle managers and supervisors were professionals with many years of experience, most of whom had MSW degrees, and many line workers were recent graduates of MSW programs. In selecting among job applicants the director stressed high energy, enthusiasm, collective effort, mutual support, esprit de corps, and competence.

From the 1960s through most of the 1990s, CCDCW built a reputation for high-quality services, a high rate of success, and a positive work environment. It was an organization other counties looked to for leadership in dealing with prominent problems of the time—not only child abuse and neglect but also domestic violence, drug and alcohol abuse, and other family-related problems.

Dismantling a Dynamic Organization. Toward the end of the 1990s, two things happened that changed the direction of the department. First, as a county in a state with one of the fastest-growing populations in the country, Canyon County doubled its population between 1985 and 2000. Increasing fiscal and political conservatism influenced decisions of the county board of supervisors, and the child welfare budget became the focus of a major budget reduction effort. Second, the original director reached retirement age.

The board of supervisors used this opportunity to appoint a person who had spent his career in the insurance industry. They saw this as an opportunity to introduce "hard-nosed business practices" into the running of human service programs. Because of its strong reputation, employment at CCDCW served as a solid reference and made staff members highly marketable in other counties and states. Many managers and supervisors took advantage of this to accept other employment offers, and their positions were filled by individuals who had political connections to the board or to the director. The team approach that had dominated for two decades was replaced by a more rigid bureaucratic structure, and collegial practices were replaced by strictly enforced administrative policies.

(continued)

VIGNETTE 1   Canyon County Department of Child Welfare (*Continued*)

By 2007, CCDCW bore little resemblance to the organization that had built such a strong reputation in prior years. The most noticeable change was in its structure. Its organizational chart reflected clearly defined work units, with reporting lines from entry level all the way to the director. Standardized workloads were assigned regardless of the difficulty or complexity of cases, and standardized performance criteria were used to judge success. Individual discretion in decision making was curtailed, and employee-oriented efforts such as job rotation, job sharing, and flex-time had been eliminated.

Involvement of the County Board. Members of the county board of supervisors began to experience mounting complaints about CCDCW. Although most child maltreatment reports were investigated, many children for whom an initial report was judged invalid were later re-reported as victims of recurring abuse or neglect. Also, annual reports revealed a steady decline in the successful resolution of problems for families served by the department. Eventually, a consultant was hired to do an organizational assessment and to make recommendations to the board of supervisors.

The consultant found that staff expressed low levels of commitment to the organization and its objectives. Line-level workers felt their opinions did not matter, so most either kept comments to themselves or complained to colleagues. When problems were identified, little effort was expended to analyze them or to propose solutions. Most staff members believed that success was defined in terms of adherence to policies and procedures rather than achievement of successful case outcomes. Ambitious staff members who sought upward mobility in the department became experts on internal policies, not on family problems or service provision.

Among those in management positions, the consultant found that most emphasized control. Virtually all decisions about cases had to pass through and be signed by a supervisor and administrator. Managers felt that staff ignored their efforts to adhere to policies and procedures, especially when it came to keeping paperwork up to date. Compliance with rules and completion of required reports and forms were the main criteria by which staff members' performance was judged, and little attention was paid to the question of whether case plans were followed or successful client outcomes achieved. An ability to "do things by the book" and "not rock the boat" was viewed as being more important in assuring positive evaluations than skill in helping clients achieve case objectives.

Professional Identity

Critical Thinking Question: What effects do you think the rigid bureaucracy and limited autonomy may have for the professional identity of committed social workers?

VIGNETTE 2   Lakeside Family Services

Historical Development. The Lakeside Family Services agency was originally incorporated as the Methodist Home for Orphaned Children in Lakeside in 1935. Begun by the Methodist Church, the home served children with no living relatives. Because it was situated on a large parcel of donated land on the outskirts of a metropolitan area, the home became the site of many church gatherings as well as fund-raising events over the years. Volunteers from the church and community were part of almost every activity at the home.

During the 1930s and 1940s, the home was the recipient of generous contributions from wealthy church and civic leaders, and it also became a Red Feather Agency. The Red Feather fund-raising campaign was the forerunner of what was now the local United Way. As campaign contributions increased, so did the scope of the home. By the mid-1950s, it had expanded to include family counseling and services for unwed mothers, and it had hired several professionally trained social workers. Originally, the fifteen-member voluntary board of directors was elected by the Annual Conference of the Methodist Church. The bylaws specified that the executive director and at least 75 percent of board members had to be members of the church. Although it was not required, most staff were also church members, and there was an active volunteer auxiliary of over one hundred persons.

Major Changes Occur. During the 1970s, the board held a number of controversial meetings to determine the future of the home. In addition to changing service needs, fewer and fewer orphans were present and in need of placement. The United Way was putting pressure on the home to merge with two other family service agencies in the same city, and the percentage of the home's budget that came from the Methodist Church dwindled each year, even though actual dollar amounts increased. Several board members were encouraging the home to rethink its mission and actively seek state and federal funding. By 1980, after a decade of controversy, the home changed its name to Lakeside Family Services (LFS), disaffiliated with the Methodist Church, and became a nonprofit provider of government contract services to children, families, and the aged. The agency relocated, and the property on which the home stood reverted to the church, which owned the land. Lakeside Family Services remained a United Way agency, and its funding allocations increased yearly. By the mid-1990s, however, a majority of the agency's budget (70 percent) came from government contracts and grants.

The remaining board members who had supported these changes in the agency's mission, funding, and structure were joined by persons carefully selected for their expertise in fund raising and politics. They chose an executive director with an MSW and hired a director of development to search for new funds.

The agency was composed of three main program components: (1) children's services, (2) family services, and (3) aging services. Each component received funds from government contracts, along with United Way funds and private contributions, and within each component there was service diversification. For example, aging services included homemaker/chore services, home health, and adult day care.

Program directors began complaining that contract dollars never covered the full cost of services and that state and federal regulations were restricting their ability to provide adequate care to their respective clientele. The executive director searched for strategies to deal with these complaints and spent considerable time conferring with directors of other nonprofit organizations.

The Search for Strategies. When the recession of the late 2000s hit, LFS witnessed a period of government retrenchment, and the result was major cutbacks in two of its program areas. In talking with other providers, the executive director detected a new sense of competitiveness that she had not noticed before. When staff suggested using volunteers to help keep services in place, the executive director realized that the active volunteer pool of earlier days had not been nurtured and maintained. In fact, only the aging services program was using volunteers—in this case to do home visits to frail elderly. Even this use was limited, because the volunteers' activities were carefully structured and greatly restricted by state regulations. At the executive director's request, the board approved a fee-for-service schedule and instructed the director of development to create a plan for recruiting fee-paying clients. Staff were angered by the agency's new focus on private fee payers, fearing this meant that the poorest clients, who were often those in greatest need, would go unserved. By 2011, the agency was in serious financial difficulty, and in desperation the executive director approached United Methodist Church officials about the possibility of taking the agency back under the church's wing.

It is not unusual for organizations, over time, to display inconsistent or counterproductive behavior such as that described in the vignettes. When this happens, it is tempting to opt for seemingly simple solutions such as changing directors (Vignette 1) or competing for high-paying clients (Vignette 2). Changes in organizational culture do not occur rapidly, however, as prevailing attitudes and behaviors tend to permeate all levels of staff. Efforts to solve problems through sudden and dramatic change are thus seldom successful, especially if the changes conflict with the mission (perceived or actual) of the agency.

The two vignettes differ in that one organization is public and exists because of a government mandate, whereas the other evolved in the private, nonprofit sector. There are also many parallels, however. Both organizations developed in growth climates, only to face severe financial and political constraints in recent years. Whereas CCDCW became more bureaucratic, LFS became more professionalized. Just as rigid rules developed within CCDCW, LFS experienced the constraints of state and federal regulations when it began receiving more and more governmental funds. Both organizations searched for answers to complex problems that could not be easily solved. In this chapter, we propose a method of conducting organizational assessments that will enable practitioners to understand more fully what is happening in agencies such as CCDCW and LFS.

Framework for Organizational Assessment

The framework we propose for assessing organizations is presented in the form of tasks to be completed and questions to be asked within each task. Although no listing of tasks can be comprehensive for every type of organization, we will attempt to cover the major elements and considerations as they relate to HSOs. Hasenfeld (1995) identifies a framework for assessing these types of agencies that examines (1) the agency and interorganizational relationships and (2) the functioning of the organization itself. The framework recommended here uses a similar "road map" in directing the organizational assessment.

Our framework aligns with models discussed in Chapter 7, such as contingency theory, which emphasize that organizations are best understood by paying attention to internal and external forces that influence organizational functioning. The tasks to be completed within the framework reflect this combined internal/external orientation and are intended to lead to a more complete and accurate understanding of the organization as a whole. It is expected that this, in turn, will facilitate change efforts. Table 8.1 provides an overview of the framework.

Task 1: Assess the Organization's Environment

The process of using the framework in Table 8.1 may be thought of as collecting information about organizations' environments, how they behave in those environments, and how they structure themselves (see Figure 8.1). The framework emphasizes (1) *identification* of the significant elements of an organization's environment and *assessment* of organization/environment relationships and (2) *understanding* the internal workings of the organization.

To understand considerations external to the organization, we will utilize the concept of an organization's *task environment.* As noted in our review of the work of James Thompson (1967) in Chapter 7, the task environment consists of elements outside an organization that enable it to operate and that set the basic context for these operations. Thompson notes that, as originally defined by Dill (1958), the task environment includes four key components: consumers,

Table 8.1   Framework for Assessing Organizations

Task	Variables	Activity
1. Assess the organization's environment	Cash and noncash revenues; resource dependence	1. Identify and assess relationships with revenue sources
	Client characteristics; client funding; organizational domain	2. Identify and assess relationships with clients and referral sources
	Environmental demand; competition vs. cooperation	3. Identify and assess relationships with other elements in the task environment
	Cultural competence	4. Identify and assess cultural competence in external relationships
2. Assess the organization internally	Corporate authority	5. Identify corporate authority and mission
	Structure; managerial style	6. Understand program structure and management style
	Accountability	7. Assess the organization's programs and services. To assess how service efficiency, quality, and effectiveness are measured and used in decision making
	Employee relations	8. Assess personnel policies, procedures, and practices
	Diversity friendliness	9. Assess whether the internal workings of the organization are diversity-friendly
	Budget management; technical resources	10. Assess adequacy of technical resources and systems

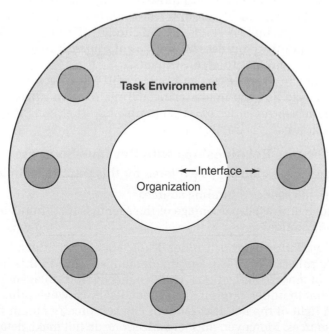

Figure 8.1
Organization, Task Environment, and Interface

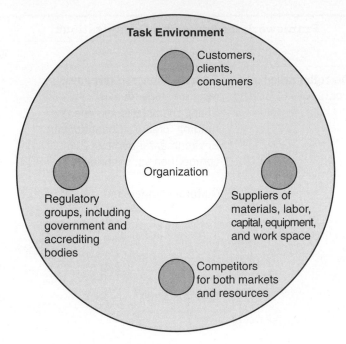

Figure 8.2
Typical Task Environment for an Organization

suppliers, competitors, and regulators (pp. 27–28). These are illustrated in Figure 8.2.

Hasenfeld (1995) proposes a slightly different model that includes three components: (1) a generalized agency environment (organizations, entities, and systems important to the agency), (2) market relations with entities that receive an agency's outputs and with those offering complementary or competing services, and (3) regulatory groups. Martin (1980) also identifies environmental entities important to HSOs. In her model, the most critical of these elements are (1) funding sources, (2) sources of noncash revenues, (3) clients and client sources, and (4) other constituents.

We will draw on these works and will distill Martin's four elements into two key variables to be used in analyzing an organization's task environment: (1) cash and noncash revenues and (2) clients and other constituents, including regulatory groups.

Identify and Assess Relationships with Revenue Sources

Cash Revenues.   Questions to be explored for this activity include:

 ◗ What are the agency's funding sources?
 ◗ How much and what percentage of the agency's total funds are received from each source?

A cynical variation on the "Golden Rule" states that "those who have the gold make the rules." There is a certain element of truth to this, especially in the operation of most organizations. Understanding how an agency is financed is often essential to understanding the agency itself. However, this process can be difficult in light of the fact that modern HSOs typically obtain funds from a multitude of sources. Moreover, most organizations do not make detailed funding information readily available except in cases where public funds are used and budget documents are, by law, a matter of public record.

Ethical Practice

Critical Thinking Question: Why do workers have an ethical responsibility to take an active interest in agency funding matters?

The first step in assessing organizational funding is to determine the sources from which funds are acquired. The following list details those sources for HSOs:

Major Cash Revenue Sources for Human Service Organizations

1. Government funds

> Direct government appropriations
>
> Government purchase-of-service contracts
>
> Government grants
>
> Matching funds
>
> Tax benefits

2. Donated funds

> Direct charitable contributions (from individuals, groups, and associations such as religious groups)
>
> Indirect contributions (e.g., via United Way)
>
> Private grants (e.g., foundation monies)
>
> Endowments

3. Fees for service

> Direct payments from clients
>
> Payments from third parties (e.g., private or public insurers)

4. Other agency income

> Investments (e.g., interest, dividends, royalties)
>
> Profit-making subsidiaries
>
> Fund-raising events and appeals

As might be expected, the sources of its funds greatly influence an organization's flexibility in how it responds to proposed change. Governmental agencies that depend entirely on direct appropriations are likely to have most of their activities rigidly specified by public policy. Nonprofit agencies usually receive funds from a wide variety of sources and thus may have greater flexibility, but they also experience greater uncertainty about the reliability of each source, and even donated funds typically come with strings attached. For-profit agencies that depend on paying clients also have greater flexibility than public agencies, but the overriding imperative in their decision making is the requirement that they return profits to their investors.

Direct appropriations are usually the only source of revenue for organizations at the federal level. This is also true for many state, county, and local agencies, but these organizations also may use a mixture of funds from higher levels of government. In general, the lower the level of government, the larger the number of funding sources organizations at that level will use. Among the most important mechanisms for dissemination are block grants (lump-sum federal appropriations in which specific allocations are left to state or local governments), matching funds (which, for example, provide a certain amount of federal funds for each dollar expended by state or local agencies), and grant programs in which funds are targeted for a specific use and are restricted accordingly. In the vignette regarding Canyon County Child Welfare Department earlier in this chapter, the agency was funded solely by government funds, although from a combination of direct appropriations, block grants, and matching funds.

Nonprofit agencies, such as Lakeside Family Services in Vignette 2, tend to have a greater range of funding sources. And though these are the agencies toward which most charitable contributions are targeted, such contributions often make up only a small portion of the annual budget of most nonprofit agencies. The most recent figures available show that in 2007, nonprofit organizations garnered an average of 22 percent of their funds from charitable contributions (down from 26 percent in 1977); 67 percent from dues, fees, and charges or government contracts (up from 65 percent in 1977); and 11 percent from other sources (Urban Institute—National Center for Charitable Statistics, 2010; Weitzman & Jalandoni, 2002).

In a study that focused specifically on nonprofit HSOs, we found the average distribution across funding sources was 34 percent from government contracts, 33 percent from charitable donations, 13 percent from client fees, 10 percent from public grants, 5 percent from private grants, and 5 percent from other sources (McMurtry, Netting, & Kettner, 1991). More recent evidence suggests that reliance on client fees has increased as funding from donors has shrunk. In a comprehensive study by the Independent Sector (2005), results showed that 31 percent of revenues of nonprofit organizations came from government contracts and other funds, 20 percent from individual givers or foundations, 11 percent from sources such as interest on investments, and 38 percent from charges to clients or individual members. It is likely that the reliance on donations has dropped further since that time, especially in the wake of the economic downturn that began in 2008. As one example, donations to nonprofit health-care organizations fell by 11 percent in just one year between 2008 and 2009 (Association of Fundraising Professionals, 2010).

It is clear from the above results that government contracts and other public funds are important sources of revenue for most organizations in the voluntary sector, and in combination with revenues from fees, they accounted for more than two-thirds of budget of organizations in the Independent Sector study. This suggests that "charitable organizations" may be more accurately viewed as quasi-public or quasi-fee-for-service organizations, and the most important elements in their task environments will be public agencies with which they contract, along with paying clients or members.

This pattern does not necessarily hold for all types of human service organizations, however. In a study of faith-based social service coalitions, Ebaugh, Chafetz, and Pipes (2005) found that these organizations obtained a relatively small share of their budgets (16.5 percent) from governmental sources while drawing the largest share (24.9 percent) from the congregation or church denomination with which they were associated. In an interesting follow-up, Scheitle (2009) found that religious-based nonprofits that receive governmental funds are more subtle in expressing their religious identity and are inclusive in their language, but this does not appear to result from the acceptance of those funds. In our study of HSOs, another major portion of their budgets (18.7 percent) came from individual donations, but some rely mostly on third-party payments (e.g., from insurance companies) for services provided to clients (Egan & Kadushin, 2004). These authors also point out that differences in revenue sources may be linked to differences in structural and operating characteristics across HSOs.

For-profit firms are a growing arena for social work practice, and among such organizations as hospitals and nursing homes they are major service providers. As of 2010, twenty-three health-related companies (not including pharmaceutical manufacturers) were on the Fortune 500 list of the largest commercial firms in the United States (CNN/Money.com, 2010), and all of these had annual revenues exceeding the $3.84 billion in charitable donations raised by United Way nationally in its 2009 campaign (Chronicle of Philanthropy, 2010). Other areas in which large human service corporations have developed include child care, home-based nursing care, and corrections. Also, private counseling firms, though traditionally small in scale, are a part of this sector. All these organizations share a principal reliance on fee-for-service revenues.

Clients themselves sometimes pay for services from HSOs, but because many are unable to pay it is more common for their costs to be covered by other organizations. This can mean that consumers themselves are a less important part of the task environment of private agencies than insurance companies and other third-party payers who establish criteria and rates for reimbursement. For example, a for-profit counseling agency may draw most of its clients from the employee assistance program of a nearby manufacturing plant; thus relationships with the manufacturer are likely to be the key environmental consideration for the counseling agency.

A critical point in understanding funding sources is that most funds come with strings attached, and decisions on how to spend them may rest much more with the funding agency than with the recipient. Using governmental organizations as an example, a county agency that appears to be subject to local decision-making processes may in fact be more accurately viewed as a local extension of the state agency that provides the bulk of its funds. A change episode that attempted to influence the use of these funds would be unlikely to succeed unless the persons seeking change recognize that decision-making power over the funds rests with organizations in the agency's task environment rather than inside its own boundaries.

Most funds come with strings attached, and decisions on how to spend them may rest much more with the funding agency than with the recipient.

The number of sources from which an agency's funds are drawn is also a key consideration. Somewhat paradoxically, an agency with many funding sources often has greater autonomy and flexibility than one with few, because the loss of any single source is less likely to jeopardize the overall viability of the organization. On the other hand, the greater the number of funding sources, the more complex the agency's operations become. With each new source comes another layer of regulatory constraints, program diversity, and accountability expectations. The agency with a single funding source may risk becoming rigid and highly specialized, but the agency with many sources may have difficulty defining or focusing on its mission.

Noncash Revenues. Questions to be asked with regard to noncash revenues include:

- Does the organization use volunteers? If yes, how many and for what purposes?
- Are appropriate efforts made to match volunteers' skills and abilities with the tasks assigned?
- What in-kind resources (e.g., food, clothing, physical facilities, etc.) does the organization receive?
- What tax benefits does the organization receive?

When considering resources it is important to remember that actual dollars coming into an HSO are not its only form of resources. Many other assets on which agencies rely are less obvious than cash revenues but sometimes equally important. Three such assets are volunteers, in-kind contributions, and tax benefits.

Volunteers have traditionally been a mainstay of HSOs. As noted in Chapter 2, the entire nonprofit human service sector originated with the activities of individual volunteers who began to work together in order to make their efforts more productive. In the Lakeside Family Services vignette, volunteers were critical to the organization's early development. Today, the contribution of these individuals to HSOs is enormous. The U.S. Bureau of Labor Statistics (BLS) reports that "about 63.4 million people, or about 26.8 percent of the population, volunteered through or for an organization at least once between September 2008 and September 2009" in the United States (2009). This number included roughly one-fourth of adult men and one-third of adult women. Volunteers spent a median of about 51 hours on volunteer activities over the course of a year. Multiplied by the total number of volunteers, this corresponds to 3.27 billion hours of volunteer work which, at an estimated value of $20.85 per volunteer hour during 2009 (Independent Sector, 2010) produces a total monetary value of $67.4 billion for all volunteering in the United States. According to the BLS report, religious organizations benefitted from the largest number of volunteer hours (34 percent of all hours), followed by educational or youth-oriented services (26.1 percent) and social or community services (13.9 percent).

The report also indicates that volunteers span almost all age ranges and perform a vast array of tasks, from serving meals in senior centers to sitting on boards of directors of counseling agencies, to staffing crisis hotlines. In the BLS study (2009), volunteering rates were highest among individuals in the 35- to 44-year-old age group, but those in the 65-and-over age group who volunteered contributed the largest average number of hours. Some agencies rely on volunteers to provide supplementary services that undergird or enhance the work of professional staff, as in hospitals, whereas in other agencies most services are provided directly by volunteers themselves, as in Big Brothers or Big Sisters programs. Volunteers also bring with them a wide range of knowledge and skills, and many organizations that rely heavily on the work of volunteers employ part-time or full-time volunteer coordinators. In addition to supervising activities, coordinators also seek to match volunteers' skills to the tasks needing to be done. Their success in achieving this can have a dramatic effect on the productivity, satisfaction, and service longevity of each volunteer.

A second type of resource is *in-kind contributions* of material goods. Examples include food, clothing, physical facilities, real estate, vehicles, and a wide variety of household and office materials. In some cases these goods are provided for use directly by the agency; in others they are donated for the purpose of resale in order to generate cash revenues, or they are simply passed through the agency for distribution directly to clients. In each circumstance, the total value of these resources to organizations is substantial. Specific figures are difficult to obtain, but one clue to the magnitude of this source of income is offered by deductions on individual income taxes claimed for noncash charitable contributions. In 2007, about 24 million individual filers claimed noncash charitable contributions, the monetary value of which totaled almost 58 billion dollars (U.S. Internal Revenue Service, 2010).

As these numbers suggest, *tax benefits* are particularly important for private, nonprofit HSOs. Indeed, one defining characteristic of nonprofit agencies is an official designation as a charitable organization under section 501(c)(3) of federal Internal Revenue Service regulations. Meeting the requirements of this section allows nonprofit agencies to avoid income taxes that for-profit firms must pay, and this can be a critical benefit in service arenas such as health care, where nonprofit and for-profit hospitals often engage in intense competition for patients and physicians. Tax laws are also important in terms of their effects on other revenue sources, especially charitable contributions. Economic analyses suggest that changes such as the Tax Reform Act of 1986 may reduce contributions to nonprofit agencies by limiting tax breaks for contributors to those who itemize deductions on their tax returns (Liu & Zhang, 2008; Uler, 2009). Still, tax deductions claimed for cash contributions (beyond the noncash contributions mentioned earlier, and including the cash portion of carryover, from prior years) totaled about $144 billion in 2007 (U.S. Internal Revenue Service, 2010), and it is likely that this source of funds for HSOs would drop precipitously if changes in tax laws were to make charitable contributions no longer deductible.

Noncash resources are important considerations in an organizational assessment because an agency's behaviors may be understood as efforts to acquire and maximize these assets. For example, an organization that relies heavily on volunteers may seek to protect this resource even if in doing so it comes into conflict with the interests of professional staff. Similarly, the structure of an agency may be altered to take advantage of one of these resources, as with the sizable number of nonprofit agencies that have begun raising funds by collecting donated material goods and reselling them through thrift stores. Attention to noncash resources may also be important in initiating change efforts. For example, some organizational problems are often left unaddressed due to pessimism about the ability to obtain revenues to add or augment services, and a change agent's awareness of the possible usefulness of noncash resources may be key to overcoming this barrier. Using a tool such as the one depicted in Table 8.2 can be helpful in assessing the status of cash and noncash resources for an organization.

Table 8.2   Tool for Assessing Cash and Noncash Resources

Sources of Cash Revenues	Percentage of Revenue	Flexibility in Using Resources
Contract with state department of social services	26	Low
Client fees	22	High
Charitable donations	14	High
Government grants	8	Low
Other	30	Depends

Sources of Noncash Revenues	Description
Volunteers	Nine members of the board of directors Thirty-three respite care volunteers for foster parents Twelve transportation providers
In-kind	One van One branch office
Tax benefits	$120,000 annually in savings from nonprofit status

Relationships with Revenue Sources.   The question to be explored for this activity is:

▶ What is the nature and quality of the relationship between funding sources and the agency?

All organizations rely on elements in their environment from which they can obtain resources needed for survival. In the terminology of systems theory, this is called *resource dependence*, and it leads organizations (1) to establish relationships with other organizations in the environment that can provide needed resources and (2) to favor relationships with organizations that can minimize uncertainty regarding availability of resources. In establishing these relationships, an organization must also consider its need for different types of resources. Cash and noncash funds represent one type of resource, but HSOs also compete for other types such as needed services (e.g., accounting or building maintenance) favorable locations, staff, and clients.

Resource dependence is a key consideration for contingency theorists, such as Thompson (1967), who contend that internal structures and processes in organizations are usually the products of forces exerted by external relationships. Research has tended to support this contention. For example, Lucas, Avi-Itzhak, and Robinson (2005) found that the stability and predictability of external funds among nursing homes was a significant predictor of whether they adopted management systems based on continuous quality improvement guidelines (as discussed in connection with the TQM movement in Chapter 7). A study by Mosley (2010) also found that HSOs' engagement in policy advocacy efforts was predicted by resource dependence—in this case the perceived importance of heightening awareness of the need for their services among key elements of their task environment.

The central issue in resource dependence is often cash funding, and organizations tend to mold themselves in ways that reflect the sources of such funds and, in particular, their predictability. Twombly (2002) compared more than 2,000 secular and faith-based organizations and found that the latter tended to have a lower diversity of services and slower rates of service expansion. This appeared to be a result of these organizations' greater dependency on private contributions, which offers less predictable funding than the more diversified funding base typical of secular organizations. In a study of service effectiveness in 127 public and independent HSOs, Mano-Negrin (2003) found that in public agencies' variations in effectiveness tended to be explained by external input from client advocates and other stakeholders. However, in independent agencies the most important determinant of effectiveness was internal factors such as structure or management practices. She attributes these differences to the fact that a public agency's dependence on public funds induces it to be more responsive to community input.

Dabelko, Koenig, and Danso (2008) examined whether the resource dependence model would predict how HSOs and for-profit firms that provide adult day services respond to rules for accessing public funding. They found that the organizations adapted by using many of the strategies discussed by contingency theorists we reviewed in Chapter 7. The tool depicted in Table 8.3 summarizes these and other points and can be helpful in assessing agencies' relationships with revenue sources.

Table 8.3	**Assessing the Relationship to Funding Sources**
Relevant Funding Sources	Nature of Communication, Length of Relationship, Changes in Funding
Contract with state department of social services	Quarterly site visits; have contracted for 12 years; funding has always stayed steady or increased
Client fees	Most clients are seen on a weekly basis; they either pay directly or through their insurance plan; client fees have declined 2 percent in the past three years
Charitable donations	Largest donations come from church groups; agency staff visit church representatives once a year; donations have increased 3.5 percent in the past year

Identify and Assess Relationships with Clients and Referral Sources

Relationships with Clients.   Questions to be explored for this activity include:

- What is the organization's domain (e.g., what criteria does it use to determine which clients it will serve)?
- Must clients be recruited or informed about the organization? Will they seek it out on their own, or will they be mandated to participate?
- How does the organization deal with clients who seek its services but do not fit the profile of those it typically serves?
- How are the costs of client services covered, and how does the organization deal with those who cannot pay?
- What are the major sources of client referrals?

No human service organization can serve all clients who may be in need of services in its area, so each organization typically establishes definitions of the types of clients it will serve. These often take the form of *eligibility criteria* that clients must meet in order to be considered a fit with the organization and its services. Clients who meet the criteria are said to be within the organization's *domain*, which may be thought of as the boundary drawn by the organization between eligible and ineligible clients (Levine & White, 1961). As we will discuss further in the next section, an organization's domain can refer both to what it does and to whom it serves, and domains are often the means by which organizations establish their role or niche within their environments.

The decision about whether a given client fits within an organization's domain is often based on a variety of factors. These may include demographic characteristics, such as age, gender, or race/ethnicity, as with organizations that focus on serving children, women, or a particular immigrant population. In other cases, eligibility may be determined by the presence of certain problems affecting clients, such as health concerns, substance use, or domestic violence. Complex problems such as poverty often require multiple services such as temporary income support, food assistance, employment counseling, and others, and it is rare for a single organization to provide all these services. In these cases, the organization may establish service eligibility based not only on the presence of a problem but also on the need for a particular service related to that problem, as might be the case with an agency that provides housing assistance.

In assessing eligibility criteria, it is important to determine whether some client groups are systematically disadvantaged by certain criteria or the manner in which they are applied. This can occur in a variety of ways. Clients may be told they are eligible for services but at only one particular site, and for those with transportation problems this may be the same as being declared ineligible. Parents with young children may be offered job training, but if child care is not made available there may be no way they can participate. Lexchin and Grootendorst (2004) describe a health services program in which a co-pay for prescriptions was imposed in order to increase clients' access to other medications, but because of the co-pay, the clients' use of necessary prescription drugs went down. Another study of eligibility criteria requiring clients to have lived in the community for a certain time showed clients who move frequently are often denied services when they need them the most, due to residency requirements (Montoya, Bell, Richard, Goodpastor, & Carlson, 1999). Some organizations and their services are well known within a community, so there is little need to recruit clients. Other organizations may be new or may have opened a new branch or initiated a new program, which means they must take steps to attract prospective clients. When assessing the organization, these steps should be evaluated in terms of whether a sufficient number of clients apply to fill the capacity available, whether many applicants are declared ineligible and turned away, and whether, even after services commence, the number of unserved clients in the community remains large.

Another important variable in understanding the client population is the financial relationship between client and agency. In commercial firms, customers usually pay directly for goods or services they receive, and the organizations carefully design their outputs to meet the needs of this group. In human service organizations, however, those who pay for services may not be the same as those who receive them. This is an important distinction, and for our purposes we will define the clients of HSOs as those who directly receive services, not necessarily those who pay for them. Clients who cover the cost of their services, either personally or through third-party reimbursement, will be termed *full-pay clients*. These clients are important resources that agencies seek to attract and are most likely to serve, because the revenues they provide can be used to offset the cost of serving other clients.

Clients who pay less than the cost of their services or who pay nothing at all are termed *non-full-pay clients* (Netting, McMurtry, Kettner, & Jones-McClintic, 1990). Because revenues for serving these clients must be generated from other sources (e.g., charitable donations or profits earned from full-pay clients), agencies often do nothing to attract these clients and may even erect eligibility barriers to restrict their numbers. A prominent example of this is the tendency of health-care providers to restrict or refuse services to Medicare or Medicaid recipients because of reimbursement rates being viewed as insufficient to cover service costs (Flint, 2006). Restrictions or refusals can also occur with clients who seek relatively costly services or services the agency does not provide. A complete agency assessment should include a determination of whether the organization makes appropriate efforts to direct clients it rejects to organizations that may be able to serve them.

Some client groups are systematically disadvantaged by certain criteria or the manner in which they are applied.

Human Rights and Justice

Critical Thinking Question: When contracting with private agencies, what are some strategies that may help to ensure that vulnerable populations still are served?

Despite these dynamics, HSOs must have clients in order to fulfill their mission and function, so sources of client referrals are important elements in their task environments. Formal and informal referral arrangements among agencies for exchange of clients are often viewed as being of equal importance as relationships with funding sources. As an example, residential treatment centers for youth are dependent on client referrals from family counseling centers, juvenile courts, school districts, and others, so they will tend to maintain close relationships with these organizations. Table 8.4 depicts a tool that may be helpful in identifying client populations and referral sources.

Table 8.4   Identifying Client Populations and Referral Sources

Client Groups Served

1. Couples/individuals relinquishing children
2. Couples wanting to adopt
3. Foster parent applications
4. Foster parents
5. Individuals in need of personal counseling
6. Families in need of counseling
7. Drug abusers

Demographic Makeup of Client Population

Age	Percentage	Ethnicity	Percentage	Gender	Percentage	Fees	Percentage
Under 20	5	American Indian	3	Female	64	Full pay	26
20–29	15	African American	14	Male	36	Some pay	38
30–39	22	Asian American	4			No pay	15
40–49	29	Hispanic	19			Contract	21
50–59	19	White	60				
60–69	8						
70+	2						

Referral Sources	Percentage
School counselors/teachers	31
Clergy	22
Social service agencies	19
Physicians and clinics	15
Attorneys	13

Relationships with Referral Sources.   Questions to be explored for this activity include:

- Does the agency claim a larger domain than it serves?
- Does demand for services outstrip supply or is there unused capacity?
- What types of clients does the organization refuse (e.g., are there disproportionate numbers of poor, elderly, persons of color, women, persons with disabilities, gays/lesbians, or other groups that are typically underserved)?

As we discussed earlier, an organization's domain refers to what the organization does and whom it serves, and it is the means by which the organization establishes its role or niche within the environment. *Domain setting* refers to the process by which organizations establish themselves and their roles among others within their task environment. One part of the process is domain legitimation, in which the organization wins acknowledgment of claims it makes as to its sphere of activities and expertise. Legitimation is not always immediately forthcoming, and there is usually a disparity between what an organization says are its boundaries, the *claimed domain*, and what these boundaries actually are, the *de facto domain* (Greenley & Kirk, 1973).

Claims regarding domains tend to evolve along with circumstances in the environment. Agencies seek to take advantage of available resources, and most are constantly adjusting their domains as a means of doing so. Funding trends from charitable or governmental sources are usually closely watched, and in order to ensure resource flow agencies may attempt to compete for funds in areas where they have little experience or expertise.

As noted earlier, clients are also resources, although an individual client may be viewed as either an asset or liability depending on whether the client fits within the agency's domain and whether he or she can pay for services. Recognizing this dynamic, a long-standing concern relative to agencies' relationships with clients is whether certain groups of clients, especially the most needy, are deliberately excluded from access to services (Cloward & Epstein, 1965). Research results have suggested that this may indeed be the case.

In one early study, Kirk and Greenley (1974) examined clients' efforts to obtain services. Their results showed that only forty-seven of every one hundred clients were served by the first two agencies they visited; the rest were either rejected or referred elsewhere. In a companion piece, Greenley and Kirk (1973) analyzed the dynamics of these outcomes and identified domain selection as a key factor. Because most agencies had larger claimed domains than de facto domains, they attracted clients that they were unable to serve. This disparity was apparently seen as desirable by many agencies, since it provided a sort of cushion and afforded the opportunity to select only the best-fitting, full-pay clients. This process is known as *creaming*. Empirical support for the existence of these dynamics has been found in studies of services for homeless adults and youth (Hunter, Getty, Kemsley, & Skelly, 1991; Thompson, McManus, Lantry, Windsor, Flynn, 2006).

Selection of clients is also driven by the types of clients an agency's contracts with governmental providers allow it to serve. Hasenfeld and Powell (2004) studied a group of nonprofit HSOs that contracted with a public welfare-to-work (WTW) agency that provided time-limited benefits to welfare recipients on the condition that the clients transition as quickly as possible to full-time employment. The study's findings showed that the agencies' environment contained elements that established detailed constraints on clients they could serve, services offered, and service outcomes. These constraints were often at odds with the service models agency staff wanted to use and were manifested in evaluation criteria established by funding and regulatory sources.

These dynamics relate to the issue of boundary control, which refers to the ability of the agency to reject clients it does not wish to serve. Greenley and Kirk (1973) found that agencies with high boundary control (usually for-profit and high-prestige nonprofit organizations) were most likely to engage in creaming, leaving clients who were rejected with the task of finding agencies that had low boundary control. This resulted in clients with the greatest difficulties and the least ability to pay having as their only option those agencies that were already the most overcrowded and had the fewest available resources. Evidence of creaming has been found in settings ranging from the admission of Medicaid-dependent clients to nursing homes (Meyer, 2001), to the awarding of training vouchers to the unemployed (Hipp & Warner, 2008), to admission of underprivileged children to charter schools (West, Ingram, & Hind, 2006).

Boundary control is generally highest in for-profit organizations, where the primary goal is making money, and lowest in governmental organizations, which are intended to provide a safety net for clients who cannot obtain services elsewhere. However, since the early 1980s, governmental policies have favored *privatization*—the shifting of more services to the private sector. A guiding assumption has been that private-sector organizations can provide services more efficiently and effectively than large governmental bureaucracies, and that, in the case of nonprofit organizations, they can also draw on their traditional commitments to the poor to ensure that these clients are served.

Unfortunately, a number of studies suggest that this trend has often led to service reductions or restrictions, particularly on the part of nonprofit agencies. Among the reasons for these cutbacks have been changes in governmental rules (Hasenfeld & Powell, 2004) and delays in reimbursement for contract services (Kramer & Grossman, 1987). In a study of the effects of changing governmental policies on nonprofit agencies in the Chicago area, Gronbjerg (1990) found that services often diminished because these policies overestimated the ability of nonprofits to provide services to the most economically disadvantaged clients.

Human service agencies adjust their boundaries according to a wide range of factors, and a misunderstanding of these may lead to critical service gaps. One key criterion in boundary setting is the nature of the clients themselves, and being poor or having complex, long-standing problems are characteristics that simultaneously increase the level of need yet decrease the likelihood of being served. Table 8.5 provides a tool that may be helpful in assessing an agency's relationship to client populations and referral sources.

Identify and Assess Relationships with Other Elements in the Task Environment

Relationships with Regulatory Bodies, Professional Organizations, and the General Public. Questions to be explored for this activity include:

> ◗ What state and federal regulatory bodies oversee programs provided by this organization?

Table 8.5	**Assessing Relationships with Clients and Referral Sources**	
Client Population	Supply vs. Demand	Unserved/Underserved
Adoptive couples/children available	Five couples for every child available	Special needs children
Foster homes/children in need	1.5 children in need for every home available	Special needs children
Families in need of counseling	Two- to three-week waiting list	Non-English-speaking families
Drug abusers	Three-month waiting list	Poor, no pay, low pay, uninsured

- ♦ With what government agencies does this organization contract for service provision?
- ♦ What professional associations, licensing and certification boards, and accrediting bodies influence agency operations?
- ♦ What are the perceptions of the "general public" in terms of the relevance, value, and quality of agency services?

Within an organization's task environment are groups that do not necessarily provide resources but that set the context in which the agency operates. One example is regulatory bodies responsible for establishing the boundaries of acceptable service practices. Some of these may be governmental licensing agencies that inspect and certify the services and physical environment of organizations such as nursing homes, child-caring institutions, and residential treatment facilities. Others may be contracting agencies that enforce adherence to detailed procedural guidelines in order for the organization to be reimbursed for services it provides. Still others may be local, state, and federal revenue departments that levy taxes and monitor financial accounting procedures. Extensive accounting and funding-usage requirements are also imposed by nongovernmental funding sources such as the United Way.

Other organizations that impose some sort of regulatory boundaries include professional associations, labor unions, and accrediting bodies. As a general rule, accrediting bodies certify the operation of organizations as a whole, whereas professional associations and licensing bodies certify the work of individuals. This means the influence of these groups may be exerted at the organizational level or through individuals within it. For example, the activities of staff who are members of the National Association of Social Workers (NASW) or the Academy of Certified Social Workers (ACSW) are governed by the NASW Code of Ethics. State licensing agencies impose similar constraints, and organizations with a high proportion of employees who meet these requirements may function differently than those with relatively few. At the organizational level, accrediting bodies such as the Joint Commission on Accreditation of Health Care Organizations (JCAHO) impose a variety of requirements for how a member agency must operate, and loss of accreditation through violation of these guidelines can threaten the agency's viability by restricting its funding and client referrals.

The "general public" is another part of this set of constituents. By their nature, HSOs are dependent on societal approval for their activities, but the views of members of the general public are not always apparent. Moreover, public opinion is seldom unanimous, so organizations must often determine which of a wide variety of expressed views represents the prevailing attitude. Finally, agencies may at times be forced to stand against public opinion, as in the case of advocacy organizations that must confront ignorance or discrimination against particular clients or client groups.

Within the task environment, public opinion is often conveyed through a bewildering diversity of elements. These include elected representatives, interest groups, civic organizations, and others. Funding sources are also indirect but important indicators of public views. For example, patterns in the ebb and flow of charitable donations may reveal issues that are considered important by donors, and the same holds true for priorities of private foundations. Finally, mass media outlets are critical purveyors of public attitudes, although they often emphasize the most extreme rather than the most typical opinions.

Child protective services offer an example of the relationship between agencies, public opinion, and mass media (as both a carrier and shaper of public opinion). Deciding whether to remove an at-risk child from his or her home involves a delicate balancing act between concern for the child's well-being and concern for parental rights. In one well-publicized case in the state of Washington, for example, fatal abuse of a child led to public outcry, which resulted in legislative changes that instructed protective service workers to favor the safety of the child in such decisions. However, publicity about cases in other locations has featured caricatures of protective service workers as "child-snatchers," leading to legislative imposition of stricter guidelines governing the removal of children.

Cordes and Henig (2001) call attention to how public opinion affects where and how funds are allocated. They note that new methods of giving allow contributors greater freedom to select specific agencies and causes they wish to support. This offers more flexibility to the giver, but it may erode the effectiveness of umbrella organizations such as the United Way in assessing community needs broadly and distributing funds based on those assessments.

The key point is that public opinion is dynamic rather than static, and similar agencies at different times or in different places may encounter widely divergent attitudes and expectations. Identifying the task environment is thus an ongoing process as public attitudes change and funding methods evolve. A tool such as the one depicted in Table 8.6 can be used to identify important elements in the agency's task environment.

Public opinion is dynamic rather than static, and similar agencies at different times or in different places may encounter widely divergent attitudes and expectations.

Relationships with Competitors and Collaborators.   Questions to be explored for this activity include:

- What other agencies provide the same services to the same clientele as this organization?
- With whom does the organization compete?
- With whom does the organization cooperate? Is the organization part of a coalition or an alliance?
- How is the organization perceived by regulatory bodies, government contracting agencies, professional organizations, accrediting bodies, and the general public in relation to its peers and competitors?

Table 8.6   Identifying Regulatory, Professional, and Media Organizations

Example Organization	Programs Affected
Regulatory bodies	
State Department of Child Welfare	Day care
County Health Department	Meals on Wheels program
Organizations issuing grants and contracts	
Federal demonstration grants (www.grants.gov)	Respite care
State Department of Developmental Disabilities	Vocational training
Professional associations	
National Association of Social Workers (www.nasw.org)	Individual and group counseling
American Association for Marriage and Family Therapy (AAMFT) (www.aamft.org)	Couple and family counseling
Accreditation organizations	
Joint Commission on Accreditation of Healthcare Organizations (JCAHO) (www.jointcommission.org)	Home care
National Association for the Education of Young Children (NAEYC)	Day care
Licensing and certification boards	
State Social Work Licensing Board	Individual and group counseling
Public media and advocacy organizations	
Local network television affiliate	Child maltreatment investigations
ARC (www.thearc.org)	Vocational training

One further critical element in an organization's environment is other service providers. Relationships among agencies that occupy each others' task environments can be competitive, cooperative, or a mixture of the two, depending on the circumstances.

In Chapter 6, Table 6.5 delineated five levels of interaction leading to improved programming. These levels were communication, cooperation, coordination, collaboration, and confederation. The levels can be used to assess how an HSO relates to other members of its task environment.

Competitive relationships characterize circumstances in which two or more agencies seek the same resources (clients, funds, volunteers, etc.) from the same sources. Nonprofit agencies compete among themselves for charitable donations as well as government and private foundation grants. McMurtry and colleagues (1991) found that nonprofit agencies reported their greatest competition for both funds and clients came from other nonprofit organizations rather than from for-profit organizations. Other studies have suggested that competition has increased between nonprofit and for-profit agencies in areas such as welfare-to-work transitions (Frumkin & Andre-Clark, 2000), and Gibelman (2007) discusses how efforts to channel government funds to faith-based agencies posed unexpected threats to those agencies due to lack of experience with marketplace dynamics. In these cases competition targets mostly contract-eligible clients, but in other settings the focus is on fee-for-service clients. Some communities have few HSOs and limited possibilities for competition, however, and a study by Van Slyke

(2003) indicated that both cost and effectiveness can be diminished when public agencies aggressively engage in service contracting within communities that lack a competitive service environment. Similarly, Rosenau and Lako (2008) found that expected benefits in containing costs did not occur in the Netherlands following the switch from a government-based system to one in which nonprofit providers competed for government funds for providing basic health care.

Direct competition for funds is not inevitable. Cooperative arrangements are also common, as in the case of referral agreements between agencies, which are used as a means of exchanging clients who do not fit the referring agency but are considered resources by the agency to which they are referred. Other agencies have implemented large-scale coalition-building efforts to improve their ability to meet client needs (Eilbert & Lafronza, 2005). Still others have developed community-oriented cooperative arrangements to ensure more complete service coverage within particular areas (Prince & Austin, 2001; Tomkins, Shank, Tromanhauser, Rupp, & Mahoney, 2005). Factors contributing to this behavior include community awareness of service needs, resource scarcity, and the capacity of local governments to coordinate these arrangements.

The final assessment of agency–community relationships has to do with how the agency is perceived relative to its peers and competitors. In what light do regulatory agencies, accrediting bodies, government contracting agencies, professional associations, the media, and the general public view this organization? Is it as a valued part of a community service network or as self-serving and unconcerned about its community? Or do community members see it as too controversial, or perhaps too timid, in responding to emerging needs? Assessing these perceptions assumes that the agency has some sort of a track record in the community and that key informants are willing to share their view of how the agency fits into the overall community service network. A tool such as the one depicted in Table 8.7 can assist in assessing an organization's relationships to others in its task environment.

Identify and Assess Cultural Competence in External Relationships
Understand Diversity in the Organizational Environment.   Questions to be explored for this activity include:

- What efforts does the organization make to familiarize itself with the diversity that exists in its environment?
- Does the organization recognize and seek to overcome barriers to service access?

Table 8.7 **Relationships with Other Service Providers**	
Other Agencies Providing Service	
State Department of Child Welfare	Collaborative
Central City Family Services	Competitive
Counseling Advocates, Inc.	Competitive
New Foundations	Collaborative
Baptist Family Services	Collaborative
Etc.	

- ♦ Does the organization take steps to ensure that its staff reflects the diversity of its clients?
- ♦ Do the organization's services fit well with the needs of minority as well as nonminority clients?

In Chapter 2 we called attention to some of the disparities in health, income, education, and other factors that affect minority populations. At the most fundamental level, an HSO that is culturally competent is one that is aware of these problems and oriented toward addressing them. Culturally competent HSOs also systematically collect information to ensure they understand the diversity of needs in their environments. This applies to prospective clients and to other groups such as donors, client advocates, and citizens' organizations. Gathering this information is usually done through needs assessments, which are carried out through methods such as soliciting input from individuals and groups via interviews, focus groups, and mail, telephone, or Internet surveys, or by examining sources such as census data or school or court records. In conducting needs assessments, the organization should demonstrate awareness that diversity arises not only from differences in race/ethnicity, gender, sexual orientation, and age, but also with respect to physical and cognitive abilities, socioeconomic background, education, receptiveness to services, and other dimensions. Recent studies offer examples of comprehensive ways to assess the needs of traditionally hard-to-reach groups (Smith, McCaslin, Chang, Martinez, & McGrew, 2010; Suarez-Balcazar, Balcazar, & Taylor-Ritzler, 2009; Sussman, Skara, & Pumpuang, 2008).

One reality a culturally competent organization must confront is that discriminatory behavior takes more subtle forms than historical examples of segregated schools and lunch counters. The organization must also recognize that it is possible to interact with members of particular groups in ways that are effectively racist (or sexist, ageist, etc.) but that are caused by ignorance or negligence rather than malice. Dovidio, Penner, Albrecht, Norton, Gaertner, and Shelton (2008) discuss how a less-direct form of aversive racism is replacing explicit prejudice (p. 479). Studies show that people who don't consider themselves racist and who oppose racial discrimination may yet retain negative stereotypes about racial groups that affect their behavior. This can happen at the organizational level as well by means of false assumptions that overestimate weaknesses while underestimating needs. Of particular concern when analyzing these dynamics are access, provider characteristics, and service characteristics.

Access.   As we discussed earlier, organizations may establish eligibility criteria that ensure a steady flow of needed resources but that exclude some clients who are most in need, including those from traditionally underserved groups. Leichter (2004) provides an example of how this occurred with regard to health-care access among low-income Hispanics in California. Other research has shown how clients from some groups are less likely than others to use services simply because they believe they are ineligible. Herbst (2008) found that low-income African Americans were significantly more likely than others not to receive child-care subsidies for which they were eligible. This was due in part to "creaming" processes in which efforts were made to make more remunerative clients aware of their eligibility, while little was done to recruit less remunerative—but no less eligible—clients. Shaefer (2010) found that low-income and minority workers accessed unemployment benefits for which they were eligible less often than others because past experiences of being denied services made them assume they couldn't qualify.

Problems of access may also be more concrete. Despite gains associated with the Americans with Disabilities Act of 1990, for example, people with physical, developmental, and other disabilities still lack physical access to many facilities and services (McColl, Jarzynowska, & Shortt, 2010). Also, evidence suggests that distance and transportation difficulties form one of the most serious barriers to access. Clients in rural areas continue to have substantially greater difficulty reaching needed services than those in urban locales (Fletcher, Garasky, Jensen, & Nielsen, 2010), while even in populous areas transit problems magnify the effect of distance. Shengelia, Tandon, Adams, & Murray (2005) summarize results showing an inverse-square relationship between distance from a service and likelihood of use. If, for example, Client A lives twice as far from an agency office as Client B, Client A is four times less likely to use services from that office as Client B. This may lead agencies to underestimate the large drop-off in access arising from small increases in distance.

These problems are especially likely to affect historically oppressed or disadvantaged populations, and culturally competent organizations take steps to avoid them. Among these are understanding the dynamics of creaming and seeking ways to provide services to those who are most in need, not just clients most able to pay. They also make outreach efforts to ensure that clients in their service area who are eligible for services are aware of this. Finally, they seek to establish neighborhood sites in areas that are convenient for clients rather than for staff or administrators, and they are active in trying to ensure that transportation options are available to clients to enable them to access services.

Provider Characteristics. One measure of an HSO's fit with its environment is whether its personnel are reasonably well matched in age, race/ethnicity, gender, and other characteristics to the clients they serve. Social workers are trained to bridge gaps between themselves and their clients, and agency personnel do not have to be identical to clients on all or even most dimensions in order to be effective. Still, research suggests that these differences may often be substantial, especially with regard to race/ethnicity. In the health-care arena, for example, 75 percent of African American patients see non-African American physicians, whereas for white patients this ratio is reversed (Chen, Fryer, Phillips, Wilson, & Pathman, 2005). Perhaps not surprisingly, white patients are significantly more likely to report satisfaction with their services. Other studies in human services also report higher satisfaction and better outcomes of services on the part of clients who see same-race providers (Martin, Trask, Peterson, Martin, Baldwin, & Knapp, 2010; Perry & Limb, 2004). Another aspect of cultural competence in an organization involves whether appropriate efforts are made to diversify its workforce. Aversive racism, which we discussed earlier, exists in the form of stereotypic attitudes that can lead to inadvertent but real discrimination. These attitudes affect behaviors such as hiring decisions, where perceptions of group characteristics may overshadow individual qualifications (Blair, 2001). Beyond race/ethnicity, research shows that hiring biases can also be based on age (Dennis & Thomas, 2007), disabilities (Shier, Graham, and Jones, 2009), and seropositivity (Rao, Angell, Lam, & Corrigan, 2008).

Chow and Austin (2008) offer guidelines for how culturally competent organizations should work to ensure that their characteristics fit well with the diversity in their environment. Adapting material from Cross and Friesen

(2005), they contend that an organization which performs best in this regard will be one that:

- Specifies the population to be served and knows their characteristics
- Ensures that staff and board members are representative of the community served
- Locates staff who reflect community characteristics and establishes staff supports (e.g., orientation, job descriptions, evaluation protocols)
- Uses guidelines for culturally competent practice
- Invests in recognizing diversity and difference in service delivery
- Offers supervision that supports and trains staff to be culturally competent
- Uses consultants who understand the cultures of service recipients.

An important asset of this model is that it calls attention to provider characteristics such as board composition, job design, and staff development to underscore the fact that cultural competence involves more than simply hiring a diverse workforce.

Service Characteristics.   Human service organizations have responded to the need to provide better services to traditionally underserved groups by developing culturally sensitive interventions (CSIs). These are defined as those in which important elements that define a culture, such as values, practices, and standards of conduct, are reflected in the ways interventions are carried out. Examples of CSIs can be found in many service arenas, including counseling, substance use, and child maltreatment, and reviews suggest they are effective (Hodge, Jackson, & Vaughn, 2010; Jackson, 2009).

A particularly important quality of a culturally competent agency is an ability to recognize and respond to high-incidence problems in client groups that are numerically small. Bubar (2010) notes that the risk of sexual assault among American Indian women is the highest of any ethnic/racial group, but few agencies, even in areas with large concentrations of American Indian women, employ counselors with special skills in treating this population. This dynamic extends to many other service needs and populations, from counseling of LGBTQ youth, to language training and housing assistance for refugees, to help with insurance premiums for people with treatable but rare and costly illnesses.

Organizations must also recognize that clients who are not part of the majority population may be reluctant to take advantage of available services, and special efforts may be needed to overcome this. Martin et al. (2010), in their study of health-care utilization by elderly African Americans, noted the presence of a number of such potential barriers, including general mistrust of dominant-culture institutions, an orientation to the use of home remedies, reluctance to use prescription medications, and concerns about cost. Services that reflect an understanding of these concerns are more likely to be utilized and completed than those that are not. Chow and Austin (2008) note that achieving this can be facilitated through inter-organizational collaborations that use existing neighborhood agencies as jumping-off points for outreach efforts.

Task 2: Assess the Organization Internally

Assessment of organizations, like assessment of communities, requires breaking down a large, complex entity into elements. The objective is to identify the points or locations within the organization that reveal its strengths as well as its weaknesses or problem areas. Each element should be approached in terms of whether and how it relates to identified problems, with the goal of understanding how interactions among elements maintain these problems or might be used to overcome them.

For an illustration of an organizational assessment, consider the examples of Canyon County Department of Child Welfare (CCDCW) and Lakeside Family Services (LFS) presented at the beginning of this chapter. When public organizations such as CCDCW experience problems in productivity, quality of client service, morale, or worker–management relationships, it would not be unusual for an oversight body, such as the county board of supervisors, to hire a management consultant to evaluate the department and its problems. Similarly, in a nonprofit organization such as LFS that has become more professional, increased its dependence on government funds, altered its mission, and is experiencing funding cutbacks, a consultant may be engaged by the board of directors to study the organization and recommend strategies for it to regain economic self-sufficiency.

A plausible scenario is that consultants, after interviewing representative staff, consumers, board members, and others, would be able to document the problems identified in the vignettes, formulate working hypotheses about their causes, and recommend solutions or remedies. Using such an approach, consultants are often misled into recommending short-term solutions such as staff development and training, employee incentive programs, morale-building activities like social events, relationship-enhancing activities between management and staff, attempts to humanize the chief executive officer, or other such actions. These steps rarely solve the kinds of fundamental problems that brought about the need for a management consultant in the first place.

An alternative approach to organizational assessment is to conduct a systematic examination of a number of organizational elements. These elements might include (1) organizational mission; (2) organizational structure, including location, management, staffing of programs and services, and workload; (3) goals and objectives of programs; (4) adequacy of funding; (5) personnel policies and practices; (6) management style; and (7) problem-solving and communication patterns, along with other such characteristics of the agency. Within each element one could examine ideal models or optimal levels of functioning, as illustrated in current theoretical or research literature. Using this ideal as a basis of comparison, the review can proceed to an examination of data that depict the actual situation, and to an examination of the gaps between ideal and real. The goal is to understand causes before proposing solutions and to solve long-term problems rather than treating present symptoms.

In this section we propose a framework for assessment that identifies elements to be examined within an organization, explores relevant theoretical frameworks, identifies the questions to be answered, and specifies information to be collected or examined. In reviewing the framework, readers may find it useful to consider how its elements might apply to an HSO with which they are familiar as an intern, employee, or even service recipient. The elements we address include:

1. Corporate authority and mission
2. Organizational and program structure
3. Administrative, management, and leadership style
4. Planning, delivery, and evaluation of programs and services
5. Personnel policies and practices
6. Adequacy of technology and resources

Identify Corporate Authority and Mission

Questions to be explored for this activity include:

- What is the basis for and extent of the organization's corporate authority?
- What is its mission?
- Is the organization operating in a manner consistent with its authority and mission?
- To what extent is the mission supported by staff who perform different roles within the organization?
- Are policies and procedures consistent with mission and authority?

As discussed earlier in this chapter, a basic step toward understanding any organization is understanding its domain. An agency's corporate authority forms the legal basis for its operations, and this represents one of the boundaries defining its domain. If the organization is public (governmental) its legal basis rests in a statute or executive order. If it is private its legal basis is in articles of incorporation. Sometimes it may be important to examine these documents firsthand, since organizations may be incorporated for one purpose (and perhaps even funded through a trust that specifies that purpose, such as operating the orphanage from which LFS arose), but over the years new populations and services, such as help for pregnant teens, are added to the mission. Although perhaps reasonable and well intentioned, these changes may still reach a point where the agency is operating outside its legal authorization.

A good statement of mission specifies the problems or needs to be addressed, populations to be served and, in general terms, client outcomes to be expected. It also serves as a statement of the reason for existence of an agency, and this should not change in fundamental ways unless the organization's reason for existence also changes. Lack of clarity in a mission statement or disparities between the mission and current activities can be signs of a problem. For example, LFS is a prime candidate for reexamining its original mission, which was established in the early 1930s when orphanages and the need for them were common. If LFS has not revised this mission, it is unlikely that its current work has any connection to its stated reason for existence. Revisiting and, if necessary, reconceptualizing the mission can begin the process of redirecting operations or sharpening their focus. Box 8.1 illustrates what the wording for the mission statement for LFS might be.

Understand Program Structure and Management Style

Organizational and Program Structure. Questions to be explored for this activity include:

- What are the major departmental or program units on the organizational chart?
- Is there a convincing rationale for the existing organizational structure?
- Is the existing structure consistent with and supportive of the mission?
- Is supervision logical and capable of performing expected functions? Are staff members capable of performing expected functions?
- Is there an informal structure (people who carry authority because they are respected by staff, and thus exert influence) that is different from those in formally designated positions of authority?

Box 8.1 Example Mission Statement for Lakeside Family Services

The mission of Lakeside Family Services is to help members of our community solve problems facing them. This includes a special concern for families, children, and elders. Our goal for families is to strengthen relationships and help each family support and care for its members. For children, we work to promote good parenting, quality education, safety, and growth. Among elders, we seek to support continued growth and to ensure basic standards for health, health care, housing, and income.

Among the characteristics of a good mission statement are that it must be available for organizational and public reference, and it must be clear and comprehensible. Busch and Folaron (2005) studied the mission statements of forty state-level child welfare agencies and found that in almost one-fourth the statements were largely inaccessible because they required higher than a 12th-grade reading level. (The example mission statement for LFS has a grade 10 reading level.) Problems such as these undermine the principle of a shared vision as fundamental to the success of an organization. Without some common understanding of mission and direction, individuals and groups will inevitably begin to work at cross-purposes.

With a shared vision there may still be differences about strategies, but a commitment to the same ends or outcomes will remain. Also, evidence suggests that mission statements are not merely symbolic but can have beneficial effects on employees. Results from a study by Clark (2007) showed that familiarity with an organization's mission statement was positively associated with job satisfaction and with behaviors that tend to strengthen relationships among employees.

Some of the more important sources of information for understanding corporate authority and mission include:

1. Articles of incorporation, statutes, or executive orders
2. Mission statement
3. Bylaws of the organization
4. Minutes of selected board meetings
5. Interviews with selected administrators, managers, and staff

Table 8.8 depicts a tool to be used as an aid in assessing agencies' corporate authority and mission.

When we think of organizational structure, we often envision a pyramid-shaped chart with boxes and lines indicating a hierarchy that extends from the top administrator's level down to many line-level positions (as illustrated in Figure 7.1). This helps us visualize the organization in terms of who reports to whom, who is responsible for which divisions of the organization, and how the chain of command proceeds from bottom to top. As noted in Chapter 7, this system is patterned after the bureaucratic model described by Weber

Table 8.8 Assessing Corporate Authority and Mission

Checklist	Yes	No
1. Are articles of incorporation on file?	___	___
2. Is there a written set of bylaws?	___	___
3. Are board members and agency director familiar with bylaws?	___	___
4. Is there a mission statement?	___	___
5. Is it one page or less?	___	___
6. Does it make a statement about expected client outcomes?	___	___
7. Are staff aware of, and do they practice in accordance with, the mission statement?	___	___

(1946). It is widely used because it is easy to understand and apply, ensures that everyone has only one supervisor, and provides for lines of communication, exercise of authority, performance evaluation, and the many other functions necessary to smooth operation.

As we also noted in Chapter 7, however, many critics of bureaucratic structure believe it is not the best design for human service agencies. Their central point is that bureaucratic structure was designed for organizations in which both inputs and operations are predictable and repetitive, whereas the individual clients and client problems served by HSOs are unique. Rules that govern the production process in manufacturing enterprises, for example, may be helpful in ensuring consistent quality of the goods produced, but in an HSO these rules may serve only to constrain workers' abilities to exercise professional judgment.

A number of terms have been used to describe the pitfalls that can accompany bureaucratic structure. Merton (1952) warned of *learned incompetence* that develops among employees in bureaucracies who rely so heavily on a policy manual to make their decisions that they lose the ability or will to think logically or creatively about their jobs (such as addressing client problems in an HSO). Lipsky (1984) used the term *bureaucratic disentitlement* to describe situations in HSOs where clients fail to receive benefits or services to which they are entitled due to decisions based on rigid and sometimes illogical internal rules rather than client needs. Jaskyte and Dressler (2005) found that innovativeness in nonprofit HSOs was negatively associated with an organizational culture that focuses mostly on stability, as is typical of bureaucratic structures.

Contingency theorists, in addressing the question of what organizational structure is best, contend that it depends on what the organization is expected to produce. Morse and Lorsch (1970) demonstrated that higher productivity in one type of organization (a container-manufacturing plant) was achieved through a traditional structure with clearly defined roles, responsibilities, and lines of supervision. A different type of organization (a research lab) achieved higher productivity through a very loose structure, which allowed researchers maximum flexibility to carry out their own work unfettered by rules, regulations, and supervision. Examples of alternative structures are depicted in Figure 8.3.

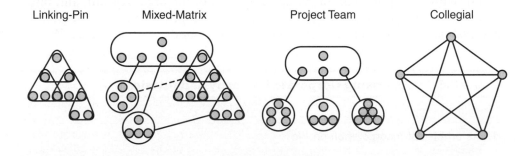

| Linking-Pin | Mixed-Matrix | Project Team | Collegial |

Stable	ENVIRONMENT	Turbulent
Fixed	GOALS	Ambiguous
Standardized	TECHNOLOGY	Unprogrammed

Figure 8.3

Human Resources Structures and Environmental Conditions

Note: This figure is based on a diagram developed by Robert Biller.

Source: R. Miles, *Theories of Management: Implications for Organizational Behavior and Development* (New York: McGraw-Hill, 1978), p. 91. Reprinted with permission of The McGraw-Hill Companies.

Miles (1975) proposed several alternatives to bureaucratic structure. One option, adapted from the work of Likert (1961), is called a *linking-pin structure*. In this approach, rigid lines of reporting and one-on-one relationships are replaced by an emphasis on work units. One or more persons within a work unit are selected to play a linking role to other work units with which collaboration is important. By serving as a fully functioning participant in both units, persons in the linking role can facilitate better communication and working relationships than are possible through traditional structures that have few links between units.

Another option is *matrix structure*, where supervision is assigned to a function rather than to a person. In this structure, staff members are likely to have more than one supervisor, and constant communication is necessary. Matrix management might be used in a ward of a mental hospital, where supervision of a social worker responsible for activities on the ward falls to a ward leader who may be a nurse, whereas supervision and evaluation of the social worker's overall performance would rest with a senior-level social worker. This approach remains relevant, and Kraus and Ray (2010) offer examples of how matrix structure can facilitate the operation of volunteer organizations.

Still another structure is the *project team structure*, in which teams working on the same effort take responsibility for different functions and work relatively independently. For example, in starting up a community project one team might conduct a needs assessment, another explore funding, another handle incorporation responsibilities, and another secure a facility. Work is coordinated by a committee of team leaders to ensure that the project teams are completing mutually supportive tasks and that their efforts are oriented toward a common end.

A final structural option proposed by Miles is the *collegial structure*. In this type of organization, individual professionals operate relatively independently and come together only in circumstances in which their work overlaps. A private counseling clinic would be a good example. Five psychologists and social workers may form a partnership to purchase a building and equipment and hire receptionists and other support staff. No single partner has more authority than any other. Each generates her or his own income and otherwise operates as an entrepreneur, except in situations in which the functioning of the organization requires overlap.

Miles continues to contribute to literature on "humanistic management" principles that can be applied within individual organizations or used as guides for external partnerships. In a study of organizational collaborations among firms in several European countries, Rocha and Miles (2009) identified assumptions that appeared to be common to successful collaborations, including mutual expectations and interests, recognition of the value of the relationships and information sharing, long-term commitments and joint pursuit of rewards, recognition of one another's contributions, and a willing collaboration. It is not difficult to see that these principles could also be used to describe organizations employing the project team, collegial, or other collaboration-oriented internal structures described in the models above.

No single organizational structure is likely to be superior to all others in all HSOs. For large public agencies, some type of bureaucratic structure may be useful because of size, predictability of operations, and accountability considerations. For a small, community-based agency, a collegial model may work very effectively. Much will depend on the mission, purpose, and goals of the organization, the services provided, and the expectations for accountability.

A related issue has to do with staff members' competence and preparation for the roles they fill and the responsibilities they hold. Human service organizations may employ staff from a wide range of specializations, including health, mental health, substance use, developmental disabilities, child welfare, services to elderly persons, residential treatment, adult and juvenile corrections, and many others. These individuals may be trained in disciplines as diverse as social work, counseling, psychology, child care, medicine, nursing, rehabilitation, and education, and their work may be supported by people from fields such as accounting, management, public relations, and finance. To bridge these differences, the organization must have clear standards governing hiring and job expectations. What, for example, are the educational requirements for each position? Does the organization adhere to these requirements? What experience is required? What licenses or certifications are necessary?

In their early work on job performance, both Taylor (1947) and Weber (1946) emphasized the importance of clearly defined job expectations, workers who were well prepared to perform expected functions, supervision, evaluation, and feedback to improve performance. Findings from a study of staff in public welfare-to-work agencies support the contention that the precision and appropriateness of job design are positively associated with job performance, even among professional-level staff (Hill, 2006). More generally, good job design contributes to increased role clarity on the part of employees, and research has linked role clarity to both increased job satisfaction and decreased turnover (Kammeyer-Mueller & Wanberg, 2003; Shim, 2010).

Still, even a well-designed and clearly defined job will be the source of problems if it rests within a rigid bureaucratic structure that is ill-suited to the organization's clients and services. The same may be true of an organization that utilizes a human relations model (such as Mayo's work discussed in Chapter 7). Although such an approach may appear more employee-oriented, constraints on professional discretion are often similar to those found in the bureaucratic model. The only differences are that a concern is expressed for the human needs of the employee, such as the desire for self-esteem. Teamwork may be emphasized in order to support employee needs for belonging, but the fundamental assumption is that managers can predict and routinize staff activities and should maintain relatively tight control of decision making.

Job design under management models such as McGregor's, where work is seen as having the potential to be intrinsically rewarding to employees, is more complex. In this type of organization employees are involved with both goal setting and decision making. Work is performed under conditions of self-direction and self-control. Information generated about individual performance and program performance is shared with the employee in the interest of promoting professional growth and development. This type of job design is ideal for the experienced employee with professional education, but it may be inappropriate for positions in which the job requires more task definition and supervision.

Documentation and data to be examined in order to understand organizational structure might include:

1. Organizational charts
2. Job descriptions
3. Relevant policy and procedure manuals
4. Interviews with selected administrators, managers staff, and representatives of each discipline

Table 8.9	Assessing Organizational and Program Structure			
	Total Organization	Program A	Program B	Program C
1. Would you describe the structure as rigid or flexible?	——	——	——	——
2. Is the structure appropriate to the needs of the organization or program?	——	——	——	——
3. Is communication primarily top–down, or in all directions?	——	——	——	——
4. Are staff competent to do the jobs expected of them?	——	——	——	——
5. Is supervision appropriate to the need?	——	——	——	——

A tool such as the one depicted in Table 8.9 can be used to assess the appropriateness of organization and program structure.

Management and Leadership Style.　Questions to be explored for this activity include:

- How is the workplace organized and work allocated?
- Is appropriate authority and information passed on along with responsibility?
- How close is supervision, and what, exactly, is supervised? Is it tasks, is it functions, or is it the employee?
- How are decisions made? Is information solicited from those affected?
- Do employees feel valued at every level? Do they believe they are making a contribution to the success of the organization?
- How is conflict handled?

A wealth of theoretical literature exists concerning approaches to administration, management, and leadership. Miles (1975) classifies managerial theories or models into one of three categories: (1) the traditional model, (2) the human relations model, and (3) the human resources model.

The *traditional model* is characterized by very closely supervising work, controlling subordinates, breaking work down into simple tasks that are easily learned, and establishing detailed work routines. Similar to McGregor's characterization of Theory X, the assumptions of this model are that people inherently dislike work, they are not self-motivated or self-directed, and they do it only because they need the money. The traditional model would include such theorists as Weber, Taylor, and others committed to the basic tenets of bureaucracy or scientific management (as discussed in Chapter 7).

The *human relations model* is characterized by efforts on the part of management to make each worker feel useful and important. Management is open to feedback, and subordinates are allowed to exercise some self-direction on routine matters. Assumptions are that people want to feel useful and important, that they have a need to belong, and that these needs are more important than money in motivating people to work. Theories that support the human relations model would include Mayo's human relations theory as well as many of the theorists who expanded on Mayo's work and focused on employee motivation.

The *human resources model* is characterized by a focus on the use of untapped resources and potential existing within employees. Managers are expected to create an environment in which all members may contribute to the limits of their abilities, full participation is encouraged on all matters, and self-direction and self-control are supported and promoted. Assumptions are that work means more than merely earning a paycheck. Because it is an important part of people's lives, they are willing to contribute to the success of the total work effort. Furthermore, people are assumed to be creative, resourceful, and capable of contributing more when they are unrestricted by the constraints of the traditional or the human relations models. The theories that support the human resources model are drawn essentially from the work on contingency theory (Burns & Stalker, 1961) and supported by a number of contemporary authors (Forcadell, 2005).

This philosophy of management is important to understand because it influences so many facets of organizational life. It can affect, for example, whether adult protective service workers are allowed merely to collect facts from a battered elderly person and then turn to a supervisor who will direct the next steps, or whether they are allowed to use professional judgment to intervene as they believe is needed. Recent research supports the validity of these principles in different types of human service organizations. Graham and Shier (2010) reported increases in subjective well-being on the part of social workers who had higher levels of perceived professional autonomy, and Knudsen, Ducharme, and Roman (2006) found that emotional exhaustion—a component of burnout—was higher among counselors at agencies in which decision-making authority is centralized.

Some more important sources of information to be examined in understanding organizational administration, management, and leadership style include:

1. Job description of the chief executive officer (CEO) and other staff in positions of leadership
2. Interviews with board members (if the agency is private) or the person to whom the CEO is accountable (if the agency is public) to determine the expectations of the CEO
3. Criteria used for performance evaluation of the CEO and other staff in positions of leadership
4. An interview with the CEO to determine expectations for other staff in positions of leadership
5. An organizational chart
6. Interviews with staff in various roles to determine perceptions about the job, the workplace, supervision, and administration

A tool such as the one depicted in Table 8.10 can be useful in assessing the agency's management and leadership style.

Assess the Organization's Programs and Services

Questions to be explored for this activity include:

- What programs and services are offered?
- Are service goals and objectives based on empirical research or evidence from past evaluations of services within the organization?

Table 8.10	**Assessing Leadership and Management Style**			
	Carried Out by Management Only	Input Allowed but Ignored	Input Solicited and Used	Group Consensus, Full Participation
1. How are organizational goals established?	——	——	——	——
2. What is the climate for supporting the achievement of goals?	——	——	——	——
3. Where are program-level decisions made?	——	——	——	——
4. How does information flow throughout the organization?	——	——	——	——
5. Who has involvement in providing feedback about performance?	——	——	——	——

▶ Are the services consistent with the goals and objectives of the program?
▶ Are staffing patterns appropriate to the services to be provided? Are workload expectations reasonable given expectations for achievement with each client and within each service and program?
▶ Is there a common understanding among management and line staff within each program about problems to be addressed, populations to be served, services to be provided, and client outcomes to be achieved?
▶ Are expected outcomes identified with sufficient clarity that program success or failure can be determined?

HSOs must typically report data on efficiency, effectiveness, and quality that reflect a commitment to providing the best services possible at the lowest cost. At the same time, government contracting agencies continue to increase requirements for HSOs to establish service standards and carry out performance monitoring as a condition of receiving public funds (Abramovitz, 2005; Polivka-West & Okano, 2008).

Standards typically emphasize three types of accountability: efficiency accountability, quality accountability, and effectiveness accountability (Martin & Kettner, 1996). *Efficiency accountability* focuses on the ratio of outputs to inputs or, more specifically, the ratio of volume of service provided to dollars expended. If Agency ABC provides 1,000 hours of counseling at a cost of $75,000 and Agency XYZ provides 1,000 hours of counseling at a cost of $100,000, Agency ABC is more efficient. Greater efficiency offers clear productivity benefits to agencies and should make them better able to compete for funds from revenue sources. Somewhat surprisingly, research evidence does not consistently support this, as in the findings of Frumkin and Kim (2001), who showed that providers of charitable funds do not necessarily reward more efficient agencies over less efficient ones. Nonetheless, most organizations that seek donated funds attempt to demonstrate efficiency by paying attention to measures such as the ratio of administrative costs to total expenditures.

Quality accountability focuses on the provision of services and differentiates between organizations that meet a quality standard and those that do not. For example, using "timeliness" as a quality standard, an organization would be required to monitor whether services were provided within a certain time frame (such as no more than 10 minutes following the scheduled time of appointment).

Assessing quality can make an important contribution to understanding HSOs. Most people have experienced the uncertainty of entering an unfamiliar organization and immediately sensing dynamics that are not easily interpreted. For example, a social work intern described her feelings about entering a particular nursing home for the first time. She stated that she "did not feel good about it," but when questioned about what that meant, she was at a loss for words to describe why she felt that way.

Several weeks later the intern was able to identify reasons for her concern. The nursing home's unpleasant odor, disturbing interactions observed between staff and residents, the receptionist's lack of interest in greeting visitors, the arrangement of furniture in the lobby in a way that was not conducive to conversations, the fact that some residents were lined up in wheelchairs in hallways, and the staff's discouragement of residents who wanted to bring personal possessions into the home were all problematic for her. These elements began to paint a picture of an organization that did not fully value its residents, staff, or visitors.

These types of concerns do not always surface when evaluating efficiency or productivity, and they are difficult to tease out in studies of service outcomes. To correct this, organizations should identify quality indicators and use them as a basis for evaluating service quality. Recent works emphasize that quality indicators must often be specific to particular services, and an increasing array of standardized quality-assessment tools are becoming available. Examples include the Framework for the Assessment of Children in Need and Their Families (FACNF; Leveille & Chamberland, 2010) for use in child protective services, the Facility Quality Indicator Profile Report for nursing homes (Castle & Ferguson, 2010), and the Lot Quality Assurance Sampling (LQAS) system in population health (Robertson & Valadez, 2006).

Effectiveness accountability focuses on the results, effects, and accomplishments of human service programs. Some of the central questions for HSOs in the 2000s include: (1) Are clients better off after coming to this organization than they were before they came? and (2) Do programs and services offered resolve the client problems they are funded to address?

These questions need to be dealt with in the context of understanding what goes into the planning, delivery, and evaluation of programs. A complete program should include a problem analysis; a review of the empirical literature, goals and objectives, and program and service design; a data-collection and management-information system; and a plan for evaluation (Kettner, Moroney, & Martin, 2008). Written plans provide the blueprints for programs and services and also serve as standards against which programs, when implemented, can be evaluated.

Each program should be based on a clear understanding of the problems it is intended to address and the populations it is intended to serve. It is not unusual to find that in some long-standing programs there has been a shift in emphasis over the years. For example, a program that was designed to deal with heroin use may have begun with an emphasis on detoxification and long-term intensive therapy, later shifting to provision of methadone, and finally to intensive self-help groups. Each of these emphases stems from a different understanding of the etiology of the problem and requires a different working hypothesis. These changes, in turn, may lead to alterations in the population served, resources, patterns of staffing, and methods of evaluating effectiveness. Such changes should be made consciously, not through "drift," and written program plans should reflect the revisions.

[Program] changes should be made consciously, not through "drift."

As suggested by the evidence-based practice model discussed in Chapter 7, programs should also be designed, monitored, and evaluated using the best available information about "what works." This may come from previous evaluations of the effectiveness of a program within the organization, and if positive with regard to service effects, those results can be used as a rationale for program continuation or expansion. The other principal source of information is research results published in social work journals and other relevant literature. In the process of program planning, this literature should be searched carefully using professional abstracts (all of which are available online at most university libraries) such as *Social Work Abstracts*, *Medline*, *PsycINFO*, and others. Whether drawn from prior agency research or the professional literature, however, the emphasis should be on data-based results from studies using the highest possible standards of scientific rigor.

Some of the more important documents and data sources to be examined to understand the planning, delivery, and evaluation of programs and services might include:

1. Program plans
2. Organizational charts
3. Roster of staff and job descriptions
4. Annual reports of programs and services
5. Needs assessment surveys
6. Evaluation findings, including client satisfaction surveys
7. Case records

A tool such as the one depicted in Table 8.11 can be useful in assessing an agency's programs and services.

Assess Personnel Policies, Procedures, and Practices

Questions to be explored for this activity include:

▶ Is there a written human resources plan?
▶ Is there a job analysis for each position?

Table 8.11	**Assessing Efficiency, Quality, and Effectiveness**		
	Program A	Program B	Program C
1. Does each program specify and monitor measures for efficiency (e.g., productivity per worker)?	____	____	____
2. Does each program specify and monitor quality measures (e.g., reliability/consistency of services)?	____	____	____
3. Does each program specify and monitor client outcomes (e.g., standardized scales that measure severity of problems before and after treatment)?	____	____	____

▶ Is there a plan for recruitment and selection?
▶ Is there a plan for enhancing agency diversity?
▶ Is there a plan for staff development and training?
▶ Is a performance evaluation system in place?
▶ Are there written procedures for employee termination?

Most organizations go to great lengths to ensure that their equipment will be in good working order, such as by purchasing maintenance contracts for their photocopy machines, computers, printers, vehicles, and other essential items. Ironically, not all agencies invest the same level of concern or resources in their employees, even though employees also have a variety of needs to be met if they are to function optimally. Perhaps one way to understand how effectively an organization is addressing its personnel needs is to understand how an "ideal" personnel system might function.

One approach recommended in the literature to ensure that personnel needs and issues are properly addressed is to develop a human resources plan (Schmidt, Riggar, Crimando, & Bordieri, 1992). Overall agency planning is referred to as *strategic planning*; it focuses on establishing goals, processes, and actions that determine future agency directions. Once these directions are established, they form the basis for human resource planning—the forecasting of personnel needs to implement the mission. The significance of a human resources plan is that it is critical to the success of an organization that new employees are brought on board in an orderly, systematic manner that maximizes the likelihood that they will be successful and productive during their tenure at the agency.

Basic to a human resources plan is a job analysis in which tasks are identified, relationships and roles are specified, and qualifications for positions are detailed (Schmidt et al., 1992). A job analysis becomes the basis for writing a job description, which in turn establishes the organizing theme for the components of the human resources plan: recruitment, selection, orientation, supervision, training and development, performance appraisal and, if necessary, termination.

The process of job analysis involves the gathering, evaluating, and recording of accurate, objective, and complete information about a given position from a variety of sources (Malinowski, 1981). It begins with an itemization of tasks carried out by those who hold a particular job. For each task or group of tasks, the job analyst must identify methods or techniques for carrying out the task(s), knowledge, and skills needed, and the results expected. The finished product should provide a complete review of the requirements and expectations associated with a particular job. From this document, a briefer, more concise job description is developed.

Once job qualifications and expectations are understood, the next step is to design a recruitment and selection plan. Effective recruitment requires a strategy, including selection of the recruitment territory (local, statewide, or national), consideration of labor market conditions, determination of recruitment audience, and the intensity of search and recruiting efforts. These decisions are crucial to successful staffing, since employee selection can be made only from the pool of applicants generated by the recruitment strategy. This is a critical point at which the agency needs to assess the diversity of its staff and give special attention to recruitment of persons from diverse racial/ethnic groups as well as women, gays and lesbians, and older and/or disabled employees, to ensure a heterogeneous and representative staff.

Selection involves a three-stage process. Recruitment typically produces applications, including résumés. In the first stage, résumés and letters of reference are reviewed to eliminate applicants who are not qualified or not a good fit for organizational needs. In the second stage, those with the highest qualifications are further narrowed down to a short list, usually a maximum of three to five applicants. In the third stage, those on the short list are interviewed, after which a job offer is made to the top candidate. Screening criteria and interview questions are developed ahead of time so they match the qualifications and expectations described in the job analysis.

After being hired, the new employee is given a complete orientation to the job, the workplace, and the community. When the orientation is completed, a plan for supervision, training, and development is initiated. This is intended to ensure a smooth entry into the job and to provide the information, knowledge, and resources necessary for successful and productive employment. Interestingly, research suggests that there is no single "personality" that fits particular types of work within the field, and job applicants of many different backgrounds and personal characteristics may adapt well to the work. Retaining quality employees appears to be most closely tied to the ability of the organization to moderate the stresses of the work through supervisor and peer support and to build commitment to the organization through participatory decision making and opportunities for advancement (Glisson, Landsverk, Schoenwald, Kelleher, Eaton Hoagwood, Mayberg, & Green, 2008; Hopkins, Cohen-Callow, Kim, & Hwang, 2010).

In order to ensure that employee performance is appropriately monitored and evaluated, a well-designed personnel or human resources system will have a performance-appraisal system based, again, on the job analysis. Tasks identified in the job analysis should be used as a basis for designing the performance-appraisal instrument. This will ensure that the job, as described at the point of recruitment and hiring, is the same job for which orientation and training have been provided, and is the same job on which the employee is evaluated. Criteria and procedures for performance evaluation should always be specified in writing and given to employees at the time of hiring. In a well-designed performance-appraisal system, it should be a rare occurrence for employees to be surprised by the written evaluation.

Policies and procedures for termination should also be clearly defined and distributed in writing at the time of hiring. At a minimum, the statements should include a description of grounds for termination. These may relate to unsatisfactory job performance or to unacceptable behavior, such as sexual harassment. In either case, criteria for determining what constitutes unsatisfactory performance or unacceptable behavior should be specified in objective, measurable terms and as clearly and unambiguously as possible. Procedures and time frames for notifying employees of poor performance long before reaching the stage of termination should also be delineated. Doing so is part of sound human resource management, but it is also a practical matter in that agencies following such guidelines are much more likely to avoid extended grievances or litigation (Bach, 2009).

In assessing an agency's effectiveness in the area of personnel policies and procedures, these are the types of elements one would want to examine. Helpful and informative documents for conducting the assessment include:

1. Manual of personnel policies and procedures
2. Copy of a human resources plan, including affirmative action/equal employment opportunity plans
3. Job analysis and job descriptions

4. Recruitment and selection procedures

5. Staff development and training plan

6. Performance evaluation forms

7. Statistics on absenteeism, turnover, usage of sick leave

8. Grievances and complaints filed with the human resources department

9. Interviews with representative staff who perform different roles

Figure 8.4 may be useful in assessing the quality of an organization's personnel or human resources system.

Assess Whether the Internal Workings of the Organization are Diversity-Friendly

Questions to be explored for this activity include:

⦁ Is the organization's structure and operation conducive to cultural competence?

⦁ Does it promote an environment that retains diverse employees?

As we discussed in Chapter 7, highly bureaucratic organizations tend to provide low levels of autonomy or decision-making authority to their staff and are oriented toward making tasks as routinized and predictable as possible. This is not a good recipe for cultural competence, which assumes that services will be ineffective or underutilized if not adapted to the customs and expectations of a diverse client population. This was demonstrated empirically by Rajendran and Chemtob (2010) who found that services provided by organizations which were bureaucratically structured and relied heavily on organizational rules and regulations were less likely to be used by clients than those provided by less-bureaucratic agencies.

A. Does the organization have a job analysis for each position within the agency that includes the following?

Responsibilities and Tasks	Methods	Knowledge and Skill	Results
Counseling			
1. Counsel individuals	One on one	Human behavior; group	Client develops
2. Counsel families	Family treatment	and family dynamics;	independent living
3. Lead groups	Group treatment	understand professional	and social skills
4. Consult with self-help groups	Occasional group meetings	role	

B. Is this job analysis consistent with the following?

1. The job description
2. The recruitment and selection plan (or procedures)
3. The plan or practices relative to hiring a diverse workforce
4. Staff development and training plans or activities
5. Performance evaluation criteria
6. Plans for involuntary termination

Figure 8.4

Assessing an Organization's Human Resources System

Chow and Austin (2008) provide a framework for agency policies and procedures to enhance cultural competence. One element is a mission statement that makes explicit the organization's commitment to being responsive to diversity. Another is to ensure that the agency's information systems gather data of sufficient variety and detail for administrators to be able to understand the diversity in the environment and within the organization. The data should allow administrators to ask and answer questions such as which services are most in demand by which groups, and which services are underutilized. Policies and procedures should also outline intake mechanisms and service standards that are culturally relevant. For example, assessment scales for measuring client problems and progress often perform differently across race/ethnicity, socioeconomic status, English proficiency, and other dimensions. In practice this might mean that a cutting score used to indicate the presence or absence of a problem among members of one group might be different for members of another group. This is of particular concern if such scores are used to determine service eligibility or termination.

Personnel management practices also play a key role in creating a productive environment within organizations. A survey of social workers by Acquavita, Pittman, Gibbons, and Castellanos-Brown (2009) found that being a member of a minority group did not predict respondents' satisfaction with their job. Instead, the important factors for predicting higher job satisfaction were whether respondents viewed their organization as being diverse and inclusive. Mallow (2010) also points to perceptions of inclusion and having a voice in decision making as critical predictors of organizations' ability to retain staff members in general and, in particular, staff members from traditionally disadvantaged or underrepresented groups.

The history of efforts to create organizations that are both diverse and diversity-friendly has often been fraught with tokenism. Success is not achieved by simply including the word "diversity" in an organizational mission statement, attracting a few minority job applicants, or promoting a lesbian woman or person with a disability to a mid-level managerial post. It is achieved only by examining the modern workforce in all its variety and making sure that the organization has a good grasp of who its members are and whom it serves. It also means creating an organizational culture that treats diversity as an asset and employees as full participants in decision making.

Assess Adequacy of Technical Resources and Systems

Questions to be explored for this activity include:

▶ Are program staff involved in a meaningful way in providing budgetary input? Do they get useful feedback about expenditures and unit costs during the year?
▶ Do program staff use budget data as a measure by which they attempt to improve efficiency?
▶ Do resources appear to be adequate to achieve stated program goals and objectives?

This task encompasses the assessment of (1) budgetary management, (2) facilities and equipment, and (3) computer technology and information management. Additional questions arise that are specific to these three categories.

Practice Contexts
_____

Critical Thinking Question:
What kind of information
about client practice can
a line worker contribute
to budget discussions?

Budget Management.   Relevant questions to be asked include:

▶ What type of budgeting system is used by the agency?
▶ How are unit costs calculated? Do staff members understand the meaning of unit costs? How are they used?

Budgeting and budget management is an activity often left to upper administration and treated as though line staff, first-line supervisors, and other persons involved in service delivery need not be included. However, good financial management practices involve all levels of staff. Fiscal soundness and budgeting practices affect programs and services in a profound way. Organizations cannot run without money, but wise use of resources make limited funds go farther, and an agency's use of good financial management practices suggest that its programs and services drive the budget, not the other way around.

For many years, human service agencies were limited to an elementary type of budgeting called *line-item budgeting.* This involved identifying expenditure categories and estimating the number of dollars needed to cover expenses in each category for one year. Categories typically included personnel; operating expenses such as rent, utilities, supplies, and travel; and other items.

Since the 1970s, increasingly sophisticated budgeting techniques have been developed for application to human service agencies (Kettner et al., 2008). These techniques, referred to as *functional budgeting* and *program budgeting*, are based on program planning and budgeting systems (PPBS) (Lee & Johnson, 1973). Both approaches to budgeting operate within the conceptual framework of programs. Both produce cost and expenditure data in relation to programs rather than in relation to the entire agency. Functional and program budgeting techniques produce data such as total program costs, cost per unit of service, cost per output (client completion of program or service), and cost per outcome (the cost of producing measurable change in a client's quality of life). Martin (2000) terms this last approach "outcome budgeting" and describes its use in state-level human service agencies. It can be useful in facilitating cost–benefit and cost-effectiveness assessments and also in helping agencies maintain a focus on measurement of outcomes.

Budget data become increasingly important in an environment of intense competition for scarce and diminishing resources. In the same manner that individuals shop for the best buy with their own personal purchases, government contracting agencies—in competitive environments—shop for the lowest unit cost. Organizations that do not have the type of budgeting system or database that permits calculation of unit costs are at a distinct disadvantage in a competitive market that is likely to remain equally or more competitive in the wake of the global economic downturn that began in 2008.

Some of the more important documentation and data sources to be examined in order to understand the agency's approach to financial management and accountability include:

1. Annual reports
2. Audit reports
3. A cost allocation plan
4. Program goals and objectives
5. Communitywide comparative studies of unit costs
6. Interviews with all levels of program staff

Facilities and Equipment.   Questions to be asked are:

▶ Is the physical work environment attractive and conducive to high productivity? Do employees feel they have enough space and space of an appropriate type?

▶ Have problems been identified with current facilities and equipment? If so, is there a plan to address the problems and to fund solutions?

▶ Are there conditions related to facilities or equipment that appear to act as barriers to productivity or work flow?

▶ Are the facilities accessible to clients?

Considerations with regard to facilities include quantity of space, physical condition and maintenance of facilities, and geographical location. In assessing physical space, client needs should be a central consideration. "Welfare offices" and other HSOs are often caricatured as dreary, fortress-like, and dehumanizing places, but successful caricatures are based on a grain of truth. Offices occupied by most HSOs will never resemble corporate boardrooms, but an organization's facilities should reflect earnest efforts to make them as pleasant as possible. They should also be located in places that maximize client access, and ongoing measures should be in place to make them safe environments. Finally, they should feature private space or interview rooms sufficient to ensure protection of client confidentially, plus areas for children if services require them to be at the agency for more than brief periods.

With regard to equipment, furniture should be comfortable, functional, and in good repair, as should vehicles if transportation is a client service. Professional staff should also have access to materials needed for their work with clients. This may include equipment ranging from audio and video recording devices to play-therapy materials to small collections of professional books and journals. Another useful resource that is often overlooked in budget planning is copies of standardized assessment scales, some of which must be purchased from commercial publishers.

Information Technology and Information Management.   Questions to be asked are:

▶ Does the agency have integrated systems for mailings, payment, case-tracking, and management data?

▶ Does the agency maintain a website, a Facebook page, a Twitter feed, or any other form of social network presence?

▶ Does the agency use external information resources for fund raising, grant applications, volunteer coordination, or other activities?

▶ Do all line staff have desktop, laptop, or tablet computers, personal data assistants (PDAs), and/or smartphones? Do they have access to the Internet, word processing, email, text messaging, data security and firewall software, and other applications? Is this technology up to date?

Advances in computer technology have made possible many of the substantial gains in productivity enjoyed by both commercial firms and HSOs during the past few decades. At the organizational level, even small agencies will need both software and hardware (such as a network server) to establish and maintain systems that allow entry and retrieval of client, management, and fiscal data; Internet access; email; and text messaging capabilities. Many will also need websites that are not merely informational but that also allow online completion of forms, provide links to resources, enable clients to communicate with staff, and offer other features. Others may also add Facebook pages or other social networking efforts.

Orsini (2010) offers examples of how agencies in one service arena, home health care, successfully applied social networking to the task of attracting clients.

Human service organizations have followed the lead of commercial firms by creating positions for information technology (IT) staff. Their responsibilities include system maintenance and security, staff training, and planning for regular upgrades of software and hardware. In addition, IT specialists are increasingly needed to serve as modern versions of reference librarians, acquainting themselves and then informing staff about the constant flow of new resources. These may range from specialized software for fund raising, website development, or production of newsletters to Internet resources such as nonprofit-agency listserves, donor databases, subscription services that track funding opportunities and assist with preparation of grant applications, and many others. Table 8.12 shows examples of websites that provide information on these and other resources for HSOs.

All professional-level employees and most support staff at HSOs should have access to a personal computer in their workplace. Laptops or PDAs may be best for those who make frequent client visits or travel to multiple office sites, and both can connect remotely to agency databases. In addition, more resources for individual professional staff are becoming available online, including access to journal abstracts, mentioned earlier in the chapter, as well as access to journal articles themselves. Subscriptions to such services may seem expensive, but the costs are often less than photocopying trips to libraries and are increasingly justifiable in an era that emphasizes evidence-based practice.

Table 8.12   Selected Internet Resources for Human Service Organizations

Web Address	Description
www.compasspoint.org	CompassPoint Nonprofit Services—a nonprofit consulting organization that serves nonprofits
www.guidestar.org	GuideStar—Web-based information clearinghouse for nonprofits
www.handsnet.org	HandsNet—news and information website for human service organizations
www.idealist.org	Action Without Borders—information source and link-builder for nonprofits
www.independentsector.org	The Independent Sector—coalition to support nonprofit organizations
www.nationalhumanservices.org	National Organization for Human Services—provides support to human service professionals
www.ncna.org	National Council of Nonprofit Associations—membership organization for nonprofits
www.aphsa.org	American Public Human Service Association—organization of public human service providers
www.techsoup.org	TechSoup—technology assistance for nonprofits

Table 8.13	**Assessing Adequacy of Technical Systems and Resources**	
	Staff Involved in Design and/or Given Access to Resource?	Up-to-Date Technology?
1. Budgeting process	——	——
2. Location/accessibility of office	——	——
3. Design/décor of office space	——	——
4. Management information system	——	——
5. Client data system	——	——
6. Use of Internet databases for fund raising, donor development, and grant writing	——	——
7. Computer hardware for line staff	——	——
8. Computer software for line staff	——	——
9. Access to Internet and email for line staff	——	——

Tools such as the one depicted in Table 8.13 can be useful in assessing the adequacy of technical resources and systems.

SUMMARY

To fully understand an organization, with all its strengths and weaknesses, one would have to spend years reviewing documents, analyzing data, and talking to people familiar with it. However, an overview of selected elements of the organization and its relationship to its environment can provide a sufficiently detailed understanding to determine the presence of problems that may need to be addressed, why they exist, and steps that might be taken to resolve them.

In this chapter we proposed that understanding an organization involves two tasks: (1) identifying the organization's environment and understanding relationships between the organization and significant elements of this environment and (2) understanding the inner workings of the organization itself.

Significant elements of the task environment include sources of needed resources such as cash funding, noncash resources, clients and client referrals, and other needed organizational inputs. Also important in the task environment are regulatory and accrediting bodies that set standards for the organization, and professional associations or licensing boards that set standards for the organization's staff. Strong and positive relationships with these entities make an important contribution to the overall strength and stability of the agency.

Assessing the internal functioning of the organization also includes understanding elements such as corporate authority and mission; management and leadership style; organizational and program structure; agency measures of efficiency, quality, and effectiveness; personnel policies and practices; and adequacy of resources. Using the tools discussed in this chapter as means of assessing the organization will enable a student or beginning practitioner to better understand the organizational context within which problems are identified and changes are proposed.

Framework for Assessing a Human Service Organization

Task 1: Assess the Organization's Environment

Identify and Assess Relationships with Revenue Sources

Cash Revenues

- What are the agency's funding sources?
- How much and what percentage of the agency's total funds are received from each source?

Noncash Revenues

- Does the organization use volunteers? If yes, how many and for what purposes?
- Are appropriate efforts made to match volunteers' skills and abilities to the tasks assigned?
- What in-kind resources (e.g., food, clothing, physical facilities, etc.) does the organization receive?
- What tax benefits does the organization receive?

Relationships with Revenue Sources

- What is the nature and quality of the relationship between funding sources and the agency?

Identify and Assess Relationships with Clients and Referral Sources

- What is the organization's domain (e.g., what criteria does it use to determine which clients it will serve)?
- Must clients be recruited or informed about the organization? Will they seek it out on their own, or will they be mandated to participate?
- How does the organization deal with clients who seek its services but do not fit the profile of those it typically serves?
- How are the costs of client services covered, and how does the organization deal with those who cannot pay?
- What are the major sources of client referrals?

Relationships with Referral Sources

- Does the agency claim a larger domain than it serves?
- Does demand for services outstrip supply, or is there unused capacity?
- What types of clients does the organization refuse (e.g., are there disproportionate numbers of poor, elderly, persons of color, women, persons with disabilities, gays/lesbians, or other groups that are typically underserved)?

Identify and Assess Relationships with Other Elements in the Task Environment

Relationships with Regulatory Bodies, Professional Organizations, and the General Public

- What state and federal regulatory bodies oversee programs provided by this organization?
- With what government agencies does this organization contract for service provision?
- What professional associations, licensing and certification boards, and accrediting bodies influence agency operations?

◗ What are the perceptions of the "general public" in terms of the relevance, value, and quality of agency services?

Relationships with Competitors and Collaborators

◗ What other agencies provide the same services to the same clientele as this organization?
◗ With whom does the organization compete?
◗ With whom does the organization cooperate? Is the organization part of a coalition or an alliance?
◗ How is the organization perceived by regulatory bodies, government contracting agencies, professional organizations, accrediting bodies, and the general public in relation to its peers and competitors?

Identify and Assess Cultural Competence in External Relationships

Understand Diversity in the Organizational Environment

◗ What efforts does the organization make to familiarize itself with the diversity that exists in its environment?
◗ Does the organization recognize and seek to overcome barriers to service access?
◗ Does the organization take steps to ensure that its staff reflects the diversity of its clients?
◗ Do the organization's services fit well with the needs of minority as well as nonminority clients?

Task 2: Assess the Organization Internally

Identify Corporate Authority and Mission

◗ What is the basis for and extent of the organization's corporate authority?
◗ What is its mission?
◗ Is the organization operating in a manner consistent with its authority and mission?
◗ To what extent is the mission supported by staff who perform different roles within the organization?
◗ Are policies and procedures consistent with mission and authority?

Understand Program Structure and Management Style

Organizational and Program Structure

◗ What are the major departmental or program units on the organizational chart?
◗ Is there a convincing rationale for the existing organizational structure?
◗ Is this existing structure consistent with and supportive of the mission?
◗ Is supervision logical and capable of performing expected functions? Are staff members capable of performing expected functions?
◗ Is there an informal structure (people who carry authority because they are respected by staff, and thus exert influence) that is different from those in formally designated positions of authority?

Management and Leadership Style

◗ How is the workplace organized and work allocated?
◗ Is appropriate authority and information passed on along with responsibility?

▶ How close is supervision, and what, exactly, is supervised? Is it tasks, is it functions, or is it the employee?

▶ How are decisions made? Is information solicited from those affected?

▶ Do employees feel valued at every level? Do they believe they are making a contribution to the success of the organization?

▶ How is conflict handled?

Assess the Organization's Programs and Services

▶ What programs and services are offered?

▶ Are service goals and objectives based on empirical research or evidence from past evaluations of services within the organization?

▶ Are the services consistent with the goals and objectives of the program?

▶ Are staffing patterns appropriate to the services to be provided? Are workload expectations reasonable, given expectations for achievement with each client and within each service and program?

▶ Is there a common understanding among management and line staff within each program about problems to be addressed, populations to be served, services to be provided, and client outcomes to be achieved?

▶ Are expected outcomes identified with sufficient clarity that program success or failure can be determined?

Assess Personnel Policies, Procedures, and Practices

▶ Is there a written human resources plan?

▶ Is there a job analysis for each position?

▶ Is there a plan for recruitment and selection?

▶ Is there a plan for enhancing agency diversity?

▶ Is there a plan for staff development and training?

▶ Is a performance evaluation system in place?

▶ Are there written procedures for employee termination?

Assess Whether the Internal Workings of the Organization are Diversity-Friendly

▶ Is the organization's structure and operation conducive to cultural competence?

▶ Does it promote an environment that retains diverse employees?

Assess Adequacy of Technical Resources and Systems

▶ Are program staff involved in a meaningful way in providing budgetary input? Do they get useful feedback about expenditures and unit costs during the year?

▶ Do program staff use budget data as a measure by which they attempt to improve efficiency?

▶ Do resources appear to be adequate to achieve stated program goals and objectives?

Budget Management

▶ What type of budgeting system is used by the agency?

▶ How are unit costs calculated? Do staff members understand the meaning of unit costs? How are they used?

▶ Facilities and Equipment

▶ Is the physical work environment attractive and conducive to high productivity? Do employees feel they have enough space and space of an appropriate type?

▶ Have problems been identified with current facilities and equipment? If so, is there a plan to address the problems and to fund solutions?

▶ Are there conditions related to facilities or equipment that appear to act as barriers to productivity or work flow?

▶ Are the facilities accessible to clients?

Computer Technology and Information Management

▶ Does the agency have integrated systems for mailings, payment, case-tracking, and management data?

▶ Does the agency maintain a website?

▶ Does the agency use external information resources for fund raising, grant applications, volunteer coordination, or other activities?

▶ Do all line staff have desktop or laptop computers? Do they have access to the Internet, word processing, email, data security and firewall software, and other applications? Is this technology up to date?

Succeed with PEARSON mysocialworklab

Log onto **www.mysocialworklab.com** and answer the questions below. (*If you did not receive an access code to* **MySocialWorkLab** *with this text and wish to purchase access online, please visit* www.mysocialworklab.com.)

1. **Read the MySocialWorkLibrary case study: Adventures in Budgets and Finances.** Pay special attention to the section entitled, "The State Budget Process."

What reasons does the author give for the fact that most legislators do not like to support funding for human service agencies?

2. **Read the MySocialWorkLibrary case study: What's Medically Wrong with This?** Consider how a clear policy about disclosure in the agency in which Sarah works could have prevented this dilemma. In what other ways may licensing boards shape agency practice?

PRACTICE TEST
The following questions will test your knowledge of the content found within this chapter. For additional assessment, including licensing-exam-type questions on applying chapter content to practice, visit **MySocialWorkLab**.

1. When supervision is assigned to functions rather than people and staff may have multiple supervisors, it is called a
   a. linking-pin structure
   b. matrix structure
   c. project team structure
   d. collegial structure

2. Research suggests that staff in organizations in which autonomy is high and decision making is decentralized and inclusive have
   a. lower levels of satisfaction among minority employees
   b. lower levels of subjective well-being
   c. lower levels of emotional exhaustion
   d. lower salaries

3. A process that identifies job tasks, determines the qualifications for a position, and examines relationships among positions is a(n)
   a. regulatory census
   b. accreditation review
   c. preliminary diversity audit
   d. job analysis

4. Human service organizations should
   a. be neat and welcoming, no matter how modest
   b. be in busy commercial areas
   c. be as upscale as possible to attract paying clients
   d. not worry about appearances at all

5. Select an agency with which you are familiar. Try to answer the questions in the Appendix in the section in Task 2 entitled "Understand Program Structure and Management Style." For questions you are unable to answer, how might you go about collecting this information?

ASSESS YOUR COMPETENCE
Use the scale below to rate your current level of achievement on the following concepts or skills associated with each competency presented in the chapter:

1	2	3
I can accurately describe the concept or skill.	I can consistently identify the concept or skill when observing and analyzing practice activities.	I can competently implement the concept or skill in my own practice.

_____ Can maintain a professional identity and uphold ethics even if working in an agency where employees have limited autonomy.

_____ Can advocate transparency and accountablity to ensure the responsible and ethical use of agency funding.

_____ Can advocate for vulnerable populations, protecting their vital services regardless of the political climate of the agency or community.

_____ Can seek opportunities to join in funding discussions, no matter what role you serve in the agency.

9

Building Support for the Proposed Change

Core Competencies in this Chapter (Check marks indicate which competencies are covered in depth)									
	Professional Identity		Ethical Practice	✓	Critical Thinking	✓	Diversity in Practice		Human Rights & Justice
	Research-Based Practice		Human Behavior	✓	Policy Practice		Practice Contexts	✓	Engage, Assess, Intervene, Evaluate

Macro practice in social work can be viewed as having four major parts: (1) understanding the important components to be affected by the change—problem, population, and arena; (2) preparing an overall plan designed to get the change accepted; (3) preparing a detailed plan for intervention; and (4) implementing the intervention and following up to assess its effectiveness. Chapters 3 through 8 focused on understanding the components. Chapters 9 and 10 concentrate on distilling the information gathered into a clearly thought-out plan to get the change accepted, and making decisions about strategy and tactics. Chapter 11 focuses on developing and implementing an intervention plan and then following up to ensure its success.

Before developing a change strategy, however, it is first necessary to be clear on the nature of the proposed intervention. Strategy and tactic planning would be premature in the absence of an understanding of what the change entails. This understanding can be achieved by developing a working intervention hypothesis.

Thus, beginning with the task of further developing and refining an intervention hypothesis, this chapter presents a series of four tasks. Together, these four tasks provide the foundation for moving toward the strategies and tactics one may choose in order to effect change.

DESIGNING THE INTERVENTION

A number of tasks need to be accomplished in the process of developing an appropriate intervention. First, in order to ensure that there are some common themes in the way participants frame the problem and proposed interventions, it is important to refine the *hypothesis of etiology* (developed in Chapter 4) and to develop a *working intervention hypothesis*. When the change agent and other participants are able to reach an agreement on these hypotheses, the second task is to identify some of the major participants who are likely to be critical to the success of the proposed change. After identifying key participants, the next task is to examine organizational and/or community readiness for change. Finally, when these tasks have been accomplished, the change agent and participants are ready to select a change approach. Table 9.1 summarizes the major tasks and activities involved in reaching consensus on an intervention.

Task 1: Develop the Intervention Hypothesis

During the early phases of problem identification, many people involved in change efforts, both paid staff and volunteers, are eager to propose a specific intervention. They may have experienced the frustration of working in what they perceive to be flawed programs, under perceived oppressive community or organizational policies, or as participants or members of communities that seem powerless to bring about meaningful change. Understandably, they are eager to propose immediate change and may be impatient with the idea of carefully thinking through the alternatives. This can be a great temptation and a potential pitfall if leaders do not insist on dealing with the findings developed to this point and avoid straying too far off course.

A well-informed, professional approach to macro-level change requires that the foregoing tasks associated with problem identification and analysis in Chapters 3 through 8 be addressed first. However, it is the unusual change

Table 9.1	Framework for Developing an Intervention Strategy
Tasks	Activities
1. Develop the intervention hypothesis	1.1 Refine the working hypothesis of etiology 1.2 Develop a working intervention hypothesis
2. Define participants	2.1 Identify the initiator system 2.2 Identify the change agent system 2.3 Identify the client system 2.4 Identify the support system 2.5 Identify the controlling system 2.6 Identify the host and implementing systems 2.7 Identify the target system 2.8 Identify the action system
3. Examine system capacity for change	3.1 Assess general openness and commitment to change 3.2 Determine availability of resources to sustain the change effort 3.4 Examine outside opposition to change
4. Select a change approach	4.1 Select a policy, program, project, personnel, or practice approach

agent who is not constantly mindful of a preferred intervention and who is not continually molding and shaping it as the analysis unfolds.

Final decisions about the design and specifics of the intervention should wait until the analytical work has been completed. When an acceptable degree of consensus is achieved about the nature of the problem and its etiology, an intervention hypothesis can be proposed.

Refine the Working Hypothesis of Etiology

The key questions to be explored are:

▶ What factors gleaned from the problem analysis, the population analysis, and the arena analysis help in understanding cause-and-effect relationships?
▶ What themes seem to fit best with the current situation?
▶ How should the working hypothesis of etiology be framed?

Study and analysis of the problem, population, and arena invariably produce a wide variety of quantitative and qualitative data. To avoid being overwhelmed with too much information, change agents must be able to identify those factors that are critical to understanding the situation at hand. It is typical that not all findings will be relevant to the immediate situation. They must be sorted out, and only those that are useful and relevant to the change effort should be retained. But how does one know what to look for, what to keep, and what to omit in this process? It may be helpful to briefly review Chapters 3 and 4, considering the tasks associated with understanding problems and populations. These considerations may provide guidance on how to refine one's thinking. Once this sorting process is complete, one is ready to frame a working hypothesis.

Take, for example, a situation where the problem identified is an increase in gang violence in a community, leading to rapid increases in the number of young men and women in the area who have become physically disabled due to gunshot wounds. A study of the problem may provide facts and figures, such as the

Engage, Assess, Intervene, Evaluate

Critical Thinking Question: When analyzing a problem, what clinical skills might help you gather meaningful information from people representing a community or population?

incidence of disabling gunshot wounds over the last five years, the demographic makeup of the community, poverty rates, high school dropout rates, comparisons with similar communities, a history of the development of gang activity in the community, and various writers' ideas about the nature and causes of violence (Bell, 2009; Bjerregaard, 2010; MacDonald, 2009; Maschi & Bradley, 2008).

A study of the population may reveal that violent youth in this community tend to cluster within lower socioeconomic strata, that many are from families having difficulty meeting basic needs, that parental neglect is common, that few have had positive experiences with education, that most are in a stage at which they are struggling to develop an identity, that peer relationships are critical to their social development, and that almost all find few incentives to conform to societal expectations.

Interviews with parents and community leaders may reveal that there is a sense of hopelessness or resignation among adults in the community, that many are unemployed and have low skill levels, that education is not highly valued, that parents rarely support the efforts of teachers, and that associations among both teens and adults are almost exclusively along ethnic lines. Patterns of participation in extracurricular activities reveal higher participation rates among white students, whereas Latino/a and African American students, who feel the programs are not relevant, are left to develop their own activities. When talking with social service leaders in the community, it may become obvious that providers' perceptions of what to do are different from those of community residents (Kissane & Gingerich, 2004).

Not everything discovered can be used. To be useful, the quantitative and qualitative data gathered in the analysis phase must be distilled into a working hypothesis about etiology (cause-and-effect relationships). In short, the change agent must ask: Having studied problem, population, and arena as well as their areas of overlap, what do I now believe to be the *most significant* contributing factors leading to the need for change? A working hypothesis of etiology, drawn from analysis of the problem, population, and/or arena, can be expressed in a statement or series of statements similar to the following example.

Example of a Working Hypothesis of Etiology

Because of the following factors (drawn from analysis of the problem, population, and/or arena):

1. A trauma that led to a disabling physical condition
2. Limited basic education and marketable skills
3. Limited job opportunities
4. The need, during the teen years, to develop a positive, socially acceptable identity while, at the same time, being denied opportunities.

The following problems have developed:

1. Limited physical activity and declining health
2. Little to offer prospective employers
3. Discouragement and hopelessness regarding prospects for developing economic and psychological independence
4. Onset of a negative, antisocial identity and behavior pattern.

This example is, of course, oversimplified for the sake of illustration. Completion of this task should result in a draft statement that reflects some level of agreement among participants regarding cause-and-effect relationships underlying the need for change.

Develop a Working Intervention Hypothesis

The key questions to be explored are:

▶ What interventions are implied by the hypothesis of etiology?
▶ Does it appear that these interventions are most likely to reduce or eliminate the problem?
▶ What results can be expected from these interventions?

Based on a distillation of the information gathered in the problem analysis phase and expressed in the working hypothesis of etiology, a working intervention hypothesis is developed. This *hypothesis* is a statement or series of statements proposing a relationship between a specific intervention and a result or outcome. It should have an "if A, then B" format, which indicates that if certain changes are made, certain results would be likely to follow. Within this framework, the statement should identify the following: (1) a target population (or specific subgroup) and problem, (2) the proposed change or intervention, and (3) the results expected from the intervention. These elements combine to form a complete package that makes clear the expected relationship between problem, intervention, and result. A working intervention hypothesis to deal with rehabilitation of physically disabled teens might read something like this example.

Critical Thinking

Critical Thinking Question: As you develop a working hypothesis, how might small changes to the way you define the target population effect the proposed intervention and expected results?

Example of a Working Intervention Hypothesis

If the following interventions are implemented for physically disabled teens:

1. Increase physical activity and exercise
2. Provide opportunities for education and development of marketable skills
3. Pair with a mentor who has overcome a physical disability
4. Work with local employers to identify job slots.

Then the following results can be expected:

1. Improved physical health and self-esteem
2. Increased incidence of acquiring a GED or equivalent
3. Development of a positive identity as demonstrated by articulation of life and career goals
4. At least a 50 percent increase in successful employment.

This would be considered a testable hypothesis. The strength of this model is that it encourages change agents to focus on a specified set of contributing factors and expected results that form a set of cause-and-effect relationships (Mullen, 2006). These understandings form the foundation on which the intervention framework is developed. If the model is followed correctly, the connections within and between hypotheses should be readily recognized. That is,

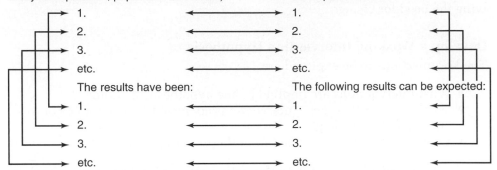

Figure 9.1
Relationship of Factors and Results in Working Hypotheses

there should be clearly understood relationships between causal factors and results in the hypothesis of etiology, and between proposed intervention and expected results in the intervention hypothesis. Furthermore, the relationships between causal or contributing factors in the working hypothesis of etiology and proposed interventions should be clear, as should the relationships between results specified in etiology and results expected of the intervention. These relationships are diagramed in Figure 9.1.

It is not necessary that each factor match precisely. The point in developing these hypotheses is that the intervention be designed to address the problems or needs specified and that the results be clearly defined so that they can be tracked. Using this format, one can establish the relationship between intervention and results. If this step is ignored or skipped, one runs the risk that the whole project cannot be evaluated or demonstrate effectiveness.

An important issue in relation to developing working hypotheses of etiology and intervention is that their development arises from findings gathered in the problem, population, and arena analyses. It is not unusual for people involved in change to attempt to impose their own perceptions and agendas on change efforts. A principal or school board member may have had a successful experience imposing strict discipline on an individual student, for example, and may firmly believe that this approach is the answer for all teens who pose disciplinary problems, regardless of findings. Every effort must be expended to resist having these pat solutions imposed. Solutions should come from well-researched analysis.

It is not necessary at this point to flesh out the intervention in detail, as that will be addressed in Chapter 11. However, for the change effort to proceed, it is necessary to make at least a preliminary decision about the nature and form of the intervention so that building support for a strategy to introduce the change may proceed.

Summary of Steps in Developing the Intervention Hypothesis

Because the information presented may be new to the reader, we recognize that these steps may seem daunting at first, but with practice, skills in writing intervention hypotheses can be developed. The following is a summary checklist reviewing the important points made so far about developing an intervention hypothesis:

1. A representative group should reexamine all relevant findings from analyses of problem, population, and arena.

2. Relevant quantitative data and other types of information should be distilled into a clear working hypothesis of etiology, establishing an understanding about cause-and-effect relationships.

3. Based on the working hypothesis of etiology, creative ideas should be generated about interventions that appear to be relevant to the need as it is currently understood.

4. Using these proposed interventions, a working intervention hypothesis should be developed. A series of statements should lay out a clear set of understandings about the nature of the intervention and the expected results or outcomes.

BUILDING SUPPORT

A broad base of support is usually critical to successful change. Building support requires planning and effort, and it begins with understanding the major participants or stakeholders (Daughtery & Blome, 2009; Fisher, 2009). A systematic effort to identify the major participants begins with understanding each of the systems to be considered. These are discussed in the following sections.

Task 2: Define Participants

Up to this point in the change process it is not unusual for the people involved to be a small core of committed individuals, possibly even close friends or colleagues, who recognize a condition or problem and are concerned enough to take action. It is appropriate for members of this group to tackle some of the early activities of problem identification and analysis, as long as they avoid becoming prematurely committed to a particular perspective.

In order for effective macro change to occur, it is necessary to have allies. A good deal of strategy development involves building coalitions. People willing to commit themselves to change rarely accept someone else's perspectives on problems and solutions without some negotiation and accommodation. Full participation should be a goal from the outset, even if the initiating group is small. It is often true that the greater the level of participation in the problem identification and analysis phases, the greater the likelihood of consensus on the problem and proposed solution (e.g., Campbell, 2009; Majee & Hoyt, 2009).

It is important that participants critical to the success of the change effort be identified in a systematic manner. One risk is that group members may assume that they represent a full range of perspectives and fail to identify everyone who needs to be included. If participation is to be representative of a wide variety of groups and interests, change agents need to understand all of the systems involved. Careful attention should be paid to insuring that a wide variety of perspectives is included throughout the process. This would include all relevant ethnic groups, women, and any other populations that are considered relevant to the change effort. A number of such systems will play critical roles in determining success or failure of the proposed change,

In order for effective macro change to occur, it is necessary to have allies.

so representatives from these systems should be selected carefully and invited to participate in designing the change or intervention.

We will use the term *system* to describe these critical participants. This term is used in the context of *systems theory*, implying that participants should be viewed as more than simply a collection of individuals with common interests and characteristics. As a system or subsystem critical to the success of the change effort, they represent a complex set of interrelationships having system-like attributes that must be recognized and attended to by the core planning group. One of these attributes, for example, is *entropy*, which refers to the natural tendency of systems to expire without input and regeneration from outside the system. The concept is directly applicable to the types of systems involved in planned change.

Given the community and organizational arenas in which change occurs, it is important to emphasize how diverse the identification of participants can be. For example, in a human service agency that has identified an unskilled and potentially insensitive staff who are unprepared to work effectively with immigrant families, it will be necessary to include persons with knowledge about immigration issues and skills in the planned change design. Although this could be initially viewed as an internal agency problem, staff members will want to include participants beyond agency walls, such as immigrants and others with expertise in this area. Another example is a grassroots community change effort in which multiple domestic violence shelters have been identified as unprepared to deal with lesbian, gay, bisexual, and transgendered clients (Crisp, 2006). In this community, participants would include representatives from multiple organizations that house shelter programs as well as interested constituencies who have an interest in solving this problem. Defining participants for both these change opportunities requires capturing persons and groups, some of whom are immediately obvious and others that may be newly identified but helpful to the change process.

The systems to be considered include the (1) initiator system, (2) change agent system, (3) client system, (4) support system, (5) controlling system, (6) host and implementing systems, (7) target system, and (8) action system. It should be noted that these terms are used here solely for conceptual purposes to assist in understanding who should be involved and why. They are not commonly used among people involved in change efforts. It is more likely that terms such as *agency, office holder, position, committee,* and *task force* will be used to designate individuals and groups, but the professional who coordinates the effort should be aware, conceptually, of which systems need to be represented and why.

Identify the Initiator System

The key questions to be explored are:

▸ Who first recognized the problem and brought attention to it?
▸ How should/can the initiators be involved in the change effort?

The initiator system is made up of those individuals who first recognize the existence of a problem and call attention to it. Note that many people inside or outside a system may see a problem that needs to be addressed, yet nothing is ever done. An individual or members of a group do not become an initiator system until they begin taking steps to bring about a change. For example, a group of citizens recognized high rates of HIV/AIDS and teenage pregnancy in their south Florida community and decided to take action

---

Box 9.1 Potential Members of an Initiator System in a Community Effort to Promote Safe Sex Practices

▶ Concerned citizens committed to change

▶ Community leaders

▶ Victims of HIV/AIDS

▶ Parents

▶ High school counselors

▶ Planned parenthood staff

▶ County health staff

▶ Other interested and committed community representatives, insuring that all relevant ethnic groups and other special populations are represented

---

(Weiss, Dwonch-Schoen, Howard-Barr, & Panella, 2010). They initiated a participatory action project that was highly successful in achieving its goals. Using this project as an example, a list of potential initiators in such a community action project might include those identified in Box 9.1.

Individuals who first raise an issue may or may not also become a part of the initial planning process. If possible, key roles in the change effort should be assigned to initiators. Having already demonstrated an interest in the issue, they may be in a position to bring other supporters along. This becomes especially important if the initiators are indigenous to the community (Meyer & Hyde, 2004). People who have lived with the problem or need are likely to be knowledgeable about the problem but may see themselves as powerless to affect the system. Empowerment strategies such as teaching, training, group counseling, or consciousness-raising efforts can pay rich dividends in the long run and can place appropriate spokespersons in leadership positions (e.g., Everett, Homstead & Drisko, 2007). In any case, it is important for change agents to be aware of the person or persons who first raised the issue and to keep in close contact as the problem or need is framed for public consumption.

Identify the Change Agent System

The key question to be explored for this activity is:

▶ Who will be responsible for leadership and coordination in the early stages of the change effort?

For a professionally assisted change effort to be successful, there must be one or more individuals designated as coordinator or coordinators of the change effort. We will refer to this person or persons as the *change agent*. The change agent, together with an initial core planning committee or task force, comprise the change agent system.

If the change activity will require drawing on the resources of an organization, it is essential that the organization sanction the change and also be identified as part of the change agent system. This may involve getting formal approval from the executive or the board and may require release time from other duties, secretarial support, use of copying machine, mailing privileges, and other such resources. Depending on the scope of the change, support may require written approval to insure that all contingencies are covered or simply an agreement among supervisor and colleagues that certain staff will be devoting some of their time to the project.

In community change efforts, approvals may be less formal than in organizational settings. For example, a grassroots organizing effort may be comprised of citizen-volunteers who are neighborhood residents but are not tied to formal organizational settings. The grassroots group may be loosely structured, not having executive committees and perhaps not having many resources. General agreement among the members of the group may be the full extent of sanctioning in this arena (Rogge, Davis, Maddox, & Jackson, 2005).

The change agent system serves as a sort of steering committee to guide the change effort in its early stages. The makeup of this system is critical to the change effort because much of what is accomplished will be framed in the perspectives of these individuals. Ideally, this system will include representation from the initiator system—people who have experienced the identified problem, people who have had experience in trying to solve the problem, and people who can be influential in getting the change accepted. Again, representation is important.

The function of the change agent system is to act as an initial coordinating or steering committee until a wider range of participants can be incorporated into the change effort. Many participants in the change effort will be taking on different activities at the same time. It is the job of the change agent system to ensure that the change effort is properly organized and carried out from its early conceptualization to the point it is turned over to others for implementation. As the major systems and perspectives are identified and the action system (discussed later in this chapter) is formed, the coordinating functions are shifted to the action system.

The work of the change agent system begins with coordinating and carrying out the problem, population, and arena analyses, as described in Chapters 3 through 8. This may involve setting up project teams, doing research, interviewing, and coordinating all of the study effort through a steering committee. Then there is the work of agreeing on a general strategy. As new participants are added, responsibilities are assigned until the analytical work is complete and a strategy is developed for getting the change accepted and implemented. Examples of people who might serve as part of the change agent system are included in Box 9.2.

Identify the Client System

The key questions to be explored for this activity are:

▶ Who will be the primary beneficiaries of change?
▶ Who will be the secondary beneficiaries of change?

The client system is made up of individuals who will become either direct or indirect beneficiaries of the change if it is implemented (Linhorst,

Box 9.2 **Potential Members of the Change Agent System in a Community Effort to Promote Safe Sex Practices**	
▶ Chair	A county staff person with good organizational skills
▶ Teens (2)	Knowledgeable about HIV/AIDS with time available to devote to the project
▶ Concerned citizens	Well known in the community; who can get others to support the effort
▶ County Board Member	Someone who can run interference and get the county to support the effort
▶ Other interested and committed community representatives	

Eckert, & Hamilton, 2005). They may desire the change but not yet be actively involved in making it happen. In Chapter 3, we pointed out that macro change efforts begin with identification of a target population and a problem. The client system is always in some way linked to the target population for whom the specific change effort is being undertaken. In some cases it is possible that the target population and the client system could even be synonymous. For example, if the target population is all homeless people in the town of Liberty, and they ask a local housing agency for help in organizing for the purpose of requesting housing and services for all homeless people in Liberty, then the target population and client system are the same. However, if drugs are being sold out of a house in a neighborhood, and if the neighborhood residents ask for help in organizing to get rid of the drug dealers, then the neighbors represent the client system, and the drug dealers become the target system.

Different terms are used for conceptual purposes. A *target population* brings focus to the population analysis and usually represents a broader spectrum of people. A *client system* refers to the people who are intended to benefit from the change effort. Sometimes they are the same, sometimes they are not.

In defining the client system, the change agent should resist the temptation to jump to the easy and obvious definition of the primary beneficiaries and should patiently and carefully analyze details. For example, if the identified problem is rising vandalism in an elementary school, the client system could include several potential beneficiaries. A partial list of those likely to benefit by eliminating vandalism from the school would include students, teachers, administrators, parents, local police, campus security, neighbors, the school board, and the community as a whole. The question, then, becomes one of establishing priorities for direct benefits and distinguishing between primary and secondary beneficiaries. The decision will have an important impact on the change effort. If "students who want a good education in a vandalism-free environment" are identified as primary beneficiaries, then the intervention may be directed toward tighter security and stricter discipline. If, on the other hand, primary beneficiaries are described as "students who commit acts of vandalism and are unable to maximize their educational opportunities due to antisocial attitudes," then the intervention may be directed toward treatment. In either case, secondary beneficiaries would be "others" on the list (teachers, parents, neighbors, etc.), who would not be the direct targets of an intervention but who would benefit from the reduction in vandalism the change effort brings about.

The boundaries for macro-level changes tend to be defined in a way that the primary focus is on a segment of a community or organization. Entire communities (such as towns, cities, or counties that have formal political boundaries) or entire organizations (from small human service agencies to large, for-profit corporations) are rarely the focus of a professionally directed change effort led by a social worker, but it is not out of the question that they could be.

No matter how the primary beneficiaries are defined, the remaining groups should be identified and listed as secondary beneficiaries. It may be important to call on secondary beneficiaries when the change effort needs public support. We will refer to secondary beneficiaries as the *support system*. Remember that systems frequently overlap, and it is possible for individuals or groups to be part of more than one system. Potential primary and secondary beneficiaries in a project to promote safe sex practices and reduce the incidence of HIV/AIDS are included in Box 9.3.

Box 9.3   Potential Makeup of the Client System in a Community Effort to Promote Safe Sex Practices

Examples of Possible Primary Beneficiaries

▶ All teens within the identified boundaries not knowledgeable about safe sex practices

▶ Selected high-risk teens within the identified boundaries

▶ All sexually active adults within the identified boundaries not knowledgeable about safe sex practices

Examples of Possible Secondary Beneficiaries

▶ Families of all who learn about and adopt safe sex practices

▶ High school teachers, administrators, and health providers

▶ The entire county-wide health provision system

▶ Community leaders concerned about HIV/AIDS

Identify the Support System

The key questions to be explored for this activity are:

▶ What other individuals and groups (in addition to the primary and secondary beneficiaries) will support the change effort?

▶ Are there associations, coalitions, alliances, or organizations (local, statewide, or national) that are particularly interested in resolving problems associated with this population group or identified problem? Can their help be solicited if needed?

The support system is a catch-all system that refers to everyone in the larger community or organization who has an interest in the success of the proposed change. Some may receive secondary benefits. This group is expected to be positively inclined toward change, and may be willing to be involved in supporting and advocating for the change if needed.

Membership in the support system is often a matter of proximity to the problem and/or to the target population or client system. People may be interested in the change because a loved one is affected by the problem, a job brings them into close contact with those affected, or their church or service organization has selected this population for assistance. They are sometimes described in terms of their nearness to the concern or issue by a phrase such as the "mental health community" or the "foster care community." People who might logically be considered a part of the support system may or may not actually be identified by name and involved in activities. Sometimes a representative is the main contact to others who may be called on at a later time to lend support. They are the people the change agent will count on to become involved if decision makers need to be persuaded that the change is necessary. Because certain types of problems may have been identified in other locations, there may be state or national groups dedicated to their resolution. For example, if there is a state or national child advocacy group interested in the problem of child abuse and neglect and it is an area you have identified, their members may be an extended support system on which one can draw (Rycraft & Dettlaff, 2009). Potential support groups and individuals in a community effort to promote safe sex practices are included in Box 9.4.

Box 9.4   Potential Support System Members and Groups in a Community Effort to Promote Safe Sex Practices

▶ Concerned citizens

▶ Teachers, counselors, and school administrators

▶ Health providers

▶ Planned parenthood

▶ High school students

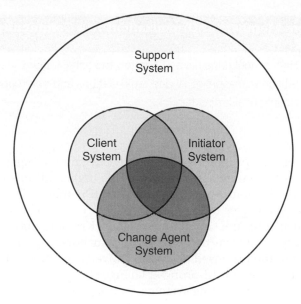

Figure 9.2
Relationship of Systems

Initiator, change agent, and client systems can be seen as incorporated within the boundaries of the support system in that they all have an interest in addressing the need for change. Initiator, client, and change agent systems may overlap or may represent separate and distinct constituencies. Figure 9.2 illustrates the relationship between initiator, change agent, client, and support systems.

Identify the Controlling System

The key questions to be explored for this activity are:

- ▶ Who has the formally delegated authority and power to approve and order implementation of the proposed change?
- ▶ Who ultimately has the authority to say "yes" to the change?

The *controlling system* is the person or group of individuals with the formally delegated authority to approve and order the implementation of the proposed change. Macro-level change almost invariably involves approval by some formally designated authority. If the change involves a public agency or publicly funded or regulated services, control may rest with a body of elected officials. If the change involves a private agency, control may rest with a board of directors. The question that must be answered in defining the controlling system is: What is the highest level to which one must appeal in order to receive sanction and approval for the proposed change? Also, because these individuals or bodies are critical for allowing the change to move forward, another important question is: What is their position on the proposed change?

The controlling system in a given episode of change is not necessarily the individual or group at the highest level of authority. It is common for a certain degree of authority to be delegated to individuals at lower levels, which means that not every proposed change must be approved at the top. For example, if staff in a domestic violence shelter find it necessary to add legal consultation to the shelter's counseling program, it is possible that the controlling system might be the organization's board of directors, but it might also be the director

Box 9.5   Potential Controlling System Members or Organizations in a Community Effort to Promote Safe Sex Practices

▶ Education of high school students	High school principal and possibly the school board
▶ Community education	Station managers of TV and radio stations and newspaper editor(s)
▶ Distribution of literature	County health director

of the shelter or the program manager of the counseling program. Much depends on the pattern of delegation within the organization and on the extent to which additional resources will be required. If residents in a long-term care facility are seeking changes in the provision of care, it may be difficult to know exactly who constitutes the controlling system (Kruzich, 2005). Some probing will be necessary to determine who has the authority to approve and order implementation of the proposed change because each situation is unique.

In some cases where multi-pronged changes are being proposed, it may be that there are several controlling systems. In this situation each will have to be approached individually to determine whether or not they will give their sanction and formal approval. Potential controlling systems in a community effort to promote safe sex practices are listed in Box 9.5

Identify the Host and Implementing Systems

The key questions to be explored for this activity are:

▶ What organization or organizational unit will be responsible for sponsoring and carrying out the activities of the change effort?
▶ What individuals will be involved in direct delivery of services or other activities necessary to implement the change effort?

The *host system* is the organization or unit with formally designated responsibility for the area to be addressed by the proposed change. If there is an organizational chart, it should provide some guidance in identifying the host system. Typically the host is located below the controlling system on the organizational chart. Within the host system is one or more employees and/or volunteers who will have day-to-day responsibility for carrying out the change. These employees or volunteers are referred to as the *implementing system*. In most instances of macro-level change, the host system will be a subunit of an organization that will be expected to implement a policy change, a new program, or a project. The listing of systems in Table 9.2 identifies controlling, host, and implementing systems. Again, as with the controlling system, there may be multiple host and implementing systems, depending on the complexity of the project.

Table 9.2   Examples of Controlling, Host, and Implementing Systems

	Controlling	Host	Implementing
School system	School board	A particular school and its principal	Teachers in the school involved in the change
Law-enforcement system	City council	Police Chief and department	Police officers involved in the change

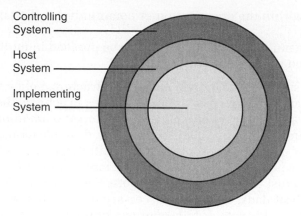

Controlling System

Host System

Implementing System

Figure 9.3
Relationships between Controlling, Host, and Implementing Systems

The change agent should be careful not to assume that the positions and perspectives about the proposed change on the part of the controlling system, host system, and implementing system are identical. It is not unusual for those involved in the execution of policy to disagree with the policymakers and vice versa. In some cases changes may be imposed upon reluctant implementers. It is, therefore, important for those in the change agent system to be sensitive to these factors and to work carefully and patiently with implementers. Figure 9.3 depicts relationships of the controlling, host, and implementing systems when structures are somewhat formalized.

In grassroots community change episodes involving coalitions and alliances or groups of volunteers, the host system may be loosely formed without a formal organizational structure. Change agents may have to assist volunteers in determining who the controlling and implementing systems are and how to access them from a position of being "outside" the system. In these cases, the "host system" may or may not be neatly nested within the concentric circles depicted in Figure 9.3. Therefore, each system should be assessed separately. Potential host and implementing system representatives in a community effort to promote safe sex practices are illustrated in Box 9.6.

The change agent should be careful not to assume that the positions and perspectives about the proposed change on the part of the controlling system, host system, and implementing system are identical.

Identify the Target System

The key questions to be explored for this activity are:

⬦ What is it that needs to be changed (e.g., individual, group, structure, policy, and practice) in order for the effort to be successful?

Box 9.6 **Potential Host and Implementing System Members in a Community Effort to Promote Safe Sex Practices**	
⬦ Education of high school students	Department chair and teachers responsible for the sex education curriculum
⬦ Community education	Persons in charge of public service announcements; News reporters and columnists willing to write articles about the project
⬦ Distribution of literature	County health supervisors and front-line personnel willing to identify patients in the target group and provide brochures and other literature

♦ Where (within the organization or community) is the target system located?

♦ Are there multiple targets that need to be pursued in multiple episodes of planned change? If so, what are they?

The *target system* is the individual, group, structure, policy, or practice that needs to be changed for the primary beneficiaries to achieve the desired benefits. The target system (not to be confused with *target population*) is a complex concept that cannot always be defined in clear and simple terms. What needs to be changed may often be philosophy, values, attitudes, practices, and policies as well as the provision of services. Another complicating factor is that many change efforts must address multiple targets. For example, in addressing the issue of "deadbeat dads," it may be necessary to educate the state legislature about the costs to the state of failure to pay child support before lawmakers are willing to support proposed legislation. The expected beneficiary is single mothers who are not receiving court-ordered child support, and the remedy is to pass legislation that allows officials to pursue delinquent parents across state lines and to seize assets until delinquent payments are made. But some reluctant legislators may resist government involvement in what they perceive as private matters, and may need to be persuaded that the proposed legislation is appropriate. In this case, reluctant legislators become the first target system and, if efforts with them are successful, passage of the legislation becomes the second target system. Finally, when the proposed legislation is passed, efforts can be focused on the third target system, delinquent parents, so that the client system, single mothers, can finally receive the child support payments due to them.

Three questions need to be answered in defining the target system: (1) What change (or series of changes) needs to take place in order for the primary beneficiaries to achieve the desired benefits; (2) what individuals or groups need to agree to the change (or series of changes); and (3) given the intervention hypothesis, what needs to be changed in order for the intervention to be successful? We have defined these individuals or groups as controlling, host, and implementing systems. The target system may lie within the boundaries of any or all of these systems, or it may lie entirely outside of any of them. The target system in a school experience may include selected school board members, a principal and assistant principals, a subgroup of teachers, or a selected group of students. The decision will be made based on what change is proposed and who needs to be convinced to support it.

For example, in the community effort to promote safe sex practices, the client system or primary beneficiaries were identified in a number of ways: (1) All teens within the identified boundaries not knowledgeable about safe sex practices, (2) selected high risk teens within the identified boundaries, and 3) all sexually active adults within the identified boundaries not knowledgeable about safe sex practices. This is an illustration where the client system and the target system would very likely be the same. The objective of this effort would be to change these groups from people who are unknowledgeable about safe sex practices into people who are knowledgeable and who adopt safe sex practices.

Identify the Action System

The key question to be explored for this activity is:

♦ Who should be represented on a central "steering committee" or decision-making group that will see the change effort through to completion?

At some point in the change effort, the central planning and steering committee moves from being the change agent system (a small group to get it started) to an action system (a larger, more inclusive group to take it through implementation, monitoring, and evaluation). Thus, as all other systems are being defined and participants selected, an action system is being formed. The *action system* is made up of individuals from other systems who have an active role in planning the change and moving it toward implementation. There may be considerable overlap between the action system and the change agent system, which was defined earlier as the professional change agent, sanctioning organization, and sometimes a core planning group. Although the change agent system often forms the core of the action system, other actors also have important roles in providing input into decision making and should be added as the change effort proceeds. The action system should include representatives from as many other systems as possible, especially those systems in need of change, if the relationship is not excessively adversarial.

Diversity in Practice

Critical Thinking Question: Ideally, an action system will include leaders, staff, community members, and families. How can you ensure all voices are valued?

For example, if the social problem under consideration is the unmet needs of homeless persons, this need might first be voiced by a person who passes by a few old men sleeping in doorways every day on her way from the bus to her place of work *(initiator)*. She finds that several other employees at her workplace have the same concern, and she takes the issue to the city council *(controlling system)*, where it is assigned to the City Department of Human Services *(change agent system* and *host system)*. The social worker from the department forms a task force that includes those who brought the issue to the council. As research and analysis proceed, more people are added to the task force. Professionals who work with homeless persons *(support system)* would be asked to join, as would some current or former victims of homelessness *(client system)* and someone from the city's political or administrative structure who understands the potentialities and limitations of the city's participation *(controlling system)*. When all significant participants have been identified, the members of this group would become the central decision-making body in the change effort and would be defined as the action system. These same principles would be applied to our ongoing example of the community effort to promote safe sex practices. As key people emerge during the change process, many will be added to form the action system. It may be necessary at some point to formalize this system in order to avoid having people join the effort late in the process and attempt to introduce completely new ideas.

Systems in Interaction

In examining these systems in interaction, it is important to remember that we distinguish among them and define them separately for conceptual purposes only. In actual practice, all systems could be within one organization or community arena, and it is probable that many systems will overlap.

Individuals and groups critical to the success of the change effort can be depicted by diagramming those identified as being included in Figure 9.2 (those assumed to be in favor of the change) and those identified as being included in Figure 9.3 (those assumed to be in control of the decisions and resources needed to make the change happen).

The target system may lie within any of these systems or even outside all of them. The action system may overlap any or all of these systems.

An example illustrating all systems within one organization would be a situation in which an organizational change is proposed. A human service agency may have a special program for "crack babies" (babies born addicted to cocaine) and their mothers *(the client system)* that includes detoxification, rehabilitation, counseling, and parent training. After six months, a community child welfare advocate *(initiator system)* notices that the case managers *(implementing system)* have been practicing "creaming"—in other words, providing the bulk of services to the most highly motivated clients and ignoring the needs of the least motivated. In this example, this practice of "creaming" is the target—that which is to be changed *(target system)*. The child welfare advocate calls the problem to the attention of the executive director (representing the *controlling system*), and the executive director directs the program supervisor *(change agent)* to form a small task group to study the problem and propose alternative solutions. The task force *(action system)* is made up of the supervisor, a case manager, a board member, an administrator, a representative of the child welfare advocacy group, and a former client now volunteering for the agency. Together they explore the problems and possibilities of directing more service to unmotivated clients.

All these have taken place within the boundaries of a single organization with some input from extra-organizational sources. Because of shifting boundaries among systems, the eventual target could become some entity completely outside the agency (e.g., focusing on working with the police to interrupt the flow of drugs to this population or supporting a community-wide drug prevention program). The reason for retaining conceptual clarity in defining the systems is that the change agent can ensure that each important perspective is represented even if the focus of the change effort changes over time.

Even though the terms *controlling*, *host*, and *implementing* may never be used, it is important that the change agent understand the domain, authority, and power of each, and that he or she keeps roles, responsibilities, and expectations for each clear and distinct. A roster such as the one illustrated in Table 9.3 may be useful in keeping track of systems and their representatives.

Task 3: Examine System Capacity for Change

As the change process unfolds, participants in the systems (defined earlier) should be assessed for their readiness to support the proposed change. An assessment of readiness should include consideration of their openness, commitments, and abilities to pursue the proposed change; availability of resources to implement the proposed change; and the degree of outside resistance likely to be encountered. These considerations should be assessed based on what is known about participants who comprise each system and their previous relationships.

Assess Openness and Commitment to Change

The key questions to be explored for this activity are:

▸ What has been the past experience with each of the system's participants with regard to organizational or community change?
▸ Does it appear that the participants in the various support systems will be able to speak with one voice and successfully work together?
▸ What levels of commitment to the proposed change and abilities to follow through are anticipated from each of the system's participants?

Table 9.3   A Roster of Systems and System Representatives

Proposed Change: To develop an orientation program and a self-help network for newly arrived immigrants who move into the local neighborhood.

System	Definition	System Representative
Initiator	Those who first brought the problem to attention.	Two women who struggled through the experience of coming to this community from another country with no help available to make the adjustment.
Change Agent	The professional social worker, agency, and others coordinating the change effort.	The social worker employed by city, initiators, and several community members.
Client	Primary and secondary beneficiaries.	Immigrant families (both adults and children); local schools; employers; neighborhood residents.
Support	Others who may be expected to support the change effort.	Churches in the neighborhood; community organizations that deal with immigrants; city officials; selected politicians; people from other, similar neighborhoods.
Controlling	The person or persons who have the power and the authority to approve the change and direct that it be implemented.	The mayor, city manager, and city council, who are being asked to extend some city services, provide bilingual staff, and donate some funding.
Host	The part of the organization or community that will provide auspices for administration of the intervention.	The City Department of Human Services, Neighborhood Services Division (NSD).
Implementing	The staff and/or volunteers who will carry out the intervention.	One staff member from the NSD (a community organizer) and ten volunteers who were once newly arrived immigrants.
Target	That which must be changed for the intervention to be successful.	The majority of the City Council opposes this effort because of the precedent they feel will be established and the number of neighborhoods that will subsequently ask for funding for special needs.
Action	The expanded planning and coordinating committee responsible for seeing the change effort through to completion.	The Coordinating Committee will be made up of the initiator system representatives, the change agent, two representatives of the client system, one City Council member, one teacher, one employer, the community organizer from NSD, and two volunteers.

Openness to change involves an informal assessment, based on experience, of how people in decision-making positions have dealt with earlier proposals. Even for those systems that are promoting the change, there are considerations. For example, does the group of people who comprise the action system have a track record of getting things done? Do they have a group identity that already bonds them over having successfully accomplished previous change episodes? If the group has not worked together before, or does not know one another well, the social worker will need to focus on team building and group development. Participants in an action system who have previously worked together have experience performing as a team and are comfortable with arguing among themselves because they have developed trust (Majee & Hoyt, 2009). It may be that some participants have worked together but others have not. Helping new participants become integrated into the group may be important so that the group functions well as a whole. This may especially be the case for recently formed community coalitions with members who come from different organizational cultures, without having yet established a jointly embraced coalition culture.

Much has been written about the difficulties of getting organizations (especially bureaucracies) to change and to collaborate (see, for example, Campbell, 2009; Guo & Acar, 2005; Perrow, 1979). Analyzing past experiences and general openness to change may be helpful in finding the subsystems or individuals that are most likely to be responsive to the proposed change. Discovering openness to change is not a simple matter of asking people in decision-making positions if they are open to change. Background information such as the position taken by an individual in response to earlier proposed changes is also needed. Other pertinent questions are: Have there been communitywide issues or initiatives that included (or could have included) this set of participants? Did the host organization participate? What was its position? Have leaders who are part of the change been willing to take stands on public issues? Or do participants prefer to keep to themselves and continue business-as-usual? Answers to these questions will help determine general openness to change.

Discovering openness to change is not a simple matter of asking people in decision-making positions if they are open to change.

Commitment to the proposed change could be examined in terms of each system's enthusiasm in endorsing the change as proposed (as identified in the intervention hypothesis). It is characteristic of community and organizational change that there will be differences in perspective on what form changes should take, even when there is strong agreement that change is needed. Low levels of commitment to the change as proposed can have a negative effect on its acceptance and eventual implementation. Assessment of commitment should involve examining the degree of enthusiasm as well as the degree of internal consensus about the design of the proposed change. Open meetings— or more refined techniques such as focus groups with parties affected by the proposed change—are useful for gaining a sense of support and degree of consensus. Ideally there should be agreement that participants in the change effort (the action system) will argue their differences in meetings but will attempt to speak with one voice in any communication with public media.

The social worker must be savvy about group development and group dynamics, recognizing who are the leaders within the action system and what they bring to the change effort.

The social worker must be savvy about group development and group dynamics, recognizing who are the leaders within the action system and what they bring to the change effort (Fisher, 2009). In organizational arenas, this assessment may be a little easier if the participants are known to one another. In community arenas, participants may be more scattered and loosely affiliated, representing constituencies that do not work together on a regular basis. Assessing the capacity of the groups that form each system to follow through with what needs to be done may make the difference in whether the proposal can successfully move forward.

Determine Availability of Resources to Sustain the Change Effort

The key questions to be explored for this activity are:

▸ From what sources will resources be solicited?
▸ What resources will be requested for the change effort?

Availability of resources, for many change efforts, will be the key issue. Although openness to change and commitment to the proposed change are helpful, availability of resources is a sine qua non. *Resources for the systems to be changed* usually refers to budgeted dollars, but they should also be understood to include staff time, volunteer time, equipment, supplies, space, and other resources of various types. Resources for the systems promoting change may be similar, but they also involve the important but difficult-to-measure resource of commitment, which includes factors such as the number of people who want the change to happen, their level of desire for it, and their willingness to persist if opposed.

An inventory of resources available to promote the change, along with a parallel inventory of resources needed to implement it, should be developed and employed as a guide for the change effort. Depending on the scope of the change, different resources will be needed. In an agency-based change, a great deal of indirect support may be available, from the use of office space and computers by the action system to permission for staff to work on the change effort as part of their jobs. However, in a policy change, when members of the action system are called to testify at legislative hearings whenever the opportunity arises (often on the spur of the moment), there may need to be additional resources available to carry out the daily work of the organization and to provide backup for those employees. Similarly, in a community change effort, volunteer time needs to be calculated into the cost, particularly if the proposal for change involves the use of volunteers over the longer term and the coordination and oversight that will entail. And if the plan calls for a programmatic intervention, a formal proposal with a justified budget that includes both cash and in-kind requests will need to be written in the planning process.

Identify Outside Opposition to Change

The key questions to be explored in this activity are:

▶ What individuals or groups outside the systems identified can be expected to oppose the change effort?
▶ What are the possible scenarios that may develop, and how will the action system deal with this conflict?

The final factor to be explored with each system is the degree of external resistance or opposition experienced. There may be instances in which a controlling system—elected local officials, for example—supports a proposed change, but the constituency it represents—certain local neighborhood groups, for example—is opposed. Almost any proposed change that requires public funds will find external resistance from groups that are competing for the funds. If pressure tactics are to be used, the change agent should ascertain whether the pressures that can be brought about through this change effort will be able to offset pressures brought by those resisting the change. Details about these tactics will be covered in Chapter 10.

For the systems promoting change, it is important to identify possible vulnerable points in its overall strategic considerations. Weaknesses in supporting data or other information, illogical arguments, or people who can be pressured to back down may represent liabilities, and those promoting change should be aware of them. A summary of considerations is illustrated in Table 9.4.

Table 9.4   Assessing System Readiness For Change

	Systems Promoting Change	Systems to Be Changed
	Initiator, Client Change Agent, Support, Action	Controlling, Host, Implementing, Target
General openness to Change	Probably not an issue, since these groups are promoting change.	If these systems have shown tendencies in the past to resist changes of this type, this should serve as an early warning.
Anticipated or Actual Response to Proposed Change	How committed are those promoting change to the type of change being proposed? What are the differences, if any? Are some committed only to a highly specific solution?	Is there consensus or disagreement about the type of change being proposed? How strong are feelings for or against it?
Availability of Resources	Do the systems promoting change have the skills and human resources to see the change effort through to completion, even if there is resistance?	Do the systems to be changed have the funding, staff, facilities, equipment, or other resources needed to implement the proposed change?
Opposition to Change	What forces outside these systems are opposing change? How strong is the opposition?	What is the source of outside opposition? How strong are the pressures to reject the proposed change? What significant actors are most vulnerable to pressures?

SELECTING AN APPROACH TO CHANGE

Task 4: Select a Change Approach

As the change agent completes the process of identifying and analyzing problem, population, and arena (as described in Chapters 3 through 8), the nature of the problem and significant supporting information should be coming into focus. This makes clear *what* needs to be changed. An important question yet to be answered is *how* the change should come about. For example, an agency's funding may be in jeopardy because its drug treatment program has been unable to demonstrate effectiveness for the past three years. Changing the ways in which these services are provided may require a policy change (e.g., redefining eligibility). Or circumstances may call for a program change (e.g., altering the type of treatment provided) or a project change (e.g., testing a new treatment approach with a limited number of clients). Changes in personnel and practices are also options, but we recommend that their use be limited to situations in which policy, program, or project approaches are determined not to be effective or feasible. These five change approaches will be discussed next.

Select a Policy, Program, Project, Personnel, or Practice Approach

The key question to be explored for this activity is:

▶ What approach (or combination of approaches) is most likely to achieve the desired change?

The professionally assisted change efforts discussed in these chapters are intended to fall into two general categories: (1) those promoting improved quality of life for the clients or communities served or (2) those promoting improved quality of work life for employees as a means of helping them provide the best possible services to clients and/or communities. In order to address these two categories, we propose five approaches to change. The approach selected determines the focus of the target system.

1. Policy. *Policy* is represented by a formally adopted statement about what is to be done and how it will happen—in other words, a course of action. Policy concerning what is to be done may include broad goals and/or specific objectives, but it should be clear in establishing a direction for operational efforts. Policy about how something will happen often takes the form of an operational manual or set of guidelines for operations. Most organizations, for example, establish policies that govern accounting, personnel matters, purchasing, and other tasks.

Policies may be established by elected representatives, boards, administrators, or a vote of the people affected. In some instances, a new policy may be needed in order to change a situation. For example, establishing a policy that outlines a grievance process for staff may be empowering to employees who feel they have no recourse when they disagree with agency practices. In other situations, existing policy may need to be amended in order to make operations more effective. For instance, a family member may be the best and most appropriate caregiver for an elderly or disabled person, but agency policy may allow for paid services for professionally licensed caregivers only.

2. Program. *Programs* are structured activities designed to achieve a set of goals and objectives. In macro practice, programs are usually intended to provide services directly to communities or groups of clients. They may also be of a supportive nature, such as fund-raising, advocacy, or public relations programs. In general, programs tend to be ongoing and long term, assuming they continue to achieve their objectives.

Program change efforts differ in the type of change being sought. Some result in the establishment of new programs to serve a special population group. For example, a coalition of child-care workers recognized a growing number of homeless, runaway youth in their urban community. No existing program served this population group. Programs for the homeless served families with children and adults but were not equipped to deal with the care of minors. Police officers could arrest the youth for loitering and curfew violations, but this was not a solution. The coalition created a new program targeted specifically to this growing population group. Other change efforts might focus on altering existing programs to make them more responsive to client or community needs. Had existing shelters been willing to accept minors, or had it been feasible to do so, the change effort might have focused on redesigning current programs to be sensitive to the special developmental and legal issues faced by the youth.

3. Project. *Projects* are much like programs but may be smaller in scale, have a time-limited existence, be more flexible, and can be adapted to the needs of a changing environment. Projects, if deemed successful and worthwhile, are often permanently installed as programs. The term *pilot project* came into use to illustrate this type of preliminary or experimental effort.

Often change agents will find that initiating a short-term project to demonstrate a new or untested intervention is more palatable to decision makers than making a long-term program commitment. For this reason it is common to select a demonstration or pilot project as a first approach, and then to attempt a more expansive program change if the project is successful.

Policy Practice

Critical Thinking Question: In addition to payment processes already mentioned, what other areas of policy may present obstacles to making practice changes in an agency?

Many communitywide, ambitious change efforts are dependent on project approaches. Because they may have multiple steps that will occur over several years, each step in the change process may need to be viewed as a pilot. For example, after two years of intensive pressure from a state organizing coalition, the state legislature enacted a statute requiring all law-enforcement officers to document the race of anyone stopped for a traffic violation. The intent was to prevent racial profiling, but the implementation of this mandate met with resistance. The coalition to prevent racial profiling conceptualized next steps as follows: First, assist officers in local communities to set up tracking systems; second, use the data generated at community–law-enforcement forums to talk about the findings; and third, follow up the forums with sensitivity training. Although the coalition had three steps in mind, they presented each sequentially as a project so that the overall plan did not overwhelm the community and also because each step was somewhat dependent on the outcome of the previous step.

4. Personnel. Communities and organizations are made up of people *(personnel)* who are constantly interacting with each other. When these interactions go well, the quality of functioning and productivity of the organization or community are enhanced. When there are problems with these interactions, however, the best policies, programs, or projects may be undermined. This means the professional change agent must be prepared to undertake change at the personnel level, which is where people in organizations and communities come together.

Problems at this level may take many different forms. Community residents or members of a unit within an organization may experience seemingly irreconcilable differences and engage in ongoing conflict. A unit supervisor or neighborhood organizer may lack the knowledge or skill to form an effective working group. Authoritarian administrators or unresponsive elected officials may engender attempts to depose them. What these situations have in common is that they require caution on the part of the professional change agent who confronts them. When doing so, certain questions should be asked. First, is the proposed personnel-related change effort being considered because of the reasons stated earlier—improvement of the quality of life of clients or communities or improvement of work life so that clients or communities can be better served? Second, will the proposed change be dealt with through regularly established channels? When the target of a change effort is an individual, there is often a temptation to proceed "underground."

Brager and Holloway (1978) suggest that under certain circumstances covert tactics may be appropriate. First, one must determine if agency officials are ignoring client or community needs in favor of their own interests. Second, the change agent must decide if the use of formal, overt sources may jeopardize self, clients, or colleagues. Third, if overt means have failed or are clearly not feasible, one may consider covert tactics. In any case, the professional change agent should recognize the potential risks, including loss of job; should be convinced that the change is worth the consequences; and should be prepared to accept them if necessary. Ethical practice is basic to social work, and ethical dilemmas often emerge in situations in which one has a conflict over who is right, with competing perspectives possibly coming from employer, colleagues, community interests, client advocates, and others. Ethical dilemmas were discussed in Chapter 1 and will be reexamined in the next chapter.

5. Practice. The fifth focus of change, *practice*, applies mostly to organizations. It refers to how the organization or individuals within it carry out basic functions in ways that are less formal than written policies. At the organizational level, for example, a domestic violence shelter may have developed a common practice of having an experienced resident serve as "big sister," and orient newly admitted residents to the daily routines at the shelter. This is not a policy; it's simply the way they choose to help new residents learn the ropes. Planned change might be needed if it is discovered that some of the more cynical experienced residents have been encouraging negative attitudes toward shelter staff and shelter programs. A study might reveal that screening is necessary for the role of "big sister," and standards might be established for selection. This all remains within the relatively informal domain of practice and does not become policy until that point is reached where there is confidence in the effectiveness of the practice, and it needs to be implemented in the same way agency wide.

Table 9.5 provides a summary of the definitions of these five approaches to change.

Approaches in Interaction

Decisions about the change approach are obviously closely tied to decisions about the nature of the problem, the target system, and the arena. The important issues to be resolved in defining the change approach are: (1) Who or what needs to be changed in order for the problem or need to be resolved? (2) What is the appropriate point of entry to address the problem or need? (3) What approaches, or combinations of approaches, are most likely to yield the desired results? (You may want to refer to Chapters 3 and 4, and the beginning of this chapter, in which the professional knowledge base was used to create hypotheses that will eventually lead to informed interventions). As we provide examples of how the approaches interact, remember that the decisions for what approach or approaches used are driven by what one has carefully learned about the problem, population, and arena (context).

Many changes can be handled in simple and straightforward ways. More day-care slots are needed for single mothers in employment training programs, and the change agent calls this to the attention of the appropriate administrator and budget director. Resources may be allocated and more day-care slots added. Parents want drug and alcohol education in the high schools; the school board agrees to provide it.

Table 9.5	**Approaches To Change**
Approach	Definition
Policy	A formally adopted statement that reflects goals and strategies or agreements on a settled course of action.
Program	Prearranged sets of activities designed to achieve a set of goals and objectives.
Project	Much like programs, but have a time-limited existence and are more flexible so that they can be adapted to the needs of a changing environment.
Personnel	Persons who are in interaction within the change arena.
Practice	The way in which organizations or individuals go about doing business. Practices are less formalized than policies and may be specific to individuals or groups.

Other changes may require multiple approaches in order to be successful. For example, a community center in a poor, Latino/a community is committed to improving the quality of life for residents. The center provides many services to the community, including a health clinic, back-to-school clothing, a food bank, after-school programs, and other community services. The social worker and several interns have completed a needs assessment to determine what the community sees as priority needs. The workers have also completed an asset assessment to determine what talents and interests community members can contribute toward strengthening the community. At an informational meeting, center staff informs community members about grants that have been applied for and about negotiations with the city to become a neighborhood targeted for specialized services. The residents express dissatisfaction that they have not been involved in these decisions and accuse the staff of having elitist attitudes about participation in decision making. Community leaders threaten to appeal to funding sources if they are not more actively involved by the center in decision making.

This issue can be approached in a number of ways. A *policy* approach would focus on creating a policy, to be passed by the board of directors, designed to ensure that community residents are involved in program and budget decisions. A policy, if monitored and enforced, would be the strongest assurance that the participation issue would be addressed, but it could become cumbersome and lead to micro-management of even small decisions within the center.

Another alternative would be to create a formal volunteer *program*, directed to continue ongoing asset assessments and to actively pursue community members to encourage and facilitate involvement in the various programs and decisions of the center. Although this approach may increase the number of residents involved in the center, it may not ensure that community members' voices are truly heard when decisions are made. Having community members present is certainly important, but the concerns are whether they are empowered to speak up and if their suggestions will be taken seriously by paid staff.

A *project* might also be undertaken, designed to survey participants periodically to determine whether they support pursuit of various special grants or contract-funded efforts. Results of surveys could be compiled and disseminated through the community newsletter. This may satisfy some of the concern about participation, but it might also eliminate some projects that require short time frames for response.

Another option may focus on *personnel*. The social worker and other staff could be sent for training to ensure that they understand how to work with community members and how to involve them at critical points in the decision-making process. Involvement of community members could be made a part of their job descriptions and could be incorporated into their annual performance evaluations.

Finally, the focus could be on the specific *practices* identified in the community meeting, such as grant writing and collaboration with the city. Community representatives could be identified to work with agency staff on an ongoing basis to ensure that appropriate local input was a part of each decision about new programs, projects, policy changes, funding or other activities of the organization.

An innovative change agent could probably come up with many more options and may even find ways to use a bit of each approach, if that is what it would take to bring about greater empowerment and participation. Deciding on who or what needs to be changed and what systems need to be involved is an important component of successful change. When these decisions have been agreed on, the change process is ready to move to selection of tactics, which will be discussed in the next chapter.

SUMMARY

As we have discussed in earlier chapters, planned change requires careful study and analysis before action is taken. We proposed in this chapter that the information compiled during the study and analysis phases be summarized into a working hypothesis of etiology and a working intervention hypothesis. This process ensures that the intervention will logically flow from an understanding of all the known factors that contribute to the problem, need, issue, or opportunity.

Once a clearly conceptualized intervention has been proposed, it is necessary to begin a systematic process of enlisting support of critical participants. We have used the term *systems* and have identified eight of these that play roles of varying importance to the success of the intervention. Change agents need to know which individuals and groups make up each of these systems, who speaks for these groups, and what the groups' positions are on the proposed change. Without this knowledge, a change agent will be severely limited in getting the change accepted. A series of assessments will help the change agent understand the positions of each of the systems on the proposed change.

Finally, before selecting among the strategies discussed in the next chapter, the change agent must select a change approach. We suggest choosing a policy, program, project, personnel, or practice approach, or some combination, based on what is known about what is likely to successfully work with the population and the problem. When these tasks have been accomplished, the change effort is ready to move toward selection of strategy and tactics.

Framework for Developing an Intervention

Task 1: Develop the Intervention Hypothesis

Refine the Working Hypothesis of Etiology

- ▶ What factors gleaned from the problem analysis, the population analysis, and the arena analysis help in understanding cause-and-effect relationships?
- ▶ What themes seem to fit best with the current situation?
- ▶ How should the working hypothesis of etiology be framed?

Develop a Working Intervention Hypothesis

- ▶ What interventions are implied by the hypothesis of etiology?
- ▶ Does it appear that these interventions are most likely to reduce or eliminate the problem?
- ▶ What results can be expected from these interventions?

Task 2: Define Participants

Identify the Initiator System

- ▶ Who first recognized the problem and brought attention to it?
- ▶ How should/can the initiators be involved in the change effort?

Identify the Change Agent System

- ▶ Who will be responsible for leadership and coordination in the early stages of the change effort?

Identify the Client System

- ▶ Who will be the primary beneficiaries of change?
- ▶ Who will be the secondary beneficiaries of change?

Identify the Support System

- ▶ What other individuals and groups (in addition to the primary and secondary beneficiaries) will support the change effort?
- ▶ Are there associations, coalitions, alliances, or organizations (local, statewide, or national) that are particularly interested in resolving problems associated with this population group or identified problem? Can their help be solicited if needed?

Identify the Controlling System

- ▶ Who has the formally delegated authority and the power to approve and order implementation of the proposed change?
- ▶ Who ultimately has the authority to say "yes" to the change?

Identify the Host and Implementing Systems

- ▶ What organization will be responsible for sponsoring and carrying out the activities of the change effort?
- ▶ What individuals will be involved in direct delivery of services or other activities necessary to implement the change effort?

Identify the Target System

▶ What is it that needs to be changed (e.g., individual, group, structure, policy, and practice) in order for the effort to be successful?

▶ Where (within the organization or community) is the target system located?

▶ Are there multiple targets that need to be pursued in multiple episodes of planned change? If so, what are they?

Identify the Action System

▶ Who should be represented on a central "steering committee" or decision-making group that will see the change effort through to completion?

Task 3: Examine System Capacity for Change

Assess Openness and Commitment to Change

▶ What has been the past experience with each of the system's participants with regard to organizational or community change?

▶ Does it appear that the participants in the various systems will be able to speak with one voice and successfully work together?

▶ What levels of commitment to the proposed change and abilities to follow through are anticipated from each of the system's participants?

Determine Availability of Resources to Sustain the Change Effort

▶ From what sources will resources be solicited?

▶ What resources will be requested for the change effort?

Identify Outside Opposition to Change

▶ What individuals or groups outside the systems identified can be expected to oppose the change effort?

▶ What are the possible scenarios that may develop and how will the action system deal with this conflict?

Task 4: Select a Change Approach

Select a Policy, Program, Project, Personnel, or Practice Approach

▶ What approach (or combination of approaches) is most likely to achieve the desired change?

Succeed with PEARSON mysocialworklab

Log onto **www.mysocialworklab.com** and answer the questions below. (*If you did not receive an access code to* **MySocialWorkLab** *with this text and wish to purchase access online, please visit* www.mysocialworklab.com.)

1. Read MySocialWorkLibrary case study: Residents' Rights to Intimacy in an Assisted Living Residence. Imagine you work at Mildred and Carter's residence and

are tasked with coming up with how the administration should approach intimacy among residents. Construct a working intervention hypothesis, including the steps you would take, and the expected results.

2. Read MySocialWorkLibrary case study: Mothers vs. The Board of Education. Identify what participant system the five women who made up the task force represent.

PRACTICE TEST The following questions will test your knowledge of the content found within this chapter. For additional assessment, including licensing-exam-type questions on applying chapter content to practice, visit **MySocialWorkLab**.

1. Which phrase below will result in a working intervention hypothesis? "Developing an adult day care program . . .
   a. and getting community support"
   b. for all levels of functioning"
   c. including occupational therapy"
   d. will provide families with respite"

2. A person or group becomes part of the initiator system when they
   a. are a member of the oppressed group
   b. become aware of the problem
   c. begin to take steps to bring change
   d. identify the action system's needs

3. The "target system" represents
   a. what needs to be changed
   b. all principal beneficiaries
   c. the full target population
   d. easily defined change goals

4. A group recommends that a time-limited trial of a new intake procedure be initiated to evaluate if the procedure is worthwhile. This is a
   a. policy change
   b. program change
   c. project change
   d. personnel change

5. Imagine being on the initial steering committee (as part of the change agent system) that is planning an intervention to help homeless teens. Who would comprise the other systems involved in this effort? What are some strategies that may improve engagement with these other systems?

ASSESS YOUR COMPETENCE Use the scale below to rate your current level of achievement on the following concepts or skills associated with each competency presented in the chapter:

1	2	3
I can accurately describe the concept or skill.	I can consistently identify the concept or skill when observing and analyzing practice activities.	I can competently implement the concept or skill in my own practice.

_____ Can engage individuals and groups using empathy and other clinical skills.

_____ Can demonstrate a logical connection between the identified problem and the proposed intervention.

_____ Can reach out to diverse groups and find ways to create room for the voices of all stakeholders to be heard and valued.

_____ Can develop policy interventions that create meaningful, system-wide change.

Buzz Words for Goal:
- partnered
- identified (opportunities)
- successfully
- influenced
- gained consensus
- explored
- developed
- incorporated
- utilized
- established
- supported
- assumed (ownership)
- collab...

10

Selecting Appropriate Strategies and Tactics

Core Competencies in this Chapter (Check marks indicate which competencies are covered in depth)				
✓ Professional Identity	✓ Ethical Practice	☐ Critical Thinking	✓ Diversity in Practice	✓ Human Rights & Justice
☐ Research-Based Practice	☐ Human Behavior	☐ Policy Practice	☐ Practice Contexts	☐ Engage, Assess, Intervene, Evaluate

In Chapter 9, we emphasized that initiating planned change can be a time-consuming process. Although many people may agree that a problem exists, getting agreement on just how the situation should be changed is seldom easy. Therefore, social workers should be open to the possibility that practices in many of the arenas in which they operate will be well entrenched and there will be a tendency to resist change.

At the community level, decision-making bodies such as city or town councils, boards of education, parks and recreation boards, or community development boards can become entrenched in their thinking and planning. Decisions made earlier may be seen as positions to be defended rather than topics for open discussion. At the organizational level, policies and practices become a part of the culture, and change may be seen as a threat. Fellow social workers may even be a part of the commitment to business-as-usual.

Selecting appropriate tactics requires recognizing the reasons that community and organizational leaders take the positions they do. At the same time, the change agent must also think analytically about how to get the proposed change accepted and implemented. Brilliant ideas don't mean much if they end up in notebooks gathering dust in some agency's archives. For this reason, it is incumbent on the change agent to study the makeup of the target system and to decide how individuals and groups can best be approached to ensure the ultimate success of the change episode.

ASSESSING THE POLITICAL AND ECONOMIC CONTEXT

The *target system* is the individual, group, structure, policy, or practice that needs to be changed for the primary beneficiaries to achieve the desired benefits. Analyzing the target system means assessing the systems involved. Given the discussion in Chapter 9 of various systems (initiator, change agent, client, support, controlling, host, implementing, target, and action) and their readiness for change, the change agent should have an increased awareness of the politics of the organization or community within which the change intervention is to occur. Even if a change agent believes she or he is in a situation in which there is little contentiousness or conflict, that view may not be held by others. For example, a school district may be overwhelmed with non-English-speaking students, and the community may have factions with divergent opinions on immigration. In this situation, attention should be focused on creating linkages among groups before any planned change can occur. However, if the organization or community system is fairly closed, with long-standing, entrenched leadership, then attention will need to be focused on changing some of the organization's or the community's policies or practices. This will require a different approach to change because change will probably not be welcomed. Some groups, organizations, and communities will be more amenable to change than others, some will be more closed, and others will be more prone to conflict. Assessing arenas and their openness to change is central to the planned change process.

No matter how one defines the problem or how one views conflict, a certain level of conflict is inevitable. Whenever change is proposed, no matter how simple it may seem, there will be resistance. Even with willing target systems that agree to collaborate, there will be points of disagreement, even

Diversity in Practice

Critical Thinking Question: How might diversity in an organization or system increase the chance of conflict when attempting change? How might diversity be a strength?

combativeness, over details or specifics of the proposed change. In any change effort, one cannot and should not expect to avoid conflict. Instead, it is the degree or level of conflict and the possibility of overcoming disagreements that will vary in each situation. Be prepared to encounter resistance, but be equally prepared to assess the consequences of the resistance for the proposed change opportunity. On the other hand, disagreement in an organization or community can also be a factor that supports change. Participants may recognize the risks of disagreement elevating to the level of dysfunction and be more ready to alter the status quo.

Task 1: Assess Political and Interpersonal Readiness

Earlier we discussed the importance of politics in bringing about change. We address these considerations more directly in this section. *Politics* as used here refers to the reasons or motivation behind the different ways individuals respond when asked to support a change effort. It is likely that those affected will respond to the prospect of change based on two main criteria: perceived self-interest and perceived responsibility within a formal or informal position they may hold. Sometimes the personal and public positions of the same person may differ or even be in conflict. For example, a city council member may have a relative who is homeless and knows the city needs better shelter, yet votes against a proposed new structure because business interests in the neighborhood are opposed. These kinds of actions may be taken for partisan reasons, or as a way of trading favors among decision makers. This includes consideration of partisan politics but is not limited to that arena.

Political and interpersonal considerations add complexity to the change effort. Dealing with the political dimensions of a change effort often comes down to negotiating among competing interests. Pooling knowledge and information among those supporting the change will help in understanding how best to approach each of the decision makers who are critical to its success. For example, tools such as the Community Readiness Assessment have been used to determine how community members perceive the need to address an identified problem. Schroepfer, Sanchez, Lee, Matloub, Waltz, and Kavanaugh (2009) used this assessment in five communities concerned about cancer health disparities. Readiness was assessed along a continuum from "no awareness" to a "high level of community ownership," providing insight into how consensus-reaching approaches might be used.

Assess Duration, Intensity, and Frequency

The key questions to be explored are:

- How long has the problem existed?
- Is the problem considered an emergency?
- If the problem is episodic or recurring, how often does it occur?

Community and organizational conditions can be referred to as varying in duration, intensity, and frequency. *Duration* is the length of time the condition or problem has existed. *Intensity* is the extent to which it is considered threatening to individual, organizational, or community survival. *Frequency* refers to the number of times the condition is likely to occur within a given time frame.

Long-standing problems are hard to change. People become desensitized, and community and organizational leaders are not easily persuaded that there is really a problem that needs attention. For example, it took a class action suit on behalf of the chronically mentally ill citizens in one state to force the legislature to address their needs. Yet, threats to immediate survival such as terrorism, contagious diseases, and natural disasters are recognized as emergencies and will receive priority attention. But even acute episodes can turn into chronic conditions, and in those situations it takes skilled advocates to keep the public's attention focused on the long-term recovery, cleanup, and rehabilitation efforts that are needed over the long haul.

Frequency of occurrence presents an interesting dilemma. One example is disaster preparedness in a community. Many experts in New Orleans raised concerns over the years about whether the infrastructure there was capable of handling the effects of a Category 4 or 5 hurricane, but such threats were so infrequent that efforts to strengthen barriers were delayed, eventually leading to disaster in 2005. Similarly, experts were always aware that offshore drilling held great risks and emergency plans had to be in place, but the push to drill for oil in the Gulf of Mexico appears to have been more important than a realistic plan in the event of an oil spill since the frequency of such occurrences are low. A problem of relatively low intensity but high frequency will often be seen by community members as a higher priority than more intense, less frequent problems.

For newly emerging or newly defined problems, the change agent should examine the issues of duration, intensity, and frequency. The closer the problem is to threatening survival needs such as food, clothing, shelter, safety, or medical care, the more likely those in a position to make changes will attend to it. Occasionally, long-standing problems can be presented in a new way, as has been done with alcohol abuse in the campaign against drunk driving over the past decades, framing it as a problem of life and death rather than simply a minor indiscretion.

Within organizations, problems that directly or indirectly affect the budget, and therefore the capacity of the organization to survive, tend to receive a relatively higher priority than nonbudget-related problems. The proposed change should be weighed in terms of its duration and urgency, with these factors used appropriately in selecting tactics for promoting the proposed change.

Address Public Image and Relationships

The key questions to be explored are:

- Who is involved in promoting the proposed change, and how are they perceived by decision makers?
- Who can serve as effective spokespersons for the proposed change?
- Who should keep a low profile when the proposed change is presented to decision makers?

Preparing a list of participants in each system and assessing the political and interpersonal strengths and liabilities of each participant can assist the change agent and action system in making the best use of each participant's skills. Some people with valuable technical expertise may be seen as highly controversial and a liability when viewed from an interpersonal/political perspective. Previous negative experiences with decision makers should serve as a warning but should not necessarily rule someone out from assuming a high-profile role. Regardless of who is designated as the public spokesperson, careful consideration should be given to whether this person is perceived positively, negatively, or as a neutral party, and by whom. This principle applies to both community and organizational change efforts, but it may be even more important in organizational change because of the closeness of working relationships and the greater likelihood of people knowing more about each other than they would in the community arena.

Task 2: Assess Resource Considerations

Cost is often decision makers' primary concern when considering a proposed change. Social workers may not agree with this value perspective, but they must face the fact that people operate within a money-oriented system and one in which decisions are made constantly regarding how to allocate scarce resources. Decision makers often consider cost even before considering the urgency or necessity of a change. This means the change agent must understand how such decisions are made and must be prepared to address cost issues in advocating for the change.

Determine the Cost of Change

The key questions to be explored are:

- What anticipated costs related to the proposed change can be itemized? What must be estimated?
- What sources of financial support or in-kind donations should be approached?

For reasons already stated, the change agent must attempt to calculate costs associated with the proposed change. This can be difficult because in many cases the details of the intervention design are not even worked out until there are some assurances that the change will be accepted. Take, for example, a situation in which the parents in a community want the school board to sponsor more organized and supervised after-school activities. Some may want arts and crafts, some athletic activities, and some drama and music programs. When the school board is approached, these details have probably not been addressed. The change agent must be prepared for a response that "the proposed change will cost too much and resources are not available." To counter this concern, some preliminary calculations must be done, at least to the point of estimating the number of staff persons, approximate salaries required, computer equipment necessary to do the job, square feet of space needed, cost per square foot, and other rough computations. Technical expertise may have to be consulted to ensure cost estimates are realistic. Although most decision makers will want to conduct their own analysis of costs, estimates by those proposing the change can at least serve as a starting point and basis of comparison.

Determine the Cost of Doing Nothing

The key questions to be explored are:

- What will this problem cost the organization or community if nothing is done?
- How can this cost be framed so that it will be persuasive to decision makers as a good investment to support the proposed change?

A valuable statistic for comparative purposes, if it can be calculated, is the cost of nonresolution of this problem or nonimplementation of the proposed change. Such calculations may start with a simple line-item budget that demonstrates what is needed to mount a program. Box 10.1 provides an

Box 10.1 Example of a Simple Line-Item Budget for an After-School Program

Personnel	Cost per Semester (in Dollars)
Arts and Crafts Instructor[1]	1,800
Music Teacher[2]	1,200
Sports and Game Supervision[3]	3,000
Operating Expenses	
Rent and Utilities	1,000
Printing and Publicity	250
Equipment & Supplies	500
Insurance	500
Total	**$8,250 per semester**

[1] 3 days per week @ 3 hours per day for 20 weeks
[2] 2 days per week @ 3 hours per day for 20 weeks
[3] 5 days per week @ 3 hours per day for 20 weeks

illustration of how one social worker constructed a budget for a much needed after-school program in an inner-city neighborhood.

It is important to impress on decision makers that there are long-term costs associated with doing nothing. For example, costs for in-patient or residential services can run as high as $6,000 to $7,000 a month. At first blush, an intensive vocational training program for high-risk adolescents costing $12,000 per participant per year may appear outrageously expensive. However, if presented side by side with data demonstrating that 90 percent of the service users who complete this program become self-sufficient and do not need residential treatment, decision makers may be persuaded that it really represents a long-term cost savings. Also, a traditional "ounce of prevention" argument may be a valid way to build support for changes designed to prevent unlikely but potentially disastrous events. As noted earlier, the cost of 2 to 5 billion dollars needed to shore up levees in New Orleans might have saved 50 to 100 billion dollars in cleanup costs from Hurricane Katrina in 2005. Likewise, the enormous human cost of lives lost in tragedies such as Columbine High School (April, 1999) and Virginia Tech University (April, 2007) might have had different outcomes had there been different perspectives on issues such as mental health assessment, right to privacy, background checks for purchase of firearms, and other related issues (Bonnie, Reinhard, Hamilton, & McGarvey, 2009). The difficulty is that too often these calculations make sense to decision makers (and taxpayers) only in hindsight.

Task 3: Weigh the Likelihood of Success

When the major participants, proposed change, and political and economic issues have been identified, the time has come to weigh the relative strength of supporting and opposing forces and to decide if the change effort is to be a "go" or a "no-go." This can be done in an orderly fashion by adapting Kurt Lewin's classic techniques of force-field analysis that was originally used in understanding planned change in organizations and then applied to the emergent field of organizational development (Medley & Akan, 2008). The issue for consideration here is whether to invest additional time, energy, and resources in seeking change. The experienced change agent recognizes that there is little value in moral victories. If a change effort is to be undertaken, it should have a reasonable chance of success. Lewin's force-field analysis model identifies three steps: unfreezing, moving/changing, and refreezing. Using this model can help determine the potential to "unfreeze" the situation and transition to moving and changing (Lewin, 1947) We propose a modification of Lewin's framework that examines two areas: (1) support from individuals, groups, and organizations; and (2) support from facts and perspectives. But first some thought should be given to the perspectives of those critical to the success of the change effort.

Ethical Practice

Critical Thinking Question: What are some possible negative consequences of pursuing a change effort that has almost no chance of success?

Identify Alternative Perspectives

The key questions to be explored are:

▶ How will opponents of the change effort frame their opposition?
▶ How much conflict or contentiousness is expected?

Perspective is an important consideration; it refers to the slant or "spin" individuals or groups choose to put on an issue. People involved in change in the field of human services are often amazed to learn that there is almost no concern raised that does not have an opposing view. For every advocate of a woman's right to make decisions about her pregnancy in consultation with her own physician, there is one who will support a fetus's right to survive. For every person concerned about child abuse or neglect, there is one who is equally concerned about perceived abuses of parental prerogatives by child welfare workers. It is tempting to dismiss opponents' views as uninformed and unenlightened, but in undertaking macro-level change it is unwise to do so. Alternative perspectives should be carefully analyzed for their merit and their potential or actual political appeal. Plotting a spectrum of opinions, together with some educated estimates of levels of public support of each, can be an informative exercise for action system participants.

Each perspective should also be weighed for the intensity of its support. The likelihood is that the closer to the extremes, the fewer the adherents but more intense the feelings. Figure 10-1 illustrates a continuum of possible perspectives on unauthorized immigration (Cleaveland, 2010). It should be noted that as one moves along the continuum, strong feelings may be accompanied by greater conflict and contentiousness.

It is tempting to dismiss opponents' views as uninformed and unenlightened, but in undertaking macro-level change it is unwise to do so.

Unauthorized migrants are trying to improve their economic status and should be encouraged to work in the United States	Unauthorized migrants are necessary to the economy and should be granted a guest worker status	Unauthorized migrants are costly to states. Since federal laws mandate services, federal funds should underwrite the costs	Employers should be fined and lose their licenses if they employ unauthorized migrants	All unauthorized migrants have broken U.S. laws by crossing borders and should be deported as quickly as possible

Figure 10-1

A Continuum of Perspectives on Issues Related to Unauthorized Immigration

Assess Support from Individuals, Groups, and Organizations

The key questions to be explored are:

- ▶ Has anyone important to the success of the change effort been left out?
- ▶ Who supports the proposed change?
- ▶ Who opposes the proposed change?
- ▶ Who is neutral about the proposed change?

The first question is particularly important from a political perspective. Failure to involve people who can help is as potentially damaging as involving people who may harm the effort. During the data-collection phase within the organization or community, efforts should be made to solicit names of those whose support is needed to succeed.

Once those with vested interests have been identified, the force-field analysis model can be applied (Medley & Akan, 2008). Support for or opposition to the change from individuals, groups, and organizations can be laid out in three columns. Column 1 represents the driving or supporting forces; column 2 represents neutral forces; column 3 represents the restraining or opposing forces. Identifying each of the systems involved, together with key individuals or groups within them, provides a graphic depiction of supporting and opposing forces and will help in determining the possibility of success if the change effort goes forward. Figure 10-2 illustrates a force-field analysis.

Assess Level of Support

The key questions to be explored are:

- ▶ What facts and perspectives gleaned from analysis of the problem, population, and arena support the proposed change?
- ▶ What facts and perspectives oppose the proposed change?

Following the identification of individuals, groups, and organizations supporting and opposing the change effort, facts and perspectives should be identified in the same way. It is unlikely that any new research or analysis is necessary at this point, although it may be worth the effort to go online to search for updates on current debates about the proposed change and how other organizations or communities are dealing with it.

Identifying supporting and opposing facts and perspectives involves drawing on everything now known and available in terms of statistics, history, theory, research, etiology, interpersonal and political factors, and resource considerations. This information is then examined for its potential driving or restraining effects on the change effort through use of the same force-field model. Figure 10-3 illustrates examples of support from facts and perspectives.

To illustrate how diverse opposition can be, Schneider and Lester (2001) identify the following categories of people from which opposition may arise: (1) individuals or groups who need more knowledge about an issue but who with adequate information might support it, (2) individuals and groups who are indifferent or neutral and would have to be convinced, and (3) those persons who are certain about their disagreement and may even be hostile (p. 125). These categories underscore the necessity of recognizing intensity of feeling, rather than just recognizing who opposes the change.

SUPPORT FROM INDIVIDUALS, GROUPS, AND ORGANIZATIONS			
System	Driving/Supporting Forces ⟶	Neutral Entities ⟵	Restraining/Opposing Forces

Initiator System	• Homeless Advocates
	  T. Johnson
	  L. Stearns		

Change Agent System	• St. Catharine's
	  Parish youth worker
	  J. Foster		

Client System	• Homeless teens in Douglas County		
Support System	• Homeless Advocates • Parents of Runaway, Inc. • Existing homeless programs		

Controlling System	• City Council
	  Members supporting
	  change
		• City Council
		  Members not yet
		  taking position
			• City Council
			  Members opposed
			  to teen shelter

Host System		• City Department of Human Services	
Implementing System	• Potential contract agencies		

Target System		• City Council member
		  votes in favor of
		  funding proposed
		  teen shelter	

Action System	• Advocates
	  (T. Johnson and L.Stearns),
	  youth worker (J. Foster),
	  two homeless teens,
	  two social workers
	  from existing shelters		

Others		• A large percentage
		  of the general public
			• Taxpayers Against
			  Increased Public
			  Social Services
			  (TAPS)
			• City Newspaper
			• Task Force on
			  CMI Homeless
			  (who are competing
			  for funding)

Figure 10-2

Force-Field Analysis of Individuals, Groups, and Organizations Supporting and Opposing a Proposed Project to Serve Homeless Teens

Using this format, action-system participants should initiate dialogue focused on making the "go/no-go" decision. One outcome might be a decision to gather more facts or to postpone deliberations until a more opportune time. This step is considered advisable only if the additional fact-gathering is highly focused and time limited. Such proposals sometimes arise simply as delaying

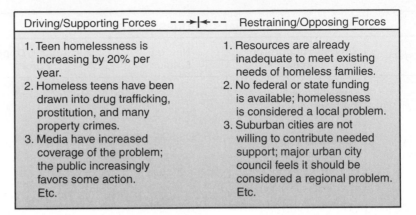

Figure 10-3

Support from Facts and Perspectives on the Problems of Homeless Teens

tactics or as ways of avoiding difficult decisions, and if so they should be recognized for what they are and rejected. It should also be noted that this may be the point at which some participants will believe the proposed change to be unattainable and will decide to drop out, whereas others may choose to continue. Here again, it should be emphasized that the professional person acting as change agent must make as sound a decision as possible in the interest of achieving the change objectives. Necessary changes that have a good chance of success should be supported. Causes that are likely to be defeated as currently conceptualized should be tabled until they are more fully developed or until the timing is better.

SELECTING STRATEGIES AND TACTICS

If, after consideration of political and economic factors, a decision is made to pursue the change, an array of approaches for achieving it can be used. We will use the terms *strategies* and *tactics* to describe these approaches.

Writers who deal with macro practice in social work sometimes use the terms *strategy* and *tactics* in different ways. Brager, Specht, and Torczyner (1987) linked strategy to long-range goals and tactics to the short-range and specific behaviors of groups. Morales (1992) identified several types of strategies and tactics used in macro practice, including building coalitions, raising consciousness, promoting awareness, and educating clients in terms of their own disempowerment.

When we use the term *strategy* in this text, we are referring to the *overall efforts* designed to ensure that the proposed change is accepted. The term *tactics* refers to the *specific techniques* and behaviors employed in relation to the target system designed to maximize the probability that the strategy will be successful and the proposed change adopted.

The development of strategies and tactics involves some critical decisions and requires careful thought. The approach(es) taken can have far-reaching effects on the success of the change effort and its impact on the problem and the target population. As will be seen, selecting strategies and their accompanying tactics is a process that requires careful, professional judgment.

Task 4: Select Strategies and Tactics

In Chapter 9 we provided guidelines on how to develop an intervention strategy based on what is known about the identified opportunity or problem. Strategies involve a long-range linking of activities to achieve the desired goal.

Consider Strategies

The key questions to be explored are:

▶ With which strategy will the change effort begin?

▶ Will it be necessary to consider sequential strategies, if a single strategy isn't working?

▶ If there are multiple, sequential targets, which strategies will be used with each target?

Change almost always involves influencing the allocation of scarce resources—authority, status, power, goods, services, or money. Decisions about strategies, therefore, must take into consideration whether the resources would be allocated willingly or whether someone must be persuaded to make the allocation. If there is agreement on the part of the action and target systems that the proposed change is acceptable and that resources will be allocated, a collaborative strategy can be adopted. If there is agreement that the proposed change is acceptable but a reluctance or refusal to allocate resources, or if there is disagreement about the need for the proposed change, then a more conflict-oriented strategy may be necessary if the change effort is to proceed.

For example, a change effort may focus on the inability of persons with physical disabilities to get around the city and travel to needed service providers. A thorough study documents the problem, and a dial-a-ride transportation service is proposed. The planning commission and city council accept the report, agree on the need, and thank the Transportation Task Force for Disabled Persons. Three city council members favor funding, three are opposed, and one is undecided. If the undecided council member can be persuaded to favor funding, then collaboration is possible. If, however, she decides to oppose funding or if a compromise would undermine the change effort, then a different strategy may be used to aggressively push for her support. For a collaborative strategy to be adopted, there must be agreement on both the proposed change and the allocation of needed resources.

Types of Strategies.   In the social work literature, strategies have been categorized under three broad headings: collaboration, campaign, and contest (Brager et al., 1987; Schneider & Lester, 2001). In this chapter, we use these strategies to describe the relationship between the action and target systems. *Collaboration* implies a working relationship where the two systems agree that change must occur. *Campaign* is used when the target must be convinced of the importance of the change, but when communication is still possible between the two systems. The effectiveness of the "campaign" may determine whether collaboration or contest follows. *Contest* is used when, because of the strength of the opposition, neither of the other two strategies is possible. Although we organize these strategies into categories, they may also be thought of as a continuum in which the lines separating one from another may sometimes blur. Change efforts that begin with one strategy may progress to others, depending on the evolving relationship between the action and target systems. The continuum along which these strategies fall is as follows:

$$\text{Collaboration} \longleftrightarrow \text{Campaign} \longleftrightarrow \text{Contest}$$

Strategies in Interaction.   In selecting an initial strategy, it almost always makes sense to begin with attempts at a collaborative strategy, and to move from left to right if it appears that collaboration will not work. Collaboration aims for win–win solutions. Once a contest strategy has been adopted, it may be difficult or impossible to recreate collaborative relationships.

What begins as a collaborative relationship may move to conflict when new issues arise during the change process. Relationships tend to ebb and flow, depending on the nature of the change proposed, the strength of the persuasive efforts, the resources required for implementation, and other competing issues.

Because of this ebb and flow in support for the change, the social worker should not take the relationship between the action and target systems for granted. To assume that the target is immovable before communication has been attempted would be poor professional judgment. To assume that the target will embrace the cause once the facts are known is naïve. Making assumptions about how members of the target system think without actually communicating with them may lead to misconceptions that will threaten the change effort with failure from the beginning.

Identify Tactics

The key questions to be explored are:

> ▸ Given the strategy most likely to succeed, what tactic (or combination of tactics) is needed first?
> ▸ As the change progresses, is it anticipated that changing strategies may lead to the use of different tactics?

Within each of the categories are tactics typically used to further those strategies. The choice of tactics is a critical decision point in planned change. Tactics are active steps taken on a daily basis that become the building blocks of a strategy and move participants toward the change effort's goal (Tropman, Erlich, & Rothman, 2001). As the change agent engages in tactical behavior, it is important not to lose sight of the intervention toward which these behaviors are directed or the overriding strategies that guide the change process (Rothman, Erlich, & Tropman, 2008).

The framework in Table 10.1 guides our discussion. Some of the following conceptualization is drawn from previous literature (Brager & Holloway 1978; Brager et al., 1987; Schneider & Lester, 2001), whereas in other areas we offer different perspectives or add new tactics. Throughout the following discussion our goal is to provide an analytical framework to guide an action system in selecting the most appropriate mix of tactics.

Consider the Pros and Cons of Collaborative Strategies

Questions to be explored include:

> ▸ Is it certain that there is little or no opposition?
> ▸ Can the desired change be achieved by identifying appropriate roles for participants and implementing the change?

Collaborative strategies include instances in which the target and action systems agree that change is needed. Using a collaborative strategy implies developing a partnership of some sort that goes beyond what one person, group, or unit could achieve alone. This process involves communication, planning, and sharing of tasks, but it goes farther. Collaboration requires

---

Making assumptions about how members of the target system think without actually communicating with them may lead to misconceptions that will threaten the change effort with failure from the beginning.

Human Rights and Justice

Critical Thinking Question: A client system may be "nonvoluntary" (e.g., clients who are batterers). Should these individuals be involved in tactical decision making? Why or why not?

Table 10.1   **Strategies and Tactical Behaviors**

Relationship of Action and Target Systems	Tactics

Collaboration
Target system agrees (or is easily convinced to agree) with action system that change is needed and supports allocation of resources
	1. Implementation
	2. Capacity building
	   a. Participation
	   b. Empowerment

Campaign
Target system is willing to communicate with action system, but there is little consensus that change is needed; or target system supports change but not allocation of resources
	3. Education
	4. Persuasion
	   a. Cooptation
	   b. Lobbying
	5. Mass media appeal

Contest
Target system opposes change and/or allocation of resources and is not open to further communication about opposition
	6. Bargaining and negotiation
	7. Large-group or community action
	   a. Legal (e.g., demonstrations)
	   b. Illegal (e.g., civil disobedience)
	8. Class action lawsuit

---

commitment among members of an action system to move toward a joint effort that will create change and achieve desired results in a community or organization. The collaboration could take a policy, program, project, personnel, or practice approach but it requires the formation of a working relationship among all members of the action system.

The definition of the term *collaboration* varies in the professional literature. It can be used to refer to informal communication, cooperation, or coordination. For the purposes of planned change, however, collaboration must be more than just a loose affiliation. This planned change strategy requires a committed partnership among action-system members to see the change process through passage, implementation, monitoring of progress, and evaluation of success.

Formal collaboration of a number of groups leads to *coalition building*. A coalition is a loosely woven, ad hoc association of constituent groups, each of whose primary identification is outside the coalition (Haynes & Mickelson, 2010). Coalitions can be especially effective in response to disasters. Responses to natural disasters such as tornados and floods often illustrate the consequences of a failure to establish working coalitions. Instead of establishing areas of responsibility and lines of communication, local, state, and federal authorities often end up pointing fingers of blame for the painfully slow pace of rescue, relocation, and rehabilitation.

There is a substantial body of literature on the varying degrees of effectiveness of collaboration in enhancing service delivery and capacity building within organizations and communities (Chen & Graddy, 2010). One study examined collaboration among ten geographically close neighborhood associations. Results showed that all ten were struggling to address the same issues with a small core of active participants. Although they expressed a commitment to collaboration, the neighborhood associations failed to translate that commitment into actual joint efforts (Knickmeyer, Hopkins, & Meyer, 2004). A second study demonstrated that coalitions can be successful when there is a neutral, external agency willing to take the lead in supporting collaboration among coalition partners (Waysman & Savaya, 2004). A third study describes successful collaboration designed to help people with disabilities live in the community. In this study, a coordinating agency brought together home buyers, financial institutions, realtors, and other agencies to successfully move people with disabilities into independent living situations (Quinn, 2004).

Studies have also indicated a number of challenges inherent in the use of collaborative strategies, such as dealing with turf issues, recognizing when organizational cultures clash, poor communication, and managing logistics. Facing these challenges can be time consuming (Takahashi & Smutny, 2002, pp. 166–167). This suggests that communication between the action and target system is only a beginning and that sustaining collaborative efforts over the time needed to complete the change may be one of the greatest challenges of their use. Nonetheless, when possible, collaborative strategies are highly desirable because they allow participants to focus their energies and resources on the change itself rather than on resolving their disagreements about what should happen.

Two primary tactics used with collaboration strategies are *implementation* and *capacity building*.

Implementation.   Implementation tactics are used when the action and target systems are willing to work together. When these systems agree that change is needed and allocation of resources is supported by critical decision makers, the change can move toward implementation. Implementation will most likely involve some problem solving, but it is not expected that highly adversarial relationships will be a concern in these types of collaborative efforts.

Schneider and Lester (2001) identify activities such as conducting research and studying the issue, developing fact sheets and alternative proposals, creating task forces or subcommittees, conducting workshops, and communicating regularly with the opposition (p. 129). Depending on how far along the change effort progresses, implementation tactics may also involve such activities as creating job descriptions for employees or volunteers and ensuring that training and other work-related arrangements are made.

Although implementation may move forward by means of communication, cooperation, and coordination occurring among systems, it is important to recognize that this does not guarantee the change will be sustained. Ongoing monitoring following initial achievement of the change should thus be considered an integral part of the overall process.

Capacity Building.   Capacity building includes the tactics of participation and empowerment. *Participation* refers to activities that involve members of the client system in the change effort. *Empowerment* refers to the steps needed to free members of the client system from real or perceived barriers to participation. Using an empowerment perspective means recognizing the power differentials within a community and working to promote positive change within all community members (Gutiérrez & Lewis, 1999). Empowerment can be viewed as both a process and an outcome in which people actually gain a psychological view that it is possible to make change happen.

For example, a problem may be defined as the exclusion of members of a neighborhood from decisions affecting them (such as rezoning, street repairs, installation of lighting, or selection of city-sponsored recreational programs for the neighborhood). The focus of the intervention is on building capacity for greater self-direction and self-control—that is, actually teaching people how to get involved in decision-making processes in their communities and taking greater control over those that affect their lives. This approach often emerges in situations where disenfranchised communities become targets for development, freeways, airport expansion, and other encroachments, or when a neighborhood is neglected and allowed to deteriorate by apathetic local authorities. Another example of the need for capacity building was reported in a study conducted by Sanders and Saunders (2009) of adult day services in a rural state. The infrastructure at both the state and local levels needed to be strengthened in order to fully provide the continuum of services needed by rural elders.

Professionally assisted change efforts in these examples would focus on bringing together selected systems. In the first example, a neighborhood social service agency may serve as the change-agent system, a neighborhood resident may represent the client system, and the city council may be the controlling (and perhaps target) system. The objective is to get all to agree that citizens should have a greater voice in developments that affect their community. The focus of the empowerment tactic, however, is not on changing the target system (city council/planning commission) but on educating, training, and preparing citizens for a fuller participation in decisions that affect their communities. This activity also involves identifying and preparing indigenous leaders. In the example provided by Sanders and Saunders (2009), the focus is bi-directional, in that both state aging services and local providers need to find simultaneous ways to build capacity with elder needs in mind.

Empowerment involves enabling people to become aware of their rights, and teaching them how to exercise those rights so that they become better able to take control of factors affecting their lives. Mobilizing the efforts of self-help groups and voluntary associations identified in Chapter 5 as well as the client system's informal support structure may also help guide the target system toward consensus with the change effort.

Consider the Pros and Cons of Campaign Strategies

The key questions to be explored are:

- Who needs to be convinced that the proposed change is needed?
- What persuasive techniques are most likely to be effective?

Campaign strategies are used when members of the target system do not necessarily agree that the change is needed but may be willing to listen to arguments on its behalf. This is likely to require a good deal of skill on the part of the change agent and action system, in part because it will first be necessary to determine why members of the target system don't agree with the change. Is it because they lack information about its need and potential benefits? Is it because they mildly disagree but are not yet immovably opposed? Or is it because they prefer to remain uncommitted until clearer evidence is available about the wishes of their community or organizational constituents?

Campaign strategies require an understanding of the target and a calculation of what tactics are most likely to succeed. Elected officials are likely to be motivated by issues important to constituents. Agency executives must be responsive to a governing board, consumers, staff, and funding sources. Understanding the context in which the target system functions can be helpful in shaping the campaign. Specific tactics most commonly used with campaign techniques address these different possibilities. They include education, persuasion, cooptation, lobbying, and mass media appeals designed to influence public opinion.

Education.   Educational tactics involve various forms of communication from members of the action system directed toward those in the target system. These communications may include face-to-face meetings, formal presentations, or written materials. The goal is to present perceptions, attitudes, opinions, quantitative data, or other information about the proposed change, and to inform members of the target system in ways that may lead them to think or act differently about the proposed change. This often involves specialized skills such as the compiling of statistics and developing PowerPoint presentations. The assumption is that more and better information will lead to a change in behavior.

Education can be a difficult tactic to use because opponents of the change can also be expected to attempt to provide decision makers with different information, and there is no absolute "truth" in dealing with complex organizational or community problems. In many cases where education fails to produce the desired result or falls short of having the desired impact, the change agent turns to persuasion.

Persuasion.   *Persuasion* refers to the art of convincing others to accept and support one's point of view on an issue. Social workers must frequently use persuasive tactics in addition to collaborative tactics because their belief that a change is worth pursuing is not always shared by decision makers. This means that the change agent must understand the motives and reasoning of the target system in order to identify what incentives or information might be considered persuasive by members of the target system.

Skillful communication requires that the action system carefully select as leaders those individuals who have the ability to persuade. Persons who are seen as nonthreatening by members of the target system and who can articulate the reasoning behind the planned change are particularly useful. For example, in a change effort certain actors may be seen as unreasonable, as troublemakers, or as chronic complainers by members of the controlling system. Although this may be an unfair characterization, it is still best not to use those individuals as primary spokespersons for the change. Credibility with representatives is an important consideration in selecting a spokesperson. Service users can sometimes be powerful spokespersons, providing both information and a viewpoint that convinces people of the need for change.

Service users can sometimes be powerful spokespersons, providing both information and a viewpoint that convinces people of the need for change.

Framing the problem statement to make it more palatable to target-system members is also a useful persuasive technique. This requires thinking as the target thinks. For example, a social worker hired as a long-term care ombudsperson was working closely with a coalition of advocates for nursing home reform to end abuse in long-term care facilities. Nursing home administrators were upset over the nursing home reform coalition and perceived the members as not understanding the difficulties with which the administrators coped on a daily basis. Although sincerely wanting to provide quality care, they were frustrated by having to hire staff who were not properly trained to work with geriatric populations. By framing the problem as a training problem designed to better prepare employees and reduce turnover, the ombudsperson was able to persuade administrators to cooperate with the action system. When the ombudsperson met with the local nursing home association, she made it clear that she believed administrators shared her goal of wanting high-quality facilities. She also noted that recent studies showed that high staff turnover rates led to lower quality care and sometimes to abuse. She explained that she and her colleagues would be willing to develop training for nurses' aides because these were the staff who interacted most closely with patients yet were most vulnerable to turnover. The result was that a key factor leading to abuse was being addressed, but it was framed as reducing an administrative problem—high staff turnover.

Cooptation.   *Cooptation* is closely related to persuasion and is defined as minimizing anticipated opposition by absorbing or including members of the target system in the action system. Once target-system members are part of the planned change effort, it is likely that they will assume some ownership of the change process and may be able to recruit others from the target system into the action system. Where there is a hierarchy of power, authority, and influence within the target system, cooptation efforts can be effective if they can find a role for influential people in the change effort. For example, allowing their names to be used in publicity materials may sway others who respect their opinions and may also give the supporter a high profile associated with a worthy cause. Cooptation is most effective as a tactic when opponents or neutral parties can be shown how supporting the change may serve their own interests as well as the interests of those who will benefit from the change.

Cooptation can be formal or informal. *Informal cooptation* refers to gaining support from an individual. *Formal cooptation* involves a group agreement, through vote or some other formal means, to support an issue. Depending on the prestige or prominence of the individual or group, a public statement of support can be helpful to the cause.

Lobbying.   *Lobbying* is a form of persuasion that targets decision makers who are neutral or opposed to a proposed change. Full-time lobbyists are paid to represent a special interest; typically, they target elected officials to get their support and their votes. Nonprofit organizations sometimes pool resources to hire a lobbyist to support or oppose legislation affecting the human services industry.

The Democracy Center (2004) identifies five types of decision makers with whom lobbyists typically deal. *Champions* are dedicated advocates for your cause. *Allies* are on your side but not outspoken advocates. *Fence sitters* are uncommitted and are key targets for lobbying. *Mellow opponents* are clear votes against your cause but not inclined to be active on the issue. *Hard core opponents* lead the opposition.

Haynes and Mickelson (2010) delineate three essential concepts for social work/lobbyists to consider. First, one should always be factual and honest. Trying to second-guess or stretching the facts to support one's position can be devastating to one's professional reputation as well as to the change effort's credibility. Second, any presentation should be straightforward and supported by the available data. The problem identification and analysis process discussed in Chapter 3 will assist the change agent in organizing the rationale for change. Third, any discussion should include the two critical concerns of decision makers: cost and social impact of what is proposed. If the cost is high,

Trying to second-guess or stretching the facts to support one's position can be devastating to one's professional reputation as well as to the credibility of the change effort.

the change agent may still be able to gain leverage by providing evidence that allowing the problem to remain unresolved will also be costly.

Mass Media Appeal.   *Mass media appeal* refers to the development and release of newsworthy stories to the print and electronic media for the purpose of influencing public opinion. This tactic is used to pressure decision makers into a favorable resolution to the identified problem. It is expected that if the proposed change can be presented to the public in a positive way and decision makers' refusal to support the change can be presented as obstructionist or somehow negative, decision makers will feel pressured to change their position. Because decision makers often occupy high-profile positions, such as elected representatives who depend on a positive public perception, this can be an effective tactic. However, it is also important to note that sometimes elected representatives want the public to know that they are opposed to a particular action, and mass media appeal may cause them to become even more firmly committed to their opposition. Initiating a mass media campaign through the print and television media will depend on convincing a reporter or editor that the proposed change is a newsworthy story.

Another option is use of the Internet. In a study of the Internet capabilities for marketing and advertising, the overall opinion about its use as a marketing tool was highly positive, especially on dimensions of consumer orientation and consumer responsiveness benefits (Patwardhan & Patwardhan, 2005). Electronic advocacy is being used more and more to rapidly reach large numbers of people. For example, Menon (2000) reports how one online discussion group developed a campaign to educate others about the issues faced by persons with severe mental illnesses. In the process of being transformed from a discussion group to a virtual community, participants learned how important it is to deal with issues while they are "hot." They also recognized the importance of having a campaign plan when numerous messages are posted in a short time frame.

Internet forums such as websites and weblogs have become increasingly important tools of communication on various issues, making members of the action system less reliant than in the past on traditional print or broadcast media. Whatever mass media option is used, professional ethics require that the change agent ensure that information on the change effort is presented accurately and that any use of media includes consideration of clients' rights to privacy.

Consider the Pros and Cons of Contest Strategies.

The key questions to be explored are:

- Is opposition to the proposed change so strong that it can only be successful by imposing the change on an unwilling target system?
- Can the proposed change be effective if it is forced?
- What are the potential consequences of conflict?

A *contest strategy* is used in situations where (1) target system representatives cannot be persuaded by the action system, (2) target system representatives refuse to communicate with the action system, or (3) members of the target system pose as being in favor of the change but do nothing to further it or secretly work against it. Use of a contest strategy means that the change effort becomes an open, public dispute as attempts are made to draw broad support and/or to coerce the target system into supporting or at least accepting the change. Once this occurs, the action system must be prepared to face open confrontation and potentially to be the subject of varying types of backlash from those in the target system.

Conflict is inevitable in social work practice. There will be times in the experience of every practitioner when formidable resistance is encountered in addressing the needs of oppressed population groups. To some extent conflict is inherent in a profession that developed in response to a basic societal conflict—the persistent antagonism between individualism and the common good. For example, schools in poor neighborhoods may be identified as failing, whereas schools in affluent neighborhoods exceed expectations. From the perspective of the common good, the issue is that *all* school-aged children need a solid educational foundation to succeed. From an individualist perspective the issue may be framed as being the result of the property tax base that funds the school, produces more revenue in some districts than in others, and therefore rewards individual achievement.

The Conflict Research Consortium distinguishes between conflict and dispute. Disputes are seen as short-term disagreements, whereas conflicts are long term. Conflicts are often value based and emerge around issues such as distribution of wealth, human needs, threats to identity, fear, and distrust. It is important to recognize, however, that conflicts can also have benefits. Without conflict there would likely be continued oppression of and injustice toward many individuals and populations, less social learning, and less participation in the political process (Burgess & Spangler, 2003).

Conflicts over the rights of individuals versus the collective have spawned violent confrontations rooted in basic value systems and beliefs. In any change episode, physical violence and terrorism cannot be condoned in a civilized society. Nonviolent confrontation, however, including civil disobedience, is an option when there is a communication stalemate between the target and action systems and when other possible avenues have been exhausted.

Schneider and Lester (2001) offer a list of specific tactics used with contest strategies that includes the following: seeking a negotiator or mediator; organizing large demonstrations; coordinating boycotts, picketing, strikes, and petition drives; initiating legal action; organizing civil disobedience and passive resistance; and arranging a media exposé. For easier discussion, we will group contest tactics into three main categories: bargaining and negotiating, large-group or community action, and class action lawsuits. The second tactic, large-group or community action, can be further divided into legal and illegal actions.

Before our discussion of these tactics, it should be noted that their use will require widespread commitment and possible participation from members of the support system. To illustrate this point, Rubin and Rubin (2008) refer to contest tactics as confrontational approaches, and confrontation implies the possibility of strong negative reactions that are less likely with other strategies. Because of these risks, it is critical to the success of contest strategies that the support system and its subsystems—initiator, client, and change agent—are comfortable with confrontation and aware of its ramifications and potential consequences. It is likely that the time and energy necessary for effective change will increase and relationships can become disrupted.

When collaborative and campaign strategies have been employed and either stalemated or failed, tactics can move toward contest. However, once a contest strategy is underway it is not likely that one can return to collaborative or campaign tactics. For these reasons, contest strategies should usually not be considered as a first option.

Bargaining and Negotiation.   Bargaining and negotiation refer to situations in which the action and target system confront one another with the reasons for their support and/or opposition to a proposal or an issue. There is typically a recognized power differential between parties, and compromises need to be made. These tactics are more formalized than persuasion and sometimes involve a third-party mediator. Members of the target system will usually agree to negotiate when the following factors are in place: (1) there is some understanding of the intentions and preferred outcomes of the action system, (2) there is a degree of urgency, (3) the relative importance and scope of the proposed change is known, (4) there are resources that facilitate the exercise of power, and (5) the action system is seen as having some legitimacy. In order to negotiate, both the action and target systems must believe that each has something the other wants, otherwise there is no reason to come together.

Schneider and Lester (2001) suggest that the involvement of a third-party mediator becomes advisable when alienation between the action and target system occurs. For example, a domestic violence shelter receives a donation of a building in a transitional area between commercial and residential areas. Both residents and business owners angrily oppose rezoning this area for this use because they fear possible violent confrontations that might erupt from angry spouses or partners. A mediator in this situation would attempt to lay out the concerns of all parties and find a middle ground that protected the interests of both sides. Perhaps the shelter could provide assurances that disgruntled spouses' or partners' concerns could be kept off the streets and managed within a "safe room" within the shelter. If a solution could not be worked out, the business owners may agree to buy a building in another area and exchange it for the one in their neighborhood.

If handled well, bargaining and negotiation can lead to win–win solutions, where both target and action systems are pleased with and fully support the outcome. However, the result can also be a win/lose, where one system is clearly the victor, or a lose/lose, where both systems give something up, are disappointed in the results, and are possibly worse off than before the change.

Large-Group or Community Action.   Large-group or community action refers to the preparing, training, and organizing of substantial numbers of people who are willing to form a pressure group and advocate for change through various forms of collective action such as picketing, disruption of meetings, sit-ins, boycotting, and other such confrontational tactics. Peaceful demonstrations are legal activities, often used by groups on either side of an issue to express their views. The pro-life and pro-choice movements are examples of groups that regularly use this tactic.

Civil disobedience activities intentionally break the law. For example, Rosa Parks deliberately defied a local ordinance when she refused to move to the back of a bus in Montgomery, Alabama, in 1955. Environmental advocates have blocked access to construction sites when forests or endangered species were jeopardized. Animal rights groups have sprayed paint on fur coats, destroying property in protest. Antiabortion activists have harassed physicians and patients at abortion clinics. A critical line, first articulated by Mohandas Gandhi while leading the struggle against British rule in India in the first half of the twentieth century, is usually drawn between illegal but nonviolent protest and actions that involve violence against others. Social work principles strictly forbid the latter but recognize the former as a legitimate tactic in cases such as the oppression of disadvantaged groups. Still, when action-system

Professional Identity

Critical Thinking Question:
What are the risks for social workers involved in direct civil disobedience? What are some indirect ways to support this tactic?

members deliberately engage in illegal activities, they must be ready to accept the consequences of their actions. The change agent is responsible for making potential participants fully aware of these risks before the decision is made to proceed.

Class Action Lawsuits.   Class action lawsuits refer to those instances where an entity is sued for a perceived violation of the law and it is expected that the finding of the court will apply to an entire class of people. These tactics are often used with highly vulnerable populations such as persons with severe mental illness, homeless persons, and children, who are unlikely to have the capacity or the resources to protect their own rights. Public interest law organizations may be resources for the action system in developing class action tactics.

Class action suits have been used by a variety of groups on behalf of many different client populations. They are a particularly common tool of advocacy and watchdog organizations seeking to ensure that certain service standards are met. In the child welfare arena, an organization called Children's Rights, Inc., has filed class action suits against child welfare agencies in more than a dozen states in the last 25 years, alleging failure to provide adequate services. The defendants have often been city, county, or state governments. When successful, these suits have forced the defendants to upgrade staff and facilities, improve or implement new programs, and invest other types of resources to correct service deficiencies. A follow-up study of a small community in New Hampshire where a class action lawsuit challenged inequitable funding for education revealed a side benefit of a sense of community empowerment through involvement and participation in the action (Banach, Hamilton, & Perri, 2004).

Weigh Relevant Considerations in Selecting Tactics
The key questions to be explored are:

- What is the purpose of the change effort, and has that purpose been altered during the change process?
- What is the perception (by those promoting change) of the controlling and host systems?
- What is the perception (by those promoting change) of the role of the client system?
- What resources are needed and available for each tactic?
- What are the ethical dilemmas inherent in the range of tactical choices?

Selecting the proper strategy and tactics is an important but difficult task, and several considerations need to be weighed in determining which approach is best. We briefly address each of these considerations next.

Purpose.   Change goals often evolve as the change process moves along; therefore, a reexamination prior to selection of tactics is in order. For example, with the problem of domestic violence, the condition may have been brought to public awareness by the perceived need for additional emergency shelter space for battered women. However, as the problem is analyzed and better understood, the purpose may shift toward consciousness-raising for all women in the community who are at risk of violence. Thus, strategy and tactics would move from advocating for service provision to educating for empowerment.

Table 10.2   Relationship of Goals to Tactics

Current Objective	Relationship of Target and Action System	Possible Tactics
1. Solving a substantive problem; providing a needed service	Collaborative	Implementation through joint action
2. Self-direction; self-control	Collaborative	Capacity building through participation and empowerment
3. Influencing decision makers	In disagreement but with open communication	Education, persuasion, mass media appeal; large-group or community action
4. Shifting power	Adversarial	Large-group community action
5. Mandating action	Adversarial	Class action lawsuit

Because tactics can change as purpose and goals change, it is worthwhile to make a final check to ensure that members of all the relevant systems are clear and in agreement with the change goals. If any system members, especially those in the action system, have concerns about the goal or nature of the change, further dialogue should take place before proceeding. Certain types of goals tend to be approached through certain types of tactics, and this can help ease the selection process. A variety of goals and their typical accompanying tactics are displayed in Table 10.2.

Controlling and Host Systems.   The controlling and host systems can be perceived in a variety of ways. If they are active supporters or sponsors of the change, it may be possible to move quickly to implementation tactics (as part of a collaboration strategy) to bring about the change. If members of these two systems are supporters but not participants in the change, capacity building (through participation and empowerment) may be the tactic of choice. If they appear to be neutral or indifferent, one or more tactics in the category of campaign strategy may be in order. Finally, if the members of these systems are oppressive or unresponsive to their primary clientele, then one or more tactics related to a contest strategy are likely to be needed. Table 10.3 illustrates the various perceptions of roles that might be assigned to the controlling and host systems, and the logical tactic for each.

Primary Client.   The role of the primary client can vary, and the way in which this role is perceived can affect selection of change tactics. Sometimes it may be difficult to determine who the primary client really is. For example, in addressing the needs of elderly persons, the change agent may learn that many caregivers are suffering from stress and fatigue and are unable to provide quality care to the elderly persons for whom they are responsible. In this situation, one must ask if the primary beneficiaries of a change effort will be the older persons themselves or their caregivers.

Table 10.3   Relationship of Controlling and Host System Roles to Tactics

Perception of Role of Controlling and Host Systems	Relationship of Controlling, Host, and Action Systems	Possible Tactics
1. Sponsors; supporters; co-participants; colleagues	Collaborative	Implementation through joint action
2. Neutrality or indifference	Collaborative	Capacity building through participation and empowerment
3. Uninformed barriers/not sure about change	In disagreement but with open communication	Education and persuasion
4. Informed barriers/opponents to successful change	Adversarial	Bargaining; large-group or community action
5. Oppressors	Adversarial	Large-group community action
6. Violators of rights	Adversarial	Class action lawsuit

If the primary client is seen as a consumer or recipient of services, an implementation tactic (as part of a collaborative strategy) will usually be the most suitable approach. When clients are primarily residents of a community or potential participants in an effort to achieve self-direction and control, then a capacity building tactic (as part of a collaborative strategy) might be preferable. If the primary client is a group in need of a particular service, but this need is not acknowledged by the controlling system, one or more tactics within the realm of a contest strategy may be needed.

For these reasons it is important to know how members of the action system perceive the primary client, how those in the client system perceive their roles, and if the perceptions are in agreement with members of the action system. Having clients as action-system members (overlapping the client and action system) can go a long way toward providing a medium for information exchange between clients and change agents. Table 10.4 displays client roles, approaches, strategies, and tactics.

Resources.   Key considerations in choosing tactics are the nature and quantity of resources available to the action system, because some tactics require more or different types of resources than others. If collaboration is the strategy of choice, for example, one necessary resource will be technical expertise capable of understanding whether the change is being properly implemented, monitored, and evaluated. In order for a capacity-building tactic to be used, grassroots organizing ability, together with some teaching and training expertise, must be available to the action system. If there is disagreement calling for a campaign or a contest strategy, either skilled persuaders, media support, large numbers of people willing to do what is necessary to bring about change, or legal expertise will be needed.

Table 10.4	**Relationship of Client System Role to Tactics**	
Perception of Role of Client System	Relationship of Client and Target Systems	Possible Tactics
1. Consumer; recipient of service	Collaborative	Implementation through joint action
2. Resident of the community in need of greater self-direction and self-control	Collaborative	Capacity building through participation and empowerment
3. Citizen/taxpayer not permitted full participation	In disagreement but with open communication	Education and persuasion
4. Victim; underserved needy person	Adversarial	Mass media appeal
5. Victim; exploited person	Adversarial	Large-group community action
6. Person denied civil rights	Adversarial	Class action lawsuit

Earlier in this chapter we discussed the importance of determining the cost of change by putting together a budget of expenditures that would be needed for the change to be successful. A similar exercise can be helpful in relation to determining the resources needed for the preferred tactics to be successful. Costs for such items as expertise, supplies and equipment, postage and mailing, training, meeting rooms, and other such needs should be itemized at this point and calculations made of anticipated costs. Volunteers and in-kind contributions should be sought to fill as many needs as possible. Resource considerations are illustrated in Table 10.5.

Professional Ethics.   In Chapter 1 we discussed the importance of values in social work practice. Ethics are the behaviors that bring values into action. An *ethical dilemma* is defined as a situation in which a choice has to be made between equally important but seemingly conflicting values. Tactical choices may often present actual or perceived ethical dilemmas in that they usually involve a clash of values between members of different systems. This is especially true in the case of conflicting action- and target-system values that can lead to the selection of contest tactics.

A number of ethical principles were highlighted in Chapter 1, including autonomy, beneficence, and social justice. These principles are of great significance to macro-level change. A clash between autonomy and beneficence can occur when members of the client system are determined to resist risking what little they have (autonomy), whereas action-system members want to push for a quality-of-life change on the clients' behalf (beneficence). When such a conflict emerges, the rights of clients take precedence over the wishes of the action system.

This clash was illustrated in a social work intern's first field experience. Working for a small community center in the Southwest, she discovered that many of her Latino clients lived in a crowded apartment complex with faulty

Table 10.5   Resources Needed by Action System for Each Tactic

Tactic	Resources Needed
1. Collaboration—joint action or problem solving	Technical expertise; monitoring and evaluation capability
2. Capacity building	Grassroots organizing ability; teaching/training expertise; opportunities for participation; some indigenous leadership; willing participants
3. Persuasion	Informed people; data/information; skilled persuaders/lobbyists
4. Mass media appeal	Data/information; newsworthy issue or slant; access to news reporters; technical expertise to write news releases
5. Large-group or community action	Large numbers of committed people (support system); training and organizational expertise; informed leadership, bargaining and negotiating skills
6. Class action lawsuits	Legal expertise; victims willing to bring action and provide information; at least enough money for court costs

wiring and inadequate plumbing. With the backing of her agency, she began talking with clients to see if they would be willing to engage in a change process directed toward correcting these problems. As she analyzed the situation, she realized that any change process would involve housing and public health personnel in the action system. Her clients begged her not to involve these authorities because many members of the client system were in the country illegally and they feared this fact would become known and could lead to their deportation, which they considered worse than the poor housing conditions. The client system's autonomy was in conflict with the change agent system's beneficence.

The clash between social justice and autonomy is exemplified when the members of the action system demand redistribution of resources and members of the target system believe that in giving up their control over valued resources they will have less freedom. Macro change frequently appeals to the principle of justice, for it is usually through the redistribution of valued resources (for example, power, money, status) that change occurs. Because social justice is a basic ethical principle that raises emotions when it is violated, change agents can become so obsessed with injustice that any tactic is viewed as appropriate if it leads to a successful end.

It is our contention that this type of thinking can lead to professional anarchy, whereby tactics are perceived as weapons to punish the target system rather than as actions to enrich the client system. In these situations it may be too easy for the change to take on a life of its own and for the professional to blindly wrap himself or herself in a cloak of beneficence while ignoring other actors. Righteous indignation may overtake sound judgment. The foregoing points should not be interpreted to mean that factors such as horrible living conditions or basic needs should be ignored because clients fear change. The issue is client system rights. If clients can be persuaded that conditions can be improved without risk or that the risk is worth it, then it is acceptable to proceed. If they cannot be persuaded, then campaign or contest strategies may need to be discontinued, unless some means of protecting clients can be identified.

Use of Covert Tactics.   The concept of "transparency" has become increasingly important in transactions that take place within both government and private organizations. *Transparency* refers to keeping actions and decision-making processes in the open and available to scrutiny by the public and the media. It is intended to protect the public against self-serving actions or ethical lapses. Scandals such as Enron in Houston and the Federal Emergency Management Administration (FEMA) response to the disaster in New Orleans in 2005 are considered, in part, to stem from a lack of transparency or openness of organizational operations to public or media review.

The question is whether the concept of transparency also applies to individuals or groups attempting to initiate change in organizations or communities. When change is being considered that requires those in power to give up some to those not in power, there may be some risk that openness or transparency will result in failure of the change effort. In situations like these, the need for secrecy must be carefully weighed against the risk of mistrust and possible charges of ethical violations. When actions are begun in secret, those involved in initiating the change episode must recognize that at some point they will be made public, and all actions should be handled in a way that they will pass the ethics test when they are brought out into the open.

An example of use of covert tactics arises when an employee feels there is a need for a "whistle blower" within the organization due to perceived unethical or illegal activities. If, for example, a child welfare worker believes that all complaints of child abuse and neglect are not being investigated in accordance with established protocols, he might begin by keeping a log and recording perceived violations. At some point the worker would compile his data and perhaps take it to the director of child welfare services. The worker may agree to a plan and a timetable for correcting the practices, while letting the director know that if deadlines were not met he would turn his data over to Children's Rights, Inc., and the issue may end up in court.

Selecting the Proper Tactics.   There are few situations in which there is clearly a "right" or "wrong" tactic. Berlin (1990) explains that thinking in terms of bi-polarizations can make people vulnerable in that they look for specific answers to what are highly complex questions. In fact, there are many gray areas in which simple answers will not suffice and in which differences must be respected. Box 10.2 raises a number of questions to guide consideration of professional ethics in selecting the proper tactics.

It is common to think dichotomously (e.g., win–lose, right–wrong, good–bad, consensus–conflict). In conflict situations it may be useful to force confrontations and bring opposing views into the open. However, dichotomous thinking about the situation may reinforce the beliefs of a radicalized change agent that the target system represents "evil" and the action system represents "good." Although this achieves the objective of fueling confrontation, it may undercut any potential progress by making it more difficult to find common ground and accept realistic accommodations. For this reason, we believe that the professional social worker has a responsibility to avoid dichotomous thinking and to

Box 10.2 **Questions to Guide Consideration of Professional Ethics**

1. What are the value conflicts between the target and action system?
2. What ethical principle(s) appear to be guiding the activities of the action system?
3. Is there the potential for a clash of ethical principles between the client and action systems?
4. If covert tactics are being considered, what conditions have led to this decision?
   a. The mission of the target agency or the community mandate is being ignored.
   b. The mission of the target agency or the community mandate is being denied for personal gain.
   c. Change efforts have been tried through legitimate channels, but the target system will not listen.
   d. Client system members are fully aware of the risks involved but are willing to take the risks.
   e. Other.

carefully analyze circumstances surrounding a change episode before making assumptions that lead directly to the use of contest tactics. This means the majority of change efforts will utilize collaboration and campaign tactics as the action and target systems attempt to achieve mutually acceptable solutions. Although collaboration–contest is a dichotomy, we believe the majority of interactions happen in the various gradations in between. When all the foregoing tasks have been completed, the proposed change should be written up in the form of a short, concise plan. Chapter 11 is devoted to a discussion of this process.

SUMMARY

In this chapter we have proposed a systematic approach for identifying strategies and accompanying tactics to bring about successful change. The approach includes a series of tasks designed to maximize participation, cover the range of possible types of change, and aid in selecting the options most likely to achieve the desired results. Planners of change consider a number of political, interpersonal, and economic factors when assessing strengths and weaknesses of the proposed change. Listing people and factors that support or oppose the change allows a systematic assessment of the likelihood of success. If it appears that the chances for success are good, the change effort moves to the stage of selecting appropriate tactics.

As with all professional practice, the approach may need to be adapted to the situation by the practitioner. If conditions dictate immediate action, some procedures may need to be abbreviated or streamlined. But if time allows, and especially if the proposed change is highly significant, best results are achieved by carrying out each task with careful attention to detail.

Some changes will always be needed in the field of human services, both in organizations and in communities. These changes, we believe, require the professional assistance and consultation of social workers knowledgeable about macro-level change. They require informed, and sometimes scholarly, participation and guidance in order to ensure that what is achieved is what is most needed to meet the needs of the target population. We believe that social workers are well positioned to lead or coordinate the planning stages of such change efforts and to bring them to the point of action and implementation. Chapter 11 is intended to assist in that process.

Framework for Selecting Appropriate Tactics

Task 1: Assess Political and Interpersonal Readiness

Assess Duration, Intensity, and Frequency

▶ How long has the problem existed?
▶ Is the problem considered an emergency?
▶ If the problem is episodic or recurring, how often does it occur?

Address Public Image and Relationships

▶ Who is involved in promoting the proposed change, and how are they perceived by decision makers?
▶ Who can serve as effective spokespersons for the proposed change?
▶ Who should keep a low profile when the proposed change is presented to decision makers?

Task 2: Assess Resource Considerations

Determine the Cost of Change

▶ What anticipated costs related to the proposed change can be itemized? What must be estimated?
▶ What sources of financial support or in-kind donations should be approached?

Determine the Cost of Doing Nothing

▶ What will this problem cost the organization or community if nothing is done?
▶ How can this cost be framed so that it will be persuasive to decision makers as a good investment to support the proposed change?

Task 3: Weigh the Likelihood of Success

Identify Alternative Perspectives

▶ How will opponents of the change effort frame their opposition?
▶ How much conflict or contentiousness is expected?

Assess Support from Individuals, Groups, and Organizations

▶ Has anyone important to the success of the change effort been left out?
▶ Who supports the proposed change?
▶ Who opposes the proposed change?
▶ Who is neutral about the proposed change?

Assess Level of Support

▶ What facts and perspectives gleaned from analysis of the problem, population, and arena support the proposed change?
▶ What facts and perspectives oppose the proposed change?

Task 4: Select Strategies and Tactics

Consider Strategies

▶ With which strategy will the change effort begin?
▶ Will it be necessary to consider sequential strategies, if a single strategy isn't working?
▶ If there are multiple, sequential targets, which strategies will be used with each target?

Identify Tactics

▶ Given the strategy most likely to succeed, what tactic (or combination of tactics) is needed first?

▶ As the change progresses, is it anticipated that changing strategies may lead to the use of different tactics?

Consider the Pros and Cons of Collaborative Strategies

▶ Is it certain that there is little or no opposition?

▶ Can the desired change be achieved by identifying appropriate roles for participants and implementing the change?

Consider the Pros and Cons of Campaign Strategies

▶ Who needs to be convinced that the proposed change is needed?

▶ What persuasive techniques are most likely to be effective?

Consider the Pros and Cons of Contest Strategies

▶ Is opposition to the proposed change so strong that it can only be successful by imposing the change on an unwilling target system?

▶ Can the proposed change be effective if it is forced?

▶ What are the potential consequences of conflict?

Weigh Relevant Considerations in Selecting Tactics

▶ What is the purpose of the change effort, and has that purpose been altered during the change process?

▶ What is the perception (by those promoting change) of the controlling and host systems?

▶ What is the perception (by those promoting change) of the role of the client system?

▶ What resources are needed and available for each tactic?

▶ What are the ethical dilemmas inherent in the range of tactical choices?

Succeed with PEARSON mysocialworklab

Log onto **www.mysocialworklab.com** and answer the questions below. *(If you did not receive an access code to **MySocialWorkLab** with this text and wish to purchase access online, please visit* www.mysocialworklab.com*.)*

1. **Watch the Core Competency video: Participating in Policy Changes.** Who represents the host system? The action system? How would you describe their relationship? Can you identify any tactics used in this video? Refer to Table 10.3.

2. **Read the MySocialWorkLibrary case study: Community to Community.** Reflect on how Catherine's work evolved from a single act of personal charity to a sustained and organized effort built around communities. What tactic(s) from the list in Table 10.5 was/were employed?

PRACTICE TEST

PRACTICE TEST The following questions will test your knowledge of the content found within this chapter. For additional assessment, including licensing-exam-type questions on applying chapter content to practice, visit **MySocialWorkLab**.

1. Lewin's "force-field analysis" approach compares
   a. intervention costs and benefits
   b. supporting and opposing forces
   c. action strategies and tactics
   d. political and economic factors

2. Which tactic involves absorbing or including people from the target system into the action system?
   a. education
   b. cooptation
   c. lobbying
   d. media appeal

3. A member of the action system claims to fully support a change but secretly works against it. Which tactic does this call for?
   a. contest
   b. blackmail
   c. cooptation
   d. persuasion

4. Intentionally breaking a law (and insisting that it be enforced) is characteristic of
   a. political demonstrations
   b. civil disobedience
   c. class action lawsuits
   d. targeted lobbying

5. In discussing the ethics of choosing a particular tactic, we refer to the importance of avoiding "dichotomous thinking." What does this mean? Give an example of a situation where dichotomous thinking may lead to one choice of tactics, whereas a more open, multifaceted review of the situation might produce a different choice.

ASSESS YOUR COMPETENCE

ASSESS YOUR COMPETENCE Use the scale below to rate your current level of achievement on the following concepts or skills associated with each competency presented in the chapter:

1	2	3
I can accurately describe the concept or skill.	I can consistently identify the concept or skill when observing and analyzing practice activities.	I can competently implement the concept or skill in my own practice.

_____ Can assess the needs and strengths of diverse constituencies while affecting change.

_____ Can assess complex contextual factors and will only attempt to affect meaningful change in a responsible, ethical manner.

_____ Can consider all aspects of human rights and social and economic justice while pursuing change.

_____ Can conduct myself according to professional social work standards when employing change tactics.

11

Planning, Implementing, Monitoring, and Evaluating the Intervention

CHAPTER OUTLINE

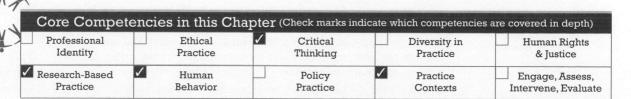

Core Competencies in this Chapter (Check marks indicate which competencies are covered in depth)				
Professional Identity	Ethical Practice	✔ Critical Thinking	Diversity in Practice	Human Rights & Justice
✔ Research-Based Practice	✔ Human Behavior	Policy Practice	✔ Practice Contexts	Engage, Assess, Intervene, Evaluate

At this point in the macro-practice planning process, it should be clear that selecting an intervention is not a simple matter of brainstorming or choosing the most popular suggestion. Macro-level intervention is a carefully researched and thoroughly planned effort. The working intervention hypothesis provides an opportunity to ensure that all participants understand the logic behind the proposed intervention and that an acceptable level of consensus has been achieved around its design. Following these activities, strategy(ies) and tactics are chosen appropriate to the levels of acceptance and/or resistance to the proposed change.

A brief written document may be prepared at this point, which includes (1) a statement that clearly explains the problem or need, (2) a description of the proposed change and its expected results, and (3) a description of strategies and tactics planned to get the change accepted. This document may be circulated among participants to provide an opportunity for review and comment as a way of achieving consensus. However, participation throughout this process should not be assumed to mean support for the final design. A final check on disagreements is appropriate and necessary before developing the details of the intervention. Final negotiations on the form the intervention is to take will come as the plan is developed. The parts of this planning process will include:

> Task 1: Setting a goal for the intervention
>
> Task 2: Developing outcome objectives
>
> Task 3: Developing process objectives
>
> Task 4: Listing activities for each process objective
>
> Task 5: Initiating the action plan
>
> Task 6: Monitoring the intervention
>
> Task 7: Evaluating the effectiveness of the intervention

PLANNING THE DETAILS OF THE INTERVENTION

It is tempting to assume that, with all the planning and consensus building that has gone into the change effort, nothing can go wrong. But even carefully planned change can fail because of lack of attention to detail during the implementation phase. As we discussed in Chapter 9, macro-level change can take place at the policy, program, project, practice, or personnel levels. Sometimes change may require planning for interventions at more than one level. In the following sections we will attempt to illustrate how a situation requiring both a policy change and a number of program or project changes might be approached. Consider the following example:

An Example: The Cedar City Volunteer Policy

Cedar City is a Midwestern town of about 30,000 people. Up until recently the town had been growing at a fairly rapid rate, with population increasing by 58 percent from 2000 to 2008. Elected officials include a mayor and town council. Town departments include a town manager, budget director, town attorney, water and sewer department, police and fire departments, parks and recreation department, and a planning and community development department. The Cedar City school system has nine elementary schools, three middle schools, and three high schools. During the years that Cedar City was growing, the number of town and school district employees increased to keep pace with the demands placed on the town and the schools. Business taxes from many small businesses, a few chain stores, restaurants and motels, property taxes, and a small sales tax supported the basic infrastructure of the town and the school district while the economy was strong.

However, the town began to notice declining resources when a serious recession hit the town, the state, and the nation. In the first year, the town council froze all hiring, swept all funds for training and travel, and cut back on some of the benefits that had been granted to town staff. By the second year of recession, officials realized that all of the easier budget reductions had been used up, and there would have to be reductions in staff. Parks and library staff were reduced first, followed by a 10 percent cut in budget from the water and sewer department, which necessitated a number of layoffs. Finally, when every other budget expense had been reduced as much as could be allowed, the town decided it would have to cut back on police and fire personnel.

To deal with this crisis, the town manager called together her department heads in an attempt to brainstorm how the town could survive this recession while maintaining acceptable levels of services. After a thorough review of available census data about the town, past services offered, past budgets, and comparable services provided in other similar towns, the department heads decided that they would focus on attempting to carry out certain functions using volunteers and part-time workers in place of full-time staff. It was agreed that this effort would be temporary and that any staff laid off during the economic recession would have rehiring rights when tax revenues once again permitted hiring. Department heads agreed to draft a proposed policy change that would allow for expanded use of volunteers and also agreed that if the policy change was accepted by the town council, each department head would initiate a program planning effort within her or his department to establish the parameters for implementation.

Based on their findings, the town manager and executive committee proposed the following working intervention hypothesis:

If a policy including the following components is accepted by the town council:

1. Current entry-level job descriptions will be examined to determine what tasks can be handled by volunteers;
2. Job descriptions for volunteers will be drafted, spelling out limits and liabilities;
3. Training sessions and certification requirements for volunteers will be prepared; and
4. A volunteer coordinator will be appointed.

Then the following results can be expected:

1. Assigned tasks will be performed by volunteers;
2. All volunteers will be trained and certified, and volunteers will operate within the scope of their job descriptions;
3. All volunteer involvement will be scheduled by a coordinator; and
4. Services to the public will be continued at no less than 90 percent of previous levels.

The Cedar City town council was made up of six members elected at large and a mayor. When the community volunteer program was first proposed, the three council members and the mayor didn't push back against it, but they expressed several concerns. First, they were worried about the precedent this might set in terms of being fully staffed in the future. Second, they expressed concerns about liability, should any volunteers or citizens being served be harmed in the process. And third, they wondered about the reliability of volunteers in fulfilling town-sponsored activities and services. The executive committee drew up the policy statement in Box 11.1 to address these concerns.

Box 11.1   A Policy to Initiate a Volunteer Program

Proposed Policy 11-326

Relating to the use of volunteers to carry out some of the functions currently assigned to selected full-time staff of Cedar City. This policy provides for analyzing job descriptions; identifying tasks that are within the scope of capability of trained volunteers; creating position descriptions that limit the responsibility and liability of the volunteer and the town; training and certifying volunteers to perform very specific functions; and assigning a volunteer the responsibility of scheduling other volunteers and insuring that there is always coverage whenever it is promised. This program will continue until such time as town revenues have recovered to the point where full-time employees can once again be hired back into their positions unless the town council chooses to terminate the program early or extend it beyond this time.

In this policy statement, unless the context otherwise requires:

1. "Volunteer" refers to a nonpaid person who is a resident of Cedar City.
2. "Functions" refers to items listed in current job descriptions of selected employees.

3. "Selected full-time staff" refers to current Cedar City employees whose employment is terminated due to loss of funding.
4. "Training and certifying" refers to programs that will be designed within each department that uses volunteers, with training content and certification standards approved by the department head.
5. "Liability" refers to assurance by the town's insurance carriers that they will cover, at a reasonable cost, the functions carried out by volunteers.

Upon approval of this policy (as amended, if necessary) department heads will be directed to:

A. Create volunteer job descriptions for their departments.
B. Create a training and certification program for volunteers.
C. Identify a volunteer coordinator.
D. Recruit, train, and certify volunteers.
E. Prepare and publish a schedule for the use of volunteers.
F. Collect monitoring and evaluation data for reporting back to the town council on the effectiveness of the program.

The Importance of Implementation

Implementation is not an event, it is a process, and it needs to be carefully planned, monitored, and evaluated.

The lesson here is that implementation is not an event, it is a process, and it needs to be carefully planned, monitored, and evaluated. In this chapter, we will discuss what goes into the detailed planning, implementation, monitoring, and evaluation of a change effort.

Practice Contexts

Critical Thinking Question: In addition to limited resources, what are some factors that may influence the political environment of a change effort?

INTERVENTION PLANNING

Whether one is taking a policy, program, project, personnel, or practice approach (as discussed in Chapter 9), it is necessary to engage in an intentional planning process. Weinbach (2010) advocates careful planning so that managers do not leave too much to chance. He points out that activities tend to get sidetracked within organizations unless someone puts into place certain vehicles designed to keep them on track.

Similarly, Hardina (2002) focuses on the community arena in which planning occurs among organizations as well as with multiple constituency groups. "Planners need political and administrative skills to ensure that plans are actually implemented. They must use all the steps in the problem-solving model—problem identification, assessment, goal setting, implementation, and evaluation—to create appropriate plans" (p. 272). Hardina reminds us that political skills must be combined with administrative skills in order to make change happen as planned.

Planning the details of the intervention includes establishing goals, writing objectives, listing all the activities that will need to be carried out, and setting time frames, due dates, and responsibilities. This plan must be in writing, with copies distributed to all participants who will be involved in implementation. These documents are then used to orient and train the implementers and later as a basis for monitoring and evaluating the effectiveness of the intervention.

Task 1: Set a Goal for the Intervention

The key question to be explored is:

▶ What is the overall outcome that is expected if the intervention is successful?

Goals provide a beacon or focal point for the change effort that serve as reminders of the real purpose of the change effort. They also provide a tool around which people with diverse views can begin the process of building consensus. Goals are stated in outcome terms and should include a target population, a boundary, and an expected result or outcome (Brody, 2005; Montana & Charnov, 2008). The processes or methods intended to achieve goals should never be included in the goal statement itself. For example, the Cedar City Volunteer Program hopes to achieve the following goal:

▶ To continue the level of services in selected departments during the period of declining resources in Cedar City

Other illustrations of goal statements might include:

▶ The goal of this project is to increase the number of Latino/a students who remain in high school and achieve their diplomas in the Jefferson School District.
▶ The goal of this program is to reduce the number of isolated elders in the town of Elwood.
▶ The goal of this change effort is to pass and implement a policy that will ensure a positive and productive lifestyle for first-time offenders in Washington County.

Note that these statements are not measurable as they are stated. Building in measurement criteria is the function of objectives.

DEVELOPING OBJECTIVES
FOR THE INTERVENTION

Objectives serve as an elaboration of goals. They spell out the details of the planned intervention in measurable terms, including expected outcomes and the processes needed to achieve them. *Activities* are lists of tasks that must be undertaken and completed in order to achieve each objective.

Setting goals and objectives requires translating the concepts and ideas generated during the analytical phase into concrete terms. The purpose of this approach to planning is to take what can be a complex undertaking and break it up into manageable subsets.

The process begins with reexamining the working intervention hypothesis and translating the proposed interventions into objectives. In order to illustrate this process we will continue with the example of a working intervention hypothesis used in the Cedar City example.

If a policy including the following components is accepted by the town council:

1. Current entry-level job descriptions are examined to determine what tasks can be handled by volunteers;

2. Job descriptions for volunteers are drafted, spelling out limits and liabilities;

3. Training sessions and certification requirements for volunteers are prepared; and

4. A volunteer coordinator is appointed.

Then the following results can be expected:

1. Assigned tasks will be performed by volunteers;

2. All volunteers will be trained and certified, and volunteers will operate within the scope of their job descriptions;

3. All volunteer involvement will be scheduled by a coordinator; and

4. Services to the public will be continued at no less than 90 percent of previous levels.

Objectives can be developed around each of the proposed interventions. Objectives are intended to lay out a clear path that moves the change effort toward the goal. Objectives are specific and measurable. There are two types: (1) outcome objectives and (2) process objectives. An *outcome objective* specifies the *result or outcome* to be achieved with and for the target population. One or more process objectives are written for each outcome objective. *Process objectives* specify the procedures to be followed in order to achieve the result. When the outcome objective and all its related process objectives are completed and written out, it should be evident that (1) the process objectives, when completed, will lead to achievement of the outcome objective; and that (2) the outcome objective, when accomplished, will move the effort toward the goal. For a more complete discussion of goals and objectives, see Kettner, Moroney, and Martin (2008), Chapter 7; and Hardina (2002), Chapter 11.

Task 2: Write Outcome Objectives

Writing objectives in outcome terms is often a tricky and elusive process for beginners. Practitioners are so conditioned to think in terms of what it is that they will be providing that it is tempting to try to use objectives to describe the services. Writing outcome objectives requires thinking in terms of the impact on clients or program participants as a result of the intervention. An outcome must be stated as a quality of life change for the client or consumer of services. For example, it is not the objective of a counseling program that clients participate in counseling, but rather that they strengthen and improve their relationships or that they avoid an impending divorce. The time will come to deal with the process, but first the expected outcome must be addressed.

A complete objective, whether outcome or process, has four parts: (1) a time frame, (2) a target, (3) a result, and (4) a criterion for measuring or documenting the result (Kettner et al., 2008). The following sections will explain how each of these parts is applied to outcome objectives.

Establish a Time Frame for the Objective

The key questions to be explored are:

- Is it possible to establish a day, month, and year when the first results should be evident?
- At what point in the future is it reasonable to expect to see measurable results from this intervention?

The time frame ideally should be stated in terms of the month, day, and year by which the result will be achieved, because this information will later be needed for monitoring purposes. The end of a fiscal or calendar year is often used ("By June 30, 20XX" or "By December 31, 20XX . . .") When a start date is unknown, the time frame may be specified in terms of time elapsed from the beginning of the change effort (for example, "within three months of the beginning of the project," or "by the end of the first year"). Once a start date is known, it is wise to go back and fill in actual dates, because objectives are often also used as monitoring tools.

A time frame in an outcome objective should not exceed one year. Funding and sponsoring sources usually expect at least annual reporting on progress and results. In situations where it is expected to take more than a year to achieve results, thought should be given to what kind of annual milestones can be established that will indicate that the project is on track. In some instances where shorter time frames are important, reporting milestones are established at the 3-, 6-, 9-, and 12-month periods.

Define the Target Population

The key question to be explored for this activity is:

- Who are the expected primary beneficiaries of the intervention?

The second part of an objective, *the target*, specifies the individuals or focal point for which the objective is written. Outcome objectives are focused on a quality of life change and identify the individuals for whom the change is intended. By the time the change agent reaches this point, there should be no doubt about the makeup of the target system. Even so, there can be complexities in writing this part of the objective.

Statements should be as precise as current knowledge will allow. An outpatient drug treatment program, for example, might specify "24 cocaine addicts at least 18 years of age and currently employed" as its target.

In the Cedar City example, it is clear from the policy statement that the ultimate desired outcome is a community that continues to receive the level of services to which it has become accustomed in spite of the economic recession. Successful work with the town council will result in a *program* that will achieve this objective. However, in order to illustrate a *policy* objective, we will focus on working with the town council, even though this step is just a prelude to achieving the ultimate objective. For reasons stated in earlier chapters in this book, the more precise the target, the greater the likelihood of a successful intervention. An example might be: "To insure unanimous support in terms of a positive vote on the volunteer initiative from all six council members and the mayor."

Specify a Result or Outcome

The key question to be explored for this activity is:

- What quality of life changes are expected for the target population from this intervention?

An outcome objective focuses on a quality of life change for the target population; that is, something must happen to make their lives better or more stable.

The third part of an objective is a phrase that specifies the expected result or outcome to be achieved when all activities are completed. An *outcome objective* focuses on a quality of life change for the target population; that is, something must happen to make their lives better or more stable. Outcome objectives refer to such factors as improved knowledge and skill, improved relationship with spouse, reduction of alcohol abuse, or more control over community decision making. The process designed to achieve the result is not the focal point at this time and is not included in the statement. That will be dealt with later. Results or outcomes for a jobs program might be stated as follows: "Improvement in computer knowledge and skills, achievement of a certificate, upgrade in job and career path, increased stability and healthy development of children, and/or improved performance in school and extracurricular activities." The way an outcome is written depends on the purpose of the program or project. Results or outcomes for the volunteer initiative in Cedar City will focus first on the intermediate outcome of securing town council support for the use of volunteers. Note that in changes that involve policy approaches, the approval or enactment of the policy is actually an intermediate step to get to an outcome. It is assumed in this situation, for example, that approval of the policy will facilitate continuing to provide a high level of good quality services in spite of the economic recession. The following wording might be used to establish an expected outcome for the volunteer project:

> "By June 30, 20XX, at least three departments will demonstrate levels of service to the citizens of Cedar City . . . ."

While this statement does focus on service provision, it is important to remember that the purpose or outcome expected of this change effort is that services continue at essentially the same level as before the intervention.

Define a Criterion for Measuring Success

The key questions to be explored are:

▶ How will the result as stated in the objective be measured?
▶ Are there observable criteria readily available for measurement, or will criteria need to be designed?

The final part of an objective is the criterion that will be used to determine whether the objective has been achieved. Objectives must be precise and measurable, yet sometimes the result to be achieved seems vague and elusive. Some programs, for example, are designed to improve self-esteem. The question is: How does one know if self-esteem has been improved? Clearly, opinion alone is not sufficiently valid or reliable.

Specifying a criterion in the objective ensures that only one standard will be used by all who monitor and evaluate the program. If improving self-esteem is the result, then improvement must be measured by a standardized test designed to measure self-esteem. The criterion for an outcome objective usually begins with the phrase, "as measured by . . . ." Increased self-esteem, for example, might be measured by the Rosenberg Self-Esteem Scale (SES) (Rosenberg, 1965). Although this scale is over 45 years old, it is still commonly used by practitioners to evaluate self-esteem and continues to be examined for its effectiveness among both adolescents and adults (Whiteside-Mansell & Corwyn, 2003).

In the Cedar City example, a successful volunteer program requires that a policy change occur in the form of approval by the town council. An enacted policy will facilitate implementation of the program or project. However, it is important to recognize that actual volume of services provided by volunteers will be the *ultimate* measure of success. Other indicators that may be used could include volunteer citizen, town employee, and town council satisfaction with the program. This two-step process is illustrated with the following objectives.

Examples of Complete Outcome Objectives

The first example focuses on securing approval of the town council.

Time Frame:	Within one month of the time the policy change is introduced
Target:	Seven members of the town council
Result:	Will support the volunteer initiative
Criterion:	As demonstrated by a vote taken by the town council

Even though all seven votes are not required, this hoped-for result might be established in the interest of focusing on every person and not eliminating anyone, and also because it will strengthen the program if it is unanimously approved. There is nothing wrong with establishing an objective that is ambitious, and if it ended up passing with only four votes, this would still be considered a success. Once approved, the following outcome objective would move the program closer to its ultimate goal:

Time Frame:	By June 30, 20XX
Target:	At least three departments
Result:	Will demonstrate levels of service to the citizens of Cedar City
Criterion:	That do not fall below 90 percent of the levels of service provided prior to implementation of this program

This objective focuses more clearly on the hoped-for outcome of the whole volunteer effort. The program, as proposed here, begins with three departments and then presumably expands to all seven over time.

Task 3: Develop Process Objectives

Each outcome objective is followed by a number of process objectives designed to spell out the ways in which the outcome objective will be achieved. Process objectives should identify the major components of a planned intervention, not the specific details. Brody (2005) points out that process objectives usually involve the interaction of people and organizations. The logic behind a process objective is that everything that needs to be changed or accomplished in order to achieve the outcome objective should be laid out in sequence. As described by Montana and Charnov (2008), an organizer breaks down an objective and delegates responsibility for those pieces to different individuals or units. When all those tasks are completed, then the objective should be successfully accomplished.

Each major component of the intervention is translated into a process objective. For example, if the outcome specified is "self-sufficiency," then the process might include such activities as (1) completion of a GED, (2) a skills training course, (3) job counseling, (4) job placement, and (5) follow-up. Details, such as setting up GED preparation or the skills training courses, become part of the *activities*, to be discussed in a following section. A complete process objective includes the same four parts: time, target, result, and criterion.

Critical Thinking

Critical Thinking Question: Why do you think it is helpful to develop outcome measures prior to process measures?

Establish a Time Frame for the Process Objective

The key question to be explored is:

> ‣ When will the actions specified in this objective begin and end?

Time frames are specified in the same way for both outcome and process objectives. Ideally, due dates or milestones are established in terms of specific dates—day, month, and year. When this information is not known, it is permissible to express a time frame in terms of the number of weeks or months from the time the intervention begins. The actual date selected for a process objective should be the date when the process is expected to be completed, such as: "By March 31, 20XX, all seven department heads will submit a plan for use of volunteers in their departments." Time frames for process objectives must, of course, be coordinated with the time frame for the related outcome objective.

Define the Target

The key question to be explored for this activity is:

> ‣ What individuals, groups, or products will be the focus of this objective?

Process objectives are used to specify the various components or phases of an intervention. The focus is on what steps need to be accomplished in order to achieve the outcome objective. For some process objectives, the target may be an individual or a group of people. For other process objectives, it may be that the target is not people at all, but rather an object, such as a training curriculum to be produced or a policy to be enacted. An example would be "a training and certification curriculum will be completed . . ." or "at least ten volunteers will be recruited . . . ." One illustrates a document as the target; the other a group of people.

Specify a Result for the Process Objective

The key question to be explored for this activity is:

> ‣ What result will provide evidence that the objective has been achieved?

Process objective results focus on completing a service or intervention process. The result must be stated in a way that is concrete and observable. If the process involves services to people, the result might be something like completion of a course, completion of at least six counseling sessions, or attendance of at least three training sessions on the political process. If the process involves changing some part of an organization or community, the result might be described as a completed report, a new strategic plan, or the design of a new data collection form. Examples would include "completion of a training plan" or "copies of agreements signed by at least ten volunteers . . ."

Define a Criterion to Be Used for Documentation Purposes

The key question to be explored for this activity is:

> ‣ What observable or measurable factor(s) can be used to determine whether the process objective has been achieved?

Process objectives typically are directed toward the completion of something. It may be the completion of a part of the process by participants (such as training or counseling sessions), or it may be the production of products (such as a policy or training manual). A wide variety of criteria can be used to measure the result of a process objective. The focus in writing process objectives is on record-keeping or documentation that clearly demonstrates that the result has been achieved. In most cases, process objectives will use the phrase "as documented by" or "as demonstrated by." Completion of a course, for example, can be documented by receipt of a certificate of completion, by attendance records, or by a formal transcript. Creation of a new form or writing of a new policy can be documented by submission of these items in writing to a specified person by a due date. The issue is that there should be some indicator that allows for complete agreement as to when the process objective has been achieved. Documentation in process objectives is usually pretty straightforward. Once the target has been specified, the criterion for measuring completion is usually simply submission of some sort of proof that the objective has been achieved. Examples would include ". . . as documented by a session outline and attached training materials for each session . . ." or "as documented by copies of agreements signed by at least ten volunteers . . ."

Examples of Process Objectives

Continuing with the example of the Cedar City volunteer program, a policy process objective might read as follows:

Time Frame:	Within one month of preparing the policy statement on use of volunteers
Target:	All seven members of the town council
Result:	Will have been visited and briefed on the proposal
Criterion:	As documented by a memo submitted by department heads to the town manager

---

When all four parts—time frame, target, result, and criterion—have been written, the objective is complete. Typically, a set of goals and objectives will include one goal, a number of outcome objectives, and several process objectives for each outcome objective. The program and policy examples are reproduced in Figure 11-1 to reinforce the understanding of the relationship between a goal and its outcome and process objectives.

Each outcome objective usually requires a series of process objectives. It is important that each of these phases of the implementation process be put into writing and become clear and visible parts of the plan. The reason for putting the plan into writing is that implementers will know precisely what was intended so that they may implement the plan as designed without skipping important elements.

Task 4: List Activities for Process Objectives

The final step in developing the intervention plan is to itemize activities. Activities represent the highest level of detail incorporated into the plan. Each activity represents a step that, when accomplished, moves the change effort closer to achievement of a process objective. Activities should specify the work to be done, the person responsible, and a time frame.

Format Activities for Easy Monitoring

The key questions to be explored for this activity are:

- What activities or tasks must be successfully completed in order to achieve the process objective?
- When should each activity begin and end?
- Who should be assigned responsibility for completion of the activity?

Example: The Cedar City Volunteer Program

Working Intervention Hypothesis: If a policy including the following components is accepted by the town council:

1. Current entry-level job descriptions are examined to determine what tasks can be handled by volunteers.
2. Job descriptions for volunteers are drafted, spelling out limits and liabilities.
3. Training sessions and certification requirements for volunteers are prepared.
4. A volunteer coordinator is appointed.

Then the following results can be expected:

1. Assigned tasks will be performed by volunteers.
2. All volunteers will be trained and certified, and volunteers will operate within the scope of their job descriptions.
3. All volunteer involvement will be scheduled by a coordinator.
4. Services to the public will be continued at no less than 90 percent of previous levels.

Goal: To continue the level of services in selected departments during the period of declining resources in Cedar City

Outcome Objective #1:

Time Frame:	Within one month of the time the policy change is introduced
Target:	Seven members of the town council
Result:	Will support the volunteer initiative
Criterion:	As demonstrated by a vote taken by the town council

Process Objective #1.1:

Time Frame:	Within one month of preparing the policy statement on use of volunteers
Target:	All seven members of the town council
Result:	Will have been visited and briefed on the proposal
Criterion:	As documented by a memo submitted by department heads to the town manager

Outcome Objective #2: (Developed once objective #1 has been met)

Time Frame:	By June 30, 20XX
Target:	At least three departments
Result:	Will demonstrate levels of service to the citizens of Cedar City
Criterion:	That do not fall below 90 percent of the levels of service provided prior to implementation of this program

Figure 11-1

Illustration of Relationship Between Hypothesis, Goal, Outcome Objective, and Process Objective

Activities should be organized in a way that allows for orderly, systematic implementation. This could include organization by individuals, by types of tasks, or by chronology of tasks. One format that can be useful in managing projects like these is the Gantt chart, developed by management pioneer Henry L. Gantt (1919). A Gantt chart is made up of columns and rows. Each row represents an activity; the columns are used to identify the activity number, the person responsible, and the beginning and ending dates. Brody (2005) points out that these charts are valuable because they provide for a hierarchy where tasks can be

Process Objective: Within one month of preparing the policy statement all seven members of the town council will have been visited and briefed on the proposal as documented by a contact form submitted by department heads.						
Activity Number	**Activity**	**Person Responsible**	**Weeks**			
			1	**2**	**3**	**4**
1.	Schedule appointment with council representatives and mayor.	All department heads E.Johnson	▬			
2.	Prepare agendas for discussion and summaries of the proposal.		▬			
3.	Meet with council members and mayor.	All department heads D.Brown			▬▬▬	
4.	Reconvene to compare notes and plan for follow-up.	All department heads				▬
5.	Hold follow-up meetings as needed.	All department heads				▬
6.	Report back to town manager on level of support and commitment from council and mayor.	All department heads				▬

Figure 11-2
Gantt Chart of Policy Change

subsumed under major activities. Beginning and ending points are projected for each task. Project managers can see at a glance what efforts must be made within a specific time period. An example of a Gantt chart is illustrated in Figure 11-2.

It is helpful in constructing Gantt charts to first list the activities chronologically and then establish time frames, beginning at the bottom of the list. The final activity must coincide with the date established in the process objective, so a due date for the final activity should be established first, and then time frames can be set for each of the previous activities.

In preparing an action plan for a macro level change, each subsection of the intervention should include an outcome objective, process objective(s), and activities. When these are developed at an acceptable level of precision, with responsibilities and time frames clearly specified, the action plan is complete. The last steps in macro-level change involve the implementation and monitoring of the plan and the evaluation of its effectiveness.

IMPLEMENTING AND MONITORING THE PLAN

Human Behavior

Critical Thinking Question: How would you increase engagement with implementers, especially if you knew several were "traditionalists" and reluctant to change?

A common oversight in planning for organizational and community change is leaving those who will ultimately be responsible for implementation of the program out of the planning process. Fogel and Moore (2011) elaborate on the importance of collaboration among community agencies. In any change effort it is common to feel that the standard approaches that have been used have not been effective in getting the job done, so something new needs to be tried. At the same time, it is not unusual for at least part of the implementing system to be made up of people who have been using standard approaches for many years. The situation described has the potential for conflict. The "traditionalists" may feel threatened by new approaches or may feel that their previous work is being discredited. The "innovators" may have reservations about long-time employees in terms of their ability to take a fresh approach. The key to addressing these potential problems is to plan for overlap between the planners and the implementers. Ideally, implementers should be involved in the planning process, but if this is not possible it is important to work with the implementing system to make certain that all facets and complexities of the change are properly understood and enthusiastically supported.

Policy implementation has been the subject of research for a number of experts in the field. A prominent theme in the findings is the potential for failure between the planning stage and implementation. One project tracked spending to educate children and support families in local communities and discovered that some available resources were not getting to their intended target populations (McCroskey, Picus, Yoo, Marsenich, & Robillard, 2004). Another project explored how elite perceptions of poverty often influence policy in ways that interfere with effective problem resolution (Reis & Moore, 2005). On the other hand, another project demonstrated that collaborative policy advocacy led by social work researchers, practitioners, advocates, and students was successful in placing an issue on the state agenda and instrumental in its passage (Sherraden, Slosar, & Sherraden, 2002). The message is that the implementation process must be managed every bit as carefully as the earlier stages of the change episode.

Task 5: Initiate the Action Plan

Putting the plan into action usually requires a number of tasks that need to be completed in advance, prior to involving clients, consumers, or participants. For change efforts, such as the ones described in this book, to be successful, it is critical that they be well organized at the point of implementation and that they have a clearly defined lead person or coordinator. The primary focus of this person is to get others to get the job done, to maintain morale, and to motivate participants (Dessler, 2011).

Up to this point the major phases of the change effort (researching the change in Chapters 3 to 8; creating the design and soliciting support in Chapter 9; and developing strategy and tactics in Chapter 10, and planning the details of implementation in Chapter 11) have been carried out by many groups of interacting and overlapping individuals and systems. In preparation for implementation it is necessary that the intervention become more formalized. Logistical considerations, such as facilities and equipment, need to be addressed. Depending on the approach to change, some type of lead or point person must be appointed. Some of the earlier participants may now form a policy-making or an advisory board to provide consultation and guidance. In the case of project or program approaches, personnel issues, including hiring, orienting, and training, must be planned. Coordination and communication among new and old participants will help ensure successful implementation.

Manage Logistics

The key questions to be explored are:

- What facilities, equipment, and other resources will need to be made available prior to implementation?
- Where will new personnel, including volunteers, be housed?
- How can the steps or phases be depicted in flowchart form?

The planned change will involve either existing staff and volunteers, new services, new staff, and perhaps new clients, consumers, or participants, or some combination. If new personnel are to be involved, appropriate accommodations will have to be identified. If existing staff and volunteers are to be used, decisions need to be made about sharing of space and equipment between the old and new programs. It may be necessary to sketch out a floor plan to make clear where all personnel will be located. Appropriate resources need to be made available, including computers, if needed, copying equipment, desk, telephone, and other necessities. It may also be helpful to prepare a flowchart that depicts client flow through the system, if the change involves services to clients. Returning to the Cedar City example, let's assume that the volunteer initiative was passed by the town council and is now in the hands of the town manager and department heads to plan for implementation. Box 11.2 describes the scenario.

From the scenario described in Box 11.2, the following intervention hypothesis was established:

⬥ If the following activities are undertaken by neighborhood residents and town volunteers:

1. The neighborhood council will commit to educating and informing residents and getting them to keep their yards and surrounding areas as clean and free of debris as possible;

2. As soon as graffiti appears on any of the surfaces in the neighborhood, the town will send a volunteer trained in spray painting techniques who will paint over the graffiti;

3. The town will send two volunteers with a truck to the neighborhood once every two weeks to pick up large items and take them to the city dump; and

4. Twice a year the town and the community will establish a clean-up day that will be staffed by community residents and volunteers.

⬥ Then the following results can be expected:

1. The neighborhood will maintain a clean appearance;

2. Volunteers will paint over graffiti on all surfaces in the community within 24 hours;

3. Large items will be placed at the curb only on pickup days; and

---

Box 11.2   The Community Development Department's Neighborhood Beautification Project

The Community Development director has had a very successful neighborhood beautification project going for several years, but now funding has been terminated. Each neighborhood involved in this project was required to form a neighborhood council and determine what services were to be made available from the town. The Broadway neighborhood was a low-income, transitional community that included many recently arrived immigrants, elderly individuals and couples living on Social Security, many homes with extended families living in single family units, and a significant number of public aid recipients living in multi-family housing. The Broadway neighborhood had long been considered one of the biggest challenges for the Community Development department. Streets were frequently littered, large pieces of old furniture and non-working appliances were frequently placed outside, many vehicles of all types were up on blocks, and many of the surfaces were covered with graffiti. The Community Development director decided that this was a neighborhood where he would test out the use of volunteers. The town would provide the vehicles and equipment, and the volunteers would haul away junk left in the street, would paint over graffiti, would pick up litter, and would attempt to educate the community about ordinances designed to keep neighborhoods clean. The neighborhood council agreed to recruit neighborhood residents to help in the cleanup projects and to try to police the neighborhood regularly and persuade residents to stop making the neighborhood unsightly.

4. The community residents will develop a pride in their neighborhood and a partnership relationship with the town, resulting in more positive use of resources for both the town and the neighborhood.

A sample goal, outcome objective, and process objective might read as follows:

Goal: To maintain a clean appearance for the Broadway neighborhood and instill a sense of pride in neighborhood residents.

Outcome Objective #1: By September 30, 20XX, all streets in the Broadway neighborhood will be free of discarded furniture and appliances, as documented by a report from the neighborhood council.

Process Objective #1.1: By June 1, 20XX, four volunteers will be trained in picking up discarded furniture and appliances, as documented by training records.

Process Objective #1.2: By July 15, 20XX, a schedule will be posted for two teams of two volunteers each, with each team driving through the neighborhood once a month and picking up discarded furniture, appliances, and other donated items.

Figure 11-3 illustrates a simple flowchart that can be used to clarify the steps in the service process. Implementation of the Broadway neighborhood project is depicted in flowchart form.

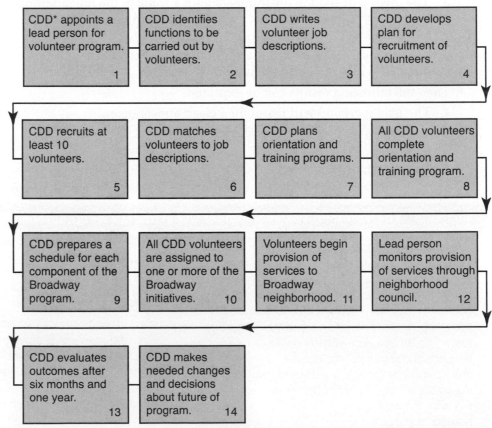

*CDD refers to Community Development Department. While a lead person may be in charge of the overall program, it should be understood that many different staff members may be called on to help with the program at various points.

Figure 11-3

Flowchart for Implementing the Cedar City Volunteer Program

Select and Train Participants

The key questions to be explored are:

- ‣ Who will have overall leadership and management responsibilities for the intervention?
- ‣ Will existing or new staff and/or volunteers be used in the intervention?
- ‣ What preparations need to be made to bring new participants on board?
- ‣ What type of orientation and training will be needed?

One of the first steps in getting the intervention underway is the selection of an overall program leader and lead persons on each of the subunits of the change effort. These individuals will be critical to the success of the intervention and should therefore be screened with great care. It may be tempting to select the most willing leaders, but in the long run the change is most likely to be successful if the most competent are selected, even if they have to be actively recruited.

If the intervention is designed as a new initiative, with its own funding and other resources, and if people filling key positions will be employed, then formal job descriptions and job announcements will need to be written. In large-scale changes, where time permits, it is desirable first to go through the recruitment, selection, and hiring process for the overall manager or coordinator, and then to have that person take a leading role in selecting other staff. Whether additional staff and volunteers will be new or drawn from current employees or from community groups, it is advisable to have a job description for each position and to go through a selection process, including interviews, even if the positions are to be filled by nonpaid volunteers. (For a more complete discussion of recruitment, selection, and hiring issues, see Dessler, 2011; Kettner, 2002; and Weinbach, 2010.)

Once personnel have been selected, an orientation is in order. It is advisable to involve as many of the early participants as possible in orientation in order to maintain continuity. Once orientation has been completed, plans for ongoing training should be addressed, based on findings from early implementation experiences and training needs expressed by staff and volunteers.

By this time it may seem that the change process is very tedious and requires lots of attention to detail. That is probably a pretty accurate perception, but the detail is important and gets easier over time. Becoming familiar with goals, outcome objectives, process objectives, and activities is a way to shape the planner's thinking and to keep the project focused on outcomes. Understanding the differences between outcomes and process is a critical skill. Once familiar with the differences, planners may be surprised how much it grabs their attention when they hear others propose new programs or changes. When someone proposes to a board of directors or a city council that they plan to "help the homeless" or "provide better services to victims of domestic violence" and planners find themselves immediately thinking "But what is the proposed result?", they can feel confident that they have mastered an understanding of the differences between outputs and outcomes.

Understanding the differences between outcomes and process is a critical skill.

Many different tracking techniques can be used to help the implementation process to succeed. Some of the more sophisticated techniques are computer based, but "old fashioned" techniques such as Gantt charting, flow charting, and PERT charting are sometimes just as effective. The bottom line is this. When planners have completed all the goals, objectives and activities, they cannot simply assume that everyone involved will be responsive to the plan. If no one puts together a volunteer schedule, volunteers will not show up when they are expected. If no one carries out training on use of town equipment such as trucks and paint sprayers, volunteers will not know how to make proper use of this necessary equipment. If no one takes the lead on planning the clean-up days, they will not happen. Whatever system works for planning and tracking the implementation is the one that should be used. Good old common sense will come in very handy in planning the implementation.

Task 6: Monitor and Evaluate the Intervention

The word *monitor* comes from the Latin *monitorius*, which means "to warn." Monitoring systems are set up to keep track of progress and to warn project and program managers about what is happening. Collecting data and information about implementation experiences will enable managers to discover how well they are meshing with the plan. For many years monitoring required the use of extensive and dreaded paper work—filling out many forms with multiple copies. Now it is possible to monitor using data collection and aggregation abilities of various software packages.

Whether data and information are collected by manual completion of forms or electronically, the basic approach to monitoring is to track the activities as they are implemented and to make judgments about their effectiveness in moving the program toward achievement of its objectives.

Evaluation is different from monitoring. *Evaluation* means to determine the value of something by careful appraisal and study. When a program or project manager is monitoring implementation, she is attempting to determine whether or not activities have happened as planned. When she is evaluating, she is attempting to determine whether the project is working and whether it is as effective and efficient as it can be.

In the first phase of developing the Cedar City Volunteer program, monitoring would involve tracking the activities listed in the Gantt chart depicted in Figure 11-2. The person(s) responsible, listed in the chart for each activity, would be expected to prepare either an oral or a written progress report at some point on or before the due date specified in the chart.

Monitoring would most likely focus on "meetings with mayor and council members as scheduled." Evaluation would involve an assessment of the success of these efforts. These concepts will be discussed in more detail in the following sections.

Monitor Technical Activities

The key questions to be explored are:

▶ What is the appropriate sequencing for the activities that must be completed in order to achieve the process objective?
▶ Who will be assigned responsibility for completion of each activity?
▶ When must each activity be completed in order for the process objective to be achieved on time?

In order to achieve a process objective, it is necessary to complete a number of activities. If activities have been carefully itemized (preferably in Gantt chart form), monitoring technical activities is greatly simplified. Activities should be designed to happen in sequence. In most cases, one activity is a prerequisite for the next and subsequent activities. When start and completion dates, together with a person responsible, have been established for each activity, monitoring simply requires confirming with the person responsible that

Research-Based Practice

Critical Thinking Question:
If a program's success is mainly measured through outcome evaluations, why should we devote extra effort to ongoing monitoring?

the activity has been started/completed as of the date specified. This provides an early warning system in case any of the activities have not or cannot be completed on time.

Where activities have not met deadlines, or where problems emerge, the lead person becomes involved in problem solving and decision making. Brody (2005) points out that *problem solving* involves formulating a problem statement and examining potential alternatives, whereas *decision making* requires choosing from among alternatives and implementing an approach to deal with the problem.

The critical issue in managing change efforts is keeping on schedule. If the due date for scheduling appointments is missed, then each subsequent due date may slip, delaying implementation and possibly resulting in an inability to complete the project on schedule. The lead person is often the only person who has an overview of all of the activities that are going on simultaneously and therefore has responsibility for integrating component parts of the change effort.

In monitoring technical activities, it may be useful to add several columns to the activity chart, such as the following: Was the activity completed? Was it completed on time? What was the quality of the product? What adjustments are needed for this activity? What adjustments are needed for subsequent activities? By tracking each of these factors, the lead person will be in a position to be more proactive in anticipating problems and needs and in making the necessary adjustments.

Monitor Interpersonal Activities

The key questions to be explored are:

- How enthusiastic and supportive are the designated implementers?
- Is there a formal or informal system for evaluating the performance of implementers?
- Is there a strategy for dealing with poor performance, apathy, or resistance?

Monitoring the implementation of a plan can be a highly rewarding experience when persons carrying out the plan are enthusiastic, hard working, competent, compatible, cooperative, and committed to a common vision. Unfortunately, such a scenario is not always the case. Some participants may have been assigned without their consent. Personalities and styles of working may clash. Competition may emerge.

Interpersonal tensions can often be traced to uncertainty about roles and responsibilities or to feelings of being overly controlled. Good management practices should be promoted, encouraging participants to use their talents and abilities to the greatest extent while the designated point person focuses on removing barriers to implementation activities. However, in spite of the manager's best efforts, competition and conflict are likely to surface at some point.

A strategy for dealing with performance problems, including interpersonal tensions, should be established and communicated to all participants. Within an organizational arena, performance should be evaluated regularly and consistently. In a larger, more permanent program, a formal appraisal will be conducted and placed in a personnel file. In a less formally structured effort (particularly with community change), regularly scheduled conferences, staff meetings, or peer review sessions can be encouraged in the interest of airing concerns before they affect morale and performance. Rewards and incentives should commensurate with performance. Identifying all of these motivational factors for each participant at the point of selection and/or hiring (if applicable) can go a long way toward preempting interpersonal problems.

Community change efforts may involve coalitions of organizations or groups of people who do not work for one organization. They may be almost totally dependent on volunteer commitment. Policy approaches to change may pull together disparate groups who are concerned about an issue but who are not formally related and who disperse once approval of the policy occurs. In some cases, employees of the organization responsible for implementing a change could not have been involved in the change process because they are not allowed to participate in advocacy efforts as part of their employment status, thus preventing the early involvement of implementers that is recommended. When facing the complexities of a diffused implementation system, it is advisable for the project manager to spend a great deal of time communicating by telephone and email, in formally written reports, and in person to keep the project on track. Persistent and personalized attention to participants in the implementation process is critical if the full extent of the change effort is to be realized.

Task 7: Evaluate the Effectiveness of the Intervention

To evaluate effectiveness, it is necessary to refer to outcome objectives. Recall that the plan includes a goal, one or more outcome objectives, a set of process objectives for each outcome objective, and a set of activities for each process objective. If all has gone according to plan, there should be a cumulative effect. When the work specified in the activities has been completed, the process objective should be completed, and when all process objectives have been achieved, the outcome objective should have been achieved.

Once all activities and processes have been completed, it is time to return to outcome objectives to determine if the intervention has been successful. In planning for change, the "bottom line" for an intervention is whether the intervention improved the condition or quality of life of the people and/or the organization or community it set out to help. This is the focus when evaluating the intervention.

Make Use of Available Resources

Evaluation can be a complex undertaking, and many resources are available to assist the change agent in evaluating project or program efficiency and effectiveness. The Community Outreach Partnership Center (COPC) program sponsored by the U.S. Department of Housing and Urban Development (HUD) supports partnerships between universities and their communities. Doe and Lowery (2004) describe such a partnership in Gary, Indiana, where logic models and telephone surveys were used to evaluate effectiveness in education, neighborhood revitalization, community organizing, and economic development programs. Rogge and Rocha (2004) describe how these partnerships can be used to support collaboration between low-income inner-city neighborhoods, social work students, and faculty.

Evidence-based practice is built on the principle that social work practice should combine knowledge and skill with research-based evidence and the values and expectations of clients (e.g. Roberts-DeGennaro & Fogel, 2011). Gambrill (2008) discusses some of the challenges in incorporating this philosophy into the culture of social service agencies. They advocate agency–university partnerships, training to support evidence-based practice, and the modification of agency cultures.

Kluger (2006) offers the program evaluation grid as a tool to assist organizations in planning and systematically evaluating programs. Programs are rated on 24 individual factors within five areas: strategic, effectiveness/quality, financial, program importance to key stakeholders, and marketing. The resulting rank-ordering provides useful evaluative information that can be used in budgetary and programmatic decision making.

Another valuable tool is the logic model, a tool that incorporates theory in the development and evaluation of programs. In earlier chapters we stressed the importance of drawing on theoretical frameworks and generating testable hypotheses. Savaya and Waysman (2005) propose the use of the logic model for assessing program readiness for evaluation, for program development, for monitoring, and for building knowledge. Carrilio, Packard, and Clapp (2003) point out that much valuable information is already available on the performance of social service programs through existing information systems, but they found that available information is underutilized even when required by funding sources. A number of factors—including leadership, attitudes, accountability expectations, and organizational culture—influenced the collection and utilization of program data and information. Any or all of the tools discussed in this section can make the tasks associated with program evaluation much more manageable and should be utilized whenever possible.

Compile Periodic Evaluation Reports

The key questions to be explored are:

- ▶ What outcome(s) or result(s) were specified in the intervention plan?
- ▶ What qualitative and quantitative data and other types of information are available for evaluative purposes?
- ▶ How shall data be aggregated and displayed in evaluation reports?

Evaluation requires collecting and compiling data and information. The performance of each client or each team needs to be tracked in a way that allows for establishment of a baseline at the outset of the intervention and periodic measurement of progress. Documenting performance and progress will require some type of data collection. If the intervention involves initiation of a large-scale program with many clients or participants, forms must be designed and data entered into a computerized system. For a small project, it is possible that records may be maintained by hand in a notebook.

Recall that our outcome objectives for the policy change and the program change were stated as follows:

The bottom line for an intervention is whether the intervention improved the condition or quality of life of the people and/or the organization or community it set out to help.

Policy Change to Incorporate Volunteers into Cedar City

Outcome Objective 1:

Time Frame:	Within one month of the time the policy change is introduced
Target:	All seven members of the town council
Result:	Will support the volunteer initiative
Criterion:	As demonstrated by a vote taken by the town council

Program Change to Improve the Broadway Neighborhood

Outcome Objective 1:

Time Frame: By September 30, 20XX

Target: All streets in the Broadway neighborhood

Result: Will be free of discarded furniture and appliances

Criterion: As documented by a report from the neighborhood council

When data for all outcome objectives have been collected, aggregated, and compiled, a brief end-of-the-year report should be prepared for funding and decision-making sources and/or other stakeholders. This report would include information such as the following:

I. Overview (Rationale behind the change effort)

II. Description (What interventions are being provided?)

III. Goals and Objectives (Briefly stated)

IV. First Year Findings (Tables, graphs, and charts plus explanations)

V. Recommendations (What should be changed in the second and succeeding years?)

Rapp and Poertner (2007) offer some useful suggestions for report writing:

1. **Establish a standard.** Numbers are meaningless if there are no standards for comparison.

2. **Avoid too much information.** Limit the presentation to major findings. Present in an uncluttered format.

3. **Pay attention to aesthetics.** Use simple, attractive graphs, charts, and tables wherever possible.

4. **Explain tables, graphs, and charts in simple English.** Avoid using jargon. Write for the uninformed reader.

5. **Make aggregation meaningful.** Make sure that users of the report will be able to identify data and information that are meaningful to them at their level in the organization or community.

Using sound techniques for collecting and aggregating data and information, clearly displaying outcomes, and reporting in a way that is useful to the intended audience will help to solidify and build support for the change effort from key stakeholders. Continual feedback and reassessment, and steady communication with all participants and supporters, will go a long way toward stabilizing the change effort in a way that it becomes a permanent, well-integrated part of the organization or community if that is the intent. This, in the end, is what the change agent hoped for when the change effort was initiated and is an indicator that the intervention has been successful.

SUMMARY

Our objective in writing this book was to help students understand the macro-practice process in social work and to develop at least some beginning skills as these principles are applied. It may strike practitioners at the beginning of their careers that this process seems overwhelmingly detailed at times. Some may still have the image of the activist that plows right into the middle of a problem and begins organizing protests or other action. That is not the role taken by change agents in a professionally assisted episode of organizational or community change.

Good planning is much more likely to lead to successful change. If all the procedures described in the first ten chapters are followed, the change agent should have the necessary ingredients to develop the final, written plan and to implement, monitor, and evaluate the intervention. The working intervention hypothesis establishes the direction and the parameters for goals and objectives. Writing goals and objectives makes the whole change effort become proactive, which is to say that the action system is in a position to make things happen rather than to simply hope that they happen.

A goal statement provides the general sense of direction for the planned change effort. It is stated in terms of expected outcomes for the target population. As the intervention is implemented, there should be some general sense of positive movement toward the goal, but goal achievement as used in this context is not actually measured.

An outcome objective is a statement of expected outcomes that is intended to operationalize the goal, and it is written in a way that the outcome can be measured, monitored, and evaluated. An objective includes four parts: time, target, result, and criterion. Process objectives are used to describe the major components of the intervention that will be necessary in order to achieve the outcome objective. Once the outcome expectations are clear, phases or components necessary to successful achievement of the outcomes should be itemized, followed by a complete process objective written for each phase or component. When examining the process objectives as a whole, the planner should be convinced that, if they are all completed as planned, their completion will add up to successful achievement of the outcome objective.

Activities are then written for each process objective. Activities or tasks should be planned sequentially so that, when all activities are completed, the process objective will have been achieved. For each activity a time frame and the person responsible for completion of the activity should be specified. Thus, the overall plan becomes an intricate set of goals, objectives, and activities designed to work together. If the plan is devised in this manner, the chances for success are greatly increased. If all the activities are completed within the specified time frame, then process objectives should be achieved. If process objectives are achieved, then outcome objectives should be achieved. Finally, if outcome objectives are achieved, the change effort will have moved toward its goal.

Implementing the intervention involves managing the logistics specified in the plan and ensuring that all technical and interpersonal problems are addressed. Evaluating the effectiveness of the intervention focuses on outcome objectives; it requires data collection and aggregation for the purpose of reporting back to funding sources and other sponsors and stakeholders. Once the first cycle of monitoring and evaluation has been completed (usually by the end of the first year), efforts should be focused on making necessary adjustments to improve the program based on findings from the evaluation and looking for ways to solidify the project and ensure ongoing support.

Framework for Planning, Implementing, Monitoring, and Evaluating the Intervention

Task 1: Set a Goal for the Intervention

▶ What is the overall outcome that is expected if the intervention is successful?

Task 2: Write Outcome Objectives

Establish a Time Frame for the Objective

▶ Is it possible to establish a day, month, and year when the first results should be evident?

▶ At what point in the future is it reasonable to expect to see measurable results from this intervention?

Define the Target Population

▶ Who are the expected primary beneficiaries of the intervention?

Specify a Result or Outcome

▶ What quality of life changes are expected for the target population from this intervention?

Define a Criterion for Measuring Success

▶ How will the result as stated in the objective be measured?

▶ Are there observable criteria readily available for measurement, or will criteria need to be designed?

Task 3: Develop Process Objectives

Establish a Time Frame for the Process Objective

▶ When will the actions specified in this objective begin and end?

Define the Target

▶ What individuals, groups, or products will be the focus of this objective?

Specify a Result for the Process Objective

▶ What result will provide evidence that the objective has been achieved?

Define a Criterion to Be Used for Documentation Purposes

▶ What observable or measurable factor(s) can be used to determine whether the process objective has been achieved?

Task 4: List Activities for Process Objectives

Format Activities for Easy Monitoring

▶ What activities or tasks must be successfully completed in order to achieve the process objective?

▶ When should each activity begin and end?

▶ Who should be assigned responsibility for completion of the activity?

Task 5: Initiate the Action Plan

Manage Logistics

▶ What facilities, equipment, and other resources will need to be made available prior to implementation?

▶ Where will new personnel, including volunteers, be housed?

▶ How can the steps or phases be depicted in flowchart form?

Select and Train Participants

▶ Who will have overall leadership and management responsibilities for the intervention?

▶ Will existing or new staff and/or volunteers be used in the intervention?

▶ What preparations need to be made to bring new participants on board?

▶ What type of orientation and training will be needed?

Task 6: Monitor and Evaluate the Intervention

Monitor Technical Activities

▶ What is the appropriate sequencing for the activities that must be completed in order to achieve the process objective?

▶ Who will be assigned responsibility for completion of each activity?

▶ When must each activity be completed in order for the process objective to be achieved on time?

Monitor Interpersonal Activities

▶ How enthusiastic and supportive are the designated implementers?

▶ Is there a formal or informal system for evaluating the performance of implementers?

▶ Is there a strategy for dealing with poor performance, apathy, or resistance?

Task 7: Evaluate the Effectiveness of the Intervention

Compile Periodic Evaluation Reports

▶ What outcome(s) or result(s) were specified in the intervention plan?

▶ What quantitative data and other types of information are available for evaluative purposes?

▶ How shall data be aggregated and displayed in evaluation reports?

Case Example: Jackson County Foster Care

The following example illustrates the major components of a written plan for a macro change effort.

Background

Jackson County incorporates a major city, several medium-sized suburbs, and a small amount of rural area. The Child Welfare Services Division of its Department of Social Services recently undertook an analysis of foster children for which it had responsibility during the past five years. The findings revealed that there were a disproportionately low number of white children in this population and a disproportionately high number of children from other racial or ethnic groups.

In response to a newspaper article that reported these results, over 30 representatives of various ethnic communities attended an open hearing held by the County Board of Supervisors. They expressed serious concerns about the findings. The County Director of Child Welfare Services was instructed to appoint a task force to study the situation and to make recommendations. The fourteen-member task force included:

- Three parents of ethnic minority foster children
- Four leaders from minority communities
- Two foster parents
- Two foster care social workers
- A foster home recruitment coordinator
- A child welfare researcher from the local university
- The top administrator from the foster care program

Analysis of the Problem

The task force began with an initial statement of the problem that focused on the fact that ethnic minority children comprised a higher proportion of children in foster care than would be expected based on the overall proportion of these children in the county. The group then started to review available literature to become familiar with issues associated with foster care and return to natural families. The literature review the group conducted uncovered the following facts:

1. Children of color were overrepresented in foster care not only in Jackson County but elsewhere in the country as well.

2. Racial or ethnic minority children can become overrepresented in foster care in two ways: (a) they can be placed in foster care at a higher rate than white children and/or (b) they can leave foster care at a slower rate than white children and thus account for a greater number in care at any given point in time.

3. Research reports suggested that ethnic minority children, once placed in foster care, were adopted or placed in other permanent arrangements at the same rate as white children. However, ethnic minority children who were returned to their parents' homes did so much more slowly than did white children.

4. Placing children in foster care may be necessary if it is the only way to ensure their safety, but all possible efforts should be made by workers to avoid the need for foster care by facilitating solutions to family problems while the child is still in the home.

5. If it still becomes necessary, foster care is supposed to be temporary. Workers should attempt to facilitate solutions to problems in the family in order to allow the child to return home as quickly as possible. If this cannot be done, the next best option is to find some other permanent placement such as an adoptive home.

Analysis of the Population

The task force members then directed their efforts toward gaining a better understanding of the population of interest, which they defined as ethnic minority children in foster care. To accomplish this, they reviewed five-year statistics from the department's child welfare division, studied in detail the findings of the division's recent report, and examined other research on minority children and families. The most important results they found were:

1. Foster care that is intended to be temporary but that continues indefinitely is harmful to children. This is because it jeopardizes their ability to form developmentally critical attachments with a parent or permanent parent surrogate.

2. For healthy development, children need to go through a series of stages and successfully complete developmental tasks. Completion of these tasks can be interrupted by going into foster care. This can result in delayed development for the child.

3. Placement of a child from an ethnic group with a foster family from another ethnic group can be detrimental to the child if the foster family is unaware of or insensitive to important cultural factors.

Based on these findings, the task force refined its problem statement to focus on the specific concerns of children of color being too likely to be placed in foster care and too unlikely to be reunited with their biological families in a timely fashion.

Analysis of the Arena

Initial findings of the research efforts of the task force also implied that the arena in which a change effort would need to take place was not the community as a whole but the Jackson County Social Services organization. Under this assumption, the task force collected the following information from records within the department and from interviews with current and former clients and professionals in other agencies in the community:

1. The proportion of persons of color who held professional positions in Jackson County's foster care services division was much lower than the proportion of children of color who were placed in foster care in the county.

2. Foster parents licensed by the division were also much less racially and ethnically diverse than the population of foster children in the county.

3. Many child welfare workers and foster parents were seen as lacking an in-depth understanding of the meaning of culture and tradition to ethnic minority families. This meant that children's behavior tended to be interpreted from a white perspective, which might be inconsistent with norms established and understood in minority communities.

4. Once child welfare services in Jackson County had commenced, white children were less likely to be placed in foster care than were nonwhite children.

5. Support services offered to help families deal with problems when a child was removed were seen as lacking the cultural sensitivity necessary to help strengthen ethnic minority families.

As shown in Figure 1-1 in Chapter 1, the change effort that task force members began planning therefore assumed that the situation was one involving an overlap of problem (too great a likelihood of children entering foster care and staying too long), population (children of color), and arena (Jackson County Social Services, its employees, its foster parents, and its clients). It was thought that biological families served by the department's foster care division needed more resources and supportive services. Also, the division's professional staff and its foster parents needed a better understanding of family norms and the variables critical to healthy family environments for minority children.

Hypothesis of Etiology

Based on the preceding findings, the task force developed the following hypothesis of etiology:

Because of the following factors:

1. The low number of staff from ethnic minority populations;
2. The low number of foster parents from ethnic minority populations;
3. The limited knowledge of culture on the part of staff and foster parents; and
4. The high number of ethnic minority children being removed from their homes.

The result has been:

1. An organizational insensitivity to and unawareness of the importance of culture in foster care;
2. A preference on the part of foster parents for white children;
3. Low levels of cultural competence throughout the agency; and
4. A disproportionate number of ethnic minority children in foster care.

Intervention Hypothesis

Based on the preceding analysis, the task force proposed the following as their intervention hypothesis:

If we can do the following:

1. Recruit a more diverse child welfare staff;
2. Recruit more ethnic minority foster parents;
3. Train staff and foster parents; and
4. Support ethnic minority families in the home.

Then we would expect the following results:

1. Improved communication and understanding between ethnic minority families and staff;
2. Families better able to meet the cultural and ethnic needs of ethnic minority foster children;
3. Increased cultural competence on the part of white staff and foster parents; and
4. Increased number of successful returns of ethnic minority children to biological families.

After proceeding through each of the tasks outlined in the earlier chapters of this book, the task force produced the following written plan.

Part I: The Problem and the Proposed Change

In the Jackson County Division of Child Welfare Services, it was recently discovered that the rate of return of minority children from foster care to their natural families was significantly less than the rates for white children. A task force was appointed and a study was undertaken. A number of causal factors have emerged from the study.

There is some evidence that minority families whose children go into foster care have more serious economic, social, and emotional problems and are in need of a network of supportive services that will enable them to strengthen the family and better parent the child. On the whole, such services, with a special emphasis on serving ethnic minority families, have generally not been available to these families.

Also, there is evidence that child welfare workers and foster parents lack knowledge about culture that could be important in the decision-making process about the needs of ethnic minority children and what should be considered realistic behavioral and performance expectations for return to natural families.

The task force proposes a series of interventions aimed at improving the cultural sensitivity of child-care workers and foster parents and strengthening families who place children in foster care.

The first set of interventions will be directed toward child welfare workers and foster care parents. Recruitment activities will include:

- Contact with graduate schools of social work
- Advertising in urban agencies where there are large numbers of ethnic minority child welfare workers

Cultural sensitivity training for child welfare workers and foster parents will include:

- Assessing one's values and perceptions as they relate to work with minority children and their families
- Understanding African American families and children
- Understanding Latino families and children
- Understanding Native American families and children
- Understanding Asian American families and children

Foster parents who complete cultural sensitivity training courses will:

- Receive a higher level of payment
- Be certified to receive ethnic minority foster children

The second set of interventions will include support services, under contract with agencies that have demonstrated an understanding of and sensitivity to ethnic minority cultures. These services will be directed toward minority families. They are:

- Individual and family assessment and counseling
- Case management
- Economic incentives
- Parent training
- Self-help groups

Part II: Key Actors and Systems

Table 11.1 provides an overview of the systems, their definitions, and the representatives of each system. Note that there is intentional overlap between systems.

Table 11.1	**Systems**	
System Representative	Definition	System
Initiator	Those who first brought the problem to attention	Black Families United, a community organization that organized the effort to meet with the County Board of Supervisors
Change agent	The professional social worker, agency, and others coordinating the change effort	The task force, staffed by an experienced child welfare supervisor
Client	Primary and secondary beneficiaries	Ethnic minority children who are placed in foster care, and their parents
Support	Others who may be expected to support the change effort	At least eight ethnic community organizations, two child welfare advocacy groups, several ethnic minority clergy and their congregations, many child welfare professionals, and the foster parents' association
Controlling	The person or persons who have the power and the authority to approve the change and direct that it be implemented	The County Board of Supervisors
Host	The part of the organization or community that will provide auspices for administration of the intervention	The Jackson County Division of Child Welfare
Implementing	The staff and/or volunteers who will carry out the intervention	Three units within the Jackson County Division of Child Welfare: (1) the foster care unit, (2) the staff development and training unit, and (3) the purchase of services contracting unit
Target	That which must be changed for the intervention to be successful	Since this will be a multiphase process, there will be phase-specific targets. The initial target will be the funding sources needed to underwrite the proposed interventions. This includes the Board of Supervisors and several local foundations. Subsequent targets include (1) child welfare workers and foster parents who need to become more ethnic sensitive and (2) ethnic minority families with children in foster care
Action	The expanded planning and coordinating committee responsible for seeing the change effort through to completion	The task force, together with key representatives from the Division of Child Welfare and potential service providers

Part III: Goals, Objectives, and Activities

This change effort is proposed as a three-year pilot project, during which time the Division of Child Welfare will experiment with and correct any problems discovered in implementing the original design. Following the three-year trial period, it is to be implemented as a permanent part of Jackson County Child Welfare Services.

Goal

To reduce the disproportionate number of ethnic minority children in foster care in the Jackson County Child Welfare system.

Outcome Objective 1

By December 31, 20XX, to increase the knowledge of four ethnic minority cultures of at least 50 trainees (including child welfare workers and foster parents), as measured by a 50 percent increase between pretest and posttest scores on tests developed for the training course.

Process Objectives

1.1 By July 31, 20XX, to present a proposal to the County Board of Supervisors for funds to develop culturally sensitive curriculum for child welfare workers and foster parents in Jackson County.

1.2 By September 30, 20XX, to develop four training courses on understanding African American, Latino, Native American, and Asian American families designed for child welfare workers and foster parents who serve ethnic minority children.

1.3 By October 31, 20XX, to produce fifty copies of all handouts associated with the training courses and distribute them to the Child Welfare Staff Development and Training Unit.

1.4 By November 30, 20XX, to recruit at least fifty child welfare workers and foster parents to take the training courses.

1.5 By January 31, 20XX, to administer pretests and to train at least fifty child welfare workers and foster parents in cultural sensitivity.

1.6 By March 31, 20XX, to administer posttests to trainees and to analyze the pretest/posttest results.

Outcome Objective 2

By September 30, 20XX, at least one hundred ethnic minority families with children in foster care will demonstrate improved family strength and parenting skills as measured by at least 30 percent higher scores on the Multidimensional Parenting and Family Assessment Inventory.

Process Objectives

2.1 By November 30, 20XX, economic, social, emotional, and family support resources needed to serve African American, Latino, Native American, and Asian American families in Jackson County will be inventoried.

2.2 By April 30, 20XX, at least one hundred ethnic minority families with children in foster care will have been initially assessed to determine what resources are currently used and what resources are needed but not available or accessible.

2.3 By June 30, 20XX, gaps between available and needed resources for minority families will be documented in writing.

2.4 By September 30, 20XX, formal proposals for funding services designed for minority families will be presented to the Jackson County Board of Supervisors and at least two local foundations.

Part IV: Tactics

It is anticipated that this change effort will proceed through a series of phases, as shown here.

Phase 1

The objective of phase 1 is to get the change accepted by potential funding sources. The focus of this phase is on the County Board of Supervisors, several private foundations interested in minority concerns, and people capable of influencing their decisions. Campaign tactics will include education, persuasion, and lobbying. In the event that campaign tactics are not successful and that funding sources are not open to change, contest tactics may be used. These tactics would include mass media appeals to mobilize the support system as well as bargaining and negotiation and large-group social action.

Phase 2

The objective of phase 2, if the project is funded, is to increase cultural awareness, knowledge, and competence. The focus of this phase is on child welfare staff and foster parents who serve minority children and their families. Collaborative tactics will include joint action, capacity building, and education.

Phase 3

The objective of phase 3 is to ensure that improved services are provided to minority families who have placed children in foster care. Services should be adapted to the unique needs, concerns, interests, and traditions of each ethnic group and will involve application of knowledge and skill gained in phase 2. The focus of this effort will be on child welfare workers, foster parents, and contracted service providers. Collaborative tactics will include capacity building and joint action.

Monitoring and Evaluation

The child welfare supervisor who served on the task force will be assigned the responsibility of monitoring the implementation of the project and producing evaluation reports. She will use the project's goal, outcome objectives, process objectives, and activities as a basis for ensuring that all tasks and activities are carried out on time and at an acceptable level of quality.

The evaluation report will focus on outcomes related to (1) increased cultural awareness, knowledge, and competence of workers and foster parents; (2) improved levels of comfort and understanding between ethnic minority families and child welfare workers; (3) strengthened families and parenting skills on the part of participating ethnic minority families; and (4) increasing rates of successful return of ethnic minority children in foster care to their biological families.

Succeed with PEARSON **mysocialworklab**

Log onto **www.mysocialworklab.com** and answer the questions below. (*If you did not receive an access code to* **MySocialWorkLab** *with this text and wish to purchase access online, please visit* www.mysocialworklab.com.)

1. **Read the MySocialWorkLibrary case study: Military Veteran Justice Outreach and the Role of a VA Social Worker Part I.** Imagine you created a program to increase the collaboration between the police and the VJO social workers. Identify the goal of the program

and several outcome objectives. How would you measure the success of your objectives?

2. **Read the MySocialWorkLibrary case study: A Community Coalition. Pay special attention to the last section.** The new goal of the group is articulated in this section. Develop a few outcome objectives for this goal. Now select one of those outcome objectives, and develop one or more process objectives that would need to occur to successfully complete this outcome.

PRACTICE TEST

The following questions will test your knowledge of the content found within this chapter. For additional assessment, including licensing-exam-type questions on applying chapter content to practice, visit **MySocialWorkLab**.

1. The relationship between the working intervention hypothesis and outcome objectives can best be described as:
   a. the hypothesis provides a rationale for the objectives
   b. the hypothesis provides the analysis, leading to proposed interventions
   c. in outcome objectives the proposed interventions are translated into specific plans
   d. outcome objectives help to avoid premature decisions about the interventions

2. The criterion that will be used to determine whether an objective has been achieved:
   a. reduces the vagueness and elusiveness that is sometimes part of outcomes
   b. breaks down the process into manageable segments
   c. helps to determine a realistic time frame
   d. helps to determine who is responsible for each objective

3. Process objectives are used in the planning process to:
   a. delegate responsibility for carrying out tasks
   b. enable supervisors and managers to track milestones
   c. ensure that everyone is using the same criterion for measurement
   d. define how the outcome objective will be achieved

4. Evidence-based practice is built on the principle that all social work practice should:
   a. collect data and information
   b. combine knowledge and skill with research-based evidence
   c. include aggregation of evaluation findings
   d. make use of both quantitative and qualitative research findings

5. Thinking back to the Cedar City example, the first outcome objective was to have all streets in the Broadway neighborhood free of discarded furniture and appliances. What are some ways to present data documenting the success of this in a final report?

ASSESS YOUR COMPETENCE

Use the scale below to rate your current level of achievement on the following concepts or skills associated with each competency presented in the chapter:

1	2	3
I can accurately describe the concept or skill.	I can consistently identify the concept or skill when observing and analyzing practice activities.	I can competently implement the concept or skill in my own practice.

_____ Can respond to political and other context that may influence change efforts.

_____ Can use critical thinking to develop measures that track activities and processes as well as measures that show the extent to which the change effort was ultimately successful.

_____ Can apply knowledge of human behavior and social environment to dynamic group processes and collaborations.

_____ Can use information gained from outcome and monitoring data to inform practice.

References

Chapter 1

Cummins, L. K., Byers, K. V., & Pedrick, L. (2011). *Policy practice for social workers: New strategies for a new era.* Boston, MA: Allyn & Bacon.

Fabricant, M. (1985). The industrialization of social work practice. *Social Work, 30*(5), 389–395.

Gilbert, N., & Terrell, P. (2010). *Dimensions of social welfare policy* (6th ed.). Boston, MA: Allyn & Bacon.

Gustafson, J. M. (1982). Professions as "callings." *Social Service Review, 56*(4), 501–515.

Hillier, A., Wernecke, M. L., & McKelvey, H. (2005). Removing barriers to the use of community information systems. *Journal of Community Practice, 13*(1), 121–139.

Itzhaky, H., & Bustin, E. (2005). Promoting client participation by social workers: Contributing factors. *Journal of Community Practice, 13*(2), 77–92.

Jansson, B. S. (2011). *Becoming an effective policy advocate: From policy practice to social justice* (6th ed.). Belmont, CA: Thomson Brooks/Cole.

Jenson, J. M. (2005). Connecting science to intervention: Advances, challenges, and the promise of evidence-based practice. *Social Work Research, 29*(3), 131–135.

Karger, H. J., & Stoesz, D. (2009). *American social welfare policy: A pluralist approach* (6th ed.). Boston, MA: Allyn & Bacon.

Reamer, F. G. (1995). *Social work values and ethics.* New York: Columbia University Press.

Reamer, F. G. (1998). *Ethical standards in social work: A critical review of the NASW Code of ethics.* Washington, DC: NASW Press.

Rothman, J., Erlich, J. L., & Tropman, J. E. (2008). *Strategies of community intervention* (7th ed.). Peosta, IA: Eddie Bower.

Sullivan, W. M. (2005). *Work and integrity: The crisis and promise of professionalism in America.* San Francisco, CA: Jossey-Bass.

Warren, R. L. (1978). *The community in America* (3rd ed.). Chicago, IL: Rand McNally.

Chapter 2

Abramovitz, M. (1991). Putting an end to doublespeak about race, gender, and poverty: An annotated glossary for social workers. *Social Work, 36*(5), 380–384.

Allen, M. (2009, September 13). Obama sees "coarsening" of national debate. *Politico.* Retrieved January 2011, from http://www.politico.com/news/stories/0909/27082.html

American Council on Education. (2010). *Gender equity in higher education: 2010.* Washington, DC: Author.

Anngela-Cole, L., & Hilton, J. M. (2009). The role of attitudes and culture in family caregiving for older adults. *Home Health Care Services Quarterly, 28,* 59–83.

Annie E. Casey Foundation. (2010). *Kids count data center—Children in single-parent families by race (Percent)—2009.* Retrieved January 2011, from http://datacenter.kidscount.org/data/acrossstates/Rankings.aspx?ind=107

Aron-Dine, A., & Shapiro, I. (2007). *New data show income concentration jumped again in 2005: Income share of top 1% at highest level since 1929.* Center on Budget and Policy Priorities.

Retrieved December 2010, from http://www.cbpp.org/cms/index.cfm?fa=archivePage&id=3-29-07inc.htm

Austin, A. (2010). *Different race, different recession: American Indian unemployment in 2010.* Washington, DC.: Economic Policy Institute. Retrieved January 2011, from http://www.epi.org/publications/entry/ib289

Axinn, J., & Stern, M. J. (2008). *Social welfare: A history of the American response to need* (7th ed.). Boston, MA: Pearson/Allyn & Bacon.

Barry, B. (2007). *Speechless: The erosion of free expression in the American workplace.* San Francisco, CA: Berrett-Koehler Publishers.

Becker, D. G. (1987). Isabella Graham and Joanna Bethune: Trail-blazers of organized women's benevolence. *Social Service Review, 61,* 319–336.

Bender, D. E. (2008). Perils of degeneration: Reform, the savage immigrant, and the survival of the unfit. *Journal of Social History, 42,* 5–29.

Benish, A. (2010). Re-bureaucratizing welfare administration. *Social Service Review, 84,* 77–101.

Bernstein, J., Mishell, L., & Brocht, C. (2000). *Briefing paper: Any way you cut it—Income inequality on the rise regardless of how it's measured.* Washington, DC: Economic Policy Institute.

Boisson, S. (2006). When America sent her own packing. *American History, 41,* 20–27.

Brager, G., & Holloway, S. (1978). *Changing human service organizations: Politics and practice.* New York: Free Press.

Brieland, D. (1987). Social work practice: History and evolution. In Ann Minahan (Ed.), *Encyclopedia of social work* (19th ed., Vol. 3, pp. 2246–2258). Washington, DC: NASW Press.

Brieland, D. (1990). The Hull-House tradition and the contemporary social worker: Was Jane Addams really a social worker? *Social Work, 35*(2), 134–138.

Broughton, C. (2010). Bringing the organization back in: The role of bureaucratic churning in early TANF caseload declines in Illinois. *Journal of Sociology and Social Welfare, 37,* 155–182.

Brown v. Board of Education of Topeka, 347 U.S. 483 (1954).

Carlton-LeNey, I., & Hodges, V. (2004). African American reform-ers' mission: Caring for our girls and women. *Affilia, 19,* 257–272.

Carnevale, A. P., Smith, N., & Strohl, J. (2010). *Projections of jobs and education requirements through 2018.* Georgetown University: Center on Education and the Workforce. Retrieved January 2011, from http://www9.georgetown.edu/grad/gppi/hpi/cew/pdfs/FullReport.pdf

Centers for Disease Control. (2010). Early release of selected estimates based on data from the January–June 2010 National Health Interview Survey, *Percentage of adults aged 18 years and over who had five or more drinks in 1 day at least once in the past year: United States, 1997–June 2010.* Retrieved January 2011, from http://www.cdc.gov/nchs/data/nhis/earlyrelease/201012_09.pdf

Chambers, C. A. (1985). The historical role of the voluntary sector. In G. A. Tobin (Ed.), *Social planning and human service delivery in the voluntary sector* (pp. 3–28). Westport, CT: Greenwood Press.

Chambers, C. A. (1986). Women in the creation of the profession of social work. *Social Service Review, 60*(1), 3–33.

ChildStats.gov. (2010). *America's children in brief: Key national indicators of well-being, 2010.* Retrieved January 2011 from http://www.childstats.gov/americaschildren/tables.asp

Coleman, M. C. (1999). The responses of American Indian children and Irish children to the school, 1850s–1920s. *American Indian Quarterly, 23,* 83–112.

Collins, G. (2010). *When everything changed: The amazing journey of American women from 1960 to the present.* Boston, MA: Back Bay.

Corsini, R. J. (2002). *The dictionary of psychology.* New York: Brunner/Mazel.

Crompton, L. (2003). *Homosexuality and civilization.* Cambridge, MA: Harvard University Press.

DuBois, E. C. (1999). *Feminism and suffrage: The emergence of an independent women's movement in America, 1848–1869.* Ithaca, NY: Cornell University Press.

Facebook Pressroom Statistics. (2011). Retrieved January 2011, from http://www.facebook.com/press/info.php?statistics

Friedan, B. (1963). *The feminine mystique.* New York: Norton.

Fukuyama, F. (1999). *The great disruption.* New York: Free Press.

Gandy, K. (2005, September 22). Editorial/Opinion: The patriarchy isn't falling. *USA Today.* Retrieved September 2006, from www.usatoday.com/news/opinion/editorials/2005–09–22-oppose_x.htm

Garvin, C. D., & Cox, F. M. (2001). A history of community organizing since the Civil War with special reference to oppressed communities. In J. Rothman, J. L. Erlich, & J. E. Tropman (Eds.), *Strategies of community intervention* (6th ed., pp. 65–100). Itasca, IL: F. E. Peacock.

Gingrich, N. (1995). *To renew America.* New York: HarperCollins.

Granado, C. (2006). "Hispanic" vs. "Latino:" A new poll finds that the term "Hispanic" is preferred. *Hispanic Magazine.* Retrieved September 2006, from www.hispaniconline.com/hh/hisp_vs_lat.html

Gray, M., & Boddy, J. (2010). Making sense of the waves: Wipeout or still riding high? *Affilia, 25,* 368–389.

Griswold del Castillo, R. (2001). *The Treaty of Guadalupe Hidalgo: A legacy of conflict.* Norman: University of Oklahoma Press.

Gutiérrez, L. M., & Lewis, E. A. (1999). *Empowering women of color.* New York: Columbia University Press

Harrington, M. (1962). *The other America: Poverty in the United States.* New York: Macmillan.

Haskins, R. (2006, July 19). *Testimony to Committee on Ways and Means, U.S. House of Representatives.* Retrieved August 2006, from www.brookings.edu/views/testimony/haskins/20060719.pdf

Hildebrand, V., & Van Kerm, P. (2009). Income inequality and self-rated health status: Evidence from the European Community Household Panel. *Demography, 46,* 805–825.

Holt, S. (2006). *The Earned Income Tax Credit at age 30: What we know.* Washington, DC: Brookings Institution. Available at www.brookings.edu/metro/pubs/20060209_Holt.pdf

Huisman, M., & Oldehinkel, A. J. (2009). Income inequality, social capital and self-inflicted injury and violence-related mortality. *Journal of Epidemiology and Community Health, 63,* 31–37.

Hutchinson, R. N., Putt, M. A., Dean, L. T., Long, J. A., Montagnet, C. A., & Armstrong, K. (2009). Neighborhood racial composition, social capital and black all-cause mortality in Philadelphia. *Social Science & Medicine, 68,* 1859–1865.

Institute for Women's Policy Research. (2010). *Fact Sheet: The Gender Wage Gap—2009.* Retrieved January 2011 from http://www.iwpr.org/pdf/C350.pdf

Jansson, B. S. (2009). *The reluctant welfare state: American social welfare policies—Past, present, and future* (6th ed.). Belmont, CA: Brooks/Cole/Thomson Learning.

Kelly, P. J., Rasu, R., Lesser, J., Oscos-Sanchez, M., Mancha, J., & Orriega, A. (2010). Mexican-American neighborhood's social capital and attitudes about violence. *Issues in Mental Health Nursing, 31,* 15–20.

Kettner, P. M., & Martin, L. L. (1987). *Purchase of service contracting.* Newbury Park, CA: Sage.

Lau, A. S., Fung, J., Wang, S., & Kang, S. (2009). Explaining elevated social anxiety among Asian Americans: Emotional attunement and a cultural double bind. *Cultural Diversity & Ethnic Minority Psychology, 15,* 77–85.

Le, C. N. (2006). *Asian-Nation: The landscape of Asian America.* Retrieved September 2006, from www.asian-nation.org/demographics.shtml

Lens, V. (2008). Welfare and work sanctions: Examining discretion on the front lines. *Social Service Review, 82,* 197–222.

Lewis, H. (1978). Management in the nonprofit social service organization. In S. Slavin (Ed.), *Social administration: The management of the social services.* New York: Council on Social Work Education.

Lindeman, E. (1921). *The community: An introduction to the study of community leadership and organization.* New York: Association Press.

MacDorman, M. F., & Mathews, T. J. (2008). *Recent trends in infant mortality in the United States.* Atlanta, GA: Centers for Disease Control. Retrieved January 2011, from http://www.cdc.gov/nchs/data/databriefs/db09.pdf

Marotta, T. (1981). *The politics of homosexuality.* Boston, MA: Houghton Mifflin.

Martin, L. L. (2005). Performance-based contracting for human services: Does it work? *Administration in Social Work, 29,* 63–77.

McCarthy, K. D. (Ed.). (1990). *Lady bountiful revisited: Women, philanthropy, and power.* New Brunswick, NJ: Rutgers University Press.

McCarthy, K. D. (2003). *American creed: Philanthropy and the rise of civil society 1700–1865.* Chicago, IL: University of Chicago Press.

McMurtry, S. L., Netting, F. E., & Kettner, P. M. (1991). How nonprofits adapt to a stringent environment. *Nonprofit Management & Leadership, 1*(3), 235–252.

Morris, P. M. (2008). Reinterpreting Abraham Flexner's speech, "Is Social Work a Profession?": Its meaning and influence on the field's early professional development. *Social Service Review, 82,* 29–60.

Murray, K. O., & Primus, W. E. (2005). Recent data trends show welfare reform to be a mixed success: Significant policy changes should accompany reauthorization. *Review of Policy Research, 22,* 301–324.

National Center for Education Statistics. (2007). *Status and Trends in the Education of Racial and Ethnic Minorities.* Retrieved January 2011, from http://nces.ed.gov/pubs2007/2007039.pdf

National Indian Gaming Association. (2010). *National Indian Gaming Association releases report on the economic impact of Indian gaming in 2009.* Retrieved January 2011, from http://www.indiangaming.org/info/NIGA_2009_Economic_Impact_Report.pdf

National Women's Law Center. (2009). *The lilly ledbetter fair pay Act.* Retrieved from http://www.nwlc.org/resource/fair-pay-frequently-asked-questions

Native American Journalists Association. (2006). *Reading Red Report 2002: A report and content analysis on coverage of Native Americans by the largest newspapers in the United States.* Retrieved September 2006, from www.naja.com/resources/publications/

Nord, M., Coleman-Jensen, A., Andrews, M., & Carlson, S. (2010). *Household food security in the United States, 2009.* Washington, DC: U.S. Department of Agriculture. Retrieved January 2011, from http://www.ers.usda.gov/Publications/ERR108/ERR108.pdf

O'Brien, G. V., & Leneave, J. (2008). The "Art" of social work and the ADA's essential functions provision: Challenges and recommendations. *Administration in Social Work, 32*, 87–99.

Ohmer, M. L. (2010). How theory and research inform citizen participation in poor communities: The ecological perspective and theories on self- and collective efficacy and sense of community. *Journal of Human Behavior in the Social Environment, 20*, 1–19.

Orgad, L., & Ruthizer, T. (2010). Race, religion and nationality in immigration selection: 120 years after the Chinese exclusion case. *Constitutional Commentary, 26*, 237–296.

Olson, M. E., Diekema, D., Elliott, B. A., & Renier, C. M. (2010). Impact of income and income inequality on infant health outcomes in the United States. *Pediatrics, 126*, 1165–1173.

Parrott, S. (2006). *Testimony before the committee on ways and means, United States House of Representatives, July 19, 2006.* Washington, DC: Center on Budget and Policy Priorities. Retrieved May 12, from www.cbpp.org/7-19-06tanf-testimony.pdf

Parsai, M., Nieri, T., & Villar, P. (2010). Away from home: Paradoxes of parenting for Mexican immigrant adults. *Families in Society, 91*, 201–208.

Patti, R. J. (2000). The landscape of social welfare management. In R. J. Patti (Ed.), *The handbook of social welfare management* (pp. 3–25). Thousand Oaks, CA: Sage.

Percy, S. L. (1989). *Disability, civil rights, and public policy.* Tuscaloosa, AL: University of Alabama Press.

Peterson, P. E., & Greenstone, J. D. (1977). The mobilization of low-income communities through community action. In R. H. Haveman (Ed.), *A decade of federal antipoverty programs: Achievements, failures, and lessons.* New York: Academic Press.

Pew Hispanic Center. (2007). *Statistical portrait of the foreign-born population in the United States, 2007.* Retrieved December 2010 from http://pewhispanic.org/factsheets/factsheet.php?FactsheetID=45

Piketty, T., & Saez, E. (2003). Income inequality in the United States: 1913–1998. *Quarterly Journal of Economics, 118*, 1–39.

Pitt, V., & Curtin, M. (2004). Integration versus segregation: The experiences of a group of disabled students moving from mainstream school into special needs further education. *Disability & Society, 19*, 387–401.

Putnam, R. D. (2000). *Bowling alone: The collapse and revival of American community.* New York: Simon & Schuster.

Rapp, C. A., & Poertner, J. (1992). *Social administration: A client-centered approach.* New York: Longman.

Redelings, M., Lieb, L., & Sorvillo, F. (2010). Years off your life? The effects of homicide on life expectancy by neighborhood and race/ethnicity in Los Angeles County. *Journal of Urban Health, 87*, 670–676.

Rehabilitation Act of 1973, Pub. L. No. 93-112, 87 Stat. 335 (1973).

Reisch, M., & Andrews, J. (2001). *The road not taken: A history of radical social work in the United States.* Philadelphia, PA: Brunner-Routledge.

Reisch, M., & Wenocur, S. (1986). The future of community organization in social work: Social activism and the politics of profession building. *Social Service Review, 60*(1), 70–93.

Richmond, M. (1917). *Social diagnosis.* New York: Russell Sage Foundation.

Rodin, J., & Steinberg, S. P. (Eds.). (2003). *Public discourse in America: Conversation and community in the twenty-first century.* Philadelphia, PA: University of Pennsylvania Press.

Shaw, H., & Stone, C. (2010). *Tax data show richest 1 percent took a hit in 2008, but income remained highly concentrated at the top.* Retrieved December 2010, from http://www.cbpp.org/cms/index.cfm?fa=view&id=3309#_ftnref1

Sherman, A., & Stone, C. (2010). *Income gaps between very rich and everyone else more than tripled in last three decades, new data show.* Retrieved December 2010 from http://www.cbpp.org/files/6-25-10inc.pdf

Shilts, R. (1987). *And the band played on: Politics, people, and the AIDS epidemic.* New York: St. Martin's Press.

Shipler, D. K. (2005). *The working poor: Invisible in America.* New York: Vintage Books.

Sigelman, L., Tuch, S. A., & Martin, J. K. (2005). What's in a name? Preference for "Black" versus "African-American" among Americans of African descent. *Public Opinion Quarterly, 69*(3), 429–438.

Sun, X., Rehnberg, C., & Meng, Q. (2009). How are individual-level social capital and poverty associated with health equity? A study from two Chinese cities. *International Journal for Equity in Health, 8*, 1–13.

Thompson, S. J., Kim, J., McManus, H., Flynn, P., & Kim, H. (2007). Peer relationships. *International Social Work, 50*, 783–795.

Toffler, A. (1980). *The third wave.* New York: Morrow.

Trattner, W. I. (1999). *From poor law to welfare state: A history of social welfare in America* (6th ed.). New York: Free Press.

U.S. Bureau of the Census. (1970). *Population of congressional districts.* Retrieved December 2010, from http://www2.census.gov/prod2/decennial/documents/42078080.pdf

U.S. Bureau of the Census. (2006d). *Health insurance coverage: 2005.* Retrieved September 2006, from www.census.gov/hhes/www/hlthins/hlthin05.html

U.S. Bureau of the Census. (2010a). *Annual estimates of the resident population for incorporated places over 100,000.* Retrieved December 2010, from http://www.census.gov/popest/cities/tables/SUB-EST2009-01.xls

U.S. Bureau of the Census. (2010b). *Current Population Survey (CPS): Annual Social and Economic (ASEC) Supplement.* Retrieved January 2011, from http://www.census.gov/hhes/www/cpstables/032010/health/h01_004.htm

U.S. Bureau of the Census. (2010c). *Large metropolitan statistical areas population: 1990 to 2008.* Retrieved December 2010, from http://www.census.gov/compendia/statab/2010/tables/10s0020.pdf

U.S. Bureau of the Census. (2010d). *Nativity Status and Citizenship in the United States: 2009.* Retrieved December 2010, from http://www.census.gov/prod/2010pubs/acsbr09-16.pdf

U.S. Bureau of the Census. (2010e). *U.S. Census Bureau announces 2010 census population counts — Apportionment counts delivered to President.* Retrieved December 2010, from http://2010.census.gov/news/releases/operations/cb10-cn93.html

U.S. Bureau of the Census. (2011a). *Historical income tables—people.* Retrieved January 2011, from www.census.gov/hhes/www/income/data/historical/people/index.html

U.S. Bureau of the Census. (2011b). *Current population survey; Table 2. Percent of Persons in Poverty, by Definition of Income and Selected Characteristics: 2009.* Retrieved January 2011, from www.census.gov/hhes/www/cpstables/032010/rdcall/2_000.htm

U.S. Bureau of the Census. (2011c). *Hispanics in the United States.* Retrieved January 2011, from www.census.gov/population/www/socdemo/hispanic/files/Internet_Hispanic_in_US_2006.pdf

U.S. Bureau of the Census. (2011d). *2011 Statistical Abstract: Black elected officials by office and state.* Retrieved January 2011, from http://www.census.gov/compendia/statab/cats/elections/elected_public_officials—characteristics.html

U.S. Bureau of Labor Statistics. (1995). *A Current Population Survey supplement for testing methods of collecting racial and ethnic information: May 1995.* Washington, DC: U.S. Department of Labor.

U.S. Bureau of Labor Statistics. (2010a). *Highlights of women's earnings in 2009.* Retrieved January 2011, from http://www.bls.gov/cps/cpswom2009.pdf

U.S. Bureau of Labor Statistics. (2010b). *Occupational employment and wages, May 2009.* Retrieved December 2010, from www.bls.gov/news.release/ocwage.t01.htm

U.S. Bureau of Labor Statistics. (2011). *Employment situation summary.* Retrieved January 2011, from http://www.bls.gov/news.release/empsit.nr0.htm

U.S. Congress. (1964). *Act to Mobilize the Human and Financial Resources of the Nation to Combat Poverty in the United States,* Pub. L. No. 88-452, 88th Cong., § 2, 78 Stat. 508 (1964).

U.S. Congressional Budget Office. (2002). *The role of computer technology in the growth of productivity.* Washington, DC: Congress of the United States, Congressional Budget Office. Available at www.cbo.gov/ftpdocs/34xx/doc3448/Computer.pdf

U.S. Department of Commerce, Bureau of Economic Analysis. (2010). *Gross domestic product by industry accounts.* Retrieved December 2010, from http://www.bea.gov/industry/gpotables/gpo_action.cfm

U.S. Department of Health and Human Services. (2010a). *Summary Health Statistics for the U.S. Population: National Health Interview Survey, 2009.* Hyattsville, MD: U.S. Department of Health and Human Services, Centers for Disease Control and Prevention, National Center for Health Statistics. Retrieved January 2011, from http://www.cdc.gov/nchs/data/series/sr_10/sr10_248.pdf

U.S. Department of Health and Human Services. (2010b). *Results from the 2009 National Survey on Drug Use and Health: Detailed tables.* Retrieved January 2011, from www.oas.samhsa.gov/NSDUH/2k9NSDUH/tabs/Sect1peTabs19to23.pdf

U.S. Department of Housing and Urban Development. (2008). *American housing survey for the United States: 2007.* Washington, DC: Author. Retrieved January 2011, from http://www.census.gov/prod/2008pubs/h150-07.pdf

U.S. Internal Revenue Service. (2010). *Earned income tax credit statistics.* Retrieved December 2010, from http://www.irs.gov/individuals/article/0,,id=177571,00.html

Wagner, D. (1989). Radical movements in the social services: A theoretical framework. *Social Service Review, 63*(2), 264–284.

Wahl, A., Bergland, A., & Løyland, B. (2010). Is social capital associated with coping, self-esteem, health and quality of life in long-term social assistance recipients? *Scandinavian Journal of Caring Sciences, 24,* 808–816.

Waller, M. A., Okamoto, S. K., Miles, B. W., & Hurdle, D. E. (2003). Resiliency factors related to substance use/resistance: Perceptions of Native adolescents of the Southwest. *Journal of Sociology & Social Welfare, 30,* 79–94.

Walter, U. M., & Petr, C. G. (2004). Promoting successful transitions from day school to regular school environments for youths with serious emotional disorders. *Children & Schools, 26,* 175–180.

Warren, R. L. (1978). *The community in America* (3rd ed.). Chicago, IL: Rand McNally.

Westmoreland, T. M., & Watson, K. R. (2006). Redeeming hollow promises: The case for mandatory spending on health care for American Indians and Alaska Natives. *American Journal of Public Health, 96,* 600–605.

Wilkinson, R. G., & Pickett, K. E. (2009). *The spirit level: Why more equal societies almost always do better.* London: Penguin.

Wilkinson, S., & Kitzinger, C. (2005). Same-sex marriage and equality. *Psychologist, 18,* 290–293.

Wing, K. T., Pollak, T. H., & Blackwood, A. (2008). The nonprofit almanac 2008. Washington, DC: Urban Institute Press.

Wolff, E. N. (2010). *Recent trends in household wealth in the United States: Rising debt and the middle-class squeeze—an update to 2007.* Annandale-on-Hudson, NY: Levy Economics Institute of Bard College.

Wright, B. A. (1988). Attitudes and the fundamental negative bias: Conditions and corrections. In H. E. Yuker (Ed.), *Attitudes toward persons with disabilities.* New York: Springer.

Wu, C.-F., & Eamon, M. K. (2010). Need for and barriers to accessing public benefits among low-income families with children. *Children and Youth Services Review, 32,* 58–66.

Wynne, B. (2006). *Mississippi's Civil War: A narrative history.* Macon, GA: Mercer University Press.

Chapter 3

Brody, R. (2000). *Effectively managing human service organizations* (2nd ed.). Thousand Oaks, CA: Sage.

Devore, W. (1998). The house on midland: From inside out. In F. Rivera & J. Erlich (Eds.), *Community organizing in a diverse society* (pp. 62–74). Boston, MA: Allyn & Bacon.

Diala, C. C., Muntaner, C., & Walrath, C. (2004). Gender, occupational, and socioeconomic correlates of alcohol and drug abuse among U.S. rural, metropolitan, and urban residents. *American Journal of Drug & Alcohol Abuse, 30,* 409–428.

Fetterman, D. (2009). Ethnograhy. In L. Bickman & D. Rog (Eds.), *Applied social research methods.* Thousand Oaks, CA: Sage.

Gambrill, E. (2008). Evidence-based (informed) macro practice: Process and philosophy. *Journal of Evidence-Based Social Work, 5*(3–4), 423–452.

Gutierrez, L., & Lewis, E. (1999). *Empowering women of color.* New York: Columbia University Press.

Hyde, C. (2004). Multicultural development in human service agencies: Challenges and solutions. *Social Work, 49*(1), 17–26.

Kettner, P. M., Moroney, R. M., & Martin, L. L. (1999). *Designing and managing programs: An effectiveness-based approach.* Newbury Park, CA: Sage.

Kettner, P. M., Moroney, R. M., & Martin, L. L. (2008). *Designing and managing programs: An effectiveness-based approach* (3rd ed.). Thousand Oaks, CA: Sage.

Lecca, P., Quervalu, I., Nunes, J., & Gonzales, H. (1998). *Cultural competency in health, social, and human services.* New York: Garland.

National Association of Social Workers (NASW). (n.d.). *Evidence-based practice.* Retrieved April 9, 2011, from http://www.socialworkers.org/research/naswResearch/0108EvidenceBased/default.asp

Netting, F. E., O'Connor, M. K., & Fauri, D. P. (2008). *Comparative approaches to program planning.* Hoboken, NJ: Wiley.

Piven, F., & Cloward, R. (1971). *Regulating the poor: The functions of public welfare.* New York: Pantheon.

Roberts-DeGennaro, M. (2003). Internet resources for community practitioners. *Journal of Community Practice, 11*(4), 133–137.

Sabol, W., Coulton, C., & Polousky, E. (2004). Measuring child maltreatment risk in communities: A life table approach. *Child Abuse & Neglect, 28,* 967–983.

Tashakkori, A., & Teddlie, C. (2009). Integrating qualitative and quantitative approaches to research. In L. Bickman & D. Rog (Eds.), *Applied social research methods.* Thousand Oaks, CA: Sage.

Trochim, W. (2006). Qualitative Data. Retrieved April 9, from http://www.socialresearchmethods.net/kb/qualdata.php

Ungar, M., Manuel, S., Mealey, S., Thomas, G., & Campbell, C. (2004). A study of community guides: Lessons for professionals practicing with and in communities. *Social Work, 49*(4), 550–561.

Chapter 4

Aguirre, A., Jr., & Turner, J. H. (2001). *American ethnicity: The dynamics and consequences of discrimination* (3rd ed.). Boston, MA: McGraw Hill.

Appleby, G. A. (2007). Dynamics of oppression and discrimination. In G. A. Appleby, E. Colon, & J. Hamilton (Eds.), *Diversity, oppression, and social functioning* (pp. 51–67). Boston, MA: Allyn & Bacon.

Armbruster, C., Gale, B., Brady, J., & Thompson, N. (1999). Perceived ownership in a community coalition. *Public Health Nursing, 16*(1), 17–22.

Ashford, J., LeCroy, C., & Lortie, K. (2006). *Human behavior in the social environment: A multidimensional perspective* (3rd ed.). Pacific Grove, CA: Brooks/Cole.

Ashford, J., LeCroy, C., & Lortie, K. (2009). *Human behavior in the social environment: A multidimensional perspective* (4th ed.). Pacific Grove, CA: Brooks/Cole.

Barker, R. (2003). *The social work dictionary* (5th ed.). Washington, DC: NASW Press.

Barrera, M., Munoz, C., & Ornelas, C. (1972). The barrio as an internal colony. *Urban Affairs Annual Review, 6*, 480–498.

Bell, L. A. (2007). Overview: Twenty-first century racism. In M. Adams, L. A. Bell, & P. Griffin (Eds.), *Teaching for diversity and social justice* (2nd ed., pp. 117–122). New York, NY: Routledge.

Bourdieu, P. (1977). *Outline of a theory of practice.* Cambridge, MA: Cambridge University Press.

Bricker-Jenkins, M., & Hooyman, N. R. (Eds.). (1986). *Not for women only.* Silver Spring, MD: NASW Press.

Brooks, F. (2001). Innovative organizing practices: ACORN's campaign in Los Angeles organizing workfare workers. *Journal of Community Practice, 9*, 65–85.

Broido, E. M. (2000). The development of social justice allies during college: A phenomenological investigation. *Journal of College Student Development, 41*, 3–18.

Busch, N. B., & Wolfer, T. A. (2002). Battered women speak out: Welfare reform and their decisions to disclose. *Violence Against Women, 8*(5), 566–584.

Casey, E., & Smith, T. (2010). "How can I not?": Men's pathways to involvement in anti-violence against women work. *Violence Against Women, 16*(8), 953–973.

Cass, V. C. (1979). Homosexual identity formation: A theoretical model. *Journal of Homosexuality, 4*(3), 219–235.

Cass, V. C. (1984). Homosexual identity formation: Testing a theoretical model. *The Journal of Sex Research, 20*(2), 143–167.

Cross, T. L., Bazron, B. J., Dennis, K. W., & Isaacs, M. R. (1989). *Towards a culturally competent system of care.* Washington, DC: Georgetown University Child Development Center, Technical Assistance Center.

Cross, W. E., Jr. (1971). The Negro-to-Black conversion experience. *Black World, 20*(9), 13–27.

Cross, W. E. (1991). *Shades of black: Diversity in African-American identity.* Philadelphia, PA: Temple University Press.

DuBois, W. E. B. (1982). *The souls of black folk.* New York, NY: New American Library.

Erickson, E. (1968). *Identity, youth and crisis.* New York: Norton.

Fellin, P. (1995). *The community and the social worker.* Itasca, IL: F. E. Peacock.

Giddens, A. (1979). *Central problems in social theory: Action, structure and contradiction in social analysis.* London: MacMillan.

Hardina, D. (2003). Linking citizen participation to empowerment practice: A historical overview. *Journal of Community Practice, 11*(4), 11–38.

Hill Collins, P. (2000). *Black feminist thought: Knowledge, consciousness, and the politics of empowerment.* New York, NY: Routledge.

Hooks, b. (1981). *Ain't I a woman? Black women and feminism.* Boston, MA: South End Press.

Hooks, b. (1989). *Talking back: Thinking feminist, thinking black.* Toronto: Between the Lines.

Hutchison, E. D. (2010a). *Dimensions of human behavior: Person and environment* (4th ed.). Thousand Oaks, CA: Pine Forge Press.

Hutchison, E. D. (2010b). *Dimensions of human behavior: The changing life course* (4th ed.). Thousand Oaks, CA: Pine Forge Press.

Jackson, A., & Scheines, R. (2005). Single mothers' self-efficacy, parenting in the home environment, and children's development in a two-wave study. *Social Work Research, 29*(1), 7–20.

Jansen, G. G. (2006). Gender and war: The effects of armed conflict on women's health and mental health. *Affilia, 21*(2), 134–145.

Johnson, Y. M., & Munch, S. (2009). Fundamental contradictions in cultural competence. *Social Work, 54*(3), 220–231.

Kohlberg, L. (1984). *Essays on moral development: Vol. 2: The psychology of moral development.* San Francisco, CA: Harper & Row.

Kondrat, M. E. (1999). Who is the "self" in self-aware: Professional self-awareness from a critical theory perspective. *Social Service Review, 73*(4), 451–477.

Leondar-Wright, B., & Yeskel, F. (2007). Classism curriculum design. In M. Adams, L. A. Bell, & P. Griffin (Eds.), *Teaching for diversity and social justice* (2nd ed., pp. 309–333). New York: Routledge, Taylor and Francis Group.

Link, B. J., & Phelan, J. (2001). Conceptualizing stigma. *Annual Review of Sociology, 27*, 363–385.

Macy, R., Nurius, P., Kernic, M., & Holt, V. (2005). Battered women's profiles associated with service help-seeking efforts: Illuminating opportunities for intervention. *Social Work Research, 29*(3), 137–150.

Marcia, J. E. (1993). The ego identity status approach to ego identity. In J. E. Marcia, A. S. Waterman, D. R. Matteson, S. L. Arcjer, & J. L. Orlofsky (Eds.), *Ego identify: A handbook for psychosocial research.* New York: Springer-Verlag.

Maslow, A. (1943). A theory of motivation. *Psychological Review, 50*, 370–396.

McInnis-Dittrich, K. (2002). *Social work with elders.* Boston, MA: Allyn & Bacon.

Mulroy, E. (2004). Theoretical perspectives on the social environment to guide management and community practice: An organization-in-environment approach. *Administration in Social Work, 28*(1), 77–96.

National Association of Social Workers. (2000). Cultural competence in the social work profession. In *Social work speaks: National Association of Social Workers policy statements* (5th ed., pp. 59–62). Washington, DC: NASW Press.

National Association of Social Workers. (2001). *NASW standards for cultural competence in social work practice.* Washington, DC: Author.

Norton, D. G. (1978). *The dual perspective: Inclusion of ethnic minority content in the social work curriculum.* New York: CSWE Press.

Nygreen, K., Kwon, S. A., & Sanchez, P. (2006). Urban youth building community. *Journal of Community Practice, 14*(1), 107–123.

Organista, K. C. (2009). New practice model for Latinos in need of social work services. *Social Work, 54*(4), 297–305.

Parham T. A. (1989). Cycles of psychological Nigrescence. *The Counseling Psychologist, 17*, 187–226.

Piaget, J. (1972). Intellectual evolution from adolescence to adulthood. *Human Development, 15*, 1–12.

Rosenblum, K. E., & Travis, T. C. (2008). *The meaning of difference: American constructions of race, sex and gender, social class, sexual orientation, and disability* (5th ed.). Boston, MA: McGraw Hill.

Ryan, W. (1971). *Blaming the victim.* New York: Pantheon.

Santrock, J. (2010). *Life-span development* (10th ed.). Boston, MA: McGraw-Hill Higher Education.

Savaya, R., & Waysman, M. (2005). The logic model: A tool for incorporating theory in development and evaluation of programs. *Administration in Social Work, 29*(2), 85–103.

Skinner, B. F. (1971). *Beyond freedom and dignity.* New York: Knopf.

Tervalon, M., & Murray-Garcia, J. (1998). Cultural humility versus cultural competence: A critical distinction in defining physician training outcomes in multicultural education. *Journal for the Poor and Underserved, 9*(2), 117–125.

Turner, R. H. (1990). Role change. *Annual Review of Sociology, 16*, 87–110.

Turner, J. C. (1982). Toward a cognitive redefinition of the social group. In H. Tajfel (Ed.), *Social identity and intergroup behavior* (pp. 15–40). Cambridge, England: Cambridge University Press.

Weil, M., Gamble, D. N., & Williams, E. S. (1998). Women, communities, and development. In J. Figueira-McDonough, F. E. Netting, & A. Nichols-Casebolt (Eds.), *The role of gender in practice knowledge* (pp. 241–286). New York: Garland.

Yan, M. C., & Wong, Y. R. (2005). Rethinking self-awareness in cultural competence: Toward a dialogic self in cross-cultural social work. *Families in Society: The Journal of Contemporary Social Services, 86*(2), 181–188.

Chapter 5

Adam, B. D. (1995). *The rise of a gay and lesbian movement.* New York: Twayne Publishers.

Aguilar, J. P., & Sen, S. (2009). Comparing conceptualizations of social capital. *Journal of Community Practice, 17,* 424–443.

Alinsky, A. (1971). *Rules for radicals.* New York: Vintage.

Alinsky, A. (1974). *Reveille for radicals.* New York: Vintage.

Balgopal, P. R. (1988). Social networks and Asian Indian families. In C. Jacobs & D. D. Bowles (Eds.), *Ethnicity and race: Critical concepts in social work* (pp. 18–33). Silver Spring, MD: NASW Press.

Balser, D. B., & Carmin, J. (2009). Leadership succession and the emergence of an organizational identity threat. *Nonprofit Management & Leadership, 20*(2), 185–201.

Blau, P. (1964). *Exchange and power in social life.* New York: Wiley.

Breton, M. (2001). Neighborhood resiliency. *Journal of Community Practice, 9*(1), 21–36.

Bricker-Jenkins, M., & Netting, F. E. (2008). Feminist issues and practices in social work. In A. R. Roberts (eds.). *The social worker's desk reference* (2nd ed., pp. 277–283). New York: Oxford University Press.

Burrell, G., & Morgan, G. (1979). *Sociological paradigms and organisational analysis.* London: Heineman.

Chaskin, R., Brown, P., Venkatesh, S., & Vidal, A. (2001). *Building community capacity.* New York: Aldine De Gruyter.

Clark, D. C. (1973). The concept of community: A reexamination. *Sociological Review, 21,* 397–416.

Cohen, A. P. (1985). *The symbolic construction of community.* London: Routledge & Kegan Paul.

Coulton, C. J. (2003). Metropolitan inequalities and the ecology of work: Implications for welfare reform. *Social Service Review, 77,* 159–190.

Delgado, M. (2000). *Community social work practice in an urban context.* New York: Oxford University Press.

Eikenberry, A. M. (2009). *Giving circles: Philanthropy, voluntary association, and democracy.* Bloomington, ID: Indiana University Press.

Fellin, P. (1995). *The community and the social worker* (2nd ed.). Itasca, IL: F. E. Peacock.

Fellin, P. (2001). Understanding American communities. In J. Rothman, J. L. Erlich, & J. E. Tropman (Eds.), *Strategies of community intervention* (6th ed., pp. 118–132). Itasca, IL: F. E. Peacock.

Finn, J. L. (2005). La Victoria: Claiming memory, history, and justice in a Santiago Problacion. *Journal of Community Practice, 13*(3), 9–31.

Gamble, D. N., & Weil, M. (2010). *Community practice skills: Local to global perspectives.* New York: Columbia University Press.

Gerloff, R. (1992). Rediscovering the village. *Utne Reader,* 93–100.

Green, P., & Haines, A. (2002). *Asset building and community development.* Thousand Oaks, CA: Sage.

Guberman, N. (2006, April). Assessment of family caregivers: A practice perspective. In *Report from a National Consensus Development Conference. Caregiver assessment: Voices and views from the field* (Vol. 2, pp. 38–57). San Francisco, CA: Family Caregiver Alliance National Center on Caregiving.

Gutierrez, L. M., & Lewis, E.A. (1999). *Empowering women of color.* New York: Columbia University Press.

Han, M. (2003). Community readiness: A promising tool for domestic violence prevention programs in the Korean community. *Journal of Community Practice, 11*(3), 55–69.

Hannah, G. (2006). Maintaining product-process balance in community antipoverty initiatives. *Social Work, 51*(1), 9–17.

Hardina, D. (2002). *Analytical skills for community organization practice.* New York: Columbia University Press.

Hardina, D. (2003). Linking citizen participation to empowerment practice: A historical overview. *Journal of Community Practice, 11*(4), 11–38.

Harrison, W. D. (1995). Community development. In Richard L. Edwards (Ed.), *The encyclopedia of social work* (19th ed., pp. 555–562). Washington, DC: NASW Press.

Hasenfeld, Y. (1983). *Human service organizations.* Englewood Cliffs, NJ: Prentice-Hall.

Hash, K. M., & Netting, F. E. (2007). Long-term planning and decision-making among mid-life and older gay men and lesbians. *Journal of Social Work in End-of-Life & Palliative Care, 3*(2), 59–77.

Hawley, A. (1950). *A human ecology: A theory of community structure.* New York: Roland Press.

Hawley, A. (1968). *Urban ecology.* Chicago, IL: University of Chicago Press.

Haynes, K. S., & Mickelson, J. S. (2006). *Affecting change: Social workers in the political arena* (6th ed.). Boston, MA: Allyn and Bacon.

Helms, J. (1984). Toward a theoretical explanation of the effects of race on counseling: A black and white model. *Counseling Psychologist, 12*(3–4), 153–165.

Hillery, G. (1955). Definitions of community: Areas of agreement. *Rural Sociology, 20,* 779–791.

Hillier, A. (2007). Why social work needs mapping. *Journal of Social Work Education, 43*(2), 205–221.

Hirshorn, B. A., & Stewart, J. E. (2003). Geographic information systems in community-based gerontological research and practice. *Journal of Applied Gerontology, 22*(2), 134–151.

Hoefer, R., Hoefer, R. M., & Tobias, R. A. (1994). Geographic information systems and human services. *Journal of Community Practice, 1*(3), 113–127.

Holley, L. C. (2003). Emerging ethnic agencies: Building capacity to build community. *Journal of Community Practice, 11*(4), 39–57.

Hunter, A. (1993). National federations: The role of voluntary organizations in linking macro and micro orders in civil society. *Nonprofit & Voluntary Sector Quarterly, 22*(2), 121–136.

Hutcheson, J. D., & Dominguez, L. H. (1986). Ethnic self-help organizations in non-barrio settings: Community identity and voluntary action. *Journal of Voluntary Action Research, 15*(4), 13–22.

Kayal, P. M. (1991). Gay AIDS voluntarism as political activity. *Nonprofit & Voluntary Sector Quarterly, 20*(3), 289–312.

Kettner, P. M., Moroney, R. M., & Martin, L. L. (2008). *Designing and managing programs: An effectiveness-based approach* (3rd ed.). Thousand Oaks, CA: Sage.

Knickmeyer, L., Hopkins, K., & Meyer, M. (2003). Exploring collaboration among urban neighborhood associations. *Journal of Community Practice, 11*(2), 13–25.

Kretzmann, J. P., & McKnight, J. L. (1993). *Building communities from the inside out.* Evanston, IL: Northwestern University, Center for Urban Affairs and Policy Research.

Lazzari, M. M., Colarossi, L., & Collins, K. S. (2008). Feminists in social work: Where have all the leaders gone? *Affilia, 24*(4), 348–359.

Lohmann, R. A. (1992). *The commons.* San Francisco, CA: Jossey-Bass.

Lynd, R. S., & Lynd, H. M. (1929). *Middletown: A study in contemporary American culture.* New York: Harcourt & Brace.

Lynd, R. S., & Lynd, H. M. (1937). *Middletown in transition: A study in cultural conflicts.* New York: Harcourt & Brace.

Lyon, L. (1987). *The community in urban society.* Philadelphia, PA: Temple University Press.

MacNair, R. H., Fowler, L., & Harris, J. (2000). The diversity functions of organizations that confront oppression: The evolution of three social movements. *Journal of Community Practice, 7*(2), 71–88.

Martin, P. Y., & O'Connor, G. G. (1989). *The social environment: Open systems applications.* New York: Longman.

Maslow, A. (1962). *Toward a psychology of being.* New York: Van Nostrand.

McIntyre, E. L. G. (1986). Social networks: Potential for practice. *Social Work, 31*(6), 421–426.

McNutt, J. G., Queiro-Tajalli, I., Boland, K. M., & Campbell, C. (2001). Information poverty and the Latino community: Implications for social work practice and social work education. *Journal of Ethnic & Cultural Diversity in Social Work, 10,* 1–20.

Meyer, M. (2010). Social movement service organizations: The challenges and consequences of combining service provision and political advocacy. In Yeheskel Hasenfeld (Ed.), *Human services as complex organizations* (pp. 533–550). Thousand Oaks, CA: Sage.

Mondros, J. B., & Wilson, S. M. (1994). *Organizing for power and empowerment.* New York: Columbia University Press.

Mulucci, A. (1995). The process of collective identity. In H. Johnson & B. Klandermans (Eds.), *Social movements and culture* (pp. 41–63). Minneapolis: University of Minnesota Press.

Nye, N., & Glickman, N. J. (2000). Working together: Building capacity for community development. *Housing Policy Debate, 11,* 163–198.

Nkomo, S. M., & Cox, T., Jr. (1996). Diverse identities in organizations. In S. R. Clegg, C. Hardy, & W. R. Nord. *Handbook of organization studies* (pp. 338–356). London: Sage.

Norlin, J., & Chess, W. (1997). *Human behavior and the social environment: Social systems theory.* Boston, MA: Allyn and Bacon.

O'Brien, G. V., & Leneave, J. (2008). The "art" of social work and the ADA's essential functions provision: Challenges and recommendations. *Administration in Social Work, 32*(4), 87–99.

Pantoja, A., & Perry, W. (1998). Community development and restoration: A perspective and case study. In F. G. Rivera & J. L. Erlich (Eds.), *Community organizing in a diverse society* (pp. 220–242). Boston, MA: Allyn and Bacon.

Park, R. E. (1983). Human ecology. In R. L. Warren & L. Lyon (Eds.), *New perspectives on the American community* (pp. 27–36). Homewood, IL: Dorsey Press.

Parsons, T. (1971). *The system of modern societies.* Englewood Cliffs, NJ: Prentice-Hall.

Portes, A. (2000). The two meanings of social capital. *Sociological Forum, 15*(1), 1–12.

Putnam, R. D. (2000). *Bowling alone: The collapse and revival of American community.* New York: Simon & Schuster.

Pyles, L., & Cross, T. (2008). Community revitalization in post-Katrina New Orleans: A critical analysis of social capital in an African American neighborhood. *Journal of Community Practice, 16*(4), 383–401.

Quinn, P. (2004). Home of your own programs: Models of community collaboration. *Journal of Community Practice, 12*(1/2), 37–50.

Rogge, M. E., David, K., Maddox, D., & Jackson, M. (2005). Leveraging environmental, social and economic justice at Chattanooga Creek: A case study. *Journal of Community Practice, 13*(3), 33–53.

Rothman, J. (2008). Multi modes of community intervention. In J. Rothman, J. L. Erlich, & J. E. Tropman, & Cox, F. (Eds.), *Strategies for community intervention* (7th ed., pp. 141–170). Peosta, IA: Eddie Bower.

Saegert, J., Thompson, P., & Warren, M. R. (Eds.). (2001). *Social capital and poor communities.* New York: Russell Sage Foundation Press.

Saleeby, D. (1997). *The strengths perspective in social work practice* (2nd ed.). New York: Longman.

Smith, D. H. (1991). Four sectors or five? Retaining the member-benefit sector. *Nonprofit and Voluntary Sector Quarterly, 20*(2), 137–150.

Smith, D. H. (2000). *Grassroots associations.* Thousand Oaks, CA: Sage.

Solomon, B. (1976). *Black empowerment.* New York: Columbia University Press.

Stanfield, J. H. (1993). African American traditions of civic responsibility. *Nonprofit and Voluntary Sector Quarterly, 22*(2), 137–153.

Tönnies, F. (1987/1957). *Community and society* [Gemeinschaft und Gesellschaft] (C. P. Loomis, Trans., Ed.). East Lansing: Michigan State University Press. (Original work published 1887)

Van Til, J. (1988). *Mapping the third sector: Voluntarism in a changing social economy.* New York: Foundation Center.

Warren, R. L. (1978). *The community in America* (3rd ed.). Chicago, IL: Rand McNally.

West, J. (1945). *Plainville, U.S.A.* New York: Columbia University Press.

Williams, C., & Williams, H. B. (1984). Contemporary voluntary associations in the urban black church: The development and growth of mutual aid societies. *Journal of Voluntary Action Research, 13*(4), 19–30.

Wineberg, R. J. (1992). Local human services provision by religious congregations. *Nonprofit and Voluntary Sector Quarterly, 21*(2), 107–118.

Wollebaek, D. (2009). Survival in voluntary associations, *Nonprofit Management & Leadership 19*(3), 267–284.

Wong, Y. I., & Hillier, A. E. (2001). Evaluating a community-based homelessness prevention program: A geographic information system approach. *Administration in Social Work, 25*(4), 21–45.

Chapter 6

Alliance of Information and Referral Systems (AIRS). (2006). Retrieved June 26, 2006, from www.airs.org/aboutairs//about/aboutairs.asp

Appleby, G. A. (2007). Dynamics of oppression and discrimination. In G. A. Appleby, E. Colon, & J. Hamilton (Eds.), *Diversity, oppression, and social functioning* (pp. 51–67). Boston, MA: Allyn & Bacon.

Appleby, G. A., Colon, E., & Hamilton, J. (2007). *Diversity, oppression, and social functioning.* Boston, MA: Allyn & Bacon.

Bailey, D., & Koney, K. M. (2000). *Creating and maintaining strategic alliances: From affiliations to consolidations.* Thousand Oaks, CA: Sage.

Barker, R. L. (1995). *The social work dictionary.* Washington, DC: NASW Press.

Bellah, R. N., Madsen, R., Sullivan, W. M., Swidler, A., & Tipton, S. M. (1985). *Habits of the heart: Individualism and commitment in American life.* New York: Harper & Row.

Brudney, J. L. (2005). Emerging areas of volunteering. *ARNOVA Occasional Paper Series, 1*(2).

Cross, T. L., Bazron, B. J., Dennis, K. W., & Isaacs, M. R. (1989). *Towards a culturally competent system of care.* Washington, DC: Georgetown University Child Development Center.

Engstrom, D. W., Piedra, L. M., & Min, J. W. (2009). Bilingual social workers: Language and service complexities. *Administration in Social Work, 33*(2), 167–185.

Green, G. P., & Haines, A. (2002). *Asset building and community development.* Thousand Oaks, CA: Sage.

Hasenfeld, Y. (2010). *Human services as complex organizations.* Thousand Oaks, CA: Sage.

Jansson, B. S. (2009). *The reluctant welfare state: A history of American social welfare policies.* Belmont, CA: Brooks/Cole Cengage Learning.

Jansson, B. S. (2011). *Becoming an effective policy advocate: From policy practice to social justice* (6th ed.). Belmont, CA: Thomson Brooks/Cole.

Karger, H. J., & Stoesz, D. (1990). *American social welfare policy.* New York: Longman.

Kettner, P. M., Daley, J. M., & Nichols, A. W. (1985). *Initiating change in organizations and communities.* Monterey, CA: Brooks/Cole.

King, S. W., & Mayers, R. S. (1984). A course syllabus on developing self-help groups among minority elderly. In J. S. McNeil & S. W. King (Eds.), *Guidelines for developing mental health and minority aging curriculum with a focus on self-help groups* (pp. 1–12). Publication Supported by National Institute of Mental Health Grant #MH 15944–04.

Kramer, R. M. (1981). *Voluntary agencies in the welfare state.* Berkeley: University of California Press.

Kretzmann, J., & McKnight, J. (1993). *Building communities from the inside out: A path toward finding and mobilizing community assets.* Chicago, IL: ACTA.

Marmor, T. R., Schlesinger, M., & Smithey, R. W. (1987). Nonprofit organizations and health care. In W. W. Powell (Ed.), *The nonprofit sector* (pp. 221–239). New Haven, CT: Yale University Press.

Marwell, N. P., & McInerney, P. B. (2005). The nonprofit/for-profit continuum: Theorizing the dynamics of mixed-form markets. *Nonprofit and Voluntary Sector Quarterly, 34*(1), 7–28.

Meenaghan, T. M., Gibbons, W. E., & McNutt, J. G. (2005). *Generalist practice in larger settings: Knowledge and skills concepts* (2nd ed.). Chicago, IL: Lyceum.

Milofsky, C. (2008). *Smallville: Institutionalizing community in twenty-first-century America.* Medford, MA: Tufts University Press.

Nartz, M., & Schoech, D. (2000). Use of the Internet for community practice: A delphi study. *Journal of Community Practice, 8*(1), 37–59.

National Association of Social Workers (NASW). (2006). *NASW standards of cultural competence in social work practice.* Washington, DC: Author. Retrieved June 26, 2006, from www.naswdc.org/sections/credentials/cultural_comp.asp

Nussbaum, M. C. (2006). *Frontiers of Justice: Disability, Nationality, and Species Membership.* Cambridge, MA: The Belknap Press of Harvard University Press.

O'Connor, M. K., & Netting, F. E. (2009). *Organization practice.* Hoboken, NJ: Wiley.

Rossi, P. H., Lipsey, M. W., & Freeman, H. E. (2004). *Evaluation: A systematic approach* (7th ed.). Thousand Oaks, CA: Sage.

Sen, A., & Williams, B. (1982). *Utilitarianism and beyond.* Cambridge, MA: Cambridge University Press.

Tannen, D. (1990). *You just don't understand.* New York: Williams Morrow.

Tilbury, C. (2007). Shaping child welfare policy via performance measurement. *Child Welfare, 86*(6), 115–135.

Tobin, S. S., Ellor, J. W., & Anderson-Ray, S. (1986). *Enabling the elderly: Religious institutions within the community service system.* New York: State University of New York Press.

Warren, R. L. (1978). *The community in America* (3rd ed.). Chicago, IL: Rand McNally.

Chapter 7

American Society for Quality. (2006). *Total quality management.* Retrieved October 2006, from www.asq.org/learn-about-quality/total-quality-management/overview/overview.html

Argyris, C., & Schön. D. A. (1978). *Organizational learning.* reading, MA: Addison-Wesley.

Argyris, C., & Schön. D. A. (1996). *Organizational learning II.* reading, MA: Addison-Wesley.

Bae, J., & Koo, J. (2008). Information loss, knowledge transfer cost and the value of social relations. *Strategic Organization, 6,* 227–258.

Bastalich, W., Franzway, S., Gill, J., Mills, J., & Sharp, R. (2007). Disrupting masculinities: Women engineers and engineering workplace culture. *Australian Feminist Studies, 22,* 385–400.

Beddoe, L. (2009). Creating continuous conversation: Social workers and learning organizations. *Social Work Education, 28,* 722–736.

Bertalanffy, L. von. (1950). An outline of general system theory. *British Journal for the Philosophy of Science, 1*(2), 493–512.

Blau, P. M., & Scott, W. R. (1962). *Formal organizations.* San Francisco, CA: Chandler.

Bolman, F. G., & Deal, T. E. (2008). *Reframing organizations* (4th ed.). San Francisco, CA: Jossey-Bass.

Borkman, T. (2006). Sharing experience, conveying hope: Egalitarian relations as the essential method of Alcoholics Anonymous. *Nonprofit Management & Leadership, 17,* 145–161.

Bowen, G. L., Ware, W. B., Rose, R. A., & Powers, J. D. (2007). Assessing the functioning of schools as learning organizations. *Social Work in Education, 29,* 199–208.

Brazzell, M. (2003). Historical and theoretical roots of diversity management. In D. L. Plummer (Ed.), *Handbook of diversity management: Beyond awareness to competency based learning.* Lanham, MD: University Press of America.

Brockner, J. (1992). The escalation of commitment to a failing course of action: Toward theoretical progress. *Academy of Management Review, 17,* 39–61.

Briggs, H. E., & McBeath, B. (2009). Evidence-based management: Origins, challenges, and implications for social service administration. *Administration in Social Work, 33,* 242–261.

Burns, T., & Stalker, G. M. (1961). *The management of innovation.* London: Tavistock.

Burrell, G., & Morgan, G. (1979). *Sociological paradigms and organizational analysis: Elements of the sociology of corporate life.* London: Heinemann.

Cameron, K.S., & Quinn, R. E. (2006). *Diagnosing and changing organizational culture: Based on the competing values framework (Rev. ed.).* San Francisco, CA: Jossey-Bass.

Carr-Ruffino, N. (2002). *Managing diversity: People skills for a multicultural workplace* (5th ed.). Boston, MA: Pearson.

Castilla, E. J. (2008). Gender, race, and meritocracy in organizational careers. *American Journal of Sociology, 113,* 1479–1526.

Champion, D. J. (1975). *The sociology of organizations.* New York: McGraw-Hill.

Chang, C. C., Chiu, C. M., & Chen, C. A. (2010). The effect of TQM practices on employee satisfaction and loyalty in government. *Total Quality Management & Business Excellence, 21,* 1299–1314.

Chenhall, R. H. (2003). Management control systems design within its organizational context: Findings from contingency-based research and directions for the future. *Accounting, Organizations and Society, 28,* 127–168.

Cohen, P. N. (2007). Working for the woman? Female managers and the gender wage gap. *American Sociological Review, 72,* 681–704.

Collins-Camargo, C., & Royse, D. (2010). A study of the relationships among effective supervision, organizational culture promoting evidence-based practice, and worker self-efficacy in public child welfare. *Journal of Public Child Welfare, 4,* 1–24.

Cross, E. Y. (2000). *Managing diversity: The courage to lead.* Westport, CT: Quorum Books.

Cyert, R. M., & March, J. G. (1963). *A behavioral theory of the firm.* Englewood Cliffs, NJ: Prentice-Hall.

Davis, K.D. (2009). Sex, gender and cultural intelligence in the Canadian forces. *Commonwealth and Comparative Politics, 47,* 430–455.

Deming, W. E. (1982). *Out of the crisis.* Cambridge, MA: Massachusetts Institute of Technology, Center for Advanced Engineering Study.

Desai, V. M. (2010). Ignorance isn't bliss: Complaint experience and organizational learning in the California nursing home industry, 1997–2004. *British Journal of Management, 21,* 829–842.

Dirsmith, M. W., Heian, J. B., & Covaleski, M. A. (1997). Structure and agency in an institutionalized setting: The application and social transformation of control in the big six. *Accounting, Organizations & Society, 22,* 1–27.

Drucker, P. F. (1954). *The practice of management.* New York: Harper.

Ecklund, E. H. (2006). Organizational culture and women's leadership: A study of six Catholic parishes. *Sociology of Religion, 67,* 81–98.

Etzioni, A. (1964). *Modern organizations.* Englewood Cliffs, NJ: Prentice-Hall.

Feigenbaum, A. V. (1951). *Quality control: Principles, practice, and administration.* New York: McGraw-Hill.

Fernandez, S., & Wise, L. R. (2010). An exploration of why public organizations 'ingest' innovations. *Public Administration, 88,* 979–998.

Follett, M. P. (2005 [1926]). The giving of orders. Reprinted in J. M. Shafritz & J. S. Ott (Eds.), *Classics of organizational theory* (6th ed.). Belmont, CA: Thomson Wadsworth.

Friedmann, P. D., Lan, J., & Alexander, J. A. (2010). Top manager effects on buprenorphine adoption in outpatient substance abuse treatment programs. *Journal of Behavioral Health Services & Research, 37,* 322–337.

Galbraith, J. R. (1973). *Designing complex organizations.* Reading, MA: Addison-Wesley.

George, C. S., Jr. (1968). *The history of management thought.* Englewood Cliffs, NJ: Prentice-Hall.

Gibson, C. B., & Zellmer-Bruhn, M. E. (2001). Metaphors and meaning: An intercultural analysis of the concept of teamwork. *Administrative Science Quarterly, 46,* 274–303.

Glisson, C., Dukes, D., & Green, P. (2006). The effects of the ARC organizational intervention on caseworker turnover, climate, and culture in children's service systems. *Child Abuse & Neglect, 30,* 855–880.

Gorman, E. H., & Kmec, J. A. (2009). Hierarchical rank and women's organizational mobility: Glass ceilings in corporate law firms. *American Journal of Sociology, 114,* 1428–1474.

Hakanen, J. J., Schaufeli, W. B., & Ahola, K. (2008). The Job Demands-Resources model: A three-year cross-lagged study of burnout, depression, commitment, and work engagement. *Work & Stress, 22,* 224–241.

Herman, R. D., & Renz, D. (2004). Doing things right: Effectiveness in local nonprofit organizations, a panel study, *Public Administration Review, 64,* 694–704.

Herzberg, F. (1966). *Work and the nature of man.* Cleveland, OH: World.

Institute for Mergers and Acquisitions. (2011). *Statistics.* Retrieved January 2011, from www.imaa-institute.org/statistics-mergers-acquisitions.html

Kang, H. R., Yang, H. D., & Rowley C. (2006). Factors in team effectiveness: Cognitive and demographic similarities of software development team members. *Human Relations, 59,* 1681–1710.

Katovich, M., Weiland, M. W., & Couch, C. J. (1981). Access to information and internal structures of partisan groups: Some notes on the iron law of oligarchy. *Sociological Quarterly, 22,* 431–445.

Katz, D., & Kahn, R. L. (1966). *The social psychology of organizations.* New York: Wiley.

Katz, H. C., Batt, R., & Keefe, J. H. (2003). The revitalization of the CWA: Integrating collective bargaining, political action, and organizing. *Industrial and Labor Relations Review, 56,* 573–589.

Kelly, M. J., & Lauderdale, M. L. (2001). Public-private mentoring for leadership and service quality. *Professional Development: The International Journal of Continuing Social Work Education, 4,* 32–41.

Kovner, A. R., & Rundall, T. G. (2006). Evidence-based management reconsidered. *Frontiers of Health Services Management, 22,* 3–22.

Landsberger, H. A. (1958). *Hawthorne revisited.* Ithaca, NY: Cornell University Press.

Latting, J. K., Beck, M. H., Slack, K. J. Tetrick, L. E., Jones, A. P., Etchegaray, J. M., & da Silva, N. (2004). Promoting service quality and client adherence to the service plan. *Administration in Social Work, 28,* 29–48.

Lawrence, P. R., & Lorsch, J. W. (1967). *Organization and environment: Managing differentiation and integration.* Boston, MA: Graduate School of Business Administration, Harvard University.

Leach, D. (2005). The iron law of what again? Conceptualizing oligarchy across organizational forms. *Sociological Theory, 23,* 312–337.

Leana, C., Appelbaum, E., & Shevchuk, I. (2009). Work process and quality of care in early childhood education: The role of job crafting. *Academy of Management Journal, 52,* 1169–1192.

March, J. G., & Olsen, J. P. (1976). *Ambiguity and choice in organizations.* Bergen, Norway: Universitetsforlaget.

March, J. G., & Simon, H. A. (1958). *Organizations.* New York: Wiley.

Martin, L. L. (1993). *Total quality management in human service organizations.* Thousand Oaks, CA: Sage.

Mathew, J., & Ogbonna, E. (2009). Organisational culture and commitment: a study of an Indian software organisation. *International Journal of Human Resource Management, 20,* 654–675.

McGregor, D. (1960). *The human side of enterprise.* New York: McGraw-Hill.

Merton, R. K. (1952). Bureaucratic structure and personality. In R. K. Merton, A. P. Gray, B. Hockey, & H. C. Selvin (Eds.), *Reader in bureaucracy* (pp. 261–372). Glencoe, IL: Free Press.

Meyer, J., & Parfyonova, N. M. (2010). Normative commitment in the workplace: A theoretical analysis and re-conceptualization. *Human Resource Management Review, 20,* 283–294.

Michels, R. (1949 [1915]). *Political parties* (E. Paul & C. Paul, Trans.). Glencoe, IL: Free Press.

Millar, J. A. (1978). Contingency theory, values, and change. *Human Relations, 31,* 885–904.

Moore, S. T., & Kelly, M. J. (1996). Quality now: Moving human services organizations toward a consumer orientation to service quality. *Social Work, 41*(1), 33–40.

Morgan, G. (1986). *Image of organizations.* London: Sage.

Morse, J. J., & Lorsch, J. W. (1970). Beyond Theory Y. *Harvard Business Review, 45,* 61–68.

Mouzelis, N. P. (1967). *Organization and bureaucracy.* London: Routledge & Kegan Paul.

O'Connor, M. K., Netting, F. E., & Fabelo, H. (2009). A multidimensional agency survey. *Administration in Social Work, 33,* 81–104.

O'Donnell, J., & Kirkner, S. L. (2009). A longitudinal study of factors influencing the retention of Title IV-E Master's of Social Work graduates in public child welfare. *Journal of Public Child Welfare, 3,* 64–86.

Ohana, M., & Meyer, M. (2010). Should I stay or should I go now? Investigating the intention to quit of the permanent staff in social enterprises. *European Management Journal, 28,* 441–454.

Ouchi, W. (1981). *Theory Z: How American business can meet the Japanese challenge.* Reading, MA: Addison-Wesley.

Parsons, T. (1960). *Structure and process in modern societies.* Glencoe, IL: Free Press.

Peters, T. J., & Waterman, R. H. (1982). *In search of excellence: Lessons from America's best-run companies.* New York: Harper & Row.

Pfeffer, J. (1981). *Power in organizations*. Marshfield, MA: Pitman.

Pfeffer, J., & Sutton, R. I. (2006). *Hard facts, dangerous half-truths, and total nonsense*. Boston, MA: Harvard Business School Press.

Pfeifer, C. (2010). Impact of wages and job levels on worker absenteeism. *International Journal of Manpower, 31*, 59–72.

Rogers, R. E. (1975). *Organizational theory*. Boston, MA: Allyn & Bacon.

Rousseau, D. M. (2006). Is there such a thing as "evidence-based management"? *Academy of Management Review, 31*, 256–269.

Saylor, J. H. (1996). *TQM simplified: A practical guide* (2nd ed.). New York: McGraw-Hill.

Schein, E. H. (2010). *Organizational culture and leadership* (4th ed.). San Francisco, CA: Jossey-Bass.

Scott, W. R. (1981). *Organizations: Rational, natural, and open systems*. Englewood Cliffs, NJ: Prentice-Hall.

Selznick, P. (1949). *TVA and the grass roots*. Berkeley: University of California Press.

Selznick, P. (1957). *Leadership in administration*. New York: Harper & Row.

Senge, P. M. (1990). *The fifth discipline: The art and practice of the learning organization*. New York: Doubleday.

Sills, D. L. (1957). *The volunteers*. New York: Free Press.

Simon, H. A. (1957). *Administrative behavior* (2nd ed.). New York: Macmillan.

Simons, K. V., & Jankowski, T. B. (2008). Factors influencing nursing home social workers' intentions to quit employment. *Administration in Social Work, 32*, 5–21.

Sutton, R. I. (2006). *Management advice: Which 90 percent is crap?* Retrieved October 2006, from www.changethis.com/23.90PercentCrap

Sykes, A. J. M. (1965). Economic interests and the Hawthorne researchers: A comment. *Human Relations, 18*, 253–263.

Taylor, F. W. (1911). *The principles of scientific management*. New York: Harper Bros.

Thomas, R. R., Jr. (1991). *Beyond race and gender: Unleashing the power of your total work force by managing diversity*. New York: AMACOM.

Thompson, J. D. (1967). *Organizations in action*. New York: McGraw-Hill.

U.S. Bureau of Labor Statistics. (2009). Labor force. *Occupational Outlook Quarterly Online, 53*(4). Retrieved January 2011, from www.bls.gov/opub/ooq/2009/winter/art3fullp1.htm

Wamsley, G. L., & Zald, M. N. (1976). *The political economy of public organizations*. Bloomington: Indiana University Press.

Weber, M. (1946). *From Max Weber: Essays in sociology* (H. H. Gerth & C. W. Mills, Trans.). New York: Oxford University Press.

Weber, M. (1947 [1924]). *The theory of social and economic organization* (A. M. Henderson & T. Parsons, Trans.). New York: Macmillan.

Weick, K. E. (1995). *Sensemaking in organizations*. Thousand Oaks, CA: Sage.

Weick, K. E., Sutcliffe, K. M., & Obstfeld, D. (2005). Organizing and the process of sensemaking. *Organization Science, 16*, 409–421.

Williams, M. S. (2004). Policy component analysis: A method for identifying problems in policy implementation. *Journal of Social Service Research, 30*, 1–18.

Chapter 8

Abramovitz, M. (2005). The largely untold story of welfare reform and the human services. *Social Work, 50*, 175–186.

Acquavita, S. P., Pittman, J., Gibbons, M., & Castellanos-Brown, K. (2009). Personal and organizational diversity factors' impact on social workers' job satisfaction: Results from a national internet-based survey. *Administration in Social Work, 33*, 151–166.

Association of Fundraising Professionals. (2010). *Trends: In 2010, expect charitable donors to keep giving through long-term pledges*. Retrieved November 2010, from http://www.afpnet.org/Audiences/ReportsResearchDetail.cfm?itemnumber=4289

Bach, S. (2009). Human resource management in the public sector. In A. Wilkinson, N. A. Bacon, T. Redmon, & S. Snell (Eds.) *The SAGE handbook of human resource management* (pp. 561–567). Los Angeles: Sage.

Blair, I. V. (2001). Implicit stereotypes and prejudice. In G. B. Moskowitz (Ed.), *Cognitive social psychology: The Princeton symposium on the legacy and future of social cognition* (pp. 359–374). Mahwah, NJ: Erlbaum.

Bubar, R. (2010). Cultural competence, justice, and supervision: Sexual assault against Native women. *Women & Therapy, 33*, 55–72.

Burns, T., & Stalker, G. M. (1961). *The management of innovation*. London: Tavistock.

Busch, M., & Folaron, G. (2005). Accessibility and clarity of state child welfare agency mission statements. *Child Welfare, 84*, 415–430.

Castle, N. G., & Ferguson, J. C. (2010). What is nursing home quality and how is it measured? *Gerontologist, 50*, 426–442.

Chen, F. M., Fryer, G. E., Jr., Phillips, R. L., Jr., Wilson, E., & Pathman, D. E. (2005). Patients' beliefs about racism, preferences for physician race, and satisfaction with care. *Annals of Family Medicine, 3*, 138–143.

Chow, J. C., & Austin, M. J. (2008). The culturally responsive social service agency: An application of an evolving definition to a case study. *Administration in Social Work, 32*, 39–64.

Chronicle of Philanthropy. (2010). *Philanthropy 400 Data*. Retrieved November 2010, from http://philanthropy.com/premium/stats/philanthropy400/index.php

Clark, R. H. (2007). A study of the relationship between job satisfaction, goal internalization, organization citizenship behavior, and mission statement familiarity. *Dissertation Abstracts International, A: The Humanities and Social Sciences, 67*(7), 2745.

Cloward, R. A., & Epstein, I. (1965). Private social welfare's disengagement from the poor. In M. N. Zald (Ed.), *Social welfare institutions* (pp. 623–644). New York: Wiley.

CNNMoney.com. (2010). *The Fortune 500—2010*. Retrieved October 2010, from http://money.cnn.com/magazines/fortune/fortune500/2010/industries/

Cordes, J., & Henig, J. R. (2001). Nonprofit human service providers in an era of privatization: Toward a theory of economic and political response. *Policy Studies Review, 18*, 91–110.

Cross, T. L., & Friesen, B. J. (2005). Community practice in children's mental health: Developing cultural competence and family-centered services in systems of care models. In M. Weil (Ed.), *The handbook of community practice* (pp. 442–459). Thousand Oaks, CA: Sage Publications.

Dabelko, H. I., Koenig, T. L., & Danso, K. (2008). An examination of the adult day services industry using the resource dependence model within a values context. *Journal of Aging & Social Policy, 20*, 201–217.

Darlington, Y., & Feeney, J. A. (2008). Collaboration between mental health and child protection services: Professionals' perceptions of best practice. *Children and Youth Services Review, 30*, 187–198.

Dennis, H., & Thomas, K. (2007). Ageism in the workplace. *Generations, 31*, 84–89.

Dill, W. R. (1958). Environment as an influence on managerial autonomy. *Administrative Science Quarterly, 2*(1), 409–443.

Dovidio, J. F., Penner, L. A., Albrecht, T. L., Norton, W. E., Gaertner, S. L., & Shelton, J. N. (2008). Disparities and distrust: The implications of psychological processes for understanding racial disparities in health and health care. *Social Science & Medicine, 67*, 478–486.

Ebaugh, H. R., Chafetz, J. S., & Pipes, P. (2005). America's non-profit sector: Funding good works: Funding sources of faith-based social service coalitions. *Nonprofit and Voluntary Sector Quarterly, 34,* 448–472.

Egan, M., & Kadushin, G. (2004). Job satisfaction of home health social workers in the environment of cost containment. *Health & Social Work, 29,* 287–296.

Eilbert, K. W., & Lafronza, V. (2005). Working together for community health: A model and case studies. *Evaluation and Program Planning, 28,* 185–199.

Fletcher, C. N., Garasky, S. B., Jensen, H. H., & Nielsen, R. B. (2010). Transportation access: A key employment barrier for rural low-income families. *Journal of Poverty, 14,* 123–144.

Flint, S. S. (2006). Ensuring equal access for Medicaid children. *Health & Social Work, 31,* 65–71.

Forcadell, F. J. (2005). Democracy, cooperation and business success: The case of Mondragon Corporacion Cooperativa. *Journal of Business Ethics, 56,* 255–274.

Frumkin, P., & Andre-Clark, A. (2000). When missions, markets, and politics collide: Values and strategy in the nonprofit human services. *Nonprofit and Voluntary Sector Quarterly, 29,* 141–163.

Frumkin, P., & Kim, M. T. (2001). Strategic positioning and the financing of nonprofit organizations: Is efficiency rewarded in the contributions marketplace? *Public Administration Review, 61,* 266–275.

Gibelman, M. (2007). Purchasing faith-based social services: Constitutional, philosophical, and practical challenges. *Public Administration Quarterly, 31,* 218–248.

Glisson, C., Landsverk, J., Schoenwald, S., Kelleher, K., Eaton Hoagwood, K., Mayberg, S., & Green, P. (2008). Assessing the organizational social context (OSC) of mental health services: Implications for research and practice. *Administration and Policy in Mental Health Services Research, 35,* 98–113.

Graham, J. R., & Shier, M. L. (2010). The social work profession and subjective well-being: The impact of a profession on over-all subjective well-being. *British Journal of Social Work, 40,* 1553–1572.

Greenley, J. R., & Kirk, S. A. (1973). Organizational characteristics of agencies and the distribution of services to applicants. *Journal of Health and Social Behavior, 14,* 70–79.

Gronbjerg, K. A. (1990). Poverty and nonprofit organizations. *Social Services Review, 64*(2), 208–243.

Gronbjerg, K. A. (2001). The U.S. nonprofit human service sector: A creeping revolution. *Nonprofit and Voluntary Sector Quarterly, 30,* 276–297.

Hasenfeld, Y. (1995). Analyzing the human service agency. In J. Tropman, J. L. Erlich, & J. Rothman (Eds.), *Tactics and techniques of community intervention* (pp. 90–98). Itasca, IL: F. E. Peacock.

Hasenfeld, Y., & Powell, L. E. (2004). The role of non-profit agencies in the provision of welfare-to-work services. *Administration in Social Work, 28,* 91–110.

Herbst, C. M. (2008). Who are the eligible non-recipients of child care subsidies? *Children and Youth Services Review, 30,* 1037–1054.

Hill, C. J. (2006). Casework job design and client outcomes in welfare-to-work offices. *Journal of Public Administration Research and Theory, 16,* 263–288.

Hipp, L., & Warner, M. E. (2008). Market forces for the unemployed? Training vouchers in Germany and the USA. *Social Policy and Administration, 42,* 77–101.

Hodge, D. R., Jackson, K. F., & Vaughn, M. G. (2010). Culturally sensitive interventions and health and behavioral health youth outcomes: A meta-analytic review. *Social Work in Health Care, 49,* 401–423.

Hopkins, K. M., Cohen-Callow, A., Kim, H. J., & Hwang, J. (2010). Beyond intent to leave: Using multiple outcome measures for assessing turnover in child welfare. *Children and Youth Services Review, 32,* 1380–1387.

Hunter, J. K., Getty, C., Kemsley, M., & Skelly, A. H. (1991). Barriers to providing health care to homeless persons: A survey of providers' perceptions. *Health Values, 15,* 3–11.

Independent Sector. (2005). *Panel on the Independent Sector: Strengthening transparency, governance, accountability of charitable organizations.* Washington, DC: Author.

Independent Sector. (2010). *The value of volunteer time.* Retrieved October 2010, from http://www.independentsector.org/volunteer_time

Jackson, K. F. (2009). Building cultural competence: A systematic evaluation of the effectiveness of culturally sensitive interventions with ethnic minority youth. *Children and Youth Services Review, 31*(11), 1192–1198.

Jaskyte, K., & Dressler, W. W. (2005). Organizational culture and innovation in nonprofit human service organizations. *Administration in Social Work, 29,* 23–41.

Kammeyer-Mueller, J. D., & Wanberg, C. R. (2003). Unwrapping the organizational entry process: Disentangling multiple antecedents and their pathways to adjustment. *Journal of Applied Psychology, 88,* 779–794.

Kettner, P. M., Moroney, R. M., & Martin, L. L. (2008). *Designing and managing programs: An effectiveness-based approach* (3rd ed.). Los Angeles, CA: Sage.

Kirk, S. A., & Greenley, J. R. (1974). Denying or delivering services? *Social Work, 19*(4), 439–447.

Knudsen, H. K., Ducharme, L. J., & Roman, P. M. (2006). Counselor emotional exhaustion and turnover intention in therapeutic communities. *Journal of Substance Abuse Treatment, 31,* 173–180.

Kramer, R., & Grossman, B. (1987). Contracting for social services. *Social Service Review, 61*(1), 32–55.

Kraus, W. E., & Ray, P. S. (2010). Increasing productivity in a volunteer organization. *AACE International Transactions,* pDEV.03.1-DEV.03.15.

Lee, R. D., & Johnson, R. W. (1973). *Public budgeting systems.* Baltimore: University Park Press.

Leichter, H. (2004). Ethnic politics, policy fragmentation, and dependent health care access in California. *Journal of Health Politics, Policy and Law, 29,* 177–202.

Leveille, S., & Chamberlain, C. (2010). Toward a general model for child welfare and protection services: A meta-evaluation of international experiences regarding the adoption of the Framework for the Assessment of Children in Need and Their Families (FACNF). *Children and Youth Services Review, 32,* 929–944.

Levine, S., & White, P. E. (1961). Exchange as a conceptual framework for the study of interorganizational relationships. *Administrative Science Quarterly, 5,* 583–601.

Lexchin, J., & Grootendorst, P. (2004). Effects of prescription drug user fees on drug and health services use and on health status in vulnerable populations: A systematic review of the evidence. *International Journal of Health Services, 34,* 101–122.

Likert, R. (1961). *New patterns of management.* New York: McGraw-Hill.

Lipsky, M. (1984). Bureaucratic disentitlement in social welfare programs. *Social Service Review, 58*(1), 3–27.

Liu H. M., & Zhang, J. (2008). Donations in a recursive dynamic model. *Canadian Journal of Economics, 41,* 564–582.

Lucas, J. A., Avi-Itzhak, T., & Robinson, J. P. (2005). Continuous quality improvement as an innovation: Which nursing facilities adopt it? *The Gerontologist, 45,* 68–77.

Malinowski, F. A. (1981). Job selection using task analysis. *Personnel Journal, 60*(4), 288–291.

Mallow, A. (2010). Diversity management in substance abuse organizations: Improving the relationship between the organization and its workforce. *Administration in Social Work, 34,* 275–285.

Mano-Negrin, R. (2003). Spanning the boundaries: A stakeholder approach to effectiveness gaps and empowerment in public and independent human service organizations. *Administration in Social Work, 27,* 25–45.

Martin, L. L. (2000). Budgeting for outcomes in state human agencies. *Administration in Social Work, 24,* 71–88.

Martin, L. L., & Kettner, P. M. (1996). *Measuring the performance of human service programs.* Newbury Park, CA: Sage.

Martin, P. Y. (1980). Multiple constituencies, dominant societal values, and the human service administrator. *Administration in Social Work, 4*(2), 15–27.

Martin, S. S., Trask, J., Peterson, T., Martin, B. C., Baldwin, J., & Knapp, M. (2010). Influence of culture and discrimination on care-seeking behavior of elderly African Americans: A qualitative study. *Social Work in Public Health, 25,* 311–326.

McColl, M. A., Jarzynowska, A., & Shortt, S. E. D. (2010). Unmet health care needs of people with disabilities: Population level evidence. *Disability & Society, 25,* 205–218.

McMurtry, S. L., Netting, F. E., & Kettner, P. M. (1991). How non-profits adapt to a stringent environment. *Nonprofit Management and Leadership, 1*(3), 235–252.

Merton, R. K. (1952). Bureaucratic structure and personality. In R. K. Merton, A. P. Gray, B. Hockey, & H. C. Selvin (Eds.), *Reader in bureaucracy* (pp. 261–372). Glencoe, IL: Free Press.

Meyer, M. H. (2001). Medicaid reimbursement rates and access to nursing homes: Implications for gender, race, and marital status. *Research on Aging, 23,* 532–551.

Miles, R. E. (1975). *Theories of management: Implications for organizational behavior and development.* New York: McGraw-Hill.

Montoya, I. D., Bell, D. C., Richard, A. J., Goodpastor, W., & Carlson, J. (1999). Barriers to social services for HIV-infected urban migrators. *AIDS Education and Prevention, 10,* 366–379.

Morse, J. J., & Lorsch, J. W. (1970). Beyond theory Y. *Harvard Business Review, 48,* 61–68.

Mosley, J. E. (2010). Organizational resources and environmental incentives: understanding the policy advocacy involvement of human service nonprofits. *Social Service Review, 84,* 57–76.

Netting, F. E., McMurtry, S. L., Kettner, P. M., & Jones-McClintic, S. (1990). Privatization and its impact on nonprofit service providers. *Nonprofit and Voluntary Sector Quarterly, 19,* 33–46.

Orsini, M. (2010). Social media: How home health care agencies can join the chorus of empowered voices. *Home Health Care Management & Practice, 22,* 213–217.

Perry, R., & Limb, G. E. (2004). Ethnic/racial matching of clients and social workers in public child welfare. *Children and Youth Services Review, 26,* 965–979.

Polivka-West, L., & Okano, K. (2008). Nursing home regulation and quality assurance in the states: seeking greater effectiveness for better care. *Generations, 32,* 62–66.

Poole, D. L. (2008). Organizational networks of collaboration for community-based living. *Nonprofit Management & Leadership, 18,* 275–293.

Prince, J., & Austin, M. J. (2001). Innovative programs and practices emerging from the implementation of welfare reform: A cross-case analysis. *Journal of Community Practice, 9,* 1–14.

Rajendran, K., & Chemtob, C. M. (2010). Factors associated with service use among immigrants in the child welfare system. *Evaluation and Program Planning, 33,* 317–323.

Rao, D., Angell, B., Lam, C., & Corrigan, P. (2008). Stigma in the workplace: Employer attitudes about people with HIV in Beijing, Hong Kong, and Chicago. *Social Science & Medicine, 67,* 1541–1549.

Robertson, S. E., & Valadez, J. J. (2006). Global review of health care surveys using lot quality assurance sampling (LQAS), 1984–2004. *Social Science & Medicine, 63,* 1648–1660.

Rocha, H., & Miles, R. (2009). A model of collaborative entrepreneurship for a more humanistic management. *Journal of Business Ethics, 88,* 445–462.

Rosenau, P. V., & Lako, C. J. (2008). An experiment with regulated competition and individual mandates for universal health care: The new Dutch health insurance system. *Journal of Health Politics Policy and Law, 33,* 1031–1055.

Scheitle, C. P. (2009). Identity and government funding in Christian nonprofits. *Social Science Quarterly, 90,* 816–833.

Schmidt, M. J., Riggar, T. F., Crimando, W., & Bordieri, J. E. (1992). *Staffing for success.* Newbury Park, CA: Sage.

Shengelia, B., Tandon, A., Adams, O. B., & Murray, C. J. L. (2005). Access, utilization, quality, and effective coverage: An integrated conceptual framework and measurement strategy. *Social Science & Medicine, 61,* 97–109.

Shier, M., Graham, J. R., & Jones, M. E. (2009). Barriers to employment as experienced by disabled people: A qualitative analysis in Calgary and Regina, Canada. *Disability & Society, 24,* 63–75.

Shaefer, H. L. (2010). Identifying key barriers to unemployment insurance for disadvantaged workers in the United States. *Journal of Social Policy, 39,* 439–460.

Shim, M. (2010). Factors influencing child welfare employee's turnover: Focusing on organizational culture and climate. *Children and Youth Services Review, 32,* 847–856.

Smith, L. A., McCaslin, R., Chang, J., Martinez, P., & McGrew, P. (2010). Assessing the needs of older gay, lesbian, bisexual, and transgender people: A service-learning and agency partnership approach. *Journal of Gerontological Social Work, 53,* 387–401.

Suarez-Balcazar, Y., Balcazar, F. E., & Taylor-Ritzler, T. (2009). Using the internet to conduct research with culturally diverse populations: Challenges and opportunities. *Cultural Diversity & Ethnic Minority Psychology, 15,* 96–104.

Sussman, S., Skara, S., & Pumpuang, P. (2008). Project Towards No Drug Abuse (TND): Needs assessment of a social service referral telephone program for high risk youth. *Substance Use & Misuse, 43,* 2066–2073.

Taylor, F. W. (1947). *Scientific management.* New York: Harper & Row.

Thompson, J. D. (1967). *Organizations in action.* New York: McGraw-Hill.

Thompson, S. J., McManus, H., Lantry, J., Windsor, L., & Flynn, P. (2006). Insights from the street: Perceptions of services and providers by homeless young adults. *Evaluation and Program Planning, 29,* 34–43.

Tomkins, A., Shank, N., Tromanhauser, D., Rupp, S., & Mahoney, R. (2005). United Way and university partnerships in community-wide human services planning and plan implementation: The case of Lincoln/Lancaster County, Nebraska. *Journal of Community Practice, 13,* 55–72.

Twombly, E. C. (2002). Religious versus secular human service organizations: Implications for public policy. *Social Science Quarterly, 83,* 947–961.

Uler, N. (2009). Public goods provision and redistributive taxation. *Journal of Public Economics, 93,* 440–453.

Urban Institute—National Center for Charitable Statistics. (2010). *Quick Facts about Nonprofits.* Retrieved October 2010, from http://nccs.urban.org/statistics/quickfacts.cfm

U.S. Bureau of Labor Statistics. (2009). *Volunteering in the United States, 2005.* Retrieved October 2006, from www.bls.gov/news.release/volun.nr0.htm

Van Slyke, D. M. (2003). The mythology of privatization in contracting for social services. *Public Administration Review, 63,* 296–315.

Weber, M. (1946). *From Max Weber: Essays in sociology* (H. H. Gerth & C. W. Mills, Trans.). Oxford, England: Oxford University Press.

Weitzman, M. S., & Jalandoni, N. T. (2002). *The new nonprofit almanac and desk reference: The essential facts and figures for managers, researchers, and volunteers.* San Francisco, CA: Jossey-Bass.

West, A., Ingram, D., & Hind, A. (2006). "Skimming the cream?": Admissions to charter schools in the United States and to autonomous schools in England. *Educational Policy, 20,* 615–639.

Chapter 9

Bell, K. E. (2009). Gender and gangs. *Crime & Delinquency, 55*(3), 363–387.

Bjerregaard, B. (2010). Gang membership and drug involvement. *Crime & Delinquency, 56*(1), 3–34.

Brager, G., & Holloway, S. (1978). *Changing human service organizations: Politics and practice.* New York: Free Press.

Campbell, D. A. (2009). Giving up the single life: Leadership motivations for interorganizational restructuring in nonprofit organizations. *Administration in Social Work, 33,* 368–386.

Crisp, C. (2006). The gay affirmative practice scale (GAP): A new measure for assessing cultural competence with gay and lesbian clients. *Social Work, 51*(2), 115–126.

Daughtery, L. G., & Blome, W. W. (2009). Planning to plan: A process to involve child welfare agencies in disaster preparedness planning. *Journal of Community Practice, 17*(4), 483–501.

Everett, J. E., Homstead, K., & Drisko, J. (2007). Frontline worker perceptions of the empowerment process in community-based agencies. *Social Work, 52*(2)*, 161–170.*

Fisher, E. A. (2009). Motivation and leadership in social work management: A review of theories and related studies. *Administration in Social Work, 33,* 347–367.

Guo, C., & Acar, M. (2005). Understanding collaboration among nonprofit organizations: Combining resource dependency, institutional, and network perspectives. *Nonprofit and Voluntary Sector Quarterly, 34*(3), 340–361.

Kissane, R. J., & Gingerich, J. (2004). Do you see what I see? Nonprofit and resident perceptions of urban neighborhood problems. *Nonprofit Voluntary Sector Quarterly, 33*(2), 311–333.

Kruzich, J. M. (2005). Ownership, chain affiliation, and administrator decision-making autonomy in long-term care facilities. *Administration in Social Work, 29*(1), 5–24.

Linhorst, D. M., Eckert, A., & Hamilton, G. (2005). Promoting participation in organizational decision making by clients with severe mental illness. *Social Work, 50*(1), 21–30.

MacDonald, J. M. (2009). Assessing the relationship between activity among serious adolescent offenders. *Journal of Research in Crime and Delinquency, 46*(4), 553–580.

Majee, W., & Hoyt, A. (2009). Building community trust through cooperatives: A case study of a worker-owned homecare cooperative. *Journal of Community Practice, 17*(4), 444–463.

Maschi, T., & Bradley, C. (2008). Exploring the moderating influence of delinquent peers on the link between trauma, anger, and violence among male youth: Implications for social work practice. *Child and Adolescent Social Work Journal, 25*(2), 125–138.

Meyer, M., & Hyde, C. (2004). Too much of a "good" thing? Insular neighborhood associations, nonreciprocal civility, and the promotion of civic health. *Nonprofit and Voluntary Sector Quarterly, 33*(3), 77S–96S.

Mullen, E. J. (2006). Choosing outcome measures in systematic reviews: Critical challenges. *Research on Social Work Practice, 16*(1), 84–90.

Perrow, C. (1979). *Complex organizations. A critical essay* (2nd ed.). Glenview, IL: Scott, Foresman.

Rogge, M. E., Davis, K., Maddox, D., & Jackson, M. (2005). Leveraging environmental, social, and economic justice at Chattanooga Creek: A case study. *Journal of Community Practice, 13*(3), 33–53.

Rycraft, J. R., & Dettlaff, A. J. (2009). Hurdling the artificial fence between child welfare and the community: Engaging community partners to address disproportionality. *Journal of Community Practice, 17,* 464–482.

Weiss, J. A., Dwonch-Schoen, K., Howard-Barr, E. M., & Panella, M. P. (2010). Learning from a community action plan to promote safe sexual practices. *Social Work, 55*(1), 19–26.

Chapter 10

Banach, M., Hamilton, D., & Perri, P. M. (2004). Class action lawsuits and community empowerment. *Journal of Community Practice, 11*(4), 81–99.

Berlin, S. B. (1990). Dichotomous and complex thinking. *Social Service Review, 64*(1), 46–59.

Bonnie, R. J., Reinhard, J. S., Hamilton, P., & McGarvey, E. (2009). Mental health system transformation after the Virginia Tech tragedy. *Health Affairs, 28*(1), 793–804.

Brager, G., & Holloway, S. (1978). *Changing human service organizations: Politics and practice.* New York: Free Press.

Brager, G., Specht, H., & Torczyner, J. L. (1987). *Community organizing.* New York: Columbia University Press.

Burgess, H., & Burgess, G. M. (2003, November). What are intractable conflicts? In G. Burgess & H. Burgess (Eds.), *Beyond Intractability.* Boulder: Conflict Research Consortium, University of Colorado. Retrieved April 9, 2011, from http://www.beyondintractability. org/essay/meaning_intractability/

Chen, B., & Graddy, E. A. (2010). The effectiveness of nonprofit lead-organization networks for social service delivery. *Nonprofit Management & Leadership, 20*(4), 405–422.

Cleaveland, C. (2010). 'We are not criminals': Social work advocacy and unauthorized migrants. *Social Work, 55*(1), 74–81.

Democracy Center. (2004). *Lobbying—The basics.* San Francisco, CA: Author.

Gutiérrez, L. M., & Lewis, E. A. (1999). *Empowering women of color.* New York: Columbia University Press.

Haynes, K. S., & Mickelson, J. S. (2010). *Effecting change: Social workers in the political arena* (7th ed.). Boston, MA: Allyn & Bacon.

Knickmeyer, L., Hopkins, K., & Meyer, M. (2004). Exploring collaboration among urban neighborhood associations. *Journal of Community Practice, 11*(2), 13–25.

Lewin, K. (1947). Frontiers in group dynamics. *Human Relations, 1,* 5–41.

Medley, B. C., & Akan, O. H. (2008). Creating positive change in community organizations: A case for rediscovering Lewin. *Nonprofit Management & Leadership, 18*(4), 485–496.

Menon, G. M. (2000). The 79-cent campaign: The use of on-line mailing lists for electronic advocacy. *Journal of Community Practice, 8*(3), 73–81.

Morales, J. (1992). Cultural and political realities for community social work practice with Puerto Ricans in the United States. In F. Rivera & J. Erlich (Eds.), *Community organizing in a diverse society* (pp. 75–96). Boston, MA: Allyn & Bacon.

Patwardhan, P., & Patwardhan, H. (2005). An analysis of senior U.S. advertising executives' perceptions of internet communication benefits. *Journal of Website Promotion, 1*(3), 21–39.

Quinn, P. (2004). Home of your own programs: Models of creative collaboration. *Journal of Community Practice, 12*(1/2), 37–50.

Rothman, J., Erlich, J. L., & Tropman, J. E. (Eds.) (2008). *Strategies for community intervention* (6th ed.). Itasca, IL: F. E. Peacock.

Rubin, H. J., & Rubin, I. S. (2008). *Community organizing and development* (4th ed.). Boston, MA: Allyn & Bacon.

Sanders, S., & Saunders, J. A. (2009). Capacity building for gerontological services: An evaluation of adult day services in a rural state. *Journal of Community Practice, 17,* 291–308.

Schneider, R. L., & Lester, L. (2001). *Social work advocacy.* Belmont, CA: Brooks/Cole.

Schroepfer, T. A., Sanchez, G. V., Lee, K. J., Matloub, J. Waltz, A., & Kavanaugh, M. (2009). Community readiness assessment: The scoring process revisited. *Journal of Community Practice, 17,* 269–290.

Takahashi, L. M., & Smutny, G. (2002). Collaborative windows and organizational governance: Exploring the formation and demise of social service partnerships. *Nonprofit and Voluntary Sector Quarterly, 31*(2), 165–185.

Tropman, J. E., Erlich, J. L., & Rothman, J. (2001). *Tactics and techniques of community intervention* (4th ed.). Itasca, IL: F. E. Peacock.

Waysman, M., & Savaya, R. (2004). Coalition-based social change initiatives: Conceptualization of a model and assessment of its generalizability. *Journal of Community Practice, 12*(1/2), 123–143.

Chapter 11

Brody, R. (2005). *Effectively managing human service organizations* (3rd ed.). Newbury Park, CA: Sage.

Carrilio, T. E., Packard, T., & Clapp, J. D. (2003). Nothing in–nothing out: Barriers to the use of performance data in social service programs. *Administration in Social Work, 27*(4), 61–75.

Dessler, G. (2011). *Human resource management* (12th ed.). Upper Saddle River, NJ: Prentice-Hall.

Doe, S. S., & Lowery, D. (2004). The role of evaluation in developing community-based interventions: A COPC project. *Journal of Community Practice, 12*(3/4), 71–88.

Fogel, S. J., & Moore, K. A. (2011). Collaborations among diverse organizations: Building evidence to support community partnerships. In M. Roberts-Gegennaro & S. J. Fogel (Eds.). *Using evidence to inform practice for community and organizational change* (pp. 99–109). Chicago, IL: Lyceum.

Gambrill, E. (2008). Evidence-based (informed) macro practice: process and philosophy. *Journal of Evidence-based social work, 5*(3–4), 423–452.

Gunti, H. (1919). *Organizing for work*. New York: Harcourt, Brace & Howe.

Hardina, D. (2002). *Analytical skills for community organization practice*. New York: Columbia University Press.

Kettner, P. M. (2002). *Achieving excellence in the management of human service organizations*. Boston, MA: Allyn & Bacon.

Kettner, P. M., Moroney, R. M., & Martin, L. L. (2008). *Designing and managing programs: An effectiveness-based approach* (3rd ed.). Thousand Oaks, CA: Sage.

Kluger, M. P. (2006). The program evaluation grid: A planning and assessment tool for nonprofit organizations. *Administration in Social Work, 30*(1), 33–44.

McCroskey, J., Picus, L. O., Yoo, J., Marsenich, L., & Robillard, E. (2004). Show me the money: Estimating public expenditures to improve outcomes for children, families, and communities. *Children and Schools, 26*(3), 165–173.

Montana, P. J., & Charnov, B. H. (2008). *Management* (4th ed.). Hauppauge, NY: Barron's Educational Series.

Rapp, C. A., & Poertner, J. (2007). *Textbook of social administration: A consumert-centered approach*. New York: Haworth.

Reis, E. P., & Moore, M. (2005). Elite perceptions of poverty and inequality. *Community Development Journal, 41*(2), 260–262.

Roberts-DeGennaro, M., & Fogel, S. J. (2011). *Using evidence to inform practice for community and organizational change*. Chicago, IL: Lyceum.

Rogge, M. E., & Rocha, C. (2004). University-community partnership centers: An important link for social work education. *Journal of Community Practice, 12*(3/4), 103–121.

Rosenberg, M. (1965). *Society and the adolescent self-image*. Princeton, NJ: Princeton University Press.

Savaya, R., & Waysman, M. (2005). The logic model: A tool for incorporating theory in development and evaluation of programs. *Administration in Social Work, 29*(2), 85–103.

Sherraden, M. S., Slosar, B., & Sherraden, M. (2002). Innovation in social policy: Collaborative policy advocacy. *Social Work, 47*(3), 209–221.

Weinbach, R. W. (2010). *The social worker as manager: A practical guide to success* (5th ed.). Boston, MA: Pearson /Allyn & Bacon.

Whiteside-Mansell, L., & Corwyn, R. F. (2003). Mean and covariance structures analyses: An examination of the Rosenberg Self-Esteem Scale among adolescents and adults. *Educational & Psychological Measurement, 63*, 163–173.

Photo Credits

Index